End-of-Life Care, Dying and Death in the Islamic Moral Tradition

أخلاق العناية في الإسلام: الرعاية الصحية عند نهاية العمر والاحتضار والموت

Studies in Islamic Ethics

Editorial Board

Mutaz al-Khatib (*Research Center for Islamic Legislation and Ethics, HBKU*)
Mohammed Ghaly (*Research Center for Islamic Legislation and Ethics, HBKU*)
Ray Jureidini (*Research Center for Islamic Legislation and Ethics, HBKU*)

Managing Editor

Abdurraouf Oueslati

VOLUME 4

The titles published in this series are listed at *brill.com/sie*

End-of-Life Care, Dying and Death in the Islamic Moral Tradition

أخلاق العناية في الإسلام
الرعاية الصحية عند نهاية العمر والاحتضار والموت

Edited by

Mohammed Ghaly

تحرير

محمد غالي

BRILL

LEIDEN | BOSTON

Cover illustration: Cover calligraphy by Nihad Nadam, 2022.

مركز دراسات التشريع
الإسلامي والأخلاق
Research Center for Islamic
Legislation and Ethics
عضو في جامعة حمد بن خليفة
Member of Hamad Bin Khalifa University

This publication is sponsored by the Research Center of Islamic Legislation and Ethics in Doha (Qatar), which is affiliated to the Faculty of Islamic Studies, Hamad Bin Khalifa University.

The Library of Congress Cataloging-in-Publication Data is available online at https://catalog.loc.gov
LC record available at https://lccn.loc.gov/2022050133

Typeface for the Latin, Greek, and Cyrillic scripts: "Brill". See and download: brill.com/brill-typeface.

ISSN 2589-3947
ISBN 978-90-04-45940-3 (hardback)
ISBN 978-90-04-45941-0 (e-book)

This book is printed on acid-free paper and produced in a sustainable manner.

To my late grandmother, Muntahā, whose love remains a great source of inspiration

Contents

Preface IX
List of Figures and Tables XI
Notes on Style, Transliteration and Dates XII
Notes on Contributors XIII

Introduction
End-of-Life Care in the Islamic Moral Tradition 1
Mohammed Ghaly

PART 1
Methodological Issues

1 End-of-Life Care, Dying and Death in Islamic Ethics
A Primer 13
Mohammed Ghaly

2 Muslim Disquiet over Brain-Death
Advancing Islamic Bioethics Discourses by Treating Death as a Social Construct that Aligns Purposes with Criteria and Ethical Behaviours 50
Aasim I. Padela

PART 2
End-of-Life Care in Islamic Studies

3 مقاربات فلسفية أخلاقية لرهاب الموت في الحضارة الإسلامية
دراسة آراء محمد بن زكريا الرازي، وأبي علي مسكويه، وصدر الدين الشيرازي 83
حامد آرضائي وأسماء أسدي

4 جلال الدين الرومي وفلسفة الألم والمعاناة 109
شهاب الدين مهدوي وأمير عباس علي زماني

5 Plague, Proper Behaviour and Paradise in a Newly Discovered Text by Zakariyyā al-Anṣārī 127
Hans Daiber

6 Islamic *Ars Moriendi* and Ambiguous Deathbed Emotions
Narratives of Islamic Saints and Scholars on the End-of-Life 152
Pieter Coppens

PART 3
End-of-Life Care as a Bioethical Issue

7 Palliative Care and Its Ethical Questions
Islamic Perspectives 175
Mohammed Ghaly

8 Suicide Prevention and Postvention
An Islamic Psychological Synthesis 202
Khalid Elzamzamy

9 Limits to Personal Autonomy in Islamic Bioethical Deliberations on End-of-Life Issues in Light of the Debate on Euthanasia 238
Ayman Shabana

10 An Islamic Bioethical Framework for Withholding and Withdrawing Life-Sustaining Treatment 282
Rafaqat Rashid

11 Artificial Nutrition and Hydration at the Terminal Stage of Dementia from an Islamic Perspective 330
Hadil Lababidi

12 Child Loss in Early Pregnancy
A Balancing Exercise between Islamic Legal Thinking and Life's Challenge 351
Beate Anam

فهرس 371
Index 375

Preface

This volume is the product of the international seminar "End-of-Life Care in the Islamic Moral Tradition," which was hosted by the Research Center for Islamic Legislation & Ethics (CILE) at Hamad Bin Khalifa University on 20–22 October 2020.[1]

The seminar was part of the CILE series of interdisciplinary seminars which attracted contributions from researchers, scholars and experts in various fields with the aim of addressing complex ethical questions from an Islamic perspective. Like previous seminars in the series, it was preceded by a call-for-papers (CFP), together with a Background Paper explaining its main themes and key questions. All submissions were reviewed by an internal committee within CILE and a limited number of the submissions was selected. Besides the CFP, direct invitations were sent to some researchers whose publication record shows interest in the main themes and questions of the seminar. Throughout the three days of the seminar, the authors of both submitted and solicited papers presented their work, received critical feedback and exchanged ideas and insights on various related issues. The post-seminar work included revising the papers based on the intensive discussions during the seminar. Additionally, some papers were written after the seminar to include some of the research areas that were not covered by the papers presented at the seminar.

Moving to the publication of this volume, each of the included chapters first went through a double-blind review process to improve each individual chapter's academic quality. Finally, the whole volume went through the usual peer-review process managed by Brill. As a result, some of the papers presented during the seminar, or included thereafter, did not find their way to this publication. Although this has been a time-consuming process, we believe that it was worthwhile, especially for such pioneering work in the field.

From the phase of having scattered ideas about this project and up to this publication, I have received invaluable help and support from a great number of colleagues and friends whose list is just too long to be included here. I received additional support for the arduous task of tidying up the language and unifying the referencing style of pieces written by different authors. Our research assistants, Rana Taher, Sara Abdelghany and Yara Abdelbasset provided great help in this regard. Also, all colleagues working at CILE were very

1 Both the call-for-papers and the background paper of the seminar were published on the CILE website (www.cilecenter.org) and also advertised via *Times Higher Education*.

supportive throughout all the elevations and depressions of this extensive journey.[2]

The last word here is for my beloved family, to whom I remain indebted. My wife, Karima, has always been a great asset in my life and I cannot imagine my life without her next to me. My children, Maryam, Khadija, Mustapha, Aisha, and Hamza, keep adding meaning to my life and the more they grow the more we learn from each other. Despite her poor health condition, my mother, Fawzia, has been following up on what each family member is doing, providing necessary support. My late father, Mustafa, remains a great source of inspiration in my life and I hope that I will be as good of a father to my children as he always was to me.

Mohammed Ghaly
Doha, Qatar
June 2022

2 The full list of CILE team is available at www.cilecenter.org/about-us/our-team.

Figures and Tables

Figures

8.1 Chapter outline 203
8.2 The *Tawheedic* paradigm in Islamic psychology and its methodological application in this chapter 205
10.1 Balancing benefits and harms of treatment 312
10.2 Flow chart showing a decision algorithm related to obligations of withholding and withdrawing LST 317

Tables

1.1 The recurrence of the term death (*mawt*) in the nine canonical collections of *ḥadīth* 36
1.2 Theme-based survey of death and related eschatological terms in *ḥadīth* 37
8.1 Responses to myths about suicide prevention (WHO 2014) 208
8.2 WHO's suicide prevention interventions (WHO 2014) 209
8.3 Islamically-informed protective measures against suicide 211
10.1 Certainty of medical intervention outcomes and their respective normative rulings 299
10.2 Maxims that relate to harm considerations 310
10.3 Quantitative and qualitative reasons which permit foregoing LST (see Larcher et al. 2015) 315

Notes on Style, Transliteration and Dates

For referencing, this volume follows the *Chicago Manual of Style* author-date in-text citation system.

Arabic words and names are transliterated according to the system used in Brill's *Encyclopaedia of Islam Three*, which is also adopted in the *Journal of Islamic Ethics* (JIE):

> Consonants: ʾ, b, t, th, j, ḥ, kh, d, dh, r, z, s, sh, ṣ, ḍ, ṭ, ẓ, ʿ, gh, f, q, k, l, m, n, h, w, y.
> Short vowels: a, i, u.
> Long vowels: ā, ī, ū.
> Diphtongs: aw, ay.
> *Tāʾ marbūṭa*: -a, -at (construct state).

While classical proper names are fully transliterated (e.g., al-Ghazālī), for modern names, i.e., since 1900, also the official or common spellings are adopted (e.g., Mohammed Ali al-Bar). The "l" of the definite article "al-" is always retained, regardless of whether it is assimilated in pronunciation to the initial consonant of the word to which it is attached (*idghām*).

If not otherwise specified, the dates given are common era (CE) dates. If two dates are provided (e.g., 505/1111), the first one is the year according to the Islamic *hijrī* calendar (AH) and the second the CE date. For dates after 1900 only the CE date is provided.

Notes on Contributors

Amir Abbas Alizamani (أمير عباس علي زماني)
is Associate Professor at the Department of Philosophy of Religion at the University of Tehran. He obtained his PhD degree in Philosophy of Religion from the University of Tehran. His publications include *Khudā, Zabān va Maʿnā: Dar Āmudī bar Falsafah Zabān Dīnī* ("God, Language and Meaning: An Introduction to the Philosophy of Religious Language," 2003) and *Zabān Dīn* ("The Language of Religion," 1996) as well as a Persian translation of John Cottingham's (b. 1943) *On the Meaning of Life* (2003) titled *Maʿnā-yi Zandagī* ("The Meaning of Life," 2019).

Beate Anam
is Research Associate at the Department of Law and Anthropology, Max-Planck-Institute for Social Anthropology, Halle/Saale and Associate at the Erlangen Zentrum für Islam und Recht in Europa (EZIRE), University of Erlangen-Nürnberg. She is the managing editor of the *Zeitschrift für Recht & Islam* ("Journal of Law and Islam"), co-editor of the *Zeitschrift für Medizin, Ethik und Islam* ("Journal of Medicine, Ethics and Islam") and co-leader of the Working Group "Medical Ethics and Islam" (Arbeitskreis "Medizinethik und Islam"). Her research focuses on applied Islamic medical ethics (especially at the beginning of life) and artificial intelligence.

Hamed Arezaei (حامد آرضائي)
is Faculty Member at the Imam Sadiq University (ISU, Tehran) and the Iran University of Medical Sciences (IUMS, Tehran), as well as member of the Academy of Medical Sciences in Iran. He obtained BA in Arabic Language and Literature from Tehran University, BA and MA degrees in Islamic Theology and Philosophy from Imam Sadiq University (ISU, Tehran 2011) and a PhD in Islamic Philosophy from Tarbiat Modares University (TMU, Tehran, 2017). Arezaei's research interests include the history of philosophy and sciences in the Islamic age, and Ibn Sīnā's (Avicenna, d. 428/1037) heritage in particular. He has published on the classification of knowledge and natural philosophy in Islamic thought – especially the Avicennian tradition – and the relationship between philosophy, medicine, alchemy and other natural sciences. Arezaei has a keen interest in the philosophical approaches of Islamic medicine.

Asma Asadi (أسماء أسدي)
is a Medical Doctor who specialises in infections. Born in Tehran, she studied at the Shahid Beheshti University of Medical Sciences (SBUMS). She obtained her medical degree (MD) in 2010. At the same university she pursued her specialisation in internal medicine and subsequently infection diseases and virology. In 2015 she obtained her PhD degree. Ever since, she is active as a medical specialist in various hospitals and performs research in both modern medicine and herbal medicine. Asadi has published a number of clinical studies on inflammatory diseases and their treatments with medicinal herbs.

Pieter Coppens
is Assistant Professor at the Faculty of Religion and Theology, Vrije Universiteit Amsterdam, where he teaches in the Spiritual Care programme. He obtained his BA and MA degrees in Arabic Language and Culture from the Radboud University Nijmegen, and his PhD degree in Islamic Studies from Utrecht University. A reworked version of his dissertation was published under the title *Seeing God in Sufi Qur'an Commentaries: Crossings between This World and the Otherworld* (2018). Coppens has published on the history of Qurʾān commentaries (*tafsīr*), Islamic hermeneutics and the history of Sufism.

Hans Daiber
was Chair of Oriental Languages at the Johann Wolfgang Goethe-Universität Frankfurt am Main from 1995 until his retirement in 2010. He obtained his PhD in 1967, and in 1980 his thesis was published under the title *Aetius Arabus*. In 1973 he finalised his monograph titled *Das theologisch-philosophische System des Muʿammar Ibn ʿAbbād as-Sulamī (gest. 830 n. Chr.)*, which granted him the qualification for teaching Arabic and Islam; the work appeared in print in 1975. Daiber taught at the Free University of Amsterdam 1977–1995, at the University of Tokyo 1992, ISTAC (International Institute of Islamic Thought and Civilization, Kuala Lumpur/Malaysia) 2001, and is member of the KNAW (Royal Dutch Academy of Arts and Sciences) since 1981. His main fields of interest are Arabic and Islam, including Islamic philosophy, theology, the history of sciences and Greek-Syriac-Arabic-Latin translations. Daiber is an expert in analysing and describing Arabic manuscripts. He is the editor of *Islamic Philosophy, Theology and Sciences* (Brill) and of *Aristoteles Semitico-Latinus* (Brill). In 1999 and 2007 he published the *Bibliography of Islamic Philosophy* in three volumes. His latest book publication (2012) is *Islamic Thought in the Dialogue of Cultures. A Historical and Bibliographical Survey*. Daiber's forthcoming book, *From the Greeks to the Arabs and Beyond* (Brill, 6 volumes), will contain thematically arranged key publications and unpublished articles.

Khalid Elzamzamy
is a Psychiatry Fellow at the Institute of Living/Hartford Healthcare in Connecticut, USA. Currently he also serves as researcher with the Family and Youth Institute, the Khalil Center and as a faculty member at The Alkaram Institute, all in the USA. Previously Elzamzamy served as a research assistant at Yale University. He received his Medical Degree from Ain Shams University, Egypt, and completed his psychiatry residency at Hamad Medical Corporation in Doha, Qatar. Elzamzamy also holds an MA degree in Islamic Studies from Hamad Bin Khalifa University in Qatar. His research interests lie at the intersection of mental health, culture, spirituality and religiosity. He has a particular focus on the integration of religion and spirituality in clinical practice, suicide in the Islamic literature and the Muslim community, contributions of Muslim intellectuals to psychology and mental health and Islamic ethics in clinical practice.

Mohammed Ghaly
is professor of Islam and Biomedical Ethics at the Research Center for Islamic Legislation & Ethics (CILE), College of Islamic Studies at the Hamad Bin Khalifa University in Doha, Qatar. He holds a BA degree in Islamic Studies from Al-Azhar University (Egypt) and MA and PhD degrees in the same field from Leiden University (the Netherlands). During the period 2007–2013, Ghaly was a Faculty Member at Leiden University. Since 2011, he has been Faculty Member at the European Master of Bioethics, part of the Erasmus Mundus Program, jointly organized by a number of European universities. Ghaly's main research area is the Islamic Ethics and how it relates to applied fields like biomedical sciences and artificial intelligence. He published on various topics from an Islamic ethical perspective, including disability, principles of biomedical ethics, GenEthics, human genome editing, infertility treatment, etc. His publications can be accessed via https://cilecenter.academia.edu/MohammedGhaly. Ghaly is the founding editor and editor-in-chief of the *Journal of Islamic Ethics* (published by Brill). He was Visiting Researcher/Professor at various institutions, including the Kennedy Institute of Ethics (Georgetown University, USA), the School of Anthropology (University of Oxford, UK) and the School of Philosophy (Erasmus University, Netherlands). Ghaly is also the Lead Principal Investigator (LPI) and research consultant of a number of funded research projects.

Hadil Lababidi
is PhD candidate in the field of Medical Ethics in Islam at the University Erlangen-Nürnberg. She holds an MA in Modern Middle Eastern Studies from

the University of Leiden. Since 2016, Lababidi is Research Assistant at the Department of Islamic-Religious Studies at the Friedrich-Alexander-Universität Erlangen-Nürnberg. Her main research interest are: dementia in Islam, medical ethics and gender-specific medicine. She co-authored an article on the compliance of psychiatry with human rights, with a focus on patients with dementia and the Islamic tradition. Furthermore, she published a chapter on the concept of legal capacity in Islam with special attention to persons with dementia. Lababidi is co-founder of the Working Group "Medical Ethics and Islam" (Arbeitskreis "Medizinethik und Islam") and the *Zeitschrift für Medizin, Ethik und Islam* ("Journal of Medicine, Ethics and Islam"). She is also member of the commission for interreligious dialogue in the archdiocese Bamberg since 2022.

Shahaboddin Mahdavi (شهاب الدين مهدوي)
is a scholar in Islamic Religion and Philosophy. He holds a BA degree in Islamic Studies from the Qom Seminary and an MA in the Philosophy of Religion from Tehran University.

Aasim Padela
is a Researcher and Lecturer in the fields of Muslim Community Health Research and Intervention Design as well as Islamic Bioethics. Using Muslim Americans and Islam as a model, he studies how (i) religion impacts patient health behaviours and healthcare experiences, (ii) informs the professional identities and workplace experiences of clinicians, and (iii) furnishes bioethical guidance to patients, providers, policymakers and religious leaders. This knowledge is subsequently mobilised towards educational and policy interventions. Methodologically Padela's expertise spans community-engaged research, religiously tailored and faith-based message design, educational interventions aimed at health behaviour change, discourse analysis, and mixed-methods research. His current projects span behaviours related to cancer screening, organ donation, end-of-life care, and the intersection of religion and science and are funded by the John Templeton Foundation, the Health Research and Services Administration, the Greenwall Foundation and the Patient Centered Outcomes Research Institute. He has authored over 120 peer-reviewed journal articles and book chapters, three books, and serves in an editorial capacity for the *Encyclopedia of Islamic Bioethics*, *American Journal of Bioethics*, *BMC Medical Ethics*, *International Journal of Islam*, *BETIM Journal of Medical Humanities*, and *TAHFIM Journal of Islam and the Contemporary World*.

Rafaqat Rashid
is a General Practitioner, Academic Director of Al Balagh Academy, a traditionally trained Sharīʿa Scholar, and an International Professional Trainer and Educator. He is the co-founder of Al Balagh Academy and Course Director of many of its courses in particular its popular international medical *fiqh* and bioethics programmes. He is also an honorary lecturer at the University of Leeds. He gained his MBChB from the University of Liverpool and his MA in Healthcare Ethics and Law from the University of Manchester. He has contributed to academic peer-reviewed chapters in volumes and journal articles on the topics of Islamic Bioethics and Islamic Medical Jurisprudence and continues to contribute to these at an international level. He has been involved with the JKN Fatawa Department in Bradford, UK, and other organisations responding to queries related to medical *fiqh* and bioethics for over a decade, having undergone continuous and ongoing training in *iftāʾ* (issuing *fatwā*s) and contributing to the collection of medical *fatwā*s published by the JKN Fatawa Department as well as leading on the Islamic medical ethics research conducted by the Sharīʿa Department of Al Balagh Academy.

Ayman Shabana
is Associate Research Professor at Georgetown University in Qatar. He received his BA degree from al-Azhar University in Egypt, his MA from Leiden University in the Netherlands, and his PhD from the University of California, Los Angeles. His teaching and research interests include Islamic legal and intellectual history, Islamic law and ethics, human rights, and bioethics. He is the director of the Islamic Bioethics Project, which has been supported by three consecutive grants from Qatar National Research Fund's National Priorities Research Program. In 2012 he received the Research Excellence Award at the Qatar Annual Research Forum and during the academic year 2013–2014 he was Visiting Research Fellow at the Islamic Legal Studies Program at Harvard Law School. Shabana is the author of *Custom in Islamic Law and Legal Theory* (2010) in addition to several book chapters and academic journal articles, which appeared in *Islamic Law and Society*, *Journal of Islamic Studies*, *Journal of Qurʾanic Studies*, *Journal of Islamic Ethics*, *Journal of Religious Ethics*, *The Muslim World*, *Zygon*, *Hawwa*, *Religion Compass*, *Sociology of Islam* and *Medicine Health Care and Philosophy*. He contributed to several reference works such as the *Encyclopaedia of Islam THREE*, *Encyclopedia of Islam and the Muslim World*, *Oxford Encyclopedia of Islam and Law*, *Oxford Handbook of Islamic Law* and *Routledge Handbook of Islamic Law*. He is also the chief editor of the forthcoming *Oxford Encyclopedia of Islamic Bioethics*.

Introduction

End-of-Life Care in the Islamic Moral Tradition

Mohammed Ghaly

Although the initial preparation for this project occurred prior to the COVID-19 pandemic, the proceedings of the research seminar "End-of-Life Care in the Islamic Moral Tradition" took place in October 2020;[1] the midst of the pandemic and its harrowing impact. As of June 2022, the virus has infected more than 500 million people, harvested the lives of more than six million, and disturbed almost all aspects of life on earth. Navigating this unpleasant situation had its complications, as participants shifted to virtual communication with each other and researchers conducted their work under the unusual circumstances of public lockdown. Yet, this context made the proceedings of the seminar and post-seminar work for this publication quite relevant, as people worldwide realised that the ethical questions related to the end-of-life phase concerned almost everybody now and they were no longer exclusive to a limited number of intensive care unit (ICU) patients.

1 End-of-Life Care and Its Ethical Questions

That all living humans eventually die is one of the empirically verified facts that has never failed throughout human history. Thus, dying and death represent an integral part of the shared human experience that cuts across our historical, cultural, ethnic and religious differences. Individuals, families, societies and nations have always been trying, in considerably different ways, to cope with the unavoidable phenomenon of death and the associated intense feelings and emotions that arise when death approaches their milieus. Some of the questions related to this phenomenon are transhistorical in nature, which have long engaged the minds of thinkers. For example, why are humans generally inclined to fear death? How must one take care of a terminal patient or dying person and secure a "good" death? Why is there an association of suffering with death? How far can, or should, medical treatment be sought to improve the health condition of terminal patients? What happens to people after they die

1 The outcome of these seminars has resulted in a number of publications, including Ghaly 2016; Ghaly 2018; Jureidini and Hassan 2019; Hashas and al-Khatib 2021.

DOI:10.1163/9789004459410_002

and where do they eventually go? How should those who are near and dear to the deceased behave when their beloved ones die? What obligations do living people have towards the dead?

With the advent of the modern biomedical revolution, the very concept of death changed and the dying process was considerably medicalised. This revolution has produced an increasing number of tools which can keep many human organs functioning for long periods, through the assistance of expensive and cutting-edge advanced medical technology. All of these developments paved the way for newer methods of "managing" the dying process that had not been available before, thus expanding the scope of end-of-life care (EoLC) and transforming its related ethical questions and dilemmas. Many of the resulting transhistorical questions assumed new dimensions and necessitated revisions of many of the key concepts and values which had long constituted people's moral world. Indeed, new questions were triggered by the modern context of medicalised dying, such that biomedical scientists and ethicists deliberated issues like forgoing life-support machines, life-sustaining treatments, and artificial nutrition and hydration.

As outlined below, this volume approaches EoLC as a rich and complex concept. It, therefore, examines the Islamic perspectives that reflect upon both the transhistorical questions that have always occupied the minds of humans and the novel shifts and questions created by the modern biomedical revolution.

2 This Volume

Against the above-sketched background, this volume is intended to be a reference work for researchers with interests in EoLC and in Islamic Bioethics in general, while also opening up new avenues for future research. The diverse pool of this volume's contributors demonstrates that Islamic bioethical discourse can, and should, be enriched by engaging different disciplines, such as biomedical sciences, psychology, social sciences, in addition to the wide range of scholarly disciplines rooted in the Islamic tradition.

In order to do justice to complexity of EoLC and to the diverse nature of related ethical questions, the volume is divided into three distinct but related parts. The first part, "Methodological Issues," includes two chapters that provide proposals for finetuning and improving certain methodological aspects in the EoLC discourse and the field of Islamic bioethics in general. The second part, "End-of-Life Care in Islamic Studies," comprises four chapters that dig into the rich Islamic tradition to unravel a number of relevant historical discussions that relate to the abovementioned transhistorical questions. The seven chapters included in the third part, "End-of-Life Care as a Bioethical Issue," examine Islamic perspectives on the modern bioethical questions that EoLC, as a scholarly field, is currently engaging with. Below, a detailed overview is provided of each part and the chapters included therein.

2.1 *Methodological Issues*

The two chapters included in this part focus on methodological issues whose consideration is key to developing a thick discourse rooted in the Islamic tradition that concurrently shows awareness of, and critically engages with, EoLC's biomedical and bioethical complexities. The main goal here is to show that the Islamic discourse on EoLC, and by extension dying, death and other bioethical issues, should be premised on consistent methodological considerations and not just sporadic quotations, without serious effort to engage with the context of the rich and vast scholarship in the Islamic tradition. Unfortunately, we have seen numerous superficial writings in the field of Islamic bioethics and that is why methodological studies are needed to help in maturing this emerging field.

In "End-of-Life Care, Dying and Death in Islamic Ethics: A Primer," Mohammed Ghaly uses EoLC as an applied example to show how the Islamic bioethical discourse can address one of its oft-repeated critiques, namely its almost exclusive focus on juristic perspectives and thus, ends up something closer to medical jurisprudence rather than bioethical discourse. He explains how an ethical discourse on EoLC can be interdisciplinary by benefiting from, and engaging with, a wide range of scholarly disciplines and genres anchored in the Islamic tradition. The chapter starts with an extended overview and typology of the main ethical questions brought forth by EoLC as a field of scholarly inquiry. The greater part of the chapter expounds on how these questions can be examined from within the Islamic tradition. Besides outlining the possible contribution from the disciplines of Islamic jurisprudence (*fiqh*) and legal theory (*uṣūl al-fiqh*), the chapter provides extensive analysis on how to engage with Qurʾān and *ḥadīth* studies, the disciplines of Islamic theology, philosophy and Sufism. The chapter also explains how the EoLC discourse can benefit from specific genres, including eschatological manuals and works written for consoling people who have been afflicted with calamities and misfortunes, known in Arabic as the *tasliyat ahl al-maṣāʾib* genre.

In "Muslim Disquiet over Brain Death: Advancing Islamic Bioethics Discourse by Treating Death as a Social Construct that Aligns Purposes with Criteria and Ethical Behaviours," Aasim Padela makes a strong case for the argument that the ethical discourse on EoLC is strongly influenced by the way that key concepts like death and dying are defined, understood and approached. He stresses that ethical deliberations on certain EoLC practices should show awareness of the particularities of our modern context, where the dying process has been medicalised. To do justice to this modern context, Padela suggests that bioethical deliberations would better approach human death as a construct that conflates various dimensions and aspects, including the purpose for death declaration, the criteria for certifying death, and what are sometimes termed as "death behaviours," the types of actions that stakeholders are to carry out when a person dies. Judging the ethical or unethical character of one dimension or aspect, he argues, should rest upon a broader ethical evaluation of the other related dimensions. The academic literature produced by bioethicists on the concept of brain death is used as an applied example to highlight the shortcomings in Islamic engagement with this modern concept and how such shortcomings can be addressed by approaching death as a construct.

2.2 *End-of-Life Care in Islamic Studies*

The four chapters included in this part examine EoLC within the broad scope of Islamic Studies. The point here is to show how the death-related moral world in the Islamic tradition looked like before the advent of the modern biomedical revolution. As outlined above, death, dying and a wide network of related concepts have all been part of the human experience throughout history. The scholarly disciplines rooted in the Islamic tradition contributed to shaping, constructing and expounding different aspects of the death-related moral world in Islam. Thus, any modern perspectives on EoLC should show awareness of, and serious engagement with, the related pre-modern perspectives as recorded in these scholarly disciplines. The chapters included in this part give detailed examples of how pre-modern philosophers, theologians, Sufis, poets, jurists and pious public figures contributed to discussions on a wide range of concepts and issues, which remain relevant to the modern EoLC context, including fear of death, plague-related (mass) deaths, pains and agonies of the dying process, etc.

In their "Muqārabāt Falsafiyya Akhālqiyya li-Ruhāb al-Mawt fī l-Ḥaḍāra al-Islāmiyya: Dirāsat Ārā' Muḥammad b. Zakariyyā al-Rāzī wa-Abī ʿAlī Miskawayh wa-Ṣadr al-Dīn al-Shīrāzī (Philosophical-Ethical Approaches to Thanatophobia in the Islamic Civilisation: A Study of the Views of Muḥammad b. Zakariyyā al-Rāzī, Abū ʿAlī Miskawayh and Ṣadr al-Dīn al-Shīrāzī)," Hamed Arezaei and Asma Asadi provide an analytical review of the contributions of three Muslim philosophers on how to understand and/or address the phenomenon of thanatophobia or fear of death. The three selected philosophers are Abū Bakr al-Rāzī (d. 313/925), Miskawayh (d. 421/1030), and Ṣadr al-Dīn al-Shirāzī (d. 1050/1640). Besides sporadic references to possible comparisons with perspectives of classical Greek and modern Western philosophers and ethicists, Arezaei and Asadi's focus is to outline the heterogeneity of perspectives within the Islamic tradition. Some of these philosophers stressed that the best approach is to avoid pondering death itself, whereas others argued that thinking, and feeling afraid, of death can be beneficial and that it is not only something natural but even indispensable for humans. One of the agreed-upon points in this regard is that overcoming the excessive fear of death is conditioned by debunking certain myths and developing the right understanding of what dying, death, and related concepts mean in the Islamic religio-moral system. It is to be noted that other Muslim scholars, not mentioned in this chapter, also contributed to these discussions – their writings are highlighted in the chapter "End-of-Life Care (EoLC) and Islamic Ethics: A Primer," which is included in the first part of this book.

In their "Jalāl al-Dīn al-Rūmī wa-Falsafat al-Alam wa-l-Muʿānāt (Jalāl al-Dīn al-Rūmī and the Philosophy of Pain and Suffering)," Shahaboddin Mahdavi and Amir Abbas Alizamani argue that Sufism represents the best candidate, among other scholarly disciplines, to constructing spiritual care tailored to Muslim terminal patients. The authors chose the prominent poet Jalāl al-Dīn al-Rūmī (d. 672/1273), because of his wide influence that crosses the boundaries of language, culture, religion and time, to represent the vast Sufi literature on pain and suffering. Following a brief overview of Sufi literature in general and al-Rūmī in particular, the chapter focuses on unfolding his multi-level and multidimensional contribution to the theme of pain and suffering. In their analysis of al-Rūmī's insights, the authors touched upon aspects related to semantics, ontology, teleology and typology, in addition to the ethics of dealing with, pain and suffering.

In "Plague, Proper Behaviour and Paradise in a Newly Discovered Text by Zakariyyā al-Anṣārī," Hans Daiber shows the particular relevance of the classical treatises on plague to EoLC discussions, especially in relationship to the appropriate conduct of a religiously and ethically committed Muslim during such overwhelming calamities. Daiber's contribution is of special relevance to the COVID-19 pandemic, which was at its peak when the seminar took place. He focuses on a text written by Zakariyyā al-Anṣārī (d. 926/1520), known as a jurist and judge who also made important contributions to the disciplines of *ḥadīth* and Sufism. Al-Anṣārī's work is not just inspired by scholarly interest, but by personal experience as well. He lost one of his sons during a plague and another son drowned in the Nile River. Daiber provides an extensive overview of the fourteen chapters of al-Anṣārī's work entitled *Tuḥfat al-Rāghibīn fī Bayān Amr al-Ṭawāʿīn* ("On the Gift for Those Who Like to Get Information on the Topic of the Plagues"). Daiber also enriches the chapter by including a number of literal Arabic quotations, together with English translations. He pays special attention to the last chapter of al-Anṣārī's work, which is dedicated to the main etiquettes (*ādāb*) that one should abide by in the face of plagues or similar calamities.

The last chapter in this part of the book is "Islamic *Ars Moriendi* and Ambiguous Deathbed Emotions: Narratives of Islamic Saints and Scholars on the End-of-Life" by Pieter Coppens. The author elaborates how deathbed stories recorded in historical sources, particularly the hagiographies that represent different epochs of Islamic history, can help our understanding of the death-related moral world in the Islamic tradition. Coppens focuses on the deathbed stories of religious luminaries in two classical sources from the 5th/11th century, namely *Ḥilyat al-Awliyāʾ* ("The Ornaments of the Friends of God") and *Risāla fī l-Taṣawwuf* ("Treatise on Sufism"), in addition to two works from the late 19th–early 20th century, namely *Ḥilyat al-Bashar* ("The Ornaments of Humanity") and *Taʾrīkh ʿUlamāʾ Dimashq* ("The History of the Scholars of Damascus"). The objective of the author is to construct something similar to the popular *ars moriendi* (art of dying) genre in Christian literature. Such a genre generally functions as a tool to teach and guide believers on how to behave and manage one's emotions in the face of an imminent death. Coppens has deliberately chosen sources from different historical periods in order to examine whether certain shifts took place between deathbed experiences from early Islamic history and those from the late era, when the Muslim world was at the verge of "modernity." In doing so, the author attempts to fill a research lacuna in the field of spiritual care and chaplaincy from an Islamic perspective.

2.3 *End-of-Life Care as a Bioethical Issue*

In addition to the transhistorical moral questions and ethical dilemmas pertinent to the phenomena of dying and death, the modern biomedical revolution brought forth its own unique contribution to this area of inquiry. As outlined above, the medicalisation and technologisation of death caused people worldwide, Muslims being no exception, to revisit their long-established moral world and look for answers to novel and complex questions. Concepts including suicide and deliberately terminating one's life to put an end to pain and suffering are to be revisited in light of "new" information and/or "novel" medical techniques, which created their own terminology like the term "euthanasia." The EoLC discourse had to address additional questions about the scope of using advanced medical interventions for terminal patients, such as life-sustaining treatments (LSTs), e.g., ventilators and cardiopulmonary resuscitation (CPR), and the (imp)permissibility of forgoing artificial nutrition and hydration

(ANH), which are examined more than once from various angles throughout the chapters included in this part.

This part starts with an overview chapter which examines one of the most discussed topics in the EoLC discourse, namely palliative care (PC). In "Palliative Care and Its Ethical Questions: Islamic Perspectives," Mohammed Ghaly starts with introductory remarks about the overarching concept of medical treatment (*tadāwī*). He explains how modern biomedical advances problematised some of the previously held ethical generalisations in this regard. These modern advances, he argues, have created morally relevant differences and nuances to the extent that *tadāwī* cannot be judged as one simple or indivisible concept. The chapter is comprised of two sections, the first section examines the possible tension between palliative treatment which focuses on treating diseases, through pain management and curative treatment, at the hand of "life-sustaining treatments" (LSTs). Within his discussion of LSTs, the author further differentiates between cardiopulmonary resuscitation (CPR) and mechanical ventilation, on one hand, and artificial nutrition and hydration (ANH), on the other. The second section is dedicated to the dilemma of balancing conflicting values, where important ethical values or virtues cannot all be honoured or implemented within the PC context. This issue is analysed at the hand of two concrete examples, the first of which is administering analgesics, typically used to relieve pain but also used to impair one's consciousness or hasten death. The second example is communicating bad/sad news and how to balance between the value of veracity and that of compassion.

In the second chapter of this part "Suicide Prevention and Postvention: An Islamic Psychological Synthesis," Khalid Elzamzamy examines how insights from modern disciplines, like psychology and mental health, interact with the classical and modern Islamic perspectives on the prevention and postvention of suicide. Elzamzamy approaches suicide as a rich, complex and multidimensional concept whose rigorous analysis necessitates interacting with a wide range of sources that belong to different scholarly disciplines from inside and outside of the Islamic tradition. Besides some introductory methodological remarks and notes about the prevalence of suicide among Muslims, the chapter is divided into two main sections. The first section focuses on suicide prevention and engages with literature from both the fields of mental health and Islamic psychology, including reports from the World Health Organization (WHO) and *fatwās*. Moreover, the author sheds light on how the role of religion is perceived in both types of sources. The second section reviews the issues related to the aftermath of suicide by adopting the same interdisciplinary and synthetic approach. By consulting various theological, juristic and psychological sources, the author discusses issues encompassing how committing suicide would affect the religio-moral status of the deceased and the obligations of the suicide's survivors towards him/her, including funerary rituals. In addition, he discussed the psychological needs of the survivors.

In "Limits to Personal Autonomy in Islamic Bioethical Deliberations on End-of-Life Issues in Light of the Debate on Euthanasia," Ayman Shabana explains that the "old" concept of self-murder, suicide, has undergone considerable shifts and revisions after the modern biomedical revolution. A distinct and technical term, viz., "euthanasia," was coined to frame discussions on the possibility of intentionally ending the life of a terminal patient as the last resort to put an end to one's suffering. Thanks to modern advances in biomedical sciences, it is claimed that the dying process would be as painless as possible. The newly introduced term is indicative of not only linguistic modifications, but more importantly, of changes in the medical, philosophical and moral landscape. Besides the impact of modern medical advances, no one can deny the parallel influence of the concept of autonomy, which plays a central role in modern philosophical and bioethical deliberations. Against this background, the chapter provides an analytical overview of the modern Islamic juristic discussions on the concept of euthanasia, in its active and passive forms, and situates these discussions within the context of classical normative discussions on "old" concepts like self-murder and suicide. The author argues for a nuanced approach where not all forms of autonomy are necessarily incompatible with the Islamic religio-moral system and that not all types of euthanasia are indiscriminately prohibited.

The fourth and fifth chapters included in this part address two of the leading EoLC issues, namely life-sustaining treatments (LSTs) and artificial nutrition and hydration (ANH). In "An Islamic Bioethical Framework for Withholding and Withdrawing Life-Sustaining Treatment," Rafaqat Rashid argues that improving the contemporary Islamic bioethical discourse on LSTs necessitates widening the narrow scope of discussions on the religious obligations assigned to healthcare providers, patients and/or their family to include a more nuanced understanding of "futility." This would eventually clarify *when* foregoing LSTs would be morally justified from an Islamic perspective. The proposed nuanced approach is premised on developing quantitative and qualitative evaluations of life. This can be achieved by prioritising the goal of serving the patients' best interests and incorporating the principle of removing harm to oneself and to others. Concurrently, the broad scope of harm that includes both physical and non-physical forms, e.g., violating bodily dignity and loss of benefit to afterlife, should also be taken into consideration. In order to enhance the applicability of the proposed approach, Rashid also explores specific clinical situations to show when forgoing the LSTs would be permissible or prohibited.

In "Artificial Nutrition and Hydration at the Terminal Stage of Dementia from an Islamic Perspective," Hadil Lababidi focuses on dementia patients and examines how introducing modern forms of medically-assisted nutrition and hydration, e.g., through a gastrostomy tube or a nasogastric tube, raises complex ethical questions in the EoLC context. The chapter sets the scene by introducing the medical and technical aspects of the main disease discussed in the chapter, dementia, and the procedures employed to feed patients with such a life-limiting and life-threatening disease, viz., artificial nutrition and hydration (ANH). The chapter further focuses on the Islamic perspectives on ANH, especially with relevance to the cases of patients who are at the terminal stage of dementia. By reviewing the diverse perspectives on ANH within the contemporary Islamic bioethical deliberations, Lababidi shows how classical concepts formed parts of this modern discourse, e.g., the "duty to feed," the higher objectives of Sharīʿa (*maqāṣid al-Sharīʿa*), and the case of killing detainees by depriving them from eating and drinking, or the so-called *qatl al-ṣabr*, which was frequently discussed in the early works of Islamic jurisprudence. The author concludes her analysis of opposing positions by calling for a nuanced approach that differentiates between different uses of ANH in various contexts. For instance, the short-term use of ANH would be morally justified in the event that a dementia patient loses their consciousness as a result of falling into a coma. On the other hand, forgoing ANH can be justified in the terminal stage of dementia when two or more physicians confirm that harms outweigh benefits and the patient or the relatives agree with the physicians' recommendation.

The last chapter in this volume "Child Loss in Early Pregnancy: A Balancing Exercise between Islamic Legal Thinking and Life's Challenge" is by Beate Anam. The chapter serves as an example that demonstrates the need to enrich the EoLC discourse by engaging some of the underrepresented voices in Islamic bioethical deliberations. In her study, Anam engages with Muslim parents, midwives, and grief counsellors to explore how the emotionally overwhelming phenomenon of spontaneous miscarriage is actually perceived and experienced by Muslims. She unfolds and analyses the dilemmas of Muslim parents, who experienced spontaneous miscarriage, by trying to balance between honouring the ethical norms of their religion, on one hand, and providing their miscarried child with the most dignified EoLC that they can afford, on the other. The chapter also touches upon the question of religious authority for Muslims in Europe and how adopting hard-line positions that ignore the diversity of perspectives within the Islamic tradition can create difficulties for such parents and obstruct paths towards an efficient religiously motivated bereavement counselling.

Indeed, we believe that the Islamic bioethical discourse in general would greatly benefit from more studies that employ the tools and methodologies of social sciences to examine similarities, differences and discrepancies in perceiving the related Islamic moral world, as theorised by religious scholars and experienced by Muslim individuals and societies.

Bibliography

Ghaly, Mohammed, ed. 2016. *Islamic Perspectives on the Principles of Biomedical Ethics*. London: Imperial College Press & World Scientific.

Ghaly, Mohammed, ed. 2018. *Islamic Ethics and the Genome Question*. Leiden: Brill.

Hashas, Mohammed and Mutaz al-Khatib, eds. 2021. *Islamic Ethics and the Trusteeship Paradigm: Taha Abderrahmane's Philosophy in Comparative Perspectives*. Leiden: Brill.

Jureidini, Ray and Said Fares Hassan, eds. 2019. *Migration and Islamic ethics: Issues of Residence, Naturalization and Citizenship*. Leiden: Brill.

PART 1

Methodological Issues

CHAPTER 1

End-of-Life Care, Dying and Death in Islamic Ethics

A Primer

Mohammed Ghaly

1 Introduction

One of the main critiques directed to contemporary Islamic bioethical deliberations is that they are reduced to a juristic discourse which aims to simply judge certain medical interventions as either permissible (*ḥalāl*) or prohibited (*ḥarām*). Consequently, the critique continues, most of these deliberations would better fit into the so-called medical jurisprudence (*fiqh ṭibbī*), with very little to do with the broad discipline of ethics that aims to unravel and analyse the very process of moral reasoning (Sachedina 2008, 25–31; Sachedina 2009, 3–23; Sartell and Padela 2015, 756). In concurrence with this critique, I argue that Islamic bioethics should not operate as a sub-discipline of Islamic jurisprudence (*fiqh*) or a sub-category of *fatwā*-literature, sometimes called medical *fatwās* (*fatāwā ṭibbiyya*). Rather, it should function as a multidisciplinary field, where bioethical deliberations engage with relevant discussions in more than one discipline, depending on the type and scope of issues at hand and the questions to be examined. Thus, there is a need to move from a thin or monodisciplinary Islamic bioethical discourse, usually dominated by a *fiqhī* approach, to a thick and multidisciplinary discourse.

Against this background, the bioethical discourse on end-of-life care (EoLC) is one of the best candidates to demonstrate that the abovementioned thick and multidisciplinary Islamic bioethical discourse is both necessary and feasible. One of the distinctive characteristics of the EoLC discourse, and cognate fields like palliative care, is underscoring the significance of addressing the needs of the "whole person" rather than those of the "patient" only. The main thesis here is that different persons may have similar health conditions with equally advanced malignant diseases, but the severity of feeling pain (viz., suffering) and quality of life would considerably vary, depending on non-clinical and non-physical factors. Thus, specialists usually discuss the need for a holistic EoLC plan that would consider not only the physical but also the emotional, social, spiritual, and religious aspects of the concerned person (Saunders 2006, 205–221; Fallon and Smyth 2008; Hutchinson 2011). Within this framework, the

DOI:10.1163/9789004459410_003

EoLC ethical discourse will naturally examine a long list of issues and questions whose scope would necessarily go beyond the single discipline of *fiqh*. That is why engaging other scholarly disciplines is indispensable, but before reviewing these relevant disciplines and how they can contribute to enriching the Islamic discourse on EoLC, a systematic overview of the key ethical issues and questions will be presented under distinct headings below.

2 Main Themes and Questions

The lists of themes and questions outlined in this section are based on consulting a wide range of published works that examined moral issues related to EoLC (Watson et al. 2009; Wittenberg et al. 2015; Youngner, Stuart and Arnold 2016). Additionally, I benefited from face-to-face discussions and consultations with experts in cognate fields, including those specialised in intensive care and palliative care.[1] Whenever necessary, specific sources will be mentioned below to document particular points or perspectives.

2.1 *Eschatology*

When people feel that their own death, or that of their beloved ones, is imminent, a wide range of existential and practical questions emerge. For instance, people will ponder: What is the nature of death, and what awaits us thereafter? Why do many people fear death, and which effective mechanisms can help in addressing this fear and/or coping with it? The availability of answers and approaches to addressing these questions, in alignment with people's moral values, largely contribute to the overall wellbeing of the terminal patients and their families.

Such questions crafted the basis of a vast literature on eschatological issues, which have always busied the minds of humans at various ages and in various contexts. During the twentieth century, significant breakthroughs in medicine and EoLC paved the way to the medicalisation, technologisation and institutionalisation of death. Thus, these questions, and closely related concepts like the "denial of death," assumed new dimensions and extra layers of complexity. Literature from various disciplines, especially psychology, sociology, and medicine, examined the phenomenon of death anxiety, or thanatophobia as named by Sigmund Freud (d. 1939), and addressed many related questions (Becker

1 I hereby especially acknowledge Dr. Randi Diamond and Dr. Azza Hassan. Besides many other physicians and healthcare workers, I have learnt much from Dr. Diamond and Dr. Hassan during our work on earlier publication (see Ghaly et al. 2018).

1975; Zimmermann and Rodin 2004; Meyers, Golden and Peterson 2009, 105; Kogan 2010; Solomon and Lawlor 2011). The long list of the examined questions included: How can EoLC teams optimally address the (terminal) patients' fears of nothingness, losing loved ones and possible divine punishment thereafter? Does the patient actually fear death, although he/she never died before, or does this fear express deeper concerns related to expected pains from deteriorating diseases that modern technologies may not be able to mitigate, or is it related to one's regret for what has (not) been done in their life before, anticipating divine punishment in the hereafter, etc.?

2.2 *Medical (Non-)Intervention*

EoLC is characterised by going beyond the routine medical interventions to employ the so-called "heroic" or "extraordinary" measures. Such measures include Life-Sustaining Treatments (LSTs), like using ventilators for patients who cannot breathe naturally, and cardiopulmonary resuscitation (CPR) to assist the heart to keep beating, etc. LSTs are quite expensive and are usually employed as life-keeping measures rather than for curing diseases. Further, the health condition of the (terminal) patient is sometimes so poor that physicians would question the likelihood of these extraordinary measures to effectuate a beneficial outcome and, thus, would rather judge some cases as medical futility (White and Pope 2016).

Such situations raise a wide range of ethical questions, including: How should the goals of EoLC be determined and prioritised, e.g., treating diseases, saving life, keeping someone alive irrespective of the quality of their life, etc.? Is there a type of life whose quality is (not) worth saving by employing extraordinary measures? How should one manage the fair allocation of such scarce and expensive resources? When would medical non-intervention be, morally speaking, the better course of action? How should the boundaries between morally significant dichotomies be demarcated, e.g., ordinary vs. extraordinary measures, withholding vs. withdrawing these measures, and natural vs. unnatural death? What are the criteria to judge a certain case as futile and who has the authority to make this judgement? Would Artificial Nutrition and Hydration (ANH) fall within the scope of LSTs, or should it be classified within the category of basic needs of life that should always be given to the patient, irrespective of the quality of his/her life?

Additionally, EoLC usually involves administering analgesics and palliative sedation meant to reduce the patient's pain. Despite this benefit, such measures can also reduce or remove the patient's awareness/consciousness, which can be considered a harm from social and religious perspectives. They may also entail the risk of "hastening" death – coming closer, in the eyes of some ethicists, to "euthanasia in disguise." The moral questions revolving around the mechanisms of harm-benefit assessment in this context are usually analysed through the lens of the moral principle "Double Effect" (DE).

2.3 *Beyond Clinical Care*

As outlined above, EoLC specialists stress the significance of addressing the needs of the "whole person" rather than those of the "patient" only. The underlying thesis here is that different patients may have similar health conditions, but their overall quality of life would considerably vary, depending on non-clinical and non-physical factors. Thus, a holistic EoLC plan should also consider the emotional, social, and spiritual aspects. It is to be noted that spirituality here does not necessarily mean religious aspects only, but it would comprise the complex web of relationships that gives coherence to one's life, including relationships with ourselves, significant others, groups, and communities, and with God. Furthermore, the EoLC team is frequently impelled to deal with theodical questions that their patients and family members struggle with, e.g., What is the wisdom behind their pains? Does God care about them and their suffering? What would this overwhelming experience tell these patients about their fate in the hereafter? The way these questions are addressed usually have substantial impact on the patients' and their families' (in)ability to cope with their difficult situations (Dein, Swinton and Abbas 2013).

Other related key questions in this regard would also touch upon specific spiritual aspects, e.g., how should the EoLC plan comprise spiritual components to assist the patient and their family in finding meaning and purpose in the remainder of the patient's life and the prospective dying process, and to facilitate and frame discussions about beliefs in what happens after death. How can EoLC holistic plans help the survivors cope with the patient's (approaching) death and associated grief, mourning, and bereavement? How can the patient's and family's intense feelings and experiences be transformed into a catalyst for spiritual growth?

2.4 *Moral Agency*

Many of the EoLC questions and dilemmas have to do with our understanding of what moral agency is and with related concepts like (mental/cognitive) decision-making capacity. Besides the role of these concepts in addressing EoLC moral dilemmas, available research reveal that restoring and/or supporting moral agency can positively impact the patients' health outcomes and their ability to cope (Kirk, Coyle and Doolittle 2015, 28; Price and Barry 2016; Fairman and Irwin 2016, 396–397).

The list of related questions here include: How far can/should support be provided to empower the patients to identify and prioritise their own values and to take decisions in alignment therewith? Which criteria should be adopted to measure the presence/absence of moral agency in an EoLC setting? Who will have this authority, and how would this affect the perception of the patient's autonomy and the whole process of informed consent? Would these criteria differ from one situation to another, e.g., decisions about withholding/withdrawing certain LSTs vs. enrolling the (dying) patient in a research trial, or the capacity to accept vs. the capacity to decline particular interventions? Who should have the right to decide on behalf of the incapacitated patients? How should the EoLC team proceed when there is more than one person (e.g., patient's family members) who disagree with each other on how to serve the patient's best interest? What is the actual moral obligation of the assigned guardian; trying to reach the right decision according to his/her own convictions, or trying to envisage what the patient would have preferred in certain scenarios, irrespective of the guardian's own convictions?

2.5 *Communication Issues*

Various researchers consider communication the *sine qua non* of EoLC and argue that effective communication among involved stakeholders, especially the patient, family, and healthcare personnel, is fundamental to good and effective EoLC (Ragan 2015).

The EoLC context is usually loaded with bad news, which can be quite sensitive and stressful for the patient and family. While communicating such news, the EoLC team find themselves divided between conflicting values that cannot be equally cherished, e.g., how to strike a balance between respecting the value of truth-telling by relaying bad news, on one hand, or cherishing the virtue of compassion by not offending the patient and his/her family, on the other hand? Should the healthcare team differentiate between communicating pieces of information related to prognosis and those related to diagnosis? What should the EoLC team do if the patient's family insists that the patient should not know all the information about his/her health condition, and what if family members disagree among themselves on this point? How should the moral worlds of each stakeholder be explained and considered to facilitate the communication process (e.g., the physician feels committed to conveying accurate information about the approaching death, whereas the patient and/or family may feel that the physician is acting like an omnipotent god who can decide the moment of someone's death)?

3 Main Scholarly Disciplines and Genres

In order to develop a thick Islamic discourse on EoLC that critically engages with the above-outlined themes and questions, insights from more than one scholarly discipline should be involved and, thus, a multidisciplinary approach becomes a must. In this section, I provide an overview of the scholarly disciplines and genres of sources that can develop such a thick and interdisciplinary discourse.

Before embarking on the detailed discussions in distinct disciplines and genres, we need to clarify that the list of disciplines and genres below is meant to be representative rather than comprehensive in nature. For reasons related to the limited space available, I selected what I believed to be relevant to the EoLC context in general and, particularly, the above-sketched themes and questions.[2] We will start with a review of the relevant references in the Qurʾān and Sunna, because they represent the core and raw material that was employed in the writings of the relevant scholarly disciplines and genres.

3.1 *Scriptural References*

The foundational scriptures in Islam, namely the Qurʾān and Sunna, are replete with references that have (in)direct relevance to many of the abovementioned EoLC issues and questions. Any of the abovementioned themes can hardly be examined from within the Islamic tradition without consulting specific references in the Qurʾān or Sunna or their overarching principles and governing philosophies. However, the abundance of relevant scriptural references widely differs from one theme to another. For instance, understanding the nature of death and post-death eschatological issues that usually raise the curiosity of terminal patients and/or their families are all central topics in both the Qurʾān and Sunna. On the other hand, deliberations on questions like withholding/withdrawing life-support machines would expectedly be less dependent on direct quotations from the Qurʾān or Sunna. In such cases, there is usually more reliance on the detailed discussions in relevant scholarly disciplines, especially Islamic jurisprudence (*fiqh*). That is why this section will focus on the scriptural references with relevance to the broad concept of death and related eschatological issues.

---

2 *Adab* is an example of one of the disciplines that were not given special attention in this chapter. Interested researchers can explore how the phenomenon of death was recorded and colorfully depicted in many writings within this discipline, e.g., the poems on laments (*rithāʾ*) (see Shahin 2016).

The phenomenon of death is usually connected with a network of eschatological concepts, including the dying process (*iḥtiḍār*), post-death time in the grave (*barzakh*), resurrection (*baʿth*), Doomsday (*yawm al-qiyāma*), the hereafter (*ākhira*), accountability before God (*ḥisāb*), and people's final destination into heaven (*janna*) or hellfire (*nār/jahannam/jaḥīm*). These interrelated topics are all central to the overall message communicated by the Qurʾān and Sunna and their broad vision of the purpose of God's creation, the position of humans in the universe, and their final destiny.

Besides providing a tentative statistical overview of relevant scriptural references, this section will also refer to the main studies that elaborated on these references. Considering the scope of this study and its main purpose of providing interested researchers with helpful tools, no detailed analysis will be given to the content of these references.

3.1.1 *Qurʾān*

Numerical surveys show the occurrence of the Arabic root of death, viz., *m-w-t*, 165 times in the Qurʾān (ʿAbd al-Bāqī 1945, 678–680; Badawi and Abdel Haleem 2008, 903–905). Additionally, one comes across various Arabic synonyms for death and their derivatives throughout the Qurʾān. Examples include *wafāt* (e.g., Q 2:281, 3:161, 22:5), *manūn* (Q 52:30), *radā* (e.g., Q 37:56, 92:11), *halāk* (e.g., Q 4:176, 26:139, 28:59), and *ajal* (e.g., Q 6:02, 6:128, 7:185, 10:11). Death as an empirically verified phenomenon was naturally accepted by the Arabs, but the focus of the Qurʾānic message was to instill the conviction that death is not the autonomous work of time and natural forces (*dahr*), but that of God, alone, who determines its appointed time (*ajal*) (e.g., Q 45:24–26). Without using our modern technical terms, the dying process, and associated agonies (*sakarāt/ghamarāt*), are extensively described in the Qurʾān. These references are often meant to stress the omnipotence of God and the helplessness of humans who cannot avert the approaching death (e.g., Q 6:93, 50:19, 56:83–87, 75:26–36). After one's death, the intermediary phase commences between one's previous life and future resurrection on the Doomsday, named *barzakh* in the Qurʾān (32:100), a term which literally means a barrier or separation, such as the one between two seas (Q 25:53, 55:20).

The multitude of Qurʾānic references to the topic of resurrection (*baʿth*) (ʿAbd al-Bāqī 1945, 124–125) shows that Arabs had strong opposition to the very idea that there could be new life after death (e.g., Q 16:38, 34:7–8, 64:7). As for the Doomsday, the exact term *yawm al-qiyāma* is mentioned about 70 times (ʿAbd al-Bāqī 1945, 581–582) besides other synonyms like *yawm al-tanād* (Q 40:32), *yawm al-ḥisāb* (e.g., Q 38:16, 38:26, 40:27), and *yawm al-taghābun* (Q 64:09). The term *al-ākhira* shows up more than 100 times, sometimes independently (e.g., Q 28:70, 29:27), other times with qualifying terms such as *al-dār al-ākhira* (abode of the hereafter, e.g., Q 2:94, 6:32, 28:38, 29:64, 33:29), and sometimes in the context of contrasting between this life (*dunyā*) and the afterlife (*ākhira*) (e.g., Q 22:11, 22:15, 24:14, 24:19, 43:35, 59:3, 59:20).

One of the recurrent themes in the Qurʾān is that the hereafter is the time of reckoning (*ḥisāb*), because people will be held accountable for their deeds, up to the minutest details, before God (e.g., Q 99:7–8). That is why Doomsday is also sometimes called the Day of Reckoning (*yawm al-ḥisāb*) (Q 38:16, 38:26, 38:53, 40:27). Some Qurʾānic verses give details about how the process of reckoning will take place. Some verses state that each person will be given a book containing one's deeds throughout his/her lifetime (e.g., Q 69:19–29, 84:6–12) and that there is the Scale (*mīzān*) to weigh these deeds (e.g., Q 21:47). The Qurʾān stresses further that the reckoning process will not entail the slightest form of injustice or unfairness (e.g., Q 17:71, 24:24–25, 41:19–22). The whole process is even much more characterised by God's benevolence than strict justice, to the extent that one good deed will be counted as ten, but one bad deed will remain in its singular form (Q 6:106). The reckoning process will eventually divide people into two main groups, namely the saved ones whose final abode will be heaven (*janna*) and the doomed ones who will end up in the hellfire (*nār/jahannam*) (e.g., Q 3:158). Both heaven, or paradise, and hell, or hellfire, are extensively mentioned throughout the Qurʾān, where each abode has more than one name. Through various Qurʾānic verses, both heaven and hellfire are graphically described, the characteristics of the inhabitants are detailed, the (mis)deeds that lead to each of these two abodes are enlisted, the types of pleasures in heaven and pains in hellfire are expounded, etc. (Kinberg 2006; Gwynne 2006).

Despite the huge number of Qurʾānic references to death and related issues, modern scholarship has produced strikingly few studies dedicated to this topic (Welch 1977; Saleh 2008; Günther 2016).[3] The *Beiträge zur Eschatologie des Islam*, published in 1895, seems to be one of the earliest studies in this regard. One chapter was dedicated to the Qurʾānic framework, as the study has a broader scope, which includes perspectives in: the Sunna, theology, philosophy, etc. (Rüling 1895). The monograph *Muhammad's Thoughts on Death* may be the only book-length contribution to the concept of death in the Qurʾān

3 Distinct chapters on death, or eschatology in general, are also missing in the famous companions to the Qurʾān (e.g., Rippin 2006; MacAuliffe 2007). The exception here is *The Oxford Handbook of Qurʾanic Studies*, which included a chapter on "Eschatology and the Qurʾan" (see Günther 2020b).

(O'Shaughnessy 1969),[4] but the author seems to have been predominantly interested in comparative religious dimensions that fall outside the scope of EoLC issues. Almost in the same vein, some later studies approached themes like *barzakh*, resurrection, and the hereafter through similar comparative lenses (Galloway 1922, 372; Tesei 2016). In his doctoral thesis on *barzakh* in the Qurʾān, for example, George Archer focused more on the intra-Qurʾānic dimensions (Archer 2015).

As for the Doomsday, the Egyptian thinker and activist, Sayyid Quṭb (d. 1966), wrote possibly the most famous work in this genre, which examined how the Qurʾān portrayed the Doomsday at the hand of specific scenes. As explained throughout the book, including the note on dedicating the book to the author's father, there is interest in showing how beliefs about the hereafter are instrumental for improving one's behaviour to achieve an overall uprightness in this life (Quṭb 2006). It seems that this work inspired other Arabic works that also studied the Doomsday and related afterlife issues in the Qurʾān (Muqbil 2011; Saʿīd 2015). Sebastian Günther has recently published a book-chapter in which he examined the Qurʾānic references to the end of time and how they formed the basis for an Islamic apocalyptic literature (Günther 2020a). Some studies particularly focused on paradise in the Qurʾān (e.g., Horovitz 1923; al-Shinnāwī 1994; Abdel Haleem 2017; Qian 2017). As for hellfire, some researchers argued that it is still awaiting more studies. One of the few available studies is a book-chapter examining the identity of Hell's angels in the Qurʾān (Lange 2016b). In *Paradise and Hell in Islamic Traditions*, Christian Lange provided a comparative overview of both heaven and hellfire in the Qurʾān (Lange 2016a, 37–70).

Various entries on death and related eschatological themes in the *Encyclopaedia of the Qurʾān* provided important insights on the concept of death and a wide range of eschatological issues in the Qurʾān, and some have also critically engaged with the abovementioned works (e.g., Borrmans 2006; Gwynne 2006; Hasson 2006; Kinberg 2006; Lalani 2006; Smith 2006; Waardenburg 2006; Zaki 2006). Also, *The Qurʾan: An Encyclopedia* included several relevant entries, some of which show more awareness of EoLC context than those published in

4 Despite the important insights provided by this study and their impact on later works, the author's main questions and overall framework of the book echoed a typically orientalist perspective of his time, e.g., was Prophet Muḥammad the author of the Qurʾān? How many unique ideas did he introduce and how much did he borrow from Judaism, Christianity, or other religious traditions, etc.? Such questions are quite far from the scope of today's EoLC ethical questions and dilemmas. Further, the publication record of O'Shaughnessy shows that he had interest in broader eschatological issues (e.g., O'Shaughnessy 1961; O'Shaughnessy 1986).

the *Encyclopaedia of the Qur'ān* (Leaman 2006, 27, 114, 170–178, 194–199, 258–263, 486–488).

3.1.2 Sunna

Concerning the Sunna, the canonical collections of Prophetic traditions (*ḥadīth*)[5] usually provide much more eschatological details than the references in the Qur'ān. For instance, the concise and indirect Qur'ānic references to *barzakh* are more elaborated in the Prophetic traditions. Besides eschatology, the Sunna also provides some important references with direct relevance to other themes, including (non-)medical intervention and communication issues.

If we follow the approach used above with the Qur'ān, viz., searching for specific terms and concepts, the famous indexed lexicon *al-Muʿjam al-Mufahras li-Alfāẓ al-Ḥadīth al-Nabawī* will be a helpful tool in this regard. For instance, the lexicon shows that the term *mawt* (death) appears 1891 times, *ajal* 245 times, *qabr* (grave) and its derivatives 775 times, *baʿth* 152 times, throughout the nine canonical collections. These figures are indicative of the quantitative omnipresence of eschatology in the Sunna (Wensinck 1936, 1:22–23, 5:222–232, 6:282–301) (see Appendix, Table 1.1).

Besides this term-based approach, the theme-based approach seems to be a more productive and convenient way of searching for material related to EoLC questions in the *ḥadīth* literature. Canonical collections of *ḥadīth*, with the exception of the work compiled by Aḥmad b. Ḥanbal (d. 241/855), are thematically ordered in chapters, where each chapter (*kitāb*) is further divided into sections (*abwāb*). This makes it straightforward to locate entire chapters or sections relevant to the above-sketched EoLC themes. The two authoritative works, compiled by the two prominent traditionists al-Bukhārī (d. 256/870) and Muslim (d. 261/875), serve as representative examples of other canonical collections for this purpose. Each of these two collections included a number of distinct chapters, almost exclusively dedicated to EoLC issues, in addition

5 The mainstream view within the Sunnī tradition is that the two collections compiled by the famous traditionists, al-Bukhārī (d. 256/870) and Muslim (d. 261/875), comprise the most authentic traditions, and are thus widely known as the "Two Authentic [works]" (*Ṣaḥīḥān*). Additionally, the collections compiled by Ibn Māja (d. 273/887), Abū Dāwūd (d. 275/889), al-Tirmidhī (d. 279/892), and al-Nasāʾī (d. 303/915) are usually held in high esteem and viewed, together with the works of al-Bukhārī and Muslim, as the six authoritative collections (*al-kutub al-sitta*). Some scholars would also add three other collections, compiled respectively by Mālik b. Anas (d. 179/795), Aḥmad b. Ḥanbal (d. 241/855) and al-Dārimī (d. 255/ 869), to have a total of nine works (*al-kutub al-tisʿa*). For further information, see Abdul-Jabbar 2020. Also, a helpful research tool to surveying these nine collections was developed by a group of researchers led by the Dutch orientalist Arent Jan Wensinck (d. 1939) (see Wensinck 1936).

to small sections that were compiled to form bigger chapters with broader scope. In the work compiled by al-Bukhārī, researchers on EoLC cannot ignore complete chapters like those on "Funerals" (*janāʾiz*), "Patients" (*marḍā*), "Medicine" (*ṭibb*), and "Softening One's Heart" (*riqāq*) (al-Bukhārī 2001, 2:71–104, 7:114–140). As shown in the Appendix, Table 1.2, similar examples also exist in the collection compiled by Muslim (Muslim n.d.).

Additionally, one comes across a great number of relevant references scattered in various sections. Examples in the collection of al-Bukhārī include sections on "Giving Charity by the Time of Death," and "Supplication for Death or Life" (al-Bukhārī 2001, 4:4, 8:76, 106–121). In the collection of Muslim, examples include sections on the "Recommendation to Seek Refuge [in Allah] from the Punishment of the Grave," the "Reprehensibility of Wishing Death because of Harm or Calamity," and on the "Vastness of God's Mercy that Prevails over His Wrath." Muslim's chapter on "Greetings" also includes various sections relevant to medical treatment. A more comprehensive overview of these chapters and sections is provided in the Appendix, Table 1.2.

Ḥadīth literature is particularly rich with references that outline the etiquettes of dealing with pre-death sickness. For the patient, these etiquettes include details about how one can seize upon the last opportunity to correct previous mistakes or misconduct. For the group around the patient, various guidelines are provided, including the necessity of using hope-giving language in communication with the patient, not forcing him/her to take specific medicine, in addition to a long list of the duties of the living towards the dying patients and dead people, etc. In the same vein of Qurʾānic references, Prophetic traditions provide graphic details about the dying process, post-death period in the grave, the resurrection, paradise, hellfire, etc.

The scholarly studies that examined relevant eschatological issues through the particular lens of the Sunna remain strikingly few. I am not aware of any study that provided analytical insights on the above-mentioned chapters and sections in the canonical collections of *ḥadīth*. As stated above, *Beiträge zur Eschatologie des Islam*, included a chapter on eschatology in the Sunna (Rüling 1895). Also, one of the few examples in this regard is the recently published Roberto Tottoli's book-chapter "Death and Eschatological Beliefs in the Lives of the Prophets according to Islam," which examined *ḥadīth* literature (Tottoli 2020).

3.2 *Eschatological Manuals*

The above-sketched scriptural references created a solid basis for a vast genre of works on eschatology that has been growing since the early history of the Islamic scholarly tradition. For reasons related to available space, I cannot provide a comprehensive survey of all works that fall within this vast genre. Therefore, I will try to give a balanced overview which is representative of both early and modern seminal works, and the different writing styles and approaches adopted therein, where our focus will be on themes and questions relevant to EoLC context.

Broadly speaking, one can differentiate between two styles of writing on death and related eschatological issues. Some of the early works adopted a writing style that was a kind of extension for the chapters included in the canonical collections of *ḥadīth*. Besides the Qurʾānic verses and Prophetic traditions, the author would also add statements and/or anecdotes attributed to early Muslim authorities, especially the Companions of the Prophet (*ṣaḥāba*) and their followers (*tābiʿūn*). In this type of work, analytical remarks or comments from the author are either minimal or simply non-existing. The eschatological works attributed to the traditionist Asad b. Mūsā (d. 212/827), the prominent Sufi al-Ḥārith al-Muḥāsibī (d. 243/857)[6] and the famous traditionists Ibn Abī Dāwūd (d. 316/929) and al-Bayhaqī (d. 485/1066) fall within this genre (Ibn Mūsā 1993; al-Muḥāsibī 1992; Ibn Abī Dāwūd 1987; al-Bayhaqī 1986).

The most prolific author for these types of works on eschatology, however, is the celebrated scholar Ibn Abī l-Dunyā (d. 281/894). He wrote a famous book on death in general, whose material addressed a wide range of topics, starting from why people hate and fear death, passing by the nature of death itself and the agonies of the dying process, and, ending with submitting condolences to the deceased's family (Ibn Abī l-Dunyā 2002). He also wrote two distinct works on the etiquettes associated with the dying process and the anecdotes of people who have gone through this overwhelming experience (Ibn Abī l-Dunyā 2012, 3:321–415, 6:309–341), in addition to one book on graves (Ibn Abī l-Dunyā 2012, 4:513–592), one book on the horrors (*ahwāl*) that will take place by the end of time and in the hereafter (Ibn Abī l-Dunyā 2012,1:499–595), and two books on how paradise and hellfire look like (Ibn Abī l-Dunyā 2012, 3:317–499). Another important work of Ibn Abī l-Dunyā that deserves special mention here, viz., *Ḥusn al-Ẓann bi-Llāh* ("Thinking Good of God"), because of its relevance to today's discussions on the psychology and psychotherapy of terminal patients and dying persons. The whole material included in the book is meant to reiterate the significance of optimism when death is approaching and to stress the idea that one should be full of hope that God's unbounded mercy in the hereafter will override human pitfalls and shortcomings in this

6 It is to be noted that the attribution of this book to al-Muḥāsibī is a disputed issue among those who wrote on him and/or edited his works (see al-Muḥāsibī 1992, 3–4; Maḥmūd 1998, 64–65).

life (Ibn Abī l-Dunyā 2012, 2:305–350). Overall, the works of Ibn Abī l-Dunyā represent a treasure trove and storehouse of eschatological material that can be of benefit in addressing many of today's EoLC questions.

Unlike the previous style of writing which heavily, or even exclusively, depends on quoted material, there is another style of writing which is characterised by providing in-depth and analytical insights. One of the seminal contributors to these types of eschatological writings is the prominent scholar Abū Ḥāmid al-Ghazālī (d. 505/1111). In his *magnum opus* on reviving the religious sciences, al-Ghazālī dedicated the last chapter to death and the afterlife (*dhikr al-mawt wa-mā baʿdah*).[7] Al-Ghazālī provided a serious, and largely successful, attempt to synthesise almost all earlier eschatological perspectives and to construct a mainstream version, which later proved to be influential within both scholarly and popular milieus (al-Ghazālī 2004a, 4:448–543; al-Ghazālī 1878; al-Ghazālī 1989; Lange 2016a, 24). The list of other influential contributors to this genre includes other encyclopedic scholars. Al-Qurṭubī (d. 621/1273) wrote one of the most comprehensive eschatological manuals in Islamic history, which was the subject of further reworkings and abridgments by later scholars up to the modern time (al-Qurṭubī 1969; al-Shaʿrānī 1880; al-Jundī 1997; Lange 2016a, 87). Ibn Rajab al-Ḥanbalī (d. 795/1393) also authored many eschatological works and was particularly influenced by the abovementioned Ibn Abī l-Dunyā (Ibn Rajab 2002; Ibn Rajab 2012; Lange 2016a, 87). Finally, al-Suyūṭī (d. 911/1505) is another productive scholar in this genre who is rightfully credited with the successful continuation of the eschatological tradition created by earlier Muslim scholars (al-Suyūṭī 1996a; al-Suyūṭī 1996b; Lange 2016a, 88).[8] Various examples show the interest of orientalists to publish, translate and analyse some of the classical works in this genre (Wolff 1872; Tottoli 2008).

Broadly speaking, these eschatological manuals represent a trove of insights that can be employed to address the questions and issues outlined under the abovementioned heading "eschatology." They provide detailed accounts of almost every single phase, starting from the dying process up to one's final destination in paradise or hellfire. This rich material can help satisfy the curiosity of terminal patients and people around them, who wonder what/where they are heading to. Besides the "is" aspects, viz., explaining how things are, this literature also elaborates on the "ought" questions, namely how patients

7 The famous work on eschatology, *al-Durra al-Fākhira* ("The Precious Pearl") is also attributed to al-Ghāzālī but this attribution is debatable (see Günther 2017, 195–196).

8 These manuals, and many others, were the subject of modern scholarship, where a great bulk of modern studies was dedicated to paradise and hellfire. Some of these studies also provided an extended list of relevant classical works (see Eklund 1941; Taylor 1968; Smith and Haddad 2002; Chittick 2008; Günther and Lawson 2016; Lange 2016a; Lange 2016b).

and/or their families should ideally behave, and the etiquettes (*ādāb*) associated with various phases. For instance, these works clarify how one can make a good end (*ḥusn al-khātima*) in leaving this life and ready themselves for the approaching death, and how people around them can be of help in this regard, e.g., by reminding him/her of the testimony of faith (*shahāda*). As for after death, the contributors to this genre also explain how far one's family and/or friends can help by doing good (e.g., fasting, pilgrimage, giving charity, etc.) in the name of the deceased. Also among the recurrent themes in this literature are themes related to the abovementioned "Communication Issues," like how to speak with terminal or dying patients and what (not) to say to them and also what (not) to say about the deceased.[9] Finally, this literature is characterised by touching upon numerous issues, many of which are addressed in more details in distinct scholarly disciplines, such as death rituals that belong to the discipline of *fiqh* (Islamic jurisprudence), the ethics of patience and repentance that relate to the discipline of Sufism, etc. Each of these issues will be elaborated in the section dedicated to the respective discipline.

Researchers interested in EoLC need to be aware that the material of these classical manuals continue to be the subjects of modern discussions, but in various ways. From the end of the thirteenth/nineteenth century onwards, roughly speaking, modernity presented a number of challenges to religious convictions, especially those related to eschatology. The response of contemporary Muslim scholars and intellectuals to these challenges was not uniform. Some just ignored these challenges and continued presenting old works but in an accessible way to a modern audience. Others tried to reconcile old eschatological material with modern rational thinking and scientific discoveries and theories, especially Darwin's theory of evolution. For instance, the detailed and graphic descriptions of the fearsome horrors of the dying process and after-death period in the grave (*barzakh*) became much less focal in many contemporary eschatological works. These authors showed much

9 Related to this theme, but coming from another genre, are the works which detailed the proper *adab* (code of conduct or etiquettes) that a virtuous physician should stick to. These works provide rich information with direct relevance to the set of questions delineated under the heading "Communication Issues." The main representative examples of the so-called *adab al-ṭabīb* (etiquettes of the physician) genre is the seminal work of the physician al-Ruhāwī, who lived in the third/ninth century (Levey 1967). Such etiquettes and related rulings were further expounded in many of the writings on regulating the work of physicians, besides other various professionals. For more information on the contribution of this genre on professional ethics (*ḥisba*) to the practice of medicine, see Levey 1963.

more interest in demonstrating the naturalness and transitional character of death and that it should not be treated as taboo or viewed as an ultimate end in itself.[10]

3.3 *Theology and Philosophy*

Belief in the hereafter (*maʿād/ākhira/qiyāma*) and related eschatological issues is integral to the main works on Islamic theology and philosophy. Although each discipline has its own distinctive approach and argumentative tools, they were grouped together here in one section because of the overlap in the relevant topics covered in both disciplines.

The hereafter is usually presented as a part of a broader worldview, where belief in the unity of God (*tawḥīd*) and prophethood (*nubuwwa*) conflate with belief in the hereafter. One can hardly think of any theological or philosophical work, where the hereafter was not one of its central themes. The agreed-upon aim was to show, through religious and/or rational modes of reasoning, that this life will necessarily come to an end and that in the hereafter people will be held accountable by God for what they did in this life (al-Baghdādī 2002, 255–270; al-Bazdawī 2003, 160–171; al-Ghazālī 2004b, 115–119; al-Bayḍāwī 1991, 220–234; al-Taftazānī 1998, 5:82–174; Ibn Khaldūn 1988, 1:580–591). Philosophical insights were particularly interested in rationalising the transition from this life to the hereafter and the process of resurrection (*baʿth*) and whether this will take place through only body, soul, or both (Ibn Sīnā 1984b; Ibn Sīnā 1984a; Ibn Sīnā 1960, 423–432; Ikhwān al-Ṣafā n.d.; Mullā Ṣadrā 1990, 9:121–381). The latter point proved to be a subject of intense disagreements between various theologians and philosophers, as exemplified in the works of al-Ghazālī and Ibn Rushd (d. 595/1198) (al-Ghazālī 1958, 282–306; Ibn Rushd 1993, 324–327).

Another relevant theme for the EoLC context is the belief that people die at a fixed moment (*ajal*), exclusively determined by the omnipotent God. Within this theme, theologians discuss the cases of homicide and whether the killer could modify the *ajal* of someone else, in addition to those who die because of terminal or malignant diseases and how far such a death could change their religious status into the commendable rank of martyr (*shahīd*) (al-Baghdādī 2002, 162–163; al-Taftazānī 1998, 4:314–317). In this sense, such theological and philosophical discussions can somehow be viewed as an extension for the parallel discussions in the abovementioned eschatological manuals, by

10 For an analytical overview of the diverse contemporary eschatological perspectives, see Smith and Haddad 2002, 99–146. For critical remarks about the study of Smith and Haddad and further insights, see Ryad 2017.

incorporating eschatology into the broader belief-system of Islam and showing how neatly these issues would fit into this system.

In his major work on Islamic theology and society, Josef van Ess provided one of the most comprehensive surveys of the diverse eschatological perspectives in early Islamic history, up to the third/ninth century (Van Ess 2017, 605–626). A great number of the studies on Islamic philosophy addressed the relevant eschatological perspectives (Michot 1986; ʿAbd al-Maqṣūd 1992; Jaffer 1998; Druart 2000; Jambet 2000; Jaffer 2003; De Callataÿ 2012; al-Kutubi 2015). Additionally, many of the publications outlined in the previous sections examined the diverse theological and philosophical perspectives on eschatology (e.g., Rüling 1895; Archer 2015; Günther 2016; Lange 2016a; Lange 2016b). As for reference works on Islamic theology and philosophy, some did not dedicate a chapter to eschatology (Adamson 2004; Schmidtke 2016; El-Rouayheb and Schmidtke 2016), whereas others did (Hermansen 2008).

Another important possible contribution from the disciplines of Islamic theology and philosophy comes from the rich discussions on theodicy. Under broad themes related to understanding the dichotomy of pain and pleasure in life, many theologians and philosophers from different schools provided a wide range of explanations on how to understand God's goodness, omnipotence, justice, and mercy in the light of the existence of pains and calamities that befall (innocent) people in this life (al-Ashʿarī 1977, 193–194; ʿAbd al-Jabbār 1996, 483–509; al-Baghdādī 2002, 264–265; al-Juwaynī 2009, 221–231; al-Zamakhsharī 2004, 14–16; Ibn Sīnā 1960, 414–422; al-Rāzī 1966, 387–400; al-Rāzī 1987, 4:411–427). Such questions have also been addressed in works on God's Names and Attributes (al-Ghazālī 1987, 64). These discussions are with direct relevance to EoLC theodical questions that both patients and their families would grapple with, as outlined above under the heading "Beyond Clinical Care" and may eventually affect their overall wellbeing.

The question of theodicy and related theological and philosophical deliberations in the Islamic tradition attracted the attention of many researchers (Ormsby 1984; Inati 2000; Shihadeh 2006, 155–170; Hoover 2007; Kalin 2007; Shihadeh 2019). Some works on disability and bioethics also touched upon the question of theodicy in a way that is more relevant to the EoLC context (Sachedina 2009, 77–100; Ghaly 2009, 17–53). The studies that contextualise the question of theodicy within EoLC are still quite few and do not show sufficient awareness of the above-mentioned rich and diverse discussions (Dein, Swinton and Abbas 2013, 202–204).

Various Muslim philosophers also provided their analyses for the question of death anxiety (*al-khawf min al-mawt*), as part of their broad interest in the phenomenon of sorrows and anxieties (*aḥzān/humūm*). Some of them also proposed practical and psychological "therapeutics" to ward off such anxiety. Examples of famous philosophers who were active in this area include al-Kindī (d. *c.*256/873), Abū Bakr al-Rāzī (d. *c.*312/925), Miskawayh (d. 421/1030) and Mullā Ṣadrā (d. *c.*1045/1635) (Badawī 1980, 6–32; al-Rāzī 1978, 120–123; Miskawayh n.d., 217–228; Mullā Ṣadrā 1990, 9:242–243; Van Riet 1963). The famous jurist Ibn Ḥazm (d. 456/1064) also wrote a concise treatise on this topic, in which he argued that death itself has no pain (Ibn Ḥazm 1983, 4:359–360). Some of these classical works were also the subject of translation and/or further analysis in modern publications (Butterworth 1992; Druart 1993; Jayyusi-Lehn 2002). It is to be noted here that some philosophers also explored the other side of the spectrum, namely those who are eager to terminate their life by committing suicide, sometimes because they feel that their human dignity is undermined or is completely missing (al-Tawḥīdī 1992, 215–221; Rosenthal 2015, 247–251).

Besides the mainstream philosophical works, insights of Muslim philosophers can be found in other types of literature, e.g., the famous allegorical work *Ḥayy Ibn Yaqẓān*, where death was depicted as one of the first lessons of metaphysics (Ibn Sīnā, Ibn Ṭufayl and Suhrawardī 1952).[11] Also, some philosophers recorded their accounts of losing their beloved ones, such as Abū l-ʿAlāʾ al-Maʿarrī (d. 449/1057) who wrote about his mother's death (al-Maʿarrī 1998, 28–33). Al-Maʿarrī also wrote the unique work, *Risālat al-Ghufrān* ("Epistle of Forgiveness"), in which he provided an imaginary and derisive depiction of the afterlife world, especially paradise and hellfire, and highlighted the significance of God's forgiveness for people's salvation (al-Maʿarrī 2012).

3.4 *Sufism*

The history and the very nature of Sufism make its contribution to the EoLC discussions self-evident, especially when it comes to the particular themes and questions outlined above under the heading "Beyond Clinical Care." Among many other distinctive aspects, this discipline is characterised by its distinctive approach to two main issues, both of which have direct relevance to the EoLC context.

The first issue has to do with the renunciation of this worldly life (*duynā*) and the necessity of keeping one's focus on the hereafter. To reflect the significance of this aspect, this discipline is known by the name of "science of the hereafter" (*ʿilm al-ākhira*) (al-Ghazālī 2004a, 1:13–16; Ibn Khaldūn 1988, 611–615). In the same vein is the famous Sufi metaphor that human beings

---

11 This work received incredible attention throughout history, including a great number of editions, translations, and analytical examinations (for examples, see Hourani 1956; Kukkonen 2016; Idris 2016; Somma 2021, 183–244).

experience this worldly life as if they are on a journey (*sayr*) whose destination is meeting God and ending up in paradise or hellfire. In this sense, humans should ideally behave as wayfarers (*sāʾirūn*) and try to collect as much provision (*zād*) as possible to avail them when they reach their destination (al-Ḥakīm al-Tirmidhī 1992, 3:123). The Sufi literature provides comprehensive, but not necessarily homogenous, analyses of the so-called states (*aḥwāl*) and stations (*maqāmāt*) that the "wayfarer" will go through during one's lifetime journey and how to excel in each phase. One of the evident purposes of this literature is to empower the believer to face and overcome difficulties in life, including sickness and facing the reality of death itself. Within this literature, the discussions on certain states and stations are quite relevant to the EoLC context, e.g., endurance and patience (*ṣabr*), contentment (*riḍā*), gratitude (*shukr*), repentance (*tawba*),[12] and trust in God (*tawakkul*) (al-Kharrāz 1988; al-Sarrāj 1960; al-Kalabādhī 1994; al-Makkī 2005; al-Kharkūshī 1999; al-Harawī n.d.; Ibn ʿAjība 2004). Some modern studies have made good attempts to approach this discourse as part of a spiritual/mystic psychology (Khalil 2012; Khalil 2014; Khalil 2016; Kaya 2016; Khalil 2018), which can be further employed in addressing specific EoLC questions.

The second distinctive issue relates to the Sufi understanding of human nature, where the significance of the inner (*bāṭin*) or spiritual component overrides that of the external (*ẓāhir*) or physical part (*jasad*).[13] While elaborating on each of the abovementioned states (*aḥwāl*) and stations, Sufi scholars highlight how the inner component of the human being can be disciplined, purified, and enhanced to overcome the various difficulties that the "wayfarer" will experience. One of the relevant psychological applications of this aspect within the EoLC context is the idea that feeling pain or pleasure is not just a physical process but something that one's soul has control over. Like one's body, which can be made stronger by doing physical exercises, one's soul can also grow stronger and become more immune to pain by performing spiritual

12 It is to be noted that the concept of *tawba* received considerable attention, from inside and outside Sufism. Some scholars dedicated distinct works to the various dimensions of this concept, some of which are closely related to the EoLC context such as deathbed repentance (see al-Muḥāsibī 1977; Ibn Abī l-Dunyā 1991a; 1991b; Maḥmūd 1998, 80, 82).

13 The inner/spiritual part was given different names, with different connotations, in Sufi literature, including *rūḥ, nafs* and *qalb* (see al-Ḥakīm al-Tirmidhī 1998; al-Ghazālī 2004a, 3:3–5). The concept of *rūḥ* received special attention, because of its close relation to the basic concept of life and death. The Ḥanbalī scholar, Ibn al-Qayyim (d. 751/1350) wrote one of the seminal book-length works on this concept in the Islamic tradition (Ibn al-Qayyim n.d.).

exercises.[14] Some works would also provide anecdotal or narrative ethics about what one may call the "etiquettes of dying," where they narrate how Sufi masters ideally faced their approaching death (al-Kharkūshī 1999, 542–550). Another benefit in this regard is the ability of the "purified" soul, developed by few saints and well-established scholars, to perceive and realise the reality of eschatological issues, which normally belong to the invisible world (*ghayb*), whose knowledge remains inaccessible to human intellect (*ʿaql*) (al-Hamadhānī 1962, 46).

Additionally, many of the statements and positions attributed to Sufi scholars about making use of medical interventions or therapeutics to cure (terminal) diseases are relevant to the above-outlined themes and questions under the heading "Medical (Non-)Intervention." As for what is written *about* Sufis, the so-called "extreme Sufis" (*ghulāt al-ṣūfiyya*) were criticised for their anti-treatment position (al-Nawawī 1972, 14:191). However, the works written *by* authoritative Sufi scholars show a much more nuanced position, where they explain that treating one's body should not be at the cost of one's spiritual well-being (al-Jīlānī 2007a, 1:94–95; al-Ḥakīm al-Tirmidhī 1992, 1:250–251, 402–406).

Sufi literature also contributed to the phenomenon of the fear of death and related anxiety, by elaborating on possible reasons and suggesting "therapeutics." One of the typically Sufi dimensions in this regard, on the one hand, is the stress on making the remembrance of, and preparing for, death an integral part of one's daily life. The one who succeeds in achieving this is usually called the smart person (*kayyis*), or the prudent (*ʿāqil*), in contrast to the one who fails to remain conscious of this fact, usually named the idiot (*aḥmaq*) (al-Ḥakīm al-Tirmidhī 1992, 1:421–425; al-Ghazālī 1964, 393–399). On the other hand, death anxiety, even when it reaches the intense level of panic (*jazaʿ*), was judged positively when the reason behind it was one's concern that death will prevent him/her from performing the religiously commendable practices (*ʿibādāt*) (Ibn al-Mubārak 2010, 1:94–95).

As for eschatology, some of the Sufi writings, which collated the relevant scriptural references and statements attributed to authoritative figures in Islamic history, were mentioned above in the section on "Eschatological Manuals." In his famous work on asceticism (*zuhd*), Ibn al-Mubārak (d. *c.*119/797) also used the same writing style, which is mainly premised on quotations, and included distinct sections on death and related eschatological issues

14 For Sufi perspectives on the relationship between body and soul, how this relationship would relate to pain and suffering, how the individual can understand the underlying theodicy and how to practically instrumentalise these difficulties for spiritual growth, see al-Ḥakīm al-Tirmidhī 1980, 56; Schimmel 1976; Ghaly 2009, 54–62; Rouzati 2018.

(Ibn al-Mubārak 2010, 2:39–42, 66–131). Furthermore, many Sufi writings provided distinctively Sufi commentaries and insights. This was sometimes done by underscoring moral messages related to the fact that this worldly life is worthless and too short to make us forget the need to work on our salvation in the hereafter (e.g., al-Muḥāsibī 1937; al-Ḥakīm al-Tirmidhī 1992, 1:88–92, 123–129, 175–187, 266–268, 284–286, 377–380, 413–414, 424–425, 2:100–106, 3:92–98, 4:159–163). Other works engaged with, and were sometimes influenced by, eschatological perspectives in other disciplines, especially theology and philosophy (e.g., al-Jīlānī 2007a, 1:140–155, 279–316; al-Hamadhānī 1962, 45–48; al-Suhrawardī 2010, 127–148).

One of the unique contributions made by Sufi literature was introducing a metaphorical use of eschatological terms, including death, *barzakh*, Doomsday, etc. The overall purpose here was creating particularly mystic connotations for these eschatological terms in order to frame a particular way of life that keeps the person continuously close to the spirit of the hereafter. For instance, "death" would mean severing one's relations with other creatures, as if he/she actually died, and only focusing instead on improving their relationship with God (al-Jīlānī 2007b, 61–62; Ibn al-ʿArabī 2010, 8:550–556). Yet, sometimes, the eschatological views of certain Sufis were considered so aberrant and heretic by other scholars to the extent that they were persecuted and even executed (al-Hamadhānī 1962).

As for modern studies, although the *Routledge Handbook on Sufism* did not have a distinct chapter on eschatology (Ridgeon 2021), many of the modern studies, which examined eschatological issues in the Islamic tradition, paid attention to the Sufi perspectives, especially their perception of paradise and hell (e.g., Günther 2016; Lange 2016a; Lange 2016b). Also, many of the studies on Sufism in general, or on specific Sufi scholars, examined relevant perspectives on eschatology (e.g., Chittick 1987; Chittick 1988; Corbin and Pearson 1990; Gianotti 2001; Papan-Matin 2010, 114–132; Csirkés 2011; Aminrazavi 2014, 41–44, 49–50; Lange 2014).

3.5 *Islamic Legal Theory* (Uṣūl) *and Jurisprudence* (Fiqh)

The health condition of the human body and one's mental capacity form part of the core interests of two interrelated scholarly disciplines, namely Islamic legal theory (*uṣūl al-fiqh*) and jurisprudence (*fiqh*). Both disciplines explore how Muslims should implement God's will, as expressed in His commandments and rulings, in their practical life. To enable individuals to live in accordance with His will, God tied the scope and volume of these commandments and rulings to one's mental capacity (*istiṭāʿa ʿaqliyya*), which enables the person to comprehend what God wants him/her (not) to do, and physical capacity (*qudra badaniyya*), which makes the individual able to execute these rulings (Ghaly 2019, 260).

Against this background, the works on Islamic legal theory, especially within the Ḥanafī school, provided extensive discussions on how one's physical and mental capacities relate to key concepts like religious obligation (*taklīf*) and legal capacity (*ahliyya*) (al-Dabūsī 2001, 420; al-Samʿānī 1999, 2:373). Further, these early discussions were represented in a way accessible to the modern reader, sometimes accompanied by showing their particular relevance to people with disabilities, comparisons with related legal and judiciary systems of healthcare in the Muslim world, and also with critical revisions of the conclusions of these early works in the light of updated knowledge produced by disciplines like physiology, psychology, and psychiatry (al-Nūrī 1954; Kīlānī 2002–2003; Arabi 2004; Hilāl 2011). Engaging with such diverse discussions is indispensable to addressing many of the questions that fall within the above-sketched theme of "Moral Agency."

As for Islamic jurisprudence (*fiqh*), one can safely say that this particular discipline has the greater share of both classical and modern works with relevance to EoLC issues. Almost all classical *fiqh* manuals have a distinct chapter entitled *al-Janāʾiz* (lit. "Funerals" or "Funerary Practices"), in addition to some modern distinct works featuring the same title, which usually provides a detailed juristic commentary on the Prophetic traditions included in a like-named chapter in the abovementioned *ḥadīth* collections. The standard contents of such a chapter usually cover a wide range of issues, starting from the moment of having a (terminal) disease and feeling that one's death is approaching, passing by the etiquettes of visiting the patients and what (not) to say to them, the rulings pertinent to washing, shrouding and burying the dead, and up to what one's close relatives, friends and wider circles should (not) do with the (terminal) patient and/or the dead (Wizārat al-Awqāf 1983–2006, 16:5–46; al-Albānī 1992; al-Qaḥṭānī 2003). EoLC researchers can thus extract substantial information for Muslim patients and families who ask how to frame their response to the tragedy of death within the parameters of their religious normativity.

Another distinctive aspect of the contributions made by the discipline of *fiqh* has to do with the interdisciplinary discussions, involving both biomedical scientists and Muslim jurists, which addressed many of the above-outlined direct EoLC questions under the heading "Medical (Non-)Intervention." These discussions form parts of the contemporary Islamic bioethical discourses facilitated by institutions like the Islamic Organization for Medical Sciences (IOMS), Islamic Fiqh Academy (IFA), and International Islamic Fiqh Academy (IIFA) (Ghaly et al. 2018).

3.6 Tasliya (*Consolation/Solace*) Genre

The EoLC context is usually marked by a multitude of "bad" news about misfortunes that many people, whether the patients or those who care about them, would name as a calamity or catastrophe (*muṣība*). Addressing the impact of such calamities on people's wellbeing necessitates engaging with people's inner concerns, values, and their broader moral world.

The Islamic tradition has a rich genre of works meant to console people with calamities (*tasliyat ahl al-maṣāʾib*), especially those related to (life-threatening) diseases, (approaching) death, and the demise of beloved ones. Broadly speaking, these works have a psychologically oriented agenda, viz., appeasing the bitter sorrow and anguish that such calamities can generate. Despite the non-clinical nature of their works, some authors would use plain medical language such as curing (*ʿilāj*) the adverse consequences of a calamity (*muṣība*), in addition to describing the afflicted person a patient (*ʿalīl*) and the one who tries to provide help a physician (*ṭabīb*) (Ibn al-Qayyim 1994, 4:173–180).

Besides chapters of varying lengths dispersed in various books (Ibn al-Qayyim 1989, 100–107; Ibn al-Qayyim 1994, 4:173–180; Ibn al-Qayyim 2011, 2:941–950), this genre has its own distinct works dedicated to the broad concept of *muṣība* (misfortune, calamity, affliction) (al-Manbijī 1929; al-Maqdisī 1993) or to a specific calamity, the most familiar of which was the death of one's child (Ibn al-Jawzī 1986; Ibn Nāṣir al-Dīn 1999; al-Dimashqī 1980; Gilʿadi 1989). Some of these works were written in response to the calamities generated by mass death events, such as plagues (al-Manbijī 1929, 3). Closely related to this genre are the works which defended the purposefulness of diseases and calamities in general, including their expiatory role and purging effect on the believers (Ibn Abī l-Dunyā 1991a; Ibn ʿAbd al-Salām 1992). The same holds true for the literary genre known as the deliverance-after-hardship (*al-faraj baʿd al-shidda*). These works are also characterised by their hope-giving and optimism-spreading agenda, which underscores the message of the Qurʾānic verse "So truly with hardship comes ease" (Q 94:5) (al-Tanūkhī 1978; al-Tanūkhī 2019; Moebius 2008; Khalifa 2010; Pomerantz 2016). All these diverse works can be utilised to develop well-tailored counseling mechanisms and other forms of psychological support for the EoLC context of today's world.

4 Concluding Remarks

Since its birth as a modern discipline in the second half of the twentieth century, End-of-Life-Care (EoLC) has always been seen as an interdisciplinary field that should pay attention not only to the medical condition of the "patient" but to the overall wellbeing of the "whole person." To properly address the various EoLC ethical questions and challenges argued in this study, Islamic ethical deliberations should be premised on an interdisciplinary approach that engages with the broad spectrum of scholarly disciplines rooted in the Islamic tradition.

In order to provide interested researchers with the necessary tools to develop such a desired interdisciplinary approach, the study started with a systematic overview of the key ethical questions and issues raised by the EoLC field. The long list of questions and issues was divided into five broad themes, namely eschatology, medical (non-)intervention, beyond clinical care, moral agency, and communication issues.

The greater part of the study was dedicated to delineating how various scholarly disciplines and genres, developed throughout the history of the Islamic tradition, can contribute to an interdisciplinary Islamic EoLC discourse. Because of their particular significance and influence on the entire Islamic scholarly tradition, this chapter began by reviewing the relevant scriptural references in the Qur'ān and Sunna. Additionally, the study elaborated on how EoLC ethical questions and issues, outlined in the abovementioned themes, can be addressed with the help of the rich literature produced respectively by eschatological manuals, the disciplines of Islamic theology, philosophy, Sufism, Islamic legal theory and jurisprudence, and the genre of works dedicated to consoling and comforting people with calamities and misfortunes. In each of these disciplines and genres, the study provided a representative repertoire of both classical sources and modern studies.

I conclude this study by stressing two main remarks with the aim of streamlining future research. First, the majority of the works reviewed in this study, although quite relevant, are still in need of "translational" studies, to borrow from the biomedical terminology, in order to integrate them within the EoLC discourse. Most of these works are written for the audience of religious/Islamic studies, not for terminal patients, their families, healthcare professionals, bioethicists, or the broader EoLC audience. Researchers interested in EoLC questions and themes should dig into these sources and re-read them through the meticulous lens of EoLC. Second, the great number of sources outlined in this study and their interdisciplinary and diverse scope demonstrate the feasibility of the repeated calls to move from the currently thin, monodisciplinary, and *fiqhī*-dominant discourse to the desired thick and interdisciplinary Islamic bioethics discourse. The hope is that further studies will undertake this venture and apply it to other bioethical topics.

5 Appendix

TABLE 1.1 The recurrence of the term death (*mawt*) in the nine canonical collections of *ḥadīth*[a]

Compiler of the collection	Number of occurrences
al-Bukhārī (d. 256/870)	241
Muslim (d. 261/875)	145
Ibn Māja (273/887)	159
Abū Dāwūd (d. 275/889)	155
al-Tirmidhī (279/892)	133
al-Nasāʾī (d. 303/915)	180
Mālik b. Anas (d. 179/795)	47
Aḥmad b. Ḥanbal (d. 241/855)	757
al-Dārimī (d. 255/869)	180
Total	1891

a The numbers given in this table are based on *al-Muʿjam al-Mufahras li-Alfāẓ al-Ḥadīth al-Nabawī*, which surveyed the nine collections of *ḥadīth* (Wensinck 1936).

TABLE 1.2 Theme-based survey of death and related eschatological terms in *ḥadīth*

Compiler of the collection	Chapter/Section title	Relevant EoLC theme
	(A) Chapters (*kutub*)	
al-Bukhārī (d. 256/870)	Funerals (*janāʾiz*)	– Eschatology – Beyond clinical care
	Patients (*marḍā*)	– Eschatology – Medical (non-)intervention
	Medicine (*ṭibb*)	– Medical (non-)intervention – Moral agency
	Softening One's Heart (*riqāq*)	– Beyond clinical care
Muslim (d. 261/875)	Funerals (*janāʾiz*)	– Eschatology – Beyond clinical care
	Characteristics of the Day of Judgment, Paradise and Hell (*ṣifat al-qiyāma wa-l-janna wa-l-nār*)	– Eschatology
	Paradise, the Characteristics of its Delights and Inhabitants (*al-janna wa-ṣifat naʿīmihā wa-ahlihā*)	– Eschatology
	Repentance (*tawba*)	– Beyond clinical care
	(B) Sections (*abwāb*)	
al-Bukhārī (d. 256/870)	Giving Charity by the Time of Death (*al-ṣadaqa ʿind al-mawt*)	– Moral agency – Beyond clinical care
	Supplication for Death or Life (*al-duʿāʾ bi-l-mawt wa-l-ḥayāt*)	– Eschatology
	Euphemisms are Safe Alternatives to Avoid Lying (*al-maʿārīḍ mandūḥa ʿan al-kadhib*)	– Communication issues
	Repentance (*tawba*)	– Beyond clinical care
Muslim (d. 261/875)	Recommendation to Seek Refuge [in Allah] from the Punishment of the Grave (*istiḥbāb al-taʿawwudh min ʿadhāb al-qabr*)	– Eschatology
	Reprehensibility of Wishing Death because of some Harm that has Befallen Him (*karāhat tamannī l-mawt li-ḍurr nazal bih*)	– Eschatology – Beyond clinical care
	Vastness of God's Mercy and that it Prevails Over His Wrath (*siʿat raḥmat Allah taʿālā wa-annahā sabaqat ghaḍabah*)	– Eschatology – Beyond clinical care
	Medicine, Sickness and Incantation (*al-ṭibb wa-l-maraḍ wa-l-ruqya*)	– Beyond clinical care
	For Every Disease there is a Remedy, and the Recommendation to Seek Treatment (*li-kull dāʾ dawāʾ wa-istiḥbāb al-tadāwī*)	– Medical (non-)intervention
	Reprehensibility to Forcibly Administer Medicine in the Side of the Patient's Mouth (*karāhat al-tadāwī bi-l-ladūd*)	– Moral agency – Medical (non-)intervention

Bibliography

ʿAbd al-Bāqī, Muḥammad. 1945. *Al-Muʿjam al-Mufahras li-Alfāẓ al-Qurʾān al-Karīm.* Cairo: Dār al-Ḥadīth.

ʿAbd al-Jabbār. 1996. *Sharḥ al-Uṣūl al-Khamsa*, edited by ʿAbd al-Karīm ʿUthmān. Cairo: Maktabat Wahba.

ʿAbd al-Maqṣūd, ʿAbd al-Ghanī. 1992. "Mushkilat al-Khulūd ʿinda Ibn Sīna wa-Atharuhā fī Fahmih lil-Maʿād." *Majallat Kulliyyat Dār al-ʿUlūm* 15: 1–48.

Abdel Haleem, Muhammed. 2017. "Quranic Paradise: How to Get to Paradise and What to Expect There." In *Roads to Paradise: Eschatology and Concepts of the Hereafter in Islam*, edited by Sebastian Günther and Todd Lawson, 47–66. Leiden: Brill.

Abdul-Jabbar, Ghassan. 2020. "Collections." In *The Wiley Blackwell Concise Companion to the Hadith*, edited by Daniel W. Brown, 137–158. Hoboken, NJ: John Wiley and Sons.

Adamson, Peter. 2004. *The Cambridge Companion to Arabic Philosophy.* Cambridge: Cambridge University Press.

al-Albānī, Muḥammad Nāṣir al-Dīn. 1992. *Aḥkām al-Janāʾiz wa-Bidaʿuhā.* Riyad: Maktabat al-Maʿārif.

Almagor, Ella A. 1973. "'*Kitab Dhamm al-Dunya*' by Ibn Abi al-Dunya edited and annotated, with an introduction." PhD diss., University of California, Los Angeles.

Aminrazavi, Mehdi. 2014. *Suhrawardi and the School of Illumination.* London: Routledge.

Arabi, Oussama. 2004. "The Regimentation of the Subject: Madness in Islamic and Modern Arab Civil Laws." In *Standing Trial: Law and the Person in the Modern Middle East*, edited by Baudouin Dupret, 264–293. London: I.B. Tauris.

Archer, George. 2015. "A Place Between Two Places: The Qur'an's Intermediate State and the Early History of the Barzakh." PhD diss., Georgetown University.

al-Ashʿarī, Abū l-Ḥasan. 1977. *Al-Ibāna ʿan Uṣūl al-Diyāna*, edited by Fawqiyya Ḥusayn Maḥmūd. Cairo: Dār al-Anṣār.

Badawī, ʿAbd al-Raḥmān. 1980. *Rasāʾil Falsafiyya lil-Kindī wa-l-Farābī wa-Ibn Bāja wa-Ibn ʿAdī.* Beirut: Dār al-Andalus lil-Ṭibāʿa wa-l-Nashr.

Badawi, Elsaid and Muhammed Abdel Haleem. 2008. *Arabic-English Dictionary of Qurʾanic Usage.* Leiden: Brill.

al-Baghdādī, ʿAbd al-Qāhir. 2002. *Uṣūl al-Dīn*, edited by Aḥmad Shams al-Dīn. Beirut: Dār al-Kutub al-ʿIlmiyya.

al-Bayḍāwī. 1991. *Ṭawāliʿ al-Anwār min Maṭāliʿ al-Anẓār*, edited by ʿAbbās Sulaymān. Cairo: Maktabat al-Turāth and Beirut: Dār al-Jīl.

al-Bayhaqī. 1986. *Al-Baʿth wa-l-Nushūr*, edited by ʿĀmir Aḥmad Ḥaydar. Beirut: Markaz al-Khadamāt wa-l-Abḥāth al-Thaqāfiyya.

al-Bazdawī. 2003. *Uṣūl al-Dīn*, edited by Hans Lenis. Cairo: al-Maktaba al-Azhariyya lil-Turāth.

Becker, Ernest. 1975. *The Denial of Death*. New York: The Free Press.

Borrmans, Maurice. 2006. "Resurrection." In *Encyclopaedia of the Qurʾān*. https://referenceworks.brillonline.com/entries/encyclopaedia-of-the-quran/resurrection-EQSIM_00356.

al-Bukhārī. 2001. *Ṣaḥīḥ al-Bukhārī*, edited by Muḥammad Zuhayr b. Nāṣir al-Nāṣir. Beirut: Dār Ṭawq al-Najāt.

Butterworth, Charles. 1992. "Al-Kindī and the Beginning of Islamic Philosophy." In *The Political Aspects of Islamic Philosophy: Essays in Honor of Muhsin S. Mahdi*, edited by Charles Butterworth, 11–60. Cambridge, MA: Harvard University Press.

Chittick, William C. 1987. "Rumi's View of Death." *Alserat* 13: 30–51.

Chittick, William C. 1988. "Death and the World of Imagination: Ibn Al-ʿArabī's Eschatology." *The Muslim World* 78(1): 51–82.

Chittick, William C. 2008. "Muslim Eschatology." In *The Oxford Handbook of Eschatology*, edited by Jerry Walls, 132–150. Oxford: Oxford University Press.

Corbin, Henry and Nancy Pearson. 1990. *Spiritual Body and Celestial Earth: From Mazdean Iran to Shīʿite Iran*. London: I.B. Tauris.

Csirkés, Ferenc. 2011. "Mystical love as the day of judgement. Eschatology in Jalāl al-Dīn Rūmī's Dīvān-i Kabīr." *Acta Orientalia Academiae Scientiarum Hungaricae* 64(3): 305–324.

al-Dabūsī. 2001. *Taqwīm al-Adilla fī Uṣūl al-Fiqh*, edited by Khalīl Muḥyī l-Dīn. Beirut: Dār al-Kutub al-ʿIlmiyya.

De Callataÿ, Godefroid. 2012. *Ikhwan al-Safaʾ: A Brotherhood of Idealists on the Fringe of Orthodox Islam*. Oxford: Oneworld.

Dein, Simon, John Swinton and Syed Qamar Abbas. 2013. "Theodicy and End-of-Life Care." *Journal of Social Work in End-of-Life & Palliative Care* 9(2–3): 191–208.

al-Dimashqī, Ibn Nāṣir al-Dīn. 1980. *Bard al-Akbād ʿinda Faqd al-Awlād*. Cairo: n.p.

Druart, Thérèse-Anne. 1993. "Al-Kindi's Ethics." *The Review of Metaphysics* 47: 329–357.

Druart, Thérèse-Anne. 2000. "The Human Soul's Individuation and its Survival after the Body's Death: Avicenna on the Causal Relation between Body and Soul." *Arabic Sciences and Philosophy* 10(2): 259–273.

Eklund, Ragnar. 1941. *Life Between Death and Resurrection According to Islam*. Uppsala: Almqvist & Wiksells.

El-Rouayheb, Khaled and Sabine Schmidtke, eds. 2016. *The Oxford Handbook of Islamic Philosophy*. Oxford: Oxford University Press.

Fairman, Nathan and Scott A. Irwin. 2016. "Depression and the Desire to Die Near the End of Life." In *The Oxford Handbook of Ethics at the End of Life*, edited by Stuart J. Youngne and Robert M. Arnold, 389–408. Oxford: Oxford University Press.

Fallon, Marie and J. Smyth. 2008. "Terminology: The Historical Perspective, Evolution and Current Usage – Room for Confusion?" *European Journal of Cancer* 44(8): 1069–1071.

Galloway, Dalton. 1922. "The Resurrection and Judgment in the Kor'an." *The Muslim World* 12(4): 348–372.

Ghaly, Mohammed. 2009. *Islam and Disability: Perspectives in Theology and Jurisprudence*. London: Routledge.

Ghaly, Mohammed. 2019. "The Convention on the Rights of Persons with Disabilities and the Islamic Tradition: The question of Legal Capacity in Focus." *Journal of Disability & Religion* 23(3): 251–278.

Ghaly, Mohammed, Randi R. Diamond, Maha El-Akoum and Azza Hassan. 2018. *Palliative Care and Islamic Ethics: Exploring Key Issues and Best Practice*. Doha: World Innovation Summit for Health.

al-Ghazālī, Abū Ḥāmid. 1878. *La perle précieuse (ad-dourra al-fâkhira) de Ghazālī. Traité d'eschatologie musulmane*, edited and translated by Lucien Gautier. Geneva: H. Georg.

al-Ghazālī, Abū Ḥāmid. 1958. *Tahāfut al-Falāsifa*, edited by Sulaymān Dunyā. Cairo: Dār al-Maʿārif.

al-Ghazālī, Abū Ḥāmid. 1964. *Mīzān al-ʿAmal*, edited by Sulaymān Dunyā. Cairo: Dār al-Maʿārif.

al-Ghazālī, Abū Ḥāmid. 1987. *Al-Maqṣad al-Asnā fī Sharḥ Maʿānī Asmāʾ Allāh al-Ḥusnā*, edited by Bassām ʿAbd al-Wahhāb al-Jābī. Limasol: al-Jaffān wa-l-Jābī.

al-Ghazālī, Abū Ḥāmid. 1989. *The Remembrance of Death and the Afterlife. Book XL of the Revival of the Religious Sciences*, translated by T.J. Winter. Cambridge: The Islamic Texts Society.

al-Ghazālī, Abū Ḥāmid. 2004a. *Iḥyāʾ ʿUlūm al-Dīn*, edited by Badawī Ṭibāna. Beirut: Dār al-Maʿrifa.

al-Ghazālī, Abū Ḥāmid. 2004b. *Al-Iqtiṣād fī l-Iʿtiqād*, edited by ʿAbd Allāh Muḥammad al-Khalīlī. Beirut: Dār al-Kutub al-ʿIlmiyya.

Gianotti, Timothy. 2001. *Al-Ghazālī's Unspeakable Doctrine of the Soul: Unveiling the Esoteric Psychology and Eschatology of the Iḥyāʾ*. Leiden: Brill.

Gilʿadi, Avner. 1989. "'Ṣabr' (Steadfastness) of Bereaved Parents: A Motif in Medieval Muslim Consolation Treatises and Some Parallels in Jewish Writings." *The Jewish Quarterly Review* 1(2): 35–48.

Günther, Sebastian. 2016. "'Die Menschen schlafen, und wenn sie sterben, erwachen sie': Eschatologische Vorstellungen im Koran." In *Gottesgedanken: Erkenntnis, Eschatologie und Ethik in Religionen der Spätantike und des frühen Mittelalters*, edited by Reinhard Feldmeier, Monika Wine tand Isabel Toral-Niehoff, 113–122. Tübingen: Mohr Siebeck.

Günther, Sebastian. 2017. "The Poetics of Islamic Eschatology: Narrative, Personification, and Colors in Muslim Discourse." In *Roads to Paradise: Eschatology and Concepts of the Hereafter in Islam*, edited by Sebastian Günther and Todd Lawson, 181–217. Leiden: Brill.

Günther, Sebastian. 2020a. "'When the Sun is Shrouded in Darkness and the Stars are Dimmed' (Qur'an 81: 1–2). Imagery, Rhetoric and Doctrinal Instruction in Muslim Apocalyptic Literature." In *Cultures of Eschatology*, edited by Veronika Wieser, Vincent Eltschinger and Johann Heiss, volume 1, 66–83. Berlin: De Gruyter.

Günther, Sebastian. 2020b. "Eschatology and the Qur'an." In *The Oxford Handbook of Qur'anic Studies*, edited by Mustafa Shah and Muhammad Abdel Haleem, 472–487. Oxford: Oxford University Press.

Günther, Sebastian and Todd Lawson, eds. 2016. *Roads to Paradise: Eschatology and Concepts of the Hereafter in Islam*. Leiden: Brill.

Gwynne, Rosalind W. 2006. "Hell and Hellfire." In *Encyclopaedia of the Qurʾān*. DOI: 10.1163/1875-3922_q3_EQCOM_00083.

al-Ḥakīm al-Tirmidhī. 1980. *Al-Masāʾil al-Maknūna*, edited by Muḥammad Ibrāhīm al-Juyūshī. Cairo: Dār al-Turāth al-ʿArabī.

al-Ḥakīm al-Tirmidhī. 1992. *Nawādir al-Uṣūl*, edited by ʿAbd al-Raḥmān ʿAmīra. Beirut: Dār al-Jīl.

al-Ḥakīm al-Tirmidhī. 1998. *Bayān al-Farq bayna al-Ṣadr wa-l-Qalb wa-l-Fuʾād wa-l-Lubb*, edited by Aḥmad ʿAbd al-Raḥīm al-Sayyāḥ. Cairo: Markaz al-Kitāb lil-Nashr.

al-Hamadhānī, ʿAyn al-Quḍāt. 1962. *Risālat Shakwā al-Gharīb*. Tehran: Tehran University Press.

al-Harawī, al-Anṣārī. n.d. *Manāzil al-Sāʾirīn*. Beirut: Dār al-Kutub al-ʿIlmiyya.

Hasson, Issac. 2006. "Last Judgment." In *Encyclopaedia of the Qurʾān*. DOI: 10.1163/1875-3922_q3_EQCOM_00105.

Hermansen, Marcia. 2008. "Eschatology." In *The Cambridge Companion to Classical Islamic Theology*, edited by Tim Winter, 308–324. Cambridge: Cambridge University Press.

Hilāl, Hudā. 2011. *Naẓariyyat al-Ahliyya: Dirāsa Taḥlīliyya Muqārina bayna al-Fiqh wa-ʿIlm al-Nafs*. Herndon, VA: al-Maʿhad al-ʿĀlamī lil-Fikr al-Islāmī.

Hoover, Jon. 2007. *Ibn Taymiyya's Theodicy of Perpetual Optimism*. Leiden: Brill.

Horovitz, Josef. 1923. *Das Koranische Paradies*. Frankfurt am Main: Hierosolymis.

Hourani, George. 1956. "The Principal Subject of Ibn Ṭufayl's Ḥayy Ibn Yaqẓān." *Journal of Near Eastern Studies* 15(1): 40–46.

Hutchinson, Thomas A. 2011. *Whole Person Care: A New Paradigm for the 21st Century*. New York: Springer.

Ibn ʿAbd al-Salām, al-ʿIzz. 1992. *Al-Fitan wa-l-Balāya wa-l-Miḥan wa-l-Razāyā*, edited by Iyād Khālid al-Ṭabbāʿ. Damascus: Dār al-Fikr and Beirut: Dār al-Fikr al-Muʿāṣir.

Ibn Abī l-Dunyā. 1991a. *Kitāb al-Maraḍ wa-l-Kaffārāt*, edited by ʿAbd al-Wakīl al-Nadwī. Bombay: al-Dār al-Salafiyya.

Ibn Abī l-Dunyā. 1991b. *Kitāb al-Tawba*, edited by Majdī l-Sayyid Ibrāhīm. Cairo: Maktabat al-Qurʾān.

Ibn Abī l-Dunyā. 2002. *Dhikr al-Mawt*, edited by Mashhūr b. Ḥasan Salmān. ʿAjmān: Maktabat al-Furqān.

Ibn Abī l-Dunyā. 2012. *Mawsūʿat Ibn Abī l-Dunyā*, edited by Fāḍil al-Raqqī. Riyad: Dār Aṭlas al-Khaḍrāʾ lil-Nashr wa-l-Tawzīʿ.

Ibn Abī Dāwūd. 1987. *Al-Baʿth wa-l-Nushūr*, edited by Muḥammad al-Saʿīd Basyūnī. Beirut: Dār al-Kutub al-ʿIlmiyya.

Ibn ʿAjība. 2004. *Miʿrāj al-Tashawwuf ilā Ḥaqāʾiq al-Taṣawwuf*, edited by ʿAbd al-Majīd Khayālī. Casablanca: Markaz al-Turāth al-Thaqāfī l-Maghribī.

Ibn al-ʿArabī, Muhyī l-Dīn. 2010. *Al-Futūḥāt al-Makkiyya*. Sanaa: Ministry of Culture.

Ibn Ḥazm. 1983. *Rasāʾil Ibn Ḥazm al-Andalusī*, edited by Iḥsān ʿAbbās. Beirut: al-Muʾassasa al-ʿArabiyya lil-Dirāsāt wa-l-Nashr.

Ibn al-Jawzī. 1986. *Al-Thabāt ʿinda al-Mamāt*, edited by ʿAbd Allāh al-Laythī l-Anṣarī. Beirut: Muʾassasat al-Kutub al-Thaqāfiyya.

Ibn Khaldūn. 1988. *Dīwān al-Mubtadaʾ wa-l-Khabar*, edited by Khalīl Shiḥāda. Beirut: Dār al-Fikr.

Ibn al-Mubārak. 2010. *Al-Zuhd wa-l-Raqāʾiq*, edited by Ḥabīb al-Raḥmān al-Aʿẓamī. Beirut: Dār al-Kutub al-ʿIlmiyya.

Ibn Mūsā, Asad. 1993. *Kitāb al-Zuhd*, edited by Abū Isḥāq al-Ḥuwaynī. Cairo: Maktabat al-Tawʿiya al-Islāmiyya and Maktabat al-Waʿy al-Islāmī.

Ibn Nāṣir al-Dīn. 1999. *Bard al-Akbād ʿinda Faqd al-Awlād*. Riyad: Dār Ibn Khuzayma lil-Nashr wa-l-Tawzīʿ.

Ibn al-Qayyim. n.d. *Al-Rūḥ*. Beirut: Dār al-Kutub al-ʿIlmiyya.

Ibn al-Qayyim. 1989. *ʿUddat al-Ṣābirīn wa-Dhakhīrat al-Shākirīn*. Damascus: Dār Ibn Kathīr.

Ibn al-Qayyim. 1994. *Zād al-Maʿād fī Hady Khayr al-ʿIbād*. Beirut: Muʾassasat al-Risāla and Kuwait: Maktabat al-Manār al-Islāmiyya.

Ibn al-Qayyim. 2011. *Ighāthat al-Lahfān fī Maṣāʾid al-Shayṭān*. Mecca: Dār ʿĀlam al-Fawāʾid.

Ibn Rajab. 2002. *Al-Takhwīf min al-Nār wa-l-Taʿrīf bi-Ḥāl Dār Ahl al-Bawār*, edited by ʿAbd Allāh Salām. Beirut: Dār al-Kutub al-ʿIlmiyya.

Ibn Rajab. 2012. *Ahwāl al-Qubūr wa-Aḥwāl Ahilhā ilā l-Nushūr*, edited by Muḥammad Niẓām al-Dīn al-Fatīḥ. Medina: Dār al-Zamān.

Ibn Rushd. 1993. *Tahāfut al-Tahāfut*, edited by Muḥammad al-ʿUraybī. Beirut: Dār al-Fikr al-Lubnānī.

Ibn Sīnā. 1960. *Al-Shifāʾ/al-Ilāhiyyāt*, edited by Jūrj Qanawātī and Saʿīd Zāyid. Cairo: Al-Hayʾa al-ʿĀmma li-Shuʾūn al-Maṭābiʿ al-Amīriyya.

Ibn Sīnā. 1984a. *Al-Aḍḥawiyya fī l-Maʿād*. Tehran: Tehran University.

Ibn Sīnā. 1984b. *Al-Mabdaʾ wa-l-Maʿād*, reviewed by ʿAbd Allāh Nawrānī. Tehran: Tehran University.

Ibn Sīnā, Ibn Ṭufayl and Suhrawardī. 1952. *Ḥayy Ibn Yaqẓān*. Cairo: Dār al-Maʿārif.

Idris, Murad. 2016. "Producing Islamic Philosophy: The Life and Afterlives of Ibn Ṭufayl's Ḥayy ibn Yaqẓān in Global History, 1882–1947." *European Journal of Political Theory* 15(4): 382–403.

Ikhwān al-Ṣafā. n.d. *Rasāʾil Ikhwān al-Ṣafā*. Online version available at www.al-mostafa .com/.

Inati, Shams C. 2000. *The Problem of Evil: Ibn Sina's Theodicy*. Global Academic Publishing.

Jaffer, Tariq. 1998. "Avicenna and the Resurrection of the Body." MA thesis, McGill University.

Jaffer, Tariq. 2003. "Bodies, Souls and Resurrection in Avicenna's *ar-Risāla al-Aḍḥawīya fī Amr al-Maʿād*." In *Before and after Avicenna: Proceedings of the First Conference of the Avicenna Study Group*, edited by David Colum Reisman, 361–174. Leiden: Brill.

Jambet, Christian. 2000. *Se rendre immortel, suivi du Traité de la résurrection de Mollâ Sadrâ Shîrâzî*. Saint-Clément: Fata Morgana.

Jayyusi-Lehn, Ghada. 2002. "The Epistle of Yaʿqūb ibn Isḥāq al-Kindī on the Device for Dispelling Sorrows." *British Journal of Middle Eastern Studies* 29(2): 121–135.

al-Jīlānī, ʿAbd al-Qādir. 2007a. *Al-Ghunya li-Ṭālibī Ṭarīq al-Ḥaqq ʿAzza wa-Jall*. Beirut: Dār al-Kutub al-ʿIlmiyya.

al-Jīlānī, ʿAbd al-Qādir. 2007b. *Futūḥ al-Ghayb*, edited by ʿAbd al-ʿAlīm Muḥammad Darwīsh. Cairo: Dār al-Hādī and Maktabat Dār al-Zāhir.

al-Jundī, Fatḥī. 1997. *Al-Tadhkira fī Aḥwāl al-Mawtā wa-Umūr al-Ākhira*. Riyad: Dār al-ʿĀṣima.

al-Juwaynī. 2009. *Al-Irshād ilā Qawāṭiʿ al-Adilla min Uṣūl al-Iʿtiqād*, edited by Aḥmad ʿAbd al-Raḥīm al-Sayyāḥ and Tawfīq ʿAlī Wahba. Cairo: Maktabat al-Thaqāfa al-Dīniyya.

al-Kalabādhī. 1994. *Al-Taʿarruf li-Madhhab Ahl al-Taṣawwuf*. Cairo: Maktabat al-Khanjī.

Kalin, Ibrahim. 2007. "Mullā Ṣadrā on Theodicy and the Best of All Possible Worlds." *Journal of Islamic Studies* 18(2): 183–201.

Kaya, Çinar. 2016. "Rumi from the Viewpoint of Spiritual Psychology and Counseling." *Spiritual Psychology and Counseling* 1(1): 9–25.

Khalifa, Nouha. 2010. *Hardship and Deliverance in the Islamic Tradition: Theology and Spirituality in the Works of al-Tanūkhī*. London: I.B. Tauris.

Khalil, Atif. 2012. "*Tawba* in the Sufi Psychology of Abū Ṭālib Al-Makkī (d. 996)." *Journal of Islamic Studies* 23(3): 294–324.

Khalil, Atif. 2014. "Contentment, Satisfaction and Good-Pleasure: *Rida* in Early Sufi Moral Psychology." *Studies in Religion/Sciences Religieuses* 43(3): 371–380.

Khalil, Atif. 2016. "The Embodiment of Gratitude (*Shukr*) in Sufi Ethics." *Studia Islamica* 111(2): 159–178.

Khalil, Atif. 2018. *Repentance and the Return to God: Tawba in Early Sufism*. New York: Suny Press.

al-Kharkūshī. 1999. *Kitāb Tahdhīb al-Asrār*, edited by Bassām Muḥammad Bārūd. Abu Dhabi: al-Majmaʿ al-Thaqāfī.

al-Kharrāz. 1988. *Kitāb al-Ṣidq*, edited by ʿAbd al-Ḥalīm Maḥmūd. Cairo: Dār al-Maʿārif.

Kīlānī, S. 2002–2003. "Ahliyyat al-Muʿawwaq lil-Taklīf bi-l-Aḥkām al-Sharʿiyya." *Riʿāyat al-Islām li-Dhawī l-Iḥtiyājāt al-Khāṣṣa: Al-Muʾtamar al-ʿIlmī l-Rābiʿ li-Kulliyyat al-Sharīʿa bi-Jāmiʿat Jarash*. Jerash: Jerash University.

Kinberg, Leah. 2006. "Paradise." In *Encyclopaedia of the Qurʾān*. DOI: 10.1163/1875-3922_q3_EQCOM_00143.

Kirk, Timothy W., Nessa Coyle and Matthew Doolittle. 2015. "Communication Ethics." In *Textbook of Palliative Care Communication*, edited by Elaine Wittenberg, Betty R. Ferrell, Joy Goldsmith, Thomas Smith, Sandra Ragan, Myra Glajchen and the Rev George F. Handzo, 27–34. Oxford: Oxford University Press.

Kogan, Ilany. 2010. "Fear of Death: Analyst and Patient in the Same Boat." In *The Wound of Mortality: Fear, Denial, and Acceptance of Death*, edited by Salman Akhtar, 79–96. Lanham: Rowman & Littlefield.

Kukkonen, Taneli. 2016. "Ḥayy ibn Yaqẓān." In *The Oxford Handbook of Islamic Philosophy*, edited by Khaled El-Rouayheb and Sabine Schmidtke, 233–254. Oxford: Oxford University Press.

al-Kutubi, Eiyad. 2015. *Mullā Ṣadra and Eschatology: Evolution of Being*. London: Routledge.

Lalani, Arzina. 2006. "Judgment." In *Encyclopaedia of the Qurʾān*. DOI: 10.1163/1875-3922_q3_EQCOM_00244.

Lange, Christian. 2014. "A Sufi's Paradise and Hell: Azīz-i Nasafīs (fl. mid-7th/13th c.) Epistle on the Otherworld." In *No Tapping Around Philology: Festschrift in Honor of Wheeler McIntosh Thackston Jr.'s 70th Birthday*, edited by Alireza Korangy and Daniel J. Sheffield, 193–214. Wiesbaden: Harrassowitz.

Lange, Christian. 2016a. *Paradise and Hell in Islamic Traditions*. Cambridge: Cambridge University Press.

Lange, Christian. 2016b. "Revisiting Hell's Angels in the Quran." In *Locating Hell in Islamic Traditions*, edited by Christian Lange, 74–99. Brill.

Leaman, Oliver, ed. 2006. *The Qur'an: An Encyclopedia*. London: Routledge.

Levey, Martin. 1963. "Fourteenth Century Muslim Medicine and the *Ḥisba*." *Medical History* 7(2): 176–182.

Levey, Martin. 1967. *Medical Ethics of Medieval Islam with Special Reference to Al-Ruhāwī's "Practical Ethics of the Physician."* Philadelphia: The American Philosophical Society.

al-Maʿarrī. 1998. *Rasāʾil Abī l-ʿAlāʾ l-Maʿarrī*, edited by Geert Jan van Gelder. Oxford: Clarendon Press.

al-Maʿarrī. 2012. *Risālat al-Ghufrān*. Cairo: Muʾassasat Hindāwī lil-Taʿlīm wa-l-Thaqāfa.

MacAuliffe, Jane Dammen. 2007. *The Cambridge Companion to the Qurʾān*. Cambridge: Cambridge University Press.

Maḥmūd, ʿAbd al-Ḥalīm. 1998. *Ustādh al-Sāʾirīn*. Cairo: Dār al-Maʿārif.

al-Makkī, Abū Ṭālib. 2005. *Qūt al-Qulūb*, edited by ʿĀṣim Ibrāhīm al-Kayalī. Beirut: Dār al-Kutub al-ʿIlmiyya.

al-Manbijī. 1929. *Tasliyat Ahl al-Maṣāʾib*. Cairo: Maktabat al-Khanjī.

al-Maqdisī, ʿAlāʾ al-Dīn. 1993. "Al-Lubāb fī Tasliyat al-Muṣāb." *Majallat al-Ḥikma* 2: 125–159.

Meyers, Karen, Robert Golden and Fred Peterson. 2009. *The Truth About Death and Dying*. New York: Facts On File.

Michot, Jean. 1986. *La destinée de l'homme selon Avicenna*. Louvain: Peeters.

Miskawayh. n.d. *Tahdhīb al-Akhlāq wa-Taṭhīr al-Aʿrāq*, edited by Ibn al-Khaṭīb. Cairo: Maktabat al-Thaqāfa al-Dīniyya.

Moebius, Marc H. 2008. "Narrative Judgments: The Qādī l-Tanūkhī and the "Faraj" Genre in Medieval Arabic Literature." PhD diss., Princeton University.

al-Muḥāsibī, al-Ḥārith. 1937. *Kitāb al-Tawahhum*, reviewed by A.J. Arberry. Cairo: Maṭbaʿat Lajnat al-Taʾlīf wa-l-Tarjama wa-l-Nashr.

al-Muḥāsibī, al-Ḥārith. 1977. *Al-Tawba*, edited by ʿAbd al-Qādir Aḥmad ʿAṭā. Cairo: Dār al-Faḍīla.

al-Muḥāsibī, al-Ḥārith. 1992. *Al-Baʿth wa-l-Nushūr*, edited by Abū l-Yazīd al-ʿAjamī. Cairo: Dār al-Arqam lil-Ṭibāʿa wa-l-Nashr wa-l-Tawzīʿ.

Mullā Ṣadrā. 1990. *Al-Ḥikma al-Mutaʿāliya fī l-Asfār al-ʿAqliyya al-Arbaʿa*. Beirut: Dār Iḥyāʾ al-Turāth al-ʿArabī.

Muqbil, Hāla. 2011. "Al-Ḥiwār fī Mashāhid al-Qiyāma fī l-Qurʾān." MA thesis, the Middle East University, Amman.

Muslim. n.d. *Ṣaḥīḥ Muslim*, edited by Muḥammad Fuʾād ʿAbd al-Bāqī. Beirut: Dār Iḥyāʾ al-Turāth al-ʿArabī.

al-Nawawī. 1972. *Sharḥ Ṣaḥīḥ Muslim*. Beirut: Dār Iḥyāʾ al-Turāth al-ʿArabī.

al-Nūrī, Ḥusayn. 1954. *ʿAwāriḍ al-Ahliyya fī l-Sharīʿa al-Islāmiyya maʿa al-Muqārana bi-l-Sharāʾiʿ al-Waḍʿiyya*. Cairo: Maṭbaʿat Lajnat al-Bayān al-ʿArabī.

O'Shaughnessy, Thomas. 1961. "The Seven Names for Hell in the Qurʾān." *Bulletin of the School of Oriental and African Studies* 24: 444–469.

O'Shaughnessy, Thomas. 1969. *Muhammad's Thoughts on Death: A Thematic Study of the Qurʾanic Data*. Leiden: Brill.

O'Shaughnessy, Thomas. 1986. *Eschatological Themes in the Qurʾān*. Manila: Cardinal Bea Institute, Loyola School of Theology.

Ormsby, Eric. 1984. *Theodicy in Islamic Thought: The Dispute over al-Ghazali's Best of All Possible Worlds*. Princeton: Princeton University Press.

Papan-Matin, Firoozeh. 2010. *Beyond Death: The Mystical Teachings of ʿAyn al-Quḍāt al-Hamadhānī.* Leiden: Brill.

Pomerantz, Maurice A. 2016. "The Play of Genre: A *Maqāma* of 'Ease after Hardship' from the Eighth/Fourteenth Century and Its Literary Context." In *The Heritage of Arabo-Islamic Learning*, edited by Maurice Pomeranz and Aram Shahin, 461–482. Leiden: Brill.

Price, Annabel and Caroline Barry. 2016. "Capacity and End of Life Decision-Making." In *Mental Capacity Legislation: Principles and Practice*, edited by Rebecca Jacob, Michael Gunn and Anthony Holland, 91–101. Cambridge: Cambridge University Press.

al-Qaḥṭānī, Saʿīd. 2003. *Aḥkām al-Janāʾiz.* Riyad: Muʾassasat al-Juraysī.

Qian, Ailin. 2017. "Delights in Paradise: A Comparative Survey of Heavenly Food and Drink in the Quran." In *Roads to Paradise: Eschatology and Concepts of the Hereafter in Islam*, edited by Sebastian Günther and Todd Lawson, 251–270. Leiden: Brill.

al-Qurṭubī. 1969. *Al-Tadhkira bi-Aḥwāl al-Mawtā wa-Umūr al-Ākhira*, edited by al-Ṣādiq b. Muḥammad b. Ibrāhīm. Cairo: Dār al-Minhāj.

Quṭb, Sayyid. 2006. *Mashāhid al-Qiyāma fī l-Qurʾān*, 16th ed. Cairo: Dār al-Shurūq.

Ragan, Sandra L. 2015. "Overview of Communication." In *Textbook of Palliative Care Communication*, edited by Elaine Wittenberg, Betty R. Ferrell, Joy Goldsmith, Thomas Smith, Sandra Ragan, Myra Glajchen and the George F. Handzo, 1–9. Oxford: Oxford University Press.

al-Rāzī, Abū Bakr. 1978. *Al-Ṭibb al-Rūḥānī.* Cairo: Maktabat al-Nahḍa al-Miṣriyya.

al-Rāzī, Fakhr al-Dīn. 1966. *Al-Mabāḥith al-Mashriqiyya fī ʿIlm al-Ilāhiyyāt wa-l-Ṭabīʿiyyāt.* Tehran: Maktabat al-Asadī.

al-Rāzī, Fakhr al-Dīn. 1987. *Al-Maṭālib al-ʿĀliya min al-ʿIlm al-Ilāhī*, edited by Aḥmad Ḥijāzī l-Saqqā. Beirut: Dār al-Kitāb al-ʿArabī.

Ridgeon, Lloyd, ed. 2021. *Routledge Handbook on Sufism.* London: Routledge.

Rippin, Andrew. 2006. *The Blackwell Companion to the Qurʾān.* Oxford: Wiley Blackwell.

Rosenthal, Franz. 2015. "On Suicide in Islam." *Journal of the American Oriental Society* 66(3): 239–259.

Ross, Heather M. 2001. "Islamic Tradition at the End of Life." *Medsurg Nursing* 10(2): 83–87.

Rouzati, Nasrin. 2018. "Evil and Human Suffering in Islamic Thought – Towards a Mystical Theodicy." *Religions* 9(47): 1–13.

Rüling, Josef B. 1895. *Beiträge zur Eschatologie des Islam.* Leipzig: Druck v. G. Kreysing.

Ryad, Umar. 2017. "Eschatology between Reason and Revelation: Death and Resurrection in Modern Islamic Theology." In *Roads to Paradise: Eschatology and Concepts of the Hereafter in Islam*, edited by Sebastian Günther and Todd Lawson, 1187–1221. Leiden: Brill.

Sachedina, Abdulaziz. 2008. "Defining the Pedagogical Parameters of Islamic Bioethics." *Quarterly Journal of Medical Ethics* 2(5): 25–44.

Sachedina, Abdulaziz. 2009. *Islamic Biomedical Ethics: Principles and Application.* Oxford: Oxford University Press.

Saʿīd, Faḍīla. 2015. *Mashāhid al-Qiyāma fī l-Qurʾān al-Karīm: Dirāsa Adabiyya.* Amman: Dār Ghaydāʾ lil-Nashr wa-l-Tawzīʿ.

Saleh, Walid. 2008. "Death and Dying in the Qurʾan." *American Journal of Islam and Society* 25(3): 97–110.

al-Samʿānī. 1997. *Qawāṭiʿ al-Adilla fī l-Uṣūl*, edited by Muḥammad Ḥasan Ismāʿīl. Beirut: Dār al-Kutub al-ʿIlmiyya.

al-Sarrāj, Abū Naṣr. 1960. *Al-Lumaʿ*, edited by ʿAbd al-Ḥalīm Maḥmūd and Ṭāhā ʿAbd al-Bāqī Surūr. Cairo: Dār al-Kutub al-Ḥadīth and Baghdad: Maktabat al-Muthannā.

Sartell, Elizabeth and Aasim I. Padela. 2015. "*Adab* and its Significance for an Islamic Medical Ethics." *Journal of Medical Ethics* 41(9): 756–761.

Saunders, Cicely. 2006. *Cicely Saunders: Selected Writings 1958–2004*, foreword by David Clark. Oxford: Oxford University Press.

Schimmel, Annemarie. 1976. *Pain and Grace: A Study of Two Mystical Writers of Eighteenth-Century Muslim India.* Leiden: Brill.

Schmidtke, Sabine, ed. 2016. *The Oxford Handbook of Islamic Theology.* Oxford University Press.

Shahin, Aram. 2016. "Reflections on the Lives and Deaths of Two Umayyad Poets: Laylā al-Akhyaliyya and Tawba b. al-Ḥumayyir." In *The Heritage of Arabo-Islamic Learning*, edited by Maurice Pomeranz and Aram Shahin, 398–443. Leiden: Brill.

al-Shaʿrānī. 1880. *Mukhtaṣar Tadhkirat al-Qurṭubī.* Cairo: Dār Iḥyāʾ al-Kutub al-ʿArabiyya.

Shihadeh, Ayman. 2006. *The Teleological Ethics of Fakhr al-Dīn al-Rāzī.* Leiden: Brill.

Shihadeh, Ayman. 2019. "Avicenna's Theodicy and al-Rāzī's Anti-Theodicy." *Intellectual History of the Islamicate World* 7(1): 61–84.

al-Shinnāwī, ʿAbd al-ʿAzīz. 1994. *Al-Janna wa-Naʿīmuhā min al-Qurʾān wa-l-Sunna.* Mansoura: Maktabat al-Īmān.

Smith, Jane. 2006. "Eschatology." In *Encyclopaedia of the Qurʾān.* https://referenceworks.brillonline.com/entries/encyclopaedia-of-the-quran/eschatology-EQCOM_00055.

Smith, Jane and Yvonne Haddad. 2002. *The Islamic Understanding of Death and Resurrection.* Oxford: Oxford University Press.

Solomon, Sheldon and Krista Lawlor. 2011. "Death Anxiety: The Challenge and the Promise of Whole Person Care." In *Whole Person Care: A New Paradigm for the 21st Century*, edited by Thomas Hutchinson, 97–107. New York: Springer.

Somma, Bethany. 2021. *Models of Desire in Graeco-Arabic Philosophy: From Plotinus to Ibn Ṭufayl.* Leiden: Brill.

al-Suhrawardī. 2010. *Hikmat al-Ishrāq.* Beirut: Dār al-Maʿārif al-Ḥikmiyya.

al-Suyūṭī, Jalāl al-Dīn. 1986. *Al-Araj fī l-Faraj*, edited by Muḥammad al-Saʿīd Basyūnī. Cairo: Maktabat al-Thaqāfa al-Dīniyya.

al-Suyūṭī, Jalāl al-Dīn. 1996a. *Al-Budūr al-Sāfira fī ʿUlūm al-Ākhira*, edited by Muḥammad Ḥasan Ismāʿīl. Beirut: Dār al-Kutub al-ʿIlmiyya.

al-Suyūṭī, Jalāl al-Dīn. 1996b. *Sharḥ al-Ṣudūr bi-Sharḥ Ḥāl al-Mawtā wa-l-Qubūr*, edited by ʿAbd al-Majīd Ḥalabī. Beirut: Dār al-Maʿrifa.

al-Taftazānī. 1998. *Sharḥ al-Maqāṣid*, edited by ʿAbd al-Raḥmān ʿUmayra. Beirut: ʿĀlam al-Kutub.

al-Tanūkhī. 1978. *Kitāb al-Faraj Baʿd al-Shidda*, edited by ʿAbbūd al-Shaljī. Beirut: Dār Ṣādir.

al-Tanūkhī. 2019. *Stories of Piety and Prayer*, edited and translated by Julia Bray. New York: New York University Press.

al-Tawḥīdī, Abū Ḥayyān. 1992. *Al-Muqābasāt*, edited by Ḥasan al-Sandūbī. Kuwait: Dār Suʿād al-Ṣabāḥ.

Taylor, John B. 1968. "Some Aspects of Islamic Eschatology." *Religious Studies* 4(1): 57–76.

Tesei, Tommaso. 2016. "The *Barzakh* and the Intermediate State of the Dead in the Quran." In *Locating Hell in Islamic Traditions*, edited by Christian Lange, 31–55. Leiden: Brill.

Tottoli, Roberto. 2008. "Muslim Eschatological Literature and Western Studies." *Der Islam* 83(2): 452–477.

Tottoli, Roberto. 2020. "Death and Eschatological Beliefs in the Lives of the Prophets according to Islam." In *Cultures of Eschatology*, edited by Veronika Wieser, Vincent Eltschinger and Johann Heiss, 467–478. Berlin: De Gruyter.

Van Ess, Josef. 2017. *Theology and Society in the Second and Third Centuries of the Hijra: A History of Religious Thought in Early Islam*, translated by Gwendolin Goldbloom, volume 4. Leiden: Brill.

Van Riet, Simone. 1963. "Joie et bonheur dans le traité d'al-Kindi sur l'art de combattre la tristesse." *Revue philosophique de Louvain* 61: 13–23.

Waardenburg, Jacques. 2006. "Death and the Dead." In *Encyclopaedia of the Qur'ān*. https://referenceworks.brillonline.com/entries/encyclopaedia-of-the-quran/death-and-the-dead-EQCOM_00049.

Watson, Max, Caroline Lucas, Andrew Hoy and Jo Wells. 2009. *Oxford Handbook of Palliative Care*. Oxford: Oxford University Press.

Welch, Alford T. 1977. "Death and Dying in the Qur'an." In *Religious Encounters with Death: Insights from the History and Anthropology of Religions*, edited by Frank E. Reynolds and Earle H. Waugh, 183–199. University Park: Pennsylvania State University Press.

Wensinck, Arent Jan. 1936. *Al-Muʿjam al-Mufahras li-Alfāẓ al-Ḥadīth al-Nabawī*. Leiden: Brill.

White, Douglas and Thaddeus Pope. 2016. "Medical Futility and Potentially Inappropriate Treatment." In *The Oxford Handbook of Ethics at the End of Life*, edited by Stuart J. Youngner and Robert M. Arnold, 65–86. Oxford: Oxford University Press.

Wittenberg, Elaine, Betty R. Ferrell, Joy Goldsmith, Thomas Smith, Sandra Ragan, Myra Glajchen, and the Rev George F. Handzo, eds. 2015. *Textbook of Palliative Care Communication*. Oxford: Oxford University Press.

Wizārat al-Awqāf wa-l-Shu'ūn al-Islāmiyya. 1983–2006. *Al-Mawsūʿa al-Fiqhiyya*. Kuwait: Wizārat al-Awqāf wa-l-Shu'ūn al-Islāmiyya.

Wolff, M. 1872. *Muhammedanische Eschatologie nach der leipziger und der dresdner Handschrift zum ersten Male Arabisch und Deutsch mit Anmerkungen herausgeben von Dr. M. Wolff*. Leipzig: F.A. Brockhaus.

Youngner, Stuart J. and Robert M. Arnold. 2016. *The Oxford Handbook of Ethics at the End of Life*. Oxford: Oxford University Press.

Zaki, Mona. 2006. "Barzakh." In *Encyclopaedia of the Qur'ān*. https://referenceworks.brillonline.com/entries/encyclopaedia-of-the-quran/barzakh-EQCOM_00023.

al-Zamakhsharī. 2004. *Al-Minhāj fī Uṣūl al-Dīn*. Sanaa: Markaz Badr al-ʿIlmī wa-l-Thaqāfī.

Zimmermann, Camilla and Gary Rodin. 2004. "The Denial of Death Thesis: Sociological Critique and Implications for Palliative Care." *Palliative Medicine* 18(2): 121–128.

CHAPTER 2

Muslim Disquiet over Brain-Death

Advancing Islamic Bioethics Discourses by Treating Death as a Social Construct that Aligns Purposes with Criteria and Ethical Behaviours

Aasim I. Padela

1 Background

There are some vigorous debates over the extent to which religion plays a role in modern healthcare. These debates includes concerns over clinicians providing religious and spiritual support (Sloan and Bagiella 2000), religious frameworks being used to inform bioethical rules and regulations (Murphy 2012; Schuklenk 2018; Duivenbode and Padela 2019; McCarthy, Homan and Rozier 2020), and religious values being used to support modifying or limiting conventional healthcare (Campbell 2018). Regardless of these important debates, religion and medicine both respond to the human condition. They address the existential questions of what we are, what will become of us, and what will be our end. While medicine and religion converge in responding to these queries, their epistemic frameworks differ and can lead to conflicts between patients, providers, and policy makers.

An area where differences in perspectives are readily observed, and where conflicts between various stakeholders may arise, is end-of-life healthcare. For example, the religious notion of "life after death" on account of a human soul may not square up with a biological notion that human life ends once organismal functioning ceases. Sometimes such differences have no bearing upon clinical care, but at other junctures different views lead to ethical conflict over when death should be declared, how the dying or dead patient should be treated, and what each stakeholder's moral duties are.

Herein, I will address this context by asserting that, at least in healthcare, death is a social construct where stakeholder purposes for death declaration, methods of death verification (or criteria for death certification), and human behaviours interact. Because the way in which we treat dead persons in society betrays how we, as a society, value life and humanity, great moral significance is attached to the behaviours that clinicians, families, religious professionals, and other stakeholders carry out post the death of an individual. This moral significance carries over and becomes attached to the criteria by which human

DOI:10.1163/9789004459410_004

death is assessed and certified, and further upstream to the purpose for which dead is declared.

Consequently, death constructs, criteria and behaviours are sites of much ethical debate and controversy. Differences in the purposes, means of assessing, and moral views on death result in multiple constructions of death within any given society. In my view, a failure to (i) recognise death as a construct and to (ii) acknowledge a plurality of death constructs, can lead to misdirected bioethical analyses and perceived conflicts between families, clinicians, religious professionals, and counsellors at the bedside.

A cursory examination of empirical studies of Muslim patients, families, clinicians, and Muslim/Islamic critiques of "brain-death"[1] attests to these phenomena. Muslims by and large are disquieted by brain-death and conflicted over ethical duties in end-of-life healthcare (Duivenbode, Hall and Padela 2019; Khalid et al. 2013; Saeed et al. 2015; Rady and Verheijde 2013; Bedir and Aksoy 2011; Arbour, AlGhamdi and Peters 2012; Farah and Al-Kurdi 2006; Khan 2009; Krawietz 2003; Miller, Ziad-Miller and Elamin 2014; Padela, Arozullah and Moosa 2013; Padela and Basser 2012; Padela, Shanawani and Arozullah 2011; Rady and Verheijde 2015; Rady and Verheijde 2016; Sarhill et al. 2001; Sheikh 1998; Kassim and Adeniyi 2010; Ahaddour, Branden and Broeckaert 2018; Khater 2005; Mohiuddin et al. 2020; Ahaddour, Broeckaert and Branden 2019; Muishout et al. 2018; Padela and Qureshi 2017; Borhani, Hosseini and Abbaszadeh 2014; Lewis, Kitamura and Padela 2020; Popal, Hall and Padela 2022). Consequently, I hold that ethical evaluation may be better undertaken when both religious and secular scholars separate the inquiries related to the ontological reality of death from the ethical evaluation of its social implications.[2] Holding human death to be a social construct facilitates such

1 I have placed the term brain death in quotations to highlight that the term is a misnomer and controversial. "Brain death" is often used colloquially to represent that neurological criteria for death have been met. Death here refers to death of the human being not of the brain because it is odd to attach the term alive or dead to organs, and that when neurological criteria for death are met all of the brain need not necessarily have ceased activity. Moreover, the term is a fact-value fusion. The medical fact that an individual who has met the neurological criteria for death will not be able to be revived to consciousness based on contemporary medical knowledge and technology is fused with the value that such a state represents a life not worth living or maintaining. Both the medical fact here and the value attributed to it are contentious. Throughout the rest of the chapter, I will not use quotation marks around the term for the sake of maintaining flow but nonetheless desire the reader to hold these controversies in his/her mind.

2 To be clear I am advocating for epistemic humility and a critical realist approach. I will offer comments on ontology, epistemology, and constructivist approaches to knowledge later in this essay.

bioethical evaluation; therefore herein I will attempt to demonstrate the merits of such an approach through a critical appraisal of selected Muslim/Islamic bioethical literature on brain-death.

Before embarking on that exercise, a few provisos are in order. With respect to Islamic bioethics discussions and literature, I will share a few examples of writings from the extant, academic bioethics literature.[3] And I will discuss these pieces with the aim of illustrating misdirected critiques of brain-death and the merit of evaluating death as a social construct. I readily acknowledge that significant Islamic bioethical discussions about brain-death and the ethics of end-of-life healthcare take place outside the confines of the published academic bioethics literature, and that a critical literature review would require dissecting the arguments the authors present in greater detail. However, given that there is no clear definition of what constitutes the field of Islamic bioethics (Shabana 2014; Padela 2013a), that there are debates over whether writings discussing religious perspectives on bioethical issues are part of academic bioethics or religious studies (Schuklenk 2018; Duivenbode and Padela 2019; Murphy 2012), and that it is methodologically impossible to canvass all writings of a bioethical nature by Muslims or those that involve Islamic frameworks given the diversity of languages and media forms they are produced in, my selection is justifiable. My exposition is simply focused on illustrating how parts of the extant discourse jumble together death purposes, criteria, and moral duties. I believe a modest review of the principal arguments of several writers suffices that aim.

Similarly, with respect to biomedicine, I acknowledge that there is no universal global biomedicine. Rather, various traditional, folk, public, and scientific models of health and healing operate within any given society to guide patient, provider and other healthcare stakeholder behaviours (Kleinman, Eisenberg and Good 1978; Kleinman 1980; Shweder 2008). In this chapter I point at ethical challenges related to end-of-life healthcare in allopathic hospitals. While ethical questions may be addressed differently in different societies, end-of-life healthcare issues are similar enough across societies, to illuminate how various cultural, religious, and biomedical views on death may be brought into alignment.

3 By the academic bioethics literature, I am referring to peer-reviewed journals indexed in Medline, which is the preeminent biomedical bibliographic database. I also include monographs and chapters from bioethics-related books produced by academic biomedical publishers, i.e., Springer, or affiliated with universities or academic medical centres, e.g., University of California, as part of the academic bioethics literature.

Finally, I would like to comment on social constructionism, realism, and moral relativism as it relates to this chapter. Social constructionism is an approach to scholarship that sees the world as being invested with meaning by human actors. While there are many different flavours to social constructionism, its supporters generally view knowledge as constructed and subjective (Burr 1998). This perspective appears to deny that there are objective realities/truths, and thus opens the door to moral relativism. Said another way, if all knowledge is constructed by the human mind, including knowledge about social phenomena or the nature and essence of things, then there are no fundamentals to constrain individuals (or societies) from refashioning categories such as race, gender, sexuality, disease, illness and the like (Burr 1998). In distinction, realists hold there to be objective truths that humans can discover, and this research approach focuses on describing such truths/realities. The camps grow more complex as some social constructionists can view knowledge as having subjective and objective poles (Andrews 2012), and critical realists readily acknowledge that what we can know (epistemology) does not fully match up with what is real (ontology) (Miller 2013). Moreover, there are interpretivists, subtle realists, positivists and other groups of scholars who variably view the social world as created, negotiated, sustained and modified by human agents, and each group takes a different position on the relationship between knowledge and reality (Berger and Luckmann 1991; Andrews 2012; Burr 1998). Notwithstanding these complexities, my assertion is that death has a subjective reality; it means something to human actors, and accordingly we must study these diverse meanings in order to make moral assessments of what it means and how we should behave around it. I am not arguing that death has no "true" or reality, rather I would argue that various aspects of death are disclosed as it is probed using social scientific, natural scientific, affective and other research methods (Padela 2022). Indeed, I more closely ally myself with subtle or critical realism than social constructionism as I find those approaches more consistent with Islamic views on the nature of human knowledge (Padela 2022). My cause for treating death as a social construct is to clarify the social contexts and moral worlds of contemporary allopathic healthcare, and thus inform cogent Islamic bioethical deliberations over the ethics of end-of-life healthcare.

This chapter will proceed as follows. In the next section, I will delineate different views on death to lay bare diverse perspectives on the ethical questions surrounding death in biomedical and religious settings. Death will be discussed as a sociological as well as a scientific entity, and the different legal, policy, biomedical, and religious purposes that death serves will be examined. Thereafter, I will use examples from the academic bioethics literature to highlight Muslim disquiet over brain-death. Specifically, I will highlight critiques offered by different stakeholders (jurists, philosophers, and clinicians) to suggest that these views are based on differing purposes for death, and that viewing death as a construct might serve to enhance moral evaluation. In the subsequent section of the chapter, I will offer a modest intervention to bring various perspectives on death into alignment. I will argue that moral evaluation must connect the purposes of death, the criteria used to adjudicate it, and the behaviours that will ensue when it is declared. I will close this piece by reflecting on the how religious, biomedical, and social scientific perspectives need to come together to address critical problems within the nascent field of Islamic bioethics.

2 What Is Death? Researching Its Realities from an "Alien" Perspective

The Qur'ān metaphorically refers to death as "[the] certainty" (Q 15:99), yet contemporary biomedical understandings and capacities have shrouded this assured occurrence with multiple uncertainties. What physiologic event marks the death of a human? Does the human body undergo multiple forms and types of deaths? What clinical procedures are sufficient to certify one has died? Is the soul's departure from the body manifested physically? How certain is the diagnosis of brain-death? Does medical care hasten or forestall death? These uncertainties work their way into clinical encounters near the end-of-life where clinicians, patients, and religious leaders contend with decisions about advanced directives, therapeutic goals, withdrawing and withholding life support, and verifying death. Ambiguities related to death also confound Islamic legists and Muslim health policy makers who debate which views align with the Islamic moral tradition.

The importance of death within religious theology, biomedical practice, and society is clear. Yet, while it may seem intuitive, death is not a straightforward concept. Defining death is a challenge and explaining the diverse symbols and behaviours surrounding human death is even more difficult. Consider for example that the Qur'ān refers to death (*mawt*) as created by God to test humankind (Q 67:2). Prophetic statements further relate that death will be brought forth of the Day of Judgement as a calf to be slaughtered by angels so that everlasting human life ensues (al-Bukhārī n.d., #6548). Thus, its reality from a religious lens is more complex than simply the absence of life. The same holds true in the secular space as Alexander Capron, the Executive Director of the US Presidential Commission on the uniform determination of death act, notes "the belief that defining human death is a medical matter misapprehends the undertaking. At issue is not a biological understanding of cells and organ systems, but rather a social formulation of humanhood. Through a formal declaration of the points at which life begins and ends society determines who is a full human being with rights and responsibilities" (Rich 2014; Capron 1995).

Relatedly, both at the bedside and at the proverbial juridical table, Muslim thinkers must appreciate that death has multiple different meanings within the house of biomedicine and of Islam. Within *medicine*, clinical guidelines for declaring death as the cessation of cardiopulmonary or brain function do not fully map onto *biological* definitions of death as the loss of integrative capacity or an inability to maintain homeostasis (Veatch and Ross 2016; Shewmon 2001; Truog and Miller 2014; Gervais 2014). Within the Islamic tradition, *metaphysical* speculations about death representing the dissolution of the soul-body connection are related to, but also separate from determinations of what physical markers should be the *legal* thresholds for human death (Krawietz 2003). In both biomedicine and Islam, discussions of human death involve social, biological, legal and ethical considerations and different understandings from within each of these disciplines are found.

In the creation story of the first human, Prophet Adam, the Qur'ān states that God taught Adam the "names of all things" (Q 2:31). Some commentators such as Abul A'la Maududi (Abū l-A'lā Mawdūdī, 1903–1979) interpret this verse to mean that the reality of things was disclosed to Adam, while others view the verse as indicating that the ability to name and label things is intrinsic to the human being. Either way, it appears that the tradition would permit us to ask and resolve for ourselves: what is death? For our purposes, I suggest we take on the following thought experiment to begin mapping out understandings of death: If we were scientists from a different planet visiting Earth, how might we investigate human death?

For one, we might seek a *biomedical* understanding of its nature. We could catalogue differences in the state of the living human and the dead one, and then observe the processes and order by which these changes occur. Additionally, we may examine clinical practices around death determination and verification across different contexts. We might also conduct experiments to ascertain whether human death is different from the death of animals and plants. These natural scientific approaches would illuminate *criteria for death* as a matter of biological and biomedical science.

Notably, in the US there are two overarching criteria by which death is declared, cardiopulmonary and neurologic. Individuals are legally declared dead based on either (i) the irreversible cessation of circulatory and respiratory functions, or (ii) the irreversible cessation of all functions of the entire brain, including the brain stem (Uniform Law Commission 1981). However, depending on the situation these criteria might be flexed. For example, in order to resolve bioethical tensions about the futile resuscitation of patients with miniscule chance of "meaningful" recovery, some ethicists note that the irreversible cessation criterion refers not to the physiological permanence of such a state, rather it should be tied to the assessment that it is likely that such a state would not be reversed even if cardiopulmonary resuscitation is undertaken (Bernat 2010). Others argue that irreversibility must be interpreted in light of ethical and practical constraints as in the case where a patient has decided they do not want to be resuscitated (Lizza 2005). In this scenario physiological permanence and irreversibility is disregarded in order to respect the patient's wishes. On the opposite spectrum, clinicians may opt to accept a cardiac notion of death over a neurological notion based on family and patient choice. These examples illustrate how various purposes for death declaration cause biomedical practice to stretch and flex the criteria by which to determine death.

Furthermore, different disciplines may arrive at their own death criteria. For example, religious frameworks may adopt a metaphysical view whereby separation of the soul from the body represents death. Should metaphysical occurrences be deemed to have physical correlates, death criteria may include observable signs reflecting the departure of the soul. Positive law, on the other hand, does not offer deliverables upon which to build up its own criteria and may instead incorporate biomedical criteria. Illustratively, the legal threshold in the US referenced above is based on accepted medical standards. In other jurisdictions, legal thresholds may involve religious or cultural norms as well. The way in which a discipline arrives at death criteria depends on its epistemic framework, and how it negotiates different claims about the reality of death.

Another investigative approach might involve observing *behaviours* surrounding death. This sociological approach aligns with treating death to be a construct. Within psychology, a construct refers to an analytic tool which facilitates an understanding of human behaviours, and in sociology a construct represents a specific interconnected set of values and beliefs that manifest in human behaviours and understandings (Thomas 1966).[4] A sociological construct is imbued with meaning by the language, symbols, and behaviours used to convey the construct's significance. Considering death to be a sociological construct would mean that different groups and cultures can hold different definitions of death, that definitions and behaviours towards death can change over time, and that there is no singular correct perspective on what death signifies. Consequently, this approach would entail examining how

4 Note that all sciences are built on systems of constructs, for example gravity is core to physics, and *istiḥāla* (essential transformation) is an operative construct within Islamic law.

people treat the dead to glean the significance of that state, and analysing how people behave when death is near, and when it is declared, to understand the importance of death and the various relational changes that ensue. These sorts of studies entail looking at *death behaviours*, and actions that can be undertaken when a human being is termed dead. A fuller sociological study may also involve reviewing the legal and policy actions taken by various parties when death occurs to glean its societal impact, as well as analysing the symbols used to describe death to glean its cultural significance.

Beyond death behaviours, another way for us to research human death would be to consider the *purposes of death*. By purposes I mean the functions death serves. For example, death serves legal purposes such as being the condition for disbursing the decedent's estate, and dissolving business and martial relationships. Relatedly, death serves policy objectives. For example, different fiscal policies and safety regulations govern the transport of dead human bodies than the transport of the living. Death also serves various biomedical purposes. Counts of human deaths are used to assess the virulence of diseases, the efficacy of clinical treatment and research protocols, and the safety of drugs. It also represents the point the decedent's tissues can be used for teaching or research purposes (with consent). At the same time, human death in the context of medical practice, represents a moral endpoint at which the duty to rescue is obviated from healthcare workers. Hence, there are indeed a host of purposes for death declaration.

Our thought experiment suggests that scientific approaches to understanding death could entail examining *death criteria, death purposes* and *death behaviours*. Taken together these inform *death constructs* that operate within society. The moral assessment of death constructs thus involves examining the "rightness" of death purposes, criteria, and behaviours. Operatively, in any given context, a specific purpose for death is identified, which then leads to the selection of criteria to verify death has occurred, and subsequently death behaviours are enacted by various stakeholders. This procedural flow is routine at the proverbial death bed in hospital where clinicians, family members, and religious leaders surround the patient in their final moments; Death criteria are identified, a physician certifies death by assessing if those criteria are met, and then the clinical care team, family members and religious professionals carry out various death behaviours.

Before proceeding further, it is critically important to recognise that there can be significant interaction between death purposes and criteria. For example, in some jurisdictions religious exemptions allow patients (and families) to object to one biomedically-sourced criterion for death in lieu of another that aligns with their religious values (Son and Setta 2018; Grodin 1994). This illustrates how religious purposes and death behaviours influence biomedical practice. Moreover, it highlights how the biomedical construction of death is multi-faceted rather than singular, and that different purposes lead to different notions of what constitutes human death in the halls of medicine.

As we move to consider Islamic bioethical approaches to death, a careful observer, be they an alien scientist or an ethicist, must acknowledge that there is multiplicity and plurality among *death behaviours*, *criteria*, and *purposes*.

3 Islamic Bioethical Disquiet over a Modern Form of Death

Over the past decades, there has been a rapid medicalisation of the dying process around the globe. In developed nations most people die in medical facilities, surrounded by machines and sterility rather than in the confines of their home surrounded by their loving relatives. Burgeoning technology and medical capacities have contributed to this shift as access to healthcare facilities has increased, and doctors are now able to use novel technologies to sustain critically injured individuals for greater periods of time. While this progress has saved many lives, it has also left many individuals befuddled as new forms of living and dying are instantiated. Brain-death has entered our collective vernacular, and the idea of physical reanimation tickles our imagination. While movements advocating releasing ourselves from the confines of the human body such as transhumanism have gained traction, so too have organisations that assist individuals with ending their own life when it is self-judged to be too cumbersome.

As biomedicine has made liminal states between traditional markers of life and death possible, and societal debates over the medicalisation of dying have taken hold, Muslim thinkers have also entered the discourse. Islamic legists are debating the concept of and criteria for brain-death. For instance, Muslim philosophers and theologians are reengaging lines of inquiry into the relationship between the soul and body, and Muslim clinicians are analysing religious bioethics discourses seeking answers about ethical duties surrounding death. These engagements reveal disquiet over the ways in which death is managed and adjudicated in biomedicine. In what follows, I use contentions over the notion of brain-death from various Muslim corners to highlight this unease and confusion over death purposes and criteria.

3.1 *Islamic Legists*

In response to the increasing calls for deceased organ donation programs and clarity over brain-death in Egypt, Muḥammad Sayyid Ṭanṭāwī (1928–2010), the former rector of al-Azhar and grand *muftī* of Egypt, declared the matter of ascertaining the occurrence of death to be a medical and not a religious affair (Hamdy 2012). Several, prominent juridical councils have since concurred that physician experts can set the legal standards for death in Islamic law (al-Bar and Chamsi-Pasha 2015). On the other hand, Ṭanṭāwī's contemporary colleague, ʿAlī Jumuʿa (Gomaa, b. 1952) also former grand *muftī* of Egypt, advocates a large role for religious scholars and sees the issue not to be about applying the label of death to a physiological state, rather it is about uncovering a reality. He notes "it is not just a technical medical issue, it's also a human and moral issue … doctors cannot say it is only for them alone to decide. We [religious scholars] must get involved … the issue is not about definitions [of death], the issue is about uncovering the truth [reality] about something" (Hamdy 2012, 73).

The Jordanian legist, Muḥammad Naʿīm Yāsīn (Muhammad Naim Yasin), an authority on Islamic medical jurisprudence envisages an interplay between religious and medical authorities on the concept of and criteria for death. He asserts that Islamic scholars should have the dominant role in identifying principles, definitions and conditions for death based on scriptural sources. Muslim clinicians, on the other hand, should apply these religiously-derived definitions to their practice (Krawietz 2003), as they bear the responsibility for certifying when life ends (Qazi et al. 2013). A similar view is advanced by the American jurist, M. Amin Kholwadia (Stodolsky and Kholwadia 2021).

These varied perspectives exemplify debates among religious scholars about the validity of neurological criteria for death in Islamic law and whether religious scholars or medical experts have the primary role in defining death. Generally speaking, scholars fall into one of two camps; some legists and juridical councils consider brain-death to satisfy legal thresholds for declaring death and implicitly give medical science a continued role in determining death criteria, while others consider brain-death to represent a human being that is dying but not dead and that the traditional criteria of cessation of heartbeat and breathing should be maintained as markers for human death (Padela, Arozullah and Moosa 2013; al-Bar and Chamsi-Pasha 2015).

The impetus for bioethical deliberations over brain-death, within both Muslim and non-Muslim circles, has been the advent of organ transplantation. Brain-dead individuals represent a source for life-sustaining and/or life-saving organs since clinical research suggests better outcomes when organs are received from brain-dead donors as compared to those declared death after cardiopulmonary cessation, though more recent data suggests comparable outcomes (Demiselle et al. 2016; De Vleeschauwer et al. 2011; Molina et al. 2019; Chen et al. 2017; Van Loo et al. 2017; Shahrestani et al. 2017; Bellingham et al. 2011; Gavriilidis and Inston 2020; Xue et al. 2017). Moreover, a greater number of organs can be procured from brain-dead donors. Consequently, the main purpose of ascertaining death in this context is to save or sustain another's life. Additionally, death also marks the moral endpoint at which the clinical care of the patient (the potential donor) can cease. It thus appears that in this scenario, death serves biomedical purposes[5] and informs the behaviour of clinicians, the dying patient, his/her relatives, and the patient afflicted within organ failure and his/her social circle.

If death purposes are restricted to biomedical practice and behaviours, then one could argue that death criteria should be derived based on biomedical science. Indeed, biomedical science reveals the optimal conditions and methods for procuring organs so that the most lives benefit, and it also reveals when continued medical care is inefficacious or harmful. Religion has no primary deliverables to offer these equations, rather religious values are applied to biomedical data about the efficacy of organ donation, transplantation, and clinical therapies. Similarly, the death behaviours that are enacted in the context of organ donation, for example the ways in which donor families and recipients interact and the tributes paid to the brain-dead donor, are unified by the biomedical death purpose(s). If the biomedical context was not present such activities would not carry meaning. As such death purposes and death behaviours in this context are connected by the biomedical conceptualisation of death.

The foregrounding of the biomedical context is what proponents of brain-death criteria as legitimate in Islamic law have in mind. Doctors are the experts in this domain and as such have the authority to setup death criteria when biomedical purposes are primary. Religious scholars, in this context and according to this view, have a different role, rather than setting up the criteria for death they should assess the moral dimensions of the human behaviours around brain-death as well as the purposes of death. Hence it is perfectly within scope for religious scholars to condemn vivisection for organ procurement, and to argue that the societal need for organs does not justify a new conception of human death.

Islamic juridical deliberations confuse, and are confusing, when criteria for death are debated without seeking logical connections between death purpose(s), criteria, and behaviours. Said differently, religious critiques of brain-death are incomplete when the entire death construct is not addressed, and evidence from religious sources that speaks to each of the three dimensions of the construct is not marshalled.

For example, some jurists heatedly debate whether the brain is the "seat" of the soul, holding this to be a prerequisite for legitimating brain-death within Islamic law (Moosa 1999; Ebrahim 1998; al-Awadhi 1985). Yet, the brain-death

5 By biomedical here, I mean purposes related to health and healthcare in society.

construct holds no metaphysical truths and such deliberations are, in my view, tangential to the ethical assessment of the death purposes and the death behaviours around brain-death.

A more appropriate question religious scholars have taken up is whether brain-death criteria are legitimate indicants for death within Islamic legal epistemology (Padela, Shanawani and Arozullah 2011; Padela, Arozullah and Moosa 2013). Here detractors argue that neurological criteria for death cannot supplant traditional indicants for human death in classical legal manuals because they are not scripturally sourced. However, the opposing camp rebuts this critique by noting that indicants for death in legal manuals, signs such as the rigidity of the body and the sinking of the temples, are also not scripturally-sourced, rather they are based on custom and observation. Rather than basing their critique of criteria upon precedent, a better tactic would be for religious scholars to raise questions about the accuracy of brain-death diagnosis. Relatedly, they could be critical of the variance of brain-death criteria around the globe (Braksick et al. 2019; Greer et al. 2008; Hornby et al. 2006; Pandey et al. 2017; Powner, Hernandez and Rives 2004). By developing such arguments, a biomedical construction (brain-death) that serves biomedical purposes would be critiqued on the basis of biomedical sciences. Given the inherent inaccuracies in diagnosis and variability in criteria, Islamic scholars could reasonably assert that the clinical foundations of brain-death are too shaky to base human death criteria upon. Unfortunately, more often than not, jurists defer to physicians and do not interrogate the probabilistic clinical practice. Nonetheless, critiquing death criteria without also examining the purpose for which these criteria are used, and the human behaviours that are involved, results in a partial moral evaluation.

If jurists were to view brain-death not as a metaphysical truth but as a construct, then they could better aim their critiques at the moral purposes brain-death serves. They would also be better able to use Islamic ethico-legal principles to opine on the behaviours that are enacted by multiple actors in the context of brain-death. And if they foregrounded the biomedical context that connects purposes with criteria and behaviours, they would be able to levy a biomedically-sourced critique of brain-death criteria.

3.2 *Muslim Philosophers*

In the academic bioethics literature several Muslim philosophers draw upon Qurʾānic exegesis and Islamic discussions about the soul's nature and function to marshal arguments for and against this notion of death.

For example, Ahmet Bedir and the late Şahin Aksoy, both philosophically trained Turkish ethicists, delve into Qurʾānic verses and Prophetic traditions describing the departure of the soul from the body and the moment of death. These scriptural evidences suggest that the human soul animates the body, and note various departure points for its separation including the feet, the throat, via breath, and from the cheek (Bedir and Aksoy 2011). Death, therefore, is a metaphysical event with physical indicators. This idea is supported by Islamic law which recognises many different physical signs as markers of human death including the bending of the nose, sagging of the skin, and others (Brockopp 2003). In their view, brain-death cannot be legitimated in Islam because this form of death disregards metaphysical realities. It is also faulty because the brain-dead patient still maintains the indicators of life noted in Islamic legal manuals (Bedir and Aksoy 2011).

In contrast, Omar Sultan Haque, a social scientist, a clinician, and a philosopher embraces brain-death. He argues that the loss of personhood should align with a notion of death, and that this idea is reflected in the Qurʾānic usage of the term *nafs* when referring to death, as in every *nafs* shall taste/endure death (Q 3:185 and 21:35). With this toehold, he refashions concepts of soul (*rūḥ*) to develop a naturalistic account of embodied consciousness as personhood drawing in works penned by Ibn Sīnā (Avicenna, d. 428/1037) and others. He argues that the brain-death both fully accords with contemporary neuroscience and philosophy of mind, and is amenable to being grafted onto the Islamic tradition as death proper (Haque 2008).

Harkening back to the idea that death constructs bring together death purposes, criteria, and behaviours, the aforementioned philosophical/theological critiques appear to address the brain-death construct incompletely. Rather than debating purposes, criteria, and behaviour, some Muslim philosophers primarily focus on the conceptual underpinnings of brain-death and how it may account for Islamic theologies of the soul. While this enterprise has scholarly merit, it fails to address clinical and bioethical challenges that lead to advent of brain-death, and thus may find little purchase in healthcare circles.

Overlooking the purpose for which brain-death was "created," in my view, leads to this neglect and a somewhat off-base critique. Firstly, the purpose of brain-death is not to account for Islamic theologies of the soul. Neither is brain-death meant to resolve critical tensions in Muslim "philosophies" of mind. Religious sources discuss the soul in order to explain the reality of human existence and to motivate living righteously. Moreover, Islamic scholarly writings on the soul, its functions, and its purposes are speculative in nature. There are multiple different, and equally legitimate, notions of the soul that represent an orthopraxy that is centuries old. From time to time, Muslim thinkers have found neuroscience to support one or more of these notions, but there has been no definitive conclusion or universally-accepted notion (Brown 2013).

Hence basing a conceptual critique of brain-death based on a speculative theology may be problematic.

What is clear however is that brain-death sheds no light on the moral life, nor does it lay claim upon the reality of human nature. Whether brain-death fits, or can be made to fit, with Islamic theologies of the soul does not directly address contextual purposes of, and criteria for, brain-death. Rather, at best, these discussions can inform death behaviours because whether the concept of brain-death aligns with traditional understandings of soul and human death, can impact how Muslims behave around it.

On the other hand, as noted in the previous section, critiques about the legal standards for verifying death, as illustrated by Bedir and Aksoy, may be valid. If Islamic legal manuals base their indicants of death upon the lack of soul-body connectivity, one may argue that an "Islamic" criterion for death in the hospital should do so as well. However, Islamic legal manuals note many different physical indicants for death based on custom and do so for purposes that are different than the purposes behind brain-death. These purposes must be foregrounded in any analysis of the dissonance between brain-death criteria and those in legal manuals.

Alternatively, brain-death's relationship with personhood can be subject to critique based on Islamic philosophical and theological frameworks. Indeed bioethics scholars debate the philosophical basis of brain-death diagnosis and whether it does/should differentiate persons from non-persons, given that there are different versions of brain-death criteria (McMahan 1995; Blain-Moraes, Racine and Mashour 2018; Rich 1997). Yet, personhood itself is a culturally-defined notion that is subject to change. There was a time when females were not considered persons, and when black people were considered lesser persons.

As we saw above with some jurists, some Muslim philosophers discuss the brain-death construct in a partial way, and neglect to address critical features of the biomedical context in their discussions. One may argue that a philosophical or a theological examination does not require delving into the biomedical dimensions of brain-death. Yet since brain-death is a product of biomedicine, biomedical stakeholders have primacy over whether the brain-death is accepted as a standard for human death in clinical practice. Muslim philosophers who write in the academic bioethics literature who neglect the biomedical dimensions of brain-death are making a critical mistake. In my opinion, Muslim philosophers would be better able to aim their critiques, or advocate for the acceptance, of brain-death, should death be viewed as a sociological construct that brings together human purposes, criteria, and behaviour. Moreover, a holistic moral evaluation of brain-death demands that human purposes and behaviours are assessed.

3.3 *Muslim Healthcare Providers*

As a group, a significant proportion of Muslim healthcare providers who might be tasked with declaring death and a host of other death behaviours express disquiet over brain-death. For example, a national survey of Muslim physicians in the United States reported that nearly half did not consider brain-death to be death proper (Popal, Hall and Padela 2021). A smaller study of Muslim healthcare professionals, including chaplains, reported that half of participants felt that families should be given choice over whether brain-dead examinations are performed given the moral significance and ethical conundrums associated with the diagnosis (Lewis, Kitamura and Padela 2020). Muslim healthcare providers unease with brain-death occurs at both the conceptual and practical levels, and they use religious and biomedical sources in their critical arguments.

Mohammed Rady, a critical care physician at Mayo Clinic in the United States represents one prominent voice among this group and levels his critique at death criteria. From a religious perspective he contends that brain-death cannot be equated with death because, according to him, the Qurʾān and Prophetic traditions unequivocally characterise death as a "single irreversible event" where the soul leaves the body (Rady and Verheijde 2016; Rady and Verheijde 2015). In his view, because individuals who are declared brain-dead retain somatic integration, either intrinsically or via supportive medical technology, such individuals cannot be considered dead because they do not meet the biological definition of death, and neither can be considered dead by religious criteria because the soul may still be attached to the body (Rady and Verheijde 2015). He asserts that leading Islamic jurists and juridical councils that consider a brain-dead state to meet the legal standards for death in Islam have erred by misinterpreting both the scriptural and medical evidences for human death (Rady and Verheijde 2013). Sherine Hamdy, an anthropologist who has studied the organ transplantation and brain-death debates in Egypt, reports that Ṣafwat Luṭfī (Safwat Lotfy), a prominent critical care physician at Cairo University, similarly critiques several Egyptian religious authorities as having misunderstood the clinical and biological bases of brain-death, as well as the scriptural texts defining death (Hamdy 2012). Rady and colleagues also harshly critique the purposes for brain-death, believing that dead donor rule is threatened by donation after brain-death, that the biomedical push for organ donation and brain-death has trampled over religious liberties and the rights of citizens (Rady, Verheijde and Yanke 2017; Rady and Verheijde 2013; Rady, Verheijde and McGregor 2006; Rady and Verheijde 2018).

Among the clinical intelligentsia, a different perspective is offered by Faisal Qazi, a neurologist and bioethicist located in California. He acknowledges uncertainties surrounding the clinical diagnosis of brain-death, but he points out that Islamic rulings are probabilistic judgements. He argues that brain-death must not be treated as a certain state because the clinical criteria have inherent false error rates. Similarly, no single juridical ruling about whether brain-death is legitimate in Islam should be treated as definitive given that the matter requires juridical exertion to extend the scriptural sources to a new phenomenon. Rather both are tentative, probabilistic conclusions (Qazi et al. 2013). Hence, he calls for embracing epistemic humility and plurality in Islamic bioethical deliberations over brain-death.

Considering again that death constructs connect purposes, criteria and behaviours, Muslim clinician discourses appear to address all three components. Rady's numerous writings certainly critique the biomedical purposes that led to the construction of brain-death, take aim at the criteria for assessing human death, and object to the clinician, family, religious professional and healthcare policymakers' behaviours that treat an individual who has met neurological criteria for death as dead. Perhaps the intimate knowledge these stakeholders have of the biomedical context, given that they are healthcare providers, generates a better conceptualisation of death in healthcare as a human construct, and brain-death as one such construct. Yet this discourse requires modest intervention as well.

Like the philosophers, Rady and others who cite scriptural evidence to oppose brain-death, fail to recognise that the religious sources they quote are not addressing the same death purpose that brain-death serves. Because the purposes are different, hermeneutical exercises are undertaken to glean how they may be relevant to the issue of brain-death. Said another way, these texts do not univocally address discussions about the lifesaving or life-sustaining technologies, nor the morality of donating organs at or near the end of one's life. Hermeneutical and ethico-legal reasoning must be employed to ascertain where the tradition lies on these issues, and, at least theoretically, a plurality of views may be legitimate. Rady's reading does not preclude other equally legitimate readings of the scriptural sources *vis-à-vis* brain-death.

Additionally, using scripture to destabilise brain-death criteria is somewhat misguided. Verses and traditions describing the moment of death as departure of the soul from the body offer multiple different indicators. It is not clear which are primary and which are secondary, and whether they are determinative or adjunctive. As such a critique of brain-death criteria would have greater foundations if it was grounded in biomedical evidence not religious manuals. Rady and others take up this tactic. They point out, as noted above, that biological definitions of death may not be sufficed by brain-death, and that clinical criteria can be faulty due to inherent limitations including what aspects of the brain are tested, variations in test procedures, and the inherent false positive rate of the diagnostic test. In their view, these deficiencies render brain-death incompatible with Islamic law because the diagnosis of death should be certain, and they contend that had Islamic scholars critically appraised the biomedical and clinical evidence related to brain-death criteria, they would have reached the same conclusion. My own reading of juridical deliberations points to several other shortcomings as some jurists fail to recognise brain-death as a prognostic rather than a diagnostic entity, and others mistakenly consider brain-death to represent total brain failure (Padela and Basser 2012).

Relatedly, suggesting that brain-death criteria do not suffice as indicants for human death in Islamic law because they do not meet the epistemic level required is appropriate. But simply critiquing these criteria because they do not square up with those mentioned in legal manuals is not an adequate criticism. Legal indicants of death within Islamic manuals are tied to religious/ social purposes for death such as when burial can commence, when the estate can be divided and when the waiting period for a widow can commence. The question to ask is how these indicants came to sanctioned by Islamic law. If customary practice or biomedical expertise were the basis upon which these standards came to be legitimated within Islamic law, then there is no reason that Islamic legal manuals cannot expand to include other indicants for death as custom and biomedical practice changes and/or if "new" purposes are identified that require different indicants. In my view, purposes and criteria should always be aligned when any death construct is developed or evaluated.

4 The Moral Assessment of Death Constructs: Foregrounding Purposes and Stakeholders, and Embracing Plurality

Bioethical issues are multidimensional because the questions addressed interface with social, legal, political, and healthcare systems. Consequently, bioethical deliberations must involve multiple disciplines coming together to map out and address the ethical problem-space to the fullest extent possible. Illustratively, leading academic bioethics institutions such as the Hastings Center convene experts from law, medicine and policy to develop ethical policy reports and positions statements, and bioethics consultancies such as the Presidential Commission on Bioethics engage with social scientists, religious leaders, as well as experts in medicine, law and policy. In Muslim circles, premier Islamic bioethics deliberations[6] whether they be at the local, national, or

6 I recognise this statement is too wide-ranging. Yet, the developing field of Islamic bioethics heavily relies on juridical academics, such as the Islamic Fiqh Academy of the Muslim World

transnational level largely involve dialogue between two disciplinary experts, Islamic jurists and Muslim physicians, and it is not clear which discipline has the upper hand in determining which actions and policies accord with Islamic morality (Ghaly 2015; Stodolsky and Kholwadia 2021; Padela 2021). As a result, various aspects of the ethical problem-space are neglected or left unaddressed. For example, juridical academies convened to address whether porcine-based medications are permissible to use for Muslims did not appreciate how their rulings would impact global pharmaceutical manufacturing and polices governing religious pilgrimages (Padela 2013b). Worse yet is when biomedical aspects of the ethical issue are inaccurately understood because key disciplinary expertise is missing. In my view, Islamic bioethical discussions over brain-death, illustrate these phenomena. As I have demonstrated elsewhere, jurists and clinicians at premier academies have not fully conceptualised the ethical problem-space and incompletely addressed the policy and practical dimensions of end-of-life healthcare surrounding brain-death (Padela, Arozullah and Moosa 2013; Padela and Basser 2012; Padela, Shanawani and Arozullah 2011).

In the preceding section I have offered a snapshot of Muslim discussions in the academic bioethics literature to illustrate further discursive challenges. Whether Muslim stakeholders are critiquing, or alternatively advocating for, brain-death critical biomedical aspects of brain-death are overlooked, and at times muddled analyses is observed. Occasionally theological critiques are levelled at the concept of brain-death as human death at the expense of evaluating the purpose for which brain-death was constructed and whether that purpose is legitimate. At other times, scriptural texts and legal manuals are used to claim that neurological criteria for death cannot be legitimated by the Islamic tradition. Yet the purposes that undergird indicants of death within scripture and legal manuals are not lifted up as part of the analytic. Islamic bioethical discussions thus appear to be incomplete discourses yielding partial answers (Padela, Shanawani and Arozullah 2011; Krawietz 2003; Arbour, AlGhamdi and Peters 2012; Padela, Arozullah and Moosa 2013; Padela and Qureshi 2017). As such the tradition's moral standpoints on various death purposes, criteria, and behaviours as it relates to end-of-life healthcare, is far from clear.

In my view, death purposes, criteria, and behaviours must be connected together in order to enable a fuller evaluation of the overarching death construct. Additionally, the roots of a specific death construct within a particular discipline (e.g., biomedicine or theology) should be made explicit in order to

League, as the "best evidence" or "highest level" of ethical opinions. My statement concerns these academies.

maintain logical coherence when evidence for, or against, the related death purposes, criteria, or behaviours construct is marshalled.[7]

The present state of affairs emerges, at least partially, from discussants desiring a singular concept of death, and a single set of universally accepted criteria by which it is adjudicated. There is also a desire to subordinate various societal purposes for death underneath a single unifying purpose. These desires, however strong, are illusory. There have always been different constructs for death operative in society because of different underlying purposes. For example, a person lost at sea is considered *for all intents and purposes* by various legal systems, Islam included, to have died, although no one ever certified or verified that cardiopulmonary or neurological criteria for death were present in that stated individual. On the other hand, patients undergoing cardiopulmonary resuscitation can be declared dead by physicians provided a pulse is not palpated, even if the heart has not ceased to beat and even if such a state is not physiologically irreversible as demanded by the Uniform Determination of Death Act (Uniform Law Commission 1981). Relatedly, in some cultures, an individual is not truly dead despite having fulfilled biomedical and legal criteria until mourning rituals are completed (Selin and Rakoff 2019; Gire 2014; Uniform Law Commission 1981). Its ultimate reality notwithstanding, human death has many different social configurations.

Given this diversity, I suggest that Islamic bioethical discussions related to end-of-life healthcare analyse death as a sociological construct that emerges from the need to suffice the specific purpose(s) of particular stakeholder(s). Once this linkage between needs and stakeholder group is made, appropriate death criteria can be advanced. I further suggest that perceived conflicts between religious and biomedical perspectives may be lessened by legitimating a plurality of death constructs. To be clear I am not suggesting that every death construct aligns with Islamic morality, rather I hold that several death constructs can be legitimated by, and operate cohesively within, the tradition. To illustrate this approach, let us consider the perspectives of three stakeholder audiences (physicians, family members, and religious professionals) and how the death of a patient impacts each of them.

7 That is not to say that cross-disciplinary or transdisciplinary ethical analysis and deliberation is not warranted. However, I caution against jumbled analysis where the evidence that is used to craft an argument is misaligned with the issue that is being critiqued. A stronger argument can be fashioned when truth claims based on deliverables of a particular science are critiqued from within the epistemic frameworks of that science. For example, when a clinical diagnosis is critiqued based on clinical and biological evidence that there are flaws in such a diagnosis.

For practicing physicians, death is a biological occurrence marked by physiological and anatomical changes in the human body. As part of their professional and societal duties, this change is certified/verified using clinical practice guidelines by physicians. To clinicians, death also represents a moral endpoint to patient care. Hence for clinicians, death is tied to biomedical understandings and moral duties.

With respect to the family members of a dying patient, death represents the point at which their caretaker role diminishes and ultimately absolves. Death also marks the transition point from concern about the patient to concern about the mourning family. For families, while death might be perceived as a biological and/or metaphysical event, the declaration of death changes their social and ethical responsibilities.

For religious professionals serving the patient in a pastoral capacity or in a community setting, death marks the point at which religious duties commence. These leaders may be charged with arranging and performing the funeral and burial, and with providing religious counsel and support to family members. While religious professionals may understand death as a metaphysical occurrence, a patient's death initiates professional, social and moral duties.

Given the varied roles each of these stakeholders have with respect to the dying patient, and the different social and moral significance the declaration of death has to each of these groups, we can say that the patient's death serves different purposes for each. We can also assert that the onset of death behaviours is marked by a different act.

Illustratively, the patient's death has at least two different purposes for the physician, it serves to bring biological and clinical closure. By biological closure I mean human death marks the cessation of the type of biological activity that can be termed life, and as such it can be correlated with physiological and organismal changes. At the same time, another purpose of human death, from the vantage-point of a clinician, is to herald the futility of further clinical intervention in restoring the patient's health. For the clinician, the absence of physiological and biological correlates for life marks death, and clinical data foretell the point at which continued interventions lack the efficacy to restore patient health. The many death behaviours that are enacted by the clinician, for example certifying patient death, removing clinical therapeutics, conveying this news to the rest of the clinical care team, supporting the patient's family whilst sharing news of the passage of their loved one, counselling, are all triggered when biomedical thresholds are met.

Closely tied to the idea of clinical closure, death can also serve as a moral end of the clinician's duty to treat. However moral duties to restore health or to treat a patient need not correlate with patient death. According to some bioethicists these obligations fall away when biomedicine offers no further beneficial treatment to a patient, others assert they are obviated when the patient can no longer be considered a person. Ethical theories, professional codes, and social contracts setup this moral endpoint not biology, and hence the biomedical determination of death does not need to be the exact point at which the clinicians' duty to restore health, or to treat a patient, ends.

Moving outside the domain of biomedicine, metaphysical frameworks for human death can only offer insight to the clinician should metaphysical occurrences have physical signs. Said another way, the religious idea that human death is the departure of soul from a body is only relevant to conversations over the criteria for death should there be a way to observe this occurrence, or to mark the difference between a souled and an unsouled human body. While many theories may abound, Islamic scholastic theology does not offer a definitive view on whether the soul resides within the world of matter, nor whether the moment of death where it disconnects from the body has definitive physical indicants (Gianotti 2001; Maghnisawi et al. 2007; Brown 2013). Thus, for the physician practice, death criteria must be biologically grounded.

For families, as noted above, the patient's death triggers changes in social and ethical responsibilities, the purpose of declaring death is to effect these changes. The biomedical sciences, by themselves, provide no deliverables on which to assess when mourning rituals should commence, or when the decedent's estate should be distributed, or when a family's ethical duties towards the newly dead person mitigate. Rather religious, cultural, and secular frameworks opine on these matters. It may be that these frameworks defer to biomedical criteria for death to trigger changes in duties and responsibilities, but it is not necessarily so.

Moreover, families mourn when someone is close to death and also after. It is certainly true that these behaviours change when death is declared, but that transition occurs when death is pronounced/communicated not when the biological and physiological correlates for death were verified by a clinician. Some clinicians declare death when there is no palpable pulse regardless of whether the heart still beats, others may use ultrasound to assess the cessation of heartbeat before declaring death. Either approach is accepted in medical practice, but neither mean anything to the family until death is vocalised. The biological occurrence of death and the sociological instantiation of death almost always stand apart in time. Thus, the criterion by which the death behaviours of a family commence is socially determined. It is linked to biology, but that biology/physiology may vary across patients.

Relatedly, law dictates when contracts can be initiated, and contracts signed close to one's death are subject to critical scrutiny in both secular and religious law. For example, in order to avoid coercion or confusion impacting contracts near the end-of-life, Islamic law recognises the concept of death illness (*maraḍ al-mawt*) and allows for family members or others to become financial caretakers of an individual with a terminal illness (Yanagihashi 1998). Notably a death illness can be declared based on an individual's perception of terminality, even if the medical prognosis is not dire. These cases illustrate how legal thresholds, ethical duties, and biology/physiology surrounding death stand somewhat apart. From the perspective of families, the enactment of death behaviours does not wholly depend on whether specific biological or religious criteria for death have been met.

Finally, for religious leaders working in a healthcare-related capacity or in a community setting, death serves ethical and professional purposes. Yet, just like for families, a religious leader's pastoral and religious duties are triggered when death is pronounced by the clinician. Certainly, Islamic law and scriptural evidence inform the timing and types of procedures a religious leader must undertake when death is declared, but they do unequivocally identify physical markers of human death. Hence religious leaders depend on customary self-evident signs of death, or on the pronouncement of medical scientists. Certainly, religious leaders may hold that death occurs when the soul departs, but biomedicine has little to say about the relationship between the body and the soul. This religious belief; however, should not stand in the way of using biological criteria to ascertain the loss of homeostasis and organising capacity of the human body. It is these sorts of concepts that buttress criteria used by clinicians to pronounce death, which in turn initiates the professional and ethical death behaviours of religious leaders.

For Islamic bioethics stakeholders, be they clinicians, patients and their families, or religious leaders, metaphysics and ontology do not have to stand in the way of assessing moral duties in end-of-life care if we understand death at the bedside to be a construct that joins specific purposes with criteria so that certain behaviours can be enacted.

5 Conclusion

At the Islamic Fiqh Academy of the Organization of Islamic Conference (now Cooperation) (OIC-IFA) meeting dedicated to discussing brain-death in 1986, Muḥammad Sulaymān al-Ashqar (d. 2008), a pre-eminent Jordanian jurist, proposed that a brain-dead individual should be considered dead for some purposes, and living for others. He offered that for the biomedical purposes of removing life support and thus ending the clinical staff's moral duty to treat, the brain-dead person was to be treated as a dead human. Similarly, for the purpose of organ procurement to save the life of another, the brain-dead patient was to be considered dead. However, he noted that the brain-dead patient was to be considered alive when it came to financial and contractual matters such that the estate was not to be distributed among heirs, and if the patient was a husband, his wife could not yet be declared a widow (Moosa 1999; Krawietz 2003). For these latter purposes, death had to be ascertained by cardiopulmonary criteria. This stance was also approved by the Senior Council of Scholars in Saudi Arabia, among other juridical academies (al-Bar and Chamsi-Pasha 2015). The fact that preeminent Islamic legists recognise different purposes for death declaration, acknowledge multiple biomedical criteria for verifying death, and specify which death behaviours are permitted when one or the other biomedical threshold is met, elucidates that multiple different death constructs can operate within the Islamic ethico-legal tradition.

In this chapter I have provocatively argued that death should be evaluated as a sociological construct, that multiple such constructs operate within society, and that death purposes, criteria and behaviours must be logically and ethically connected. I have suggested that extant Islamic bioethical discussions over brain-death have misfired, in part, because they do not analyse death constructs, i.e. death purposes, criteria, and behaviours, as a unit nor seek logical connections between criteria and purposes. This critical failure, in my view, is related to the lack of multidisciplinary engagement over end-of-life care ethics in Muslim circles.

As a provisional remedy, I advocate Islamic bioethicists legitimate a plurality of death constructs based on different death purposes because allowing for different constructs to "live" alongside each other may help resolve ethical tensions in end-of-life healthcare. Obviously, the utility of such an approach must deserve further attention and must be tested through application. Some may wonder if I deny that death has a singular, knowable reality. My response to such interlocuters is that I do not. Rather I assert that death serves functions in society and cogent bioethical analysis must begin by acknowledging these functions which are at the root of pressing ethical issues at the bedside and in society.

Finally, this chapter also highlights the need for social scientific engagement in Islamic bioethics. Thus far the field has centred around medical scientists and Islamic jurists, both vying for dominance in framing the ethical questions and delivering Islamic responses. However ethical questions arise in social contexts and emerge against the backdrop of social history. Without social scientists alongside, doctors and jurists may not fully appreciate the origin of the ethical question and the implications of their responses to them. Moreover, social scientific perspectives may indicate how to negotiate between different versions of the ethical. It is past time for the field of Islamic bioethics to fully embrace social scientific approaches. Indeed, the phenomenon of "twice dead" is here to stay (Lock 2002). Since brain-death is a fusion of biomedical facts with ethical and social values, Islamic bioethical deliberations must involve those who can speak to the biomedical, the ethical, and the social dimensions of the issues.

Bibliography

Ahaddour, Chaïma, Bert Broeckaert and Stef Van den Branden. 2019. "'Every Soul Shall Taste Death.' Attitudes and Beliefs of Moroccan Muslim Women Living in Antwerp (Belgium) toward Dying, Death, and the Afterlife." *Death Studies* 43(1): 41–55.

Ahaddour, Chaïma, Stef Van den Branden and Bert Broeckaert. 2018. "Between Quality of Life and Hope. Attitudes and Beliefs of Muslim Women toward Withholding and Withdrawing Life-Sustaining Treatments." *Medicine, Health Care and Philosophy* 21(3): 347–361.

Andrews, Tom. 2012. "What is Social Constructionism?" *Grounded Theory Review* 11(1).

Arbour, Richard, Hanan M. AlGhamdi, and Linda Peters. 2012. "Islam, Brain Death, and Transplantation: Culture, Faith, and Jurisprudence." *AACN Adv Crit Care* 23(4): 381–394. DOI: 10.1097/NCI.0b013e3182683b1e.

al-Awadhi, Abd El-Rahman Abdulla. 1985. *Human Life: Its Inception and End as Viewed by Islam*. Kuwait: Islamic Organization for Medical Sciences.

al-Bar, Mohammed Ali and Hassan Chamsi-Pasha. 2015. *Contemporary Bioethics: Islamic Perspective*. Cham: Springer.

Bedir, Ahmet and Şahin Aksoy. 2011. "Brain Death Revisited: It Is Not 'Complete Death' according to Islamic Sources." *Journal of Medical Ethics* 37(5): 290–294. DOI: 10.1136/jme.2010.040238.

Bellingham, Janet M., Chandrasekar Santhanakrishnan, Nikole Neidlinger, Philip Wai, Jim Kim, Silke Niederhaus, Glen E. Leverson, Luis A. Fernandez, David P. Foley, and Joshua D. Mezrich. 2011. "Donation after Cardiac Death: A 29-year Experience." *Surgery* 150(4): 692–702.

Berger, Peter L. and Thomas Luckmann. 1991. *The Social Construction of Reality: A Treatise in the Sociology of Knowledge*. London: Penguin.

Bernat, James L. 2010. "How the Distinction between "Irreversible" and "Permanent" Illuminates Circulatory – Respiratory Death Determination." *Journal of Medicine and Philosophy* 35(3): 242–255.

Blain-Moraes, Stefanie, Eric Racine and George A. Mashour. 2018. "Consciousness and Personhood in Medical Care." *Frontiers in Human Neuroscience* 12: 306.

Borhani, Fariba, Seyed H. Hosseini and Abbas Abbaszadeh. 2014. "Commitment to Care: A Qualitative Study of Intensive Care Nurses' Perspectives of End-of-Life Care in an Islamic Context." *International Nursing Review* 61(1): 140–147.

Braksick, Sherri A., Christopher P. Robinson, Gary S. Gronseth, Sara Hocker, Eelco F.M. Wijdicks and Alejandro A. Rabinstein. 2019. "Variability in Reported Physician Practices for Brain Death Determination." *Neurology* 92(9): e888–e894. DOI: 10.1212/WNL.0000000000007009.

Brockopp, Jonathan E. 2003. *Islamic Ethics of Life: Abortion, War, and Euthanasia*. Columbia, SC: University of South Carolina Press.

Brown, Jihad. 2013. *The Problem of Reductionism in Philosophy of Mind and its Implications for Theism and the Principle of Soul: Framing the Issue for Further Islamic Inquiry*. Abu Dhabi: Tabah Foundation.

al-Bukhārī. n.d. *Ṣaḥīḥ al-Bukhārī*, edited by M. Muhsin Khan, *ḥadīth* #6548. www.sunnah.com.

Burr, Vivien. 1998. "Overview: Realism, Relativism, Social Constructionism and Discourse." In *Social Constructionism, Discourse and Realism*, edited by Ian Parker, 13–26. Manchester: Manchester Metropolitan University.

Campbell, Courtney S. 2018. "Imposing Death: Religious Witness on Brain Death." *The Hastings Centre Report* 48(S4): S56–S59. DOI: 10.1002/hast.957.

Capron, Alexander Morgan. 1995. "Legal Issues in Pronoucing Death." *Encyclopedia of Bioethics, Revised Version*, edited by Stephen G. Post, 534–540. New York: Macmillan.

Chen, Guodong, Chang Wang, Dicken Shiu-Chung Ko, Jiang Qiu, Xiaopeng Yuan, Ming Han, Changxi Wang, Xiaoshun He and Lizhong Chen. 2017. "Comparison of Outcomes of Kidney Transplantation from Donation after Brain Death, Donation after Circulatory Death, and Donation after Brain Death Followed by Circulatory Death Donors." *Clinical Transplantation* 31(11): e13110.

De Vleeschauwer, Stéphanie I., Shana Wauters, Lieven J. Dupont, Stijn E. Verleden, Anna Willems-Widyastuti, Bart M. Vanaudenaerde, Geert M. Verleden and Dirk E.M. Van Raemdonck. 2011. "Medium-Term Outcome after Lung Transplantation is Comparable between Brain-Dead and Cardiac-Dead Donors." *The Journal of Heart and Lung Transplantation* 30(9): 975–981.

Demiselle, Julien, Jean-François Augusto, Michel Videcoq, Estelle Legeard, Laurent Dubé, François Templier, Karine Renaudin, Johnny Sayegh, Georges Karam and Gilles Blancho. 2016. "Transplantation of Kidneys from Uncontrolled Donation after Circulatory Determination of Death: Comparison with Brain Death Donors with or without Extended Criteria and Impact of Normothermic Regional Perfusion." *Transplant International* 29(4): 432–442.

Duivenbode, Rosie and Aasim I. Padela. 2019. "Contextualizing the Role of Religion in the Global Bioethics Discourse: A Response to the New Publication Policy of

Developing World Bioethics." *Developing World Bioethics* 19(4): 189–191. DOI: 10.1111/dewb.12242.

Duivenbode, Rosie, Stephen Hall and Aasim I. Padela. 2019. "Assessing Relationships Between Muslim Physicians' Religiosity and End-of-Life Health-Care Attitudes and Treatment Recommendations: An Exploratory National Survey." *American Journal of Hospice and Palliative Medicine* 36(9): 780–788.

Ebrahim, Abul Fadl Mohsin. 1998. "Islamic jurisprudence and the end of human life." *Medicine and Law* 17: 189–196.

Farah, Samir and Ashraf Al-Kurdi. 2006. "Brain Death: Definition, Medical, Ethical and Islamic Jurisprudence Implications." In *FIMA Year Book 2005–2006*, edited by Hossam E. Fadel, Muhammed A.A. Khan and Aly A. Mishal, 33–48. Amman: Jordan Society For Islamic Medical Sciences.

Gavriilidis, Paschalis and Nicholas G. Inston. 2020. "Recipient and Allograft Survival Following Donation after Circulatory Death versus Donation after Brain Death for Renal Transplantation: A Systematic Review and Meta-Analysis." *Transplantation Reviews* 34(4): 100563.

Gervais, Karen G. 2014. "The Social Construction of Death, Biological Pausibility, and the Brain Death Criterion." *The American Journal of Bioethics* 14(8): 33–34.

Ghaly, Mohammed. 2015. "Biomedical Scientists as Co-Muftis: Their Contribution to Contemporary Islamic Bioethics." *Die Welt des Islams* 55(3–4): 286–311. DOI: 10.1163/15700607-05534p03.

Gianotti, Timothy J. 2001. *Al-Ghazālī's Unspeakable Doctrine of the Soul: Unveiling the Esoteric Psychology and Eschatology of the Iḥyāʾ*. Leiden: Brill.

Gire, James. 2014. "How Death Imitates Life: Cultural Influences on Conceptions of Death and Dying." *Online Readings in Psychology and Culture* 6(2): 3. DOI: 10.9707/2307-0919.1120.

Greer, David M., Panayiotis N. Varelas, Shamael Haque and Eelco F.M. Wijdicks. 2008. "Variability of Brain Death Determination Guidelines in Leading US Neurologic Institutions." *Neurology* 70(4): 284–289. DOI: 10.1212/01.wnl.0000296278.59487.c2.

Grodin, Michael A. 1994. "Religious Exemptions: Brain Death and Jewish Law." *Journal of Church and State* 36(2): 357–372.

Hamdy, Sherine. 2012. *Our Bodies Belong to God: Organ Transplants, Islam, and the Struggle for Human Dignity in Egypt*. Berkely, CA: Univiversity of California Press.

Haque, Omar S. 2008. "Brain Death and Its Entanglements: A Redefinition of Personhood for Islamic Ethics." *Journal of Religious Ethics* 36(1): 13–36. DOI: 10.1111/j.1467-9795.2008.00334.x.

Hornby, Karen, Sam D. Shemie, Jeanni Teitelbaum and Christopher Doig. 2006. "Variability in Hospital-Based Brain Death Guidelines in Canada." *Neuroanesthesia and Intensive Care* 53(6): 613–619.

Kassim, Puteri Nemie Jahn and Omipidan Bashiru Adeniyi. 2010. "Withdrawing and Withholding Medical Treatment: A Comparative Study between the Malaysian,

English and Islamic Law." *Medicine and Law* 29(3): 443–461. www.ncbi.nlm.nih.gov/pubmed/22145563.

Khalid, Imran, Wasfy J. Hamad, Tabindeh J. Khalid, Mazen Kadri and Ismael Qushmaq. 2013. "End-of-Life Care in Muslim Brain-Dead Patients: A 10-year Experience." *American Journal of Hospice and Palliative Care* 30(5): 413–418. DOI: 10.1177/1049909112452625.

Khan, Abrar. 2009. "Brain Death Legislation and Organ Transplantation in the Islamic World." *Middle East Health Magazine.*

Khater, Wejdan Abdelkareem. 2005. "United States Muslim Physicians' Attitudes toward Withholding and Withdrawing Life-Sustaining Treatment: A Qualitative Study." PhD diss., The University of Kansas. http://search.proquest.com.proxy.uchicago.edu/docview/304990688/abstract.

Kleinman, Arthur. 1980. *Patients and Healers in the Context of Culture: An Exploration of the Borderland between Anthropology, Medicine, and Psychiatry*. Berkeley, CA: University of California Press.

Kleinman, Arthur, Leon Eisenberg and Byron Good. 1978. "Culture, Illness and Care: Clinical Lessons from Anthropologic and Cross-Cultural Research." *Annals of Internal Medicine* 88(2): 251–258. www.ncbi.nlm.nih.gov/pubmed/626456.

Krawietz, Birgit. 2003. "Brain Death and Islamic Traditions: Shifting Borders of Life?" In *Islamic Ethics of Life: Abortion, War, and Euthanasia*, edited by Jonathan E. Brockopp, 194–213. Columbia, SC: University of South Carolina Press.

Lewis, Ariane, Elizabeth Kitamura and Aasim I. Padela. 2020. "Allied Muslim Healthcare Professional Perspectives on Death by Neurologic Criteria." *Neurocritical Care* 33(2): 347–357.

Lizza, John P. 2005. "Potentiality, Irreversibility, and Death." *The Journal of Medicine and Philosophy* 30(1): 45–64.

Lock, Margaret M. 2002. *Twice Dead: Organ Transplants and the Reinvention of Death.* Berkeley, CA: University of California Press.

Maghnisawi, Ahmad ibn Muhammad, Abdur-Rahman Ibn Yusuf, Abu Hanifah, and Ali ibn Sultan Muhammad Qari al-Harawi. 2007. *Imam Abu Hanifa's Al-Fiqh Al-Akbar Explained.* London: White Thread Press.

McCarthy, Michael, Mary Homan, and Michael Rozier. 2020. "There's No Harm in Talking: Re-Establishing the Relationship between Theological and Secular Bioethics." *The American Journal of Bioethics* 20(12): 5–13. DOI: 10.1080/15265161.2020.1832611.

McMahan, Jeff. 1995. "The Metaphysics of Brain Death." *Bioethics* 9(2): 91–126.

Miller, Andrew C, Amna Ziad-Miller and Elamin M. Elamin. 2014. "Brain Death and Islam: The Interface of Religion, Culture, History, Law, and Modern Medicine." *Chest* 146(4): 1092–1101.

Miller, Kris Allen. 2013. "Participating in the Knowledge of God: An Engagement with the Trinitarian Epistemology of TF Torrance." PhD diss., Durham University. http://etheses.dur.ac.uk/7369/.

Mohiuddin, Afshan, Mehrunisha Suleman, Shoaib Rasheed and Aasim I. Padela. 2020. "When Can Muslims Withdraw or Withhold Life Support? A Narrative Review of Islamic Juridical Rulings." *Global Bioethics* 31(1): 29–46.

Molina, María, Félix Guerrero-Ramos, Mario Fernández-Ruiz, Esther González, Jimena Cabrera, Enrique Morales, Eduardo Gutierrez, Eduardo Hernández, Natalia Polanco and Ana Hernández. 2019. "Kidney Transplant from Uncontrolled Donation after Circulatory Death Donors Maintained by nECMO Has Long-Term Outcomes Comparable to Standard Criteria Donation after Brain Death." *American Journal of Transplantation* 19(2): 434–447.

Moosa, Ebrahim. 1999. "Languages of Change in Islamic Law: Redefining Death in Modernity." *Islamic Studies* 38(3): 305–342.

Muishout, George, Hanneke W.M. van Laarhoven, Gerard Wiegers and Ulrike Popp-Baier. 2018. "Muslim Physicians and Palliative Care: Attitudes towards the Use of Palliative Sedation." *Supportive Care in Cancer* 26(11): 3701–3710.

Murphy, Timothy F. 2012. "In Defense of Irreligious Bioethics." *The American Journal of Bioethics* 12(12): 3–10. DOI: 10.1080/15265161.2012.719262.

Padela, Aasim I. 2013a. "Islamic Bioethics: Between Sacred Law, Lived Experiences, and State Authority." *Theoretical Medicine and Bioethics* 34(2): 65–80. DOI: 10.1007/s11017-013-9249-1.

Padela, Aasim I. 2013b. "Islamic Verdicts in Health Policy Discourse: Porcine-Based Vaccines as a Case Study." *Zygon* 48(3): 655–670.

Padela, Aasim I., ed. 2021. *Medicine and Shariah: A Dialogue in Islamic Bioethics*. Notre Dame, IN: University of Notre Dame Press.

Padela, Aasim I. 2022. "Integrating Science and Scripture to Produce Moral Knowledge: Assessing Human Interests and Necessities in Islamic Bioethics and the Case of Organ Donation." In *Islam and Biomedicine*, edited by Afifi Al-Akiti and Aasim I. Padela. Dordrecht: Springer.

Padela, Aasim I. and Omar Qureshi. 2017. "Islamic Perspectives on Clinical Intervention near the End-of-Life: We Can But Must We?" *Medicine, Health Care and Philososphy* 20(4): 545–559. DOI: 10.1007/s11019-016-9729-y.

Padela, Aasim I. and Taha A. Basser. 2012. "Brain Death: The Challenges of Translating Medical Science into Islamic Bioethical Discourse." *Medicine and Law* 31(3): 433–450. www.ncbi.nlm.nih.gov/pubmed/23248843.

Padela, Aasim I., Ahsan Arozullah and Ebrahim Moosa. 2013. "Brain Death in Islamic Ethico-Legal Deliberation: Challenges for Applied Islamic Bioethics." *Bioethics* 27(3): 132–139. DOI: 10.1111/j.1467-8519.2011.01935.x.

Padela, Aasim I., Hasan Shanawani and Ahsan Arozullah. 2011. "Medical Experts & Islamic Scholars Deliberating over Brain Death: Gaps in the Applied Islamic Bioethics Discourse." *The Muslim World* 101(1): 53–72. DOI: 10.1111/j.1478-1913.2010.01342.x.

Pandey, Ashutosh, Pradeep Sahota, Premkumar Nattanmai and Christopher R. Newey. 2017. "Variability in Diagnosing Brain Death at an Academic Medical Center." *Neuroscience Journal* 2017: 6017958. DOI: 10.1155/2017/6017958.

Popal, Sadaf, Stephen Hall and Aasim I. Padela. 2021. "Muslim American Physicians' Views on Brain Death: Findings from a National Survey." *Avicenna Journal of Medicine* 11(2): 63. DOI: 10.4103/ajm.ajm_51_20.

Powner, David J., Michael Hernandez and Terry E. Rives. 2004. "Variability among Hospital Policies for Determining Brain Death in Adults." *Critical Care Medicine* 32(6): 1284–1288.

Qazi, Faisal, Joshua C. Ewell, Ayla Munawar, Usman Asrar and Nadir Khan. 2013. "The Degree of Certainty in Brain Death: Probability in Clinical and Islamic Legal Discourse." *Theoretical Medicine and Bioethics* 34(2): 117–131. DOI: 10.1007/s11017-013-9250-8.

Rady, Mohamed Y. and Joseph L. Verheijde. 2013. "Brain-Dead Patients Are Not Cadavers: The Need to Revise the Definition of Death in Muslim Communities." *HEC Forum* 25(1): 25–45. DOI: 10.1007/s10730-012-9196-7.

Rady, Mohamed Y. and Joseph L. Verheijde. 2015. "Brain Death and the Moral Code of Islam." *Chest* 147(2): e69.

Rady, Mohamed Y. and Joseph L. Verheijde. 2016. "A Response to the Legitimacy of Brain Death in Islam." *Journal of Religion and Health* 55(4): 1198–1205. DOI: 10.1007/s10943-016-0221-z.

Rady, Mohamed Y. and Joseph L. Verheijde. 2018. "Legislative Enforcement of Nonconsensual Determination of Neurological (Brain) Death in Muslim Patients: A Violation of Religious Rights." *Journal of Religion and Health* 57(2): 649–661. DOI: 10.1007/s10943-017-0512-z.

Rady, Mohamed Y, Joseph L. Verheijde and Greg Yanke. 2017. "Nonconsensual Determination of Neurologic (Brain) Death: Is It a Violation of Constitutional Rights?" *Chest* 152(4): 903–904.

Rady, Mohamed Y, Joseph L. Verheijde and Joan McGregor. 2006. "Organ Donation after Circulatory Death: The Forgotten Donor?" *Critical Care* 10(5): 1–3.

Rich, Ben A. 1997. "Postmodern Personhood: A Matter of Consciousness." *Bioethics* 11(3-4): 206–216. DOI: 10.1111/1467-8519.00059.

Rich, Ben A. 2014. "Structuring Conversations on the Fact and Fiction of Brain Death." *The American Journal of Bioethics* 14(8): 31–33. DOI: 10.1080/15265161.2014.925158.

Saeed, Fahad, Nadia Kousar, Sohaib Aleem, Owais Khawaja, Asad Javaid, Mohammad Fasih Siddiqui and Jean L. Holley. 2015. "End-of-Life Care Beliefs among Muslim Physicians." *American Journal of Hospice and Palliative Medicine* 32(4): 388–392. DOI: 10.1177/1049909114522687.

Sarhill, Nabeel, Susan LeGrand, Ramez Islambouli, Mellar P. Davis and Declan Walsh. 2001. "The Terminally Ill Muslim: Death and Dying from the Muslim Perspective."

American Journal of Hospice and Palliative Medicine 18(4): 251–255. DOI: 10.1177/104990910101800610.

Schuklenk, Udo. 2018. "On the Role of Religion in Articles this Journal Seeks to Publish." *Developing World Bioethics* 18(3): 207. DOI: 10.1111/dewb.12210.

Selin, Helaine and Robert M. Rakoff. 2019. *Death across Cultures: Death and Dying in Non-Western Cultures*. Dordrecht: Springer.

Shabana, Ayman. 2014. "Bioethics in Islamic Thought." *Religion Compass* 8(11): 337–346. DOI: 10.1111/rec3.12137.

Shahrestani, Sara, Angela C. Webster, Vincent Wai To Lam, Lawrence Yuen, Brendan Ryan, Henry Claud Capron Pleass and Wayne John Hawthorne. 2017. "Outcomes from Pancreatic Transplantation in Donation after Cardiac Death: A Systematic Review and Meta-Analysis." *Transplantation* 101(1): 122–130.

Sheikh, Aziz. 1998. "Death and Dying – a Muslim Perspective." *Journal of the Royal Society of Medicine* 91(3): 138–140.

Shewmon, Daniel Alan. 2001. "The Brain and Somatic Integration: Insights into the Standard Biological Rationale for Equating 'Brain Death' with Death." *The Journal of Medicine and Philosophy* 26(5): 457–478. DOI: 10.1076/jmep.26.5.457.3000.

Shweder, Richard A. 2008. "The Cultural Psychology of Suffering: The Many Meanings of Health in Orissa, India (and Elsewhere)." *Ethos* 36(1): 60–77. DOI: 10.1111/j.1548-1352.2008.00004.x.

Sloan, Richard P. and Emilia Bagiella. 2000. "Should Physicians Prescribe Religious Activities?" *New England Journal of Medicine* 342(25): 1913–1916.

Son, Rachel Grace and Susan M. Setta. 2018. "Frequency of Use of the Religious Exemption in New Jersey Cases of Determination of Brain Death." *BMC Medical Ethics* 19(1): 76.

Stodolsky, Muhammed Volkan Yildiran and Mohammed Amin Kholwadia. 2021. "A Jurisprudential (*Uṣūlī*) Framework for Cooperation between Muslim Jurists and Physicians and Its Application to the Determination of Death." In *Medicine and Shariah: A Dialogue in Islamic Bioethics*, edited by Aasim I. Padela, 71–86. Notre Dame, IN: University of Notre Dame Press.

Truog, Robert D. and Franklin G. Miller. 2014. "Changing the Conversation about Brain Death." *The American Journal of Bioethics* 14(8): 9–14.

Uniform Law Commission. 1981. *Uniform Determination of Death Act*, approved by the American Bar Association 10 February 1981.

Van Loo, Ellen S., Christina Krikke, Hendrik S. Hofker, Stefan P. Berger, Henri G.D. Leuvenink and Robert A. Pol. 2017. "Outcome of Pancreas Transplantation from Donation after Circulatory Death Compared to Donation after Brain Death." *Pancreatology* 17(1): 13–18.

Veatch, Robert M. and Lainie F. Ross. 2016. *Defining Death: The Case for Choice*. Washington, DC: Georgetown University Press.

Xue, Wujun, Puxun Tian, Heli Xiang, Xiaoming Ding, Xiaoming Pan, Hang Yan, Jun Hou, Xinshun Feng, Linjuan Liu and Chenguang Ding. 2017. "Outcomes for Primary Kidney Transplantation from Donation after Citizens' Death in China: A Single Center Experience of 367 Cases." *BMC Health Services Research* 17(1): 250.

Yanagihashi, Hiroyuki. 1998. "The Doctrinal Development of "*Maraḍ Al-Mawt*" in the Formative Period of Islamic Law." *Islamic Law and Society* 5(3): 326–358.

PART 2

End-of-Life Care in Islamic Studies

الفصل 3

مقاربات فلسفية أخلاقية لرهاب الموت في الحضارة الإسلامية

دراسة آراء محمد بن زكريا الرازي، وأبي علي مسكويه، وصدر الدين الشيرازي

حامد آرضائي وأسماء أسدي

1 تمهيد

يُعدّ رهاب الموت (thanatophobia) أو ما يُسمّى بقلق الموت (death anxiety) وطرق التعامل معه من القضايا ذات الأهمية البالغة في الرعاية التلطيفية. فمن الأهمية بمكان أن ندرك طرق التعامل مع المرضى الذين يعانون من أمراض عضال ومستعصية والتي قد تؤدّي إلى وفاة المريض خلال فترة زمنية محدّدة. كما يهمّ الطاقم الطبّي معرفة كيفية المواجهة مع المرضى المصابين برهاب الموت وعوائلهم في مراحل الاحتضار. وهنا تطرح أسئلة ذات طابع فلسفي وأخلاقي نفسها.

يُعدّ الموت وما يحوم حوله من مسائل من القضايا الأساسية التي لفتت انتباه عدد كبير من المفكرين منذ بدء التاريخ حتى يومنا هذا. هناك عدد كبير من القضايا التي تثير اهتمام المفكرين قديمًا وحديثًا حول الموت لعلّ من أهمها مسألة قلق الموت والخوف منه. فقد كانت هذه القضية وطرق علاجها من القضايا الشائكة التي تجلّت منذ ظهور الفلسفة في كتاباتها التاريخية الأولى؛ انطلاقا من محاورات أفلاطون (ت. 347 ق.م.) ومرورًا بنظريات لأبيقور (ت. 270 ق.م.) ولوكريتيوس (ت. 55 ق.م.) ووصولًا برواقيين كسينيكا (ت. 65 م.) وابيكتتوس (ت. حوالي 135م) وأورليوس (ت. 180م)؛ ومنذ ذلك اليوم وحتى يومنا هذا، أخذ كثير من العقول البشرية يناقشون هذه القضية ويكتبون عنها.

يمكن الإشارة كنماذج إلى أوغسطينوس في بدايات العصر الوسيط وإلى ليوناردو دا فينشي (ت. 1519م) وباروخ سبينوزا (ت. 1677م) في القرنين 15 و16 للميلاد وبعد ذلك أرتور شوبنهاور (ت. 1860م) ونيتشه (ت. 1900م) وشلر (ت. 1805م) وخصوصًا الفلاسفة الوجودين من أمثال كيركيجارد (ت. 1855م) وسارتر (ت. 1980م) وهيدجر (ت. 1976م) واونامونو (ت. 1936م) وغيرهم. وفي العقود الماضية، انصبّ اهتمام الباحثين على قضايا فلسفية أخرى حول الموت تتعلّق أحيانًا بقضايا أخلاقية عامّة (Steffen and Cooley 2014) وأحيانًا بأخلاقيات الطب (medical ethics) والقانون الطبي (medical law) (Edwards 1967; Laing 2002).

2 النظريات التاريخية

يمكن تصنيف أهمّ النظريات عن خوف الموت في القرون السابقة عن الحضارة الإسلامية في ثلاث محاور رئيسة:

1.2 النظرية السقراطية-الأفلاطونية

تتجلّى هذه النظرية بوضوح في العبارات الأخيرة من محاورة «**محاكمة سقراط**» وهي آخر ما قاله سقراط (ت. 399 ق.م.) في محكمته بعد إدانته بالموت برواية أفلاطون:

> وأنتم أيضًا أيها المواطنون القضاة يجب أن تكونوا على أمل قوي بإزاء الموت وأن تعتبروا شيئًا حقًا، وهو أن رجل الخير لا يستطيع الشرّ أن يلحقه، لا فى حياته ولا بعد مماته، وأن الآلهة لا تهمل أمره. وما يحدث لي ليس وليد المصادفة، بل إنه واضح أمامي أن الموت والتخلص من كل العلائق هو الأفضل لي. ولهذا السبب فلم تظهر لي العلامة الإلهية في أية لحظة... ولكن ها قد حانت الساعة للرحيل، أنا لأموت، وأنتم لتعيشوا. من منا يذهب إلى المصير الأفضل؟ الأمر غير واضح أمام الجميع باستثناء الإله.
>
> أفلاطون 2001، 136

صحيح أنّ سقراط كعادته في محاوراته الجدلية لا يعطينا الإجابة النهائية ولكنّ الأمر يبدو جليًا حينما نقرأ عباراته الأولى حيث يشير إلى أنّ الموت خير بالنسبة إلى أهل الخير كما يذكر في قسم آخر من المحاورة نفسها أن من الأمور التي يمكن أن يلام عليها أهل أثينيا في الحكم بإعدامه هو التصور الخاطئ بأنهم بإماتته يلحقون به الأذى (أفلاطون 2001). على أساس هذا الرأي، يكون الموت جيدًا لصاحب الحياة الطيبة والمرافقة للفضيلة. وفي محاورة فايدون (أفلاطون 2001، 141/1 وما بعدها؛ اعتمادى فرد وحسينى 2015؛ شفيع‌بيك 2015).

واقتفى عدد من المفكرين الآخرين هذا الرأي، ومن أبرزهم دافنشي الذي منح لنا بعبقريته الفنية تمثيلًا أدبيًا يقرّب إلى نفوسنا هذه النظرية، فشبّه الموت بعد حياة طيبة بنوم عميق بعد يوم مفعم بالنعم والهدوء والسكينة. ويأتي بعده كندورسة ومن ثمّ يلحق بهم فلاسفة المدرسة البراغماتية (pragmatism) وبرتراند راسل ليوسعوا من نطاق هذه النظرية لتشمل النظريات التي لا تعتقد بالحياة بعد الموت. وفي المقابل، يعترض مفكرون من أمثال شوبنهاور ونيتشه بأنّ الموت شرّ دائمًا ولا يمكن اعتباره خيرًا في أيّ من الحالات خلافًا لسقراط لكنّ هذا الشرّ يجب استقباله بجفاوة وجرأة على حدّ قول هذين الفيلسوفين.(شورون 1984).

2.2 النظرية الأبيقورية

هذه النظرية والتي تجلّت في بعض رسائل أبيقور نفسه (Epicurus 2016; Saunders 1997) وأحد أتباع مدرسته لوكريتيوس (Carus 1994)، حظيت باهتمام الكثير من الباحثين في العقود الأخيرة والذين تناولوا هذه النظرية ذودا عنها أو احتجاجا عليها (Taylor 2013). لفهم هذه النظرية لابدّ أن نلقي نظرة عابرة على النظرية الأبيقورية عن اللذة والشرور. في النظرية الأبيقورية، الإنسان طالب اللذة واللذة المطلوبة كلّما كانت أدوم كانت أحسن. واللذة عدم الألم والشرّ هو ما يمنعنا من اللذة (Luper 2009).

بعد هذه المقدمات، يطرح هذا السؤال نفسه: هل الموت شرّ أم يمكن اعتباره خيراً؟. في الوهلة الأولى يتبدّى لنا أنّ الموت شرّ لأنّه يمنعنا من ملذات الحياة لكنّ أبيقور ولوكريتيوس يستدلان بأنّ هذا التصور خاطئ. اللذة ليست إلا عدم الألم. والألم هو الشيء الذي نهرب منه. فمن يخاف الموت فإنه في الحقيقة يخاف أن يلحق به ألم أو أذى. لذلك من المهم فحص حالة الميت كي نرى هل الموت يُلحق به أذى أو ألمًا ليستحق بذلك أن يُخاف منه. الموت حالة بعد الحياة والإنسان في حياته يتمتع بالإدراك وتُمكّنه القوى الإدراكية من إدراك الملذات والآلام على حدّ سواء. فلا يُحسب الأذى أذىً ولا يُعدّ الألم ألمًا إلا إذا أدركه مُدرِك. لنشاهد الآن هل الميت يمكن أن يلحق به أذى أو ألم ؟ كلّا، حيث أنّ الميّت يفقد الإدراك فلا يدرك شيئا من الآلام والأذى. على هذا، لا داعي أن نخاف الموت لأنّ الألم هو الذي يسفر عن الخوف بينما لا يوجد هناك ألم بعد الموت، فمن غير المنطقي أن نخاف منه (May 2009).

هذه النظرية توحي بأنّه يتوجب علينا أن نبيّن هذه القضية الأساسية للمصابين برهاب الموت من أجل إنقاذهم من وسواس الخوف. ولكنّ الأبيقوريين يقدمون لمصابي رهاب الموت وصفة أخرى، هي تجنب التفكير بالموت. على هذا، للتخلص من قلق الموت لا بدّ أن نفكّر بالحياة وليس الموت. هذا ما يقترحه الأبيقوريون وباروخ سبينوزا على حدّ سواء، ويعترض عليهم آخرون بأنّ الخوف من الموت ليس عملًا إراديًا لكي نوصي المصابين به بتجنبه والاحتراز منه ولابدّ أن تكون هناك حلول أكثر كفاءة لعلاج هذه القضية (May 2009).

3.2 النظرية الرواقية (*Stoicism*)

الرواقيون قاموا بتقديم نظرية أخرى حول قلق الموت. نظرية الرواقيين تستمدّ بعض مبادئها من النظريات السابقة لها، لكنّها تأتي بالجديد في المدرسة الرواقية المتأخرة والرومانية عند مفكرين كسينيكا وإبيكتتوس وماركوس أوريليوس (Kuczewski and Polansky 2002; Stephens 2008). يقول سينيكا أنّه للخلاص من قلق الموت لابدّ للإنسان أن يُطيل التفكير في الموت ويظلّ يتأمّل فيه بطريقة عقلانية. لابدّ أن ندرك حقيقة بأنّنا جزء من الطبيعة وأن نرضى بالدور الذي

نقوم به في الحياة. يشبّه سينيكا الحياة بضيافة لابدّ لنا أن نغادرها في لحظة ما بوقار وأدب، أو يشبّهها بمسرح يتوجّب على كلّ الممثلين فيه أن يقبلوا بالمحدوديات التي يفرضها عليهم دورهم في المسرحية (Motto 1955; Nietmann 1966; Noyes Jr 1973).

حسب الرواقيين، انّ القلق من ذكر الموت والخوف من مواجهته لا يليق بتاتا بسالك الفلسفة والذي تعلّم في سلوكه الفلسفي أن يتحرّر من القيود والعلائق المادية. ليست الفلسفة إلّا تدريبا للموت، بمعنى أنّ التفكير الفلسفي يجعلك في مواجهة مباشرة للحقيقة الأبدية، الأمر الذي يدلّنا على أهمية التفكير بالموت وعدم التهرّب منه.

3 نظريات مواجهة قلق الموت في الحضارة الإسلامية

انصبّ اهتمام المفكرين المسلمين على موضوع الموت والقضايا المتعلقة به منذ بدايات الحضارة الإسلامية وخاصة بالنسبة إلى حقيقة الموت والحياة الأخروية (پيتركراوس 2005؛ خدري 2020؛ قائمي وواعظي 2014؛ مهري، منصفي، ومصلح 2018). أمّا مسألة الخوف من الموت وطرق علاجه فنراها في عدد أقلّ من الكتابات. وعلى سبيل المثال يمكن الإشارة إلى عدد من كتب الأخلاقيات التي ألّفها علماء منهم أبو بكر محمد بن زكريا الرازي (ت. 925/313) وأبي علي أحمد بن محمد مسكويه (ت. 1030/421) ومن ثمّ نصير الدين الطوسي (ت. 1274/672) والنراقيَين وغيرهم. ومن بين الفلاسفة الكبار نُسبت رسالة مستقلة في هذا الموضوع إلى ابن سينا (ت. 1037/428) واهتمّ صدر الدين الشيرازي (ملا صدرا، ت. 1636/1045) بهذه المسألة في طيات كتبه.

1.3 نظرية الرازي حول قلق الموت

عُرف محمد بن زكريا الرازي طبيباً وصيدلياً شهيراً في القرنين الثالث والرابع للهجرة وقدّم مؤلفات هامة منها «**المنصوري**» (الرازي 1408) و«**الحاوي في الطب**» (الرازي 1422) على هذا الصعيد، أمّا اهتماماته الفلسفية فقد تجلّت في عدد من آثاره منها «**السيرة الفلسفية**» (الرازي 2005) و«**الشكوك على جالينوس**» (Koetschet 2019؛ الرازي 1426) و«**الطب الروحاني**» (الرازي 2005؛ 1978). يتطرّق الرازي في كتاب «**الطبّ الروحاني**» الذي ألّفه في علم الأخلاق إلى الموضوع الذي نحن بصدد البحث عنه (محمد 1986).

بشكل عام، يمكن اعتبار الرازي قريباً من المدرسة الأبيقورية من خلال دراسة آثاره الفلسفية (Goodman 2015; 1971)، حيث ينصبّ اهتمامه الفلسفي إلى مفهوم اللذة والألم أكثر من اهتمامه بأي موضوع آخر ويتناوله بطريقة أبيقورية وإن كان له اتجاه أفلاطوني ظاهر في جوهر أفكاره (Adamson 2008; 2021). من هذا المنطلق، نراه يدرس موضوع رهاب الموت

على أسس أبيقورية وأفلاطونية في الوقت نفسه، علاوة على بعض التفاصيل الأخرى نقف عندها ههنا.

يخصّص الرازي الفصل العشرون من كتاب «**الطبّ الروحاني**»، وهو الفصل الأخير منه، بموضوع الخوف من الموت. يستهلّ الرازي الفصل بالإشارة إلى أنّ الطريقة الوحيدة للخلاص من رهاب الموت هو أن يصل المصاب بهذه الحالة إلى قناعة بأنّ نفسه تصير من بعد الموت إلى ما هو أصلح مما كانت فيه. ولإثبات هذا المرام يحجم عن ذكر التفاصيل متذرعًا بأنّه بابٌ يطول فيه الكلام، إذ كان الحديث في هذا الأمر بحاجة إلى النظر في جميع الديانات والمذاهب التي تعرض نظريات عن حالة الإنسان بعد موته، والحكم بعد لمحقّها على مُبطلها. بدلًا من ذلك يلجأ إلى إقناع من يعتقد أن النفس تفسد بفساد الجسد، أما الذي يجعل لمن مات عاقبة يصير إليها بعد الموت فهو إذا كان إنسانًا خيرًا فاضلًا حسب الشريعة المحقّة فلا داعي أن يخاف الموت. ويشبه رأيه النظرية السقراطية هنا ويأتي بتفاصيل أخرى لمن شك في الديانة المحقة فيوضح انّه إذا "أفرغ وسعه وجهده غير مقصر ولا وانٍ فإنه لا يكاد يعدم الصواب. فإن عدِمه – ولا يكاد يكون ذلك – فالله تعالى أولى بالصفح عنه والغفران له إذ كان غير مطالب بما ليس في الوسع بل تكليفه وتحميله عزّ وجلّ لعباده دون ذلك كثير" (الرازي 1978).

ويستمرّ الرازي بتقديم رأيه في إطار الآراء التي لا تقبل ببقاء النفس بعد الموت:

> أما من يعتقد أن النفس تفسد بفساد الجسد، فإنه متى أقام على الخوف من الموت كان مائلًا عن عقله إلى هواه. فنقول: إن الإنسان على قول هؤلاء ليس يناله من بعد الموت شيء من الأذى بتةً، إذ الأذى حس والحس ليس إلا للحي وهو في حال حياته مغمور بالأذى منغمس فيه، والحالة التي لا أذى فيها من الحالة التي فيها الأذى، فالموت إذًا أصلح للإنسان من الحياة.
>
> الرازي 1978

وهذه هي النظرية الأبيقورية الشهيرة عن قلق الموت (Luper 2019). ولكنّ الرازي لا يتوقف عند ذكر هذه النقطة ويبدأ بتحليلات ثانوية خطيرة يتوصّل فيها نهاية بأنّ الموت أفضل من الحياة كلّيا. في طريق الوصول إلى هذه النتيجة الأبيقورية، تُثار إشكالية وهي أنّ الإنسان وإن كان يصيبه في حال حياته الأذى فإنه ينال من اللذات ما ليس يناله في حال موته. ردًّا على هذا السؤال يبيّن الرازي أنّ اللذة المرغوب فيها والمتنافس عليها، هي في الحقيقة أمر عدمي وليست إلا راحة من المؤلم ودفعًا للأذى، فهل الميت يدرك أذى حتى يطالب بتلافيه الذي هو لذته؟ كلّا، إذ الأذى إنما يلحق الحيَّ دون الميت. فليس يضرّه أن لا ينال اللذات وليس بالميت إليها حاجة ولا له إليها نزوع ولا عليه في أن لا ينالها أذىً كما ذلك للحي (الرازي 1978).

هنا يبدأ الرازي بمقارنة بين حالتي الحياة والموت على أساس اللذة التي تدركها النفس الإنسانية فيأتي بقاعدة فلسفية جوهرية وهي أن التفاضل إنما يكون بين المحتاجين إلى شيءٍ ما إذا كان لأحدهما فضل مع قيام الحاجة إليه، فأما أن يكون المحتاج على غنى فلا. وعلى أساس هذه القاعدة فإنّ حالة الموت أصلح للإنسان إذ أنّه لا يدرك أذى حتى يريد أن يدفعها بالملذات. والرازي لا يتوقف عند هذه النقطة أيضًا ويعرض تحليلًا منطقيًا وفلسفيًا في جواب من يحتجّ ولا يرى جدوى في استدلاله إذ أنّ الإنسان الميت غير موجود فلا يمكن المقارنة بين حالة معدومة هي الموت وحالة موجودة هي الحياة؛ فيوضّح الرازي بأنّ هذه المعاني نضعها متوهمة متصورة لنقيس شيئًا على شيء ونعتبر شيئًا بشيء.

يقوم الرازي بعد ذلك بتحليل معرفي نفساني ليوضّح الأسباب التي قد تسفر عن عدم قبول البعض للتبيين العقلاني الذي قدّمه لحلّ المسألة. إذ أنّ هذا رأي تدعمه الحجة المنطقية ويقتضيه العقل السليم ولكن الرأي الذي يتبعه الهوى يُجتبى ويؤثر ويُتبع ويتمسك به؛ لا بحجة بينة ولا بعذر واضح وإنما يكون عن ضرب من الميل إلى ذلك الرأي والموافقة له في النفس وأما الرأي العقلي فإنه يجتبى بحجة بينة وعذرٍ واضح وإن كانت النفس كارهة له. فلابدّ أن نربّي النفوس على حبّ الحقيقة واعتناقها مهما كانت مخالفة لميولنا ونزعاتنا، وهذا المنحى الذي ينحو به الرازي يحتوي على إتّجاه بيداغوجي معرفي وتثقيفي ملحوظ.

في النهاية، يأتي الرازي بنظريته المعاكسة للمذهب الوجودي إذ يعتقد أن الموت لا بدّ منه ومن وقوعه. فالاغتمام به والخوف منه أمر زائد لا جدوى فيه ومن ثمّ التلهي عنه والتناسي له ربح وغنم. ويستمر الرازي قائلًا بأنّا نحن معاشر البشر بذلك صرنا نغبط البهائم من أجل عدم ذكرهم للموت إذ لها بالطبع هذه الحالة كاملة.

1.1.3 تحليل رأي الرازي ومقارنته بنظريات أخرى

الرأي بعدم التفكير بالموت هو الذي أبداه عدد من الفلاسفة أشهرهم سبينوزا في مقولته الشهيرة "إنّ آخر ما يفكر فيه الرجل الحرّ هو الموت؛ لأنّ حكمته ليست تأملًا للموت، بل تأملًا للحياة" (سبينوزا 2009). يتبدّى لأوّل وهلة أنّ نظرية الرازي تشبه رأي سبينوزا، ولكنّ نظرة أخرى إلى عباراته تدلّنا أنّ الرازي يختلف عن سبينوزا والأبيقوريين في بعض النقاط. وفقًا لسبينوزا، كلّ شيء من حيث وجوده يودّ ويسعى أن يبقى في الوجود دومًا والنفس الإنسانية بطبيعتها المدركِة تتجه نحو الخلود - الأمر الذي يستقبله سبينوزا في رأيه عن الحياة بعد الموت. في هذا السياق، يتوصّل الفيلسوف الهولندي إلى نتيجة أنّ النفس البشرية في محاولتها للبقاء لاتنفك تدرك البدن فإدراكها للبدن أمر واجب وكراهيتها من مغادرة البدن والخوف الحاصل منها أمر ضروري لها.

هنا يأتي دور الفيلسوف الإيراني أن يعبّر عن رأيه في هذا الحقل، حيث يرى بأنّ التفكير العقلاني عن الموت ليس سيئًا، بل يوصلنا إلى نتيجة أنّ الموت أصلح للنفس حيث لا يوجد

أذى وبالتبع ليس هناك حاجة للملذات. تحدث الإشكالية من تأثر الرأي بالهوى والذي يسبّب التوجس من الموت بلا سبب وجيه عقلاني. هنا يبدأ الرازي بوصف المصابين برهاب الموت، فهو لامحالة كطبيب سريري قابل هؤلاء، فيقول بأن الخائف من الموت حينما يتصوره كأنّما يموت في كلّ تصويرةٍ موتة، فتجتمع عليه من تصوره له مدة طويلة موتات كثيرة. وهكذا يصف لنا الرازي بجلاء مدى المعاناة التي يعاني منها هؤلاء علماً بأنّه يقول في مؤلفاته الطبية بأنّ الأعراض النفسانية لها تأثير في الحالات الجسدانية من الصحة والمرض وما يتبعهما (الرازي 1408).

الوصفة التي يصفها الرازي للمصابين برهاب الموت تختلف عن مقولة سبينوزا بأنّ الخوف من الموت أمر طبيعي لكن «الإنسان الحر لا يفكر بالموت». انتقد الكثيرون سبينوزا على أنّ نظريته تفتقد الدقة الكافية حيث أنّ المصاب برهاب الموت لا يخاف منه إراديًا ليكفّ عن التفكير به إراديًا (May 2009). في المقابل، يرى الرازي بأننا لسنا قادرين على نبذ الاغتمام الحاصل بتصور الموت إلا بالحيلة لإطراح الأفكار العارضة في الذهن. "فالأجود والأعود على النفس، التلطف والاحتيال لإخراج هذا الغم عنها. وذلك يكون كما قيل إن العاقل لا يغتم بتّة. وذلك أنه إذا كان لما يغتم به سبب يمكنه دفعه جعل مكان الغم فكرًا في دفع السبب، وإن كان مما لا يمكن دفعه أخذ على المكان في التلهي والتسلي عنه وعمل في محوه وإخراجه عن نفسه" (الرازي 1978).

من الواضح أنّ الرازي يحاول جاهدًا أن يأتي ببديل لذكر المسائل النظرية الفلسفية للذين يعانون من رهاب الموت بشكل مرضي ويتألّمون بسببه؛ ويسوقه تفكيره إلى أنّ الحلّ الأمثل هو صرف الفكر عن الموت بإشغاله بأمور مختلفة، قد تكون الاهتمام بفنون مختلفة أو صناعات يتعلّمها الإنسان، أو قراءة كتاب مفيد أو رواية ممتعة أو ممارسة رياضة مسلّية أو الاستمتاع بقطعة موسيقية رائعة أو مشاهدة فيلم رائع في زماننا المعاصر. ثمّ إنّ الرازي يختلف عن الأبيقوريين حيث أنّهم يلخصون أدلة الخوف من الموت في دليلين أولّهما الاعتقاد بأنّ الموت مؤلم، والثاني أنّ النفس باقية بعد فساد البدن ويمكن أن تتألّم في الآخرة. ومن هنا يبدأون ببيان زيف القضيتين (Saunders 1997). حيث أنّ الإنسان لا يشعر بألم في الموت لأن الميت لا يشعر بألم إذ أنّه غير موجود، والثاني أنّ الإنسان يفسد بفساد البدن فلا يوجد هناك حياة بعد الموت حسب رأيهم (Luper 2008).

اتضح لنا خلال عرض عبارات الرازي أنّه لا يساير الأبيقوريين مسايرة تامّة وإن كان يتفق معهم أحيانًا ويستلهم منهم نظرياته الأساسية. بالنسبة إلى القضية الأولى والتي بحث عنها الفلاسفة كثيرًا – ولاسيما في الفلسفة التحليلية المعاصرة (Luper 2019; Taylor 2013) – السؤال الذي يطرح نفسه هو: ما الموت الذي تقولون أنّه غير مؤلم؟ هل هي لحظات الاحتضار أو لحظة مفارقة الإدراك؟ وهل مفارقة الإدراك هي الموت أو الموت شيء آخر؟ هناك عدد كبير من الأسئلة تُطرح في هذا المجال (DeGrazia 2017). ولكنّ تصنيف الرازي لا يُدخله في دوّامة

هذه الأسئلة حيث أنّه يختار متعمدًا أن يتكلّم عما يحدث بعد مفارقة النفس للجسد. وبالنسبة إلى القضية الثانية فإنّ الرازي يحاول في جدلية سقراطية-أفلاطونية أن يرينا جوانب الموضوع المختلفة ويبحث في نظريات شتى ليخلص إلى نتيجة واحدة: سواء أكانت تعتقد بالحياة الأخروية أم لا، فإنّ الخوف من الموت منشأه الهوى، وللحيلولة من تأثير الهوى لا بدّ من اتباع الحياة العقلانية السليمة والتي يفسّرها لنا في رسالته «**السيرة الفلسفية**» (الرازي 2005). هذه الإستراتيجية كما يصرّح الرازي تُلزم أتباع وجهات نظر مختلفة بتبني النتيجة ويسدّ الباب أمام اعتراضات غير سديدة.

وأخيرًا، نلقي نظرة سريعة إلى بعض النظريات المخالفة للرازي. يختلف نيتشه وشوبنهاور عن الرازي بأنّهما يعتقدان أنّ الموت شرّ وسوء (شورون 1984) ويوافقهما الفيلسوف المعاصر توماس ناغل (Thomas Nagel) (Nagel 2012, 1898) في أنّ الموت شرّ مهما حلّ بالإنسان. ولكنّ الفيلسوفين الألمانيين يعتقدان أن هذا الموت الذي يعدّ شرًّا بالذات لا بدّ أن نتقبّله بقوة وأن نفكّر به مليًا. والرازي يختلف عنهما أوّلًا في اعتقاده بأنّ الموت أصلح للإنسان من الحياة وثانيًا بأنّ الذي لم يتعوّد على الحياة العقلية السليمة وأصيب برهاب الموت فالأحرى له أن يتسلّى عن ذكر الموت منشغلًا بأمور أخرى، فما الفائدة من الاغتمام بأمر حاصل لا محالة.

يقول بوسويه أنّ اهتمام الناس بدفن أفكارهم عن الموت قد لا يقلّ شأنًا عن اهتمامهم بدفن موتاهم، فخوف الناس من الموت هو الذي حدا بهم إلى تجاهل التفكير في الموت أو العمل على تناسيه، حتى جاءت الفلسفة الوجودية فأصبح الموت من موضوعاتها الرئيسة. حسب الوجوديين، لا يحق لنا أن نتناسى ونتسلّى عن الحالات النفسانية العميقة مثل قلق الموت والتفكير بالانتحار، معتقدين أنّ هذا القلق الوجودي هو الذي يكوّن الوجود الإنساني وإذا هربنا منه فإنّنا هربنا من أنفسنا. سواءًا إن آلمنا التفكير في مثل هذه المواضيع أم لا، فليس هناك طريقة ثانية غير المواجهة المباشرة مع هذه القضايا الجوهرية في الحياة البشرية. فالإنسان الذي رُمي به في هذا العالم لابدّ أن يواجه هذا القلق شخصيًا وفردانيًا ليتمكّن من تحقيق ذاته في الفرصة المتاحة له في هذه الدنيا (Crowell 2020; Flynn 2006). على هذا، فإنّ الفلاسفة الوجوديين سواء من يرى أنّ الإنسان يُعدم بانعدام حياته منهم جان بول سارتر ومارتن هيدجر وسواءًا من يعتقد بالحياة بعد الموت كسورن كيركيغارد وميجل ديه أونامونو فانّ جميعهم يرون بأنّ التفكير في الموت أمر جوهري للإنسان (Hasker and Taliaferro 2019). فلا يحقّ للإنسان، الذي من أهمّ ميزاته التفكير بالموت الذي يضفي على حياته معنى ومغزى، أن ينبذ فكرة الموت جانبًا متناسيًا متلهيًا (شورون 1984).

ولمراجعة هذه النظرية يمكن مثلًا الرجوع إلى عبارات هيدجر في كتابه الشهير «**الكينونة والزمان**» (هيدجر 2013) حيث يرى أنّ الكينونة الأصيلة تستتبع حياة ذات معنى والتي بدورها

لا تتحقّق إلا عبر القلق الوجودي تجاه الموت وتستلهم معناها من التفكير المرافق للاضطراب حول الموت (عسكري يزدي وميرزايي 2018). وفي مقابل نظرة الأبيقوريين في عدم التفكير بالموت ووصية الرازي المشابهة للمصابين برهاب الموت يقول أونامونو: "إنّ اكتشاف الموت هو الذي ينتقل بالشعوب والأفراد من مرحلة النضج العقلي أو البلوغ الروحي" ويذهب غيره من الوجوديين إلى أن ما يسمى بالموقف «الصحي» تجاه الموت، وهو تجاهله، ليس إلا حالة هروبية غير صحية! (شورون 1984).

ونختم الحديث عن النظرة المقابلة للرازي برأي الفيلسوف الإيراني المعاصر ابراهيمي ديناني والذي يعتقد منتقدًا المدرسة الأرسطية المشائية بأنّ الفصل المقوّم للإنسان لا يمكن أن ينحصر في كونه ناطقًا، بل في كونه مفكّرًا بالموت فيكون الحدّ المنطقي للإنسان والذي يميزه عن سائر الحيوانات أنه هو الحي المتأمّل في الموت.

2.3 قلق الموت عند أبيعلي مسكويه

أبوعلي أحمد بن محمد بن يعقوب مسكويه مؤرخ وعالم موسوعي، ولد في الري وسكن أصفهان وتوفي بها. اشتغل بالعلوم الفلسفية والمنطق مدة، ثم أولع بالتاريخ والأدب والإنشاء (مسكويه 1424). وقد كان لمؤلّفه في الأخلاقيات الفلسفية الحظّ الأوفر ليكون نقطة انطلاق لعدد كبير من مؤلفات علم الأخلاق في الحضارة الإسلامية (مسكويه 2011). كتاب «**تهذيب الأخلاق وتطهير الأعراق**» هو مؤلَّف في الأخلاقيات الفلسفية سجّل فيه مسكويه قمة إبداعاته الفلسفية بمنهجية مترابطة ومتآلفة مصرّحا بأنّه تأثّر فيه بآراء أرسطو (ت. 322 ق.م.) حيث ينقل عنه مباشرة في عدة مواضع من الكتاب (مسكويه 1426). لقد اعتنى الكثير من الباحثين بكتاب «**تهذيب الأخلاق وتطهير الأعراق**» فتمّت ترجمته أكثر من مرّة إلى الفارسية على يد علماء كبار. ومن الترجمات المعروفة لهذا الكتاب يمكن الإشارة إلى «**الأخلاق الناصرية**» («**أخلاق ناصري**») لنصيرالدين الطوسي وترجمة أبيطالب الزنجاني («**كيميای سعادت**») (زنجاني 1996)، وترجمتين معاصرتين إحداهما للسيدة نصرت أمين (مسكويه 1990)، والثانية لعلي‌أصغر حلبي (مسكويه 2002).

من بين هذه الترجمات كان لترجمة نصير الدين الطوسي (الطوسي 1400) انتشار أوسع حيث تداولتها الأوساط العلمية وتم تدريسها في مدارس علمية ودينية خلال عدّة قرون (Lameer 2015) وتم تعريب «**أخلاق ناصري**» مرّتين (جهانبخش 2018) فاكتسى مرّة الزي العربي على يد رُكن الدّين الجرجاني (ت. بعد 1320/720) (Lameer 2015) وقام محمّد صادق فضل الله بتعريبه بلغة معاصرة ونشره في بيروت (الطوسي 2008). يقول الطوسي في ديباجة كتابه بأنه قام بترجمة كتاب أبي علي مسكويه للأخلاقيات وتتميمًا للفائدة أضاف جزئين مختصرين في تدبير المنزل وتدبير المدن ليتمّ

بذلك أجزاء الحكمة العملية. قام نصيرالدين الطوسي بتلخيص كتابه باسم «**أوصاف الأشراف**» وقام العالم الهندي عبد الرحمن بن عبد الكريم برهانپورى الغياثي (ت. بعد 1683/1094) بشرح «**أخلاق ناصري**» لأورنج زيب (ت. 1707/1118) في كتابه المسمّى «**مفتاح الأخلاق**» (الطوسي 1994). ثمّ شرحه علاء الدين حسين الآملي (ت. 1654/1064) بعبارات أوضح للشاه صفي (ت. 1642/1052) في كتاب «توضيح الأخلاق» (كازروني 2007). وكذلك فعل أبو المعالي العاملي (ت. 1646/1055) للسلطان عبد الله قطب شاه (ت. 1672/1082) وسمّي كتابه «**بتوضيح الأخلاق**» وهناك شرح آخر كتبه السيد عليم الله جالندهري (ت. 1787/1202) أسماه «**شرح أخلاق ناصري**» (كازروني 2007). كما كان لكتاب أخلاق ناصري تأثير منقطع النظير على الكتب المدوّنة في الأخلاقيات الفلسفية في القرون التالية (قربان خانى وابن الرسول 2012) سواءا الفارسية منها كـ«**درّة التاج**» لقطب الدين الشيرازي (ت. 1311/710) (قطب الدين شيرازي 1990) و«**معراج السعادة**» لأحمد النراقي (ت. 1830/1245) (نراقي 1999) والعربية منها كـ«**الأخلاق الجلالية**» لجلال الدين الداوني (ت. 1503/908) (خراساني 2008) و«**الأخلاق المنصورية**» لغياث الدين الدشتكي (ت. 1542/928) (پشت دار 2010) و«**جامع السعادات**» للمولى مهدي النراقي (ت. 1795/1209) (نراقي 2006). وقد تُرجم «**أخلاق ناصري**» إلى الإنجليزية على يد ويكنز ونشر في لندن (Ṭūsī 2011).

بناءًا على هذا، كان لكتاب مسكويه تأثير مباشر من جهة وغير مباشر من جهة أخرى عبر «**أخلاق ناصري**» وترجماته وشروحه، على صعيد الأخلاقيات في الحضارة الإسلامية (ميرزامحمد 2007). وهذا الكتاب بالذات هو الذي أورد فيه مسكويه نظريته عن قلق الموت. لقد ألّف مسكويه كتابه في سبع مقالات هي: 1. تعريف النفس 2. الأخلاق والطبائع 3. الفرق بين الخير والسعادة 4. أعمال الإنسان 5. أنواع المحبة 6. الأمراض النفسية 7. الطب النفساني. وفي القسم الأخير خصّص صفحات بموضوع خوف الموت (مسكويه 1426).

تجدر الإشارة هنا إلى أنّ هذه الرسالة نُسبت خطأً إلى ابن سينا، والذي كان معاصرًا لمسكويه، تحت عنوان «**الشفاء من خوف الموت ومعالجة داء الاغتمام به**» أو «**دفع الغمّ من الموت**» ونشرت في مجموعة رسائل ابن سينا كما ترجمت إلى الفارسية ضمن رسائله (ابن سينا 1994؛ 2009). إثر ذلك اهتمّ عدد من الباحثين بدراسة آراء ابن سينا عن رهاب الموت ونشروا دراساتهم بناءًا على فحوى هذه الرسالة (آزادي و لانتركوشه 2016؛ سليماني 2008؛ شه گلي 2012؛ طاهري أخوان 2011). خلال دراستنا هذه، انتبهنا إلى انّ بعض الدارسين أشار إلى أنّ نصير الدين الطوسي تأثّر برسالة ابن سينا في كتابه «**أخلاق ناصري**». من المعلوم أنّ «**أخلاق ناصري**» ليس إلّا ترجمة حرّة لـ«**تهذيب الأخلاق**» لمسكويه، والدراسات الحديثة تثبت بوضوح إلى أنّ الرسالة اقتطعت من كتاب مسكويه ثمّ نسبت إلى ابن سينا عن طريق الخطأ – لا سيما أنّ كنية كليهما أبوعلي – أو عمدًا لاشتهار هذا الثاني وإمكانية بيع مؤلفاته أكثر من الآخرين (آرضائي

2020). اهتمّ ابن سينا في كتبه الفلسفية بمسألة الموت وحقيقته وأسبابه ومايجري للإنسان بعده (أحمدي زاده 2012؛ أرشد رياحي 2002؛ أكبري 2009؛ خادمي 2013؛ خاني، چنگي آشتياني، وميرديلمي 2019؛ رازي‌زاده 2019؛ رحيم‌پور وزارع 2013)، كما قام بتنظير فسيولوجي عن الموت في كتبه الطبية (أمجديان وديرباز 2014؛ رحيم‌پور 2014؛ شه گلی 2012؛ فرامرز قراملكي وهمتي 2008)، أمّا هذه الرسالة فلا تمّت له بصلة إطلاقًا. علمًا بأنّ هناك وجوهًا أخرى تدلّنا بأنّ هذه الرسالة لا يمكن أن تُنسب إلى ابن سينا، فقد غامرتني شكوك حينما رأيت نظرة أفلاطونية جلية في الرسالة ونحن نعلم قلة اهتمام ابن سينا بآراء أفلاطون كما أنّ تصنيف هذه الرسالة للمصابين برهاب الموت يخلو من التدقيق المنطقي. واعترض بعض الباحثين بأن الأصناف المقدمة متداخلة (سليماني 2008؛ شه گلی 2012)، بينما يُعرف ابن سينا بتصنيفاته المنطقية الدقيقة جدًا ويمكن القول أنّ عبارات الرسالة ليست بمستوى التدقيق العلمي الذي نألفه عند ابن سينا. إنّ مقارنة سريعة ونظرة خاطفة لرسالة دفع «**الغمّ من الموت**» من جهة و«**تهذيب الأخلاق من جهة أخرى**» تدلّنا بوضوح أنّهما نص واحد وكما استدللنا في مقال آخر، أنّها اقتطعت من كتاب مسكويه والأصل له وليس العكس.

خصّص مسكويه في المقالة السابعة من «**تهذيب الأخلاق**» بعنوان الطبّ النفساني فقرات حول موضوع الخوف وأنواعه (مسكويه 1405). وبعد أنّ تكلّم في الخوف المطلق يصل الأمر به إلى معالجة خوف الموت والذي يراه أعظم أنواع الخوف الذي يلحق الإنسان. يتناول مسكويه في هذا القسم من كتابه، أسباب قلق الموت والاغتمام الحاصل منه وأساليب مواجهته، محاولا إحصاء أسباب خوف الموت والتي يعرضها في سبعة أسباب (أميد 2013). ومن ثمّ، يصنّفها في خمسة محاور رئيسة ويسعى أن يصف أحسن علاج لكلّ منها. من حيث المبدأ، وعلى غرار أي مفكّر مهتمّ بالجوانب الفلسفية واللاهوتية يرى مسكويه أن العلاج الأنجع لهذه الحالات هي تبيين الحقائق المعرفية للمرضى وأسرهم (مسكويه 1405). على هذا، يمكن أن نعتبر معالجته لقضية رهاب الموت وقلقه ذات مقاربة فكرية تثقيفية أكثر منها ذات توجّه علاجي وتطبيقي.

يعرّف مسكويه حقيقة الموت على الطريقة المشائية بأنّها "مفارقة النفس للبدن" ويستنتج في تعلّة فلسفية تدفعه للإرجاع إلى الدراسات الفلسفية في إطار الأفلاطونية المحدثة بأنّ "الموت إذن ليس برديّ وإنما الرديّ هو الخوف منه؛ فإن الذي يخاف منه هو الجاهل به وبذاته." ومن هنا، يبدأ بتبيين المفاهيم الخاطئة التي أسفرت عن الأسباب المذكورة أدناه لقلق الموت والاغتمام بذكره (مسكويه 1405).

يقوم مسكويه بتحليل نفساني للمصابين برهاب الموت ليرينا الأسباب التى تؤدّي بهم لهذا الخوف، فيسرد لنا سبعة أسباب؛ فإنّ الخوف من الموت لا يحدث إلا لمن:

1. لا يدري حقيقة الموت.
2. لا يعلم مصير نفسه وعاقبته بعد الموت.
3. يظنّ أنه إذا انحلّ وبطل تركيبه فقد انحلّت ذاته وبطلت نفسه بطلان عدم ودثور.
4. يظنّ أن للموت ألمًا عظيمًا غير ألم الأمراض التي ربما تقدمته وأدّت إليه وكانت سبب حلوله.
5. يعتقد بعقوبة تحلّ به بعد الموت.
6. متحيّر لا يدري على أي شيء يقدم بعد الموت.
7. يأسف على ما يخلفه من الثروات والأموال.

وينهي كلامه عن ذكر الأسباب التي بسببها يخاف المصابون برهاب الموت بعبارة «وهذه كلّها ظنون باطلة لا حقيقة لها» (مسكويه 1424). من ثمّ يبدأ مسكويه بتقديم حلول لكلّ هذه الحالات بعد أن يلخّصها في خمس حالات رئيسة:

1. من جهل الموت ولم يدر ما هو؟
2. من لا يعلم إلى أين تصير نفسه أو يظنّ أن بدنه إذا انحلّ وبطل تركيبه فقد انحلّت ذاته وبطلت نفسه ويجهل بقاء النفس وكيفية المعاد.
3. من يظنّ انّ للموت ألمًا عظيما غير ألم الامراض المؤدّية إليه.
4. من يخاف الموت لأجل العقاب.
5. من يحزن على ما يخلّفه من أهل وولد ومال ويأسف على ما يفوته من ملاذّ الدنيا وشهواتها (مسكويه 1424).

يقوم مسكويه بعرض حلّ لكلّ حالة من الحالات المذكورة آنفا:

الحالة الأولى: علاج هذه الحالة باختزال، هو تبيين حقيقة الموت. هنا يأتي مسكويه بنظريته عن الموت وهي نظرية الفلاسفة المشائيين قائلين أن الموتَ ليس شيئًا أكثر مِن ترك النفس استعمال آلاتها التي هى أعضاء البدن. فكما يترك الصانع آلاته فإنّ النفس تغادر أعضاء البدن. ويضيف أنّ النفس جوهر غير جسمانى، غير قابلة للفساد (مسكويه 1424).هنا يُرجع مسكويه القارئ إلى تحليله عن النفس والذي بينّه باختصار ضمن المقالة الأولى من هذا الكتاب كما تحدّث عنه باستيعاب في سائر كتبه. فقد ألّف مسكويه كتابًا آخر حول السعادة الإنسانية والذي يمكن عدّه توأمًا لـ«**تهذيب الأخلاق**» وهو كتاب «**الفوز الأصغر**» (مسكويه 1402). في «**الفوز الأصغر**»، يفصّل مسكويه الحديث عن النفس الإنسانية فيكتب فصولًا في تحديد نسبة النفس والموت. يكفي مثلًا أن نطالع الفصول الخامسة والسادسة والسابعة لنعرف نظريته حول هذه المسألة والعناوين تشير إلى فحوى الفصول بوضوح؛ الفصل الخامس في أن النفس جوهر حي باق لا يقبل الموت ولا الفناء وأنها ليست الحياة بعينها بل تعطي الحياة كلّ ما توجد فيه،

والفصل السادس في اقتصاص مذاهب الحكماء والوجوه التي أثبتوها في أنّ النفس لا تقبل الموت، والسابع في ماهية النفس والحياة التي لها وما تلك الحياة التي تحفظها عليها حتى تكون دائمة البقاء سرمدية، ويعود في الفصل العاشر إلى الموضوع نفسه ليوضح كيفية حال النفس بعد مفارقتها البدن وما الذي يحصل لها بعد موت الإنسان (مسكويه 1402). يعرض مسكويه مبادئه للتنظير في حقيقة الموت في كتاب «**الفوز الأصغر**» وفي «**تهذيب الأخلاق**» يكتفي بعرض موجز للنظرية ويرجعنا إلى كتبه الأخرى ولعلّ مؤلفه المفقود «**الفوز الأكبر**» كان يضمّ تفاصيل أكثر عن الموضوع (مسكويه 1424؛ 2011).

ملخص كلام مسكويه هو أنّ الذي يخاف من الموت لجهله بحقيقة الموت فلا بدّ أن يعرف أنّ النفس جوهر روحاني لا يقبل استحالة ولا تغيرًا فى ذاته فلا يتصور فيه العدم والتلاشي.

الحالة الثانية: وهي عدم المعرفة بحال معاد النفس بعد موتها. يعتقد مسكويه بأنّ السبب الحقيقي للخوف في هذه الحالة هو الجهل وليس الموت. وأخذ يبين أهمية العلم عند الفلاسفة وأنّ الفيلسوف الذي يعرف أنّ الجهل هو الألم الحقيقي يسعى جاهدًا للتخلّص من هذا الألم، ولهذا لن يصاب سالك الفلسفة بمحنة هذا الخوف. ويؤسس لهذه القاعدة المعرفية الهامّة "إنّ التعب الحقيقي هو تعب الجهل لأنّه مرَض فى النفس والبرء منه خلاص وراحة سرمدية ولذة أبدية"، وبعبارة أخرى، "حيث كانت الراحة في الحقيقة هي الخلاص من الألم والألم الحقيقيّ هو الجهل، لا جَرَمَ كانت الراحة الحقيقية هي العلم" (خادمي 2015). ثمّ يسرد لنا أحوال الحكماء والعلماء الذين صغرت الدنيا الفانية في أعينهم واقتصروا منها على قدر الضرورة ويأتي بأسلوب أفلاطوني جلي -وهو الذي يختلف عن أسلوبه الأرسطي - ويمزجه بالأفلوطينية المحدثة ليفسّر لنا المقولة الأفلاطونية الشهيرة "مُت بالإرادة تحيا بالطبيعة." وصولًا إلى هذه الغاية يقسّم الموت إلى قسمين والحياة مثلهما، فهناك موت طبيعي وموت إرادي وحياة طبيعية وحياة إرادية. الأمر الذي تمّ تداوله بعد ذلك في الخطاب الصوفي الإسلامي ممّا جعل نصيرالدين الطوسي يضيف في ترجمة هذا القسم مقولة المتصوفة المشهورة "موتوا قبل أن تموتوا" ليتمّ تفسيرها في هذا السياق (الطوسي 1400).

ومجمل القول هنا ذكر أهمية نبذ العلائق الدنيوية جانبًا في سياق فلسفي. وفي تعلّة فلسفية يستدل فيلسوفنا الرازي أنّ حدّ الإنسان في الحقيقة هو الحي الناطق المائت وتمامية الإنسان بموته. "فمن أجهلُ ممّن يخلف تمام ذاته ومن أسوأ حالًا ممّن يظنّ أنّ فناءه بحياته ونقصانه بتمامه؟"

بناءًا على هذا، "يجب على العاقل أن يتوحش من النقصان و يأنس بالتمام و يطلب كلّ ما يتمّمه ويكمّله ويشرّفه ويُعلي منزلته ويحلّ رباطه من الوجه الذي يأمن به الوقوع في المخاوف ... ويثق

بأن الجوهر الشريف الإلهي إذا تخلص من الجوهر الكثيف الجسماني خلاص نقاء وصفاء، لا خلاص مزاج وكدر، فقد صعد العالم الأعلى وسعد وعاد إلى ملكوته، وقرب من بارئه وفاز بجوار ربّ العالمين، وخالطته الأرواح الطيّبة من أشكاله وأشباهه ونجا من أضداده وأغياره. ومن ههنا نعلم أنّ من فارقت نفسه بدنه وهي مشتاقة إليه، مشفقةً عليه، خائفة من فراقه، فهي في غاية الشقاء والألم من ذاتها وجوهرها، سالكةً إلى أبعد جهاتها من مستقرها، طالبةً قرارها والاستقرار به" (مسكويه 2002).

الحالة الثالثة: وهي حالة من يظنّ أنّ للموت ألمًا عظيمًا غير ألم الأمراض المؤدية إليه. يرى مسكويه بطريقة أبيقورية واضحة (عويضه 1414) كمواطنه الرازي أنّ هذا الظنّ خاطئ لأنّ الألم إنما يكون بالإدراك والإدراك إنما يكون للحي والحيّ هو القابل أثرَ النفس؛ والجسم الذي ليس فيه أثر النفس فإنه لا يألم ولا يحس، فالموت الذي هو مفارقة النفس للبدن لا ألم له لأن البدن إنما كان يألم ويحس بالنفس وحصول أثرها فيه؛ فإذا صار جسمًا لا أثر فيه للنفس فلا حس ولا ألم له. ومن الجدير بالذكر أنّ الفلاسفة التحليلين المعاصرين قاموا بتحليل لغوي لهذه القاعدة الأبيقورية وفسّروها بعدّة طرق مختلفة (Luper 2008; 2019; Nagel 2012).

الحالة الرابعة: وهي حالة من يخاف العقاب بعد الموت. يقول مسكويه بأنّ سبب خوف المصاب برهاب الموت في هذه الحالة هو العقاب ليس إلا؛ والعقاب إنما يكون على شيء باق معه بعد الموت؛ فهو لا محالة يعترف بذنوب وأفعال سيئة له يستحق عليها العقاب؛ وهو مع ذلك معترف بحاكم عدل يعاقب على السيئات. على هذا، يمكن اعتبار هذا الشخص خائفًا من ذنوبه لا من الموت؛ ومن خاف عقوبته على ذنب وجب عليه أن يحترز من ذلك الذنب ويجتنبه. ثمّ إنّ الذنوب هي رذائل منشأها الجهل ويعود مسكويه ليذكر أهمية العلم الذي يمكن أن يفسَّر هنا بالأخلاقيات. وبالنسبة إلى حالة المحتار الذي لا يعرف ماذا سيحدث بعد الموت فإن وصفة مسكويه له اكتساب العلم والمعرفة أيضا (مسكويه 2002).

الحالة الخامسة: وهي حال من يخاف ويتأسّف من ترك الأهل والأولاد والأموال والممتلكات. هذه الحالة في الحقيقة تنشأ من حزن على ما لا فائدة من التحسّر عليه. ولعلاج المصاب لهذه الحالة يرجعنا مسكويه إلى قسم آخر من كتابه في معالجة الحزن (مسكويه 2002).

1.2.3 تحليل ومقارنة

يتبدّى لنا أنّ مسكويه قام بجهود مشكورة من أجل تقديم نظرة عامّة وشاملة عن وجوه الخوف من الموت ومن ثمّ تقديم حلول نظرية لكلّ واحد من الأصناف المقدّمة. من نافلة القول أنّ هذا التصنيف يمكن اعتباره أوّل نواة للبحوث التالية في هذا المضمار ولذا له أهمية بالغة، إلا أنّ الباحث الناظر بنظرة نقدية يلاحظ خللًا منطقياً في تنضيد الأقسام المقدّمة وقد يلام على هذا

التصنيف على أنّها متداخلة كما نلاحظ عمومًا وخصوصًا من وجه في أصناف المصابين برهاب الموت والعلاجات المقترحة لهم. وليس هذا موضع قدح ههنا إذ لا يوجد تصنيف منطقي سابق على مسكويه يستند عليه وإنما ذكرنا النقص المنطقي لتقديم رؤية أكثر واقعية إلى عبارات مسكويه هنا.

بالنسبة إلى الجاهل بحقيقة الموت، يقترح مسكويه تبيين حقيقة الموت له. تجدر الإشارة هنا أنّ كلّ الناس ليسوا بمستوى من القدرات العقلية تمكّنهم لفهم القضايا الفلسفية العميقة ومن ثمّ إنّ هناك اختلافًا واضحًا بين الفلاسفة نفسهم، فلابدّ أن يكون الشخص قادرًا على تمييز النظريات الفلسفية المحقة من الباطلة. كما ينبغي الانتباه إلى أنّ الموت قضية ذات تشعبات كثيرة حيث اقترح بعض الفلاسفة إقامة مذهبٍ فلسفي شامل على أساس مشكلة الموت ينقسم إلى أربعة أقسام رئيسة: الأول بعنوان «ظاهريات الموت» ويتناول الناحية النفسية، الثاني بعنوان: «تقويمية الموت» ويتناول الناحية الأخلاقية، الثالث بعنوان «إلهيات الموت»، والرابع يتناول الناحية الوجودية ويحمل عنوان «وجوديات الموت» (بدوي 1945). وإنشاء مثل هذا المذهب مشروط لديه بأن تكون الناحية الوجودية هي الأساس في كل بحث. الأمر الذي نرى بداياته عند هيدجر حيث يؤكد على أن "الوجود الإنساني وجود متناه، وهذا التناهي هو مصدر القول والفعل. وإننا نمارس القول والفعل بالرغم من الموت. فالموت ليس شيئًا عارضًا، بل هو نسيج الوجود الإنساني" (هيدجر 2013). فليس الموت إذًا حادثًا يطرأ على الحي، بل الحي يحمل الموت بين جوانحه منذ أن بدأ حياته. وإنما يوهم الناس أنفسهم بالفرار من الموت، وذلك بإحالته إلى مجرد وقائع إحصائية لعدّ الوفيات، أو بردّه إلى اليقين بأن كل نفس ذائقة الموت، وكأن الموت يهمّ الناس ولا يهمّ أحدًا بالذات، مع أنه "في الموت يتم الشعور بالفردية إلى أقصى درجة إذ يشعر من يموت أنه يموت وحده لا يشاركه في موته أحد" (پيتركراوس 2005؛ عسكري يزدي وميرزايي 2018).

والنظريات عن الموت كثيرة سواءًا في الغرب أو في الشرق؛ فيمكننا مثلًا أن نعرض النظرية الهيجلية التي ترى الموت تصالحاً مع الذات (Singer 2001) حيث نظر هيجل إلى الخلود على أنه يقف شاهدًا على "لا تناهي الروح والقيمة المطلقة للفردية الروحية" فعنده أنّ "الخلود صفة حاضرة في الروح وليس واقعة أو حدثًا مستقبلًا" (هيجل 2006) وأنّ الموت "هو الحب ذاته، ففي الموت يتكشف الحبّ المطلق، إنّه وحدة ما هو إلهي مع ما هو إنساني" (Houlgate 2005)؛ ومن البديهي أن هناك بون شاسع بين التنظير الهيجلي ونظريات أتباع المذهب الفيزيائي (physicalism) حيث تقول أطروحتهم الفلسفية بأن كل شيء فيزيائي ولا يوجد شيء ما وراء المادة الفيزيائية (Stoljar 2017) وعلى هذا يقدّمون تفسيرًا بيولوجيًا بحتًا للموت أو مذهب

شوبنهاور الذي يعتقد "أنّ الموت بالنسبة إلى لشخص المحتضر هو لحظة الانشطار التي يتوقف فيها وعيه فهو شعور يشبه الإغماء وليس سوى مشهد كريه" (بدوي 1942).

ماذا يفعل الشخص الذي لا يعرف الحقيقة بين هذه النظريات؟ فهل يتوجّب عليه أن يتبنى نظرة فويرباخ الذي يخاطب الموت قائلا "أيها الموت! ليس بمقدوري انتزاع نفسي من التأمل العذب في طبيعتك الرقيقه، المرتبطة ارتباطًا وثيقًا بطبيعتي، يا مرآة روحي وانعكاس وجودي. من قلب انفصال الوحدة البسيطة للطبيعة عن ذاتها تنشأ الروح الواعية وينهض هذا النور المتأمل لذاته على نحو ما يسطع القمر في المجد المنعكس عن الشمس. وكذلك أنت أيضًا لا تعكس في توهجك الرقيق إلا اللهب المتقد للوعي أنت نجمة المساء في الطبيعة ونجمة الصباح للروح" (Feuerbach 1981) أو يقبل الرأي القائل بأنّ الموت شرّ حلّ بالإنسان فنغّص عيشه سواء عند الاتجاهات الدينية لأمثال أغسطينوس الذي يرى الموت شرًّا عرض على البشرية برمتها ودخل العالم بسبب خطيئة آدم التي أدت إلى طرده من عالم الخلد فأصبح لأول مرة قابلًا للفناء والزوال (كاكائى 2019، 2016) أو النظرة الإلحادية لأمثال نيتشه الذي ينشد "إن المقاتل ليكره الموت الساخر" (شورون 1984).

في الحالة الثانية نرى توجهًا أفلوطينيا بارزا عند مسكويه يجمعه مع المدرسة الرواقية الإغريقية والرومانية التي ترى انّ الفيلسوف الحقيقي يواجه الموت ويعرض عن الدنيا كما يتشبّه في ذلك بديوجانس الكلبي الذي قيل عنه "كان حكيمًا فاضلًا متقشفًا لا يقتني شيئًا ولا يأوى إلى منزل." وفي الحالة الثالثة يلجأ إلى آراء الأبيقوريين ليستدلّ على عدم إدراك الألم في حالة الموت لكن هذه المرّة بدون ذكر مقدمات تلزم عليك هذا القول كما فعل مواطنه الرازي. وفي الحالة الرابعة تظهر النظرية السقراطية أو النظرية المعروفة بالموت الطيب بعد حياة طيبة (May 2009) والتي ذكرناها عند ذكرنا لليوناردو دافنشي. والحالة الخامسة إرجاع إلى حالة الحزن ولكنّه يقترب إلى قول بعض الفلاسفة الماديين المتأخرين الذين يرون ان لا فائدة في التحسّر بما لا يمكننا دفعه وبهذا يحاولون دفع الاغتمام الحاصل من ذكر الموت.(شورون 1984، مسكويه 1405).

على كلّ، تحظى عبارات مسكويه بأنها اكثر اتساعًا في ذكر أسباب خوف الموت لكن بحوثه وإن كانت مستفيضة شيئًا ما لكنها ليست دراسة نسقية متشابكة بل يتبدى لنا أنّه حاول أن يتمسك بعدة نظريات مختلفة المنشأ ومتفاوتة المنبت لتستقصي جوانب البحث، فعمله أشبه بجمع نظريات إلى جعلها في نظام مترابط متّسق لتخرج منها نظرية متآلفة منطقيًا ومحبوكة بانتظام فلسفيا. وليس هذا نقدًا موجّها لفيلسوفنا فحسب حيث يقول روبرت أولسن (Robert Olson) عن سائر الفلاسفة "على الرغم من أن معظم الفلاسفة الكبار درسوا مشكلة الموت بطريقة أو بأخرى فإنّ قلة منهم هم الذين درسوه دراسة نسقية مستفيضة." ولعلّ هذا يعود إلى كراهية

الإنسان للفناء وحبّه للبقاء لمن يظنّ أنّ الموت فناء، ومن هنا قال أحد المفكرين المعاصرين "أن ثمة شيئين لا يمكن أن يحدق فيهما المرء: الشمس والموت!" (Olson 2017).

بغضّ النظر عن وجوه الخلل، يبدو أنّ معالجة مسكويه لهذه القضية كانت أوسع الجهود المبذولة في الحضارة الإسلامية والتي انتشرت عبر ترجمات وشروح مباشرة وغير مباشرة إلى مختلف أنحاء العالم الإسلامي وطوال قرون متتالية.

3.3 صدر الدين الشيرازي والخوف من الموت

محمد بن إبراهيم القوامي الشيرازي المشهور بصدر المتألهين وملا صدرا الشيرازي، فيلسوف مؤسس ينسب إليه نهج الجمع بين الاستدلال العقلي والشهود العرفاني والتفسير الديني ويسمي طريقته الفلسفية بالحكمة المتعالية. فهو كمن سبقه من فلاسفة الإسلام بل وأكثر منهم بكثير حاول دراسة جوانب الحياة الأخروية كما أبرز هذه النقطة الفيلسوف الفرنسي هنري كوربين (Corbin 2008; Jambet 2006). تكلّم فيلسوفنا الشيرازي باستفاضه في موضوع الموت وأسبابه وحقيقته (ارشد رياحى 2002، رحيم پور وزارع 2013، شايانفر ومقدم للكلو 2015، شه گلى 2012، عارفي 2005، فرامرز قراملكي وهمتي 2008) سواءًا في كتبه المتعلّقة بعلم النفس أو كتبه عن المعاد وخاصة المجلدين الأخيرين من كتابه الموسوعي «**الحكمة المتعالية في الأسفار الأربعة العقلية**»، ولكنّه قلّما تكلّم عن رهاب الموت والقلق الحاصل من ذكره. نقوم هنا بعرض عبارات ملا صدرا في هذا المضمار لتتبين نظريته لنا. يطرح صدر الدين الشيرازي في المجلد السابع من الحكمة المتعالية سؤالًا يستتبع الخوض في المسألة المطروحة هنا والسؤال هو "ما العلة في محبة الحيوانات الحياة وكراهيتها الممات؟"، يجيب الشيرازي عن هذا السؤال قائلًا:

> لعلل شتى، إحداها أن الحياة تشبه البقاء والممات الفناء والبقاء محبوب والفناء مكروه في طباع الموجودات إذ كان البقاء قرين الوجود والفناء قرين العدم والوجود والعدم متقابلان والباري عزّ شأنه لما كان علة الموجودات وهو باق أبدًا صارت الموجودات كلّها تحب البقاء وتشتاق إليه لأنه صفة لعلتها والمعلول يحب علته وصفاتها ويشتاق إليها ويتشبه بها.
>
> الشيرازى 1989

يتبدى لنا اتجاه الشيرازي الصوفي جليًا ليدخلنا في منظومة من أفكار ومبادئ عرفانية سبق وتكلّم عنها فيلسوفنا في المجلدات السابقة عن هذا المجلّد ويستمرّ الشيرازي في إجابته عن هذا السؤال بذكر دليلين آخرين هما: "وثانيها ما يلحقها من الآلام والأوجاع والفزع والجزع عند مفارقة نفوسها الأبدان، وثالثها أن نفوسها لا تدري بأن لها وجودًا خلوا من الأجسام." نراه مرّة أخرى يطرح

السؤال نفسه ويجيب عنه في المجلد التاسع من كتابه بعد أن يصنف أسباب رهاب الموت إلى نوعين قائلا:

> نقول في كراهة الموت البدني للنفوس الإنسانية سببان: فاعلي وغائي، أما السبب الفاعلي فهو أن أول نشئات النفس هي هذه النشأة الطبيعية البدنية ولها الغلبة على النفوس ما دامت متصلة بالبدن متصرفة فيه، فيجري عليها أحكام الطبيعة البدنية ويؤثر فيها كلما يؤثر في الجوهر الحسي والحيوان الطبيعي من الملائمات والمنافيات البدنية ولهذا تتألم وتتضرّر بتفرق الاتصال والاحتراق بالنار وأشباه ذلك لا من حيث كونها جواهر نطقية وذواتًا عقلية بل من حيث كونها جواهر حسية وقوى تعلقية فتوحشها من الموت البدني وكراهتها إنما يكون لحصة لها من النشأة الطبيعية وهي متفاوتة بحسب شدة الانغمار في البدن والانكباب فيه على أنا لا نسلم الكراهة عند الموت الطبيعي الذي يحصل في آخر الأعمار الطبيعية دون الآجال الاخترامية وأما ما يقتضيه العقل التام وقوة الباطن وغلبة نور الإيمان بالله واليوم الآخر وسلطان الملكوت فهو محبة الموت الدنيوي والتشوق إلى الله ومجاورة مقربيه وملكوته والتوحش عن حياة الدنيا وصحبة الظلمات ومجاورة المؤذيات ...
>
> الشيرازي 1989

أمّا السبب الثاني في كراهية الناس للموت له أهمّية في الحياة نفسها وهو أمر غريزي في الأحياء قبل أن يكون أمرًا إراديا ويكتب الشيرازي عن هذا:

> وأما السبب الغائي والحكمة في كراهة الموت هو محافظة النفس للبدن الذي هو بمنزلة المركب في طريق الآخرة وصيانته عن الآفات العارضة ليمكن لها الاستكمالات العلمية والعملية إلى أن يبلغ كمالها الممكن وكذا إرادة الله تعالى تعلقت بإبداع الألم والإحساس به في غرائز الحيوانات والخوف في طباعها عمّا يلحق أبدانها من الآفات العارضة والعاهات الواردة عليها حثًا لنفوسها على حفظ أبدانها وكلالة أجسادها وصيانة هياكلها من الآفات العارضة لها إذ الأجساد لا شعور لها في ذاتها ولا قدرة على جر منفعة أو دفع مضرة فلو لم يكن الألم والخوف في نفوسها لتهاونت النفوس بالأجساد وخذلتها وأسلمتها إلى المهالك قبل فناء أعمارها وانقضاء آجالها ولهلكت في أسرع مدة قبل تحصيل نشأة كمالية برزخية وتعمير الباطن وذلك ينافي المصلحة الإلهية والحكمة الكلية في إيجادها.
>
> الشيرازي 1989

ويذكر صدر المتألهين أنّ خوف الموت إذا زاد عن الحدّ الضروري الحافظ للبقاء فمصدره جهل الإنسان ويصف لنا وصفة الحكماء السابقين لمعالجة رهاب الموت وهو المعرفة والعلم (سليماني 2008).

1.3.3 تحليل لرأي الشيرازي ومقارنته بنظريات أخرى

مجمل القول في رأي الشيرازي أنّه يعتقد أوّلًا أنّ الموت مرحلة انتقالية من عالم إلى عالم آخر حيث يقسم الموت إلى موتين: طبيعي واخترامي(شايانفر ومقدم للكلو 2015؛ شه گلی 2012؛ فرامرز قراملكي وهمتي 2008) فالموت الطبيعي يحلّ بالإنسان حينما تنضج نفسه كما تنضج الفاكهة التي حان وقت قطوفها والموت في هذه الحالة هو انقطاع الإنسان عن العلائق الدنيوية بشكل طبيعي والموت الاخترامي الذي يحلّ بالإنسان قبل ذلك بحاجة إلى تفسيرات درس الشيرازي جوانبها في كتبه(أسعدي 2016؛ قوانلو، ناجي إصفهاني وأفشاركرماني 2017). في هذا السياق، لا يمكن اعتبار الموت شرًّا على الإنسان والحيوانات إذ أنّ هناك أنواعًا من الحشر بعد الحياة الدنيوية وهي كلّها مراحل في الوجود أرقى من هذه الدنيا (الشيرازي 1419؛ ديباجي وشوبكلائي 2012؛ زماني خارائي والهبداشتي 2014). علاوة على ذلك، يرى ملا صدرا أنّ التفكير في الموت هو أمر إيجابي وله فوائد جمّة لحفظ حياة الحيوانات والإنسان معتقدًا أنّ الخوف من الآلام منشأها الخوف من الفناء والموت وهو الذي اقتضت الإرادة الإلهية أن يجعله في كيان الحيوانات وليس حكرًا على الإنسان (رامين 2019).

بناءًا على هذا، وإن كان الشيرازي يعتقد بأنّ هذه الفكرة صالحة لبقاء الإنسان ويشبهه مارتن هيدجر في هذا المجال ولكنّ الثاني يختصر أهمية قلق الموت لإعطاء المعنى لحياة الإنسان ولا يتكلّم عن إمكانية البقاء بعد الموت خلافًا للشيرازي (أبطحي 2019؛ صالحي وأكبرزاده 2015؛ مهري، منصفي ومصلح 2018). ونظرة هيدجر المؤكدة على فردانية الإنسان في مواجهة الموت تختلف بدورها عن النظرة الطاوية (Taoism) الشرقية حيث تعتقد الأخيرة أنّ الموت خروج عن الفردانية وأنّ الأمواج تعود إلى البحر مرّة أخرى عند حضيضها (Hansen 2020). ولعلّها أشبه بنظرية الشيرازي والنظريات الصوفية في العالم الإسلامي حيث يصرّحون بأنّ الإنسان يرجع إلى العالم الأعلى في قوس الصعود (رحيم‌پور وزارع 2013؛ عارفي 2005؛ كاكائي وناصرو 2019)، وفي هذه السياق أنشد جلال‌الدين الرومي:

ما ز بالاییم و بالا می‌رویم　　ما ز دریاییم و دریا می‌رویم
ما از اینجا و از آنجا نیستیم　　ما ز بی‌جاییم و بی‌جا می‌رویم
مولوی 2005

نحن من العالم الأعلى وسنعود إلى العالم الأعلى
نحن من البحر وسنعود إلى البحر
نحن لسنا من هنا وهناك
نحن من اللامكان وسنعود إلى اللامكان

4 النتائج والتوصيات

قمنا في هذه الدراسة بتقديم نظريات ثلاثة من مفكّري الحضارة الإسلامية الذين اهتّموا بمسألة رهاب الموت كما حاولنا تحليل عباراتهم ومقارنتها بآراء بعض الفلاسفة المتقدمين والمتأخرين. خلال هذه الدراسة تبدى لنا بوضوح أنّ نظريات رهاب الموت عند مفكري الحضارة الإسلامية تتسم بمقاربة فلسفية أخلاقية جلية وانتشرت هذه المقاربة المعرفية في العالم الإسلامي عبر مؤلفات الأخلاقيات الفلسفية. يمكن أن ننظر إلى المساعي المبذولة في هذا الجانب بأنها جهود مشكورة حيث كانت واسعة النطاق نسبياً بالمقارنة مع آراء فلاسفة الإغريق وان كانوا مصدر استلهام الفلاسفة المسلمين لكنّ الرازي الأبيقوري ومسكويه الأرسطي والشيرازي الصوفي ساهموا في تقديم آراء ونظريات بديعة لحدّ ما على هذا الصعيد.

علاوة على ذلك، لا بدّ أن نشير إلى انّ مقاربات فلاسفة الحضارة الإسلامية واتجاهاتهم المعرفية مع أهميتها المعرفية وتألقها الفلسفي في عصرها، تفتقر إلى الجانب التطبيقي والعلاجي. يمكن القول أنّ هذه المقاربات تتسمّ بطابع معرفي وبيداغوجي تثقيفي بامتياز، وفي الوقت نفسه خليق بنا أن نطوّرها نظريا وتطبيقيا إذا أردنا استخدامها في حقل الرعاية التلطيفية. ولا ينبغي غضّ النظر عن هذه النظريات بحجة أنّها تفتقر إلى الجانب التوظيفي اذ تكوّن كمثيلاتها في الفلسفات الغربية رصيدا ثقافيا ومعرفيا يمثل دور مبادئ سابقة وأمر قبلي (*a priori*) بالنسبة إلى كلّ اتجاه تطبيقي يمكن تقديمه.

من نافلة القول أن نؤكد على أنّ الوصول من المبادئ النظرية والفلسفية إلى الجانب التطبيقي ليس عملية فردانية يقوم بها الفيلسوف نفسه، وفي عالمنا المعاصر وفي ظلّ الانتشار المتسارع للتخصصات المتعدّدة في ميادين العلم والمعرفة انصرف كلّ علم من العلوم تعمقًا في تخصصاته الدقيقة محققًا اكتشافات علمية مبهرة ولكن هذه الكنوز المعرفية شابها التشتت وعدم وجود روابط تحقق الاستفادة التكاملية بين العلوم المختلفة. وللحيلولة دون ذلك ولتكوين عقلية علمية أكثر شمولية وتكاملية أصبحت الدراسات المتعددة التخصصات (multidisciplinary) والدراسات البينية (interdisciplinary) مطلباً عالميًا للجامعات والمراكز البحثية. ونظراً إلى أهمية الدراسات البينية بين العلوم المختلفة ومحاولةً لتجسير الفجوة بين العلوم النظرية والتطبيقية، بعد أن تشعَّبت وتشَّظت على هذا النحو غير المسبوق، يُقترح عادة وضع استراتيجيات بحثية لدراسة القضايا

الفلسفية الإنتزاعية ومدى إمكانية تحققها في الحياة المعاصرة بحيث يساهم فيها تخصصات معرفية شتى ومن وجوه نظر متنوعة. وتجنباً لإغفال دور العلوم الإنسانية النظرية والفلسفية في إثراء سائر مجالات المعرفة والبحث العلمي يمكن أن يتكوّن فريق بحث من المختصين في المجالات المختلفة من قطاع العلوم الإنسانية وقطاع العلوم الطبيعية والتطبيقية كعلم النفس وعلم الاجتماع والطب النفسي والفلسفة ونظرية التربية وغير ذلك ليتم إعادة صياغة هذه النظريات ومثيلاتها لتقديم حلول ناجعة للمصابين برهاب الموت على صعيد الرعاية التلطيفية. إذ يمكن لكلّ واحد من التخصصات المعرفية أن تبحث عن الموضوع من وجهات نظر مختلفة وتساهم في إثراء المداولات المعرفية ونضج الخطاب الفلسفي لتلبية احتياجات المجتمعات والحياة البشرية.

والحمد لله أولًا وآخرًا

المصادر والمراجع

آرضائي، حامد. 2020. «ابن سينا و هراس از مرگ، تصحيح يک اشتباه درباره تک‌نگاری منسوب به ابن سينا». **حکمت سينوی** 64(24): 77–93.

آزادي، محمود، وسيد محمد كلانتر كوشه. 2016. «اضطراب مرگ از ديدگاه ابن سينا و اليس: رهيافتی مقايسه‌ای-التقاطی». **انديشه نوين دينی** 47(12): 59–72.

أفلاطون. 1994. **أفلاطون – المحاورات الكاملة**، ترجمة شوقي داود تمراز. بيروت: الأهلية للنشر والتوزيع.

أفلاطون. 2001. **محاكمة سقراط: محاورات أوطيفرون، الدفاع، أقريطون**، ترجمة عزت قرني. القاهرة: دار قباء.

أفلاطون. 2002. **محاورة فيدون أو في خلود النفس**، ترجمة عزت قرني. القاهرة: دار قباء.

أبطحي، صديقه، غلامحسين خدري، هادى وكيلي، ومهدي دهباشي. 2019. «سنجش مرگ‌انديشی با معنای زندگی از منظر حکمت متعاليه». **الهيات تطبيقی** 21(10): 63–78.

ابن سينا. 1994. **رسائل ابن سينا (بيدار)**، ج. 1. قم: بيدار.

ابن سينا. 2009. **مجموعه رسائل شيخ الرئيس ابن سينا**. طهران: آيت اشراق.

أحمدي زاده، حسن. 2012. «مقايسه ديدگاه ابن سينا و ارسطو درباره ماهيت نفس و نتايج اين ديدگاه ها در زندگی پس از مرگ». **انديشه نوين دينی** 31(8): 147–64.

أرشد رياحي، علی. 2002. «تحليل و نقد نظر نفوس انسانی با يکديگر پس از مرگ از ديدگاه سه حکيم مسلمان (فارابی-ابن سينا-صدرالمتألهين)». **علوم انسانی دانشگاه الزهرا(س)** 41(12): 1–16.

أسعدي، عليرضا. 2016. «ملاصدرا و مسئله مرگ». **نقد و نظر** 21(81): 92–123.

اعتمادي فرد، اعظم، ومالک حسيني. 2015. «سقراط افلاطون: رابطه خودشناسی با زندگی و مرگ راستين». **پژوهش‌های اخلاقی** 21(6): 5–23.

أفلاطون. 2001. **محاورات أفلاطون**، ترجمة زكي نجيب محمود، ج. 1. محاورات أفلاطون. القاهرة: الهيئة المصرية العامة للكتاب.

أكبري، رضا. 2009. «تصوير زندگی پس از مرگ در فلسفه ابن سینا». **فلسفه و کلام اسلامی** 1(2): 11–28.

أمجديان، قاسم، وعسكر ديرباز. 2014. «نقد دیدگاه صدرالمتألهین در باب مرگ انسان با تکیه بر آرای ابن سینا». **معرفت فلسفی** 45(12): 121–142.

أميد، مسعود. 2013. «تخفیف و تسکین هراس از مرگ». **اطلاعات حکمت و معرفت** 92(8): 29–34.

بدوي، عبد الرحمن. 1942. **شوپنهور**. بيروت لبنان: دار القلم.

بدوي، عبد الرحمن. 1945. **الموت والعبقرية**. القاهرة: مكتبة النهضة المصرية.

پشت‌دار، علي محمد. 2010. «اخلاق منصوری و ارزش‌های ادبی آن». **پیام بهارستان** 89(2): 77–95.

پيتركراوس. 2005. «مرگ و ما بعد الطبیعه؛ نیستی و معنای هستی در فلسفه هستی هایدگر»، ترجمة محمد سعيد حنايي كاشاني. **ارغنون** 26–27 (6): 273–294.

جهانبخش، جويا. 2018. «أخلاق ناصري در کهن جامه‌ای تازی؛ یادداشتی با شادمانگی انتشار کتابی ارزنده». **آینه پژوهش** 174(29): 87–100.

خادمي، عين الله. 2013. «وضعیت طبقه‌بندی نفوس پس از مرگ (مقایسه دیدگاه ابن سینا و سهروردی)». **حکمت سینوی** 49(17): 114–134.

خادمي، عين الله. 2015. «چیستی لذت از منظر مسکویه». **شناخت** 72(1): 35–55.

خاني، مريم، مهری چنگي آشتياني، وسيدحسن ميرديلمي. 2019. «مرگ از دیدگاه ابن‌سینا و فلوطین». **معرفت** 259(28): 63–74.

خدري، غلامحسين. 2020. «تبیین و تحلیلی انتقادی بر رابطه «مرگ‌اندیشی» با «معنای زندگی» در فلسفه کرکگور». **فلسفه دين** 43(17): 235–258.

خراساني، محبوبه. 2008. «اخلاق نامه‌نویسی در ایران و جایگاه اخلاق جلالی». **پژوهش‌های ادبی** 20(5): 9–24.

ديباجي، سيد محمد علي، ومسلم شوبكلائي. 2012. «واکاوی مسئله حشر حیوانات از دیدگاه ملاصدرا». **فصلنامه علمی پژوهشی آیین حکمت** 3(زمستان 90-مسلسل 10): 33–66.

الرازي، محمد بن زكريا. 1408. **المنصوري في الطب**. كويت: المنظمة العربية للتربية والثقافة والعلوم، معهد المخطوطات العربية.

الرازي، محمد بن زكريا. 1422. **الحاوي في الطب**، ج. 1. بيروت: دار إحياء التراث العربي.

الرازي، محمد بن زكريا. 1426. **الشكوك للرازي على كلام فاضل الأطباء جالينوس في الكتب التي نسبت إليه**، ج. 1. القاهرة: دار الكتب والوثائق القومية، الإدارة المركزية للمراكز العلمية، مركز تحقيق التراث.

الرازي، محمد بن زكريا. 1978. **الطب الروحاني**. القاهرة: مكتبة النهضة المصرية.

الرازي، محمد بن زكريا. 2005. **الدراسة التحليلية لكتاب الطب الروحاني للطبيب الفيلسوف محمد بن زكريا الرازي**. طهران: انتشارات انجمن آثار ومفاخر فرهنگی.

الرازي، محمد بن زكريا. 2005. **رسائل فلسفية (رازي)**. دمشق: بدايات.

رازي‌زاده، فاطمه. 2019. «استكمال نفس پس از مرگ از منظر ابن سينا». **حكمت سينوى** 61(23): 118–132.

رامين، فرح. 2019. «تأملی بر چيستی مرگ در فلسفه شوپنهاور و ملاصدرا». **حكمت معاصر** 28(10): 111–136.

رحيم پور، فروغ. 2008. «تحليلی بر نقش بدن در ابتدا و انتهای حيات دنيوی از منظر ابن سينا». **انديشه دينی** 53(14): 3–32.

رحيم پور، فروغ السادات، وفاطمه زارع. 2013. «فرجام نفوس انسانی پس از مرگ بدن در انديشه ابن سينا، سهروردی و ملاصدرا». **انسان پژوهی دينی** 29(10): 109–134.

زماني خارائي، علي، وعلي اله بداشتي. 2014. «عوالم سه گانه‌ی وجود و نقش آن در حشر انسان از ديدگاه ملاصدرا». **دوفصلنامه علمی ـ پژوهشی حكمت صدرايی** 5(1): 67–76.

زنجاني، ميرزا ابوطالب. 1996. **كيميای سعادت: ترجمه طهارة الأعراق ابوعلي مسكويه رازي**. طهران: ميراث مكتوب.

سبزه آراي لنگرودي، ميلاد، نادر حاجلو، سجاد بشرپور، وعباس ابوالقاسمي. 2016. «مرگ آگاهی تجربه ای بيدار كننده: دو مطالعه بر اضطراب مرگ و ارزش گذاری آرزوهای بيرونی». **پژوهش در سلامت روانشناختی** 28(10): 21–30.

سبينوزا، باروخ. 2009. **علم الأخلاق**، ترجمة جلال الدين سعيد. بيروت: المنظمة القومية للترجمة.

سليماني، فاطمه. 2008. «ترس از مرگ با تكيه بر ديدگاه ابن سينا و ملاصدرا». **حكمت سينوى** 40(12): 75–101.

شاهيني، علي رضا، ومحمد رضا نصر إصفهاني. 2011. «مرگ انديشی هدايت نگرشی فلسفی يا روان شناسانه؟!». **پژوهش زبان و ادبيات فارسی** 23(10): 79–100.

شايان فر، شهناز، وزهرا مقدم للكلو. 2015. «تبيين وجودی مرگ از ديدگاه ابن سينا و ملاصدرا». **پژوهش‌های هستی شناختی** 8(4): 39–56.

شفيع بيک، إيمان. 2015. «تعريف «فلسفه» و «فيلسوف» در فايدون افلاطون». **فلسفه** 31(43): 21–40.

شه گلي، أحمد. 2012. «علت مرگ از ديدگاه ابن سينا و ملاصدرا». **آينه معرفت** 31(10): 95–118.

شورون، جاك. 1984. **الموت في الفكر الغربي**، ترجمة كامل يوسف حسين. الكويت: عالم المعرفة.

الشيرازي، صدر الدين. 1419. **رساله الحشر فارسی-عربی**، ترجمة وتصحيح محمد خواجوي. طهران: مولی.

الشيرازي، صدر الدين، ومحمد بن إبراهيم. 1989. **الحكمة المتعالية فى الأسفار العقلية الأربعة**. قم: مكتبة المصطفوی.

صالحي، اكبر، وفهيمه اكبرزاده. 2015. «تحليل تطبيقی ديدگاه اسلامی و آرای مارتين هايدگر در زمينه مرگ آگاهی و پيامدهای آن بر سبک زندگی». **پژوهش در مسائل تعليم و تربيت اسلامی** 26(23): 59–84.

طاهري أخوان، زهرا. 2011. «اندر حكايت بوعلی سينا ...». **كتاب ماه فلسفه** 48(4): 33–38.

الطوسي، نصير الدين محمد. 1400. **أخلاق ناصري**، ج. 1. طهران: علميه اسلاميه.
الطوسي، نصير الدين محمد. 1994. **أوصاف الأشراف**. طهران: وزارت فرهنگ و ارشاد اسلامی، سازمان چاپ و انتشارات.
الطوسي، نصير الدين محمد. 2008. **أخلاق ناصري**. ترجمة محمد صادق فضل الله. بيروت: دار الهادي.
عارفي، محمد إسحاق. 2005. «مرگ و بقای نفس: نقد و بررسی دیدگاه ابن سینا، سهروردی و ملاصدرا». **الهيات و حقوق** 18(5): 51–72.
عسكري يزدي، علي، ومسعود ميرزايي. 2018. «مرگ‌اندیشی و معنای زندگی در هایدگر». **فلسفه دين** 34(15): 25–49.
فرامرز قراملكي، أحد، وحيدر همتي. 2008. «چيستی و انواع مرگ از ديدگاه ابن سينا و ملاصدرا». **رهنمون** 27–28(7): 19–40.
قائمي، محمّد مهدي، وأحمد واعظي. 2014. «حقيقت مرگ، مرگ انديشی ومعنای زندگی». **آيين حكمت** 20(6): 155–183.
قربان خاني، مرضيه، وسيد محمّدرضا ابن الرسول. 2012. «مقايسه ی دو كتاب «أخلاق ناصري» و اخلاق «محتشمی»». **اخلاق** 28(2): 199–244.
قطب‌الدين شيرازي، محمود بن مسعود. 1990. **درة التاج**، ج. 1. تصحيح محمد مشكوة. طهران: حكمت.
قوانلو، فاطمه، حامد ناجي اصفهاني، وعزيزاله أفشاركرماني. 2017. «مرگ از نظر ملاصدرا در نگره تفسير فلسفي تعابير موت و نفس». **پژوهش ديني** 35(17): 107–119.
كازروني، آسيه. 2007. «توضيح الأخلاق خليفه سلطان تحريری از أخلاق ناصري خواجه نصيرالدين طوسی». **فرهنگ** 61–62(20): 575–594.
كاكايي، قاسم، ومحبوبه جباره ناصرو. 2016. «بررسی و نقد ارتباط مرگ و گناه در آثار آگوستين قديس». **الهيات تطبيقی** 16(7): 1–18.
كاكائي، قاسم، ومحبوبه جباره ناصرو. 2019. «بررسی تطبيقی مرگ‌انديشی از ديدگاه آگوستين قديس و ملاصدرا». **تأملات فلسفی** 22(9): 11–41.
محمد، عبد اللطيف. 1986. **إصلاح النفس بين الرازي في الطب الروحاني، والكرماني في الأقوال الذهبية**. القاهرة: دار الثقافة العربية.
محمد عويضه، محمد. 1414. **أبيقور مؤسس المدرسة الأبيقورية**، ج. 1. بيروت: دار الكتب العلمية.
مسكويه، أبو علي أحمد. د.ت. **تهذيب الأخلاق وتطهير الأعراق**، ج. 1. اصفهان: مهدوی.
مسكويه، أبو علي أحمد. 1402. **الفوز الأصغر**، ج. 1. بيروت: دار مكتبه الحياة.
مسكويه، أبو علي أحمد. 1405. **تهذيب الأخلاق لإبن مسكويه في التربية**. بيروت: دار الكتب العلمية.
مسكويه، أبو علي أحمد. 1424. **تجارب الأمم وتعاقب الهمم**. ج. 1. بيروت – لبنان: دار الكتب العلمية.
مسكويه، أبو علي أحمد. 1426. **تهذيب الأخلاق وتطهير الأعراق**، ج. 1. قم: طليعه النور.
مسكويه، أبو علي أحمد. 1990. **اخلاق و راه سعادت: اقتباس و ترجمه از طهاره الاعراق ابن مسكويه**، ج. 1. طهران: فيض كاشاني.

مسكويه، أبو علي أحمد. 2002. **تهذيب الاخلاق**، ترجمة علي اصغر حلبي. طهران: اساطير.

مسكويه، أبو علي أحمد. 2011. **تهذيب الأخلاق وتطهير الأعراق**. بيروت: منشورات الجمل.

كمپاني زارع، مهدي، ومنيره پنج تني. 2013. «دفتر ماه: مرگ انديشي و مرگ آگاهی». **اطلاعات حكمت و معرفت** 92(8): 6–10.

مهري، هژير، عليرضا منصفي، وعلي‌اصغر مصلح. 2018. «مرگ‌انديشي در پرتو ديدگاه‌هاى اسلامى و غربى: مقايسه تطبيقى ديدگاه‌هاى ملاصدرا و هيدگر با توجه نظرات هانرى كربن». **جستارهای فلسفه دين** 15(7): 45–65.

مولوي، جلال الدين محمد بن محمد. 2005. **كليات شمس تبريزى**، ج. 1. طهران: طلايه.

ميرزامحمد، علي رضا. 2007. «انديشه هاى اخلاقى ابن مسكويه در أخلاق ناصري». **فرهنگ** 61–62(20): 595–626.

نراقي، احمد بن محمدمهدي. 1999. **معراج السعادة**، ج. 1. قم: هجرت.

نراقي، مهدي بن أبي ذر. 2006. **جامع السعادات**. بيروت: موسسة الأعلى للمطبوعات.

هيجل. 2006. **فنومينولوجيا الرّوح**، ترجمة ناجي المؤنلي. بيروت: المنظمة العربية للترجمة.

هيدجر، مارتن. 2013. **الكينونة والزمان**، ترجمة فتحي المسكيني. بيروت: دار الكتّاب الجديد.

Adamson, Peter. 2008. "Platonic Pleasures in Epicurus and Al-Razi." In *In the Age of al-Farābī: Arabic Philosophy in the Fourth-Tenth Century*, edited by Peter Adamson, 71–97. London: Warburg Institute.

Adamson, Peter. 2021. *Al-Rāzī*. Oxford: Oxford University Press.

Carus, Titus Lucretius. 1994. *On the Nature of the Universe*. London: Penguin Books.

Corbin, Henry. 2008. *History of Islamic Philosophy*. London: Routledge.

Crowell, Steven. 2020. "Existentialism." In *The Stanford Encyclopedia of Philosophy*, edited by Edward N. Zalta. Stanford: Stanford University Press.

DeGrazia, David. 2017. "The Definition of Death." In *The Stanford Encyclopedia of Philosophy*, edited by Edward N. Zalta. Stanford: Stanford University Press.

Edwards, Paul. 1967. *The Encyclopedia of Philosophy*. New York: Macmillan.

Epicurus. 2016. *Principal Doctrines*. London: Independent Publishing Platform.

Feuerbach, Ludwig. 1981. *Thoughts on Death and Immortality: From the Papers of a Thinker*, translated by James A. Massey. Oakland, CA: University of California Press.

Flynn, Thomas. 2006. *Existentialism: A Very Short Introduction*. Oxford: Oxford University Press.

Goodman, Lenn E. 1971. "The Epicurean Ethic of Muḥammad Ibn Zakariyâ' Ar-Râzî." *Studia Islamica* 34: 5–26.

Goodman, Lenn E. 2015. "How Epicurean was Rāzī?" *Studia Graeco-Arabica* 5: 247–280.

Hansen, Chad. 2020. "Daoism." In *The Stanford Encyclopedia of Philosophy*, edited by Edward N. Zalta. Stanford: Stanford University.

Hasker, William and Charles Taliaferro. 2019. "Afterlife." In *The Stanford Encyclopedia of Philosophy*, edited by Edward N. Zalta. Stanford: Stanford University Press.

Houlgate, Stephen. 2005. *An Introduction to Hegel Freedom, Truth and History*. London: Wiley-Blackwell.

Jambet, Christian. 2006. *The Act of Being*, translated by Jeff Fort. New York: Zone Books.

Koetschet, Pauline. 2019. *Abū Bakr al-Rāzī, "Doutes sur Galien": Introduction, édition et traduction*. Berlin: De Gruyter.

Kuczewski, Mark G. and Ronald M. Polansky. 2002. *Bioethics: Ancient Themes in Contemporary Issues*. Cambridge, MA: MIT Press.

Laing, John. 2002. "Life and Death in Healthcare Ethics: A Short Introduction: H Watt. Routledge, 2000, £7.99, vii + 97pp. ISBN 0-415-21574-9." *Journal of Medical Ethics* 28(5): 331–332.

Lameer, Joep. 2015. *The Arabic Version of Ṭūsī's* Nasirean Ethics*: With an Introduction and Explanatory Notes*. Leiden: Brill.

Luper, Steven. 2008. *The Cambridge Companion to Life and Death*. Cambridge: Cambridge University Press.

Luper, Steven. 2009. *The Philosophy of Death*. Cambridge: Cambridge University Press.

Luper, Steven. 2019. "Death." In *The Stanford Encyclopedia of Philosophy*, edited by Edward N. Zalta. Stanford: Stanford University Press.

May, Todd. 2009. *Death*. London: Routledge.

Motto, Anna Lydia. 1955. "Seneca on Death and Immortality." *The Classical Journal* 50(4): 187–189.

Nagel, Thomas. 1989. *The View from Nowhere*, revised edition. Oxford: Oxford University Press.

Nagel, Thomas. 2012. *Mortal Questions*. Cambridge: Cambridge University Press.

Nietmann, William D. 1966. "Seneca on Death: The Courage to Be or Not to Be." *International Philosophical Quarterly* 6(1): 81–89.

Noyes Jr, Russell. 1973. "Seneca on Death." *Journal of Religion and Health* 12: 223–240.

Olson, Robert. 2017. *An Introduction to Existentialism*. New York: Dover Publications.

Saunders, Jason L., ed. 1997. *Greek and Roman Philosophy After Aristotle*. New York: Free Press.

Singer, Peter. 2001. *Hegel: A Very Short Introduction*. Oxford: Oxford University Press.

Steffen, Lloyd and Dennis R. Cooley. 2014. *The Ethics of Death: Religious and Philosophical Perspectives in Dialogue*. Minneapolis, MN: Fortress Press.

Stephens, W.O. 2008. "Epictetus on Fearing Death: Bugbear and Open Door Policy." *Ancient Philosophy* 34(2): 365–391. DOI: 10.5840/ancientphil200834227.

Stoljar, Daniel. 2017. "Physicalism." In *The Stanford Encyclopedia of Philosophy*, edited by Edward N. Zalta. Stanford: Stanford University Press.

Taylor, James Stacey. 2013. *The Metaphysics and Ethics of Death: New Essays*. Oxford: Oxford University Press.

Ṭūsī, Naṣīr ad-Dīn. 2011. *The Nasirean Ethics*, translated by G.M. Wickens. London: Routledge.

الفصل 4

جلال الدين الرومي وفلسفة الألم والمعاناة

شهاب الدين مهدوي وأمير عباس علي زماني

1 تمهيد

لقد كان الألم ولا يزال توأم الإنسان وقرينه، فإنّ الإنسان يُولَد في العناء ويعيش في العناء ويموت في العناء. ولذلك فقد شغلت فكرة الألم والمعاناة أذهان البشر دائمًا. ورغم أنّ الألم هو ظاهرة عامّة تشمل جميع أفراد النوع الإنساني إلا أنّه قد يكون أحيانًا أكثر قوةً وتأثيرًا في بعضهم، وبالتالي تحتاج مواجهته إلى تفكير وتركيز أكثر. وخير نموذج لهذه الفئة من الناس هم المرضى المشرفون على الموت أو الذين يعانون من مرض عضال لا يرجى تماثلهم للشفاء منه؛ حيث إنّهم لا يكابدون أصعب الآلام الجسدية فقط، بل يعيشون أيضًا في أغلب الأحوال حالة من الخوف تجاه معنى الحياة أو مصيرهم في المستقبل، وهي بدورها تزيد من معاناتهم وتُضاعف آلامهم في نهاية الحياة. بالإضافة إلى ذلك، قد تساور المريض شكوك بشأن معتقداته الدينية، ويتساءل عما إذا كان الله محقًّا وعادلًا وحكيمًا في إنزال البلاء عليه؟! الأمر الذي قد يؤدّي إلى سلب إيمانه أو إضعافه قُبيل وفاته. لذا ومن منطلق المسؤولية الإنسانية والإسلامية يقع على عاتقنا مساعدة هؤلاء لكي يواجهوا الحياة بقلوب مؤمنة ووجوه باسمة.

ولا شك أنّ الدين الإسلامي الحنيف يزخر بكثير من المعاني العميقة والصافية عن فلسفة الألم والعناء وما يعتري الإنسان من المحن والابتلاءات، كما أنّه يطفح بالمفاهيم الأخلاقية عن كيفية العلاقة بين الإنسان وربّه من الصبر والشكر والرضى والتسليم وما إلى ذلك، وهذا من شأنه أن يمكّن الإنسان من مواجهة المحن ويساعده في إضفاء المعنى على حياته والمحافظة على استقراره والتغلب على تقلباته النفسية والروحية، ويمهّد الأرضية اللازمة للوصول إلى تأصيل إسلامي للرعاية الروحية في رعاية نهاية الحياة، بل وفي الرعاية التلطيفية بشكل عامّ أيضًا. ولكن استنباط هذه المعاني لا يتسنّى إلا بإعمال الاجتهاد والنظر، وهذا ما قام به فعلًا علماء الإسلام من الفقهاء والمحدّثين والفلاسفة والعرفاء والمتكلمين، فنهلوا من معين الإسلام واغترفوا منه علومًا فياضة متنوعة، إلا أنّه لا غرو إذا ما ادعينا بأنه ليس شيء من هذه الجهود يُطَمئن القلب، ويُريح النفس، ويشرح الصدر، ويُقنع العقل، مثلما يفعل الأدب الصوفي، حيث يلتقي هؤلاء الفقه والحديث والفلسفة والعرفان والكلام، فيمتزج بالفنّ والأدب، ويكتسي صورة عذبة بديعة

تؤثّر في الإنسان تأثيرًا بالغًا، وتمنحه القابلية للتحرّر من الجمود وامتلاك القدرة على الانطلاق نحو اللانهاية.

إنّ الفكرة المركزية لهذا البحث هي أنّ الأدب الصوفي يحظى بقوّة أكثر مقارنةً بغيره من المناهج الفلسفية والكلامية والنفسية في تكييف الإنسان مع حالات الألم والمعاناة. ودليلنا على ذلك هو أنّ الألم، بمثابة موقف حدّي (boundary situation) للإنسان، يشاركه في أعمق مراتب وجوده ويتحوّل إلى قضية وجودية بالنسبة إليه. وعندئذٍ فلم يَعُد الألم وما يُفرزه من الأسئلة والحالات نابعًا عن عقلية المريض، بل الصواب أنّه نتيجة طَبيعية للواقع العاطفي الذي يعيشه. وهنا يظهر الدور البارز للأدب في معالجة القضية حيث يمكن له من خلال ما يقدّمه من صور الخيال والإبداع الأدبي أن يؤثّر في مشاعر المريض، ويعدّل الصورة المركوزة في ذهنه عن الكون، ويساعده في السيطرة على سلوكه.

ومن الواضح أنّ تناول الأدب الصوفي على شموله ورحابته هو أمر لا يسعه هذا البحث. وبناءً عليه، فقد قرّرنا أن نقتصر في دراستنا على شخصية جلال الدين الرومي (ت. 1273/672)، مسلّطين الضوء على بعض آرائه عن الألم وفلسفته، ونقف على شطر من عطاءاته الفكرية والروحية التي يمكن أن نستفيد منها في واقعنا المعاش. ولقد انطلقنا في هذا الاختيار من مبرّرات عدّة، الأول هو أنّ الرومي يعتبر من الشخصيات القليلة عبر التاريخ التي تمكنت من اجتياز حاجز اللغة والثقافة والدين، ليذيع صيته في جميع أرجاء العالم. وهذا يدلّ على أنّ كلماته تنطبق بنفس القدر على عالمنا اليوم مثلما كانت في القرن السابع الهجري. والثاني أنّ جلال الدين الرومي يتميّز عن غيره من الأدباء الصوفيين ببراعته المنقطعة النظير في صبّ بنات أفكاره ومواجده في القوالب الأدبية. وذلك قد جعل منه شخصية فريدة فذة في الأدب الصوفي. والثالث أنّ مشكلة الألم والمعاناة كانت لأسباب تاريخية – وفي رأسها اجتياح المغول للبلاد الإسلامية وما خلّف من القتل والدمار والخراب – محطّ نظر عامّة الناس في عصر جلال الدين، وقد عكس الرومي ذلك في مؤلفاته أيضًا، ودرسه بعناية فائقة، وقدّم لنا منظورًا فريدًا عن الكون يمكننا أن نستلهم منه معاني الحياة. والأخير أنّ منهج الرومي في التعاطي مع قضايا الإنسان يكون قائمًا على استخدام الأمثال والتشبيهات والقصص والحكايات، وبذلك يعرض أعمق المفاهيم العرفانية في أبسط الأشكال الأدبية، فتكون قابلةً للفهم لدى الناس عامةً.

2 لمحة عن الأدب الصوفي

الأدب الصوفي هو أدب المتصوّفة الذين كتبوه ودوّنوه وخلّدوه في آثارهم، شعرًا ونثرًا، حكمةً، ونصيحةً، وموعظةً، ومثلًا، وعبرةً. وقد تناول الصوفيون في أدبهم الكثير من دقائق الحكمة

والتجربة والفكر والمعاني والأخيلة وأعمق مشاعر الإنسان، وحفل أدبهم بروائع المناجاة والحبّ الإلهي (خفاجي د.ت.، 66). يُقصد بالتصوف في الاصطلاح تلك التجربة الروحانية الوجدانية التي يعيشها السالك المسافر إلى ملكوت الحضرة الإلهية والذات الربانية من أجل اللقاء بها وصالًا وعشقًا. ويمكن تعريفه كذلك بأنه تحلية وتخلية وتجلٍّ، كما يمكن القول أيضًا بأن التصوف هو محبة الله والفناء فيه والاتحاد به كشفًا وتجليًا من أجل الانتشاء بالأنوار الربانية والتمتع بالحضرة القدسية (أمين 2013، 173).

ولقد شهد الأدب الصوفي في الجغرافيا الإسلامية مراحل مختلفة اتسمت في بعضها بالازدهار، وفي الأخرى بالتوقف والتراجع، وأحيانًا بالجمود والانحطاط. وقد يصعب رسم معالم عصور واضحة للأدب الصوفي، إلا أنّ المعروف هو أنّ الأدب الصوفي القديم مرّ بثلاث مراحل، أولاها من فجر الإسلام إلى أواسط القرن الثاني الهجري، وكل ما بين أيدينا منها هو طائفة كبيرة من الحكم والمواعظ الدينية والأخلاق تحثّ على كثير من الفضائل، وتدعو إلى التسليم بأحكام الله ومقاديره، وإلى الزهد والتقشّف وكثرة العبادة والورع، والثانية تمتدّ إلى أواخر القرن الرابع، وتتّسم بظهور آثار التلاقح بين الجنس العربي والأجناس الأخرى واتساع أفق التفكير اللاهوتي، والأخيرة تستمرّ إلى أواسط القرن الثامن الهجري، وهي العصر الذهبي في الأدب الصوفي (أمين 2013، 769). وأما بعد ذلك فيمكن القول بأنّ الأدب الصوفي بدأ مرحلة الفتور والتدهور.

إنّ الموضوعات التي طرقها الأدب الصوفي غنيّة ومتنوّعة مثل التجربة الصوفية نفسها، فالصوفي بين صحو وسكر، ومدّ وجزر، وطيّ ونشر، ونشوة وهجر، والأدب الصوفي هو الترجمان المعبّر عن مواجد الصوفيين في أحوالهم التي تعتريهم ويتقلّبون فيها نتيجةً للمجاهدات التي يزاولونها، والتي من شأنها أن ترقّق مشاعرهم نحوها، وترهف أحاسيسهم (محمد د.ت.، 57). وأمّا بالنسبة إلى الأغراض التي يحملها الأدب الصوفي فيمكن اختزالها في ثلاثة محاور رئيسة وهي:

1. الدعوة إلى الزهد والتقشف والتعبير عن التبرّم من الحياة الدنيا.
2. تحديد معالم الطريق إلى الله وما يتقلب فيه الصوفي من مقاماتٍ وأحوالٍ.
3. بيان الرؤية الصوفية بما فيها الحب الإلهي والسُكر الصوفي والمعرفة والفناء والشهود وما إلى ذلك (العوادي د.ت.،157–222).

وإذا كان للأدب العربي دور ريادي في نشأة الأدب الصوفي وازدهاره بفضل أدبائه المبدعين مثل ابن الفارض (ت. 632/1235) والجنيد (ت. 297/910) ورابعة العدوية (ت. 184 أو 185/801) وذي النون المصري (ت. 245/859) وعبد القادر الجيلاني (ت. 544/1166) وغيرهم، إلا أنّه فيما بعد أبدى الأدب الفارسي اهتمامًا كبيرًا بفكر الصوفية وتجاربهم وظهر عباقرة الشعر الفارسي نظير الحكيم السنائي (ت. 545/1150) وفريد الدين العطار (ت. 618/1221) وجلال الدين الرومي

وحافظ الشيرازي (ت. 1390/792) وعبد الرحمن الجامي (ت. 1492/898) ومحمود الشبستري (ت. 1339/720) وغيرهم. وفي هذا السياق يقول عبد الوهاب عزام: "فبلغوا في هذه السبيل غايةً لم يدركها شعراء أمة أخرى، فأخرجوا المعاني الظاهرة والخفية والدقيقة في صور شتّى معجبة مطربة وقد فُتح عليهم في هذا فتحًا عظيمًا، فكان شعرهم فيضًا تضيق به الأبيات والقوافي حتى يمسك القارئ أحيانًا حائرًا كيف تجلّت لهم هذه المعاني، وكيف استطاعوا أن يشقّقوا المعنى الواحد إلى معانٍ شتّى" (عزام 2013، 38–37).

3 من هو جلال الدين الرومي؟

وُلد الشاعر جلال الدين محمد في مدينة بلخ في السادس من ربيع الأول سنة 604 للهجرة (7 أكتوبر 1207م) (براون 1954، 654)، واشتهر وعُرف في الأوساط العلمية بمولانا جلال الدين الرومي أو المولى الرومي نسبة إلى بلاد الروم؛ حيث قضى الشطر الأكبر من حياته الحافلة بالخصب والإنتاج (غالب 1982، 12). وقد كان أبوه محمد بن الحسين بهاء الدين ولد، الملقّب بسلطان العلماء، متكلمًا إلهيًا مشهورًا وصوفيًا منتميًا إلى مدرسة الغزّالي (شيمل 2016، 52).

وقد كان عصر الرومي من أقسى ما مرّ على البشرية من عصور؛ حيث تزامن مع الغزو المغولي، الأمر الذي أدّى -إلى جانب بعض العوامل الداخلية الأخرى- أن ترحل أسرة جلال الدين بعيدًا عن الدمار والخراب والقتل الذي لحق بالبلاد وأهلها. بدأت الرحلة سنة 1220/617 وكانت المحطة الأولى في نيسابور، حيث التقت الأسرة بالشاعر الصوفي فريد الدين العطّار الذي أدرك قابليات جلال الدين وقدراته، فأهداه نسخة من كتابه «**أسرار نامه**»، وقال عنه: "إنّه سيؤجّج النار في قلوب العشّاق الصوفيين." ولدى مرورهم بالعراق نزلوا في بغداد، والتقوا الصوفي الكبير شهاب الدين السهروردي صاحب كتاب «**عوارف المعارف**»، وحين حطّ بهم الرحال في مدينة دمشق التقوا شيخ الصوفية وفيلسوفها محي الدين ابن عربي الذي ما إن رأى جلال الدين يسير خلف والده حتى قال: "سبحان الله، محيط يمشي خلف بحيرة" (محمد 2010، 178–179). وفي السنوات التي أعقبت سنة 617هـ وصل بهاء الدين ولد وأسرته إلى أواسط الأناضول، وبعد مكوث في مدينة لارَندَه طال عدة سنوات، تلقّى بهاء الدين دعوة من السلطان السلجوقي الذي جمع حوله العلماء والصوفية من كلّ مكان في العالم للإقامة في قونية، ولبّى بالفعل هذه الدعوة، واستقرّ فيها حوالي سنة 1230/627، وبدأ بفعّاليات وعظه وتعليمه، وبعد سنتين فقط توفّي وعُيّن ابنه جلال الدين خليفة له (شيمل 2016، 55–56).

بعد مضيّ عام على وفاة بهاء ولد، قدم إلى قونية برهان الدين محقق الترمذي لرؤية شيخه وأستاذه بهاء الدين، ولكنّه وجده قد توفّي وخلفه ابنه جلال الدين في التدريس والفتوى

بالمدينة (حسن د.ت.، 35). كان وصول برهان الدين إلى قونية حدثًا جللًا بالنسبة إلى جلال الدين الرومي، والذي كان في الخامسة والعشرين من عمره حينذاك؛ حيث أشرف على تربيته وتوجيهه، وعرّفه على أعمق درجات الفكر الصوفي والخبرة الصوفية، والذي كان سببًا رئيسًا في نضج جلال الدين الرومي روحانيًا (شيمل 2006، 352).

وفي سنة 1233/630 اتجه إلى حلب، وأقام هناك في المدرسة الحلاوية -التي كانت تعدّ من أهم مراكز العلم المعروفة في حلب-، واشتغل بالتحصيل. لقد تتلمذ جلال الدين الرومي في هذه المدرسة على يد كمال الدين أبي القاسم عمرو بن أحمد المعروف بابن العديم (ت. 1262/660) في الفقه الحنفي وسائر العلوم الدينية. وبعد سنوات عديدة انتقل إلى المدرسة المقدسية في دمشق، وأقام فيها أربع سنوات. وقد التقى فيها بالشيخ محي الدين ابن عربي (ت. 1240/638) كما التقى بكلّ من سعد الدين الحموي (ت. 1251/649) وأوحد الدين الكرماني (ت. 1238/635) وصدر الدين القونوي (ت. 1274/672) الذين تركوا أثرًا كبيرًا في تفكير جلال الدين الرومي، ثمّ عاد الرومي فيما بعد إلى قونية تلبيةً لدعوة مريدي والده فاشتغل بالوعظ والإرشاد (محمد 2010، 179).

أما سنة 642هـ، فقد كانت علامة فاصلة في حياة جلال الدين، حيث التقى بشمس الدين التبريزي (ت. 1248/645)، وقد غيّر هذا اللقاء حياة شاعرنا إلى حدّ يعبّرون عنه بالانقلاب في حياة مولانا (رفعت جو 2008، 55). ويذكر عطاء الدين تدين أنّ الشمس قد همس إلى مولانا في لقائهم الأول قائلًا: "جئت إلى هنا من جهة مرشدي وشيخي، ركن الدين السّجاسيّ (ت. القرن السابع/ القرن الثالث عشر)، وقد قال لي اذهب إلى قونية ففيها محترقٌ لا بد من إضرام النار في طينته" (تدين 2015، 101). لقد كانت آراء شمس المتفرّدة وغير المألوفة سببًا في انجذاب جلال الدين الرومي إليه، كانجذاب العطشان إلى الماء. وقد عبّر جلال الدين عن ذلك بقوله: "إذا كان العطاش ينشدون الماء، فإنّ الماء أيضًا ينشد العطاش في العالم." هذه الكلمات تختصر فلسفة العشق والشوق في فكر جلال الدين الرومي (محمد 2010، 181).

إنّ تعليم شمس الدين لجلال الدين أشبه ما يكون بفصله عن حالة السبات التي يغطّ فيها، ويدفعه للبحث عن الله سبحانه، ولذلك فقد ظلّ جلال الدين يعترف له بحبٍ وعرفانٍ لا حدود لهما طوال حياته. يقول جلال الدين: "إنّ الشمس هو الذي أراني طريق الحقيقة وهو الذي أدين له في إيماني ويقيني." لقد فتح عينيه على نافذة الحياة، وكان ذلك إيقاظًا وتفتّحًا في ذهن الرومي واتساعًا في إدراكه وفهمه. كان ذلك ثورة على الداخل وإعادة صياغة للعقل والتفكير عند جلال الدين (محمد 2010، 183).

لقد كان حبّ جلال الدين للشمس حبًّا مطلقًا ملأ كل جوانبه، وجعله يهمل عائلته وتلامذته لأشهر، حتّى احتجّوا على ذلك في النهاية، فاضطرّ الشمس أن يرحل عن قونية واغتمّ

الرومي لذلك غمًّا لا شيء يواسيه. غير أنّه بعد فترة من الزمن، وبينما كان جلال الدين يصبّ شوقه في قصائد حزينة، وجد الشمس مجدداً، حيث أعاده ابنه سلطان ولد إلى قونية. وقد ازداد قربهما ثانيةً وأصبح لا يمكن التغلّب عليه، لدرجة قرّر بعض تلامذة الرومي بالاشتراك مع ابنه علاء الدين إرسال الشمس إلى مكان لا يعود منه أبدًا (شيمل 2006، 353). وقد أدرك جلال الدين حينئذٍ أن لا عودة تُرجى لأستاذه الراحل، وأنّ الموت غيّب أحبّ الناس إليه وأقرب العقول إلى عقله، فغرق في حزن عميق. وفي النهاية فقد لقي الرومي حتفه في الخامس من جمادي الثاني سنة 672هـ (26 أكتوبر 1273م)، وقد اشترك فيه جميع أهل قونية بما فيه النصارى واليهود في تشييعه وتأبينه والبكاء عليه (رفعت جو 2008، 35).

إنّ إنجاز الرومي في الأدب هائل؛ وله أعمال أدبية متعدّدة، منها المنظوم، ومنها المنثور. أمّا المنظوم من أعماله فهو «**المثنوي المعنوي**» وهو أكثرها صيتاً، و«**ديوان شمس التبريزي**» و«**الرباعيات**» والمنثور منها هو «**فيه ما فيه**» و«**المجالس السبعة**» و«**الرسائل**» (حسن د.ت.، 39–46).

4 الألم والمعاناة من منظور جلال الدين الرومي

لا ريب أنّ السؤال عن الآلام البشرية وأسبابها والحِكَم الكامنة وراءها والمسؤولية الأخلاقية تجاهها كان ولا يزال من الأسئلة المقضّة لمضجع الإنسان، وشكّل هاجسًا فكريًا ووجدانيًا مقلقًا لدى أصحاب الفكر عبر التاريخ، وقد حاول كلّ منهم أن ينظر إليه من منظاره الخاصّ، ويشفي غليله بما يدلي به من رؤية يظنّها حلًّا لهذه المعضلة التاريخية. ولا شك أنّ هذا الموضوع البالغ الأهمية لم يغب عن فكر مفكّر فيلسوف وشاعر مبدع مثل جلال الدين الرومي الذي يقدّم نفسه طبيباً حاذقاً للأمراض الروحية والأخلاقية، بل قد أعار بالفعل اهتمامًا بالغًا بالألم وأسبابه وآثاره وطرق تداويه في مؤلفاته المختلفة وخاصة كتابه «**المثنوي**»، وفيما يلي سنشير إلى أبرز معالم فكر مولانا بهذا الخصوص وطرق معالجته لقضية الألم والمعاناة لدى الإنسان.

1.4 الألم والمعاناة دلاليًا

الألم والمعاناة هو تجربة عامة وقضية مشتركة لكافّة أبناء الإنسان، ورغم كونه أمرًا ملموسًا للجميع إلا أنّه على مستوى المفهوم يعتبر من أغمض المفاهيم وأكثرها تجريدًا، بحيث لا يمكن تقديم تعريف دقيق عنه يتّفق عليه الجميع. ولعلّ الارتكاز العامّ يميل أن يصنّف كلّ ما يوجب تعباً على الإنسان في دائرة الآلام، بينما الغريب أنّ هناك آلامًا تنهك الإنسان وهو يستطيبها. ويذكر الرومي ألم الحبّ مثالًا لهذا النوع من الآلام ويقارن بين العاشق والمريض، حيث يطلب الأخير الدواء ويستزيد الأول الداء (الرومي 1994، 539/3). ومهما كان فيبدو بديهياً أنّ الخطوة الأولى في معالجة المفاهيم – ولا سيما التجريدية منها – هي معالجتها دلالياً وبيان حقيقتها وتحديد المقصود منها، وذلك

أنّ المعالجة الدلالية تؤثّر مباشرة على نتائج الأبحاث الأخرى التي تتبعها. والسؤال الذي يطرح نفسه هنا هو: ماذا يعني الألم والمعاناة في فكر جلال الدين الرومي؟

لم يتطرّق مولانا في مؤلفاته إلى المعنى اللغوي لمفردتي «الألم» و«المعاناة»، وبدلًا من ذلك فقد حاول أن يقدّم صورة ملموسة منهما تارةً عن طريق عرض بعض المصاديق الواضحة والمفاهيم ذات الصلة من قبيل الوحدة واليأس والغمّ والكآبة والحُرقة وما إلى ذلك، وتارةً عبر بيان المفاهيم المضادّة لهما نظير الفرح والخلاص والوصال وما إلى ذلك. بالإضافة إلى ذلك، قام الرومي أحيانًا بتعريف الألم عبر ذكر مكوّنات الألم - باعتباره أمرًا مركبًا من الأجزاء - وأحكامه وميزاته وآثاره وعلاقته مع غيرها من المفاهيم المماثلة نظير الموت والوحدة والذنب، فيقول مثلًا إنّ اغتراب الإنسان وابتعاده عن أصله هو الوجه الآخر لألم الإنسان ومعاناته. وهذه الرؤية وإن كانت تعتبر رؤية أنطولوجية إلى الألم - ونحن سندرسها في القسم الآتي - إلا أنّه في نفس الوقت يتمّتع عند الرومي بأهمية دلالية أيضًا، حيث إنّ الاغتراب والافتراق من وجهة نظره ليس فقط سببًا للألم، بل هو الألم نفسه أيضًا؛ إذ يكون الألم في جوهره وماهيته هو فراق الإنسان عن موطنه الأصلي (غرجي 2012، 145).

على ذلك، يجب القول بأنّ الرومي عند بيان ماهية الألم، بدلًا من الإتيان بتعاريف منطقية أو لغوية، يؤكد دائمًا على المفاهيم المتاخمة أو المضادّة. وهذا ما يُعسّر تقديم تعريف دقيق ومقبول عند الجميع للألم وفقًا لرأي الرومي، وأقصى ما يمكن قوله هو أنّ الألم والعناء عنده أمر نسبيّ يختلف من شخص إلى آخر حسب وجهة نظره ومستوى إدراكه (غرجي 2012، 146).

2.4 الألم والمعاناة وجوديًا

تهدف الدراسة الوجودية للألم والمعاناة إلى معالجة موقف جلال الدين الرومي تجاه ظاهرة الألم من الناحية الأنطولوجية وبيان أنواعها وأسباب حدوثها وطرق التخلّص منها، وهي تشكل حجر الزاوية في جميع كلمات الرومي عن الألم، وفيها أيضا يكمن سرّ جاذبيته؛ وذلك أنّ جلال الدين يتميّز عن غيره من العلماء والمفكرين بنظرته الفريدة والمتحدّية تجاه الألم، فبينما الإنسان بطبعه يهرب من الألم، ويبذل كلّ جهده للتخلّص منه، ينظر الرومي من منظوره الصوفي إلى الألم نظرة إيجابية، ويدعو قارئيه إلى استقباله واحتضانه. إنّ الرومي يعتبر الألم لطفًا من قبل الله سبحانه وتعالى مختبئًا تحت أنواع القهر، (الرومي 1994، 106/3) ويؤمن إيمانًا راسخًا بأنّ البلاء للولاء كما أنّ اللهب للذهب، وإنّ الله يجرّع عباده من كأس البلاء على قدر قربهم منه، ومن هو المبتلى فلا شك أنّه قد شمّ أريج العناية الربانية (الرومي 1994، 39/1). فالألم، من وجهة نظر مولانا، أمارة على سموّ مكانة العبد عند الرب، والعكس صحيح أيضًا، فإنّ من لا ألم له فهو -حسب تعبيره- بمثابة ميّت يتحرّك في نعش جسده (الرومي 1994، 336/3). وبعبارة أخرى، يمكن القول: إنّ الألم

لدى مولانا هو موقف حدّي بالنسبة إلى الإنسان، وهو مصطلح أبدعه الفيلسوف الوجودي كارل ياسبرز (Karl Jaspers، ت. 1969م) إشارةً إلى مواقف تعتري الإنسان فيها حالة من القلق والهلع، ويُدرك من خلالها تمام الإدراك مكامن القصور فيه. ويذكر ياسبرز الموت والمرض والذنب والألم أمثلة على تلك المواقف (ياسبرز 1995، 238–239) ويعتقد الرومي أنّ هذا الخوف والقلق هو أمر ضروري ونافع للإنسان إذ يَنزل الإنسان من عرش الانبهار بالذات إلى فرش الافتقار إلى الله، وتُحطّم العقبات التي تقف حائلةً بينه وبين رُقيّه الوجداني والإنساني.

ويرى الرومي أنّ الألم في كافة أشكاله يتمتّع بسمتين مشتركتين:

الأولى: أنّ الألم قد يختلف من شخص إلى آخر، فقد تؤدّي تجربة واحدة إلى مشاعر شتّى في أشخاص مختلفين (محمودي ودادبه 2013، 166). ويروي الرومي لذلك حكاية الرجل الزاهد الذي يعتبر الجفاف جنّةً، بينما يراه الآخرون محنةً (الرومي 1994، 2/470).

والثانية: أنّ الألم – وكذلك الراحة – هو مقولة ذاتية (subjective) بمعنى أنّه موجود ما دام مدرَكًا، ويتبخّر عندما يقع خارج نطاق الإدراك (همايي 1987، 709). ولذلك ينصح الرومي أن يبحث الإنسان عن الراحة في ذاته وليس في القصور والحصون؛ فإنّ الإنسان قد يكون قابعًا في زاوية المسجد ثملًا فرحًا، وفي وسط البستان كئيبًا حزينًا (الرومي 1994، 3/467).

3.4 أسباب الألم والمعاناة

إنّ موقف مولانا من الأسباب الكامنة وراء الألم والمعاناة يتجذّر في النموذج الأفلاطوني الحديث، حيث «الأنا» الإنساني – أي البعد الروحي للوجود الإنساني الذي به الإنسان هو هو – يكون حبيسًا في سجن الجسد، وليس هناك أيّ اتحاد ذاتيّ بين الجسد والروح، وتكون الروح منقطعة عن الجسد تمامًا (علمي وصابري 2013، 146). يقول الرومي: "ما تعلّقك بهذا الجسد؟ وأنت قائمٌ من دونه. أنت دائمًا من دونه. في الليل لا تُعنى بالجسد، وفي النهار تكون منهمكًا دائمًا بالأعمال، ولستَ مع الجسد. وهكذا لِمَ ترتجف على هذا الجسد وأنت لا تكون معه ساعة واحدة، بل تكون دائمًا في أمكنة أخرى؟ أين أنت، وأين الجسد؟ أنت في واد وأنا في واد" (الرومي 2002، 328).

إنّ الروح وجوهر الوجود الإنساني، برأي الرومي، كانت تسكن في الأزل في عالم روحاني يتميز بوحدة لا كثرة فيها، فتنزّلت من ذلك العالم العُلوي «قوس النزول» وتلبّست في لباس الجسد، وأصبحت رهينة له (الرومي 1998، 304). وقد كان هذا الافتراق عن مألفه ومأواه مبدأ شقاءه والسبب الرئيس لبُؤسه (الرومي 1994، 1/42–43). ويمكن بشكل عامّ تصنيف مصادر الألم من وجهة نظر مولانا في العوامل الثلاثة التالية:

التركب والتكثّر: موطن النفس الإنسانية هو عالم الوحدة، ولكنّها هبطت إلى عالم الكثرة. وهذا التكثر والتركب هو مصدر القلق والألم المعنوي والنفسي لديه (الرومي 1994، 1/191).

أسر الزمان: المصدر الثاني للألم هو همّ الإنسان لما فاته في الماضي وما سيأتيه في المستقبل، ويعتقد مولانا أنّ أسر الزمان يقيّد وجود الإنسان ويجب التحرّر منه (الرومي 1994، 134/1).

سُكر الوجود: إنّ النرجسية والنظرة الاستقلالية إلى «الأنا» ونشوة الوجود هي الأخرى مصدرًا أساسيًا للألم في الإنسان، فطالما الأنا هو الأنا، يكون الإنسان في قيد الكثرة والكثرة يتبعها الألم. "إنّ الآلام كلّها تنبعث من أنّك تريد شيئًا ثمّ لا يتيسّر لك ذلك الشيء، وعندما لا تريد لا يبقى هناك ألم" (الرومي 2002، 192).

وبناءً على ذلك، فإنّ الرومي يرفض جميع الاتجاهات المادّية بشأن قضية الألم ومصدره، ويعتبره خطأً منهجيًا، وبدلًا من ذلك، يؤكد على محورية الروح العُلوية في تحليل القضايا الإنسانية، ويعتقد أنّ الألم ليس أمرًا طارئًا على الإنسان وناتجًا عن حياته الفردية والاجتماعية، بل هي مشكلة أنطولوجية بالنسبة إليه، حيث إنّه ينتمي إلى عالم الوجود الوحداني ويعيش في جوهره غربة التنافر والاضطراب. وعلى رأي الرومي حتّى إذا ما توفّرت كافة حاجاته النفسية والاقتصادية والاجتماعية، فإن الإنسان مازال يبقى معانيًا من اغترابه الأنطولوجي ويظلّ باحثًا عن سعادته الحقيقية (علمي وصابري 2013، 147–148).

4.4 أنواع الألم

في فكر الرومي هناك نوعان من الألم، أحدهما هو ما يسبّبه الإنسان لنفسه، والثاني هو ما يُنزله الله على الإنسان لحكمة يعلمها. ويرى الرومي أنّ الآلام من النوع الأول هي آلامٌ مذمومةٌ وعلى الإنسان أن يتصدّى لها، ويحرّر نفسه منها، ويحصل على الراحة والسكينة؛ أمّا النوع الثاني منها فهي آلامٌ هادفةٌ ومقدّسةٌ ليس فقط لا ينبغي الهروب منها، بل يجدر بالإنسان أن يستقبلها بحفاوة، لما لها من أثر بالغ في تكوين شخصية الإنسان والارتقاء بها. إنّ معظم كلمات الرومي تختصّ بالنوع الثاني من الآلام، وهو يحاول أن ينظر إليه بنظرته التوحيدية المعتادة إلى الكون، ويعدّه مقبولًا ومبرّرًا. حيث يؤمن أنّ الله على كلّ أمر قدير، وبكلّ شيء عليم بصير، وهو أعلم بمصالح العباد، ولا يصدر الفعل منه عبثًا، ولا ريب أنّ ما يقوم به إله كهذا حتّى إذا كان في لباس الألم والقهر فهو في صالح الإنسان، ومن هذا المنطلق يعتبر ذلك هدية من الله (شهبازي 2007، 172).

وللرومي تقسيم آخر للألم أيضًا، وهو تقسيمه إلى الأصيل والطارئ؛ والألم الأصيل ليس سوى ألم الفراق والابتعاد عن المعشوق الأزلي. ويشرح الرومي هذا الألم من خلال قصيدته الشهيرة «أنين الناي» التي يبدأ بها كتابه «**المثنوي**». فالناي عنده هو أصل النفس البشرية والإنسان الذي يبحث عن سرّ وجوده، ومنبت الغاب يرمز إلى أصل تلك النفس وعالمها الأول، وأنين الناي هو رمز لحنين النفس للابتعاد عن أصلها. وقد وجد مولانا في هذه الأداة الموسيقية خير من يمثّله في

التعبير عن حاله، فكلاهما يعاني الانفصال عن موطنه، واللوعة والحرقة التي تصدر من أنين الناي هي خير تعبير عمّا يعانيه الناس من هموم مختلفة، وسرّ نُواحه يكمن في البحث الدائم عن الأصل، من أين أتى، وإلى أين يذهب، كيف كان المبدأ وكيف يكون المعاد؟ (محمد 2010، 190–189) ويعتقد الرومي أنّ ألم الفراق هو الألم الحقيقي، وأصل كلّ ألم في الإنسان، ودواء هذا الداء هو اللقاء (الرومي 1994، 1/339–340).

وأمّا الألم الطارئ فهو ما يسمّيه العرف العامّ عادةً بالألم، وهو في رأي مولانا ليس ألمًا في الحقيقة، بل هو لطف تستّر في لباس القهر، وذلك أنّه يُعين الإنسان على علاج ألمه الأصيل، وهو الفراق من الله (محمودي ودادبه 2013، 168). فالوصال لا يقع إلا بالحبّ، والحبّ لا يتسنّى بالغفلة عن ذكر الحبيب، والنفس الإنسانية مشوبة بألوان الغفلة وأنواع الرذائل، وتطهيره هو الألم. ولا يتبدّد هذا الألم والحزن الذي يتبعه إلا بعلاج ألم الفراق، وعندئذ سوف يسمو الإنسان عن عالم الكثرة، وتخرج أفراح الدنيا وأتراحها عن قلبه، ويدخل في جملة أولياء الله الذين لا خوف عليهم ولا هم يحزنون.

إنّ طريقة مواجهة الرومي للألم ونظرته الربانية له تُظهر لنا أنّه يحلّق في ملكوت العشق الإلهي، ولا يرى ما يقاسيه الإنسان الأرضي في حياته الرتيبة مستحقًّا للحزن والاكتئاب. فالحياة الدنيا عند جلال الدين تشبه الأساطير الملحمية، فكما تُهرق فيها دماء الآلاف من الناس دون أن يترك أثرًا على نفسية القارئ، وفي نفس الوقت ينعكس فيها قتل البطل بل جرحه بشكل مؤثّر جدًا، فكذلك في نظرته الصوفية تنصهر جميع آلام الإنسان في بوتقة الرحمة الإلهية، وتُعتبر أمرًا لا يستحقّ الوقوف عنده (شهبازي 2007، 172).

5.4 الألم وشعور المتألّم بالحرمان

إنّ الشعور بالإهمال والخذلان من قبل الله سبحانه وتعالى هو من العوامل الرئيسية التي تبعث القلق في نفوس المرضى المصابون بما لا يُرجى شفائهم منه، وتزيد من آلامهم، وقد قال الله سبحانه وتعالى عن حالة شعور الإنسان بالخذلان عند نزول البلاء في الآية الكريمة: ﴿وَأَمَّا إِذَا مَا ابْتَلَاهُ فَقَدَرَ عَلَيْهِ رِزْقَهُ فَيَقُولُ رَبِّي أَهَانَنِ﴾ (الفجر: 16) واعتبر ذلك فكرة خاطئة.

ويحاول الرومي عبر ما يذكر من ألوان التمثيل وأنواع التشبيهات أن يُقنع القارئ بأنّ الألم هو أمارة على اهتمام الربّ بالعبد، فيذكر في أحد تشبيهاته أنّ الإنسان المبتلى هو كالأسد المكبّل، فالأسد لا يلحق به عار إذا كان هناك سلسلة على رقبته، فإنّه أمارة على قيمته وقوّته، ولذلك ينصح المؤمن ألا يشكو من قضاء الله وقدره، فإنّه ليس إهمالًا منه في حقّهم (الرومي 1994، 1/195). وفي تشبيه آخر يذكر أنّه لا أحد يجعل الطوق في رقبة الكلب العقور، بل يُجعل الطوق دائمًا في رقبة كلب الصيد، والطوق وإن كان قيدًا إلا أنّه يدلّ على مدى اهتمام صاحب الكلب إليه (الرومي 1994، 2/239).

وفي هذا السياق يذكر الرومي حكاية مفادها أن أحد الزهّاد ذات ليلة كان يدعو ربّه ويهتف «يا الله»، فقال له الشيطان: لطالما دعوت ربّك وناديته فهل أتاك «لبيك» من الله؟ فانكسر قلبه وطأطأ رأسه، فرأى في منامه النبي الخِضْر، وحذّره عن انصرافه عن الذكر وندمه على الدعاء، فأجاب الزاهد بأنّي أخاف أن أكون مردودًا عن الباب، حيث لم يأتني جواب من الله، فجاء الجواب: أنّ قولك «يا الله» هو نفسه «لبيك» منّا، وذلك أنّ الله لا يأذن لأيّ أحدٍ أن ينادي ربّه، بل قد يعطي العبد الدنيا بأسرها ويمنعه الألم والتعب لكيلا يشكو عند الله سبحانه وتعالى عندما يحلّ به أذى (الرومي 1994، 2/13–15). ويستنتج من ذلك الرومي أنّ العناية الربانية قد تكمن في نفس ما نظنّه إهمالًا وخذلانًا من الله، وكذلك البلاء في نفسه هو نعمة من الله على العبد حيث يجعل الإنسان متضرّعًا وملتجئًا إليه.

6.4 الله مصدر الألم والراحة

يؤمن الرومي كأيّ مسلم صادق الإسلام أنّ الله سبحانه وتعالى هو مصدر الخير والشر، وليس هناك في الكون للشرّ أصل آخر. ونظرة الرومي هذه تشبه نظرة الفيلسوف الألماني غوتفريد لايبنتس (Gottfried Leibniz، ت. 1716)، ويعتقد أنّ الشرّ لا ينافي حكمة الله سبحانه وتعالى، فإنّ مَثَل الشرّ هو مَثَل صورة عفريت قبيح يرسمها رسّام بارع، فكما أنّ رسم القبيح يدلّ على براعة الرسّام وأنّه يُحسن الرسمَ سواء كان المرسوم يوسفَ أو عفريتًا، فكذلك الله سبحانه وتعالى هو الخالق القادر على كلّ شيء سواء كان خيرًا أو شرًا، ووجود الشرّ ليس منقصة فيه، بل هو ينمّ عن كماله (الرومي 1994، 1/387). ومع ذلك يؤكد الرومي دائمًا أنّ الله لا يرضى بابتلاء عباده، ولكنّه يُنزل عليهم البلاء لحكمة يعلمها. إنّ الله يصف نفسه بالطبيب، وهذا لا يعني أنّه يحبّ أن يرى عباده مرضى، إذ لو كان كذلك لمنعهم من الدواء ولكنّه كما أعطى السمّ، أعطى الترياق أيضًا (الرومي 1994، 2/232).

5 أخلاقيات الألم والمعاناة

من الأبحاث الهامة التي تُطرح في موضوع الألم والمعاناة هو تحديد السلوك الأخلاقي الأنسب تجاه الألم. لقد أعطى التراث الإسلامي بشكل عام أهمية قصوى إزاء الوظيفة الأخلاقية للإنسان، ولا سيّما في الظروف الاستثنائية، سواء على مستوى علاقته مع الله أو مع أخيه الإنسان أو مع الكون. ولا شك أنّ المتألّم يعيش أزمة روحية في داخله قد تؤثّر على سلوكه الأخلاقي، والسؤال المطروح هنا هو: ما هو الموقف الذي ينبغي للإنسان أن يتخذه في حالات الألم والمعاناة وما هو السلوك الأنسب عند مواجهة البلاء؟

ويعتقد الرومي أنّ المسؤولية الأولى للإنسان هي المقاومة والنضال -سواء داخليًا أو خارجيًا- من أجل التخلّص من الألم، وذلك فيما إذا كان الألم قابلًا للعلاج (غرجي 2012، 157). ويرى مولانا وفقًا لرؤيته الصوفية، أنّ الأنا الإنساني -أي النفس- هو مصدر لميول نفسانية تنغّص عيش الإنسان وتكدّر صفو حياته ولذلك يعتبر النفس سببًا لأوساخٍ تعيث الفساد في كلّ زمانٍ ومكانٍ (الرومي 1994، 289/1). وطريق الخلاص من هذه الآلام ليس سوى جهاد النفس (الرومي 1994، 14/2). وأما فيما يتعلّق بالآلام غير القابلة للعلاج، فيدعو الرومي إلى مواجهتها عبر التزام أمور ثلاثة: الصبر، ويذكر أنّ الصبر هو شهوة الأذكياء والحلوى - كناية عن الأمر السهل الوصول - هو أمنية الأطفال (الرومي 1994، 98/1)، والتسليم بقضاء الله، ويعتقد أنّ الإنسان إذا سلّم بقضاء الله وفوّض أمره إليه، أصبحت إرادته إرادة الله وحينئذٍ جرى العالم بأسره بإرادته (الرومي 1994، 108/2-110) ، والتضرع إلى الله، ويبيّن ذلك من خلال تشبيه هطول السحاب وبكاء الطفل بدعاء المتضرّع، فكما أنّ السحاب ما لم يبك لم تضحك الرياض، وأنّ الطفل ما لم يبك لم يجِش اللبن من ثدي الأم، فكذلك ما لم يتضرّع الإنسان ويدعو ربّه باكيًا منتحبًا لا يأتيه الفرج (الرومي 1994، 11/3).

6 الحِكم الكامنة وراء الألم

من الأسئلة المتكرّرة لدى المرضى المشرفين على الموت أو المصابين بالمرض العضال هو السؤال عن الحكمة وراء الألم والمعاناة، فإذا كان الله سبحانه وتعالى مصدرًا للخير ومنبعًا للعطاء، فما الذي يجعله يصبّ على عباده البلاء ويفتنهم بالبأساء والضراء. ونحن قد أشرنا فيما سبق بإيجاز واقتضاب إلى بعض الفوائد المترتبة على الألم والعناء من وجهة نظر مولانا، إلا أنّنا سنستوفي الكلام هنا عن ذلك، ونذكر أهمّ الآثار الإيجابية للألم.

1.6 الألم مقدمة لاستكمال الإنسان

إنّ ارتقاء الإنسان في مدارج الكمال لا يحصل إلا بمكابدة الآلام والمتاعب، فإن الإنسان في مسيره إلى الكمال يشبه القمر الذي يصير بدرًا فكما أنّ الأخير لا يكتمل إلا بعد النقصان ودخوله في طور المحاق، فكذلك الإنسان لا يبلغ كماله إلا بعد أن يتحمل الآلام والشدائد (الرومي 1994، 195/1). وفي هذا السياق يعتقد الرومي أنّ الإنسان يمرّ في حياته بمراحل وأطوار من كونه جمادًا وحيوانًا وإنسانًا وملكًا، وفي كل مرحلة يذوق موتًا مريرًا يمكّنه من الوصول إلى المرحلة القادمة، وهذا الموت والحياة لا يخلو من التعب والألم، ولكنّ النتيجة تستحق تحمل ذلك -كوجع المخاض الذي تتحمله الأم لما تترتب عليه من النتائج (الرومي 1994، 386/1)، وعليه فينبغي للإنسان، أن يهوّن هذه المتاعب على نفسه لكي يحصل على المكانة الإنسانية الشامخة (الرومي 1994، 222/2).

ويحاول الرومي عبر ما يقدّمه من تشبيهات لا مثيل لها أن يُفهم القارئ أنّ الألم أمر إيجابي للإنسان، ففي تشبيه حبّات الحمّص والسيدة، تقفز حبّات الحمّص في القدر المغلي صعودًا وهبوطًا محاولةً الخلاص منه والهرب، ولكن السيدة تضرب بالملعقة على رأسها، وتنزلها إلى قاع القدر. فتهتف حبّات الحمّص وتشكو السيدةَ لأنّها أشعلت بها النار، ولكنّ السيدة لا تأبه شيئًا، وتقول لها "إنّ ذلك ليس كراهةً لك، بل ليطيب مذاقك وطعمك، وتصيرينَ غذاءً، وتصلين إلى غايتك، فإنّ كلّ ما تحمّلت في البستان كان لتتهيّئين لهذه النار، فتصلينَ من خلالها إلى ذروة كمالك" (الرومي 1994، 2/237–238). ويستخلص الرومي من هذه الحكاية أنّ البلاء الإلهي هو رحمة من الله على عباده ليُبلغهم مرتبة الكمال الإنساني، ولكنّ العباد لعدم صبرهم يرون ذلك جفاءً من الحبيب في حقّهم.

وفي تشبيه آخر، يقول الرومي أنّ حبّة الحنطة تُحبس تحت التراب لتتحوّل شطأً، وتستوي على ساقها، وهذا يعني أنّ نموّ الحنطة رهينة بتحمّل البرد والظلمة في قلب التراب، والأمر لا يقف عند ذلك، بل الحنطة بعد أن سنبلت يجب أن تُسحق في البيدر، وتُطحن في الطاحونة، وتُعجن في المعاجن، وتُرمى في النار لتتحوّل إلى خبز يؤكل، كما أنّ الخبز أيضًا ما لم يُمضغ تحت الأسنان لا يصير غذاءً نافعًا للإنسان وقوّة ممدة له وعلاجًا لمرضه ونورًا لبصره وركيزة لحياته (الرومي 1994، 1/195). وغرض الرومي من سرد هذه الرواية هو أنّ الإنسان أيضًا – كحبة الحنطة – ما لم يتحمل الشدائد والمصائب في حياته لا يصل إلى كماله.

وكثيرًا ما يستشهد الرومي في كلماته بقاعدة «الضدّ يتولّد من الضدّ» ويذكر لها شواهد متعدّدة: فإنّ رسول الله صلّى الله عليه وآله وسلّم حارب المشركين وانتهت تلك الحروب في النهاية إلى السلام، والبستاني يهذّب الأغصان والفروع ويقتلع الأعشاب الضارة، ويؤدي ذلك إلى تقوية الأشجار وتحسين جودة ثمارها، والطبيب يخلع الضرس المنخور، ويحصل بذلك تخلّص الضرس من الألم والمرض، والشهيد يُقطع حلقه، ولكنّه يأكل بذلك الرزق عند ربّه. ويطبّق الرومي هذه القاعدة على قضية الألم والمعاناة أيضًا ويستنتج أنّ الألم وإن كان في الظاهر نقصانًا فإنه وفقًا لقاعدة «الضدّ يتولّد من الضد» سوف يؤدّي إلى الكمال (الرومي 1994، 1/238).

2.6 الألم محرّك الإنسان نحو صلاحه وإصلاحه

إنّ الألم هو سبب شحذ الهمم وإيقاظ العزائم وتحريك الإنسان نحو ما هو صلاحه وإصلاحه، وبدون الألم قد لا يندفع الإنسان نحو العمل. يقول مولانا: "إن الألم هو الذي يوجّه الإنسان في أي عملٍ. وما لم يظهر في داخله ألم ذلك الشيء، وهوسه وعشقه، فلن يقصد إليه، ولن يتيسّر له ذلك الشيء دون ألم، سواءٌ أكان ذلك الشيء نجاحًا في هذه الدنيا أم نجاة في الآخرة، وسواء أكان تجارة أم مُلكًا، وسواء أكان علمًا أم نجومًا. ولو لم تظهر آلام الوَضع لمريم لما قصدت إلى

تلك الشجرة المباركة: فأجاءها المخاض إلى جذع النخلة، ألجأها ذلك الألم إلى الشجرة، والشجرة التي كانت جافّة غدت مثمر" (الرومي 2002، 54–53).

ويروي مولانا في حكاية النائم والحية أنّ رجلًا كان نائمًا تحت ظل إحدى الأشجار وقد فتح فاه فإذا بحيّة متّجهة نحوه حتّى وصلته ودخلت إلى بطنه، وفي تلك الأثناء صادف أن مرّ من هناك رجل صالح ممتطيًا فرسه، ولم يجد الفارس بدًّا أن ينهال عليه يضربه بعصاه، فاستيقظ النائم وهرع مسرعًا نحو شجرة كان قد سقط تفاحها، فأمره الفارس بأكله حتّى التخمة، ثمّ عاد يضربه بالعصى مجدّدًا، فاستمر الرجل بالركض وهو يصيح شاكيًا: "أيها الجبان، لم تضربني وتظلمني، لينتقم الله منك،" حتى تقيّأ كلّ ما في بطنه بما فيه تلك الحية، وعندما شاهد تلك الحية قد خرجت من فمه، أدرك رأفة وشهامة ذلك الفارس الصنديد، فوقف أمامه بكل احترام وتواضع وشكره على لطفه ونسي كلّ ذلك الضرب المبرّح والألم والأنين (الرومي 1994، 1/349–352). وأراد الرومي أن يعلّمنا عبر سرد هذه الحكاية أنّ الآلام والمحن وإن كانت بغيضة في ظاهرها فإننا إذا أمعنّا النظر فيها سنجد أنّها جاءت لتدفعنا نحو ما هو فيه صلاح أمرنا وإصلاح سريرتنا.

3.6 الألم يصقل القلب

يذكر مولانا في كثير من حكايات «**المثنوي**» أنّ مكابدة الآلام وتحمّل المصائب تؤدّي إلى نقاء القلب وصفاء النفس، ويشبه ذلك إلى بوتقة ينصهر فيه الوجود الإنساني لتزول عنه الشوائب. وفي ذلك، يسرد الرومي حكاية حيوان يسمّى **بالأشغر**، وهو كلّما ضُرب على رأسه بالعصا أكثر، كلما صار أكثر قوة وسمنة، ثمّ يخلص إلى أنّ نفس المؤمن تشبه **الأشغر**، حيث إنّ الألم والبلاء يزيدها قوة ومنعة (الرومي 1994، 2/283). وفي تشبيه آخر يذكر الرومي أنّ الإنسان بمنزلة الجلد الذي إذا دُبغ بالعقارات المُرّة تحوّل إلى الأديم الطائفي، وإذا لم يُدبغ صار منتنًا وعفنًا (الرومي 1994، 2/283)، وعلى ضوء هذا التشبيه، ينصح الإنسان أن يروّض نفسه بالمتاعب والصعوبات ليصير طاهرًا ولطيفًا وذا بهاء، وإن كان لا يتجرّأ على ذلك، فعليه أن يرضى بما يُصبّ عليه من البلاء، فإنّ البلاء هو تطهير للقلب من الأوساخ (الرومي 1994، 2/284).

4.6 الألم ينزل الرحمة

يرى الرومي أنّ كلّ بلاء تتبعه نعمة، ولو أعطيت الربّ حَمَلًا – أي: سلبه منك بالبلاء – فسيعطيك قطيعًا (الرومي 1994، 3/354)؛ فإنّه سبحانه وتعالى ليس ذلك المليك الذي يصفع الإنسان ثم لا يهبه شيئًا، وخير شاهد على ذلك الأنبياء، فإنّهم تحمّلوا في حياتهم بلاءً مريرًا، ولكنّ الله عوّضهم عن ذلك (الرومي 1994، 3/366). ويضرب الرومي على ذلك مثال الطفل والحجّام، حيث يرتعد الطفل فَرَقًا من مبضع الحجّام، ولكن أمّه فرحة بذلك، لأنّها تعلم أنّه سيزيد من صحّة الطفل

وسلامته (الرومي 1994، 17/1). يقول الرومي: إنّ الله لو كسر رِجلًا فسيعطي جناحًا، ولو رمى في بئر فسيفتح بابًا في قاع البئر (الرومي 1994، 275/2). ويقول أيضًا: السبب في أنّ أولياء الله لا يعترضون على الله هو أنّهم يؤمنون بأنّ العوض سيأتي أعظم من المفقود (الرومي 1994، 107/2). ويذكر الرومي في هذا السياق أنّ العوض قد لا يكون نعمة مادّية، بل قد يكون نعمة روحية، وهي تأصيل الأخلاق الحسنة في وجود الإنسان (الرومي 1994، 355/3). كما قد لا يكون العوض في الدنيا بل في الآخرة، ويقدّم الرومي لذلك قصة خيالية لامرأة كانت تضع كل سنة ابنًا ولكنّه لم يكن يبقى أكثر من ستّة شهور، وكانت المرأة تبكي وتشتكي إلى الله من ذلك، وقد استمرّ الوضع هكذا حتّى مات منها عشرون ولدًا واحترقت قلوب الأهل بذلك. حينئذٍ حَلِمَت المرأة ذات ليلة ورأت جنة في منتهى الروعة والجمال وكان اسمها قد كتب على قصرٍ، فعلمت أنّه لها، فقيل لها: "هذا جزاء من يفدي نفسه مخلصًا فينا، وأما أنت فقد كنت تتكاسلين عن الالتجاء إلى الله، فأعطاك هذه المصائب لتقبلي إليه،" فقالت المرأة: "لا أبالي إن ابتليتني مائة سنة أو أزيد، فما دام هذا عطاءك، فيحقّ لك أن تسفك دمي،" وعندما دخل الجنة رأت فيها أبناءها العشرين لتدرك أنّهم وإن ضلّوا عنها، ولكنهم لا يضلّون عن الله سبحانه وتعالى (الرومي 1994، 194/2–195).

5.6 الألم يزيل الغفلة

الألم يُشعل ذكر الله في نفس الإنسان، فإنّه هو حبل يربط في عنق المحبّ، فيجرّه إلى باب الحبيب لينكبّ بوجهه الشاحب على عتبته، ويبكي منتحبًا، ويدعوه لكشف ما ألمّ به من البلاء. وعن ذلك، يقول الرومي: إنّ الفيل إذا لم يُضرب على رأسه، فسيحلم بالهند – الذي هو موطنه – ويتمرّد على الفيّال، وكذلك الإنسان إذا كان في الراحة والغنى صار طاغيًا عاصيًا، ولذلك فإنّ الله يصبّ عليه أنواع البلاء والمصائب ليكسر شوكته ويكبح جماحه ويزدهر التواضع والخشوع في نفسه (الرومي 1994، 239/2). ويعتقد الرومي أنّه ثمة حجابان بين الإنسان وربّه هما الصحة والثروة، ومادام الإنسان ينعم بهما، فهو غافل عن الله سبحانه وتعالى، وعندما يفقدهما ينتبه إليه (الرومي 2002، 333). وعلى ذلك، فمن رحمة الله أن يبتلي عبده بالآلام ليتوجّه إليه، ولا غرو إذن إن قلنا بأنّ الألم من الله هو أفضل من ملك الدنيا، والمثال على ذلك هو فرعون؛ حيث يذكر لنا الرومي أنّ الله قد أعطاه ملكًا عظيمًا ومالًا وفيرًا، ووقاه طيلة عمره حتّى من ألمٍ بسيطٍ كالصداع، والسبب أنّ الله كره أن يراه متضرعًا متبتّلًا إليه (الرومي 1994، 13/2–14).

ويذكر الرومي في الدفتر الثاني حكاية عن رجل اعتلّ، فعاده رسول الله –صلّى الله عليه وآله وسلّم– فشكر المريضُ الله على ما وهبه في الكبر من السقم لكيلا ينام جميع الليل، بل ينهض من النوم ويعبد الله في جوف الليل (الرومي 1994، 372/1). كذلك يروي الرومي في حكاية الملك وابنه أنّ ابن الملك تحت عناية أبيه يحصل على حالات عرفانية وروحية، وعندئذٍ يصيبه الغرور

ويشعر بالاستغناء عن أبيه ويطغى عليه، فحينئذ يقطع الأب نظره عن الابن ليعتريه القبض ويعود إلى رشده (الرومي 1994، 3/548–560). ويحاول الرومي عبر سرد هذه الروايات أن يُظهر للقارئ أنّ الآلام والأسقام لها وجه آخر حسنٌ أيضًا، إذا ما انتبه الإنسان إليه وهو تطهير قلبه من أدران الغفلة والغرّة.

6.6 الألم يُهيّئ الإنسان للموت

من وجهة نظر الرومي، كل ألمٍ هو قطعة من الموت، لأنّ الموت ليس حدثًا يقع في لحظة، بل هو حدث مستمر طيلة حياة الإنسان، وكل ألم وتعب يمثّل جزءًا من ذلك، ومن استطاع أن يصبر أمام ما يواجهه من الآلام، ويجتازها بقوة، فإنّه يستعدّ لمواجهة الموت، ويمكنه أن يعتنق الموت في غاية السرور والحبور (الرومي 1994، 1/141–142). وإذا رأينا العرفاء يأمنون الموت، فذلك لأنّهم اجتازوا بحر الدمّ "كناية عن مكابدة المصاعب" بنجاح (الرومي 1994، 3/525). ويتحدّى الرومي في أحد غزلياته الموت قائلًا: "إذا كان الموت باسلًا فقل له تعال إليّ حتّى احتضنه بقوة، وعندئذٍ فأنا سأسلب منه لنفسي الحياة، وهو سيسلب مني خرقتي (كناية عن البدن)" (الرومي 1998، 516). وهنا يتفق الرومي مع الأديب الألماني هرمان هيسه حيث يقول: "أنا مقتنع جدًّا بسعادتي الحالية، ويمكنني أن أتحمّلها لفترة، ولكن أتمنّى أن أتألّم قليلًا، وأريد أن يكون ألمي أجمل وأعظم من ذي قبل، فأنا متعطّش لتلك الآلام والمصائب التي تهيّئني للموت" (هيسه 1975، 277).

7.6 الألم يميّز الخبيث من الطيّب

إنّ الآلام والمصائب – بل الألطاف والنعم أيضًا – هي اختبار للإنسان ليميز الخبيث من الطيب، كما قال سبحانه وتعالى: ﴿وَلَنَبْلُوَنَّكُمْ حَتَّىٰ نَعْلَمَ الْمُجَاهِدِينَ مِنكُمْ وَالصَّابِرِينَ﴾ (محمد: 31). لكن ينبغي أن لا نغفل أنّها تكون لطفًا ونعمة إذا ما صبر الإنسان وقاوم في وجهها، أمّا إذا تخلّى عن مسؤوليته وجزع عندها فهي ستتحوّل فعلًا إلى البلاء، وقد شبّه الرومي ذلك بنهر النيل حيث كان لأتباع موسى رحمة ونعمة وعلى أتباع فرعون نقمة وشقاوة (الرومي 1994، 2/454).

7 حصيلة البحث

إنّ التأصيل الإسلامي لرعاية نهاية الحياة لا يتيسّر إلا بالرجوع إلى تراثنا الإسلامي الزاخر، وجلال الدين الرومي هو أحد الشخصيات الإسلامية العظيمة التي يمكن الرجوع إليها لتوظيف عطاءاته الفكرية في مجال مساعدة المرضى المشرفين على الموت، ولا سيّما فيما يخصّ كيفية مواجهة الألم والمعاناة، حيث أنّه عاش عصرًا ذاق طعم الألم إثر اجتياح المغول وحاول أن يقدّم وصفة ناجحة للإنسان في سبيل التغلب على آلامه. بالإضافة إلى ذلك، إن صبّ المفاهيم اللاهوتية

ومزجها مع الإحساس في الأدب الصوفي يمكن أن يعتبر نموذجًا موفّقًا في تقديم الرعاية الروحية للمرضى وإقناعهم الفكري والروحي. وفي هذا السياق يعتقد الرومي أنّ أصل الآلام الإنسانية يتجذّر في انقطاع الإنسان عن موطنه الأصلي وأما سائر الآلام فهي تجليات لألم الفراق، ويقترح للتخلص منها أن يعود الأنا الإنساني إلى عالمه الروحاني، وخروجه من سُكر الوجود كحلٍّ وحيدٍ لجميع الآلام الإنسانية. إنّ الله يصبّ على الإنسان أنواع الألم والبلاء تمهيدًا لخروج الإنسان من قفص سجنه وتحليقه في الملكوت الإلهي، وعلى ذلك فإنّ الموقف الأخلاقي الذي ينبغي للإنسان أن يتّخذه في مثل هذه الظروف الاستثنائية هو الصبر والتسليم والتضرّع. ومن جملة الأمور التي قد أعارها الرومي اهتمامًا زائدًا ويمكن توظيفها في مجال رعاية نهاية الحياة هي الحكم الكامنة وراء الآلام الإنسانية، ويذكر الرومي استكمال الإنسان، ودفعه إلى القيام بما يكون فيه صلاحه وإصلاحه، نقاء القلب، وإنزال الرحمة الإلهية، وإزالة الغفلة وتهيئة الإنسان للمواجهة مع الموت كآثار إيجابية للآلام البشرية.

المصادر

أمين، أحمد. 2013. **ظهر الإسلام**. القاهرة: مؤسسة هنداوي للتعليم والثقافة.

براون، إدوارد جرانفيل. 1954. **تاريخ الأدب في إيران من الفردوسي إلى السعدي**، ترجمة إبراهيم أمين الشواربي (من الإنكليزية إلى العربية). القاهرة: مطبعة السعادة.

تدين، عطاء الله. 2015. **بحثًا عن الشمس من قونية إلى دمشق**، ترجمة عيسى علي العاكوب. دمشق: دار نينوى للدراسات والنشر والتوزيع.

حسن، هاشم أبو الحسن علي. د.ت. **الله والإنسان عند جلال الدين الرومي**. القاهرة: مكتبة الثقافة الدينية.

خفاجي، محمد عبد المنعم. د.ت. **الأدب في التراث الصوفي**. القاهرة: دار غريب للطباعة.

رفعت جو، فرح ناز. 2008. **العرفان الصوفي عند جلال الدين الرومي**. بيروت: دار الهادي للطباعة والنشر.

الرومي، جلال الدين. 1994. **مثنوي معنوي**، 4 ج. طهران: انتشارات علمي فرهنگي.

الرومي، جلال الدين. 1998. **كليات شمس تبريزي**. طهران: انتشارات أميركبير.

الرومي، جلال الدين. 2002. **كتاب فيه ما فيه**، ترجمة عيسى علي العاكوب. دمشق: دار الفكر.

شيمل، آنا ماري. 2006. **الأبعاد الصوفية في الإسلام وتاريخ التصوف**، ترجمة محمد إسماعيل السيد ورضا حامد قطب. بغداد: منشورات الجمل.

شيمل، آنا ماري. 2016. **الشمس المنتصرة**، ترجمة عيسى علي العاكوب. دمشق: دار التكوين للتأليف والترجمة والنشر.

شيرازي، إيرج. 2007. «رنج از نگاه مولانا» (العنوان بالعربية: «الألم من وجهة نظر الرومي»). **پژوهش نامه فرهنگ وأدب** 3(4): 167–186.

عزام، عبد الله. 2013. **التصوف وفريد الدين العطار**. القاهرة: مؤسسة هنداوي للتعليم والثقافة.

علمي، قربان وحسن صابری ورزنه. 2013. «ارزيابي مولانا از أقسام إيمان در پاسخ به مسأله رن» (العنوان بالعربية: «تقييم الرومي لأقسام الإيمان عند الردّ على قضية الألم»). **حكمة إسراء** 5(1): 143–169.

العوادي، عدنان حسن. د.ت. **الشعر الصوفي**. بغداد: د.ن.

غالب، مصطفى. 1982. **جلال الدين الرومي**. بيروت: مؤسسة عزّ الدين.

غرجي، مصطفى. 2012. «بررسي وتحليل ماهيت درد ورنج در مثنوي معنوي» (العنوان بالعربية: »دراسة تحليلية لماهية الألم والمعاناة في المثنوي المعنوي»). **مطالعات عرفاني** 1(15): 139–162.

محمد، نظمي عبد البديع. د.ت. **في الأدب الصوفي**. القاهرة: د.ن.

محمد، أملا. 2010. «نار العشق في ناي جلال الدين الرومي». **ثقافتنا للدراسات والبحوث** 23(6): 177–194.

محمودي، حسين وأصغر دادبه. 2013. «رنج از ديدگاه مولانا با نگاهي به مسأله شر» (العنوان بالعربية: «الألم من وجهة نظر الرومي، مع الاهتمام بمشكلة الشر»). **پژوهش نامه فلسفة دين** 11(2): 163–188.

همايي، جلال الدين. 1987. **مولوي نامه: مولوي چه مى گويد؟** (العنوان بالعربية: **رسالة مولانا: ماذا يقول الرومي؟**). 2 ج. طهران: نشر هما.

هيسة، هرمان. 1975. **گرگ بيابان** (العنوان بالعربية: **ذئب البراري**)، ترجمة كيكاووس جهانداري (إلى الفارسية). طهران: بنگاه ترجمة ونشر.

ياسبرز، كارل. 1975. **زندگي نامه فلسفي من** (العنوان بالعربية: **سيرتي الفلسفية**)، ترجمة عزت الله فولادوند (إلى الفارسية). طهران.

CHAPTER 5

Plague, Proper Behaviour and Paradise in a Newly Discovered Text by Zakariyyā al-Anṣārī

Hans Daiber

1 Introduction

At the end of his life the Egyptian scholar Zakariyyā b. Muḥammad al-Anṣārī (d. 926/1520) wrote his treatise *Tuḥfat al-Rāghibīn fī Bayān Amr al-Ṭawāʿīn* ("On the Gift for Those Who Like to Get Information on the Topic of the Plagues"). He intended to facilitate the study of Ibn Ḥajar al-ʿAsqalānī's (d. 852/1449) book *Badhl al-Māʿūn fī Faḍl al-Ṭāʿūn* ("The Grant of an Instrument for a Meritorious Plague").

We will analyse al-Anṣārī's text, as it allows interesting conclusions with regard to "end-of-life care." The treatise does not only address people afflicted with plagues, but also every invalid and all who die "for the cause of God" (*fī sabīl Allāh*) – be it during the fight against infidels or through a plague or because of both. It gives practical advice and provides information concerning duties and preconditions for the Muslim believer. The text is an admonition to believers intended to pave the way to paradise, consoling them and giving them relief. Unlike the usual consolation texts, al-Anṣārī's text is a consoling guide for the believer who is asked to be sincere, to have good "intentions" (*niyya*), to repent (*tawba*), to be patient (*ṣabr*), to pray to God (*duʿāʾ*), to seek God's "acceptance" (*marḍāt*) and to fight against enemies and kill them, including infidels. Plagues can be considered as "temptations" (*fitan*) which test a person and his patience. At this point the text differs from the consolation literature written e.g., "for bereaved parents." Its notion of a transient world full of misfortunes is replaced in the Anṣārī-text by a concept of the world where the believers are tested. Through prayers and with patience the believers find their way to paradise. Here, al-Anṣārī does not exclude practical medical recommendations which he found in texts by Ibn Sīnā (Avicenna, d. 428/1037) and Ibn al-Nafīs (d. 687/1288) (ch. 13). There is no "thanatophobia." The reason (*ḥikma*) for pains, in al-Anṣārī's view (ch. 5) caused by the "piercing" by "pricking" by the *jinn*, is a test for those who "search for God's acceptance (*marḍāt*)." The ill person can receive help from the proper behaviour of his healer. Every healer should have time for his patient, should have qualities like "kindness" and "generosity", should lay his hand on the side or hand of the patient or stroke with his hand over his face and breast, should ask him about his health and pray to God, the Healer, for the health of his patient.

These measures "beyond clinical care" betray religious-spiritual and ethical aspects. God "removes the harm" and "restores the health" and clearly restricts the influence of the physician as a decision-maker. Al-Anṣārī uses theological concepts of the almighty and all-determining God; of God's reward and punishment; of God's "mercy" (*raḥma*), "favour" (*niʿma*), "goodness" and "independence" (*ghaniya*) of man, God's "servant" (*ʿabd*), a "miserable" (*ḥaqīr*) sinful being that should obey God and repent his sins. In his fight against unbelievers he can be killed or die through the plague and enter as a martyr into paradise. The consolation offered to the ill by referring the dying person to the eternal world of the intellect is not discussed.

Al-Anṣārī's Islamic theology, as it appears in his text on the plague, shares with Islamic creeds some fundamental concepts which betray sympathy with the Ḥanbalī-Sufi school. Al-Anṣārī shares with the Ḥanbalī theology the following concepts: "submission" (*taslīm*) to God's "divine decree" (*qaḍāʾ*) by following God's orders and prohibitions; "belief" (*īmān*) as "confessing (*qawl*), acting (*ʿamal*) and intention (*niyya*)"; the belief can "increase by obedience and decrease by disobedience"; punishment in the grave; the "mediation" (*shafāʿa*) of the Prophet; paradise and hell; "holy war" (*jihād*) and "Antichrist" (*dajjāl*). The Ḥanbalī background of al-Anṣārī's theology is confirmed by his recourse to the Prophetic tradition of the *ḥadīth*, the dominating role of the Prophet and finally by al-Anṣārī's recourse to Sufism. Al-Anṣārī's *Tuḥfat al-Rāghibīn* confirms the spiritual function of the Prophet as a healer and mediator between God and His creation. Here too, al-Anṣārī appears to be a Ḥanbalī and a Sufi.

2 The Life and Scholarship of al-Anṣārī

The Egyptian Shāfiʿī judge and scholar Zakariyyā b. Muḥammad al-Anṣārī (Ingalls 2011, 39) was already more than 90 years old when he wrote his treatise *Tuḥfat al-Rāghibīn*. He wrote it after the plague which he recorded as the last epidemic that happened in the years 918/1512 and 919/1513.

Al-Anṣārī had lost his son Muḥyī l-Dīn Yaḥyā (Ingalls 2011, 81 and 86) in the plague of the year 897/1492 in Cairo and seven years later (904/1499) his son Muḥammad b. Zakariyyā drowned in the Nile (Ingalls 2011, 85). Moreover, in the year 903/1497 Cairo was again hit by the plague, and as a consequence social and political unrest dominated the streets of Cairo (Ingalls 2011, 84). After these heavy blows and because of his increasing infirmity and deteriorating vision, al-Anṣārī retired in 906/1501 (Ingalls 2011, 90), at the age of 78, from his teaching posts and his position as a judge and dedicated the last 19 years of his life to scholarship (Ingalls 2011, 96). His main interest was Sufism and *ḥadīth*; besides books on Islamic law, he wrote among others a commentary on al-Bukhārī's (d. 256/870) *Ṣaḥīḥ* ("Authentic") in which he used earlier commentaries (Ingalls 2011, 97) and a commentary on al-Qushayrī's (d. 465/1072) *al-Risāla al-Qushayriyya* ("The Qushayrian Treatise") on Sufism, called *Iḥkām al-Dalāla ʿalā Taḥrīr al-Risāla* ("The Perfect Guide to the Epistle") (Ingalls 2011, 125 and 139ff.; 2022, ch. 3 and 4).

The impressive list of teachers and texts which shaped al-Anṣārī's education (Ingalls 2011, 255–260) explain his combination of Sufism and Islamic law in a mystical worldview[1] that is based on texts by al-Qushayrī and also al-Ghazālī (d. 505/1111) (Ingalls 2011, 130) or Abū Ḥafṣ ʿUmar al-Suhrawardī (d. 632/1234) (Ingalls 2011, 49 and 130).

One of al-Anṣārī's teachers was the *ḥadīth*-scholar Ibn Ḥajar al-ʿAsqalānī. He was al-Anṣārī's shining example in the science of *ḥadīth*, but also in a treatise on the plague: Ibn Ḥajar's book *Badhl al-Māʿūn fī Faḍl al-Ṭāʿūn*,[2] which was shortened, supplemented and shaped into a new literary version in al-Anṣārī's *Tuḥfat al-Rāghibīn fī Bayān Amr al-Ṭawāʿīn*. Al-Anṣārī found his teacher's book too elaborate and too verbose and therefore, difficult to comprehend **(D 1 v–D 2 r 1)**.[3] We will edit and translate some selected passages and analyse the whole text, as it allows interesting conclusions about the "end-of-life care" project. Al-Anṣārī differs from Ibn Ḥajar's text, which consists of five chapters (*bāb*s), each containing four, nine, four, ten and five sections (*faṣl*s). Al-Anṣārī divided his text into fourteen sections, with titles partly differing from Ibn Ḥajar. He took over most literally essential passages from Ibn Ḥajar and added short supplements and critical remarks. The Anṣārī-text is approximately 12% of the Ibn Ḥajar-text (325 pages in the edition) and the additions by al-Anṣārī might be 10%. The result is an intelligent and valuable selection in the footsteps of al-Anṣārī's teacher Ibn Ḥajar.

---

1 Ingalls speaks of "a Sufism of the Law" (Ingalls 2011, 122ff.) and on of "cross-fertilization and overlap between Sufism and Islamic Law" (Ingalls 2011, [illegible]).

2 Dols presents a survey of the chapters and their contents, as an example for "religious interpretation" (Dols 1977, 109–121).

3 The references given between brackets refer to the MS D, on which see below n. 5.

3 Contents and Main Ideas of al-Anṣārī's *Tuḥfat al-Rāghibīn fī Bayān Amr al-Ṭawāʿīn*

We shall give an overview of the main ideas, allowing us to classify the text as a guidebook for the fatally ill who look for consolation. Like Ibn Ḥajar, the text often refers to Prophetic traditions. Al-Anṣārī wrote his treatise as he was confronted with plagues during which he had lost one of his sons.

The **first chapter** gives a survey of the meanings of "plague" (*ṭāʿūn*), which include "pain" (*wajaʿ*), epidemic (*wabāʾ*), but also includes a religious colouring, like "act of God's mercy" (*raḥma*), "martyrdom" (*shahāda*), religious exhortation (*mawʿiẓa*) for believers, the Muslim and "punishment" (*ʿadhāb, rujz, rijz*) or "indignation" (*sukhṭ*) for infidels **(D 2 r 3–18).**

The **second chapter** gives a historical example of a plague in Israel: Prophet David chose from the three options famine, enmity and plague the epidemic with seventy thousand or hundred thousand dead. After this trial (*balāʾ*) David implored God, who saved his people in an act of mercy. **(D 2 r 23–D 2 v 3).**

The **third chapter** describes the peculiarities of the plague and its manifestations, quoting besides *ḥadīth* also Ibn Sīnā **(D 2 v 8–14)** and Ibn al-Nafīs **(D 2 v 14–18).** Al-Anṣārī considers "plague" (*ṭāʿūn*) to be "a more specific (term)" than *wabāʾ* (epidemic); in his view *wabāʾ* can be cured, but not *ṭāʿūn*. In the footsteps of Ibn Ḥajar (Dols 1977, 116–118; Stearns 2011, ch. 3)[4] *ṭāʿūn* is a "piercing" (*ṭaʿn*) by the *jinn*. For this reason, bad air cannot be the only reason of the plague (*ṭāʿūn*) **(D 2 v 24–3 r 4).**

The **fourth chapter** takes up the explanation of plague as "piercing" (*ṭaʿn*) or "pricking" (*wakhz*) by the *jinn*. Al-Anṣārī says that the Prophet "chose for most (of the companions of the Prophet) the martyrdom (*shahāda*) through the piercing (*ṭaʿn*) for the cause of God (*fī sabīl Allāh*) and through the plague (*ṭāʿūn*), which occurred in their time and through which the remainder of them died" **(D 3 r 22–23; D 3 v 10–12).** The Prophet has the function to invoke God on behalf of the believers and to ask for forgiveness (*maghfira*). Those who should be punished can leave hellfire through the mediation (*shafāʿa*) of the Prophet. The Prophet's mediation can avoid the splitting up of the people into different parties (*shiyaʿ*), and can avoid harmfulness (*baʾs*) and opposition between brothers "in religion" or friends **(D 3 r 19–21; 29–30).** Sins in religion however cannot be forgiven **(D 3 v 12).** Interestingly, there is, according to al-Anṣārī, no pricking by the *jinn* during Ramaḍān, because during that time Satans "are hindered from most of their work." Al-Anṣārī speaks of "fettering"

4 On the *jinn* as a source of maladies see Nünlist 2015, 269–272, with a reference to a parallel in the *New Testament* (Nünlist 271, n. 126).

(*taṣfīd*) of Satans **(D 3 r 23–24)**. Al-Anṣārī's formulation follows an old tradition (see Nünlist 2015, 229, n. 206).

The **fifth chapter** "on the reason (*ḥikma*) of giving the *jinn* power over mankind" discusses the reason, why people are "pierced" or "pricked" by the *jinn*, thus causing plagues. The "piercing" or "pricking" of the *jinn* is a test for those who search for God's "acceptance" (*marḍāt*) **(D 3 v 14)**. The successful believer will achieve "happiness" (*sarrāʾ*), is "grateful" (*shakara*) and it is "good" (*khayr*) for him; the believer who has distress (*ḍarrāʾ*) is "patient" (*ṣabara*) and this too is "good" for him **(D 3 v 21–22)**.

[5] قال ابن القيِّم: فيه حكمة بالغة فإنّ اعداءنا منهم / شياطينهم واهل[6] الطاعة منهم[7] إخواننا، والله امرنا بمعاداة أعدائنا من الجنّ والإنس[8] طلباً لمرضاته، [د ٣ ب ١٥] فأبى أكثر الناس إلّا مسالمتهم وموالاتهم[9]، فسلطهم الله[10] عليهم عقوبة[11] لهم حيث اطاعوهم[12] حين اغروهم[13] / وامروهم بالمعاصي والفجور والفساد في الأرض[14]، فاقتضت الحكمة تسليطهم[15] عليهم بالطعن فيهم[16] كما سلّط عليهم [د ٣ ب ١٧] أعداءهم من الانس حيث[17] افسدوا في الأرض ونبذوا كتاب الله وراء ظهورهم،

---

5 The Arabic passages, published here and in the following, are taken from our edition and translation (published in Daiber 2021), based on three MSS and on the excerpts from Ibn Ḥajar al-ʿAsqalānī's *Badhl al-Māʿūn*:
1) **D** = د = Daiber Collection III MS 115 (copied 1035/1626), fol. 1 v–7 v.
2) **T** = ت = MS dr. Muḥammad Ibn Turkī l-Turkī, copied in 1300/1883 from the manuscript in al-Maktaba al-Baladiyya in Alexandria (which is apparently Egyptian National Archive 56, Taṣawwurāt Ḥalīm, ʿArabī 443547).
3) **B** = ب MS Berlin, Landberg 380 (Ahlwardt 1887–1899, no. 6370), undated (according to Ahlwardt copied *c.*1200/1785), fol. 1 r–8 r.–4. **Ḥ** = ح= Ibn Ḥajar 1997. The excerpts from Ibn Ḥajar are written in cursive.

6 واما اهل Ḥ 153, 5.

7 + فهم Ḥ 153, 5.

8 + وأن نحاربهم Ḥ 153, 6.

9 – Ḥ 153, 7.

10 – Ḥ 153, 7.

11 عقوبة T B Ḥ 153, 8 : عقابة D.

12 استجابوا لهم Ḥ 153, 8.

13 اغووهم Ḥ 153, 8.

14 فأطاعوهم Ḥ 153, 9.

15 أن يسلطهم Ḥ 153, 9.

16 منهم B.

17 حيث B Ḥ 153, 10 : حين T D.

.......وهو[18] تعالى[19] [٣ ب ٢١] للمؤمن حافظ وناصر ولأعدائه مخزٍ قاهرٌ، والمؤمن هو
الذي إن اصابته سرّاء شكر فكان خيراً / له وإن اصابته ضرّاء فصبر[20] فكان خيراً له،

Ibn al-Qayyim[21] said: "In it is a strong reason, because to our enemies belong their Satans and to the obedient people belong our brothers. God has ordered us to disobey our enemies, namely the *jinn* and the people (*al-jinn wa-l-ins*), in search for (God's) acceptance (*marḍātihī*). **/D 3 v 15/** Most of the people insisted on keeping peace with (with the *jinn*) and being friends with them (*muwālātuhum*). Therefore, God gave them power to punish (the people), inasmuch as they obey (the *jinn*) when (the *jinn*) induce (the people) and order them to sin and to do immoral and wicked things. Therefore, reason requires that (the *jinn*) are given power over (the people) through piercing (*ṭaʿn*) among them, just as it gave **/D 3 v 17/** their enemies among the people power about them when they in addition to their appearance act wickedly on earth and reject God's book (*Kitāb Allāh*)."

Another (person) said: ... "He **/D 3 v 21/** protects and helps the believer and He humiliates and defeats his enemy. The believer is someone who is grateful, if upon him falls happiness (*sarrāʾ*) and so it is something good to him; and he is someone who is patient (*ṣabara*), if upon him falls distress (*ḍarrāʾ*) and so it is something good to him" (see the text D 7 r 10–12 and below 17).

The **sixth chapter** introduces an important tool which man can use against "piercing" or "pricking" by the *jinn*: The quotations (*adhkār*) of verses in the Qurʾān which glorify God – can be used as a remedy **(D 4 r 1–14)**; moreover, the prayers **(D 4 r 14–18)**, which play a central role in the footsteps of al-Anṣārī's source, Ibn Ḥajar al-ʿAsqalānī and his Islamic traditions (Dols 1977, 121ff). Al-Anṣārī adds a long annotation (*tanbīh*) which he almost literally took over from Ibn Ḥajar al-ʿAsqalānī's *Badhl al-Māʿūn* (Ibn Ḥajar 1997, 171, 1ff.; 170, 10ff. and 170, 16f) and in which he mentions four preconditions for getting welfare (*nafʿ*) through Qurʾānic quotations and prayer **(D 4 r 18–19)**:

1) The "purification" of the soul (*ṣuffiya qalbuhū*) from "grief" (*kadar*).
2) "Sincerity" in the repentance (*akhlasa fī l-tawba*).
3) Regret of what someone neglected (*nadima ʿalā mā farraṭa fīhi*).
4) Regret of what escaped someone inadvertently (*nadima ʿalā mā ... faraṭa minhū*).

---

18 وقوله T.
19 عز وجل Ḥ 154, 8 : سار B.
20 D B Ḥ : صبر T.
21 Ibn Qayyim al-Jawziyya (d. 751/1350) (see *GAL* II: 127–129, and *S* II: 126–128). On Ibn Qayyim's concept of the *jinn* in the frame of his "medicine of the Prophet" (*al-ṭibb al-nabawī*) see Wessel 2022, 52ff.

The **seventh chapter** gives a detailed answer to the question whether and how martyrdom – the death of a believer for the cause of God (*fī sabīl Allāh*) – is possible during the plague. Al-Anṣārī provides us with a doxographical list of the characteristics of martyrs, many are based on *ḥadīth*-collections. His selection gives evidence of the existence of martyrdom also in a combination with the "piercing" (*ṭaʿn*) by *jinn* and with the plague (*ṭāʿūn*). Preconditions are sincerity (*ṣidq*) **(D 4 v 1–2)**, good intention (*niyya*) **(D 4 v 3–4)**, and death in the war against infidels **(D 4 v 3)**. Al-Anṣārī adds, that someone with "bad intention" will be a martyr only in this world. He says – quoting Abū ʿĪsā Muḥammad Ibn ʿĪsā Ibn Sawra al-Tirmidhī (d. 279/892): The martyr in the hereafter, "in front of God" has six characteristics that grant him God's forgiveness: 1) He seeks the help of the people for finding his seat in paradise; 2) He looks for protection from the punishment in the grave; 3) He is safe from the very great fear (*al-fazaʿ al-akbar*); 4) On his head is put down the crown of dignity (*tāj al-waqār*); 5) He marries 72 of the virgins in paradise; 6) He mediates for seventy of his relatives **(D 4 v 4–7)**.

In the **eighth chapter al-Anṣārī** discusses the relation between martyrdom and plague. "The plague is the place of origin (*manshaʾ*) of God's mercy and also of the martyrdom" – but it is neither God's mercy itself nor man's martyrdom itself **(D 4 v 23–24)**. The reason is as follows: The plague can lead to man's martyrdom and man's prayer for the abolition of the plague can result in the act of God's mercy.

The **ninth chapter** discusses different degrees of the martyrdom and the prerequisites of martyrdom in the plague. The real martyr is the faithful person, who fights against the enemy, the infidel, for the cause of God and is killed. His sins can be wiped out through fighting against his enemies and through hi being killed **(D 4 v 26–30)**. However, the hypocrite (*munāfiq*) who is killed in the fight against his enemy will be in hell **(D 4 v 30–31)**. If the martyrdom happens during a plague, the martyr will be rewarded with paradise, even if he dies because of the plague **(D 5 r 3–6)** and not directly in the fight against the infidel. But "if he did not die through plague, the grace (*faḍl*) of God is great and the intention (*niyya*) of the believer is more profound than his actions" **(D 5 r 6–7)**. "The degree of the martyrdom is specific for someone who possesses (good) qualities, is afflicted by the plague (*ṭuʿina*) and therefore dies" **(D 5 r 16)**.

[22] فالأول / نكبر القتل، ثلاثة: {١} رجل جاهد بنفسه وما له في سبيل الله حتى إذا لقِيَ العدو قاتلهم حتى يُقْتَل، [د ٤ ب، ٢٧] فذلك الشهيد الممتحن في خيمة[23] الله عزّ

---

22 /e = Ḥ 194, 4–13.

23 خيمة D B Ḥ 194, 6 : حنة T.

وجلّ تحت عرشه لا يُفضِله النبيون الا بدرجة النبوة، {٢} ورجل / مؤمن قَرِف[24] أي إكتسب[25] على نفسه من الذنوب والخطايا جاهَد بنفسه وما له في سبيل الله حتى [د ٤ ب ٢٩] إذا لقِيَ[26] العدو قاتل حتى يُقْتَل، فأنمحت خطاياه: إنّ[27] السيف محّاءٌ للخطايا وأُدْخِل من أي[28] أبواب الجنّة شاء، فإنّ لها ثمانية أبواب وبعضها افضل من بعض، {٣} ورجل منافق جاهدٌ بنفسه [د ٤ ب ٣١] وما له حتى إذا لقِيَ العدو قاتَل[29] حتى يُقْتَل فهو في[30] النار: إنّ السيف لا يمحو[31] النفاق،[e] رواه الامام / احمد وصحّحه ابن حبان،

والثاني[32] خبر البخاري عن عائشة، قالت: سألتُ رسول الله صلى الله عليه وسلمّ [د ٥ ا ١] عن الطاعون، فأخبرني أنه كان عذابا بعثه[33] الله على من[34] يشاء وجعله رحمةً للمؤمنين فليس من رجلٍ يقع / في[35] الطاعون فيمكث في بيته – وفي رواية: في بلده – صابراً محتسباً يعلم أنه لا يصيبه الا ما كتب الله [د ٥ ا ٣] له الا كان له[36] مثل أجر شهيد،[37e] فدلّ على أنّ اجر الشهيد انما يُكتَب لمن لم [ت ٩ ب] يخرج من البلد الذي[38] به الطاعون قاصداً[39] / بذلك ثواب الله[40] عارفاً بأنّه[41] ان[42] وقع به[43] او[44] صُرِف عنه فهو

24 اقترف T.
25 أي إكتسب : – Ḥ 194, 8.
26 لقيه B.
27 إنّ Ḥ T B : اي D.
28 T B Ḥ 194, 10 : + باب من D.
29 D B Ḥ 194, 12 : وقاتل T.
30 من B.
31 D T Ḥ : يحرم B.
32 /e = Ḥ 199, 5–8; cf. 199, 11–16.
33 يبعثه Ḥ 199, 7.
34 – T.
35 – Ḥ 199, 8.
36 – D.
37 /e = Ḥ 200, 1–5.
38 + يقع Ḥ 200, 2.
39 + وأن يكون في حال اقامته Ḥ 200, 2f.
40 + راجيا صدق موعوده وأن يكون Ḥ 200, 3.
41 أنه Ḥ 200, 4.
42 T B Ḥ 200, 4 : اذا D.
43 له Ḥ 200, 4 : + فهو بتقدير الله Ḥ 200, 4.
44 وإن Ḥ 200, 3.

بتقدير الله[45] غير متضجّر به[46]، إنّ[47] [د ٥ ا ٥] لو وقع به[48e] وعلى أنّ من اتصف بهذه الصفات يحصل له اجر شهيد وإن مات[49] بغير الطاعون[e] / ويكون كمن خرج من بيته بِنِيّة القتال في سبيل الله فمات بغير القتل كما مرّ،[50]وكذا إنْ لم يمت [د ٥ ا ٧] في الطاعون وفضل الله واسع[51] ونية[52] المؤمن ابلغ من عمله[e]،

......[53]وعن ابي [د ٥ ا ٩] عتبة[54] الخولاني: حدثنا أصحاب محمد صلى الله عليه وسلم أنّ شهداء الله في الارض أمناء الله / على خلقه قُتِلوا او ماتوا[55e] ولا يعكّر[56] على هذا انّه يلزم منه[57] أنّ من اتصف بهذه الصفات[58] ثمّ [د ٥ ا ١١] مات مطعوناً أن يكون له اجر شهيدَين لأنا[59] قدمنا أنّ درجات الشهداء متفاوتة، فأرفعها[60] من / اتصف بالصفات وطُعِن[61] فمات به، ودونه[62] مَن اتصف بها وطُعِن ولم[63] يمت، وقريبٌ منه مَن [د ٥ ا ١٣] اتصف[64] بها ثمّ مات بغير الطاعون، ودون الجميع مَن اتصف بها ولم يُطعَن ولم يمت، ويحتمل التعدّد / اذا تغايرت أسباب[65] الشهادة كما لو مات غريباً بالطاعون مع الصبر والاحتساب وكما لو طُعِنت [د ٥ ا ١٥] النفساء في نِفاسها وماتت فيه[66]،[e] ويمكن أن

45 + وأن يكون Ḥ 200, 5.
46 – T.
47 أن T B Ḥ 200, 5.
48 /e Cf. Ḥ 200, 6f.
49 End of MS B fol. 8 r 25. B adds تمت بهذه المشابهة لأنه صار حينئذ بمنزلة الشهداء، والله اعلم.
50 /e Cf. Ḥ 201, 1f.
51 – T.
52 وبنية T.
53 /e = Ḥ 188, 10–12.
54 عتبة Ḥ 188, 10; D; T : عنبة corrected the editor of Ḥ.
55 /e = Ḥ 201, 8–16.
56 يعكس D.
57 D Ḥ : مثله T.
58 بهذه الصفات : بالصفات المذكورة Ḥ 201, 8f.
59 + بما نتفصل عن ذلك Ḥ 201, 9f.
60 + درجة Ḥ 201, 10.
61 ثم طعن Ḥ 201, 11.
62 دونها T.
63 ثم لم 201, 12.
64 – وطعن ولمم يمت وقريب من اتصف بها T.
65 الأسباب المرتب عليها Ḥ 201, 14.
66 فيه (ـ فيه د) في نِفاسها وماتت : D T (– B) ثم ماتت في نفاسها Ḥ 201, 16.

يقال: درجة الشهادة شيء ودرجة اجرها شيء، فدرجة / الشهادة تختصّ بمن اتصف بالصفات وطُعِن ومات به،

The first point is, e.g., the report about the killing. (There are) three (kinds of men):

(1) A man who fights (*jāhada*) for himself (*bi-nafsihī*) and in favour of himself, for the cause of God (*fī sabīl Allāh*), so that he – if he meets the enemy – fights against him until he is killed. /**D 4 v 27**/ This is the martyr who can be proud of God's tabernacle (*khayma*) under His throne, for only the Prophets provide (the martyr) with the degree of prophecy.

(2) A faithful man who feels disgust to commit a crime (*qarifa*), i.e. to acquire (*iktasaba*) against himself crimes (*dhunūb*) and sins (*khaṭāyā*), (a faithful man) who fights (*jāhada*) for himself and in favour of himself, for the cause of God (*fī sabīl Allāh*), so that he /**D 4 v 29**/ – if he meets the enemy – fights until he is killed – then his sins are wiped out, i.e. the sword strongly wipes out the sins, so that he is admitted to any entrance to paradise he wants. (This paradise) has eight entrances, some are better than others.

(3) A hypocrite man (*munāfiq*) who fights (*jāhada*) for himself /**D 4 v 31**/ and in favour of himself, so that he – if he meets the enemy – fights until he is killed and then will be in hell: The sword does not wipe out the hypocrisy (*nifāq*). This is reported by **Imam Aḥmad** (Ibn Ḥanbal, d. 241/855) and certified by **Ibn Ḥibbān** (d. 354/965).

The second point is, e.g., the report of **al-Bukhārī** from **'Ā'isha** (d. 58/678) who said: "I asked the Messenger of God about /**D 5 r 1**/ the plague. He told me that it is a punishment which God forwarded to anyone He wants. He made it (an act of) mercy (*raḥmatan*) for the believers and it is not a part of someone who is affected by the plague and then resides in his house – in (another) report: In his place – and who is patient and detained (*ṣābiran muḥtasiban*), by knowing that on him alone befalls what God has destined /**D 5 r 3**/ for him (*kataba Llāhu lahū*), but only if he is qualified for getting something like the reward of a martyr."

He showed that the reward of a martyr is destined (*yuktabu*) for someone who did not /**T 9 v**/ leave the country in which the plague (*al-ṭāʿūn*) exists, seeking hereby God's reward (*thawāb*) and knowing the following: If (the plague) occurs in it or is turned away from it (*ṣurifa ʿanhū*) – he is through God's destination (*bi-taqdīr Allāh*) not grieved by it (*ghayr mutaḍajjir bihī*). /**D 5 r 5**/ (This is also the case) if (the plague) exists in (the country), based on the fact that someone possessing these qualities does acquire the reward (*ajr*) of a martyr, even if he dies /**end of MS B**/ without (being afflicted by the) plague and if he is like someone who left his house with the intention (*niyya*) to fight (*qitāl*) for the cause of God (*fī sabīl Allāh*) and if he dies then without killing (*qatl*), in the manner as told.

Similarly, if he did not die **/D 5 r 7/** through the plague, the grace (*faḍl*) of God is great and the intention (*niyya*) of the believer is more profound (*ablagh*) than his actions (*ʿamaluhū*)....

/D 5 r 9/ From **Abū ʿUtba al-Khawlānī:**[67] The companions of **Muḥammad** told us: The martyrs of God on earth are God's curators of His creation (*umanāʾ Allāh ʿalā khalqihī*), they are killed (*qutilū*) or died (*mātū*).

There is no trouble about the fact that the following necessarily (results) from it: Who can be described with these qualities and then **/D 5 r 11/** dies afflicted by the piercing (*maṭʿūnan*) will have the reward of two martyrs, because we have already mentioned earlier that the degrees (*darajāt*) of the martyrs are different (*mutafāwita*). The highest degree (have those) who possess (good qualities), are afflicted by the piercing (*ṭuʿina*) and then die therefore; below (the highest degree) are all those, who possess (good qualities), are afflicted by piercing (*ṭuʿina*) and do not die.

Close to it (*qarībun minhū*) **/D 5 r 13/** are all those who possess (good qualities), who die thereupon without (being afflicted by) the plague.

Below all (degrees) are all those who possess (good qualities), are not afflicted by a piercing (*lam yuṭʿan*) and do not die (*lam yamut*).

A great number (*taʿaddud*) is possible, if the causes of the martyrdom differ (*taghāyarat*), as it is the case, if (the Muslim) dies as a stranger (*gharīban*)[68] through the plague (*ṭāʿūn*) with patience (*ṣabr*) and anticipating God's reward in the hereafter (*iḥtisāb*); and as it is the case, if **/D 5 r 15/** "the woman in childbed" (*nafsāʾ*) is afflicted by the piercing (*ṭuʿinat*) in her childbed (*nifāsihā*) and dies there.

It is possible to say: The degree of the martyrdom is something and the degree of its reward is something else. – The degree of the martyrdom is specific to someone who possesses (good) qualities, is afflicted by piercing (*ṭuʿina*) and therefore dies.

The **tenth chapter** discusses examples of plague in Mecca and Medina and mentions the "universal plague" (*al-ṭāʿūn al-ʿāmm*) i.e. the pandemic in the year 749/1348 and afterwards in Mecca **(D 5 v 2–3)**. Al-Anṣārī wants to show that martyrdom and plague do not contradict each other. Plague, like "temptations"

67 Cannot be identified. Perhaps it was Abū Muslim al-Khawlānī (d. *c.*62/682), from the generation after the Companions of the Prophet?

68 On the term *gharīb* see Daiber 1981, 124f.

(*fitan*), earthquakes and killing can be God's punishment in this world, e.g., if people abandon a friendly admonition (*naṣīḥa*) **(D 5 r 7–10)**. "Who has the purpose to get a degree nearer to God (*al-manzila ʿind Allāh*), which he does not reach with his work, will continue to be tested (by God) with what he dislikes, until He will let him attain (that degree)" **(D 5 v 11–12)**.

The **eleventh chapter** discusses the question, whether it is allowed to flee from the country with plague or to enter it. Al-Anṣārī explains that it is allowed for three reasons: 1) In case it is necessary for the cure; 2) If it is normal that people leave the country affected by a plague, because they usually leave the country with the aim to "return to the usual and to the habit" **(D 6 r 22)**; 3) If it is "an act of sympathy for the people" and "in fear" of an infection **(D 6 r 24)**.

The **twelfth chapter** argues that someone might remain in the country of the plague, because it is God's predestination (*qadar*). God ordered (*amara*) to endure (*ṣabr*) it and God granted in the death through plague the reward of a martyr. **(D 6 r 31–32)**. This requires "patience" (*ṣabr*) and "trust (in God)" (*tawakkul*) **(D 6 v 2)**.

Interestingly, the views of al-Anṣārī – which he shares with his teacher Ibn Ḥajar al-ʿAsqalānī – on the obligation to remain in the country of the plague and the circumstances that allow to flee from it, mirror a controversial discussion of their time. A contemporary of al-Anṣārī, the Kurdish scholar Idrīs al-Bidlīsī (d. 926/1520) clearly opposes in his unpublished *Risālat al-Ibāʾ ʿan Mawāqiʿ al-Wabāʾ* ("Treatise on Avoiding the Locations of the Plague") to the traditional standpoint, that fleeing from the plague is fleeing from God's decision and contradicts martyrdom (Stearns 2017, esp. 170ff. and 175ff.). Al-Anṣārī and before him Ibn Ḥajar al-ʿAsqalānī did not go so far and explain the reasons, why people flee from the country of plague or remain in it. Plagues are not only a pricking of the *jinn* and God's test of the believer. Medical measures, the striving for cure and the fear of an infection are indications of human responsibility within a frame of God's *qaḍāʾ wa-qadar*.

The **thirteenth chapter** contains remarks on the proper behaviour during the plague, supplementing recommendations mentioned in previous chapters:

The believer must hurry to turn from his sins.

The invocation of God for elimination of the plague is prescribed. The plague belongs to the calamities (*nawāzil*) **(D 6 v 3–5)**.

The invocation of God during the plague or diseases or during terrible situations, demolition etc. or in the face of death requires a good "reason" (*mūjib*) **(D 6 v 6–9)**.

Only that person should survive who is useful (*manfaʿa*) for the Muslims. He is entrusted with the invocation of God **(D 6 v 10)**.

Man having strong "conviction" (*yaqīn*), "trust in God" (*tawakkul*) "is in the best position (*afḍal al-maqāmāt*), in order to get full power (*fa-yufawwaḍ*) and to be protected against harm (*yusallam*). He knows: What occurred to him did not happen in order to accuse him for a mistake and what he made wrong did not happen in order to hit him. Truly, if he is restored to health (*ʿūfiya*), he is thankful (*shakara*); and if he is not cured, he is patient (*ṣabara*) and sometimes even ascends (*irtaqā*) from one step and tries to obtain the martyrdom, as it has occurred to many" **(D 6 v 13–15)**.

In a separate section al-Anṣārī gives practical recommendations, like "removal of the superfluous humidities, the diminution of nourishment, the refrain from physical exercise, the staying in the bath, constant rest and (the recommendation) not to increase the inhalation of air which is decayed" **(D 6 v 22–23)**. Al-Anṣārī adds an explanation by Ibn Sīnā on the medical treatment of the plague through incision (*sharṭ*) and bloodletting (*faṣd*) **(D 6 v 23–26)**. Interesting is al-Anṣārī's observation that "the physicians in our time and before have neglected this regulation (of Ibn Sīnā). Thereupon a very lax attitude occurred with regard to their agreement – due to loss of attention to the person afflicted by the plague – in the removal of blood, so that this dominated among them, inasmuch as the masses of them believed in its prohibition" **(D 6 v 26–28)**.

ينبغي لكل أحد المبادرة إلى / التوبة من ذنوبه والوصية، وطلبها فيه متأكد كما في سائر الامراض المخوفة ويُشرَع الدعاء برفعه إجتماعاً[69] [د ٦ ب ٥] وانفراداً في القنوت خاصّةً بناءً على أنه من جملة النوازل، ......

فمن قوى يقينه وغلب توكّله فمقامه أفضل / المقامات فيفَوّض ويُسَلّم ويعلم أنّ ما أصابه لم يكن ليخطئه وما اخطأه لم يكن ليصيبه، وإنه[70] إن عوفِيً شكر وإنْ لم [د ٦ ب ٥١] يعافَ صبر بل ربما إرتقى عن ذلك درجةً فطلب[71] الشهادة كما وقع ذلك لِكثيرٍ[72]، .....

[73] فرعٌ: ذكر الزركشي أن بعض السلف كان يدعو / عَقِبَ صلاته لمنازله:[74] اللهم انا نعوذ بك من عِظَم البلاء في النفس والاهل والمال والولد،[e] الله اكبر ثلاثا [د ٦ ب ١٩] مما نخاف ونَحذَر! الله أكبر ثلاثاً [ت ١٤ ا] عدد ذنوبنا حتى تُغْفَر! اللهم كما شفَّعتَ لنبينا

69 اجماعا D.
70 ولانه T.
71 – D.
72 كثير D.
73 /e Cf. Ḥ 334, 5f.
74 للمنزله D : للنازله T : – Ḥ : correxi (cf. D 6 v 20).

محمداً صلى الله عليه وسلم[75] فينا / فأمهلْنا وعَمِّر بنا منازلَنا ولا تُؤاخذنا بسوء افعالنا ولا تهلكنا بخطايانا يا ربّ العالمين!

[76]فرعٌ: يُستنبط من [د ٦ ب ٢١] الأدلّة الدالّة على مشروعية الدواء والتحرُّز في أيام الوباء عن[77] أمور أوصى بها حُذّاق الاطبّاء مثل إخراج / الرطوبات الفضلية[78] وتقليل الغذاء وترك الرياضة والمكث في الحمام وملازمة السكون[79] وأن لا [د ٦ ب ٢٣] يُكَثَّر من استنشاق الهواء الذي عَفِن،

وصرح الرئيس أبو علي بن سينا بأنّ اول شيء يبدأ[80] به في علاج الطاعون / الشرطُ إن امكن فيسيل ما فيه ولا يترك حتى يَجمُد فتزداد سميته....

قال: [د ٦ ب ٢٥] «ويعالَج الطاعون بما يَقبُض ويبرُد وبالفصد[81] وبإسفنجة مغموسة في خلّ وماء او دُهن وَرْدٍ او / دُهن تُفّاح او دُهن آس[82]»، [e] انتهى،[83]وقد اغفل الاطبّاء في عصرنا وما قبله هذا التدبير، فوقع التفريط [د ٦ ب ٢٧] الشديد من تواطُئِهم على عدم التعرُّض لصاحب الطاعون بإخراج الدم حتى شاع[84] ذلك فيهم[85] بحيثُ / صار عامّتهم يعتقد[86] تحريم ذلك، وهذا النقل عن رئيسهم يخالف بالفعل[87] ما[88] اعتمدوه [89e]بل قال رئيسهم – لما [د ٦ ب ٢٩] ذكر العلاج بالشرط او الفصد – إنه واجبٌ،[e]

It is proper for everyone to hasten to repent (*tawba*) of his sins (*dhunūbuhū*) and (to speed up) his instruction (*waṣiyya*). The demand (for speed) regarding (the plague) is urgent (*muta'akkid*) as well as with regard to all dangerous (*makhūfa*) diseases. The prayer for the elimination (of the plague) is prescribed (*yushraʿu*), (the prayer) either in a group **/D 6 v 5/** or individually, in particular

75 صلى الله عليه وسلم : – T.
76 /e = Ḥ 340, 5–14.
77 من T.
78 T Ḥ 340, 6 : الفضيلة D.
79 + والدعة Ḥ 340, 8.
80 يبدؤ T.
81 – Ḥ 340, 12.
82 + ويعلج بالاستفراغ بالفصد Ḥ 340, 13f.
83 /e = Ḥ 341, 3–6.
84 D Ḥ 341, 5 : يشاع T.
85 + وذاع Ḥ 341, 5.
86 D Ḥ 341, 5 : يعتقدون T.
87 D : الفعل T : – Ḥ 341, 6.
88 وما T.
89 /e = Ḥ 341, 8f.

with regard to the obedience to God (*fī l-qunūt*) – in accordance with the fact that (the plague) belongs to the group of the calamities (*al-nawāzil*)……

/D 6 v 13/ Those whose conviction (*yaqīnuhū*)[90] is strong and whose trust (in God) prevails, are in the best position (*afḍal al-maqāmāt*), in order to get full power (*fa-yufawwaḍ*) and to be protected against harm (*yusallam*). They know: What occurred to them did not happen in order to accuse them for a mistake and mistakes they made did not happen, in order to scourge them. Truly (*wa-innahū*), if he is restored to health (*ʿūfiya*), he is thankful (*shakara*); and if he is not **/D 6 v 15/** cured (*lam yuʿāfa*), he is patient (*ṣabara*) and sometimes even ascends (*irtaqā*) from one step and tries to obtain the martyrdom, as it has occured to many.

/D 6 v 17/ Section: **al-Zarkashī** (d. 794/1392, see *GALS* II, 108) mentioned: One of the ancestors was praying immediately after (*ʿaqiba*) his prayer for his houses: “O God, we seek your protection (*innā naʿūdhu bi-ka*) from a great distress (*min ʿiẓam al-balāʾ*) in the soul, among the people (*ahl*), in the property (*māl*) and among the children (*walad*). God is the greatest three times **/D 6 v 19/** our fear and caution! God is the greatest three times **/T 14 r/** the quantity of our sins, so that they were forgiven! O God, just as you made our Prophet Muḥammad a mediator among us, give us time and let us build our houses! Do not blame us for our bad deeds, do not ruin us for our mistakes (*khaṭāyānā*), o Lord of the inhabitants of the world (*rabb al-ʿālamīn*)!”

Section: Deriveable from **/D 6 v 21/** the indications that show the legitimacy of the medication is the wariness (*taḥarruz*) during the time of the epidemic (*wabāʾ*) in the things which were recommended by the skillful physician, e.g., the removal of the superfluous humidities, the diminution of the nourishment, the refrain from physical exercise (*riyāḍa*), the staying (*makth*) in the bath, constant rest, and (the recommendation) **/D 6 v 23/** not to increase the inhaling (*istinshāq*) of polluted (*ʿafina*) air.

Al-Raʾīs Abū ʿAlī Ibn Sīnā explained that the first thing which he would start in the medical treatment (*ʿilāj*) of the plague (*ṭāʿūn*) would be the incision (*sharṭ*), if possible, so that its content could flow (out) and he did not desist, until it (the content) coagulated so that its poisonous (material) (*sammiyyatuhū*) increased (*tazdādu*).

He (**Ibn Sīnā**) said: **/D 6 v 25/** “The plague (*ṭāʿūn*) can be treated through something that contracts (*bi-mā yaqbuḍu*) and becomes cold (*yabrudu*), through bloodletting (*faṣd*), with a sponge (*isfanja*) which is immersed in

90 On the term *yaqīn* and its Sufi connotation in al-Anṣārī see Ingalls 2022, ch. 3.

vinegar (*khall*) and water or oil of the rose (*duhn ward*) or oil of the apple (*duhn tuffāḥ*) or oil of the myrtle (*duhn ās*)." End of (the quotation).[91]

The physicians in our time and in previous times have neglected this regulation (*tadbīr*). Thereupon a very lax attitude (*tafrīṭ*) occured **/D 6 v 27/** with regard to their agreement (*min tawāṭu'ihim*) – due to the loss of attention (*taʿarruḍ*) to the person afflicted by the plague (*ṭāʿūn*) – in the removal of blood, so that this was dominant among them, inasmuch as (*bi-haythu*) they altogether believed in its prohibition (*taḥrīm*). This report from their leader differs in fact from what they used as a basis – although their leader said – after **/D 6 v 29/** he had mentioned the medical treatment through incision (*sharṭ*), or bloodletting (*faṣd*) – that it was necessary (*wājib*).

The **fourteenth chapter**, the last section, gives advice regarding those afflicted by the plague or by any other illness. Some advices has already been mentioned in previous chapters. Al-Anṣārī describes four kinds of "good manner" (*adab*):

1) The prayer or request to God for health. The request includes repetitions of man's wishes, his prayer to God. In a Prophetic tradition, reported by the *ḥadīth*-scholar Muslim (d. 261/875), the Prophet advises ʿUthmān Ibn Abī l-ʿĀṣ (d. 51/671), who had pain in his body: "Lay your hand on what is painful in your body and say: 'In the name of God' three times and say seven times 'God and his power save me'!" **(D 7 r 3–4).**
2) The second good manner is patience (*ṣabr*) and consent (*riḍan*) to God's divine decree (*qaḍā'*) and predestination (*qadar*). Al-Anṣārī refers to a report by Ṣuhayb (d. 38/644) transmitted by Muslim, according to which "happiness" (*sarrāʾ*) and "distress" (*ḍarrāʾ*) can be "good" (*khayr*) for the believer, in one case he will be thankful (*shakara*) and in the other case he will be patient (*ṣabara*). In a report by "the two shaykhs" (al-Bukhārī and Muslim) for the believer illness, pain, grief, sorrow, grievance and sadness are not disturbances but on the contrary ways of God, to forgive him his mistakes (*khaṭāyā*) **(D 7 r 10–12).**
3) The third good manner is the recommendation to the ill to have "a good belief in God" (*ḥusn al-ẓann bi-Llāh*). It "is mandatory for someone who falls victim to fear of diseases. Its way is to call to mind that (the ill person) is a miserable being (*ḥaqīr*) among God's creatures; that God's mercy (*raḥma*) is great enough for what is similar to the similarities of what is similar to Him; that God is independent (*ghaniya*) in punishing him; (that man) recognises his sins and his inferiority (*taqṣīruhū*) and (that he) should believe that only God is beneficial to him (*yanfaʿuhū*)" **(D 7 r 14–16).**

91 On bloodletting in Ibn Sīnā see Dols 1977, 105, and above n. 573.

This is al-Anṣārī's interpretation of "the most beautiful saying on the good opinion (of God)" which he found in a Prophetic quotation, mentioned in a report by Shaddād Ibn Aws (d. 58/677),[92] transmitted in the *Ṣaḥīḥ* by al-Bukhārī. The Prophet, "the master in asking God's forgiveness (*sayyid al-istighfār*)" says: "O God, You are my Lord, there is no other God than You! You have created me and I am Your servant (*ʿabd*), I am persevering in the observance of the covenant with You (*ʿahduka*) and in the observance of the promise to You (and to assert Your unity) (*waʿduka*), as far as I am able (*mā staṭāʿtu*). I seek Your protection because of the evil (*sharr*) I have done (*ṣanaʿtu*). I come back on Your behalf, i.e. I acknowledge my sins (*aʿtarifu bi-dhunūbī*) and I come back with Your favour towards me (*bi-niʿmatika ʿalayya*). Forgive me and my calamities (*nuwabī*)! Only You can forgive my sins!" **(D 7 r 16–19)**.

Al-Anṣārī adds: "Who says (these Prophetic words), when he is awaking and then is dying right away, will enter paradise. Who says (these Prophetic words), when he is entering into the evening and then is dying right away, (also) will enter paradise" **(D 7 r 19–20)**.

The fourth good manner, the etiquette of the physician, concentrates "on the visit of a patient (*ʿiyāda*) and its merit" with references to Prophetic traditions that introduce the Prophet as a model healer: "When the Prophet had under his treatment a person who was ill, he stroke with his hand over his face and breast and said: 'Remove the harm (*baʾs*), Lord of the people, and restore to health! You are the healer! There is no healing besides Your healing, a healing that does not leave an illness, i.e. does not desist from it" **(D 7 r 29–30)**, transmitted from "the two shaykhs" (al-Bukhārī and Muslim). Following the Prophet's example al-Anṣārī describes the good manner of a healer with qualities like "kindness" (*raḥma*, **D 7 r 25**), "generosity" (*wassaʿū*, **D 7 r 28**), having time for the patient and sitting near him **(D 7 r 24–25)**, laying his hand on his side or his hand and "asking: How is it?" **(D 7 r 31)** or "stroking with his hand over his face and breast" **(D 7 r 29)**. This and short prayers to God, the real healer, will help to bring relief (*fa-tunaffisū*, **D 7 r 28**).

[93] **والرابع**[94] في العيادة وفضلها، قال رسول الله صلى الله عليه وسلم: [د ٧ ا ٢١] من عاد مريضاً ناداه منادٍ من السماء: «طِبْتَ وطاب ممشاك وتبوّأتَ من الجنّة منزلاً»، رواه الترمذي / وحسّنه وابن حبان وصحّحه،[e]

92 Companion of the Prophet.
93 /e = Ḥ 352, 18–353, 2.
94 الادب الرابع 352, 18.

......وقال صلى الله عليه وسلم: من عاد مريضاً لم يزل يخوض [د ٧ ا ٢٥] في الرحمة حتى
يجلسَ، فإذا جلس اغتمس[95] فيها، رواه ابن حبان وصحّحه،
وقال صلى الله عليه وسلم: من عاد / مريضاً لم يحضر أجله فقال عنده سبع مرات «أسأل
اللهَ العظيم ربَّ العرش العظيم أنْ يشفيك» – [د ٧ ا ٢٧] الإ عافاه الله من ذلك المرض،
رواه أبو داود وغيره وصحّحه ابن حبان[96]،
وروَىَ الترمذي وغيره خبر: «إذا / دخلتم على المريض فنفِّسوا» – أي وسّعوا له في اجله !
فإنّ ذلك لا يردّ[97] شيئا وهو يطيب نفس المريض،[e]
[د ٧ ا ٢٩][98] *وروى الشيخان : خبر: كان رسول الله صلى الله عليه وسلم إذا عاد[99] مريضاً*
مسح على[100] وجهه وصدره بيده وقال: / «اذهب البأس ربّ الناس واشفِ! انت الشافي
لا شفاء الا شفاؤك شفاء لا يغادر [ت ١٦ ا] سقما أي لا يتركه»[101]،[e]
[د ٧ ا ٣١][102] *وروى الترمذي خبر:[103] تمام عيادة المريض أنْ يضع احدكم يده على جهته*
او على يده فيسأل: «كيف هو؟»[e]

The fourth (good manner) is on the visit of a patient (*ʿiyāda*) and its merit. The Messenger of God said: **/D 7 r 21/** "Who visits an ill person (*marīḍan*), is called by someone from heaven (with the following words): 'You are good (*ṭibta*) and good (*ṭāba*) is your way. You have settled down in a house of paradise.'" – This is reported by **al-Tirmidhī** – he put it into a better form (*wa-ḥassanahū*) – and by **Ibn Ḥibbān** – he certified it (*wa-ṣaḥḥaḥahū*).

(The Prophet) said: "Who has under his treatment an ill person (*marīḍan*), constantly becomes absorbed **/D 7 r 25/** by kindness (*lam yazal yakhūḍu fī r-raḥma*), so that he sits down (*yajlisa*). And when he has taken his seat, he is immersed in (kindness)." – This is reported by **Ibn Ḥibbān**, who certified it.

(The Prophet) said: "If someone has under his treatment an ill person (*marīḍan*) whose death (*ajaluhū*) is not yet present (*lam yaḥḍur*), and if he says in his presence seven times: 'I beg God the Great, the great owner of the throne, that He may heal you' – **/D 7 r 27/** verily (*a-lā*) God releases him (*ʿāfāhu*)

95 T Ḥ 354, 2 : انغمس D.
96 – D.
97 Ḥ 355, 2 : يزيد TD.
98 /e = Ḥ 355, 7–9.
99 D Ḥ 355,7 : دعا T.
100 – Ḥ 355, 8.
101 أي لا يتركه : – Ḥ 355, 9.
102 /e = Ḥ 356, 14–16.
103 خبرا T.

from that illness." – This is reported by **Abū Dāwūd** (d. 275/889)[104] and others. It is certified by **Ibn Ḥibbān.**

It is reported by **al-Tirmidhī** and others as follows: "If you come to see the ill, bring to him relief (*fa-tunaffisū*) – i.e. be generous toward him during his appointed time (*fī ajalihī*)!" This does not drive away something (of the illness), but it is pleasant for the soul of the ill person.

/D 7 r 29/ The two shaykhs (al-Bukhārī and Muslim) reported as follows: When the Prophet had under his treatment a person who is ill (*marīḍan*), he stroked (*masaḥa*) with his hand over (*ʿalā*) his face and breast and said: "Remove (*adhhib*) the harm (*baʾs*), Lord of the people (*rabb al-nās*), and restore to health! YOU are the healer! There is no healing, a healing that does not depart (*yughādiru*) **/T 16 r/** an illness, i.e does not desist from it – besides Your healing."

/D 7 r 31/ al-Tirmidhī reported as follows: The perfect treatment of an ill person (*tammām ʿiyādat al-marīḍ*) is, if one of you lays his hand on the side or on the hand (of the ill) and asks: "How is it (*kayfa huwa*)?"

At the end of his treatise al-Anṣārī adds as an epilogue (*khātima*) a list of all plagues during Islam until the years 918/1512 and 919/1513,[105] the *terminus post quem* of the composition of his treatise.

4 Al-Anṣārī's *Tuḥfat al-Rāghibīn* as a Text on "End-of-Life Care"

Al-Anṣārī's *Tuḥfat al-Rāghibīn fī Bayān Amr al-Ṭawāʿīn* does not only address people afflicted with plagues, but also every ill person and every person who dies "for the cause of God" (*fī sabīl Allāh*) either during the fight against infidels or through the plague or because of both. It gives practical advice and advises about duties and preconditions for the Muslim believer. For this reason, al-Anṣārī's text is a mine of information on "end-of-life care." In the face of death by the plague or any other illness, the believer is reminded of his duties.

---

104 Died 275/888. The author of the *Kitāb al-Sunan*, [illegible] 148ff.

105 D 7 r 32–7 v ult. / T 16 r 3–17 v ult. This epilogue is not edited here, as it is based – with some shortenings and supplements to the time after the death of Ibn Ḥajar al-ʿAsqalānī – on Ibn Ḥajar al-ʿAsqalānī 1997, 361–370.

5 Al-Anṣārī's *Tuḥfat al-Rāghibīn* as a Guide for Believers

Al-Anṣārī's treatise is nothing less than an admonition to the believer that should pave the way to paradise, console him and give him relief. Different from usual consolation texts al-Anṣārī's text is a consoling guide for the believer who is asked to follow the example of the Prophet, to be sincere, to have good intentions (*niyya*), to repent (*tawba*), to be patient (*ṣabr*), to pray to God (*duʿāʾ*), to seek God's "acceptance" (*marḍāt*) and to fight against enemies and kill them, including infidels. Their killing is a martyrdom, if some preconditions are fulfilled.[106] Paradise is the ultimate aim and consoles, not the eternal world of intellect – different from that which is propagated in a small treatise by Ibn Sīnā on the causes of sorrow. I quote the text by Ibn Sīnā, who himself is inspired by Kindī's (d. *c.*256/870) *Risāla fī l-Ḥīla li-Dafʿ al-Aḥzān* ("Treatise on the Stratagem of Dispelling Sorrows"), an adaption of a lost late-Greek text on consolations:

> Therefore, man should not desire the ephemeral and earthly things, but the constant and lasting from the world of the intellect. Because you never lose them because nobody can touch them and there is no damage to them ... So, it is not necessary to be sad about something; rather (man) should be satisfied with his particular condition so that, God willing, he is spared from sadness.
>
> IBN SĪNĀ 1937[107]

Plagues can be "temptations" (*fitan*) which test a person and his patience (ch. 11 and 14). Herewith, the text differs from the consolation literature written, e.g., "for bereaved parents" (Gildaki 1993). Its notion of a transient world full of misfortunes is replaced in the Anṣārī-text by a concept of the world where the believers are tested and through prayers and with patience find their way to paradise. Here, al-Anṣārī does not exclude practical medical recommendations which he found in texts by Ibn Sīnā and Ibn al-Nafīs (ch. 13). He combined them with the "Prophetic remedies," like prayers, recitations of the Qurʾān, patience etc. as mentioned above and herewith, follows the traditional "Prophetic medicine" (Wessel 2022, 50).

---

106 See section 7–9. – The main condition is the right intention (*niyya*). The genuine battlefield martyr is "one whose actions proceed from the right intention (*niyya*)" (see Kohlberg 2002, 104f.).

107 The quoted passage in German translation can be found in Gätje 1956, 224. On the history of the text see the references in Daiber 1996, n. 24.

6 The Theological-Mystical World-View of al-Anṣārī

Al-Anṣārī gives an optimistic evaluation of a world of fate and divine decree *qaḍāʾ wa-qadar*, in which the infidel is punished, but the believer with proper behaviour and patience can find the way to paradise; his mistakes are forgiven by God's act of mercy (*raḥma*), if he repents. The ill are recommended to have "a good belief in God" (*ḥusn al-ẓann bi-llāh*) (**D 7 r 13–14**).

There is no "Thanatophobia", the believer is safe from "the very great fear" (*al-fazaʿ al-akbar*) (**D 4 v 6**). The reason (*ḥikma*) of pains, in al-Anṣārī's view (ch. 5) and – based on a quotation from Ibn Qayyim al-Jawziyya – caused by the "piercing" or "pricking" of the *jinn*, is "a test for those who search for God's acceptance (*marḍāt*)" (**D 3 v 14**).

The ill person can receive help from the proper behaviour of the healer. Al-Anṣārī mentions as fourth good manner the example of "visiting a patient" (*ʿiyāda*) by the Prophet, the model healer. Accordingly, every healer should have time for his patient, should have qualities like "kindness" and "generosity", should lay his hand on the side or hand of the patient or stroke with his hand over his face and breast, should ask him about his health and pray to God, the Healer for the health of his patient (**D 7 r 20–31**).

These measures "beyond clinical care" betray religious-spiritual and ethical aspects: God "removes the harm" and "restores the health" (**D 7 r 29–30**) and clearly restricts the influence of the physician as a decision-maker.

The Islamic orientation of al-Anṣārī's treatise on plagues has become clear. It uses theological concepts of the almighty and all-determining God, of God's reward and punishment, of God's "mercy" (*raḥma*), "favour" (*niʿma*), "goodness" and "independence" (*ghaniya*) from man who is God's "servant" (*ʿabd*), who is a "miserable" (*ḥaqīr*) sinful being that should obey God and repent his sins. In his fight against unbelievers he can be killed or die through the plague and enter as a martyr into paradise.

The plague or any other illness are ways of God's testing and were not caused by God, who is the Good. They remain man's responsibility. This is al-Anṣārī's answer to the theodicy. The consolation of the ill with a reference of the dying person to the eternal world of the intellect was not discussed. On the contrary, in al-Anṣārī's treatise – as well as in other Islamic treatises on plagues until the 20th century – are dominant religious-ethical aspects, based on the *ḥadīth* literature (Dols 1977, 31 and esp. 109ff.). Illness, plagues etc. are signs of disobedience against God and can be abolished, if God's "servant" repents, prays to God, is patient and endures the trials and even dies "for the sake of God" (*fī sabīl Allāh*), in the fight and the killing of unbelievers.

Al-Anṣārī's Islamic theology, as it appears in his text on the plague, shares with Islamic creeds some fundamental concepts which cannot be attributed with certainty to a theological school. More likely, it appears to me to have some sympathy with the Ḥanbalī-Sufi-school. Al-Anṣārī shares with the Ḥanbalī theology, as it is echoed in the *ʿAqīda* ("Creed") of the Ḥanbalī Ibn Qudāma al-Maqdisī (d. 620/1223), the following concepts: The submission (*taslīm*) to God's divine decree (*qaḍāʾ*) by following God's order and prohibition (Daiber 1981, 113 and 114); "belief" (*īmān*) as "confessing (*qawl*), acting (*ʿamal*) and intention (*niyya*)"; the belief can "increase by obedience and decrease by disobedience" (Daiber 1981, 113); punishment in the grave (Daiber 1981, 118); the mediation (*shafāʿa*) of the Prophet (Daiber 1981, 119); paradise and hell (Daiber 1981, 120); Holy War (*jihād*) and Antichrist (*dajjāl*) (Daiber 1981, 122; al-Anṣārī, ch. 10, and English trans., ch. 9, end, note).

The Ḥanbalī background of al-Anṣārī's theology is confirmed by al-Anṣārī's recourse to the Prophetic tradition of the *ḥadīth*, the dominating role of the Prophet and finally by al-Anṣārī's recourse to Sufism.

Echoes of Sufism, its terminology and concepts already exist in Ḥanbalī theology. I can mention the concept of "intention" (*niyya*) in **D 4 v 3–4** and **D 5 r 6–7** and the Ḥanbalī parallel in Ibn Qudāma al-Maqdisī's *ʿAqīda* (Daiber 1981, 113f); the search of the believer after nearness to God (*al-manzila ʿind Allāh*) in **D 5 v 11–12** (Daiber 1995, 54 n. 94.); the virtues "patience" (*ṣabr*) and "trust in God" (*tawakkul*) (Q 14:12; Reinert 1968, index s.n. *riḍā*, *ṣabr* and *tawakkul*; Daiber 1995, 53, n. 55); if the believer combines it with strong "conviction" (*yaqīn*), he can reach "the best position" (*afḍal al-maqāmāt*) **(D 6 v 13)** – it is not astonishing to find the above-mentioned terms discussed in al-Anṣārī's *al-Futūḥāt al-Ilāhiyya fī Nafʿ Arwāḥ al-Dhawāt al-Insāniyya* ("Divine Revelations for the Benefit of the Spirits of Human Beings"), a small manual of Sufism (Harley 1924, 131, 3ff.; 133, 1ff. and 135, 1ff.). In this small treatise, which used al-Qushayrī, *al-Risāla al-Qushayriyya* as main source, we find more Sufi terms which reappear in al-Anṣārī's text on plagues; like *tawba* **(D 4 r 18–19)**, *dhikr* **(D ch. 6**, "quotation") and *riḍan/riḍāʾ* **(D 7 r 10)** (Harley 1924, 130, ult.ss., 131, ult.ss. and 133, 13ff., 141f.).

Al-Anṣārī's *Tuḥfat al-rāghibīn* sometimes differs from the terminology of his *al-Futūḥāt al-Ilāhiyya*, apparently because he did not want to write a Sufi guide for the novice (*murīd*), but a religious orientation for people affected with plague. We do not find subtleties of the *Futūḥāt al-Ilāhiyya* in the *Tuḥfat al-Rāghibīn*. The Sufi terms *saʿāda* and *shaqāwa* (Harley 1924, 137, 8ff.) are replaced in the *Tuḥfat al-Rāghibīn* by *sarrāʾ* and *ḍarrāʾ* **(D 7 r 10–12)**. However, the *Futūḥāt al-Ilāhiyya* confirms the spiritual function of the Prophet as healer and mediator between God and His creation, a spiritual function which is not explicitly mentioned in a similar passage at the end of chapter 14 of the *Tuḥfat al-Rāghibīn* **(D 7 r 29–30)**. However, in his *Futūḥāt al-Ilāhiyya* al-Ansārī writes: "… (the Prophet) is a mediator (*wāsiṭa*) between God and His creation. (The

Prophet) places his right hand on the right hand of the novice through imposing the palm of his hand (*rāḥatuhū*) on the palm of the hand (of the novice) (*rāḥatuhū*), through holding the thumb (of the novice) with his fingers and saying: 'I seek the protection of God from the damned Satan in the name of God the Merciful and Compassionate. Praise be to God, the Lord of the worlds. I ask the forgiveness of the mighty God, there is no other God than He, the Living and the Eternal. I turn to Him in repentance.' God bless (the Prophet) and grant him salvation!" (Harley 1924, 139, 1–6). Interestingly, the word *rāḥa* has not only the meaning "palm of the hand", but also means "rest," "calm," "tranquillity."

This passage and its parallel in al-Anṣārī's treatise on plagues emphasise the eminent role of the Prophet as a healer and mediator and as a shining example for the novice and for the ill person. Here too, al-Anṣārī appears to be a Ḥanbalī and a Sufi.

Bibliography

Ahlwardt, Wilhelm. 1887–1899. *Verzeichnis der arabischen Handschriften*, 10 vols. Berlin: Schade.

Benedictow, Ole. 2010. *What Disease was Plague? On the Controversy over the Microbiological Identity of Plague Epidemics of the Past*. Leiden: Brill. Contains a bibliography on pp. 693–704.

Byrne, Joseph P.P.D. 2012. "al-Asqalani, Ibn Hajar (1372–1449)." In *Encyclopedia of the Black Death*, by Joseph Byrne. Santa Barbara, CA: ABC-CLIO.

Daiber, Hans. 1981. "The Creed (*'Aqīda*) of the Ḥanbalite Ibn Qudāma al-Maqdisī. A newly discovered Text." In *Studia Arabica et Islamica. Festschrift for Iḥsān 'Abbās*, edited by Wadād al-Qāḍī, 105–125. Beirut: American University of Beirut. Also published in Hans Daiber. 2021. *From the Greeks to the Arabs and Beyond. Volume 3: From God's Wisdom to Science*, 159–188. Leiden: Brill.

Daiber, Hans. 1995. "Literarischer Prozess zwischen Fiktion und Wirklichkeit. Ein Beispiel aus der klassisch-arabischen Erzählliteratur." *Annals of Japan Association for Middle East Studies* 10: 27–67. Also published in Hans Daiber. 2021. *From the Greeks to the Arabs and Beyond. Volume 3. From God's Wisdom to Science*, 36–78. Leiden: Brill.

Daiber, Hans. 1996. "Political Philosophy." In *History of Islamic Philosophy*, edited by Seyyed Hossein Nasr and Oliver Leaman. London: Routledge. Also published in *Routledge History of World Philosophies*, edited by Seyyed Hossein Nasr and Oliver Leaman, 2 volumes, 841–885. London: Routledge. Also published in Hans Daiber. 2021. *From the Greeks to the Arabs and Beyond. Volume 2: Islamic Philosophy*, 90–145. Leiden: Brill.

Daiber, Hans. 2021. *From the Greeks to the Arabs and Beyond. Volume 3: From God's Wisdom to Science*. Leiden: Brill.

Dols, Michael Walters. 1977. *The Black Death in the Middle East*. Princeton, NJ: Princeton University Press. Compare also Michael Walters Dols. 1974. "The Second Plague Pandemic and Its Recurrences in the Middle East: 1347–1894." *Journal of the Economic and Social History of the Orient* 22(2): 269–287.

GAL and GALS = Carl Brockelmann. 1937–1949. *Geschichte der arabischen Literatur*. 2., den Supplementbänden angepaßte Auflage, volume 1.2 and Supplement 1–3. Brill: Leiden.

GAS = Fuat Sezgin. 1967–1995. *Geschichte des arabischen Schrifttums*, volumes I–X. Leiden: Brill.

Gätje, Helmut. 1956. Avicenna als Seelenarzt. In *Avicenna Commemoration Volume*, 225–228. Calcutta: Iran Society.

Gildaki, A. 1993. "'The Child Was Small … Not So the Grief for Him': Sources, Structure, and Content of Sakhawi's Consolation Treatise for Bereaved Parents." In *Poetics Today* 14: 367–386.

Harley, A.H. 1924. "A Manual of Ṣūfism: Al-Futūḥātu'l-'ilāhīyatu fī Naf'i 'Arwāḥi'dh-dhawāti 'l-'Insānīyati. By Zaynu 'd-Dīn Abū Yaḥyā Zakarīyā' b. Muḥammad al-'Anṣārī ash-Shāfi'ī." In *Journal & Proceedings of the Asiatic Society of Bengal. New Series* 20: 123–142.

Ibn Ḥajar al-ʿAsqalānī. 1997. *Badhl al-Māʿūn fī Faḍl al-Ṭāʿūn*, edited by Aḥmad ʿIṣām ʿAbd al-Qādir al-Kātib. Riyad: Dār al-Āṣima. An older edition, by Abū Ibrāhīm Kaylānī Muḥammad Khalīfa, appeared in 1413/1993 in Cairo. On this edition see Lawrence I. Conrad. 1995. "Ibn Ḥajar al-ʿAsqalānī, Abū l-Faḍl Aḥmad ibn ʿAlī, *Badhl al-Maʿūn fi Faḍl al-Ṭāʿūn*, edited by Abū Ibrāhīm Kaylānī Muḥammad Khalīfa, Cairo, Dār al-Kutub al-Atharīya, 1413/1993, pp. 246, No Price Given." *Medical History* 39(3): 391–393.

Ibn Sīnā. 1937. *Risāla fī Māhiyat al-Ḥuzn wa-Asbābih*, edited with Turkish translation by Mehmet Hazmi Tura. In *Büyük türk filozof ve tib üstadı ibni Sina* (separate pagination). Istanbul: İstanbul Muallim Ahmet Halit Kitabevi.

Ingalls, Matthew B. 2011. "Subtle Innovation Within Networks of Convention: The Life, Thought, and Intellectual Legacy of Zakariyyā al-Anṣārī (d. 926/1520)." PhD diss., Yale University, New Haven, CT.

Ingalls, Matthew B. 2022. *The Anonymity of a Commentator: Zakariyyā al-Anṣārī and the Rhetoric of Muslim Commentaries*. New York: The State University of New York Press.

Kohlberg, Etan. 1992. *A Medieval Muslim Scholar at Work: Ibn Ṭāwūs and His Library*. Leiden: Brill.

Kohlberg, Etan. 2002. "Martyrs and Martyrdom." In *Religion and Cultures*. First International Conference of Mediterraneum, edited by Adriana Destro and Mauro Pesce, 91–120. Binghamton, NY: Global Publications.

Nünlist, Tobias. 2015. *Dämonenglaube im Islam*. Berlin: De Gruyter.

Reinert, Benedikt. 1968. *Die Lehre vom Tawakkul in der klassischen Sufik*. Berlin: De Gruyter.

Stearns, Justin K. 2011. *Infectious Ideas. Contagion in Premodern Islamic and Christian Thought in the Western Mediterranean*. Baltimore, MD: John Hopkins University Press.

Stearns, Justin K. 2017. "Public Health, the State, and Religious Scholarship. Sovereignty in Idrīs al-Bidlīsī's Arguments for Fleeing the Plague." *The Scaffolding of Sovereignty: Global and Aesthetic Perspectives on the History of a Concept*, edited by Zvi Ben-Dor Benite, Stefanos Geroulanos and Nicole Jer, 163–185. New York, NY: Columbia University Press.

Wessel, Felix. 2022. "Tipping the Scales Towards an Islamic Spiritual Medicine. Ibn Qayyim al-Jawziyya on *Jinn* and Epilepsy." In *Islam, Migration and Jinn. Spiritual Medicine in Muslim Health Management*, edited by Annabelle Böttcher and Brigitte Krawietz, 45–63. Basingstoke: Palgrave Macmillan.

CHAPTER 6

Islamic *Ars Moriendi* and Ambiguous Deathbed Emotions

Narratives of Islamic Saints and Scholars on the End-of-Life

Pieter Coppens

1 Introduction

In the master course "Theory of Islamic Spiritual Care," I have my students read Lev Tolstoy's (d. 1910) classic *The Death of Ivan Iljitsch*. Through this work students become acquainted with the types of life questions someone may be confronted with in the crisis of an approaching death. Together we analyse how a spiritual caregiver may be of assistance in navigating the complex emotions provoked by these questions, often theological. Iljitsch poses penetrating questions about the meaning of his suffering, wonders whether it is a form of divine punishment, feels abandoned by God, and is plagued by anxiety, anger, and sadness. He also finds a form of happiness, however, in his friendship with his simple-minded servant. The picture Tolstoy offers of the thoughts and emotions attached to the end-of-life are rather raw and honest, and do not seem to reflect specific religious values. He is not presenting a religious or civilisational ideal to the readers, not what one *ought* to feel on one's death bed. He rather tries to offer what *is* the case for many, and shows the full scale of highly ambiguous and unstable emotions and attitudes, sometimes even blasphemous, towards dying one can encounter on one's deathbed. The genre of the novel is of course very suitable for this: the author can "hide" one's own not always socially acceptable thoughts behind the characters. The tumultuous inner life of characters can be described with an honesty and depth that one is unlikely to encounter in real life due to social conventions and religious and cultural expectations.

Why do I have Muslim students, specifically aspiring to become Islamic spiritual caregivers, read a classic from Russian literature, shaped by struggles with tenets of faith of Russian Orthodoxy and cultural expectations of Russia's nineteenth-century upper class and nobility? First, I consider this an important training in empathy and interreligious and intercultural sensitivity. An Islamic spiritual caregiver in the Netherlands seldom gives care to fellow Muslims only, but is expected to give care to anyone demanding it, especially in health care

(Liefbroer et al. 2019). One may thus encounter people on their death beds with very different religious and cultural expectations concerning their emotions and meaning-making when coming to terms with their approaching death. Secondly, an Islamic equivalent of Tolstoy's masterpiece is hard to find in a language accessible to students. No novel from the modern or contemporary Islamicate world is thus far available to us in a European language that deals with the topic of end-of-life in a similar manner, with such honesty about the emotions as well as religious and meaning-making questions involved.[1]

The field of Islamic Spiritual Care is still very much in development and, some notable exceptions aside (Isgandarova 2019; Ghaly 2014), suffers from a significant lack of theory to build one's practice on. This is also the case in the context of terminal care. In contrast, Christian spiritual caregivers can appeal to a long tradition of literature and theological reflection on *ars moriendi* (the art of dying) that even until this day plays a significant role in models of palliative care (Leget 2007; 2017; Vermandere et al. 2015). Islamic spiritual caregivers at the moment mainly have to improvise when confronted with end-of-life care, and do not yet have a body of sophisticated theory to refer to, other than a set of primary sources. Although attitudes towards death and dying do play a role in early renunciant literature, mainly *kutub al-zuhd* (books on renunciation) (Yaldiz 2016), a similar genre of literature as the *ars moriendi*, that is equally specific in teaching believers how to die and how to behave and manage their emotions on their death beds, is not available. With this contribution I aim to offer historical reflection on repertoires of resilience when confronted with the end-of-life in Islamic traditions, that may contribute to the development of such specific literature on *ars moriendi* in an Islamic context that is also suitable for an interfaith context.

In his work on the application of values from the Christian *ars moriendi* tradition in contemporary spiritual care in a secularised and plural context, Leget (2007; 2017) has opted for a balance between the values and vices propagated in it. The medieval tradition warned against the temptations of loss of faith and confidence in salvation, clinging to this-worldly life, lack of endurance of pain and suffering as well as pride, and stimulated the dying person towards the virtues of faith, hope, patience and humility. The normative choice was clear and typical for a theist worldview. Leget states that in the current secularised and plural context, that lacks an overarching view on death and dying, it is better for spiritual caregivers to recognise that both poles are present within

1 This does not mean it does not exist of course. It is rather a problem of reception in European languages, which shows how important it is that world literature keeps being translated.

the "inner space" of the person. The task of the spiritual caregiver, then, is to help the dying person navigate these conflicting emotions and values, through focus on five tension fields: autonomy, pain control, attachment and relations, guilt, and death and the afterlife. Do Islamic ideas on *ars moriendi* as presented in this chapter offer starting points for a conversation on the possibilities for Islamic spiritual caregivers to make a similar move towards the "inner space" with clients, and to assist them in exploring their ambiguous emotions and attitudes towards death and dying? Is such a move even necessary? Was it perhaps not already present in premodern sources, and is the loss of tolerance for ambiguity (*Ambiguitätstoleranz*) (Bauer 2011; Ahmed 2015, 81–82, 171–173, 219–220, 521; Kateman 2020; Coppens 2021) and the strict regulation of deathbed emotions perhaps rather a modern phenomenon?

The objective of this chapter is thus twofold, combining engaged practical theology with religious and cultural history. On the one hand, it offers material for further normative reflection on end-of-life care in the field of practical theology, more specifically Islamic spiritual care. On the other hand, it invites to deeper reflection on the history of deathbed emotions from the perspectives of the humanities and religious studies. The discipline of history of emotions is thriving and gaining in importance (Scheer 2012; Matt and Stearns 2014). The field of Islamic studies does not participate in that development sufficiently yet, with some notable exceptions (Bauer 2017; Osborne 2019). I aim to show how the theories articulated in this discipline may enrich the study of Islamic ethics in particular, as well as Islamic studies in general.

2 History of Emotions and Hagiographic Sources

One of the main premises of the academic discipline of the History of Emotions is that, beside an evolutionarily determined universal "hard-wired" bottom layer, emotions are partly constructed: not only the way feelings are expressed and performed, but also the feelings themselves are partly learned in interaction with one's social, religious and cultural environment (Scheer 2012; Rosenwein 2015, 1–3; Plamper 2017, 1–39). As stated by Barbara Rosenwein in her seminal *Generations of Feelings*,

> there is a biological and universal human aptitude for feelings and expressing what we now call "emotions." But what those emotions are, what they are called, how they are evaluated and felt, and how they are expressed (or not) – all those are shaped by "emotional communities".
>
> ROSENWEIN 2015, 3

When one accepts this premise, this has consequences for the way one analyses the emotions generated and expressed at the end-of-life in an Islamic context. They contain performative aspects, are shaped by implicit and explicit normative expectations, and thus, most importantly, vary through the ages depending on certain historical variables, also in an Islamic context (Scheer 2012).

To understand the formation and maintenance in the Islamicate world of what Rosenwein calls emotional communities with "their own particular values, modes of feeling, and ways to express those feelings" (Rosenwein 2015, 3), the attitudes expressed by the Islamic scholarly class may be a rewarding resource. The class of scholars (*ʿulamāʾ*) and "friends of God" (*awliyāʾ*) may be considered narrowly delineated emotional communities in themselves throughout Islamic history. These had an exemplary function for other classes within society in the regulation and performance of emotions. Islamic biographical and hagiographical literature contains many stories of Islamic scholars and sages on their deathbeds. Many of these stories contain normative tropes that resurface throughout Islamic history, like repentance (*tawba*), steadfastness (*ṣabr*), trust in God (*tawakkul*) and contentment with His decree (*riḍā*). There may however also be emotional elements specific to certain ages and regions. Which elements of continuity and change do these deathbed narratives contain throughout the centuries? What does that teach us on the construction of emotions concerning the end-of-life in Islamic societies?

This chapter pays specific attention to biographical dictionaries on Islamic scholars and sages in late nineteenth/early twentieth century Damascus (ʿAbd al-Razzāq al-Bīṭār's (d. 1335/1916) *Ḥilyat al-Bashar fī Tārīkh al-Qarn al-Thālith ʿAshar* ("The Ornaments of Humanity on the History of the Thirteenth Century") and Muḥammad Muṭīʿ al-Ḥāfiẓ (b. 1359/1940) and Nizār Abāẓa's (b. 1366/1946) *Taʾrīkh ʿUlamāʾ Dimashq* ("The History of the Scholars of Damascus")), in comparison to Islam's formative period, represented mainly by related stories in Abū Nuʿaym al-Iṣfahānī's (d. 430/1038) *Ḥilyat al-Awliyāʾ wa-Ṭabaqāt al-Aṣfiyāʾ* ("The Ornaments of the Friends of God and Generations of Pure Persons") and Abū l-Qāsim al-Qushayrī's (d. 465/1072) *Risāla fī l-Taṣawwuf* ("Treatise on Sufism"). We juxtapose these early sources to the late nineteenth/early twentieth century era specifically, because this latter era is at the verge of a perceived "Islamic modernity," in which emotionally ecstatic forms of Sufism, that can be abundantly found in al-Isfahānī's *Ḥilyat al-Awliyāʾ* (al-Isfahānī 1932–1938), became more and more discredited, and certain "rational," "sober" and "purist" conceptions of Islam are said to have gained more ground due to the rise of Islamic reform (Bauer 2011; Ahmad 2016). Can a shift indeed be witnessed in the type of deathbed stories shared in this literature, the emotions expressed both by the dying persons and their loved ones in this age? How are these deathbed narratives employed to shape normative expectations concerning end-of-life emotions? Can we draw conclusions from this sample on shifts in these normative expectations in Islamic history? The study of religion and emotion can be typified by a spectrum with "the role of ambiguity and mystery at one end and the importance of clarity and meaning on the other" (Corrigan 2014, 157). This study aims to shed light on this whole spectrum.

Taking the narratives as presented in biographical and hagiographical literature of scholars and sages as point of departure makes this study vulnerable for the criticism of proponents of a focus on popular religion, who generally hold that the field of religious studies has long been plagued by a bias towards "orthodoxy." These sources obviously focus on a learned elite in society in that period, from a hagiographical perspective. The descriptions of deathbed emotions should thus be considered normative in its core, and not necessarily an example of lived religion among the common people. The material presented here is thus not so much about how people died in reality, but rather about how it was perceived and how one *ought* to die. Still a lot can be learned from that, especially in this early stage of exploring Islamic traditions from the perspective of emotion studies.

3 Deathbed Emotions in the Formative Period

Descriptions of deathbeds appear to be rich and diverse in this particular period. Two themes emphatically stand out: (1) that wishing for death and refusing medication and nutrition was quite common out of pious considerations; (2) that emotions could be very ambiguous, sometimes even within the same person, from anxiety to joy, from sadness to contentment, and that there was not one specific model to follow. However, these emotions were always God-centred and religiously motivated; the emotions may have been ambiguous, the motivation for these emotions were not, as one can expect from hagiographical Sufi sources.

3.1 *Wishing for Death*

Actively wishing for death is a recurring theme in end-of-life narrations of early pious figures. Some Prophetic narrations that explicitly prohibit wishing for death place its prohibition in the context of wishing to end one's suffering, which is considered a form of weakness. However, they do not forbid it categorically; they do explicitly allow wishing for death if one fears a form of tribulation (*fitna*) in one's religion (al-Nawawī 2016, 244). The number of sayings on pious people and renunciants wishing for death are overwhelming, and are indeed mostly motivated by fear of a tribulation in one's religion, either due to the temptation of this-worldly desires, or due to a lack of strength to keep fulfilling one's religious obligations. They thus found scriptural justification in such Prophetic narrations. A third common motivation is a strong desire to meet God and to be close to Him, which Sufi scholars from early on considered a legitimate motivation for wishing for death; they only differed which of three is better: the one who wishes for death to meet God, the one who wishes to stay alive to be able to obey God as much as possible, or the one who does not prefer either of the two and is completely content with God's decree (Gramlich 1994, 2:425–426).[2]

Both al-Iṣfahānī's well-known *Ḥilyat al-Awliyāʾ* and al-Qushayrī's *Risāla* contain several sayings attributed to pious persons from the first centuries of Islam that express a wish for death at the end-of-life.[3] Here I will only mention few of them to illustrate the ideas they contain. Some stories related about early pious figures may still fit within the category of Prophetic narrations of fearing tribulation in one's religion. The reason for wishing for death is often related to a fear of losing one's religion, of sinning, or not being able to fulfil one's religious duties properly anymore. Illustrative in this regard is a statement from Sufyān al-Thawrī (d. 161/778), explaining that, if God would ask him about it, he would defend his wish for death towards God by saying: "Because of my confidence in You, o Lord, and my fear of the people." He then recited lines of poetry that stress how death means salvation from trickeries of fellow humans, and safety in the company of God:

> I have said to those who praise life excessively,
> Death contains a thousand virtues we don't know about.
> It contains the safety of meeting Him through meeting Him,
> And separation from every companion who is unfair.
>
> IBN ʿAJĪBA 2010, 8:43

Moreover, ʿAbd al-Raḥmān b. Mahdī (d. 198/814) is said to have been asked about a person who wishes for death. He answers that he sees no harm in it, as

2 I owe the reference to this discussion in Abū Ṭālib al-Makkī's (d. 386/996) *Qūt al-Qulūb* ("Nourishment of the Hearts") to one of the anonymous reviewers.

3 There is a modern edition of *Ḥilyat al-Awliyāʾ* in which all sayings are ranked according to theme. One of the themes is *dhikr al-mawt wa-sakarātuhu* (the mention of death and its intoxicating symptoms) (Habdan 2005, 849–70). This makes it comfortable to navigate and to see the richness of ideas it contains on wishing for death. Al-Qushayrī has a separate chapter on deathbed stories from Sufi sages (al-Qushayrī 2007, 312–318).

long as it is out of fear for tribulation concerning his religion. It would be wrong, however, to wish it because one is lethally hit, or lives in deep poverty. ʿAbd al-Raḥmān points out how also Abū Bakr (d. 13/634) and ʿUmar b. al-Khaṭṭāb (d. 23/644) wished for death to befall them. When he was at a funeral, he once said: "I smell the scent of tribulation. I ask God to take me before it occurs." ʿAmr b. Maymūn (d. 74/693) never wished for death until Yāzīd b. Abī Muslim (d. 102/721), an assistant of the infamous governor al-Ḥajjāj b. Yūsuf (d. 95/714), known for his cruelty, put him under hardship and distress. He wished for death so intensely that he supplicated: "Oh God, make me belong to the pious, do not leave me behind with the wicked, and let me drink from the best river" (Habdān 2005, 858, 864).

A deep longing to meet God and a complete detachment from worldly affairs is mentioned frequently as well. These are intertwined: love for death is inherent to longing to meet God and to be a renunciant (*zāhid*) in this world. To speak in the words of the famous renunciant Bishr b. al-Ḥārith (d. 227/841): "Anyone who loves this world, does not love death, and anyone who is renunciant in this world, loves death, until he meets his Lord" (Habdān 2005, 863). According to hagiographical literature people were surprised to find Makḥūl al-Shāmī (d. *c.*112/730), known to be a sad person, laughing at his deathbed. He explained how happy he was to finally leave the world that he was always so afraid to become attached to, and that he would now finally attain what he always hoped for (al-Qushayrī 2007, 313). There was no complete agreement on this, however. When Salama al-Ghuwayṭī (death date unknown) expressed how he longed for death so that he could meet his Lord, Abū Sulaymān al-Dārānī (d. 215/830) was critical of this. The possibility to obey God would then be taken away as well after all, and one would be imprisoned in the intermediate plane between death and resurrection (*barzakh*), still not capable of meeting God.[4] It would be easier to figuratively meet God during this-worldly life, through remembrance (*dhikr*) of Him (Habdān 2005, 864).[5]

Weakness to perform pious acts is frequently mentioned as well. On the second Caliph ʿUmar b. al-Khaṭṭāb, it is related that at the end of his life he supplicated: "Oh God, I have become old, I have become weaker, my herd has spread, so take me to You." The Companion Abū l-Dardāʾ (d. 32/652) expressed his love for three things: death, because he missed his Lord; poverty, because it made him humble towards his Lord; and illness because it would expiate his sins. On the Companion Muʿādh b. Jabal (d. 17/639), it is related that on his deathbed

4 On *barzakh* see Tesei 2015; Lange 2016, 122–128.

5 On the idea of *dhikr* as a mean to meet God during this-worldly life, see Karamustafa 2007, 19; Coppens 2018, 14–16.

he stated: "Welcome to death, welcome, long absent visitor, beloved that came in neediness." Thābit b. Aslam al-Bunānī (d. *c.*127/744–745) expressed to his friends how he regretted that he was no longer able to pray, fast, and visit his companions for the remembrance of God as he was used to. He then supplicated: "Oh God, since you have imprisoned me from praying as I wish, from fasting as I wish and from remembering you as I wish, do then not keep me in this world one hour longer." He then passed away (Habdān 2005, 849–850; Gramlich 1995, 1:39–40).

ʿAṭāʾ al-Salīmī (d. *c.*140/757) is said to have combined a cultivation of fear for punishment with a deep wish to die. This was not only on his deathbed, but also during his life in good health, so that he would no longer be able to sin. His fear of Hell exceeded his hope for Paradise, he meditated frequently over death and the grave, and was so anxious before prayer that he would shiver. This attitude of fear for punishment and longing for death that he cultivated all his pious life, reached its zenith on his deathbed. He remained anxiously restless until the very end. When he saw a friend sighing at his death bed, he asked him what was wrong with him. When his friend answered him that it was because of him, he answered: "By God, I wish that my spirit would continuously move back and forth between my uvula and my throat until the Day of Resurrection, because I fear it will only go out in Hellfire." After his death, someone claimed to have seen him in a dream, finally at rest in the hereafter. He claimed it was exactly his anxious restlessness in this-worldly life that brought him peace in the hereafter (Gramlich 1995, 1:124, 127, 133). Something similar is related about Ḥātim al-Aṣamm (d. 237/851–852). Three good acts were attributed to him: fleeing from this-worldly life (*dunyā*), compassion for God's creation, and longing for death, ready and prepared for it (Gramlich 1995, 2:66).

Refusal of medication and nutrition is more common in the death stories of early sages than one would expect given the prevailing attitude among Muslims in our contemporary time to prolong treatment as long as possible (Qureshi and Padela 2016; Muishout et al. 2018; Oueslati 2018). It is a recurring theme, even in the sources describing the fourteenth/twentieth century, as we shall see later. Examples of refusing medication are even ascribed to the Companions of the Prophet and are thus a trope present since the formative period of Islam, related to themes of trust in God, contentment, and gratitude (Khalil 2014, 374).[6] When al-Rabīʿ b. al-Khaytham (d. *c.*65/684) was asked whether he wished for a doctor, he allegedly had to think deeply. He pondered a verse on preceding perished peoples (Q 25:38) that clung to this-worldly life, concluded there were doctors and sick people among them as well, but that

6 I owe this reference to one of the anonymous reviewers.

it was of no avail to them: "I see that neither the one giving medicine, nor the one given medicine have remained. They have both perished, so I am not in need of it" (Habdān 2005, 854). On Mālik b. Dīnār (d. *c.*131/749), it is related that on his deathbed he refused meat offered to him as medication against his stomach-ache. He allegedly said: "O God, You know that I do not wish to stay in this world, neither for the sake of my stomach, nor for the sake of my genitals" (Gramlich 1995, 1:67–69). Abū Muḥammad al-Jurayrī (d. 311/923) was a witness to the attack of the Qarmaṭiyya sect on Mecca when he was over 100 years old, and heavily injured. When he expressed his great thirst, someone brought him water. He refused to drink however, because others were also in need, and that would be a form of greed. He then died right away. He allegedly also refused to pray to God to alleviate the situation, despite his saintly powers. He stated this was a time for contentment (*riḍā*) and forgiveness, not for supplication (Gramlich 1995, 1:490).

3.2 *Ambiguous and Extreme Emotions*

The emotions related to this wish for death are often ambiguous. Sometimes sadness and anxiety are reported, sometimes outright joy, sometimes a mixture of emotions. Al-Qushayrī was well aware of these ambiguities when he wrote the chapter in his *Risāla* specifically dedicated to the subject. He did not consider these varying emotions, among the pious, problematic at all:

> Know that the conditions of Sufis at the time of dying vary. Some are overwhelmed by awe (*hayba*), while others experience hope (*raja'*). To others, things are revealed that bring them serenity (*sukūn*) and a beautiful trust [in the favourable outcome in the Hereafter].
>
> AL-QUSHAYRĪ 2007, 312

ʿAmr b. ʿUthmān al-Makkī (d. *c.*291/903–904) was asked how he was doing on his deathbed, and answered: "I find my head as undecided as water: it neither chooses to leave nor to stay" (Gramlich 1995, 1:353). People were surprised to see how Bishr al-Ḥāfī (d. 227/841–842) did not show joy on his deathbed, while he was known to long for death and to be a renunciant of this worldly-life. Did he suddenly like life after all? He explained that entering in the presence of God was harder than he expected (al-Qushayrī 2007, 313). Ḥudhayfa (d. 36/656) is said to have complained to God that all his life he felt that if death would come to him he would not doubt, but now that it has really come he is left in confusion about his own state (Habdān 2005, 852). The same Ḥudhayfa is also said to have begged God to strangle him on his death bed, so that he could finally go to his Beloved (Gramlich 1994, 2:421). Sufyān al-Thawrī (d. 161/778) is said to have longed for death all his life, but to have found it extremely hard when it finally came. Al-Ḥasan b. ʿAlī (d. *c.*49/669) was said to be crying because of the joyful anticipation of meeting God, because He was still unknown to him. The famous Companion Bilāl b. Rabāḥ (d. 20/640) allegedly argued with his wife on his deathbed over which emotion was appropriate to the occasion: his wife considered his deathbed a painful affliction and cried, while Bilāl showed his joy over meeting his beloved Muḥammad the next day. Some pious men were said to hope for a difficult death bed. To ʿUmar b. ʿAbd al-ʿAzīz (d. 101/720) it is attributed that he wished for his deathbed to be heavy upon him, because it is the very last thing a Muslim is rewarded for and by which his sins are expiated (Habdān 2005, 560). Abū Bakr al-Shiblī (d. 334/945) was in ambiguity between appreciating two "winds" of God, His grace (*lutf*) and His power (*qahr*), ultimately embracing both. Considering the comprehensive nature of divine unity, he understood that they are both from his beloved God:

> When the wind of grace blows over someone, he reaches the goal. When the wind of power blows over him, he is held in separation [from God]. (…) If the wind of grace reaches me, I can bear all this discomfort and misery in my hope for Him. If the wind of power will come blowing, then this misery now will be nothing compared to what I will undergo then.
>
> GRAMLICH 1995, 1:572

Al-Shiblī was not afraid to be humorous on his deathbed, reminding his friends through jokes that in the spiritual sense he was to become alive, while they were all dead. When someone whispered the testimony of faith in his ear, he joked: "A dead man has come to bring a living person back to life." The same joke he made about death prayers said for him: "How exceptional! A group of dead people have come together, to say the prayer of death over someone living." His anxiety on his deathbed was ultimately extinguished by a sense of deep love for God. When he was asked how he was doing, he said that he had arrived at his Beloved, and passed away (Gramlich 1995, 1:575).

Even outright ecstasy (*wajd*) is reported to have occurred. Abū Saʿīd al-Kharrāz (d. 286/899) was so excited about finally leaving this world that he fell into ecstasy (al-Qushayrī 2007, 313). Ecstasy provoked by deep love of God was not only the result of approaching death, sometimes it was even the cause of death. Abū l-Ḥusayn al-Nūrī (d. 295/907–908) is said to have walked into a stubble field while in ecstasy after hearing a verse of love poetry and died of his wounds. Another narration of the same incident claims it was after hearing a blind man saying the name of God, with the question "Do you know Him? And if you know Him, will you stay alive then?" (Gramlich 1997, 1:387). Such cases of extreme emotions causing death are not only related to ecstasy, but also intense sadness or shame. Mālik b. Dīnār is said to have fallen ill after a friend asked him about the face of a pious person who had already passed away. After having answered, he started crying and became aroused. He subsequently fell terminally ill (Gramlich 1995, 1:68). Dāwūd al-Ṭāʾī (d. *c.*165/781–782) was allegedly so overwhelmed by a particular verse on Hellfire, that he kept repeating it all night. The next morning, he was found dead (Gramlich 1995, 1:290–292).[7]

4 The Sobering Effect of Modernity? Continuities and Changes in the Thirteenth/Nineteenth and Fourteenth/Twentieth Centuries

In the preceding section we have focused on Sufi hagiographies from the formative period, which despite their common origin in Sufi circles painted a very diverse picture of emotions experienced at the deathbed. We will now juxtapose these to fourteenth/twentieth-century deathbed stories as narrated in two biographical dictionaries from Damascus. These sources and the era they represent are too different to validly make an analogous comparison to the formative period that leads to conclusive arguments on the development of deathbed emotions. Juxtaposing them still has value for a different reason. The sources on the fourteenth/twentieth century in Damascus deal with a much more diverse group of Muslims than the Sufi hagiographies of the formative period: beside Sufi figures, they encompass preachers, scholars, and political activists. They thus offer a wider palette of deathbed narratives, covering more diverse segments of Islamic society than the earlier Sufi hagiographical literature. They are thus suitable to see whether a trend of homogenisation and standardisation that is associated with Islamic modernity can be witnessed in these deathbed stories: do they still contain similar tropes despite the heterogeneity of the religious backgrounds of the religious authorities? Although conclusive arguments cannot be made based on this admittedly narrow selection of narratives, it can form a building brick for further *longue durée* analyses that may lead to stronger claims.

7 His deathbed stories are a case of ambiguity themselves. Some reports say his deathbed lasted for days, and was extremely heavy for him, due to his fear of Hellfire. He is also related to have died through a heavy heart attack, in which he screamed harder than a raging bull. To his mother it is attributed that he died in deep silence and loneliness, after praying all night. His mother found him in prostration (Gramlich 1995, 1:290–292). There is a whole literary genre of stories of people who found death through heavy emotions when reading the Qurʾān, the *qatlā l-qurʾān* (those killed by the Qurʾān), see Kermani 1999, 376–385.

As late as the thirteenth/nineteenth century, stories of actively wishing death were still quoted with approval. The Moroccan Sufi scholar Ibn ʿAjība (d. 1224/1809) included some of them in his Qurʾān commentary on Q 62:6 ("then wish for death if you are truthful"), among which earlier mentioned sayings attributed to ʿUmar b. al-Khaṭṭāb and Sufyān al-Thawrī (Ibn ʿAjība 2010, 8:43). Something seems to have changed in the fourteenth/nineteenth century, however. When we look at deathbed stories, wishing for death has completely left the stage, no ambiguous or extreme emotions are related, nor excessive anxiety or hardship. Most scholars are reported to have been content with their fate, to have undergone their suffering without complaining or wishing for death, and to have remained steadfast in their pious acts until the very end. A certain sense of sobriety indeed seems to have become dominant, and experiences rather unambiguous. Let us have a look at some examples.

A popular theme in hagiographies from the thirteenth/nineteenth and fourteenth/twentieth century, that is hardly mentioned in the formative period, is remaining steadfast in acts of obedience and teaching until the very end. This is perhaps the most frequently mentioned deathbed narrative even. Where the sages from the formative period, often with an implicit or explicit Sufi background were allowed to have complex emotions, often with an extreme love for God or fear of Hellfire involved, scholars in the hagiographical dictionary on the thirteenth/nineteenth century of ʿAbd al-Razzāq al-Bīṭār, the central figure of the emerging Salafī-reformist movement of Damascus, were without exception merely supposed to be sober teachers, steadfast in obedience, void of extreme emotions (al-Bīṭār 1993, 7, 13, 45, 95, 176, 179, 183–184, 189, 217, 281, 303). This also pertained to Sufi scholars. In describing the death of a Tījānī *shaykh* from Fes, for example, following the prescriptions of prayer and lying down on the right side as Prophetic practice demands, is central in the narrative, and emotions are not mentioned at all. Al-Bīṭār relates:

> He passed away in 1230[/1815] and lived 80 years. His death was on the morning of Thursday 17 Shawwāl[/21 September], after he prayed the obligatory morning prayer in a complete manner. He then lied down on his right side, asked for water and drank from it. Then he lied down again in this condition and his noble spirit rose instantly and ascended to its most sacred abode.
>
> AL-BĪṬĀR 1993, 303

This trope of ritual ablutions, prayer, remembrance of God and lying on one's right side reoccurs until late into the fourteenth/twentieth century (al-Ḥāfiẓ and Abāẓa 2016, 2:817). Steadfastness in prayer and remembrance of God are mentioned frequently, reflecting a sober pious ideal. On ʿAbd al-Ḥakīm al-Afghānī (d. 1326/1908) the following is related:

> The night that he passed away one of his students stayed with him. He constantly asked about the call to morning prayer: "Did the call for prayer sound?" He answered him "No." He then said: "Bring me [water for] ritual ablutions." He would then make ritual ablutions and pray. That happened several times, then he surrendered his spirit.
>
> AL-ḤĀFIẒ and ABĀẒA 2016, 1:275

The brothers Ṣāliḥ Kuftārū (d. 1355/1936) and Muḥammad Amīn Kuftārū (d. 1357/1938), both Naqshbandī scholars of Kurdish descent, whose family would rise to prominence in the later Syrian republic, both had a relatively sober death as well according to the reports, remembering God and admonishing others to do so as well. The last words of Ṣāliḥ, who died of the plague, were: "Prepare yourselves to meet God all alone, safely." His brother kept repeating: "O God, the Highest Companion" (*Allāhumma al-Rafīq al-Aʿlā*) on his death bed, until he gave up his spirit with a joyful expression on his face (al-Ḥāfiẓ and Abāẓa 2016, 1:579, 601). The deathbed of Ṣāliḥ al-Ḥumṣī (d. 1362/1943) follows a similar trope, stressing his great sense of contentment despite his great pain, and remembering God:

> At the end of his life, he used to repeat the noble verse "Peace be upon you for the patience that you have shown. How excellent is the final abode!" (Q 13:24). He did not stop with this until only few minutes before his death, when he started repeating the words "Allāh, Allāh." On his deathbed he was very patient. Those frequently visiting him asked him whether he was in pain. He answered them "no," while the fever was making him shake heavily in the beginning of his illness.
>
> AL-ḤĀFIẒ and ABĀẒA 2016, 1:673

Many scholars are said to have kept teaching until the very end. Badr al-Dīn al-Ḥasanī (d. 1354/1935), for example, was ill for a long time, stayed in bed most of the time, but ignored the advice of his doctor and kept teaching his Friday lessons in the Umayyad mosque until the day before he passed away. The Qurʾān scholar ʿAbd al-Qādir Quwaydir (d. 1369/1950) is said to have kept teaching while he was ill for several months. When he was struck by blood poisoning, he surprised his doctor when he came himself for the results of a blood test: "The subject of this investigation should be in his bed, not able to move" (al-Ḥāfiẓ and Abāẓa 2016, 1:569, 2:766, 1279; al-Bīṭār 1993, 7, 13, 45, 95, 176, 179, 183–184, 189, 217, 281).

Investing in relations with family and friends until the very end also occurs and dying alone is never mentioned. The famous Salafī scholar, book collector and belletrist Ṭāhir al-Jazāʾirī (d. 1338/1920) frequently repeated to his friends on his deathbed that they should all note down the names of everyone who ever stood by them in times of hardship, "so that you do not forget them, and mention them at every opportunity, and be dedicated to them as you are dedicated to the Most Magnificent." Muḥammad al-Usṭuwānī's (d. 1354/1925) last words were asking his parents whether they were satisfied with him, and an embrace of the divine decree and his mortality: "Destiny has come, so welcome to the meeting with God. This world did not last for Muḥammad, so who am I compared to him, while he is the master of mankind?" One scholar was so invested in taking care of the dogs on the graveyard, feeding them daily, that one dog even visited him on his deathbed at home every day when he no longer showed up, and followed the funeral ceremony back to the grave yard once the scholar had passed away. In 1971, Ṣalāḥ al-Dīn al-Zaʿīm travelled all the way to Beirut one day before his death, despite being very ill and weak, and despite warnings from his doctor, to visit his friends there and ask about their situation (al-Ḥāfiẓ and Abāẓa 2016, 1:411, 450, 2:909, 2:1187–1188).

Making up one's testament is mentioned frequently as well, as an act of piety when death approaches. Bakrī l-ʿAṭṭār (d. 1320/1902), the most influential scholar of Damascus in the thirteenth/nineteenth century, died of the plague. He spent his time remembering God and making up his testament once he realised the medication against the plague was not helping him. ʿAbd al-Ḥakīm al-Afghānī (d. 1326/1908), a dedicated teacher with a renunciant lifestyle, distributed all his books and his furniture among his students. The testament of Ṣāliḥ al-ʿAqqād (d. 1390/1970) shows great concern with regulations and rituals around his deathbed, forbidding extreme expressions of emotions as excessive sadness, raising one's voice and ripping one's clothes. He does not want to be visited by menstruating women, and people who have abandoned the habit of regular ritual prayer (*tārik al-ṣalāt*), does not want medication, and wants the remembrance of the unicity of God (*lā ilāha illā Llāh*) to be repeated constantly by visitors (al-Ḥāfiẓ and Abāẓa 2016, 1:225, 275, 293, 2:1193).

When forms of emotions are mentioned, they are either moderately expressed sadness or equally moderately expressed joyful contentment, always in a context of pious acts and remembrance of God. On the deathbed of a preacher from the well-known al-Khaṭīb family, who used to teach and preach in the Umayyad mosque, who passed away in 1303/1886, the following is related: "His last words before he gave up his spirit were "Allāh, Allāh." He then looked towards another scholar in his company, cried, and turned his head towards him while the tears were in his eyes. His kin, friends and neighbours were all sad about him." One scholar first felt very sad on his deathbed, but this was soon over when people around him started taking care of him. He then used to say: "God is the one who has given and He is the one who takes." People around him felt that this was motivated by his great humility, and that he did not want to be a burden to anyone, not even on his deathbed. Lines of poetry from 1309/1891 describe how a scholar who passed away gave up life easily, in anticipation of meeting his beloved Prophet:

> In this world, he was a hidden friend of God,
> Today in Paradise, he has become a banner.
> When the inviter of God came to him, he went,
> Rejoicing at the meeting with the modest beloved.

Contentment and not showing sadness or anxiety remained the norm, however. In the 1950s, ʿAbd al-Ḥamīd al-Qanawātī (d. 1376/1957) is praised for remaining steadfast during tribulations, being content with the decree of God, neither complaining nor crying. The founder of the Muslim Brotherhood in Syria, Muṣṭafā l-Sibāʿī (d. 1384/1964), is said to have kept smiling on his deathbed, without complaint or grief, while he had severe pain in his entire body and heavy seizures that made his nerves and muscles cramp up. A friend described how he visited him in the hospital to offer him some comfort: "He turned towards me with a yellow face from a night spent in exhausting pain and said: 'Thank you for offering such good comfort. But if you only knew how content I am'" (al-Ḥāfiẓ and Abāẓa 2016, 1:64, 125, 2:746, 1049).

Refusal of medication and nutrition as a sign of acceptance of one's destiny to die reoccurs in this time period as well. None other than Maḥmūd Ḥamza (d. 1305/1887), the official Ḥanafī *muftī* of the city of Damascus with close relations to the Ottoman state, is said to have refused medication. After having seen the Prophet in a dream and reaffirming the testimony of faith with him, he accepted that his appointed time had come. The Sufi scholar ʿAbd al-Qādir al-Khānī (d. 1354/1935) was afflicted by malaria during one of his many journeys abroad. He refused medication and only wanted to drink water with blessings (*baraka*). When his body turned yellow, he kept shouting "*Ḥaqq, Ḥaqq*" (God, God!). His deathbed lasted sixteen days. The grand *ḥadīth* scholar Badr al-Dīn al-Ḥasanī, the most important scholar of Damascus in the early twentieth century, completely stopped eating a week before his death, and only took small sips of milk because a doctor kept trying. The Qurʾān scholar

ʿAbd al-Wahhāb Dibs wa-Zayt (d. 1389/1969) is said to have refused medication as well, instead taking refuge in recitation of the Qurʾān and invoking blessings upon the Prophet for pain relief, and to have said: "My medication is not prepared with you, but with my Lord in Paradise" (al-Ḥāfiẓ and Abāẓa 2016, 1:83, 551, 569, 2:1137).

5 Conclusion

Based on the above analysis, it becomes clear that our – admittedly limited – sample of Sufi narratives from the first four centuries of Islam paint a much more ambiguous picture of deathbed emotions than later Damascene narratives from the verge of an Islamic modernity in the thirteenth/nineteenth-fourteenth/twentieth century. They are thus witness to a fascinating paradox in Islam's modernity: while the Sufis from the formative period all shared a mystical vision on Islam, the forms this vision took were plural, leading to a great diversity in attitudes towards death and attached emotions. The sample from the fourteenth century is much more diverse with regards to visions on Islam, from textual scholars to charismatic leaders, from Sufis to Salafīs, but expresses a larger degree of concurrence in attitudes and emotions expressed. Although further comparative research is needed and this sample has its obvious limitations, the impression that a sense of what Thomas Bauer calls *Vereindeutigung* (disambiguation), typical of Islam's modernity, at the cost of the alleged *Mehrdeutigkeit* (ambiguity) and *Vielfalt* (pluriformity) of premodern Islam (Bauer 2011; 2018), can also be witnessed in the expressed ideal of deathbed emotions. Main differences can be found in the extremity of the emotions expressed: where ambiguity on the deathbed and heavy emotions were not an exception, even considered a form of piety in sources on the formative period, by the thirteenth/nineteenth and fourteenth/twentieth centuries sobriety in emotions, steadfastness and contentment had become the absolute norm.

This chapter has of course only scratched the surface of a much larger history that has to be told from a *longue durée* perspective. The difference between the two epochs are obvious in this particular sample, but still we do not know when and how exactly this paradigm shift took place in the preferred norms and expression of emotions, and whether this is only a regional phenomenon (all examples here are from the MENA region, the modern examples even only from Damascus), or whether they can also be witnessed in other regions of the Islamic world. We cannot exclude the possibility that it was not the exclusive result of a confrontation with modernity, but that earlier internal movements of discrediting more ecstatic forms of Sufism in favour of more sober understandings of Sufism have played a role as well. More research is needed for this. This modest study may form a first onset for further comparative *longue durée* studies on deathbed emotions.

Let us in conclusion return to the study of Carlo Leget and his concept of "inner space." Can all these narratives offer fertile ground for the approach that Leget proposes, and is this necessary? I would argue that an adaptation of premodern *ars moriendi* models in the case of Islam is not necessary. It may suffice for spiritual caregivers to realise how recent a phenomenon this sobriety and disambiguation in emotions actually is, and that premodern Islamic tradition offers a vast reservoir of emotions and ambiguities, despite, or perhaps even due to, the very pious milieu from which they emerged. This, in itself, is a humbling realisation. It also shows that the history of religion as a discipline may be a very good training in empathy, since it forces us to place ourselves in the shoes of people that not only have different religious convictions, but even come from different eras and areas altogether. History of religion, I would argue, should therefore be a significant and default part of the education of spiritual caregivers. Practical theology, in itself, is not enough and should always be informed by keen historical consciousness. The same goes for the ethics of end-of-life care: the flexibility shown in historical sources in matters pertaining to medication, nutrition, and preferring to die over prolonging the deathbed, invites to reflection on the ethical norms one proposes and cultivates in Islamic modernity, and whether a certain disambiguation and ethical rigidity alien to premodern norms is not undeservedly upheld.

This chapter initially originated from a teaching reflection in the field of practical theology, aiming to offer Islamic spiritual caregivers a theoretical framework for their end-of-life care. It emphatically aims higher in its ultimate goal, however. Western academia does not only have a rich tradition of reflection on dying in theology and religious studies, also in the realm of the humanities, valuable studies are available, that also reflect upon changing attitudes and emotions towards death and dying in art and literature (Taylor 2007, 65ff; Marchant 2014; McNamara and McIlvenna 2014; Sherlock 2017). Similar studies should also become available on Islamicate cultures in the broadest sense, so that more encompassing narratives of the history of culture and mentality around death and dying in the Islamicate world can become possible. It is about time that the "affective turn" in history and anthropology also fully reaches the field of Islamic studies, and that scholars of Islam become fully integrated in the growing community of emotion studies.

Acknowledgement

This work is part of the research program "The origins, growth and dissemination of Salafī Qur'ān interpretation: the role of al-Qāsimī (d. 1914) in the shift from premodern to modern modes of interpretation," with project number 016.Veni.195.105, financed by the Dutch Research Council (NWO).

Bibliography

Ahmad, Shahab. 2016. *What is Islam? The Importance of being Islamic*. Princeton: Princeton University Press.

Bauer, Karen. 2017. "Emotion in the Qur'an: An Overview." *Journal of Qur'anic Studies* 19(2): 1–30.

Bauer, Thomas. 2011. *Die Kultur der Ambiguität: Eine andere Geschichte des Islams*. Berlin: Verlag der Weltreligionen.

Bauer, Thomas. 2018. *Die Vereindeutigung der Welt: Über den Verlust an Mehrdeutigkeit und Vielfalt*. Ditzingen: Reclam Universal Library.

al-Bīṭār, ʿAbd al-Razzāq. 1993. *Ḥilyat al-Bashar fī Taʾrīkh al-Qarn al-Thālith ʿAshar*, edited by Muḥammad Bahjat al-Bīṭār. Beirut: Dār Ṣādir.

Christian, William A. 2004. "Provoked Religious Weeping in Early Modern Spain." In *Religious Organization and Religious Experience*, edited by John Corrigon, 33–55. Oxford: Oxford University Press.

Coppens, Pieter. 2018. *Seeing God in Sufi Qur'an Commentaries: Crossings between This World and the Otherworld*. Edinburgh: Edinburgh University Press.

Coppens, Pieter. 2021. "Did Modernity End Polyvalence? Some Observations on Tolerance for Ambiguity in Sunni *Tafsīr*." *Journal of Qur'ānic Studies* 23(1): 36–70.

Corrigan, John. 2014. *Religion and Emotions*. In *Doing Emotions History*, Susan J. Matt and Peter N. Stearns, 143–162. Urbana, IL: University of Illinois Press.

Ghaly, Mohammed. 2014. "Muslim Theologians on Evil: God's Omnipotence or Justice, God's Omnipotence and Justice." In *Theologie der Barmherzigkeit? Zeitgemässe Fragen und Antworten des Kalam*, edited by Mouhanad Khorchide, Milad Karimi and Klaus von Stosch, 147–172. Münster: Waxmann.

Gramlich, Richard. 1994. *Die Nahrung der Herzen: Abū Ṭālib al-Makkīs Qūt al-qulūb eingeleitet, übersetzt und kommentiert*, 4 vols. Stuttgart: Franz Steiner Verlag.

Gramlich, Richard. 1995. *Alte Vorbilder des Sufitums*, 2 vols. Wiesbaden: Harrasowitz Verlag.

Habdān, Muḥammad b. ʿAbd Allah. 1426/2005. *Al-Tahdhīb al-Mawḍūʿī li-Ḥilyat al-Awliyāʾ*. Riyad: Dār Ṭayba lil-Nashr wa-l-Tawzīʿ.

al-Ḥāfiẓ, Muḥammad Muṭīʿ and Nizār Abāẓa. 2016. *Taʾrīkh ʿUlamāʾ Dimashq fī l-Qarn al-Rābiʿ Ashar*, 2 vols. Damascus: Dār al-Fikr.

Ibn ʿAjība, Aḥmad. 2010. *Al-Baḥr al-Madīd fī Tafsīr al-Qurʾān al-Majīd*, 8 vols. Beirut: Dār al-Kutub al-ʿIlmiyya.

al-Isfahānī, Abū Nuʿaym. 1932–1938. *Ḥilyat al-Awliyāʾ wa-Ṭabaqāt al-Aṣfiyāʾ*, 10 vols. Cairo: Maṭbaʿat Dār al-Saʿāda.

Isgandarova, Nazila. 2019. *Muslim Women, Domestic Violence, and Psychotherapy: Theological and Clinical Issues*. London: Routledge.

Karamustafa, Ahmet. 2007. *Sufism: The Formative Period*. Edinburgh: Edinburgh University Press.

Kateman, Ammeke. 2020. "Fashioning the Materiality of the Pilgrimage: The *ḥajj* Travelogue of Muḥammad Labīb al-Batanūnī." *Die Welt des Islams* 60(4): 384–407.

Kermani, Navid. 1999. *Gott ist Schön: Das Ästhetische Erleben des Koran*. München: Verlag C.H. Beck.

Khalil, Atif. 2014. "Contentment, Satisfaction and Good-Pleasure: *Rida* in Early Sufi Moral Psychology." *Studies in Religion/Sciences Religieuses* 43(3): 371–389.

Lange, Christian. 2016. *Paradise and Hell in Islamic Traditions*. Cambridge: Cambridge University Press.

Leget, Carlo. 2007. "Retrieving the *Ars Moriendi* Tradition." *Medicine, Health Care and Philosophy* 10: 313–319.

Leget, Carlo. 2017. *Art of Living, Art of Dying: Spiritual Care for a Good Death*. London: Jessica Kingsley Publishers.

Liefbroer, Anke I., Ruard Ganzevoort and Erik Olsman. 2019. "Addressing the Spiritual Domain in a Plural Society: What is the Best Mode of Integrating Spiritual Care into Health Care?" *Mental Health, Religion & Culture* 22(3): 244–260. DOI: 10.1080/13674676.2019.1590806.

Marchant, Alicia. 2014. "Narratives of Death and Emotional Affect in Late Medieval Chronicles." *Parergon* 31(2): 81–98.

Matt, Susan J. and Peter N. Sterns. 2014. *Doing Emotions History*. Urbana, IL: University of Illinois Press.

McNamara, Rebecca F. and Una McIlvenna. 2014. "Medieval and Early Modern Emotional Responses to Death and Dying." *Parergon* 31(2): 1–10.

Muishout, George, Hanneke W.M. van Laarhoven, Gerard Wiegers and Ulrike Popp-Baier. 2018. "Muslim Physicians and Palliative Care: Attitudes towards the Use of Palliative Sedation." *Supportive Care in Cancer* 26: 3701–3710.

al-Nawawī, Muḥyī l-Dīn Yaḥyā. 2016. *Al-Adhkār min Sayyid al-Abrār*. Jedda: Dār al-Minhāj.

Osborne, Lauren E. 2019. "The Qur'an and Affect: Introduction to Special Issue." *Body and Religion* 3(1): 1–4.

Oueslati, Roukayya. 2018. "Dying with a Clear Mind: Pain and Symptom Control in Palliative Care for Dutch Moroccan Patients in the Netherlands." In *Women and Social Change in North Africa: What Counts as Revolutionary?*, edited by Doris H. Gray and Nadia Sonneveld, 237–259. Cambridge: Cambridge University Press.

Plamper, Jan. 2017. *The History of Emotions: An Introduction*. Oxford: Oxford University Press.

Qureshi, Omar and Aasim I. Padela. 2016. "When Must a Patient Seek Healthcare? Bringing the Perspectives of Islamic Jurists and Clinicians into Dialogue." *Journal of Religion and Science* 51(3): 592–625.

al-Qushayri, Abu 'l-Qasim. 2007. *Al-Qushayri's Epistle on Sufism: Al-Risala al-Qushayriyya fi 'Ilm al-Tasawwuf*, translated by Alexander D. Knysh. Reading: Garnet Publishing.

Rosenwein, Barbara. 2015. *Generations of Feeling: A History of Emotions, 600–1700*. Cambridge: Cambridge University Press.

Scheer, Monique. 2012. "Are Emotions a Kind of Practice (and is that what makes them have a history?): A Bourdieuian Approach to Understanding Emotion." *History and Theory* 51: 193–220.

Sherlock, Peter. 2017. "Death." In *Early Modern Emotions: An Introduction*, S. Broomhall, 220–224. London: Routledge.

Stearns, Peter N. 2014. "Modern Patterns in Emotions History." In *Doing Emotions History*, edited by Susan J. Matt and Peter N. Stearns, 17–40. Urbana, IL: University of Illinois Press.

Taylor, Charles. 2007. *A Secular Age*. Cambridge, MA: Harvard University Press.

Tesei, Tommaso. 2015. "The *Barzakh* and the Intermediate State of the Dead in the Quran." In *Locating Hell in Islamic Traditions*, edited by Christian Lange, 29–55. Leiden: Brill.

Vermandere, Mieke, Franca Warmenhoven, Evie Van Severen, Jan De Lepeleire and Bert Aertgeerts. 2015. "The Ars Moriendi Model for Spiritual Assessment: A Mixed-Methods Evaluation." *Oncology Nursing Forum* 42(4): 294–301.

Yaldiz, Yunus. 2016. "The Afterlife in Mind: Piety and Renunciatory Practice in the 2nd/8th- and Early 3rd/9th-Century Books of Renunciation (*Kutub al-Zuhd*)." PhD diss., Utrecht University.

PART 3

End-of-Life Care as a Bioethical Issue

CHAPTER 7

Palliative Care and Its Ethical Questions

Islamic Perspectives

Mohammed Ghaly

1 Situating Palliative Care (PC) within the Broad Context of Medical Treatment (*Tadāwī*)[1]

Recent advances in biomedical sciences have added new layers of complexity to the concept of medical treatment – in Arabic *tadāwī* or *ʿilāj* (Wizārat al-Awqāf 1983–2006, 11:116–118; al-Qaradāghī and al-Muḥammadī 2006, 88–196; Qureshi and Padela 2016, 595–605). That is why this concept cannot be approached as one single block anymore, because there are different types, with sometimes blurred borderlines, whose ethical judgment would naturally vary from one to the other. In order to capture its moral nuances, the broad concept of medical treatment can, roughly speaking, be divided into five types, namely predictive, preventive, curative, rehabilitative and finally palliative treatment.

- **Predictive** treatment forecasts the probability of developing a certain disease. There is now a distinct branch of medicine called "predictive medicine," which aims to predict the probability of developing a certain disease, especially among at-risk individuals and groups. Such prediction facilitates either preventive or early curative treatment of the respective disease. The testing tools developed by fields like genetics and genomics to predict one's disposition to life-threatening diseases, including cancer, fall within the category of predictive treatment (Grech and Grossman 2015).
- **Preventive** treatment is meant to improve people's health conditions by preventing the disease before its onset. Preventive treatment, or prophylaxis, includes vaccinations, controlling air and water pollution, and encouraging

1 An earlier version of this study was published as the third chapter in *Palliative Care and Islamic Ethics: Exploring Key Issues and Best Practice* (see Ghaly et al. 2018). The chapter was mainly directed to non specialists in Islamic Studies, especially healthcare providers and policymakers who are engaged in the field of Palliative Care (PC). That is why the study included a distinct dedicated "executive summary," which outlined the key recommendations and conclusions of the study.

people to adopt healthy lifestyles. Various secular and religious traditions, including Islam, usually give preference to preventive over curative treatment (al-Zuḥaylī 2006, 2:861; Thompson and Upshur 2018, 121–127).

- **Curative** treatment is often perceived as the main function of medicine, and it is usually the supposed meaning whenever "treatment" is used as an unqualified term. Thanks to important advances made by the end of the nineteenth century in understanding and treating infectious diseases, modern medicine could achieve a revolution in therapeutic treatments. Besides pharmacotherapy, the most frequently used form of curative treatments, the spectrum of these treatments also includes others forms such as surgery, physical therapy and herbal medications (Marcum 2008, 79–80; Thompson and Upshur 2018, 134–137).
- **Rehabilitative** treatment is the specialisation of a distinct branch of medicine known as "physical and rehabilitation medicine" (PRM). Specialists in this branch of medicine treat a wide variety of medical conditions affecting muscles, brain, spinal cord, nerves, bones, joints and other parts of the body (Didier and Bigand 2010).
- **Palliative** treatment differs from the previous types of treatment in many ways. Palliative care (PC) is a form of medical care for people living with serious illnesses. It focuses on providing relief from the symptoms and stresses of a serious illness. Generally speaking, it is appropriate at any age and at any stage in a serious illness, including, but not exclusive to, terminal illness. So, one can say that end-of-life care is part of PC, but PC is not necessarily always part of end-of-life care. Keeping this background in mind, the aim of PC is not to cure diseases but to manage pain through, among other tools, the administration of drugs, while also improving the overall quality of life through non-medical measures, which are supposed to enhance the patient's and family's social, psychological and spiritual wellbeing. As to be explained below, many ethical dilemmas arise when employing palliative treatment, which would mean forgoing other types of treatment, especially the curative type, and sometimes even patients' basic needs, like medically administered nutrition and hydration, although this is not usually the case in the PC context. But in such cases, the question which arises is whether palliative treatment should be given priority or whether curative treatment should continue even if this may increase the patient's pains, whose management and minimisation is the main target of PC.

It is to be noted that the pre-modern Islamic tradition was dominantly inclined towards a generalist moral position when it comes to medical treatment (*tadāwī*), which did not capture the abovementioned nuances. The intensive discussions within the Islamic tradition has shown internal disagreements regarding whether the right position is to consider *tadāwī* permissible (morally neutral), recommended, obligatory, or morally inferior to forgoing treatment, and having, instead, to trust in God (*tawakkul*), considering that He is the true Healer (*al-Shāfī*) (al-Ḥakīm al-Tirmidhī 1992, 1:250–251, 402–406; al-Nawawī 1972, 14:191; Wizārat al-Awqāf 1983–2006, 11:116–118; al-Qaradāghī and al-Muḥammadī 2006, 88–196; Qureshi and Padela 2016, 595–605). The abovementioned typology of medical treatment (*tadāwī*) problematises the accuracy of adopting such a generalist position, which would indiscriminately judge medical treatments from an ethical perspective without keeping in mind the various nuances and complexities that have been brought forth by modern biomedical advancements. The inconsistencies inherent in such a generalist position becomes especially clear when one has to choose between, and prioritise among, different types of medical treatment, as is the case sometimes between curative and palliative treatments. For instance, some curative treatments, which may be judged as recommended or even obligatory in principle, can be seen by certain physicians or ethicists as unfavourable or even undesirable in the context of PC. As to be explained below, modern Islamic bioethical discussions, especially the interdisciplinary deliberations hosted by transnational Islamic institutions, are much more nuanced than the early discussions when it comes capturing certain particularities of the PC.

2 Overall Structure and Literature Review

Against the above-sketched background, this chapter is divided into two main sections. The first section "Life-Sustaining Treatments" (LSTs) will address the ethical dilemmas resulting from the possible tension between palliative treatment and one of the above-mentioned other types of treatments, especially curative treatment. Such dilemmas are analysed at the hand of two main examples, namely (a) cardiopulmonary resuscitation (CPR) and mechanical ventilation, and (b) artificial nutrition and hydration (ANH). The second section "Navigating Conflicting Values" addresses the ethical dilemmas resulting from having two or more ethical values or virtues, which are all significant and relevant but cannot be equally honoured or implemented in a PC setting. The dilemmas of these conflicting values are also analysed at the hand of two representative examples. The first example is the analgesics, which are instrumental to relieve the patient's pains but may impair consciousness or hasten death. The second example is communicating bad/sad news about the potentially approaching deaths of PC patients and how to combine between the value of veracity and that of compassion.

The distinctively practical nature of these themes and related ethical questions have made them the subject of intensive contemporary discussion within the discipline of Islamic jurisprudence (*fiqh*). Because of the conflation of both ethical and biomedical aspects of these topics, contemporary Muslim jurists collaborated with biomedical scientists. Thus, these discussions would naturally fit within the field of "juristic ethics," with a strong interdisciplinary tincture. In alignment with this focus, the main sources which were frequently consulted throughout this study belong to the discourse of contemporary bioethics, which heavily relies on *fiqh*. Sources coming from other disciplines, like theology, philosophy and Sufism, are only mentioned when they intersect with juristic ethics. The plan is to examine the contribution of these other disciplines to the ethics of PC in future distinct studies.

Against this backdrop, the main sources of this chapter come from the publications of transnational Islamic institutions, whose beginnings go back to the 1980s, which have been facilitating interdisciplinary bioethical deliberations by engaging both Muslim religious scholars and biomedical scientists. The Islamic Organization for Medical Sciences (IOMS), based in Kuwait, and officially established in 1984, has been the most active organisation in this regard and all their symposia exclusively focus on bioethical issues. Additionally, two other institutions should be mentioned because of their significant contributions to the contemporary Islamic bioethical deliberations, although their interest in bioethics was just part of their broader work on the role of Sharīʿa in the modern world. One of these two institutions is the Islamic Fiqh Academy (IFA), established in 1977, which is affiliated with the Muslim World League and based in Mecca, Saudi Arabia. The other institution is the International Islamic Fiqh Academy (IIFA), established in 1981, based in Jedda, Saudi Arabia, and affiliated with the Organization of Islamic Cooperation (OIC). An additional fourth institution with work specific to the PC context is the Dublin-based European Council for Fatwa and Research (ECFR) established in 1997.

These interdisciplinary bioethical deliberations are part of the broader phenomenon in the Islamic tradition, known as the collective religio-ethical reasoning (*al-ijtihād al-jamāʿī*), where Muslim religious scholars closely collaborate with specialists in fields from outside the conventional scope of religious sciences (*al-ʿulūm al-sharʿiyya*), viz., biomedical scientists in our case (Ghaly et al. 2016, 27–29). This mechanism of collective *ijtihād* produced two important documents for the field of Islamic bioethics, including addressing issues related to PC, namely the Islamic Code of Medical Ethics (*al-Dustūr al-Islāmī lil-Mihna al-Ṭibbiya*), issued in 1981 (IOIM 1981) and the International Islamic Code for Medical and Health Ethics (*al-Mīthāq al-Islāmī l-ʿĀlamī lil-Akhlāqiyyāt al-Ṭibbiya wa-l-Ṣiḥḥiyya*), issued in 2004 (al-Jundī 2005). The IOMS and IIFA provided important insights with relevance to PC-related issues in their publications on the concept of brain death, issued in January and December 1985 respectively (al-Madhkūr et al. 1985, 677–678; IIFA 2020,

50–51). The most relevant contribution to these discussions, however, comes from the IFA. During its 22nd session held in May 2015, the IFA discussed the theme "Withholding Treatment for the Patient of Incurable Condition" (*Īqāf al-ʿIlāj ʿan al-Marīḍ al-May'ūs min Bur'ih*), where both religious scholars and biomedical scientists deliberated on PC related issues (see IFA 2015a).

Other important types of sources for this study come from the *fatwā*s issued by national *fatwā* institutions. Examples of such institutions include the Permanent Committee for Scholarly Research and Issuing *Fatwā*s (al-Lajna al-Dā'ima lil-Buḥūth al-ʿIlmiyya wa-l-Iftā') and its sub-organ, the Council of Senior Religious Scholars (Hay'at Kibār al-ʿUlamā'), both from Saudi Arabia, as well as the *Fatwā* Department (Idārat al-Iftā') at the Kuwaiti Ministry of *Awqāf* and Islamic Affairs. The added values of the *fatwā*s issued by these institutions is that they sometimes address some detailed issues that are not covered in the recommendations or resolutions adopted by the transnational institutions. Additionally, these *fatwā*s sometimes have a direct impact at their national level, where hospitals affiliated with the Ministry of Health sometimes consult these institutions for religious advice.

Works published by individual Muslim scholars, specialists in Islamic Studies or biomedical scientists are also consulted, whenever relevant. Besides works published by Muslim physicians, like the Saudi Muḥammad ʿAlī l-Bārr (Mohammed Ali Al-Bar, b. 1939) (al-Bārr 1995; al-Bārr 2001; Al-Bar and Chamsi-Pasha 2015), the field of Islamic studies has witnessed an increasing number of publications in this area, mostly in Arabic (Abū Zayd 1996, 1:213–236; Barakāt 2006; al-Smāʿīl 2010; Ghaly et al. 2018; Ḥumayd and al-Mabrūkī 2019; ʿAnqāwī 2020; Ismāʿīl 2021). The authors of these publications provide important insights on how and where to find relevant classical discussions, but they are usually less competent when it comes to PC and its biomedical complexities and nuances. As for English language publications, the authors do rectify various misconceptions and fill serious gaps in English language scholarship on PC. However, one hardly finds in-depth engagement with the above-outlined three types of sources in most of these publications (Sachedina 2005; Zahedi et al. 2007; Bülow et al. 2008; Choong 2015; Kassim and Alias 2016; Padela and Qureshi 2017).

3 Life-Sustaining Treatments (LSTs)

One of the great biomedical advances of which modern medicine can be proud is introducing a range of medical interventions meant to keep patients with life-threatening conditions alive, or to forestall the moment of death, although they do not necessarily reverse the underlying condition. The umbrella term for these interventions is life-sustaining treatments (LSTs), which include famous examples like mechanical ventilation and cardiopulmonary resuscitation (CPR). In normal scenarios of reversible diseases and injuries, LSTs can be a life-saving treatment and would naturally be an integral part of the category of curative treatment. Within the Islamic tradition, this can be one of the rare cases where treatment can be judged as obligatory because the medical condition is life-threatening and the efficacy of the procedure to save the patient's life is certain or quasi-certain. However, these LSTs trigger serious ethical dilemmas within the context of life-limiting conditions. As explained above, the main target of PC is to minimise pain and improve the overall quality of the patient's life. In certain PC cases, the end of patient's life is approaching, and physicians estimate that death is imminent and unavoidable. Using LSTs in such cases can be a source of additional and prolonged pain and distress for the patient, something which goes contrary to the very aim of PC. On the other hand, many physicians estimate that the possible medical benefits of CPR and mechanical ventilation in such cases are minimal, almost non-existent, and thus their employment would be closer to medical futility and will eventually inflict harm rather than actual treatment or achieving benefit (al-Bārr 2015; Albar and Chamsi-Pasha 2018).

The ethical dilemmas in such cases revolve around key questions like: What should be done in such cases (forgo these LSTs and focus on minimising pain or initiate/continue them) and how should the decision-making process be managed in such situations? Muḥammad ʿAlī l-Bārr, one of the frequently participating physicians in the collective bioethical deliberations organised by the aforementioned IOMS, IFA and IIFA, stated that these questions represent some of the most vexing dilemmas for physicians working in the Arab and Muslim word, especially those who do not have an Islamic background (al-Bārr 2015, 13). In the analysis of the responses given to these questions within the Islamic tradition, this chapter differentiates between two main categories of LSTs, namely (a) CPR and mechanical ventilation, whose withdrawal for patients with terminal and life-threating diseases was supported by many authoritative voices in the contemporary Islamic bioethics field and (b) artificial nutrition and hydration (ANH), whose withdrawal remains controversial and more in-depth discussions are still needed.

Before delving into the details of these two categories, a word on some LSTs which received much less attention in the contemporary Islamic bioethical discourse is due. Few religious scholars or biomedical scientists expressed their views on withholding or withdrawing measures like renal dialysis and chemotherapy for patients with terminal diseases. The abovementioned *Fatwā*

Department in Kuwait held that patients with terminal and incurable diseases can forgo treatment when they contract new curable diseases, even if one of these new diseases may eventually lead to death. The reasoning provided by the *fatwā* for this position, with which some individual Muslim scholars and biomedical scientists agree, is that treatment in such cases remains a matter of probability and thus the act of seeking treatment would fall into the category of morally neutral or permissible acts rather than that of obligatory ones (al-Khādimī 2015, 27; al-Bārr 1995, 104; al-Bārr 2015, 30). The Jordanian Institution for issuing *fatwās* (*Dār al-Iftā'*) reached the same conclusion about the permissibility of forgoing dialysis for cancer patients, arguing that such procedures have no impact on either prolonging life or hastening death and they remain futile when it comes to achieving the aspired objective of recovery (*shifā'*) (Ismā'īl 2021, 163).

3.1 *Cardiopulmonary Resuscitation* (CPR) *and Mechanical Ventilation*

As explained above, the Islamic Fiqh Academy (IFA) is the main institution which dedicated a distinct session, held in 2015, to discussing the ethical issues related to (not) using LSTs like CPR and mechanical ventilation for terminal patients. The proceedings of this session show the existence of two main positions, which also dominate in the discussions of individual scholars. Before explaining the two positions and the religio-ethical reasoning developed by the advocates of each position, we need to realise that the participants in these IFA proceedings, and the majority of Muslim religious scholars, did not recognise morally significant differences between withholding and withdrawing these LSTs, although withdrawing (Ar., *īqāf*) was more frequently used in these discussions than withholding (Ar., *imtināʿ*).[2]

The advocates of the first position, consisting mainly of some individual religious scholars, like ʿAbd Allāh al-Jabūrī from the College of Islamic and Arabic Studies at Dubai, argued that withdrawing LSTs is categorically forbidden, and they equated it with intentional homicide (*al-qatl al-ʿamd*). The

2 The chapter included in this volume on withholding and withdrawing LSTs by Rafaqat Rashid also defended the same position. For the positions adopted by individuals, rather than institutions, some argued that withholding would be less controversial than withdrawing. Thus, they showed more flexibility in permitting the former but stressed that withdrawing LSTs, like mechanical ventilation, is only permissible under strict conditions. This holds true to the extent that some argued that withdrawing LSTs would only be permitted if the death of the respective patient has been firmly verified by a group of physicians. According to the advocates of this position, this conditional permission will not apply to the case of brain-dead patients, because brain death is not consensually recognised by medical professionals, they argued (see al-Smāʿīl 2010, 3760–3767; ʿAnqāwī 2020, 726–727).

governing perception here, argued the advocates of this position, is that LSTs should be approached as a life-saving measure and, thus, the juristic rulings pertinent to saving someone from death or life-threatening situations, included under terms like *inqādh* (saving) or *dafʿ al-halaka* (warding off death), should apply. Furthermore, employing medical treatments known to be effective in saving one's life are judged as an obligatory act by different Muslim jurists. Some religious scholars went as far as saying that this position even applies to braindead patients, especially the scholars who did not recognise death from an Islamic perspective, like the Kuwaiti ʿAbd Allāh Muḥammad ʿAbd Allāh and the Egyptian Tawfīq al-Wāʿī (d. 2019). The key arguments advanced by the advocates of this position revolved around two interrelated points. On one hand, they stressed the sanctity of human life by arguing that its preservation is not an option but rather an obligation imposed by God. On the other hand, they questioned the supposed irreversibility of the patient's medical condition or that his/her disease is incurable (*la yurjā bar'uh*). According to them, both the irreversibility and incurability of a health condition are relative in nature and these medical judgments are also timebound. Many diseases that used to be categorised as incurable, they explained, can later be easily cured. Some of them added the element of the physicians' fallibility and their susceptibility to make a mistaken diagnosis, thus judging a certain disease as incurable or life-threatening, even if this is not the case in reality. Additionally, the advocates of this position usually recalled the necessity of remaining optimistic and hopeful, especially for Muslims who believe in an Omnipotent God who is the true Healer (*al-Shāfī*). According to them, financial arguments related to forgoing LSTs as part of an "efficient" management of scarce resources is not in alignment with the value system inherent in the Higher Objectives of Sharīʿa (*maqāṣid al-Sharīʿa*), where preserving life is assigned higher priority than preserving money (al-Jabūrī 2015, 13–23; Jāb Allāh 2015, 13–14; ʿAnqāwī 2020, 659–661, 674–675).

The advocates of the second position comprised of both individual religious scholars and biomedical scientists, it was also included in the collective *fatwā*s issued by some of the above-mentioned institutions. According to the aforementioned physician, Muḥammad al-Bārr, almost all physicians advocated for this position (al-Bārr 2015, 27). The early document "Islamic Code of Medical Ethics," which was issued in the First International Conference on Islamic Medicine held in Kuwait in 1981, includes some phrases whose purport imply agreement with this position:

> In his defence of life, however, the Doctor is well advised to realise his limit and not transgress it. If it is scientifically certain that life cannot be

> restored, then it is futile to diligently keep on the vegetative state of the patient by heroic means of animation or preserve him by deep-freezing or other artificial methods. It is the process of life that the Doctor aims to maintain and not the process of dying. In any case, the Doctor shall not take a positive measure to terminate the patient's life.
>
> IOIM 1981, 67

Within this position, the perception of LSTs is different from that of the first position. According to advocates of the second position, LSTs are not life-saving measures because we are dealing with patients who either already died or on their irreversible way to die, with no possibility to re-wheel their health condition and bring them back to normal life. Against this background, withdrawing LSTs like CPR will not be approached as intentional homicide but as forgoing optional treatment whose harms usually override possible benefits, if any (Abū Zayd 1996, 1:233–234; al-Bārr 2015, 15–18; ʿAnqāwī 2020, 676–677).

Withdrawing LSTs from patients diagnosed with brain death, in particular, was already discussed and approved by institutions like the IOMS, IIFA and IIFA, whose position preceded the 2015 IFA deliberations. The IOMS and IIFA recognised brain death from an Islamic perspective in 1985. The resolution adopted by the IIFA clearly stated that resuscitation can be withdrawn in case of braindead patients, even if some organs keep working because of mechanical life-sustaining interventions. In its 10th session held in October 1987, the IFA reached the same conclusion about withdrawing LSTs although they did not recognise brain death as real death from an Islamic perspective (al-Madhkūr et al. 1985; 677–678; Jāb Allāh 2015, 8–9; al-Khādimī 2015, 25–27; IIFA 2020, 50–51). The 22nd session of the IFA held in 2015 focused on the cases of patients who suffered from life-threatening and incurable diseases but were not diagnosed with brain death. Besides declaring that euthanasia is strictly forbidden, the resolution adopted by the IFA stated that treatment can be withdrawn on the condition that three competent and trustworthy physicians decide that the respective treatment causes harm for the patient, instead of contributing to or improving his/her health condition. The resolution added that it is necessary, however, not to forgo the overall care for these patients by continuing nutrition and minimising pain as much as possible.[3] The same position was

3 The English translation of the exact wording of this item in the resolution would read, "It is not permissible to stop treating the patient unless three trustworthy specialist physicians decide that the treatment causes harm for the patient and has no effect on improving his condition. However, it remains significant to continue providing care for the patient represented in feeding him and removing or minimising pain as much as possible." The full text of the resolution is available in Arabic (see IFA 2015).

also adopted by the Dublin-based European Council for *Fatwā* and Research (ECFR) during its eleventh session, held in Stockholm on 1–7 July 2001, and by the International Islamic Code for Medical and Health Ethics, as clearly stated in article no. 62 (al-Jundī 2005, 96). Besides the *fatwā*s issued by these transnational institutions, other *fatwā*s issued by national committees in specific Muslim countries like Saudi Arabia and Kuwait also adopted the same position (al-Bārr 2015, 23–26; Jāb Allāh 2015, 12–18; al-Jibrīn 2015, 41–46; al-Khādimī 2015, 20–27). As we will see below, some of these *fatwā*s were impactful and had direct influence on how clinical care was regulated in national hospitals.

The advocates of the second position employed various arguments to defend their theses. For those who recognised brain death from an Islamic perspective, the ethical soundness of withdrawing LSTs like mechanical ventilation and CPR was straightforward, because there would be no benefit in keeping a dead person artificially alive through such mechanical tools. For patients who are still alive but suffer from life-threatening and incurable diseases, medical futility was a key argument. With the exception of critical remarks raised by some researchers about the vagueness of "futility" as a technical term (ʿAnqāwī 2020, 644–651), the mainstream discourse among the advocates of this position hardly questioned the issue. They argued that medical treatment (*tadāwī*) in the Islamic tradition is, in principle, optional or permissible but not obligatory, especially when the efficacy of the treatment is doubtful. In the case of patients with terminal diseases, they added, there is either certitude (*yaqīn*) or preponderant probability (*ẓann rājiḥ*) that employing these LSTs is futile (*ʿadīm al-jadwā*) in the sense that they will not treat the cause of the approaching death, viz., the life-threatening condition, and thus will not help restore the previously normal health condition or stabilise the patient's life. They argued that forgoing treatment (*tark al-tadāwī*) in such cases will not raise any ethical complications, and they quoted the works of early prominent religious scholars to support their position. Of particular significance to these modern discussions is al-Ghazālī's (d. 505/1111) explanation of the triple division of treatments whose efficacy will be either (a) certain (*maqṭūʿ bih*), (b) probable (*maẓnūn*) or (c) dubious (*mawhūm*). Only using treatments that fall within the first category will be obligatory in case of life-threatening conditions. Using LSTs, like CPR for patients, with terminal and incurable diseases would normally fall within the third category, and thus is usually discouraged (al-Ghazālī 2004, 4:283; Ghaly 2009, 118). In order to minimise the margin of mistaken medical diagnosis, the advocates of this position stipulated having a report signed by a team of three competent physicians. Additionally, they enumerated a list of possible harms, which would accrue from continuing LSTs in such cases. They spoke about financial losses which would either afflict the patient, his/her family, and/or the national healthcare system because the expenses of these LSTs are usually very high. They also hinted at the ethical aspects of the allocation of scarce resources, as hospitals usually have a limited number of LSTs like mechanical ventilators. If these LSTs would continue despite their medical futility in patients whose death is imminent, they explained, this will eventually be at the cost of other patients whose life can be saved by using such medical interventions. Another argument mentioned by some of the advocates of this position had to do with the concept of the dying process (*iḥtiḍār*) from an Islamic perspective. The process of *iḥtiḍār* is usually characterised with pains and agonies and continuing the LSTs will do nothing but prolong this process, although this is not in the best interest of the patient, even from the perspective of those who are eager to behave compassionately towards the patient (Abū Zayd 1996, 1:231–234; al-Bārr 2015, 10–11, 18–20, 45; Jāb Allāh 2015, 13–14; al-Jabūrī 2015, 19–20; al-Jibrīn 2015, 37–47; al-Khādimī 2015, 24–31).

One of the relevant and thorny questions in this context is about the identity of those who should be involved in the decision-making process about withdrawing LSTs and whose decision should override in case of disagreement. The collective *fatwā*s issued by the IOMS, IFA and IIFA are mostly silent about these questions. The modern studies, which examined the relevant dimensions of this issue in the pre-modern juristic discussions, argued that Muslim jurists have always given this right to the patient who has legal capacity, and if incapacitated, then to members of one's family in accordance with a specific order detailed in the *fiqh* manuals (ʿAnqāwī 2020, 837–858). On the other hand, the national *fatwā* committees and some biomedical scientists expressed relatively homogenous opinions, where the treating physicians were assigned a central role in the decision-making process. The Saudi physician Muḥammad al-Bārr spoke about different parties who needed to be involved, but he was inclined to entrust the treating physician with the authority of taking the ultimate decision. However, al-Bārr added, the treating physician should consult with at least two other physicians, who should all formally sign the decision to be included in the patient's file. Before implementing the decision, al-Bārr stressed, the idea of continuing or withdrawing LSTs should be consulted with the patient or, in case of incapacitation, the legally authorised guardian, who should have the right to refuse CPR, in addition to consulting with other family members (al-Bārr 2015, 31–32). Al-Bārr formulated his position in line with a number of *fatwā*s issued in Saudi Arabia by the abovementioned Council of Senior Religious Scholars and the Permanent Committee for Scholarly Research and Issuing *Fatwā*s. The most relevant example in this regard is *fatwa* no. 12086, issued in 1989 by the Council of Senior Religious Scholars whose full text was quoted by al-Bārr. Besides advocating the abovementioned second position, the *fatwā* univocally stated that the authority of taking CPR-related decisions should be exclusive to a medical team comprised of three physicians. The opinions expressed by the patient's family members, the *fatwā* issuers added, are not to be considered because continuing or withdrawing LSTs fall outside the scope of their expertise (al-Bārr 2015, 23–25).

Based on first-hand experience of palliative care (PC) physicians and intensivists working in the Gulf region, *fatwā*s which supported the above-outlined second position were embraced by various hospitals in the region and were taken into consideration when these hospitals developed their "do not resuscitate" (DNR) or "do not attempt resuscitation" (DNAR) policies.[4] Just as examples, one can refer to the Hamad Medical Corporation (HMC) in Qatar, North West Armed Forces Hospital (NWAFH) and King Faisal Specialist Hospital and Research Center in Saudi Arabia. The DNR policies adopted by these hospitals and all DNR documents drafted by these medical institutions all named the above-mentioned *fatwā* no. 12086, which was issued in response to a question raised by the NWAFH medical vice-president, as one of their main religious references.[5] Although they all adopted the standpoint that the medical team has the authority to take the ultimate decision, the written policies adopted by these hospitals, and their actual practices, underscore the significance of involving patients and their families in the decision-making process (al-Ayed and Rahmo 2014; Bharani 2018).

3.2 *Artificial Nutrition and Hydration* (ANH)[6]

The formulation of the aforementioned IFA resolution adopted in May 2015 was generic in nature and even vague on certain points. The third item of the resolution reads:

> It is not permissible to stop treating the patient unless three trustworthy specialist physicians decide that the treatment causes harm for the patient and has no effect on improving his condition. However, it remains

4 For more details about this topic, especially as it relates to patients with dementia, see the chapter in this volume written by Hadil Lababidi.

5 As part of the research conducted while working on an earlier publication (Ghaly et al. 2016), I had access to the DNR documents developed by the Hamad Medical Corporation (HMC) in Qatar and the North West Armed Forces Hospital (NWAFH) in Saudi Arabia. The NWAFH is undated whereas the HMC document had two versions, the first one goes as far back to August 2004 and the updated version was dated October 2017.

6 For more details about this topic, especially as it relates to the patients with dementia, see Hadil Lababidi's chapter in this volume.

> significant to continue providing care for the patient represented in feeding him and removing or minimising pain as much as possible.[7]

Based on the papers submitted to the IFA session, one can conclude that the resolution was surely referring to the possibility of withdrawing CPR and mechanical ventilation. The phrase "it remains significant to continue providing care for the patient represented in feeding him," would possibly refer to the thesis that forgoing artificial nutrition and hydration (ANH) should be judged as unethical or, at least, not the best practice from an Islamic perspective. In all cases, the formula "it remains significant to continue providing care" is not the standard language in Islamic jurisprudence (*fiqh*) employed to reveal a juristic ruling (*ḥukm fihqī*). This implicit standpoint was explicitly phrased and defended by Muḥammad al-Bārr in his paper submitted to the IFA session (al-Bārr 2015, 31, 48). In the book he co-authored with the Saudi-based cardiologist Ḥassān Shamsī Bāshā (Hassan Chamsi-Pasha, b. 1951), *Contemporary Bioethics: Islamic Perspective* (Al-Bar and Chamsi-Pasha 2015), the unethical character and outright prohibition of withdrawing ANH was also reiterated. The authors held that this procedure would lead to a terrible death, even worse than euthanasia, because it would take the patient ten to fourteen days suffering from hunger and thirst before their actual death. They strongly disagreed with those who classify ANH as a medical procedure, which can be judged as futile in certain cases (Al-Bar and Chamsi-Pasha 2015, 126, 246). In agreement with two law professors from Malaysia and Nigeria, al-Bārr and Shamsī Bāshā viewed ANH as part of human's basic necessities to survive and a mandatory part of comfort care. That is why they concluded that preventing ANH is a clear-cut case of homicide (Kassim and Adeniyi 2010, 457–458; Al-Bar and Chamsi-Pasha 2015, 246).

Concerning the medical aspects, there are PC physicians, with experience as practicing physicians and authors in this field, who disagreed with the thesis that withdrawing ANH would increase the suffering of the patient. To support this position, they referred to the role of the gastrointestinal (GI) tract; the organ in human bodies responsible for taking in food, digesting it to extract and absorb energy and nutrients, and then expelling the remaining waste as faeces. They argued that this organ becomes dysfunctional in some patients with advanced terminal illnesses, including cancer and advanced progressive dementia. Also, patients with diseases like end stage cancer often suffer difficulty in mobilising fluid from their bodies and it eventually accumulates in unwanted places such as the abdomen and lungs. This means that

7 The full text of the resolution is available in Arabic (see IFA 2015).

ANH for such patients may exacerbate their already failing health conditions. Strikingly enough, providing the benefit of alleviating the symptom of hunger also becomes doubtful because most dying patients do not experience hunger, as their overall organ systems are, simply, shutting down (Ghaly et al. 2018, 11–12, 32–33).

As for the religio-ethical dimensions, some researchers argued that both withholding and withdrawing ANH is equally prohibited. They argued that this position is in line with the agreement of many early Muslim jurists that eating and drinking is obligatory and feeding the patient should be implemented, even if this was against his/her will, whenever it is necessary for saving human life or warding off an approaching death (ʿAnqāwī 2020, 385, 706–707, 732). As outlined above, drawing an analogy between classical discussions on saving life by having food and drinks, on one hand, and ANH for terminal patients, on the other hand, is, medically speaking, problematic because the likelihood of saving life, or achieving medical benefit for patients, is not the same in both cases.

As for the position adopted by al-Bārr and Shamsī Bāshā, they based it on an analogy drawn between withdrawing ANH and a paradigm case addressed in pre-modern works of Islamic jurisprudence (*fiqh*), namely detaining a person in an isolated place and denying him/her food and drink, till death occurs. In this paradigm case, the majority of pre-modern Muslim jurists stated that the detainer will be held liable for the death of the detainee (Kassim and Adeniyi 2010, 458). However, the soundness of this analogy can be questioned at various points. The classical juristic discussions on this paradigm case, sometimes called *qatl al-ṣabr*, was discussed within the context of differentiating between various types of homicide and the scenarios that would make the perpetrator liable to the death penalty (*qiṣāṣ*) or paying blood money (*diya*), depending on different factors, including the perpetrator's intention to terminate the victim's life (al-Kāsānī 1986, 7:234–235; al-Ramlī 1984, 7:251–253; al-Dasūqī n.d., 4:242–243).

These classical sources speak about detaining someone with normal health conditions in a house or a closed area and preventing this person from food and drink till death occurs. In this paradigm case, there is no doubt about that the perpetrator's evil intention of harming the victim by depriving him from food and water. However, the treating physician in the case of the patient with terminal disease has no intention of harming. On the contrary, PC teams always stress that the main aim of all measures administered by them is to minimise the pains of the patient. Also, the victim with a normal health condition in the paradigm case, who could have lived further had he had access to food and water, cannot be equated with the patient admitted to the PC unit. The latter is approaching the end-of-life anyhow, with no hope of restoring normal health condition. Instead of using homicide or *qatl al-ṣabr* as the governing frame, other approaches would be more appropriate. One of these approaches is the Prophetic tradition (*ḥadīth*) which reads "Do not force your patients to [consume] food or drinks. Truly, God feeds and waters them." Pre-modern Muslim jurists used to quote this *ḥadīth* within the context of their discussions on medical treatment (*tadāwī*). The point of quoting this scriptural reference is to indicate that patients should not be forced to take medication or nutrition because this may cause harm to them and thus eventually lead to an unfavourable outcome (al-Ramlī 1984, 3:19; Wizārat al-Awqāf 1983–2006, 31:80). Indeed, some of these pre-modern jurists, like Ibn al-Qayyim (d. 751/1350), stated that physicians of their time agreed with this conclusion (Ibn al-Qayyim n.d., 68–71).

Against the above-sketched backdrop, the thesis advocated by some voices in contemporary Islamic bioethics that withdrawing ANH is, morally speaking, equal to murder does not do justice to the complexity of this topic. The reasoning advanced for defending this argument is not flawless and there are other potential, possibly even more well-argued, venues for approaching this topic. Further interdisciplinary research is direly needed to come up with nuanced and well-argued positions that take into consideration both the medical aspects and the religio-ethical dimensions of related issues.

4 Administering Analgesics: Dying without Pain or with a Clear Mind?

Helping people minimise their pains has been seen as a great value throughout human history, not only in the Islamic tradition but in almost all other religious and non-religious ethical traditions. Biomedical sciences have made invaluable contributions to this noble value by developing various mechanisms, including analgesics or pain-relieving drugs. Within the context of PC, especially for terminally ill patients when the medical condition cannot be reversed through curative drugs, controlling the symptoms and minimising the patient's pains become much more valuable and needed. The more the pain gets severe, intractable and unbearable, the more complex the process of pain management becomes. In simple cases, non-opioids like regular aspirin or paracetamol can do the job. In difficult and extreme cases, however, opioid drugs like morphine may be necessary to relieve pain. At certain doses, besides the benefit of relieving or minimising pain, such drugs can also induce decreased awareness or cause the complete loss of one's consciousness, which can be considered harmful from social and religious perspectives. Additionally, the so-called "palliative sedation" or "terminal sedation" process is sometimes initiated as the last resort to manage intractable pain. Usually this happens shortly before death, for a period which can range between few hours and few days. Besides the harm of suppressing one's consciousness, high doses of these analgesics or administering palliative sedation also entail the risk of eventually hastening death or shortening the patient's life and thus comes closer, in the eyes of some ethicists, to "slow euthanasia" or "euthanasia in disguise."

This section addresses two key questions within the context of PC: How does one strike balance between achieving the benefit of managing pain, on one hand, while avoiding the harm of suppressing consciousness, on the other hand? Would the foreseen, although unintended, effect of shortening one's life make the administration of pain-relieving drugs or analgesics unethical, despite the benefit of relieving the intractable pain of a dying patient?

Concerning the first question, heroic anecdotes about pious figures in Islamic history relate their preference to bearing pain, no matter how intense, in order to keep their consciousness intact. The story of ʿUrwa b. al-Zubayr (d. *c.*95/713) is exemplary in this regard. When doctors wanted to amputate his gangrenous foot before the gangrene spread throughout his body, they advised him to use an anaesthetic tool (*murqid*), which would make him temporarily unconscious so that he would not feel the excruciating pain of amputation. ʿUrwa refused taking the *murqid* and insisted on remaining conscious so that he would receive God's reward for being patient with these agonies (al-Dhahabī 1993, 6:427). ʿUrwa's story represents the ideal that some Muslims may want to reach, rather than the norm whose violation will be unethical from an Islamic perspective. Both pre-modern and contemporary Muslim jurists agreed that intentional suppression of one's consciousness is, in principle, forbidden. However, they stated that the legal maxim "necessity overrides prohibition" (*al-ḍarūrāt tubīḥ al-maḥẓūrāt*) entails permitting drugs which undermine consciousness in case of medical necessity, which encompasses a wide range of medical procedures including surgeries (al-Shinqīṭī 1994, 273–288). This means that it is in principle ethically defensible, from an Islamic perspective, to sacrifice, to an extent, mental consciousness when the medical condition cannot be treated otherwise.

Against this background, the default rule within the context of PC would be as following: in order to ethically justify reducing the patient's level of consciousness, which is in principle a harm, there should be a proportionately serious or compelling reason, which will be seen as a benefit. In this regard, the so-called "pain ladder" or "analgesic ladder" developed by the World Health Organization (WHO) can be helpful. This classification is increasingly gaining wide recognition among medical professionals for the management of all types of pain. According to this classification, the physician starts with drugs placed at the bottom (non-opioid), then climbs the ladder to the middle point (mild opioid) if pain persists, and then prescribes the drugs placed at the top of the ladder (strong opioids), if there are compelling medical reasons (Watson et al. 2009, 228–230). The influences of escalating doses of opioid drugs on the patient's consciousness widely vary; starting from partial and temporary loss of consciousness, and then escalating in volume and length until it reaches the top, namely total and permanent abolition of consciousness. Partial and temporary loss of consciousness can be justified on the ground of much less compelling reasons than is the case of total but temporary or partial but *permanent* loss of consciousness. In all these scenarios, the PC interdisciplinary team need to keep in mind the significance of practicing religious rituals for the patient. For instance, performing ritual prayer five times a day is a religious obligation on adult Muslims, no matter how poor their physical health condition may be. The poor health condition can entitle patients to certain concessions like performing the prayers in a shortened form (*qaṣr*) and/or combining two prayers at one time (*jamʿ*) or exempting some patients from standing, bowing, prostrating or other physical movements which can be a source of hardship for them. While planning the process of pain management, the PC team needs to schedule enough time for this religious ritual, whose performance necessitates the consciousness of the patient.

Terminal sedation in particular, which would result in total and permanent loss of consciousness, is the most controversial procedure in this regard. On one hand, one may argue that terminal sedation does not greatly differ from the general anaesthesia, which also induces total loss of consciousness, in some surgeries. Especially when it is administered only for the last few hours before death, terminal sedation used to relieve a dying patient from intractable and unbearable pain, can be analogous to the use of general anaesthesia during open heart surgery. General anaesthesia has been widely accepted by Muslim religious scholars and, so, terminal sedation, under certain conditions, can be tolerated too. On the other hand, one can still note significant differences between these two procedures which would make the moral judgment of general anaesthesia, and that of terminal sedation, far from being similar. Although the loss of consciousness in both procedures is total and can even continue for a longer period in the case of general anaesthesia than in terminal sedation, it remains temporary in the case of general anaesthesia. In the case of terminal sedation, however, loss of consciousness can be permanent if it continues till the patient's death. This permanent character of the total abolition of consciousness has its own costs at the religious and social levels. For instance, the patient is usually recommended to utter the formula of *shahāda*, by saying "There is no god but God and that Muḥammad is the Messenger of God," when one feels that he/she is at death's door. At the social level, both the patient and the family will not have the opportunity to be in conscious contact with each other during the very last hours, and to say goodbye; a situation which can be quite distressful for all of them.

Now, we move to the second question; Would the foreseen, although unintended, effect of shortening one's life make the administration of analgesics unethical despite the benefit of relieving the intractable pain of a dying patient? In mainstream bioethical literature, the double effect principle (DEP), originally developed within the Catholic tradition, is usually invoked to address this question. The starting point here is that almost all actions, including the morally sound ones, can produce a plurality of results, not all of which are necessarily good and not all of them are always intended. The purport of the DEP is that if doing something morally good has a morally bad side-effect, it will be ethically accepted to do it as long as the bad side-effect is not intended, even if this side-effect was already foreseen (Boyle 2015). Within the context of administering analgesics for PC patients, the morally good act is reducing the patient's pain whereas the foreseen, although unintended, morally bad side-effect can be hastening the patient's death or shortening his/her life. Ethicists disagree on the validity of the DEP in general and on its relevance to the PC context as well. Within the Islamic tradition, the European Council for Fatwa and Research (ECFR) and the abovementioned Islamic Organization for Medical Sciences (IOMS) organised discussions on this question. The ECFR addressed this question in its resolution on "Euthanasia," which was adopted in the eleventh session held in May 2003. Without providing details about the rationale of their position, the scenario outlined in the abovementioned question was classified in the ECRF resolution as one of the forbidden categories of euthanasia, titled "Indirect Euthanasia," even if it was approved or recommended by the treating physicians (Jāb Allāh 2015, 16; Ghaly 2015). Also, the aforementioned Permanent Committee for Scholarly Research and Issuing *Fatwā*s issued a *fatwā* that goes in line with this position (ʿAnqāwī 2020, 828). On the other hand, the IOMS reached a different conclusion, which was recorded in the aforementioned International Islamic Code for Medical and Health Ethics. In its sixty-second article, the Code mentioned three cases, which should not be equated with the prohibited euthanasia and are thus considered permissible. The third case was "intensifying the administration of a strong medication to prevent a severe pain, despite knowing that this medication may ultimately end the patient's life." No detailed reasoning was provided to justify this position from an Islamic perspective. Just in the form of straightforward bullet-points, reference was made to three of the Higher Objectives of Sharīʿa, namely preserving life, intellect and honour, in addition to two broad principles, viz., lifting hardship from Muslim communities (*umma*) and achieving benefits and avoiding harms (al-Jundī 2005, 96).

The modern studies which examined the use of LSTs from an Islamic perspective showed that classical works on Islamic jurisprudence and more particularly, the Higher Objectives of Sharīʿa can be of benefit in finetuning and tightening these discussions and also in narrowing the gap between these different perspectives by drafting more nuanced positions (Ghaly et al. 2016, 33–35; ʿAnqāwī 2020, 800–803, 823–824; Ismāʿīl 2021, 160). To start with, administering high doses of opioids to relieve severe pain as part of end-of-life care may not necessarily entail hastening death but other possible side-effects like respiratory depression and hypotension. In such cases, the benefit-harm assessment can be done more easily than in the case of hastening death, and the decision of administering these drugs can be taken. In the case of hastening death as a possible side-effect, the (un)likelihood of the occurrence of this side-effect plays a significant role in the process of benefit-harm assessment. When the side effect of hastening death is almost an inevitable outcome, then the mere absence of intending this result will not weigh heavily in this process. The paradigm case mentioned in classical juristic sources of digging a water well in the middle of a public road can be of relevance in this regard. Digging a water well is a morally good act, especially in the pre-modern context of water scarce areas like the Arabian Peninsula, but doing this in the middle of a public road can lead to injuries and even deaths among people and animals who would make use of the road. The harm of causing injuries or deaths cannot tolerated, Muslim jurists explained, by arguing that the good act of getting water was the intended one, whereas harming others was unintended. This is because the unintended harm is very likely to happen in the case of a public road. The ethical judgement would be different if digging the water well was inside one's house because the possibility that people and animals would fall in it is unlikely (al-Kāsānī 1986, 7:23, 224). Some of the practicing PC physicians held that appropriate use of analgesics is actually the most effective way of achieving pain and dyspnoea control and may even reduce the incidence of unwanted and unintended side effects, including hastening death (Ghaly et al. 2016, 11). By recalling the terminology of the abovementioned paradigm case, it seems that the appropriate use of analgesics within the PC context will make it closer to digging the water well inside one's house rather than in the public road.

5 Communicating Bad/Sad News: Truth or Compassion at the Sick/Death Bed?

Some of the complex questions that sometimes create vexing dilemmas in the PC context include: Which health-related information should the PC physician communicate, to whom, and how? What adds to the complexity of these questions is that they not only have to do with specific religious precepts and values but with cultural mores and traditions and, also, with intergenerational and individual differences. Below, this chapter addresses the ethical issues related to such questions from an Islamic ethical perspective.

Although the Eastern-Western dichotomy of moral values is a contested division, available literature, supported by empirical evidence, shows different responses and attitudes to the abovementioned questions in "Western" countries like the United States of America and Europe, compared to "Eastern" countries like Japan, Korea and China (Schapira and Steensma 2013, 36–37, 39). Even if we accepted this dichotomy, the problems of dealing with the treatment issues of Muslim patients still persist because they live not only in Muslim-majority countries, most of which fall under the "Eastern" category; yet they also live in the US and Europe where many of them were born and raised and thus their cultural identity, at least partially, would have "Western" components. Thus, physicians need to be careful of such possible cultural nuances when they deal with Muslim patients and try to avoid stereotyping, or use essentialist postulations, how a Muslim patient would behave.

As far as the Islamic tradition is concerned, there are certain values to which Muslims, irrespective of their cultural background, are to be committed. To start with, deliberate communication of incorrect information is a violation of the virtue of truthfulness (*ṣidq*), or in bioethical terms the principle of veracity, that physicians are expected to cultivate and to abide by in their relationship with the patient (al-Shinqīṭī 1994, 459–462). This means that being compassionate for, and caring about, the patient's feelings, in principle, does not make a sufficient ethical ground for lying to the patient. Having settled this point, would it be ethically acceptable to communicate factual information related to the patient's approaching death? If we extract normative morality from the famous incident of the murder of the second Muslim caliph, ʿUmar b. al-Khaṭṭāb (d. 23/644), then the answers to this question will be yes. When the caliph was stabbed six times by his assassin, the physician[8] examined him and then came to the conclusion that the injury was fatal, with no survival chance. So, the physician said to the caliph: "Make your will (*awṣi*). I believe that it is just one or two days before you die." The caliph commented by saying: "He told me the truth and had he said something else, I would not have believed him" (al-ʿAsqalānī 1960, 7:64–65). This anecdote shows that neither ʿUmar b. al-Khaṭṭāb nor the people around him, including family members

8 In some historical reports, it is related that he was examined by more than one physician.

and prominent Companions of the Prophet of Islam, were offended by the way the physician conveyed such bad news. In the literature produced within the Islamic tradition about the etiquettes of the physician (*adab al-ṭabīb*), it has been reiterated that there is no harm that the physician, when observing the signs of approaching death, communicates such news to the patient. However, the recommendation was to do this in a gentle way, e.g., by saying: "Make you will (*awṣi*)," in reference to the will that Muslims must prepare before their death. This ethical position remains the dominant one among contemporary Muslim religious scholars and biomedical scientists (IIFA 1993, 8:1179, 1251, 1443).

The recognised virtue of telling the truth in the Islamic tradition does not mean that other virtues, like compassion, should be assigned an insignificant role in the physician-patient relationship, to the extent that bad news is communicated in a blunt and compassionless way. Being compassionate to, and considerate of, the feelings of patients is instrumental in keeping them hopeful and able to cope with their poor health condition. According to a tradition attributed to the Prophet of Islam, people who pay a visit to a patient are recommended to be cautious about their words, and to select hope-giving words because they would relieve the patient's agony (al-ʿAsqalānī 1960, 10:122). As mentioned above, bad/sad but truthful information about the patient's approaching end-of-life should be communicated through gentle words (*luṭf min al-qawl*). The above-mentioned expression "make your will (*awṣi*)" was a culturally accepted metaphorical reference to the approaching death. This phrase can always be replaced with other (metaphorical) expressions, which can communicate the physician's disturbing message in a culturally accepted way. The exact wording is something to be left to the prudence of the physician and the palliative care (PC) team. However, it is important to make sure that using a metaphor is not negatively obscuring the truth. Sharing expectations about an exact survival time, or numerical estimates of life expectancy, can be negatively perceived by some Muslims. Although such information was communicated in the aforementioned historical incident of ʿUmar b. al-Khaṭṭāb, it remains problematic and, sometimes, even shocking for some Muslims who may think that making such estimations goes contrary to their belief that the exact moment of someone's death is exclusively known to God. The points outlined above are premised on the following statement in the above-mentioned Islamic Code of Medical Ethics:

> The Doctor shall comply with the patient's right to know his illness. The Doctor's particular way of answering should, however, be tailored to the particular patient in question. It is the Doctor's duty to thoroughly study the psychological acumen of his patient. He shall never fall short

> of suitable vocabulary if the situation warrants the deletion of frightening nomenclature or coinage of new names, expressions or descriptions.
> IOIM 1981, 68

Finally, to whom should this bad/sad news be communicated? The straightforward response should be the patient in the first instance. Within the Islamic tradition, the real owner of the human body is the One who Created it, namely God but each individual behaves in the capacity of a trustee (*mu'taman*) for his/her body. Based on this understanding and the famous legal maxim "Nobody is allowed to dispose what belong to others without their consent," the mainstream position among both pre-modern and contemporary Muslim religious scholars is that gaining the patient's consent is mandatory before examining his/her body (Ghaly et al. 2016, 38). Further, one needs to be aware that patients have the right *to know* about their health condition but, equally, also have the right *not to know*, or to assign someone else as a focal point for discussions with the treating physician. That is why the PC team needs to show a certain degree of cultural humility and not to think that empowering patients should mean that they have to know everything about their health. It is always recommended that physicians make an exploratory conversation with the patient first, in order to discuss what each party can expect from the other. As long as the patient has the capacity to effectively communicate with the treating physician, then priority should be given to the patient's wishes. Family members can always be engaged in discussions and their opinions can be considered, but not at the cost of what the patient wants. If the patient is unable to communicate, then a discussion with the family should take place. Both classical and modern juristic discussions provided a list of family members, in a prioritised order, who are entitled to be the legally representative guardian, or proxy decision maker. All these discussions demonstrate that there is flexibility in determining who should be on the list and who should have a higher priority in decision-making than others ('Anqāwī 2020, 853–858). That is why the recommended course of action for the PC team, in this particular context, is to ask the family members to appoint one specific representative whose opinion, including the case of knowing or not knowing, will be followed whenever there is internal disagreement within the family.

6 Conclusion

Contemporary Islamic bioethical deliberations display diverse perspectives on the themes that were examined throughout this chapter. These concluding remarks provide a concise overview of these perspectives and how they can be situated within the broad spectrum of the Islamic bioethical discourse, especially in light of the authoritative, but still non-binding, positions adopted by transnational Islamic institutions. For life-sustaining treatments (LSTs), forgoing the medical interventions of cardiopulmonary resuscitation (CPR) and mechanical ventilation was conditionally permitted by almost all institutions and Muslim biomedical scientists whose contributions were examined in this chapter, in addition to many individual religious scholars. The scope of support for this position was wider in the case of brain-dead patients. Forgoing artificial nutrition and hydration (ANH), however, proved to controversial, where institutions were silent on this issue, and some individual biomedical scientists and religious scholars held that it is equal to homicide. This study argued for the need to critically revise this generalised position and that permitting ANH can be defended in some exceptional cases, including when the patient's whole organ system has shut down, to the extent that food and water cannot be digested and the patient would not feel hungry or thirsty and, thus, ANH will be more of a burden or harm than benefit.

Concerning the dilemma of managing conflicting values in the PC context, the chapter examined two themes. For using analgesics or pain-relieving drugs, it is clear that the higher the need for reducing severe pain, the more likely religious scholars will permit using such drugs, even if they would result in temporary or partial loss of consciousness. Further, it is advised to design culturally and religiously sensitive PC plans that would accommodate the desires of patients to maintain a reasonable state of consciousness for a period long enough to perform religious rituals or properly bid farewell to family and friends. That is why the terminal sedation that causes permanent and full loss of consciousness remains controversial and would only be permitted under quite exceptional circumstances. The last theme examined in this chapter was the dilemma of balancing between the value of veracity and that of compassion while communicating bad/sad news about the patient's deteriorating health or approaching death. Both classical and contemporary deliberations show clear preference for prioritising the value of truthfulness. On one hand, without having compelling reasons to do otherwise, lying is categorically prohibited in Islam. On the other hand, not revealing certain information to the patient at his/her own request is morally justified out of respect for his/her right of "not willing to know." To honour the value of compassion, the agreed-upon moral obligation is to communicate such bad news in a "gentle way" to keep the possible side effect of offending others to the minimum, but the exact formula to be used differs from time to time and from place to place, depending on different circumstantial and cultural factors.

Finally, a rigorous anatomy of the differing Islamic perspectives on the themes examined in this chapter shows that a great deal of these differences has to do with (not) perceiving significant particularities of palliative medicine. Unlike the mainstream curative medicine, at least an important part of palliative medicine deals with patients whose life is departing and death is approaching, according to available medical knowledge. Thus, the main, or possibly even the only realistic, objective of this branch of medicine is to make this in-between phase of the patient's life as comfortable as possible. Sometimes, certain medical interventions might contradict this very philosophy of palliative medicine because they will just prolong this in-between phase, with all its agonies. Judging any of the dilemmas related to palliative medicine should be preceded by determining first whether this perception applies to the question at hand. If it is the case, then jumping to classical discussions about saving a drowning person and building up possible analogies with modern LSTs or analgesics will be of no avail. Pre-modern discussions that can be of relevance here, I argue, would be the explanation provided by al-Ghazālī for the phenomenon of refusing treatment among many pious Muslims. According to him, one of the possible reasons behind this phenomenon is that one would come to know about their imminent death that cannot be defended by medical treatment. Although al-Ghazālī explained that these pious Muslims usually receive such information, by way of visionary experience (*mukāshafa*), from God, the possibility of reaching the same conclusion through other channels that would convey less certain information, e.g., intuition (*ḥads*) and guesswork (*ẓann*), should not be crossed out (al-Ghazālī 2004, 4:287).

Bibliography

Abū Zayd, Bakr. 1996. *Fiqh al-Nawāzil*. Beirut: Mu'assasat al-Risāla.

ʿAnqāwī, Ṭāriq. 2020. *Aḥkām Qarārāt al-ʿIlājāt al-Musānida lil-Ḥayāt*. Riyad: Dār Rakā'iz lil-Nashr wa-l-Tawzīʿ.

al-ʿAsqalānī, Ibn Ḥajar. 1960. *Fatḥ al-Bārī: Sharḥ Ṣaḥīḥ al-Bukhārī*. Beirut: Dār al-Maʿrifa.

al-Ayed, Tareq and Nabil Rahmo. 2014. "Do Not Resuscitate Orders in a Saudi Pediatric Intensive Care Unit." *Saudi Medical Journal* 35(6): 561–565.

al-Bārr, Muḥammad ʿAlī. 1995. *Aḥkām al-Tadāwī wa-l-Ḥālāt al-May'ūs Minhā*. Jedda: Dār al-Manāra lil-Nashr wa-l-Tawzīʿ.

al-Bārr, Muḥammad ʿAlī. 2001. *Mawt al-Qalb aw Mawt al-Dimāgh*. Jedda: al-Dār al-Saʿūdiyya lil-Nashr wa-l-Tawzīʿ.

al-Bārr, Muḥammad ʿAlī. 2015. "Al-Tadāwī Qurb Nihāyat al-Ḥayāt wa-l-Inʿāsh al-Qalbī l-Ri'awī." Paper submitted to the 22nd session of the Islamic Fiqh Academy (IFA),

Mecca, 10–13 May. An online version is available at http://ar.themwl.org/sites/default/files/Fiqh220405.pdf.

Al-Bar, Mohammed Ali and Hassan Chamsi-Pasha. 2015. *Contemporary Bioethics: Islamic Perspective*. Dordrecht: Springer.

Albar, Mohammed Ali and Hassan Chamsi-Pasha. 2018. "Futility of Medical Treatment." *International Journal of Human and Health Sciences* 2(1): 13–17.

Barakāt, Ḍirār. 2006. "Al-Imtināʿ ʿan al-ʿIlāj wa-l-Muʿālaja." MA thesis, Yarmouk University, Jordan.

Bharani, Tina, Y. Li, I. Helmy, L. Menon, S.M. Arachchige, M. Soliman, Y. Wen, K. Silla, Y. Othman, G. Sadek, A. Bashir, H. Eltahir, S. Eziada, A. Allam and A. Hassan. 2018. "Palliative Care in Qatar, 2008–2016." *Journal of Palliative Care & Medicine* 8(1): 1–8.

Boyle, Joseph. 2015. "The Relevance of Double Effect to Decisions About Sedation at the End of Life." In *Sedation at the End-of-life: An Interdisciplinary Approach*, edited by Paulina Taboada, 55–71. Dordrecht: Springer.

Bülow, Hans-Henrik, Charles L. Sprung, Konrad Reinhart, Shirish Prayag, Bin Du, Apostolos Armaganidis, Fekri Abroug and Mitchell M. Levy. 2008. "The World's Major Religions' Points of View on End-Of-Life Decisions in The Intensive Care Unit." *Intensive Care Medicine* 34(3): 423–430.

Choong, K.A. 2015. "Islam and Palliative Care." *Global Bioethics* 26(1): 28–42.

al-Dasūqī, Ibn ʿArafa. n.d. *Ḥāshiyat al-Dasūqī ʿalā al-Sharḥ al-Kabīr*. Beirut: Dār al-Fikr.

al-Dhahabī, Shams al-Dīn. 1993. *Tārīkh al-Islām*, edited by ʿUmar ʿAbd al-Salām al-Tadmurī. Beirut: Dār al-Kitāb al-ʿArabī.

Didier, Jean-Pierre and Emmanuel Bigand. 2010. *Rethinking Physical and Rehabilitation Medicine: New Technologies Induce New Learning Strategies*. Dordrecht: Springer.

Ghaly, Mohammed. 2009. *Islam and Disability: Perspectives in Theology and Jurisprudence*. London: Routledge.

Ghaly, Mohammed. 2015. "Euthanasia." *Encyclopaedia of Islam, Three*, 2015–1: 117–118. Leiden: Brill. DOI: 10.1163/1573-3912_ei3_COM_26254.

Ghaly, Mohammed, Eman Sadoun, Fowzan Alkuraya, Khalid Fakhro, Ma'n Zawati, Said Ismail and Tawfeg Ben-Omran. 2016. *Genomics in the Gulf Region and Islamic Ethics*. Doha: World Innovation Summit for Health. www.wish.org.qa/wp-content/uploads/2021/08/023E.pdf.

Ghaly, Mohammed, Randi R. Diamond, Maha El-Akoum and Azza Hassan. 2018. *Palliative Care and Islamic Ethics: Exploring Key Issues and Best Practice*. Doha: World Innovation Summit for Health.

al-Ghazālī, Abū Ḥāmid. 2004. *Iḥyāʾ ʿUlūm al-Dīn*, edited by Badawī Ṭibāna. Beirut: Dār al-Maʿrifa.

Grech, Godfrey and Iris Grossman, eds. 2015. *Preventive and Predictive Genetics: Towards Personalised Medicine*. Dordrecht: Springer.

al-Ḥakīm al-Tirmidhī. 1992. *Nawādir al-Uṣūl*, edited by ʿAbd al-Raḥmān ʿUmayra. Beirut: Dār al-Jīl.

Ḥumayd, Bāsim and al-Ṭayyib al-Mabrūkī. 2019. "Aḥkām al-Imtināʿ ʿan Muʿālajat al-Amrāḍ al-Mayʾūs min Shifāʾihā." *Majallat al-Rāsikhūn* 5(1): 29–58.

Ibn al-Qayyim. n.d. *Al-Ṭibb al-Nabawī*. Beirut: Dār al-Hilāl.

IFA (Islamic Fiqh Academy). 2015a. "Īqāf ʿIlāj al-Marīḍ al-Mayʾūs min Barʾih." *Al-Muslim*. https://almoslim.net/node/233659.

IFA (Islamic Fiqh Academy). 2015b. "Jadwal Aʿmāl al-Dawra al-Thāniya wa-l-ʿIshrūn." *Al-Majmaʿ al-Fiqhī l-Islāmī*. https://ar.themwl.org/node/138.

IIFA (International Islamic Fiqh Academy). 1993. *Majallat Majmaʿ al-Fiqh al-Islāmī* 8. Jedda: International Islamic Fiqh Academy.

IIFA (International Islamic Fiqh Academy). 2020. *Qarārāt wa-Tawṣiyyāt Majmaʿ al-Fiqh al-Islāmī l-Dawlī*. Jedda: Islamic International Islamic Fiqh Academy.

IOIM (International Organization for Islamic Medicine). 1981. *Al-Dustūr al-Islāmī lil-Mihna al-Ṭibbiya*. Kuwait: International Organization for Islamic Medicine.

Ismāʿīl, Ardwān. 2021. "Riʿāyat Nihāyat Ḥayāt al-Marīḍ min Manẓūr al-Akhlāq al-Islāmiyya." *Majallat Zankū lil-ʿUlūm al-Islāmiyya* 25(2): 153–167.

Jāb Allāh, Aḥmad. 2015. "Īqāf al-ʿIlāj ʿan al-Marīḍ al-Mayʿūs min Burʾih." Paper submitted to the 22nd session of the Islamic Fiqh Academy (IFA), Mecca, 10–13 May. An online version is available at http://ar.themwl.org/sites/default/files/Fiqh220404.pdf.

al-Jabūrī, ʿAbd Allāh. 2015. "Īqāf al-ʿIlāj ʿan al-Marīḍ al-Mayʿūs min Burʾih." Paper submitted to the 22nd session of the Islamic Fiqh Academy (IFA), Mecca, 10–13 May. An online version is available at http://ar.themwl.org/sites/default/files/Fiqh220403.pdf.

al-Jibrīn, ʿAbd Allāh. 2015. "Īqāf al-ʿIlāj ʿan al-Marīḍ al-Mayʿūs min Shifāʾih." Paper submitted to the 22nd session of the Islamic Fiqh Academy (IFA), Mecca, 10–13 May. An online version is available at http://ar.themwl.org/sites/default/files/Fiqh220402.pdf.

al-Jundī, Aḥmad. 2005. *Al-Mīthāq al-Islāmī l-ʿĀlamī lil-Akhlāqiyyāt al-Ṭibbiya wa-l-Ṣiḥḥiyya*. Kuwait: Islamic Organization for Medical Sciences.

al-Kāsānī, ʿAlāʾ al-Dīn. 1986. *Badāʾiʿ al-Ṣanāʾiʿ fī Tartīb al-Sharāʾiʿ*. Beirut: Dār al-Kutub al-ʿIlmiyya.

Kassim, Puteri and Omipidan Adeniyi. 2010. "Withdrawing and Withholding Medical Treatment: A Comparative Study between the Malaysian, English and Islamic Law." *Medicine and Law* 29(3): 443–461.

Kassim, Puteri Nemie Jahn and Fadhlina Alias. 2016. "Religious, Ethical and Legal Considerations in End-of-Life Issues: Fundamental Requisites for Medical Decision Making." *Journal of Religion and Health* 55(1): 119–134.

al-Khādimī, Nūr al-Dīn. 2015. "(Qatl al-Raḥma) wa-Īqāf al-ʿIlāj ʿan al-Marīḍ al-Mayʾūs min Burʾih: Ḥukmuh wa-Mudrakātuh." Paper submitted to the 22nd session of the Islamic Fiqh Academy (IFA), Mecca, 10–13 May. An online version is available at http://ar.themwl.org/sites/default/files/Fiqh220401.pdf.

Leong, Madeline, Sage Olnick, Tahara Akmal, Amanda Copenhaver and Rab Razzak. 2016. "How Islam Influences End-of-Life Care: Education for Palliative Care Clinicians." *Journal of Pain and Symptom Management* 52(6): 771–774.

al-Madhkūr, Khālid, ʿAlī l-Sayf, Aḥmad al-Jundī and ʿAbd al-Sattār Abū Gudda. 1985. *Al-Ḥayāh al-Insāniyya: Bidāyatuhā wa-Nihāyatuhā min Manẓūr Islāmī*. Kuwait: Islamic Organization for Medical Sciences.

Marcum, James. 2008. *An Introductory Philosophy of Medicine: Humanizing Modern Medicine*. New York: Springer.

al-Nawawī. 1972. *Sharḥ Ṣaḥīḥ Muslim*. Beirut: Dār Iḥyāʾ al-Turāth al-ʿArabī.

Padela, Aasim and Omar Qureshi. 2017. "Islamic Perspectives on Clinical Intervention near the End-of-Life: We Can but Must We?" *Medicine, Health Care and Philosophy* 20(4): 545–559.

al-Qaradāghī, ʿAlī and ʿAlī l-Muḥammadī. 2006. *Fiqh al-Qaḍāyā al-Ṭibbiyya al-Muʿāṣira*. Beirut: Dār al-Bashāʾir al-Islāmiyya.

Qureshi, Omar and Aasim Padela. 2016. "When Must a Patient Seek Healthcare? Bringing the Perspectives of Islamic Jurists and Clinicians into Dialogue." *Zygon: Journal of Religion and Science* 51(3): 592–625.

al-Ramlī, Shams al-Dīn. 1984. *Nihāyat al-Muḥtāj ilā Sharḥ al-Minhāj*. Beirut: Dār al-Fikr.

Sachedina, Abdulaziz. 2005. "End-of-Life: The Islamic View." *Lancet* 366(9487): 774–779.

Saeed, Fahad, Nadia Kousar, Sohaib Aleem, Owais Khawaja, Asad Javaid, Mohammad Fasih Siddiqui and Jean L Holley. 2015. "End-of-Life Care Beliefs Among Muslim Physicians." *American Journal of Hospice & Palliative Medicine* 32(4): 388–392.

Schapira, Lidia and David P. Steensma. 2013. "Truth Telling and Palliative Care." In *The Handbook of Pain and Palliative Care: Biobehavioral Approaches for the Life Course*, edited by Rhonda Moore, 35–41. Dordrecht: Springer.

al-Shinqīṭī, Muḥammad. 1994. *Aḥkām al-Jirāḥa al-Ṭibbiyya wa-l-Āthār al-Mutarttiba ʿalayhā*. Jedda: Maktabat al-Ṣaḥāba.

al-Smāʿīl, ʿAbd al-Karīm. 2010. "Al-Imtināʿ ʿan Isʿāf al-Marīḍ." *Al-Sijill al-ʿIlmī li-Muʾtamar al-Fiqh al-Islāmī l-Thānī*, vol. 4, 3721–3786. Riyadh: Imam Mohammad Ibn Saud Islamic University.

Thompson, R. Paul and Ross E.G. Upshur. 2018. *Philosophy of Medicine: An Introduction*. London: Routledge.

Watson, Max Caroline Lucas, Andrew Hoy and Jo Wells. 2009. *Oxford Handbook of Palliative Care*, 2nd edition. Oxford: Oxford University Press.

Wizārat al-Awqāf wa-l-Shuʾūn al-Islāmiyya bi-l-Kuwayt. 1983–2006. *Al-Mawsūʿa al-Fiqhiyya*. Kuwait: Ministry of Endowments and Islamic Affairs.

Zahedi, Farzaneh, Bagher Larijani and Javad Tavakkoly Bazzaz. 2007. "End of Life Ethical Issues and Islamic Views." *Iran Journal of Allergy Asthma and Immunology* 6(5): 5–15.

al-Zuḥaylī, Muḥammad. 2006. *Al-Qawāʿid al-Fiqhiyya wa-Taṭbīqātuhā fī l-Madhāhib al-Arbaʿa*. Damascus: Dār al-Fikr.

CHAPTER 8

Suicide Prevention and Postvention

An Islamic Psychological Synthesis

Khalid Elzamzamy

1 Introduction

Self-preservation is one of the strongest human instincts. This instinct is manifested in the continuous endeavour to attain food, water, shelter, and safety. Various religious traditions, including Islam, emphasised this notion of preservation of life through encouraging, and sometimes mandating, seeking help and cure from life-threatening illnesses. These religious traditions also prohibited all forms of violence against one's body (self-harm or suicide) and against others (homicide).

However, data shows that a significant number of people accelerate their departure from this life by engaging in suicidal thoughts and behaviours. The World Health Organization (WHO) (2019) reports that humanity loses one person to suicide every forty seconds, which brings the total number of lives lost to suicide annually to approximately one million. Suicide ranks as the second leading cause of death among young adults (15–29 years), second only to traffic accidents. Among Muslims, previous studies indicated overall lower rates of suicide. However, a more recent report showed that, in certain contexts, Muslims might exhibit more suicidal behaviours than their counterparts from other religious groups (Awaad et al. 2021).

The main research question that this chapter attempts to address is: How do Islamic and psychological literatures address the complex phenomenon of suicide? The chapter will focus on two main domains:

1. Suicide prevention: What approaches do Islamic and psychological literature propose in order to prevent suicide and protect people against it?
2. Suicide postvention and aftermath: In the aftermath of a suicide, what issues, concerns, and questions pertaining to suicide victims and survivors arise in Islamic and psychological literatures?

The chapter will shed some light on the prevalence of suicide among Muslims. This will be followed by two sections tackling suicide prevention and suicide postvention based on psychological and Islamic literatures. Each section will

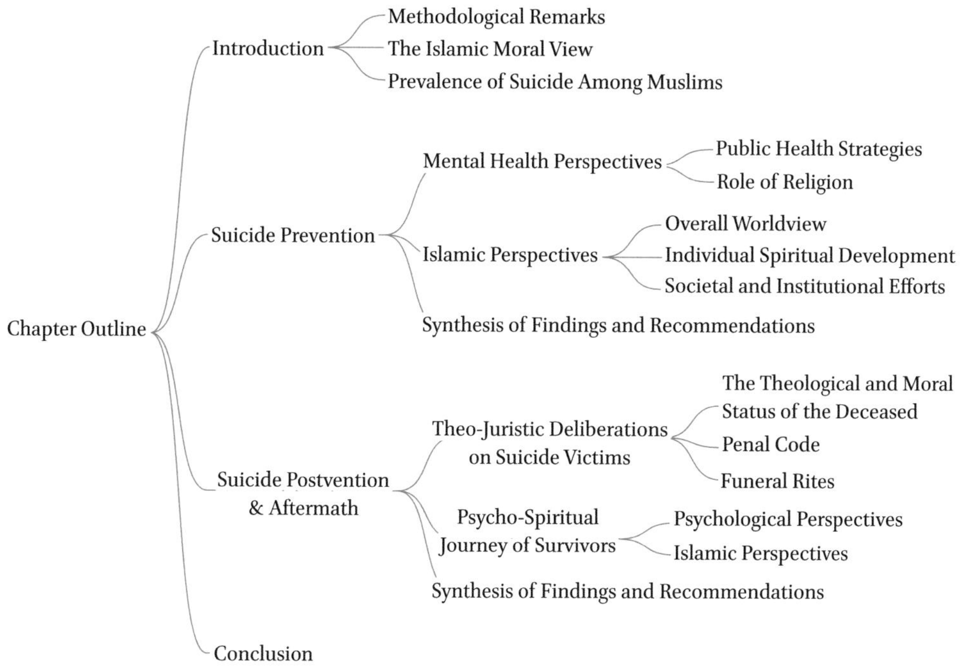

FIGURE 8.1 Chapter outline

conclude with a synthesis of the findings and recommendations. See Figure 8.1 for an overall outline of the chapter.

Although suicide is a loss of life like all other losses and deaths, it, by no means follows a similar path, nor is it followed by a similar emotional healing journey for survivors. In palliative care settings, the end-of-life experience is frequently preceded by an emotional journey endured by the family and/or the individual. In cases of suicide, on the other hand, the emotional journey endured by survivors only starts after the person is gone. The lack of preparedness and the trauma associated with suicide complicates the healing journey of survivors. Additionally, what makes suicide stand out among other end-of-life experiences is that it is the only cause of death that may be associated with strong community reactions and debates about the rites of the deceased. The attention after suicide is frequently shifted from the much-needed support for the family of the deceased to juristic and theological debates about the fate and the rites of the victim. Finally, compared to other forms of death, suicide is considered one of the most preventable.

Suicidal thoughts and behaviours represent a multifactorial phenomenon that seems to be associated with various biological, psychological, social, and spiritual factors. Mental health practice is rooted in scientific determinism and has relied primarily on secular foundations. In clinical practice, religion has long been considered foreign, or at times harmful. Earlier studies highlighted the little attention given by psychiatrists to the effects of religion on patients (Neeleman and Persaud 1995). Kehoe and Gutheil (1994), examined how various scales assessing suicidal risk almost totally fail to include questions on religion and spirituality. Moreover, religion was described by Kung, a Danish Theologian, as "psychiatry's last taboo" (Neeleman and Persaud 1995). Traditional scholars of religion and religiously committed groups and individuals also tend to view mental illness as a taboo. They frequently attribute mental illnesses to weakness of faith or sinful lifestyles, resulting in the underutilisation of mental health services (Al-Krenawi 2019; Ahmed and Reddy 2007; Cinnirella and Loewenthal 1999).

This dichotomy between the discourse on the soul (religion and spirituality) and the discourse on the psyche (psychology and mental health) creates a narrative that does not encompass the full spectrum of the human experience and suffering. This chapter aims to critically examine this dichotomy between religious, more specifically Islamic, and psychological perspectives on suicidal thoughts and behaviours. This examination of the interface between Islam and psychology regarding suicidal thoughts and behaviours is instrumental in developing culturally sensitive prevention and postvention models of care. It is worth noting that this chapter addresses suicide and its manifestations as they pertain to health and wellbeing. Certain phenomena, such as suicide bombings, do not fall under this category. Hence, they are not covered in this chapter.

1.1 *Methodological Remarks*

In order to address the questions mentioned above, this chapter will employ an inductive discourse analysis utilising a wide range of interdisciplinary psychological literature and Islamic scholarly literature to address the complex nature of the topic. In inductive analysis, the study starts with "no preconceived categories or hypotheses, thereby allowing the data to speak for themselves rather than serve as examples supporting or refuting existing theory" (Engler 2022, 308).

This study is situated within the broader field commonly referred to as Islamic Psychology. Islamic Psychology as a discipline has been emerging since the 1970s and has witnessed significant developments in the last decade. Al-Karam defines Islamic Psychology as an "interdisciplinary science where psychology subdisciplines and/or related disciplines engage scientifically about a particular topic and at a particular level with various Islamic sects, sources,

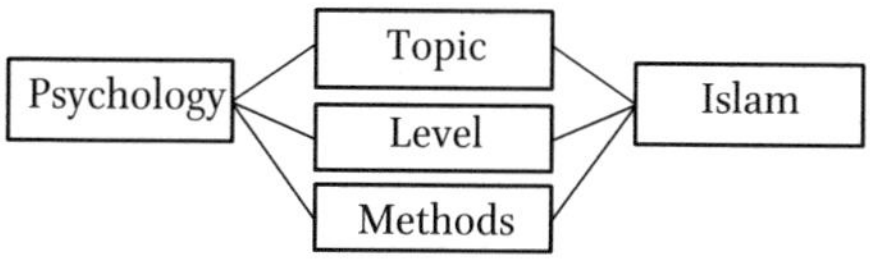

The *Tawheedic* Paradigm for Islamic Psychology (Al-Karam 2020)

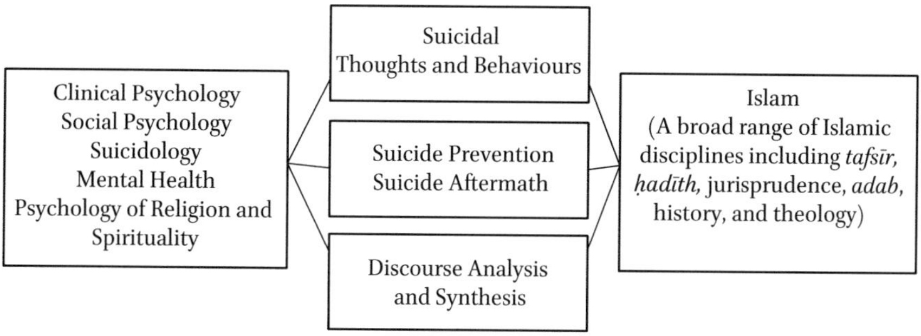

The *Tawheedic* Paradigm for Islamic Psychology as applied to this paper

FIGURE 8.2 The *Tawheedic* paradigm in Islamic psychology and its methodological application in this chapter

sciences, and/or schools of thought using a variety of methodological tools" (Al-Karam 2018b, 101–102). Al-Karam advocated for using the Multilevel Interdisciplinary Paradigm (MIP), or as she later termed it "the Tawheedic Paradigm," as a template for conceptualising interdisciplinary studies in Islamic Psychology such as this chapter (Al-Karam 2020). See Figure 8.2 for an illustration of the application of the Tawheedic Paradigm to the field of Islamic Psychology and to the topic of this chapter. It is worth noting that the Islamic perspectives presented in this chapter are rooted primarily in the Sunnī Islamic tradition.

1.2 *The Islamic Moral View*

In the Islamic worldview, human beings have an honourable status among all creatures. God has perfected their creation to befit their mission in this world to worship Him and propagate justice and truth. God forbade any form of violation that hinders the fulfilment of this mission, including violations against one's religion, life, wealth, family, and intellect. Violations against life, including suicide and homicide, are considered among the gravest transgressions. One's body is considered a trust bestowed by God. It is also the vehicle through which they establish God's mission on earth. It is established in the Qur'ān and the Sunna that God is the source of the soul; the Creator of life and death; and that one's lifespan on earth is pre-determined by God (Q 38:72, 67:2, 3:145). Therefore, human beings are not granted full autonomy over their bodies. Any violation against human life, including homicide and suicide, is considered a transgression against a territory that is divine and divinely predestined. The Islamic worldview considers this life the "sowing ground" for the next life. Many people contemplating suicide in moments of helplessness and hopelessness may feel as though it is the only escape from life's most challenging moments. However, in the Islamic view, one would be quitting their suffering in one life only to begin a journey of wrath and punishment in another, a realisation which Muslim scholars believe to deter people from committing suicide (al-Tawḥīdī 1992, 219–220).

In light of the above moral view, it becomes clear why killing oneself is juristically considered one of the gravest levels of sins, second to none but polytheism. Many scholars inferred that suicide is even graver than homicide (Ibn ʿĀbdīn 1992, 2:211; Wizārat al-Awqāf 2008, 6:283). Although the Qurʾānic discourse on suicide is limited, the *ḥadīth* tradition contains many references to suicide, its rulings, its methods, and the Prophetic handling of suicide cases. Muslim scholars unanimously agree that committing suicide is prohibited. This applies to all cases of suicide regardless of the cause, trigger, or motivation, with a very few exceptions discussed in juristic manuals and *fatwā* literature. The prohibition of suicide is established based on evidence from the Qurʾān and the Sunna, as well as the consensus of Muslim scholars.

1.3 *Prevalence of Suicide among Muslims*

Historically, suicide occurred in Muslim society as well as in pre-Islamic Arab society. However, there is not enough information to determine the magnitude of the problem or its prevalence. During the time of the Prophet Muḥammad, a few incidents of suicide were reported. One of these incidents was from a Companion who, after migrating to Medina, felt unwell psychologically and physically and killed himself by cutting his fingers (Muslim 1991, book 1, *ḥadīth* 218). Other incidents were reported on the battlefield. Multiple genres of classical Muslim literature, such as historical, philosophical, and romance literature, documented incidents of suicide in the Muslim community (al-Tawḥīdī and Ibn Miskawayh 2019, 149–150; al-Qārī n.d.; Ibn al-Jawzī n.d.; al-Shaykh 1989). In the last century, the increase of Muslim female suicide emerged as a matter of social and public concern in early Republican Turkey from the 1910s to the 1930s (Maksudyan 2015).

Recent data shows that Muslim-majority countries and Muslim diaspora communities have low suicide rates. This is partly due to how data is collected and reported. Officially reported data might misrepresent or underestimate the magnitude of a problem in a given society. There are cultural, legal, religious, and pragmatic challenges facing the reporting of suicide in Muslim-majority countries and communities. Suicide may commonly go unreported or misclassified as death due to homicide, accident, or other unknown reasons (Pritchard and Amanullah 2007). Many Muslim-majority countries have underdeveloped healthcare systems and vital registration systems, which do not allow for the production of good-quality demographic and mortality data in general, including data on suicide. In addition, suicide remains a sensitive issue surrounded by religious prohibition, stigma, and criminalisation, all of which may contribute to the intentional or unintentional concealment or under-reporting of suicide (WHO 2014; Shah and Chandia 2010). That being said, a negative statistical correlation between Islam and suicide appears in demographic literature and remains true even when cross-national investigations are undertaken. These correlations do not establish a causal relationship between Islam and suicide and require further study and investigation (Lester 2006; Raleigh et al. 1990; Shah and Chandia 2010).

2 Suicide Prevention

Suicide is a complex phenomenon that seems to be associated with and caused by a myriad of factors. Although it always seems sudden and shocking, the majority of suicides are preceded by warning signs. Identifying suicide warning signs and protective factors is the first step in developing suicide prevention strategies.

In recent decades, both health professionals and scholars of religion have paid attention to suicide prevention. This section will examine the multi-level prevention strategies proposed by the World Health Organization (WHO), including the role of religion in suicide prevention. The section will then explore the Islamically-informed preventive approaches recommended by Muslim scholars.

2.1 *Mental Health Perspectives*

2.1.1 Public Health Strategies

With the goal of reducing suicide globally by 10% by 2020, the WHO set forth its Mental Health Action Plan in 2013, with suicide prevention being an integral part of the plan. In order to achieve this goal, the WHO put together a report titled *Preventing Suicide: A Global Imperative* (2014). The report aimed at raising awareness of suicide as a *public health issue,* advancing the global knowledge on suicide, acting as a resource for developing national prevention strategies (WHO 2014, 7).

The WHO's report emphasised a few central notions pertaining to suicide prevention. First, suicide takes a high toll, yet it is preventable. Second, suicide prevention requires visions, plans, and strategies that are informed by evidence and data. Third, suicide prevention requires coordination and collaboration among multiple stakeholders in society, including health and non-health sectors. Fourth, ministries of health play a leadership role in coordinating between these various sectors and stakeholders. Finally, suicide prevention is not only about countering risk factors. It can be additionally strengthened by cultivating protective factors such as healthy close relationships, protective spiritual beliefs, and positive coping strategies.

The WHO's report attempted to dispel critical myths related to suicide and its preventability (see Table 8.1).

TABLE 8.1 Responses to myths about suicide prevention (WHO 2014)

Myth	Fact
"People who talk about suicide do not mean to do it."	"People who talk about suicide may be reaching out for help or support. A significant number of people contemplating suicide are experiencing anxiety, depression, and hopelessness and may feel that there is no other option" (WHO 2014, 15).
"Most suicides happen suddenly without warning."	"The majority of suicides have been preceded by warning signs, whether verbal or behavioural. Of course, there are some suicides that occur without warning. But it is important to understand what the warning signs are and look out for them" (WHO 2014, 29).
"Someone who is suicidal is determined to die."	"On the contrary, suicidal people are often ambivalent about living or dying. Someone may act impulsively by drinking pesticides, for instance, and die a few days later, even though they would have liked to live on. Access to emotional support at the right time can prevent suicide" (WHO 2014, 43).
"Once someone is suicidal, he or she will always remain suicidal."	"Heightened suicide risk is often short-term and situation-specific. While suicidal thoughts may return, they are not permanent and an individual with previously suicidal thoughts and attempts can go on to live a long life" (WHO 2014, 47).
"Only people with mental disorders are suicidal."	"Suicidal behaviour indicates deep unhappiness but not necessarily mental disorder. Many people living with mental disorders are not affected by suicidal behaviour, and not all people who take their own lives have a mental disorder" (WHO 2014, 53).
"Talking about suicide is a bad idea and can be interpreted as encouragement."	"Given the widespread stigma around suicide, most people who are contemplating suicide do not know who to speak to. Rather than encouraging suicidal behaviour, talking openly can give an individual other options or the time to rethink his/her decision, thereby preventing suicide" (WHO 2014, 65).

TABLE 8.2 WHO's suicide prevention interventions (WHO 2014)

Type of intervention	**Target group**	**Interventions**
Universal	The entire population	1. Mental health policies 2. Policies to reduce the harmful use of alcohol 3. Access to health care 4. Restriction of access to means 5. Responsible media reporting 6. Raising awareness about mental health, substance use disorders, and suicide
Selective	Vulnerable groups	1. Interventions for vulnerable groups 2. Gatekeeper training 3. Crisis helplines
Indicated	Vulnerable individuals	1. Follow-up and community support 2. Assessment and management of suicidal behaviours 3. Assessment and management of mental and substance use disorders

The WHO proposed three layers of prevention interventions, each targeting a different group in society in an escalating manner. Population-wide "universal" interventions are general measures that target the entire population, aiming to reduce suicide risk for the society at large. "Selective" interventions target vulnerable groups while "indicated" interventions target vulnerable individuals who are at an increased risk of suicide compared to the rest of the society (see Table 8.2). The prevention strategies comprehensively address a wide spectrum of factors contributing to suicide, including biological, psychological, social, and, to an extent, spiritual. Mental health and well-being seem to be at the centre of the WHO's suicide prevention strategy, with most interventions addressing one or more mental health domains.

2.1.2 Role of Religion

The WHO's model pointed to the critical yet complex role of religion in understanding suicide and its prevention. The potential of a given faith, spiritual tradition, or belief system to act as a protective factor against suicide depends on the practices and beliefs of each tradition and their interaction with suicidality.

One of the earliest known studies on the relationship between religion and suicide was undertaken by the French sociologist Emil Durkheim in the 19th century. The study essentially found that rates of suicide were lower among Catholic individuals compared to their Protestant counterparts due to factors related to social integration and regulation (Durkheim 1951). Research in this domain continued afterward, exploring various associations between religious factors and suicidal thoughts and behaviours. However, most large-scale studies in this domain took place in Western societies with dominantly Christian participants. Overall, the majority of studies suggest that religion is a protective factor against suicidality and that religions may protect against suicide through various means: (a) a strong moral and theological prohibition, (b) honouring the gift of life, (c) social integration and support within the religious community, (d) prohibition of harmful lifestyles such as alcohol and substance use, (e) offering a sense of meaning and purpose, and (f) providing role models in acceptance and coping with suffering (Chen and VanderWeele 2020, 28; Koenig 2009, 288).

In specific religious contexts, the typical notion of religion being protective may be reversed. For example, a religious belief that encourages self-immolation (self-burning) for women who lost their husbands is not protective against suicide (Rezaeian 2013). Another nuanced context in which religious beliefs may facilitate suicide, as shown in one *fatwā*, is in the case when belief in God's mercy and His knowledge of one's suffering brings about hope of forgiveness if one were to commit suicide (IslamWeb 2012). Experiences of guilt, shame, and abuse, which at times can happen within a religious context, may be a pathway towards vulnerability, depression, and, eventually, suicide. Developing and implementing suicide prevention strategies rely on reporting data on suicidality. In religious communities where suicide is considered prohibited and illegal, high levels of stigma might surround suicide reporting. Stigma might also hinder help-seeking and suicide prevention efforts. Thus, increasing the risk of suicide (WHO 2018).

In the religious context of suicide prevention, it is important to differentiate two facets to the stigma related to suicide. First, the religious prohibition creates a stigma that might be protective against suicide. This stigma is based on suicide being a violation against an inviolable human soul and an individualistic act that violates the right of society. Second, the stigma towards suicide and other mental health issues might hinder help-seeking behaviours which could increase suicide risk.

2.2 *Islamic Perspectives*

The Islamic worldview promotes life and lifesaving behaviours and prohibits any actions that might lead to the contrary. This worldview is believed to act as a protective factor against suicidal thoughts and behaviours (Ṣāliḥ 2019, 2003; BūKardīd 2013, 89; Shaḥāta 2015, 776–789). Based on the author's review of classical Islamic literature, it seemed to lack explicit discussions on suicide prevention. Contemporary Muslim scholars and *muftīs*, on the other hand, addressed suicide prevention. They attempted to highlight how the Islamic worldview and teachings play a protective role in addressing both direct and indirect etiological factors associated with suicidal thoughts and behaviours. Muslim scholars drew upon scriptural references and developed Qur'ān- and *ḥadīth*-based suggestions for suicide prevention (al-Ḥammūdī 2018; Shaḥāta 2015; al-Ṭarāwna 2010). They described Islamic preventive and protective measures that must be undertaken by individuals, communities, institutions, and governments.

Based on numerous studies and *fatwās* written by Muslim scholars, three main pillars are believed to form the foundation of the Islamic protective model against suicidal thoughts and behaviours: (a) overall Islamic worldview, (b) individual spiritual development, and (c) societal and institutional efforts (see Table 8.3).

TABLE 8.3 Islamically-informed protective measures against suicide

Domain	Components
Overall worldview	– Sanctity of human life – Prohibition of suicide – Hardships and tribulations as reflections of God's predestination
Individual spiritual development	– Strengthening faith and belief – Performing acts of worship – Cultivating positive spiritual states – Avoiding sinful behaviours
Societal and institutional efforts	– The family unit – Educational institutes – Mosques and religious organisations – The media – Healthcare professionals – The government

2.2.1 Overall Worldview

The Islamic teachings emphasise the value and sanctity of human life and warn against inflicting harm towards God's creatures, including oneself. Many scholars emphasised that these teachings are the seeds for all suicide prevention efforts. Islam encourages seeking food, shelter, and cure from illnesses in order to preserve one's life. It also warns against death wishes in the face of trials and tribulations (Ṣāliḥ 2019, 2001–2003; al-Rashūd 2006; Muslim 1991, book 48, *ḥadīth* 10).

In addition to the above notions of life preservation, Muslim scholars hypothesised that the Islamic unequivocal prohibition and condemnation of suicide acts as a critical protective factor against suicidal thoughts and behaviours (al-Ṭarāwna 2010; Shaḥāta 2015, 776–786; BūKardīd 2013, 89; al-Ḥammūdī 2018, 1203–1209; Ṣāliḥ 2019, 2004–2005).

The final element in the Islamic worldview that is perceived to play a role in preventing suicide is understanding the spiritual meaning of trials and tribulations and their reflection of God's attributes and His predestination (*qadar*) (Ḥabīb 2017, 112–115; Ṣāliḥ 2019, 2005; ʿĪsā 2019, 1324–1328).

Al-Ṭarāwna (2010) proposed that the following Qurʾānic verses summarised the Islamic protective worldview against suicidal thoughts and behaviours:

> And you shall not kill yourselves [or one another]. Indeed, God is ever merciful to you. And whoever does this with aggression and injustice, We shall most surely drive him into the Fire. And that, for God, is ever easy. If you keep away from the great sins from which you are forbidden, we shall absolve you of your misdeeds. And We shall admit you to a noble entrance [into Paradise].
>
> Q 4:29–31

According to his analysis, the verses conveyed various meanings: (a) promoted life preservation, (b) prohibited suicide, (c) prescribed punishment in the hereafter for ending one's life, (d) promised reward for avoiding sins, and (e) reminded people of the correct attitude towards God and His destiny. All of these meanings may bring about a state of hope that prevents suicide.

2.2.2 Individual Spiritual Development

Embracing the above Islamic worldview, practicing the Islamic rituals, and embracing Islamic morals were all perceived by Muslim scholars as significant steps towards suicide prevention. Achieving such a state requires spiritual development, which in turn requires seeking religious knowledge and seeking avenues for development. Scholars focused on four main domains of individual spiritual development *vis-à-vis* suicide prevention: (a) strengthening one's belief and faith, (b) fulfilling the acts of worship such as prayer, fasting, *dhikr*, and supplication (*duʿāʾ*), (c) cultivating positive spiritual states, such as patience, gratitude, and hope, through the process of self-purification (*tazkiyat al-nafs*), and (d) abandoning sinful behaviours (Ḥabīb 2017, 417–426; al-Zarw al-Tamīmī 1996, 15; Ṣāliḥ 2019, 2007; Shaḥāta 2015, 790–799; ʿĪsā 2019, 1287–1296; al-Saʿdūn 2006; Saʿdāt 2015, 9; Al-Sawy 2005; IslamWeb 2001; 2002b; 2003).

2.2.3 Societal and Institutional Efforts

A limited number of studies and *fatwā*s viewed suicide prevention partly as a societal and governmental responsibility. This literature ascribed roles to various institutes and entities in preventing suicidal thoughts and behaviours, including families, educational institutes, religious organisations, media outlets, healthcare organisations, law enforcement agencies, and governments (Ḥabīb 2017, 427–434; al-Saʿdūn 2006; Saʿdāt 2015, 10; al-Zarw al-Tamīmī 1996, 16; Shaḥāta 2015, 801; IslamWeb 2013; 2010a). Muslim scholars perceived the role of the family in preventing suicidal thoughts and behaviours to be central. A close-knit, nurturing family was perceived as the first line of protection against suicide. Parents act as role models for their kids. Their role is crucial in providing the kids with avenues for psycho-spiritual development and protecting them from engaging in risky behaviours (Ḥabīb 2017, 427–428; al-Saʿdūn 2006; Saʿdāt 2015, 9). Educational institutes, from pre-school up to university level, play a role in shaping behaviours and attitudes as well. Al-Saʿdūn (2006) emphasised the role of the teachers, school administrations, and curricula in establishing a foundation that addresses suicidal thoughts and behaviours from the roots. Teachers are in a position to detect any signs of behavioural concerns and offer guidance and interventions. School administrations guide the whole process of education and establish the goals, visions, and strategies. Incorporating the Islamic teachings and values in the school's vision, curriculum, and teacher recruitment is postulated as a suicide preventive measure.

2.3 *Synthesis of Findings and Recommendations*

The mental health and Islamic religious discourses on suicide prevention display a dichotomy with a few convergences, many divergences, and plenty of opportunities for reconciliation. Both sides of the dichotomy portray a sense of dominance and custodianship over the topic. The WHO and the health discourse, in general, conceptualise suicide prevention as primarily a "public health" effort, which needs to be at the top of the agenda as a "major public health problem." On the other hand, Muslim scholars conceptualise suicide prevention as primarily a spiritual and a religious undertaking that protects people from falling into a "major sin." While the WHO places the ministries of health as focal points in coordinating suicide prevention efforts, Muslim scholars emphasise the centrality of spiritual development in suicide prevention efforts. This is a reflection and an extension of the debate on suicide aetiology as perceived by each camp. Each camp proposes protective measures that address the central etiological factors in their worldview. That being said, each discourse engaged with the other to a variable extent and displayed a degree of responsiveness and overlap. Moreover, a specific domain exists within the psychological literature that attempts to address the interaction between religion and suicidality.

The interaction between religion and suicide is complex in nature as highlighted above. Most of the data supports the protective role of religion. However, some studies show a neutral or even an inverse relationship (Van Praag 2009, 7; Koenig et al. 2012, 136–143). Some empirical evidence from the Muslim world suggests a protective role played by the Islamic faith (al-Khaṭṭābī and Bū'l-Filfil 2008; al-Zuʿbī 2013; Al-Shihri 2010; ʿAbd Allāh 2009; Ozdel et al. 2009). Additionally, some empirical studies that compared Muslim samples with other ethnic and religious groups found lower suicide acceptability and stronger reasons for living expressed by Muslims (Foo et al. 2014; Kamal and Loewenthal 2002).

Despite the WHO's acknowledgment of the protective effect of certain religious practices and beliefs, they exerted caution in making blanket statements about spiritual recommendations. Koenig (2016) and Chen and VanderWeele (2020) also recommended caution in this regard. For example, it seemed acceptable to them to recommend attending religious service and engaging with one's faith community. However, they encouraged clinicians to remain vigilant and screen for signs of past negative religious experiences, which might make individuals spiritually vulnerable. Clinicians should also be cautious if they lack training in integrating spirituality in therapy.

A few observations can be made regarding contemporary Islamic literature. Despite the numerous established risk factors for suicide and the global conversation on risk-mitigating prevention strategies, the recommendations proposed by Muslim scholars were mainly targeting the cultivation of spiritual protective factors while giving less attention to other biological, psychological, and social risk factors. Muslim scholars' emphasis on spiritual development as the primary strategy for suicide prevention can, at the surface, appear to undermine the substantial risk posed by other factors. Most of the Islamic literature and *fatwā*s were published in the last two decades, and more so in the last few years. The WHO highlighted that our understanding of suicidal behaviours and the associated risk and protective factors progressed significantly in recent decades, leaving us in a much better position to devise comprehensive prevention strategies (WHO 2014). The association between mental disorders and suicide, in particular, received significant attention. This does not seem to have reflected upon the preventive proposals of many Muslim scholars to the extent of a total absence at times of any mention of mental health in the Islamic suicide discourse. For example, a Friday sermon (*khuṭba*) prepared by the Egyptian Ministry of Religious Affairs and delivered across all the mosques of Egypt in 2015 on the topic of suicide focused totally on the spiritual dimensions and religious underpinnings. It offered no recommendation regarding help-seeking for vulnerable individuals or groups (Wizārat al-Awqāf al-Miṣriyya 2015). This was also the case in the recommendations offered by some scholars (al-Saʿdūn 2006; Ḥabīb 2017). Even when some of the literature or *fatwā*s made references to psychological distress, there was an element of misrepresentation of the nature of mental illnesses and a reduction of their treatment to spiritual interventions (Ṣāliḥ 2019, 1997–2000; ʿĪsā 2019; 1284–1303; Ḥabīb 2017, 417–433).

The firm stance and unequivocal prohibition expressed in Islamic literature are understood in light of the normative state of suicide in Islamic scriptures. This has seemingly led *muftī*s to focus on emphasising the prohibition rather than showing empathy or counselling. This also suits the role of *muftī*s and their scope of work. *Muftī*s are essentially consulted for religious verdicts and opinions. However, when it comes to suicide prevention, it is "everyone's business" (Rosenberg 2018).

Although a counselling approach may be seen as falling beyond the scope of *muftī*s, it is a critical role in questions related to suicide. The Prophet Muḥammad portrayed such an approach when he addressed a young man who approached him asking for his permission to commit adultery (*zinā*). The Prophet tapped into the young person's emotions and attempted to offer an alternative cognitive framework through which his desire can be seen. When people around the Prophet turned to rebuke that young man, the Prophet stopped them and asked him to come closer to him and started asking questions such as "Would you like that for your mother?," "… for your daughter?," "… for your sister?," and the man's reply to each was "No, by Allāh, may I be sacrificed for you." Then, the Prophet placed his hand on him, and he said, "O Allāh, forgive his sins, purify his heart, and guard his chastity" (Aḥmad b. Ḥanbal 2001, *hadīth* 21708). This counselling approach is suitable for vulnerable individuals. The inevitability of *muftī*s receiving questions about suicide highlights the need for what the WHO called "gatekeepers training." Gatekeepers are professionals who are able to identify people contemplating suicide. *Imāms* and *muftīs* are perfect examples of gatekeepers. Gatekeepers' training helps them develop the skills necessary to offer initial crisis support and counselling for suicidal individuals. It also trains them to recognise when individuals may need to be referred to mental health professionals (WHO 2014, 38; Burnette et al. 2015). Studies have shown that Muslims tend to seek support first from *imāms* and faith healers before considering seeking a mental health professional (Ali et al. 2005, 402). This highlights the importance of *imāms* and *muftīs* receiving such training (Syed et al. 2020).

Moreover, the large number of *fatwā*s on the topic of suicide underscores the need to establish another service recommended by the WHO, which is "crisis helplines" (WHO 2014, 39). *Muftīs* may suggest and recommend to questioners asking about suicide to call a helpline, visit the hospital, or see a mental health clinician. A very limited number of *muftīs* suggested very briefly seeking a medical doctor or visiting the "consultations" section on the *fatwā* website. In contrast, some suggested supernatural causes for distress. Questioners offer *muftīs* a window of opportunity to help, which should be utilised to prevent suicide. *Fatwā* entities and websites should be prepared to deal with suicide-related questions with due diligence and urgency.

That being said, Muslim scholars offered a rich spiritual discourse on suicide which can lay a solid foundation for developing spiritually integrated models for suicide prevention for Muslim communities. On a public level, Muslim scholars advocated for integrating spirituality and religiosity into parenting, schooling, education, and media strategies. They called for facilitating opportunities for spiritual development and growth for individuals. On a clinical level, Muslim scholars offered recommendations that included a myriad of cognitive, behavioural, emotional, and spiritual strategies that may be incorporated into therapy with suicidal individuals. Although a plethora of evidence supports the protective role of religion against suicide, spirituality and religiosity are not often integrated in clinical psychological practice but rather alienated (Chen and VanderWeele 2020, 36). Incorporating spirituality in a manner that is consistent with professional guidelines may be associated with better assessment, management, and outcomes in suicidal patients. Many efforts are underway to develop Islamically-integrated models of psychotherapy for working with Muslim clients struggling with various mental health difficulties (Keshavarzi et al. 2020; Al-Karam 2018a). Islamically-informed suicide prevention and postvention models are emerging and need to be developed further (Awaad 2021).

Thus far, minimal work has been done in the Muslim community to bridge this gap and offer much-needed insights in this domain. ʿAbd Allāh (2009) conducted a study in Algeria that found Islamically-informed social work interventions to effectively reduce suicidal tendencies in patients. ʿĪsā (2019) proposed Islamic cognitive and emotional spiritually-oriented interventions that address a wide range of risk factors. Al-Saʿdūn (2006) offered a detailed and comprehensive institutional-level, policy-oriented, and Islamically-informed suicide prevention model. These remain theoretical and small-scale efforts that need further development and implementation; however, they are steps in the right direction. As Sherman et al. noted, "Models need to be developed for suicidal persons that address various aspects of spirituality, religion, and meanings in life" (Sherman et al. 2014, 266). Such models that integrate Islamic spirituality into therapy have been developed for other mental disorders and are currently being studied for effectiveness (Al-Karam 2018a; Keshavarzi et al. 2020). The development of such models requires a rigorous process to establish feasibility and efficacy (Chen and VanderWeele 2020, 37–38). It also involves collaboration between mental health professionals and scholars of religion.

Finally, there have been significant research achievements in suicide prevention in the last few decades. This research shed light on various risk and protective factors (WHO 2014). The data coming out from the Muslim world is limited due to many challenges. Suicide prevention requires interventions on multiple levels, including community and individual levels. Public interventions are as equally important as individual clinical interventions. Islamic spiritual interventions could play a critical role; however, it is a domain that is not well studied yet. The Islamic literature offers a rich foundation for developing Islamically-informed models for suicide prevention. Muslim scholars are considered "first responders" by many and, thus, should be prepared to respond to crises such as suicide.

3 Suicide Postvention and Aftermath

While suicide might be perceived to put an end to somebody's suffering in this world, it is the beginning of suffering for so many of those left behind. Suicide leaves behind many survivors, including family members, friends, and therapists, all of whom must endure a journey of emotional turmoil and hopefully, recovery. Suicide also leaves behind the corpse of the deceased whose funeral rites were a topic of legal and juristic discussions throughout history. In addition, suicide raises theological and moral questions pertaining to the fate of the suicide victim. This section examines the aftermath of suicide from psychological, spiritual, legal, juristic, and theological perspectives.

3.1 *Theo-Juristic Deliberations on Suicide Victims*

Historically speaking, civil and religious laws had many mandates pertaining to the permissibility and punishment of suicide as well as the funeral rites of suicide victims. Civil and religious law throughout history were practically inseparable. During the Middle Ages through the 18th century, two main penalties for suicide victims were prevalent: (a) punishment against the corpse by degradation and (b) punishment against the properties of the suicide victim by confiscation. In some parts of Europe, the body of the suicide victim was placed on a sled and dragged through the streets. Some laws decreed that the body was then thrown into a sewer or the dump. Denying suicide victims burial and funeral rites was a common practice. It was not until the 1800s when some of these laws were repealed in many countries including the UK and the US (Evans and Farberow 2003, 148).

Islamic literature pertaining to the aftermath of suicide addresses several theological, moral, and juristic questions. In classical literature, these questions were dispersed in various chapters of *fiqh* manuals as well as *ḥadīth* commentaries. In contemporary literature, such as the Kuwaiti *al-Mawsūʿa al-Fiqhiyya* ("Encyclopaedia of Islamic Jurisprudence"), these topics were discussed thematically under the topic of suicide. In addition, graduate dissertations and *fatwās* issued by *fatwā* committees and individual scholars addressed post-suicide theo-juristic issues, including the moral status of the deceased and their funeral rites.

Three major themes appear in classical and contemporary Islamic literature regarding the post-suicide period:
- theological and moral status of the deceased
- penal code
- funeral rites.

3.1.1 The Theological and Moral Status of the Deceased

Scholars debate the theological and moral status of suicide victims. The views on this matter are binary. On the one hand, traditional Sunnī theologians consider suicide victims as sinful Muslims whose fate is to be determined by God's will. On the other hand, Muʿtazilī theologians consider a person who commits a major sin and dies without repentance destined for eternal punishment (al-ʿAsqalānī 1960, 3:227; al-ʿUtaybī 2016, 56). The consequential argument that arises from both these views is whether the suicide victim is doomed to eternal punishment in Hellfire.

The difference between Muʿtazilī and traditional Sunnī theologians is based on scriptural as well as ideological foundations. One of the main principles of the Muʿtazilī school of thought is the "state between two states," which is an intermediate state between the states of belief and disbelief. They ascribe this state to those who commit major sins and die without repentance. In their view, a person who commits a major sin and dies without repentance is destined for eternal punishment (al-Isfarāyinī 1983, 68). Traditional Sunnī theologians, on the other hand, despite agreeing that suicide is a punishable major sin, unanimously agree that a Muslim who commits a major sin will not be punished in the Hellfire eternally. Moreover, they agree that whether they will be punished at all or not is determined by God's will and mercy. According to them, there is only one state in which a suicide victim is considered outside the fold of Islam, that is when the person in question insists that categorically forbidden acts, such as suicide, are rather permissible (*istiḥlāl*) (Wizārat al-Awqāf 2008, 6:292).

A Prophetic tradition in *Ṣaḥīḥ Muslim* ("The Authentic of Muslim") supports the position held by many Sunnī scholars. It was narrated:

> When the Prophet, peace and blessings be upon him, migrated to Medina, al-Ṭufayl al-Dawsī (d. 11/633) migrated with a friend from his tribe. The climate of Medina did not suit his friend. He fell sick, very uneasy, and distressed. Consequently, he took hold of an arrow, cut his finger-joints, and shed blood till he died. Al-Ṭufayl saw him in a dream in a good state with his hands wrapped. Al-Ṭufayl said to him, "How has Allāh treated you?" He replied, "Allāh granted me pardon because I migrated to the Prophet." Al-Ṭufayl asked, "Why do I see you wrapping up your hands?" He replied, "I was told, 'We would not set right anything of yours which you damaged yourself.'" Al-Ṭufayl narrated this dream to the Prophet, peace and blessings be upon him, upon which he prayed, "O Allāh, also forgive his hands!"
>
> MUSLIM 1991, book 1, *ḥadīth* 218

Imām Muslim titled the chapter containing this *ḥadīth* in his book as, "Evidence that the one who kills himself is not considered *kāfir*" (Muslim 1991, book 1, *ḥadīth* 218).

In *fatwā* literature, the moral status of the deceased was frequently inquired about. *Muftī*s emphasised that a Muslim suicide victim remains within the fold of Islam and is not destined for eternal punishment in the Hellfire (al-Majlis al-Islāmī lil-Iftā' 2009; Salmān 2012; Dār al-Iftā' al-Miṣriyya 2015; Tilīma 2019; Al-Sawy 2009). The only exception to this is the case of *istiḥlāl* as highlighted above (IslamWeb 2015a; ECFR 2003; Al-Qudah 2009).

The spiritual and moral responsibility of survivors towards the deceased was explored in several *fatwā*s. Many scholars encouraged survivors to stay spiritually connected to the deceased by offering prayers, supplicating for their forgiveness, and offering charity on their behalf (IslamWeb 2002a; Tilīma 2019). Scholars also encouraged offering condolences to the family of the deceased (al-Lajna al-Dā'ima lil-Buḥūth al-ʿIlmiyya wa-l-Iftā' 1996, 9:24). Some *muftī*s encouraged survivors to think positively of the deceased and not to accuse them of committing suicide even if there was some evidence to indicate such. Survivors were encouraged not to share the cause of death with the community to protect both the community and the deceased (IslamWeb 2010b; 2003a). Some *fatwā*s portray a collective community refrainment from offering any form of support, rites, or condolences in cases of suicide. A questioner highlighted how an entire Muslim community in a village refused to conduct a funeral prayer for a suicide victim (IslamWeb 2015b).

3.1.2 Penal Code

Suicide constitutes a violation against an inviolable soul as is the case in murder and manslaughter. However, there are no prescribed (*ḥadd*) or retaliatory (*qiṣāṣ*) punishments ascribed to suicide in Islamic scriptures. The only form of punishment for suicide discussed in *fiqh* manuals is discretionary punishment (*taʿzīr*). The nature and severity of discretionary punishments are left to the Muslim judge or ruler to determine based on the nature of the violation, its circumstances, the public interest, and the offender's background and motivations (al-Zarw al-Tamīmī 1996, 90–91). *Al-Mawsūʿa al-Fiqhiyya* reports an agreement among Muslim scholars that there should be a discretionary punishment for the person who attempts suicide (Wizārat al-Awqāf 2008, 292–293). However, al-Zarw al-Tamīmī (1996, 90–91) offers a nuanced perspective on the issue. He highlights that classical sources did not address the punishment of suicide attempters in-depth due to the lack of a prescribed punishment (*ḥadd*) as well as the scarcity of suicide attempts in society back then. He argues that suicide and murder, despite being major violations against inviolable souls, should not be dealt with equally, given the notable difference in the offenders' circumstances and motivations in each. Murder is fuelled by malicious intentions and represents unrestrained, aggressive impulses towards society. On the other hand, suicide victims are frequently people who suffer physical or mental illnesses or struggle with difficult social situations. Committing suicide is a desperate act by which the person feels they are putting an end to their suffering. Therefore, the circumstances of suicide attempters should be taken into consideration for any discretionary punishment to be effective rather than counterproductive. The circumstances of the suicide attempter might necessitate prescribing a mandatory psychiatric treatment or a direly needed social intervention. Once these circumstances are addressed, a discretionary punishment might be proposed if deemed to have a deterring effect for the attempter and the society at large. This nuanced approach was inspired by the Prophetic tradition of adapting punishments to the circumstances of the offenders. Prophet Muḥammad is reported to have postponed the implementation of the *ḥadd* on a pregnant woman who committed adultery, until her baby was delivered and fed until he was weaned (Muslim 1991, book 29, *ḥadīth* 36).

One of the questions discussed in juristic manuals is whether blood money (*diya*) and/or an expiation (*kaffāra*) apply to suicide. In terms of blood money, the majority of Sunnī jurists, including Ḥanafīs, Mālikīs, and Shāfiʿīs, agree that no blood money is indicated in the case of suicide. This is also an opinion in the Ḥanbalī school (Wizārat al-Awqāf 2009, 293). In terms of *kaffāra* (expiation), the majority of Sunnī jurists, including those affiliated with the Ḥanafī, Mālikī, Ḥanbalī schools, agree that no *kaffāra* is indicated in the case of suicide. This is one opinion in the Shāfiʿī school as well.

3.1.3 Funeral Rites

In Islamic jurisprudence, funeral rites of the deceased are determined by the theological and moral status ascribed to them. It has already been established that unless a suicide victim regarded suicide as permissible, they remain within the fold of Islam. Therefore, there is a consensus among Muslim jurists that suicide victims shall be washed, shrouded, and buried according to the Islamic norms and rites. Al-Ramlī (d. 957/1550) states, "washing, shrouding, offering a funeral prayer, carrying the body to the grave, and burying are all *furūḍ kifāya* (communal obligations, sing. *farḍ kifāya*) by consensus … and this includes murderers and suicide victims" (al-Ramlī 1984, 2:441).

The only area where a debate developed among Muslim jurists was whether a funeral prayer (*ṣalāt al-janāza*) should or should not be performed for a suicide victim. Three opinions existed on this matter, one of which is an opinion of a minority of scholars. First, most scholars believed that a funeral prayer should be offered for suicide victims like any other Muslim (Islamweb 2015b; Al-Qudah 2009). This opinion is held by Ḥanafī, Mālikī, and Shāfiʿī jurists (Ibn ʿĀbdīn 1992; al-Ramlī 1984; al-Muhayzaʿ 2013, 271). Second, a tiny minority held that no funeral prayer should be offered for a suicide victim. ʿUmar Ibn ʿAbd al-ʿAzīz (d. 101/720), al-Awzāʿī (d. 157/774), and the Ḥanafī leading figure, Abū Yūsuf (d. 82/798), expressed this opinion. Third, an intermediary opinion is expressed by the Ḥanbalī school. Ḥanbalī jurists hold that the community shall perform a funeral prayer; however, the "*Imam*" may not participate (Ibn Qudāma 1968, 2:415; Ibn Bāz n.d.).

The above opinions were based on the scholars' understanding and interpretation of the various Prophetic traditions related to the matter. The Prophet is reported to have refrained from leading the funeral prayer on a person who died by suicide (Muslim 1991, book 11, *ḥadīth* 138), saying in one narration, "As for me, I will not conduct the prayer on him" (al-Nasāʾī 1986, book 21, *ḥadīth* 148). Scholars attempted to interpret the Prophet's position in different ways. Some postulated that this position is unique to the Prophet and does not apply to anyone else. Others understood it as a form of disapproval for the act of suicide to deter the rest of the community from committing suicide (al-Nawawī 1972, 7:47; al-Muhayzaʿ 2013, 266–271). Ḥanbalī scholars, as discussed earlier, opined that the Prophetic example concerning funeral prayer is to be followed by *Imāms*.

The word "*imām*," when used in juristic literature, may denote multiple meanings. The linguistic meaning of the word implies someone who is in a leadership position or in a position of being followed by others. Prophets are called "*a'imma*" (plural of *imām*) in the Qur'ān (Q 21:73). Muslim scholars in the past were also addressed using the word *Imām*. That is, others are following them and following their opinions. Technically speaking, two distinct usages of the verbal noun (*maṣdar*) *imāma* exist: (a) *imāma ṣughrā* (minor imamate) which refers to leading the prayer or the mosque, and (b) *imāma kubrā* (major imamate) which refers to leading the Muslim State (Wizārat al-Awqāf 2008, 6:201). In the context of funeral prayers, it seems that the word *imām* used by Ḥanbalī scholars refers to the latter meaning, which is the major *Imām* or the State *Imām*. The Prophet was the Head of the State when he abstained from offering the prayer; however, he commanded his community to offer it (Ibn Qudāma 1968, 2:415).

As evident from the above, multiple theo-juristic questions are discussed in Islamic literature regarding suicide victims. Suicide also leaves behind many suicide survivors, a vulnerable group in society that has increasingly received attention in the last few decades.

3.2 *Psycho-Spiritual Journey of Survivors*

In the context of suicide, the term "survivor" has a double meaning. It could mean a person who survived a suicide attempt. It could also mean a person who continued to live after the death of a loved one. In suicidology, there is a growing agreement on using the term *survivor* to denote those who are left behind, that is, any person who is bereaved and significantly impacted by the suicide of someone in their network. They are also known as "suicide-loss survivors" (Andriessen 2005; Jordan 2008). This is the meaning denoted by *suicide survivors* in this chapter.

3.2.1 Psychological Perspectives

Each suicide leaves behind numerous survivors with various levels of physical, psychological, kinship, and professional ties with the deceased, such as family members, friends, teachers, students, and healthcare providers. The impact of suicide on each person in the social network of the deceased varies depending on the psychological closeness to the deceased and other factors (Mitchell et al. 2004, 16; Cerel et al. 2013, 418). Unlike other forms of death, suicide is almost always sudden, frequently violent, and carries the additional layer of being self-inflicted. These, as well as other, factors may make suicide-loss bereavement complicated by layers of distinct emotions and psychological experiences (Jordan and McIntosh 2015).

Suicide survivors may experience emotional reactions towards oneself, towards the deceased, and towards society. Internally, they may experience anger, intense guilt, self-blame, a sense of responsibility, shock, disbelief, and hopelessness (Grad and Andriessen 2016, 665–667). Their reactions towards the deceased may include a sense of abandonment and rejection, anger, and a search for meaning (Saha et al. 2017, 405). Emotions and reactions towards society are notable for a sense of shame, feeling stigmatised, isolated, confused, and uncomfortable (Jordan and McIntosh 2015).

The above highlights the vulnerability of this population and the need to create avenues of support for them. Postvention is a term coined by Shneidman to denote efforts and activities aiming at mitigating the detrimental emotional impact of suicide among survivors and promoting recovery and resilience (Jordan 2015). *Grief therapy* offered by a mental health professional is the most common form of postvention offered for survivors (Saha et al. 2017, 417). Grief therapy is the form of therapy usually offered to survivors of any form of death, especially those with pathological grief reactions (Worden 2018, 86–87). Spiritual and religious counselling could play a role in recovery as well. Spiritual interventions focus on inspiring optimism, encouraging forgiveness, meaning-making, and exploring coping skills and inner strengths (Saha et al. 2017, 420).

In addition to the above emotional and psychological experiences, theological and juristic discussions frequently surface during the aftermath of suicide. Regardless of their religious orientation, survivors might have concerns about the deceased being destined to some form of eternal punishment. Survivors may need reassurance about the fate of the deceased. Clergy members are likely to be the first responders responsible for arranging the funeral proceedings after suicide. Their reactions could have a significant positive or negative impact on survivors. They may themselves show signs of social ineptitude as described above. As the last act the living can perform for the deceased, a funeral, whether appropriately done or not, may impact the grieving process. Although funerals act like a reality check emphasising the end of a person's life, they can also be the place where healing begins (Wertheimer 2014, 94).

3.2.2 Islamic Perspectives

Numerous classical and contemporary Islamic works addressed themes of grief and bereavement. Although classical literature did not address suicide loss explicitly, it offered spiritual advice that applies to all forms of hardships and tribulations (al-Maqdisī 1994; al-Dimashqī 1993; Ibn Abī l-Dunyā 1991). On the other hand, some modern literature briefly addressed Muslim suicide survivors (Mehraby 2003, 5–6). This section highlights some of the common themes of healing and recovery in this Islamic grief literature, both classical and contemporary.

An overarching notion emphasised by the Islamic scriptures is that loss, trials, and difficulties are inevitable (Q 2:155). However, these trials are seen from a theistic lens as opportunities to get closer to God, exercise patience and forbearance, and experience spiritual growth. Expressing patience in the face of tribulations is considered one of the noblest and most rewarded deeds in Islam (Q 39:10). That being said, grief and sadness are also seen as inevitable, even natural, emotions. Islam acknowledges and validates the intense sorrow one experiences following the loss of a loved one. This is manifested in the immense reward promised to a person who expresses patience when their loved ones die (al-Bukhārī 2001, book 81, *ḥadīth* 13). Crying and expressions of sorrow over the death of a loved one are permissible; however, only extreme self-destructive forms of grief are forbidden, such as slapping one's cheeks or tearing one's clothes (Muslim 1991, book 1, *ḥadīth* 191; book 11, *ḥadīth* 15). In his book *al-Hamm wa-l-Ḥazan* ("Sadness and Grief"), Ibn Abī l-Dunyā (d. 281/894) reports on the importance of crying and releasing one's internal emotions and warns against suppressing such emotions (Ibn Abī l-Dunyā 1991, 95).

For grieving people, role modelling of positive bereavement reactions and coping can be derived from the life of the Prophets as portrayed in the Qurʾān and the Sunna. Muslims are reminded in the Qurʾān and the Sunna about the losses and grief of Prophet Yaʿqūb (Jacob) and Prophet Muḥammad. Prophet Yaʿqūb is reported to have felt intense sorrow after losing his son, Yūsuf (Joseph), and to have recurrently cried to the extent that his eyes turned blind, according to some Qurʾān exegetes (Q 12:84). Prophet Muḥammad exemplified to bereaving people that sadness and crying are basic human emotions and natural reactions when he was faced by the death of his son Ibrāhīm (Muslim 1991, book 43, *ḥadīth* 83). During his lifetime, Prophet Muḥammad lost most of his first-degree relatives, including his grandfather, mother, wife, uncle, six children, and many of his beloved Companions (Mehraby 2003, 32).

Supporting the bereaving individuals is considered a communal obligation in Islam. In the aftermath of a loss, Islam encourages visiting and comforting the bereaved persons, supporting them, reminding them about the nature of life and God's destiny, and providing food for them, especially food with inherent chemical qualities that uplifts one's mood such as *talbīna* (Muslim 1991, book 39, *ḥadīth* 121). Offering funeral prayers is a collective obligation (*farḍ kifāya*). It is a form of support to the grieving family and a compassionate offering for the deceased (Q 9:103; Muslim 1991, book 11, *ḥadīth* 76; al-Maqdisī 1994, 133–135).

The above offers an overall framework to understand grief from an Islamic perspective. The Islamic worldview on God, destiny, life, death, and the afterlife could lend a useful lens for meaning-making in the processing of loss during grief therapy. The bereaved may turn to faith and spirituality for coping and navigating negative reactions. Certain beliefs and traditions can be used in a therapeutic setting to address maladaptive cognitions and behaviours (Wortmann and Park 2009; Mohamed Hussin et al. 2018).

3.3 *Synthesis of Findings and Recommendations*

After surveying the psychological and Islamic literature relevant to the post-suicide period, the following observations and recommendations can be put forth.

There is a lack of public awareness about fundamental Islamic concepts pertaining to suicide, some of which are matters of consensus among scholars. *Fatwā*s and anecdotal reports highlight some of the prevalent misconceptions in the community about the Islamic perspectives on suicide. Numerous *fatwā*s addressed the question of whether a suicide victim is a believer or not. This might reveal an underlying assumption or confusion, to say the least, about such a fundamental core Sunnī Islamic belief. This core belief is that a person who commits a major sin remains within the fold of Islam and is by no means considered a *kāfir* (disbeliever). *Fatwā*s highlighted incidents where community members rejected and distanced themselves from suicide survivors. This could deprive suicide survivors of the much-needed support of the community. It may also result in bitter debates about offering funeral prayers and condolences. It was highlighted earlier how each of these elements are key to positive recovery and bereavement.

In addition to the lack of awareness, the Muslim community's reactions and questions show a need to balance the Islamic prohibition of suicide with core

Islamic values, such as empathy and compassion. At their outset, the Islamic laws and norms were already much more lenient and accommodating than the religious and civil laws that predated Islam as well as the European laws up until modern times. In addition, empathetic attitudes towards suicide victims can be derived from the Prophetic tradition. The Prophet Muḥammad was reported to have prayed for the forgiveness of al-Ṭufayl's companion who died by suicide, as highlighted earlier. Al-Ṭufayl's narration underscored that the fate of a suicide victim is subject to the divine will. Allāh forgave this individual because of the noble deed of migrating with the Prophet. The Prophet's compassionate supplication may indicate that a person's moral status is not determined by a single sin or deed but rather by the sum of one's internal states and external actions. Such compassionate empathy is an attitude that scholars of religion and the community at large need to embody when dealing with suicide victims and survivors.

Appreciating the connection between suicide, psychological distress, and mental illnesses may lead to more compassionate stances towards victims and survivors. In contemporary *fiqh* literature, some researchers heavily considered the impact of mental illnesses while addressing suicide questions. This was reflected in their juristic preferences (*tarjīḥāt*). For example, al-Muhayzaʿ (2013, 271), despite living and studying in the predominantly Ḥanbalī Saudi Arabia, leaned towards the opinion of the other juristic schools on the question of funeral prayers for a suicide victim. The nuanced approach of al-Zarw al-Tamīmī (1996, 90–91) in handling the question of "discretionary punishments" based on the individual's and public's best interest was discussed above. A similar nuanced understanding of the connection between depressive symptoms, capacity, and suicide was offered by the jurist-psychiatrist, Ibn ʿAwf (2016, 117), who called for treatment and support rather than punishment for suicide attempters. Elias (2013) also called for consideration of the public's best interest when the *Imām* decides whether to lead a funeral prayer for a suicide victim. It is arguable that the survivors' best interest shall be taken into consideration as well. Al-Ḥijjāwī (d. 968/1560), a Ḥanbalī jurist, indicated that while it is preferred for the *Imām* not to participate in the funeral prayer, there is no harm if they chose to (al-Ḥijjāwī n.d., 1:228). This leniency might allow *Imām*s following the Ḥanbalī opinion to conduct the funeral prayer if it was deemed in the best interest of survivors without compromising the public interest. This is supported by the views of the Ḥanbalī jurists, ʿAbd al-Raḥmān b. Muḥammad b. Qāsim (d. 1392/1972) and Ibn Taymiyya (d. 728/1328). Ibn Qāsim reports that there is no harm for the *Imām* to join the community in offering the funeral prayer for a suicide victim. Ibn Taymiyya preferred that the *Imām* refrains from leading the funeral prayer in order to send a public disapproval message. However, he added, "if he [decides to] pray [to] ask for Allāh's forgiveness [for the deceased] and there isn't a superior benefit in refraining then it is better" (as cited in Ibn Qāsim 1986, 2:69). It is worth noting that, while Ibn Qāsim used the word "*imām*" in the singular form which may indicate the head of State, Ibn Taymiyya rather used the term "*a'immat al-dīn*" (religious leaders).

Such considerations towards suicide victims and survivors were sympathetically expressed by Yūsuf al-Qaraḍāwī (d. 2022) in the aftermath of Muḥammad al-Būʿazīzī's (Mohammed Bouazizi) suicide.[1] Al-Qaraḍāwī invoked an important principle relevant to post-suicide deliberations, that is "the ruling after an incident had already happened is different than the ruling prior to it happening." In other words, scholars must express unequivocal prohibition of suicide to deter people from falling into it; however, if someone already committed suicide, the situation then requires more delicate and sensitive handling (Ḥasanīn 2011). Delicate handling is critical in order to balance between expressing compassion towards the deceased and support to the survivors while maintaining the prohibitive position towards the act. *Imām* Fakhr al-Dīn Ibn ʿAsākir (d. 620/1223), a famous Syrian Shāfiʿī jurist, handled a similar situation. His community experienced the suicide of a righteous schoolteacher who struggled with social and economic hardships. When the rest of the community refused to offer a funeral prayer, *Imām* Ibn ʿAsākir himself went ahead and led the prayers, encouraging other community members to join (al-Shaykh 1989, 158).

Literature on grief and bereavement provided critical insights into the moral significance of funerals in the bereavement process. Funerals bring the family to the reality and finality of the loss by seeing, washing, and burying the body. This would foster acceptance of the loss, which is a *major task* of mourning and recovery. In addition, funerals being considered a *farḍ kifāya* (collective communal obligation), indicates their social significance. It is a form of tribute offered by the religious community to a member who once belonged in that community. A funeral also provides an opportunity to express social support that would ease and facilitate grief (Worden 2018, 118–119; Wertheimer 2014,

1 Yūsuf al-Qaraḍāwī was a prominent Muslim jurist and the chairman of al-Ittiḥād al-ʿĀlamī li-ʿUlamāʾ al-Muslimīn (International Union of Muslim Scholars). In 2011, anti-government uprisings, demonstrations, and revolutions hit many regions of the Arab world in what was later known as the "Arab Spring." The Tunisian revolution took place first and is believed to have triggered the waves of unrest that spread across the region. The death of Mohammed Bouazizi sparked the uprisings in Tunisia. Bouazizi was a fruit street vendor who set himself on fire in front of a municipal office in December 2010, which led to his death a few weeks later. Bouazizi's suicide was prompted by the confiscation of his goods by law enforcement officers on arbitrary grounds with subsequent disregard of his appeal by local authorities.

90–94; Clark and Goldney 2000, 477–478). At the graveside, mosque *imāms* and scholars often offer brief reminders and advice to the congregation attending the funeral. These reminders can be opportunities for correcting misconceptions, instilling hope, and encouraging empathy and compassion. These are critical points for jurists to consider when deliberating on funeral rites of suicide victims.

It was evident that some Muslim jurists adopted the opinion that the *Imām* should refrain from offering the funeral prayer. It was also reported that the Prophet did so himself. The Prophet was also reported to have refrained from offering funeral prayers for someone who died before paying his debts. This indicates that funeral prayers represented much more than just a tribute to an individual person. Rather, they had additional communal dimensions and meanings attached to them, such as *public messaging*. In this situation, it is a message of disapproval toward harming oneself or harming the society by committing suicide or not paying back one's debts.

That being said, it is from this same perspective that compassion can be derived. As mentioned earlier, the funeral rites are described in *fiqh* manuals as *farḍ kifāya* (collective obligation). The term *farḍ* denotes that these acts are beloved and pleasing to God; thus, they are made mandatory (al-Bukhārī 2001, book 81, *ḥadīth* 91). The term *kifāya* indicates a sense of "calling" on people in the community to hasten to fulfill this duty towards the deceased brother or sister. In this regard, Ibn Ḥazm (d. 456/1064) in *al-Muḥallā* ("The Adorned") made a relevant statement:

> And every Muslim, whether righteous or corrupt, shall receive a funeral prayer … by the *Imām* and others, even if (the deceased) he is the evilest person on this planet, as long as he dies in a state of Islam. This follows the universality of the command of the Prophet, peace and blessings be upon him, "Offer the funeral prayer for your companion," and a Muslim is our companion. Allāh says: "The believers are but brothers" (Q 49:10) … and whoever denies a Muslim a funeral prayer has said a grave saying. A sinful deceased is more in need of the prayer of the righteous people than a righteous deceased.
>
> IBN ḤAZM n.d., 3:399

Finally, the Islamic worldview on grief and bereavement can provide useful frameworks that could be incorporated into models of care for survivors. Exploring the relevant Islamic beliefs and practices in a therapeutic setting can facilitate the process of meaning-making; can assist in cognitive reframing; can help address the overwhelming guilt, shame, and anger; and can bring a sense of reassurance to survivors (Mehraby 2003). Muslim mental health professionals are encouraged to explore this domain in order to develop culturally sensitive, religiously-oriented grief therapy models of care for Muslim suicide survivors.

4 Conclusion

This chapter demonstrated that psychological and Islamic literature both reflected their respective governing worldviews in their proposed approaches, strategies, and recommendations. In Islamic literature, the centrality of God, spirituality, and religious teachings was predominant, as is evident in the Islamically-informed preventive measures and the concerns raised in the post-suicide period. On the other hand, in the psychological literature, the centrality of mental health notions dominated the WHO's proposed preventive interventions and the postvention recommendations for suicide survivors. Despite a dichotomy between both discourses, there was also a degree of responsiveness, overlap, and convergence, particularly in contemporary Islamic literature. Each discourse is rich with insights that may inform the development of more comprehensive theories and models of care.

There is ample evidence that religion acts as a protective factor against suicide. The Islamic worldview has a lot to offer in that regard. Islam advocates for compassionate, supportive social systems; encourages seeking healing and well-being; provides meaning for suffering and hardships; and instils a wealth of psycho-spiritual coping strategies. These aspects and others can inform the development of Islamically-oriented, life-promoting healing approaches for suicidal individuals, the applications of which may extend beyond the Muslim population.

Suicide prevention is everyone's business. It requires a collaborative effort targeting the society at large, and more importantly, vulnerable groups and individuals. Many Muslims perceive *imāms* and *muftīs* as first responders to whom they turn during times of distress and tribulations. Although the scope of their work is, at times, purely juristic or advisory, they inevitably come across vulnerable individuals in vulnerable moments. Therefore, Muslim-majority countries and communities should develop suicide prevention strategies that include gatekeepers' training for religious professionals. Such training equips them with the necessary understanding to be able to address suicide before it happens and during the unfortunate times when it actually happens. Examples of such religiously sensitive prevention and postvention strategies are emerging and need to be developed further (Awaad 2021; Sarwari and Saraceno 2015).

Immediately after suicide, many survivors navigate their own and their community's juristic and theological concerns about the fate and the funeral of the deceased. Hence, there is a rising number of Islamic juristic studies and *fatwās* addressing post-suicide issues. However, this attention to the juristic aspects is not always paralleled with full comprehension of the intricate overlap between suicide, mental illness and *fiqh*.

This chapter was primarily written with religious and mental health professionals and stakeholders in mind. Examining the interface between Islam and psychology regarding suicidal thoughts and behaviours is instrumental in developing culturally sensitive prevention and postvention models of care. The chapter highlighted specific gaps and areas of potential improvement and offered suggestions for best practice and ideas for development. The author hopes that this chapter will inspire future works and studies to build upon the synthesis provided here. On a theoretical level, certain genres of Islamic literature pertaining to suicide require further independent and in-depth exploration, especially literature pertaining to religious risk and protective factors, grief literature, and *fatwā* literature. On a practical level, the Muslim community is in need of developing Islamically-oriented prevention and postvention models of care.

Bibliography

ʿAbd Allāh, ʿUraywa. 2009. "Ṭuruq al-Wiqāya wa-l-ʿIlāj li-Ẓāhirat al-Intiḥār fī l-Mujtamaʿ al-Jazāʾirī min Manẓūr al-Khidma al-Ijtimāʿiyya al-Islāmiyya: Dirāsa Maydāniyya bi-Minṭaqat al-Ḥaḍna Wilāyat al-Misīla." MA thesis, University of Algiers, Algeria.

Aḥmad b. Ḥanbal. 2001. *Musnad Aḥmad*. Beirut: Muʾassasat al-Risāla.

Ahmed, Sameera and Linda A. Reddy. 2007. "Understanding the Mental Health Needs of American Muslims: Recommendations and Considerations for Practice." *Journal of Multicultural Counseling and Development* 35(4): 207–218.

Al-Karam, Carrie Y., ed. 2018a. *Islamically Integrated Psychotherapy: Uniting Faith and Professional Practice*. West Conshohocken, PA: Templeton Foundation Press.

Al-Karam, Carrie Y. 2018b. "Islamic Psychology: Towards a 21st Century definition and Conceptual Framework." *Journal of Islamic Ethics* 2(1–2): 97–109.

Al-Karam, Carrie Y. 2020. "Islamic Psychology: Expanding Beyond the Clinic." *Journal of Islamic Faith and Practice* 3(1): 111–120.

Al-Krenawi, Alean. 2019. "Attitudes, Beliefs, and Stigma toward Mental Health Issues among Palestinian Citizens in Israel." In *Mental health and Palestinian citizens in Israel*, edited by M.M. Haj-Yahia, O. Nakash and I. Levav , 165–173. Bloomington, IN: Indiana University Press.

Al-Qudah, Main Khalid. 2009. "*Salaatal Janaaza*," *fatwā* ID 79235. *Assembly of Muslim Jurists of America*, 20 June 2009. www.amjaonline.org/fatwa/en/79235/.

Al-Sawy, Salah. 2005. "A Young Man Who Has Sex Appeal Towards Males," *fatwā* ID 747. *Assembly of Muslim Jurists of America*, 24 August 2005. www.amjaonline.org/fatwa/en/747/.

Ali, Osama, Glen Milstein and Peter M. Marzouk. 2005. "The Imam's Role in Meeting the Counseling Needs of Muslim Communities in the United States." *Psychiatric Services* 56(2): 202–205.

Andriessen, Karl. 2005. "A Reflection on 'Suicide Survivor.'" *Crisis: The Journal of Crisis Intervention and Suicide Prevention* 26(1): 38–39. DOI: 10.1027/0227-5910.26.1.38.

al-ʿAsqalānī, Aḥmad ʿAlī. 1960. *Fatḥ al-Bārī: Sharḥ Ṣaḥīḥ al-Bukhārī*. Beirut: Dār al-Maʿrifa.

Awaad, Rania. 2021. "How to Respond to Suicide in Muslim Communities." *Muslim Matters*, 8 April 2021. https://muslimmatters.org/2021/04/08/how-to-respond-to-suicide-in-muslim-communities/.

Awaad, Rania, Omar El-Gabalawy, Ebony Jackson-Shaheed, Belal Zia, Hooman Keshavarzi, Dalia Mogahed, and Hamada Altalib. 2021. "Suicide attempts of Muslims compared with other religious groups in the US." *JAMA psychiatry*.

BūKardīd, Nūr al-Dīn. 2013. "Manhaj al-Sharīʿa al-Islāmiyya fī Muḥārabat al-Intiḥār." *Dirāsāt wa-Abḥāth* 5(11): 87–94. DOI: 10.12816/0001166.

al-Bukhārī, Muḥammad b. Ismāʿīl. 2001. *Ṣaḥīḥ al-Bukhārī*. Beirut: Dār Ṭawq al-Najāt.

Burnette, Crystal, Rajeev Ramchand and Lynsay Ayer. 2015. "Gatekeeper Training for Suicide Prevention: A Theoretical Model and Review of the Empirical Literature." *Rand Health Quarterly* 5(1): 16.

Cerel, Julie, Myfanwy Maple, Rosalie Aldrich and Judy van de Venne. 2013. "Exposure to Suicide and Identification as Survivor: Results from a Random-Digit Dial Survey." *Crisis* 34(6): 413–419. DOI: 10.1027/0227-5910/a000220.

Chen, Ying and Tyler VanderWeele. 2020. "Spirituality, Religion and Suicide." *Handbook of Spirituality, Religion, and Mental Health*, edited by D.H. Rosmarin and H.G. Koeni 27–40. San Diego, CA: Academic Press.

Cinnirella, Marco, and Kate Miriam Loewenthal. 1999. "Religious and Ethnic Group Influences on Beliefs about Mental Illness: A Qualitative Interview Study." *British Journal of Medical Psychology* 72(4): 505–524. DOI: 10.1348/000711299160202.

Clark, Sheila E. and Robert D. Goldney. 2000. "The Impact of Suicide on Relatives and Friends." In *The International Handbook of Suicide and Attempted Suicide*, edited by K. Hawton and K. Van Heeringen, 467–484. New York: Wiley.

Dār al-Iftāʾ al-Miṣriyya. 2015. "Al-Muntaḥir wa-Takfīnuh wa-l-Ṣalāt ʿalayh wa-Dafnuh fī Maqābir al-Muslimīn," *fatwā* no. 13320, 9 March 2015. www.dar-alifta.org/Home/ViewFatwa?ID=13320.

al-Dimashqī, Muḥammad. 1993. *Bard al-Akbād ʿind Faqd al-Awlād*. Amman: Dār al-Nafāʾis.

Durkheim, Émile. 1951. *Suicide: A Study in Sociology*, translated by J.A. Spaulding and G. Simpson. New York: Free Press.

ECFR (European Council for Fatwa and Research). 2003. "Eleventh Ordinary Session of the European Council for Fatwa and Research." *Al-Majlis al-Ūrūbbī lil-Iftāʾ wa-l-Buḥūth*, 1–7 July 2003. www.e-cfr.org/eleventh-ordinary-session-european-council-fatwa-research/.

Elias, Abu Amina. 2013. "Is it Permissible for Muslims to Pray over a Muslim who Committed Suicide?" *Abuaminaelias*. https://abuaminaelias.com/is-it-permissible-for-muslims-to-pray-over-a-muslim-who-committed-suicide/.

Engler, Steven. 2022. "Grounded theory." In *The Routledge Handbook of Research Methods in the Study of Religion*, edited by M. Stausberg and S. Engler, 300–313. London: Routledge.

Evans, Glen and Norman L. Farberow. 2003. *The Encyclopedia of Suicide*. New York: Facts on File.

Foo, Xiang Yi, Muhd. Najib Mohd Alwi, Siti Irma Fadhillah Ismail, Normala Ibrahim and Zubaidah Jamil Osman. 2014. "Religious Commitment, Attitudes toward Suicide, and Suicidal Behaviors among College Students of Different Ethnic and Religious Groups in Malaysia." *Journal of Religion and Health* 53(3): 731–746. DOI: 10.1007/s10943-012-9667-9.

Grad, Onja and Karl Andriessen. 2016. "Surviving the Legacy of Suicide." In *The international handbook of suicide prevention*, edited by Rory C. O'Connor and Jane Pirkis, 663–680. New York: Wiley.

Ḥabīb, Asmāʾ. 2017. *Al-Aḥkām al-Mutaʿalliqa bi-Jarīmat al-Intiḥār fī l-Sharīʿa al-Islāmiyya: Dirāsa Fiqhiyya Muqārana*. Alexandria: Maktabat al-Wafāʾ al-Qānūniyya.

al-Ḥammūdī, Fahd. 2018. "Al-Wiqāya min al-Intiḥār fī Ḍawʾ al-Sunna al-Nabawiyya." *Majallat al-ʿUlūm al-Sharʿiyya – Jāmiʿat al-Qasīm* 11(3): 1189–1236.

Ḥasanīn, Muḥammad. 2011. "Al-Qaraḍāwī: Sūʾ Fahm li-Ḥadīthī ʿan al-Būʿazīzī ... Wa-Adʿū Shabāb al-Muslimīn li-ʿAdam Ḥarq Anfusihim." *Al-Sharq al-Awsaṭ*, 20 Januari 2011. https://archive.aawsat.com/details.asp?section=4&issueno=11741&article=604649#.YGh5WegzbIV.

al-Ḥijjāwī, Mūsā. n.d. *Kitāb al-Iqnāʿ fī Fiqh al-Imām Aḥmad b. Ḥanbal*, edited by ʿAbd al-Laṭīf Muḥammad Mūsā Sabakī, vol. 1. Beirut: Dār al-Maʿrifa.

Ibn ʿĀbdīn, Muḥammad. 1992. *Radd al-Muḥtār ʿalā al-Durr al-Mukhtār*. Beirut: Dār al-Fikr.

Ibn Abī l-Dunyā, ʿAbd Allāh. 1991. *Al-Hamm wa-l-Ḥazan*, edited by Majdī Fatḥī l-Sayyid. Cairo: Dār al-Salām.

Ibn ʿAwf, Anas. 2016. *Al-Aḥkām al-Fiqhiyya lil-Amrāḍ al-Nafsiyya wa-Ṭuruq ʿIlājihā: Dirāsa Muqārana*. Doha: Wizārat al-Awqāf wa-l-Shuʾūn al-Islāmiyya.

Ibn Bāz, ʿAbd al-ʿAzīz. n.d. "Ḥukm al-Ṣalāt ʿalā l-Muntaḥir," *fatwā* no. 5401. Majmūʿ Fatāwā wa-Maqālāt al-Shaykh Ibn Bāz. https://binbaz.org.sa/fatwas/5401/حكم-الصلاة-على-المنتحر-.

Ibn Ḥazm, ʿAlī. n.d. *Al-Muḥallā bi-l-Āthār*, vol. 3. Beirut: Dār al-Fikr.

Ibn al-Jawzī, ʿAbd al-Raḥmān. n.d. *Dhamm al-Hawā*, edited by Muṣṭafā ʿAbd al-Wāhid. Cairo: Dār al-Kutub al-Ḥadītha.

Ibn Qāsim, ʿAbd al-Raḥmān. 1986. *Al-Iḥkām Sharḥ Uṣūl al-Aḥkām*, vol. 2. n.p.

Ibn Qudāma, Muḥammad. 1968. *Al-Mughnī*. Cairo: Maktabat al-Qāhira.

ʿĪsā, Muḥammad. 2019. "Al-Intiḥār Dawāfiʿuh wa-ʿIlājuhu fī Ḍawʾ al-Sunna al-Nabawiyya." *Ḥawliyyat Kulliyyat Uṣūl al-Dīn wa-l-Daʿwa bi-l-Munūfiyya* 38: 1255–1340.

al-Isfarāyinī, Ṭāhir. 1983. *Al-Tabṣīr fī l-Dīn*, edited by Kamāl Yūsuf Ḥūt. Beirut: Dar ʿĀlam al-Kutub.

IslamWeb. 2001. "Al-Intiḥār … Laysa ʿIlājan," *fatwā* no. 10397, 19 September 2001. www.islamweb.net/ar/fatwa/10397/.

IslamWeb. 2002a. "Al-Muntaḥir … Muʾmin am Kāfir," *fatwā* no. 12658, 14 January 2002. www.islamweb.net/ar/fatwa/12658.

IslamWeb. 2002b. "Ḥall al-Mashākil bi-l-Ṣabr Lā bi-l-Intiḥār," *fatwā* no. 12722, 17 January 2002. www.islamweb.net/ar/fatwa/12722.

IslamWeb. 2003a. "Ajwiba Tataʿallaq bi-l-Intiḥār," *fatwā* no. 33667, 23 June 2003. www.islamweb.net/ar/fatwa/33667.

IslamWeb. 2003b. "Al-Intiḥār Hurūb min Kabīrat al-Yaʾs ilā Kabīrat Qatl al-Nafs," *fatwā* no. 33789, 28 June 2003. www.islamweb.net/ar/fatwa/33789.

IslamWeb. 2010a. "Al-Muntaḥir Yahrub min Shaqāʾ al-Dunyā ilā Shaqāʾ al-Ākhira," *fatwā* no. 138191, 31 July 2010. www.islamweb.net/ar/fatwa/138191.

IslamWeb. 2010b. "Iḥsān al-Ẓann bi-l-Mayyit huwa l-Aṣl," *fatwā* no. 144759, 14 December 2010. www.islamweb.net/ar/fatwa/144759.

IslamWeb. 2012. "Qatl al-Nafs min al-Dhunūb al-Kabīra wa-ʿAwāqibuh Khaṭīra," *fatwā* no. 175043, 6 March 2012. www.islamweb.net/ar/fatwa/175043.

IslamWeb. 2013. "Al-Intiḥār li-Tajannub al-Wuqūʿ fī l-Maʿāṣī Suqūt fī l-Maʿṣiya," *fatwā* no. 220918, 23 September 2013. www.islamweb.net/ar/fatwa/220918.

IslamWeb. 2015a. "Ḥukm man Iʿtaqada anna l-Intiḥār Kufr wa-Mata Muntaḥiran," *fatwā* no. 287275, 1 March 2015. www.islamweb.net/ar/fatwa/287275.

IslamWeb. 2015b. "Aḥkām al-Muntaḥir wa-l-Ṣalāt ʿalayh," *fatwā* no. 293341, 21 April 2015. www.islamweb.net/ar/fatwa/293341.

Jordan, John R. 2008. "Bereavement after Suicide." *Psychiatric Annals* 38(10). DOI: 10.3928/00485713-20081001-05.

Jordan, John R. 2015. "Grief after Suicide: The Evolution of Suicide Postvention." In *Death, Dying, and Bereavement: Contemporary Perspectives, Institutions, and Practices*, edited by J.M. Stillion and T. Attig, 349–362. Dordrecht: Springer.

Jordan, John R. and John L. McIntosh. 2015. "Is Suicide Bereavement Different? A Framework for Rethinking the Question." In *Grief after Suicide*, edited by J.R. Jordan and J.L. McIntosh, 49–72. London: Routledge.

Kamal, Zein and Kate M. Loewenthal. 2002. "Suicide Beliefs and Behaviour among Young Muslims and Hindus in the UK." *Mental Health, Religion & Culture* 5(2): 111–118. DOI: 10.1080/13674670210141052.

Kehoe, Nancy C. and Thomas G. Gutheil. 1994. "Neglect of Religious Issues in Scale-Based Assessment of Suicidal Patients." *Hospital & Community Psychiatry* 45(4): 366–369. DOI: 10.1176/ps.45.4.366.

Keshavarzi, Hooman, Fahad Khan, Bilal Ali and Rania Awaad, eds. 2020. *Applying Islamic Principles to Clinical Mental Health Care: Introducing Traditional Islamically Integrated Psychotherapy*. London: Routledge.

al-Khaṭṭābī, Aḥmad and Ibrāhīm Bū'l-Filfil. 2008. "Muqāraba Susyulūjiyya lil-Sulūk al-Intiḥārī bi-l-Jazā'ir: Dirāsa Taḥlīliyya li-Iḥṣā'iyyāt al-Intiḥār bi-l-Jazā'ir." *Majallat al-Dirāsāt al-Ijtimā'iyya* 13(26): 13–68.

Koenig, Harold G. 2009. "Research on Religion, Spirituality, and Mental Health: A Review." *Canadian Journal of Psychiatry* 54(5): 283–291. DOI: 10.1177/07067 4370905400502.

Koenig, Harold G. 2016. "Association of Religious Involvement and Suicide." *JAMA Psychiatry* 73(8), 775–776. DOI: 10.1001/jamapsychiatry.2016.1214.

Koenig, Harold G., Dana King and Verna B. Carson. 2012. *Handbook of Religion and Health*. Oxford: Oxford University Press.

al-Lajna al-Dā'ima lil-Buḥūth al-'Ilmiyya wa-l-Iftā'. 1996. *Fatāwā al-Lajna al-Dā'ima lil-Buḥūth al-'Ilmiyya wa-l-Iftā'*, vol 9. Riyad: al-Ri'āsa al-'Āmma li-Idārat al-Buḥūth al-'Ilmiyya wa-l-Iftā'.

Lester, David. 2006. "Suicide and Islam." *Archives of Suicide Research* 10(1): 77–97. DOI: 10.1080/13811110500318489.

al-Majlis al-Islāmī lil-Iftā'. 2009. "Mā Ḥukm al-Muntaḥir fī l-Sharī'a al-Islāmiyya?," *fatwā* no. 404. *Al-Majlis al-Islāmī lil-Iftā' al-Dākhil al-Filisṭīnī 48*. www.fatawah.net /Fatawah/404.aspx.

Maksudyan, Nazar. 2015. "Control over Life, Control over Body: Female Suicide in Early Republican Turkey." *Women's History Review* 24(6): 861–880. DOI: 10.1080/ 09612025.2014.994858.

al-Maqdisī, 'Alī. 1994. ""Al-Lubāb fī Tasliyat al-Muṣāb," edited by 'Abd al-Qādir Aḥmad 'Abd al-Qādir." *Majallat al-Ḥikma* 2: 131–166.

Mehraby, Nazar. 2003. "Psychotherapy with Islamic Clients Facing Loss and Grief." *Psychotherapy in Australia* 9(2): 30–37.

Mitchell, Ann M., Yookyung Kim, Holly G. Prigerson and MaryKay Mortimer-Stephens. 2004. "Complicated Grief in Survivors of Suicide." *Crisis* 25(1): 12–18. DOI: 10.1027/ 0227-5910.25.1.12.

Mohamed Hussin, Nour Atikah, Joan Guàrdia-Olmos and Anna Liisa Aho. 2018. "The Use of Religion in Coping with Grief among Bereaved Malay Muslim Parents." *Mental Health, Religion & Culture* 21(4): 395–407. DOI: 10.1080/13674676.2018.1500531.

al-Muhayza', Khulūd. 2013. *Aḥkām al-Marīḍ al-Nafsī fī l-Fiqh al-Islāmī*. Riyad: Dār al-Ṣumayʿī.

Muslim. 1991. *Ṣaḥīḥ Muslim*. Beirut: Dar Iḥyā' al-Turāth al-ʿArabī.

al-Nasāʾī, Aḥmad. 1986. *Sunan al-Nasāʾī*. Aleppo: Maktab al-Maṭbūʿāt al-Islāmiyya.

al-Nawawī, Yaḥyā. 1972. *Al-Minhāj fī Sharḥ Ṣaḥīḥ Muslim Ibn al-Ḥajjāj*, vols. 2 and 7. Cairo: Dār Iḥyā' al-Turāth al-ʿArabī.

Neeleman, Jan and Raj Persaud. 1995. "Why do Psychiatrists Neglect Religion?" *British Journal of Medical Psychology* 68(2): 169–178. DOI: j.2044-8341.1995.tb01823.x.

Ozdel, Osman, Gulfizar Varma, Figen C. Atesci, Nalan K. Oguzhanoglu, Filiz Karadag and Tarkan Amuk. 2009. "Characteristics of Suicidal Behavior in a Turkish Sample." *Crisis: The Journal of Crisis Intervention and Suicide Prevention* 30(2): 90–93. DOI: 10.1027/0227-5910.30.2.90.

Pritchard, Colin and S. Amanullah. 2007. "An Analysis of Suicide and Undetermined Deaths in 17 Predominantly Islamic Countries Contrasted with the UK." *Psychological Medicine* 37(3): 421–430. DOI: 10.1017/S0033291706009159.

al-Qārī, Jaʿfar. n.d. *Maṣāriʿ al-ʿUshshāq*. Beirut: Dār Ṣādir.

Raleigh, V. Sonni, L. Bulusu and R. Balarajan. 1990. "Suicides among Immigrants from the Indian Subcontinent." *The British Journal of Psychiatry* 156(1): 46–50. DOI: 10.1192/bjp.156.1.46.

al-Ramlī, Muḥammad. 1984. *Nihāyat al-Muḥtāj ilā Sharḥ al-Minhāj*, vol. 2. Beirut: Dār al-Fikr.

al-Rashūd, ʿAbd Allāh. 2006. *Ẓāhirat al-Intiḥār: al-Tashkhīṣ wa-l-ʿIlāj*. Riyad: Jāmiʿat Nāyif al-Amniyya.

Rezaeian, Mohsen. 2013. "Epidemiology of Self-Immolation." *Burns* 39(1): 184–186. DOI: 10.1016/j.burns.2012.05.022.

Rosenberg, Linda. 2018. "Suicide Prevention is Everyone's Business." *The Journal of Behavioral Health Services & Research* 45(4): 530–532. DOI: 10.1007/s11414-018-9637-4.

Saʿdāt, Maḥmūd. 2015. "Al-Asbāb al-Dāfiʿa lil-Intiḥār wa-Ṭuruq al-Wiqāya minhā." Paper presented at the 5th Conference of the College of Islamic Studies, Najāḥ University, Nablus, Palestine, 3 June 2015. https://repository.najah.edu/handle/20.500.11888/10396.

al-Saʿdūn, Walīd. 2006. "Al-Juhūd al-Daʿawiyya lil-Wiqāya min al-Intiḥār." MA thesis, al-Imām Muḥammad Ibn Suʿūd University, Riyad, Saudi Arabia.

Saha, Ayesha, Samridhi Ahuja, and Updesh Kumar. 2017. "Those Left Behind: The Process of Bereavement for Suicide Survivors and Postvention." In *Handbook of Suicidal Behaviour*, edited by U. Kumar, 403–427. Dordrecht: Springer.

Ṣāliḥ, Muḥammad. 2019. "Ẓāhirat al-Intiḥār wa-Aḥkāmuhā fī l-Fiqh al-Islāmī." *Ḥawliyyat Kulliyyat al-Dirāsāt al-Islāmiyya lil-Banīn bi-Aswān* 2(2): 1985–2066. DOI: 10.21608/FISB.2019.65786.

Salmān, Nūḥ ʿAlī. 2012. "Hal al-Muntaḥir fī l-Dunyā Yakhlud fī Nār Jahannam," *fatwā* no. 2613, 6 August 2012. *Dāʾirat al-Iftāʾ al-ʿĀmm al-Mamlaka al-Urduniyya al-Hāshimiyya*. www.aliftaa.jo/Question3.aspx?QuestionId=2613.

Sarwari, Bashir. 2015. "National Suicide Prevention Strategy for Afghanistan." MA thesis, NOVA Medical School, Lisbon. https://run.unl.pt/bitstream/10362/17073/1/Sarwari%20Bashir%20TM%202015.pdf.

Shah, Ajit, and Mahmood Chandia. 2010. "The Relationship between Suicide and Islam: A Cross-National Study." *Journal of Injury and Violence Research* 2(2): 93–97. DOI: 10.5249/jivr.v2i2.60.

Shaḥāta, Muḥammad. 2015. "Al-Intiḥār wa-Asbābuh wa-ʿIlājuh: Dirāsa fī Ḍawʾ al-Sunna al-Nabawwiya." *Majallat Kulliyyat Uṣūl al-Dīn wa-l-Daʿwa bi-Asyūṭ* 33(1): 754–827.

al-Shaykh, Khalīl. 1989. "Ẓāhirat al-Intiḥār fī l-Turāth al-ʿArabī." *Al-Majalla al-ʿArabiyya lil-ʿUlūm al-Insāniyya* 9(36): 140–163.

Sherman, Regina M., Barbara D'Orio, Miesha N. Rhodes, Stephanie Gantt Johnson and Nadine J. Kaslow. 2014. "Racial/Ethnic, Spiritual/Religious, and Sexual Orientation Influences on Suicidal Behaviors." In *The Oxford Handbook of Suicide and Self-Injury*, edited by Matthew K. Nock, 265–285. Oxford: Oxford University Press.

al-Shihrī, Muḥammad. 2010. "Ḍaʿf al-Tadayyun wa-l-Qalaq wa-l-Iktiʾāb wa-l-Shuʿūr bi-l-Wiḥda al-Nafsiyya Munabbiʾāt lil-Muyūl al-Intiḥāriyya." PhD diss., Imām Muḥammad Ibn Suʿūd University, Riyad, Saudi Arabia.

al-Shirbīnī, Muḥammad. 1994. *Mughnī l-Muḥtāj ilā Maʿrifat Maʿānī Alfāẓ al-Minhāj*, vol. 5. Beirut: Dār al-Kutub al-ʿIlmiyya.

Syed, Farhad, Sara Keshavarzi, Naushin Sholapur and Hooman Keshavarzi. 2020. "A Survey of Islamic Clergy & Community Leaders Regarding Muslim Mental Health First Responder Training." *Journal of Muslim Mental Health* 14(2). DOI: 10.3998/jmmh.10381607.0014.201.

al-Ṭarāwna, Ziyād. 2010. *Al-Intiḥār: Asbābuh, Aʿrāḍuh, Anwāʿuh, wa-Ṭuruq ʿIlājih.* Amman: Muʾassasat al-Ṭarīq.

al-Tawḥīdī, Abū Ḥayyān. 1992. *Al-Muqābasāt*. Kuwait: Dār Suʿād al-Ṣabāḥ.

al-Tawḥidī, Abū Ḥayyān and Aḥmad Ibn Miskawayh. 2019. *Al-Hawāmil wa-l-Shawāmil.* Windsor: Hindawi.

Tilīma, ʿIṣām. 2019. "Al-Muntaḥir Yarḥamuh al-Raḥmān." *Aljazeera*, 6 December 2019. https://mubasher.aljazeera.net/opinions/2019/12/6/المنتحر-يرحمه-الرحمن.

al-ʿUtaybī, Nasir. 2016. "*Al-Aḥkām al-Fiqhiyya al-Mutaʿalliqa bi-Qatl al-Marʾ Nafsih: Dirāsa Muqārana.*" MA thesis, Āl al-Bayt University, al-Mafraq, Jordan.

Van Praag, Herman M. 2009. "The Role of Religion in Suicide Prevention." In *Oxford Textbook of Suicidology and Suicide Prevention*, edited by D. Wasserman and C. Wasserman, 7–12. Oxford: Oxford University Press.

Wertheimer, Alison. 2014. *A Special Scar: The Experiences of People Bereaved by Suicide*. London: Routledge.

Worden, J. William. 2018. *Grief Counseling and Grief Therapy: A Handbook for the Mental Health Practitioner*. Dordrecht: Springer.

WHO (World Health Organization). 2014. *Preventing Suicide: A Global Imperative*. Geneva: World Health Organization. www.who.int/publications/i/item/9789241564779.

WHO (World Health Organization). 2018. *National Suicide Prevention Strategies: Progress, Examples and Indicators*. Geneva: World Health Organization. www.who.int/publications/i/item/national-suicide-prevention-strategies-progress-examples-and-indicators.

WHO (World Health Organization). 2019. "Suicide: One Person Dies Every 40 Seconds." *World Health Organization News*, 9 September 2019. www.who.int/news-room/detail/09-09-2019-suicide-one-person-dies-every-40-seconds.

Wizārat al-Awqāf al-Miṣriyya. 2015. "Al-Intiḥār wa-Mawqif al-Islām Minh." https://ar.awkafonline.com/?p=16659.

Wizārat al-Awqāf. 2008. *Al-Mawsūʿa al-Fiqhiyya*, 45 vols. Kuwait: Wizārat al-Awqāf wa-l-Shuʾūn al-Islāmiyya.

Wortmann, Jennifer H. and Crystal L. Park. 2009. "Religion/Spirituality and Change in Meaning after Bereavement: Qualitative Evidence for the Meaning Making Model." *Journal of Loss and Trauma* 14(1): 17–34. DOI: 10.1080/15325020802173876.

al-Zarw al-Tamīmī, ʿImād. 1996. "Aḥkām al-Intiḥār fī l-Sharīʿa al-Islāmiyya." MA thesis, University of Jordan, Amman.

al-Zuʿbī, Ibrāhīm. 2013. "Mushkilāt al-Intiḥār fī l-Urdunn min Wijhat Naẓar Islāmiyya wa-Nafsiyya: Dirāsa Maydāniyya." *Muʾta lil-Buḥūth wa-l-Dirāsāt: Silsilat al-ʿUlūm al-Insāniyya wa-l-Ijtimāʿiyya* 28(5): 121–144.

CHAPTER 9

Limits to Personal Autonomy in Islamic Bioethical Deliberations on End-of-Life Issues in Light of the Debate on Euthanasia

Ayman Shabana

1 Introduction

Islam's foundational texts emphasise free choice in matters of faith as well as individual responsibility for one's actions. On the other hand, they also highlight the importance of submission to the divine will, which is captured in the meaning of the term "Islam" itself. Both freedom and submission feature prominently in the scriptural sources and they shape and influence the believer's experience as well as encounter with the divine. These two dimensions of the Islamic religious experience represent one of the important religious-moral tensions that have inspired extensive and extended debates across the Islamic normative tradition and its various genres. Similarly, while several Islamic injunctions emphasise the notion of individual rights, several others underscore communal rights and collective responsibility. In general, one can argue that Islamic norms envision personal freedom and agency within a larger framework that also includes divine and collective considerations. Within Islamic normative discussions, these three sets of rights (individual, divine, and collective) constitute a trilogy within which individual rights should be balanced and reconciled against the other two sets of rights. Moreover, these discussions also include the assumption that worldly actions should be evaluated in terms of ultimate consequences, both in this world and in the Hereafter.

This chapter examines the trilateral relationship within the Islamic religious-moral framework between personal autonomy and individual rights, on the one hand, and divine as well as collective rights, on the other, in light of the debate on euthanasia. The choice of this example is meant to highlight the perceived tension between individual freedom and religious norms and the extent to which personal autonomy is or ought to be qualified by such norms. Concentration on personal autonomy in investigating the religious-moral status of euthanasia does not rule out the relevance and potency of other ethical principles.[1] This chapter, however, addresses the issue from the perspective of personal autonomy in an effort to investigate whether any form of induced death can be accepted. It explores whether a decision to end the life of a terminally ill person can be justified or qualified by certain restrictions from a normative Islamic perspective. In other words, the main focus here is whether religious values can place restrictions on one's capacity to act freely with regard to end-of-life (EoL) decisions either on the basis of, or apart from, medical or professional standards. A related point would be the extent to which adherence to a religious principle would amount to infringement of one's autonomy. The chapter argues that an Islamic assessment of EoL decisions, especially in the case of euthanasia, does not depend solely on personal autonomy but has also to include other considerations stemming from pertinent divine, as well as communal, rights-claims.

A quick review of Islamic literature on euthanasia shows the prevalence of a general attitude against any form of deliberately induced death, in view of the fundamental Islamic principle upholding the sanctity of human life. However, despite this general attitude, closer examination reveals an important development in Islamic discourses on death and EoL choices. Pursuant to the changing conception of death on the basis of brain function and the introduction of advanced life-sustaining medical technology at EoL stages, a distinction is often made between active and passive euthanasia. While the former is strictly condemned, the latter could be admitted in certain situations.

The example of euthanasia reveals the scope of personal agency in making life and death decisions against the religious ethic of submission to the divine will at times of distress. The chapter investigates how the religious-moral tension between freedom and submission applies to the debate on the different types of euthanasia. The main concerns within this debate range from questions of responsibility and culpability to questions about the meaning of life and the role of faith in advanced cases of illness when all therapeutic methods are exhausted. In particular, discussions on active forms of euthanasia often involve questions of competence and liability as a consequence of an independent decision to end one's life, or the life of someone else in the case of assisted

1 In fact, bioethical discussions on euthanasia are often undertaken in light of principles such as beneficence and nonmaleficence (Beauchamp and Childress 2019, 171–194). The appeal to different principles has to do with the different conceptualisations of life and the moral grounds on the basis of which it is evaluated. For example, John Keown distinguishes three main values: vitalism, sanctity/inviolability of life, and quality of life (Keown 2018, 37–44).

suicide. The chapter places these discussions within classical juristic views on suicide and murder and explores the degree to which these classical views inform modern views on active euthanasia. On the other hand, discussions on passive forms of euthanasia reveal the role of the religious ethic of submission to the divine will in dealing with the impact of life-sustaining technologies on blurring the boundaries between life and death.

The chapter aspires to contribute to scholarly investigations on the two topics of autonomy and euthanasia in light of the ongoing developments highlighted above. In particular, it seeks to contribute to ongoing discussions on the evaluation of personal autonomy as a paramount principle in bioethical deliberations pertaining to EoL decisions within the Muslim context. Contemporary deliberations on bioethical principles often highlight the difficulty of a general assessment of such principles, especially in the case of autonomy (Ghaly 2016, 375–376). Examining such principles in relationship to concrete ethical questions can reveal helpful insights on the theoretical and substantive prospects of such principles. More broadly, this example can be useful for assessments of the universal scope of ethical principles and also the boundaries of a universal common morality. With regard to the debate on euthanasia, the chapter seeks to highlight the need for conceptual clarity in discussions about this topic, which are usually marred by terminological confusion concerning the various types of euthanasia, along with other procedures at EoL situations. Highlighting the role of personal autonomy is meant to address cases involving competent individuals who are capable of making free and independent decisions. The chapter underscores the role of classical discourses in the Islamic ethical-legal heritage on topics such as murder and suicide in shaping contemporary views, especially in the case of active euthanasia. For example, juristic views on liability in the case of prior forgiveness or consent by the victim shed light on understanding how liability in these cases were determined. With regard to passive forms of euthanasia, the chapter highlights the extent to which a patient can choose to refuse futile medical treatment. As empirical research shows, personal autonomy is hardly the sole factor in the formulation of treatment decisions in EoL situations because it often has to be understood in relationship to a host of other social and, sometimes, economic factors. It also points out the religious significance of pain and the illness experience as a whole in opening new venues and allowing possible alternatives to euthanasia. Finally, the chapter highlights the need for further research to facilitate deeper understanding of the role of life-sustaining technologies in (re)drawing the boundaries of life and death.

Before proceeding further, I would like to make two remarks about the scope of this chapter. First, the chapter investigates the limitations of personal autonomy in decisions pertaining to EoL issues, but it does not claim to introduce an extensive conceptualisation of autonomy from an Islamic perspective. While it touches on the broader contours of such a conceptualisation, a comprehensive treatment of the topic would require an independent undertaking. Second, the chapter emphasises the multifaceted as well as multilayered nature of Islamic moral discourses. The Islamic ethical heritage draws on a multiplicity of philosophical, theological, juristic, literary, and mystical sources and genres (Hourani 1985; Fakhry 1994; Zargar 2017; Ayubi 2019). While all these genres include important sources on both autonomy and euthanasia, this chapter concentrates mainly on relevant theological and juristic formulations, with possible occasional references to the other genres. The chapter is divided into two main sections, covering the two issues of autonomy and euthanasia respectively. The first section provides an overview of the concept of autonomy in modern secular ethics and bioethics, and then examines the Islamic view of autonomy in light of classical as well as contemporary contributions. The second section also provides an overview of euthanasia before examining the Islamic perspectives on the topic in light of both classical as well as modern Islamic, mainly juristic, discussions.

2 Personal Autonomy: Secular and Islamic Perspectives

The term *autonomy* is derived from a Greek origin that indicates self-rule or self-governance of independent city-states, but its meaning has also been extended to individuals. In this sense the actions of an autonomous individual proceed from a self-chosen plan in the same way an independent state manages its own affairs. By contrast, persons of diminished or reduced autonomy are those who, due to influence by others, cannot act on the basis of their own plans (Beauchamp and Childress 2019, 99). In modern Western philosophy, autonomy is associated with liberal thought, in general, and liberal political thought, in particular, to the extent that it is considered the cornerstone of political liberalism. The notion of autonomy is often emphasised as one of the main defining characteristics of Western modernity itself.[2] From this perspective the ultimate goal of an ideal political system is to enhance people's ability

2 For example, Armando Salvatore notes: "The dominant model of modernity – combining economic factors linked to the rise of capitalism, socio-political dynamics related to the formation of increasingly centralised and homogeneous national states, and cultural orientations putting a premium on individual and collective autonomy – reflects the historical experience of European societies or, better, of some key fragments of north-western Europe" (see Salvatore 2009, 26; MacIntyre 2007).

to make their own decisions in accordance with what they consider valuable in life. Notwithstanding this emphasis on the importance of autonomy and the strong appeal of liberalism, there is no agreement on the definition of either concept.[3]

Despite the importance of autonomy and its centrality in modern Western thought, a quick survey of the philosophical literature would reveal a significant degree of ambiguity that engulfs the basic idea of autonomy and its various conceptualisations. In general, three conceptions of autonomy are often distinguished. The first gives primacy to the rational definition of autonomy, which is often traced to Kantian thought. According to this conception an autonomous action is one that is determined by a self-ruling will in accordance with the categorical imperative. This means that one's actions must be derived from pure reason to the exclusion of all alien causes, which include not only the agency of others but also personal lawless actions that derive from particular contingent circumstances such as desires, impulses, and other types of pressures. Kant (d. 1804) argued that in order for moral requirements to be valid, they must adhere to a supreme moral criterion, which he referred to as the categorical imperative. He provided several formulations for the categorical imperative that underscore the intrinsic human value, the universality of moral principles, and independent capacity for freedom of choice (Timmons 2013, 232–233). This Kantian version of autonomy is sometimes described as moral autonomy, which is contrasted with personal autonomy. The second conception of autonomy is based on a structural hierarchy of personal motivations, as developed by Harry Frankfurt (b. 1929) and Gerald Dworkin (b. 1937). Accordingly, self-rule is defined in terms of structuring motivations and attitudes (preferences, desires, and wishes) in a certain way by aligning first-order attitudes in accordance with higher-order desires (e.g., a desire for healthy diet conforms to a higher order desire to maintain a healthy lifestyle). The third conception of autonomy focuses on the notion of self-creation, as developed by Joseph Raz. In this view an autonomous person is one who is seen as being in charge of his own life and who takes responsibility for his own destiny through successive conscious decisions (Colburn 2010, 5–20). These various conceptualisations show the range of diversity in the different definitions of autonomy. While most share an emphasis on freedom (absence of external pressures) and agency (ability to make conscientious decisions) (Beauchamp 2005, 310), they would vary in terms of emphasis on other factors such as the moral grounds of an autonomous action or the subjective perspective of an autonomous person.

3 For more on the various theories and conceptualisations of autonomy, see Taylor 2005.

2.1 *Autonomy and Bioethics*

The prominence of autonomy in modern Western thought explains the special place it has occupied in the realm of secular bioethics, and also the transformation of the traditional paternalistic attitude of physicians into a new attitude in modern medical practice that emphasises respect for individual patients. Nowhere can this be more visible than in the emergence of Principalism in the late 1970s as a practical approach for moral analysis in biomedical ethics consisting, according to the most famous formulation, of four fundamental principles: autonomy, nonmaleficence, beneficence, and justice (Beauchamp and Childress 2019). Within this framework ethical analysis consists mainly in balancing competing claims on the basis of these four principles. Given the prominent place that autonomy occupies within this framework, some scholars speak of a triumph of personal autonomy in Western secular bioethics, which usually refers to respect for the patient's autonomy (Wolpe 1998). The most famous articulation of the principle of respecting the patient's autonomy in mainstream Western bioethics equates it with the right to self-determination, which can then be implemented through the mechanism of informed consent – despite the growing realisation that such a mechanism does not always ensure the full coverage of the rich concept of autonomy (Kukla 2005, 35). The triumph of autonomy in this outlined sense, therefore, is questioned by other researchers who point out significant problems with the exaggerated emphasis on this principle (O'Neill 2003; Stammers 2015). Reservations have often, though not exclusively, been grounded in religious perspectives. For example, several Catholic bioethicists argue that overemphasis on personal autonomy has the potential of impoverishing bioethics. On the other hand, some philosophers warn that exaggerated emphasis on personal autonomy negatively affects other ethical principles associated with communal or feminist considerations (May 2005). Moreover, some physicians argue that upholding personal autonomy as the paramount ethical consideration in medical practice may thwart some of the main goals of medicine such as restoring health and reducing suffering. Other concerns that critics raise against the predominance of autonomy in bioethics include its conflict with conscientious objection and professional judgement (Barry 2012, 113).

Another important problem with personal autonomy is the absence of a universal understanding of this principle. For example, several empirical studies reveal divergent attitudes among people of different ethnic groups towards medical practice and procedures that place less emphasis on personal autonomy in favour of more familial and collective considerations (Padela et al. 2015). These studies question not only the centrality of personal autonomy but also the continued dominance of the principalist approach, which is seen as a product of particular historical and socio-cultural circumstances.

An important dimension of autonomy within modern liberal thought is its role in defining one's identity, particularly as far as such definition is deemed authentic. Authentic definition of identity denotes the ability to express who we are or who we want to be rather than having such expression imposed by external forces. For some individuals such expression does not exclude religious ideas, beliefs, or expectations. The relationship between religion and autonomy in this sense would depend on one's view of the role of religion in either enhancing or hampering authentic self-expression. Moreover, this also requires balancing individual and communal considerations. Ultimately, in order for a person's identity to be recognised, such recognition often requires a reciprocal and communal setting. The connection between autonomy and identity should, therefore, as Ros Hague argues, be seen in relational terms. It should be understood as a process that can be enjoyed with varying degrees within a larger reciprocal framework that recognises others' aspirations towards authentic expression of their identity (Hague 2011, 7).[4]

Within the medical field the relationship between personal autonomy and religion is quite complex. For example, personal autonomy can be used to support a decision by an adult and competent member of Jehovah Witnesses to refuse blood transfusion on the basis of religious convictions, as long as such a decision is taken voluntarily (Barry 2012, 79).[5] On the other hand, the application of personal autonomy in everyday medical practice, especially with regard to certain reproductive or EoL questions, can be problematic as they often reveal the difficulty of reconciling appeals to conscientious objection by medical professionals, and individual decisions by patients acting on the basis of their personal freedom (Barry 2012, 113–114). In order to address some of the issues that an unrestrained implementation of personal autonomy can give rise to, some bioethicists, including those examining bioethical questions

4 Hague approaches autonomy as a complex concept that includes several important themes such as "individuality, self-development, emphasis on autonomy by degrees, recognition, agency and authenticity" (Hague 2011, 8).

5 Some researchers make a distinction between mere desires and rational desires in the evaluation of autonomous actions. For example, Julian Savulescu argues that only rational desires can be used as grounds to characterise an autonomous action. He deems a decision by a member of Jehovah's Witnesses to refuse blood transfusion to be irrational and therefore should not be considered autonomous. Other researchers suggest other criteria to define an autonomous action. For example, Tom Beauchamp argues that autonomous actions can include not only everyday choices but also wilfully adhering to beliefs that are based on institutional authority (Beauchamp 2005, 313–314).

from a religious perspective, have suggested a number of offsetting principles. Examples of these principles include the ecological principle, the vital institution principle, the theonomy principle, the participated theonomy principle, and the principle of the inviolability of life (Barry 2012, 117–120; Keown 2018, 53).

Some researchers make a distinction between negative (thin) and positive (thick) conceptions of autonomy. While the first denotes "freedom from," which is usually associated with liberty, the second conception emphasises one's ability to lead a meaningful life in harmony with one's values (Bredenoord 2016, 137). Others emphasise the need to formulate richer accounts of autonomy, which do not reduce autonomy to the mere practice of informed consent. For example, Rebbeca Kukla underscores the need to develop a more holistic view of autonomy on the basis of conscientiousness. Accordingly, this conscientious construction of autonomy does not limit itself to isolated or atomistic medical decisions but takes into account individuals' choices in light of their life journeys, ongoing commitments, and deeply held values (Kukla 2005, 38). Within the context of EoL decisions, some researchers highlight the importance of this distinction in as far as it involves others in the execution of one's autonomous decisions to end their lives. For example, a negative construction of autonomy does not imply obligations on others (e.g., medical professionals) to facilitate the implementation of one's chosen actions. On the other hand, a positive construction of autonomy would not only denote individuals' ability to make their own independent decisions but also the expectation to receive help from others to carry out those decisions. This second interpretation, however, raises serious tensions concerning impact on the autonomy of those expected to provide help, especially in light of considerations associated with other moral principles such as the principle of avoiding killing (Veatch and Guidry-Grimes 2020, 159–160). As the following section illustrates, Islamic discussions on euthanasia are premised on the view that claims to personal autonomy have to be balanced with divine and collective demands emanating from Islamic values.

2.2 *Personal Autonomy in Islamic (Bio)Ethics*

Despite the general impression that the rise of personal autonomy with its concomitant emphasis on freedom, agency, rationality, and self-rule is an achievement of modern (Western) moral thought, significant links are often traced to pre-modern moral traditions, both philosophical and religious. In the case of the Islamic normative tradition, important precursors range from theological discussions on the concept of viceregency (*khilāfa*) or human freedom and destiny, philosophical psychology of the soul, juristic discussions on legal responsibility, and mystical Sufi reflections on the self and ways to edify one's moral character.[6] Theoretically there is no absolute divorce between these genres as they all evolved and developed side by side within the Islamic normative tradition. An extensive survey of these discussions lies beyond the limited scope of this chapter but, in keeping with the ethical-legal concentration in the subsequent discussion on topics such as suicide and murder, I will give a brief overview of some of the important juristic underpinnings of the concept of autonomy in Islamic ethics, as rooted in the trilateral relationship mentioned above between individual, divine and collective claims-rights.

One of the most important topics that undergird an Islamic conceptualisation of autonomy is the concept of rights, which usually includes two main sets of rights: those that belong to God and those that belong to man. Over time, the jurists devised different typologies, which would include also mixed rights between God and man. This last category is further divided into those in which the right of God is larger than that of man and those in which the right of man is larger than that of God. The rights of God include divine commands and prohibitions, especially in the domain of devotional deeds as well as areas that are of public concern. The rights of man include rights owed to people, especially in the domain of transactions such as debts and other financial claims. The mixed rights with a larger share for God include examples such as the punishment for slander because it affects the individual being slandered but also involves a right of God in the sense that: a) it violates a divine stipulation against the act of slander; and b) it also affects public morality. The mixed rights with a larger share for man include examples such as retaliation, which involves the right of the victim as well as that of the community. One main criterion that is used to distinguish a right of God from a right of man is the possibility of dropping claims associated with the right in question such as pardoning or forgiving such claims. In the case of mixed rights, even if the person involved forgives the perpetrator, that still does not remove the moral sin attached to the act in light of the share owed to God, which would require another form of expiation or discretionary punishment (al-Qarāfī 2001, 1:269; Wizārat al-Awqāf 2008, 18:14; Kamali 2003, 448–449; Abou El Fadl 2014, l–lii). This issue is of great importance in the realm of bioethics because of the added sensitivity surrounding any procedure that impacts life or the human body in light of the Qurʾānic references to the inherent dignity bestowed on

6 In a recent study, Muhammad U. Faruque examines the notion of the self from an Islamic and comparative perspectives. He highlights the multiplicity of the dimensions from which the notion of the self can be addressed and distinguishes two main approaches: descriptive (scientific, social, cognitive) and normative (philosophical, spiritual) (Faruque 2021, 1–58).

man (Q 17:70) and also the sanctity of human life (Q 5:32). Due to this divine bestowal of dignity, as well as the sanctity of human life, the jurists understood the right to protect life and the human body to be a mixed right between God and man (Sharaf al-Dīn 1987, 26). This in turn explains the reluctance of some jurists to sanction certain medical procedures that impact the integrity of the human body, as evident in the debate on organ donation (Hamdy 2012). As noted below, important parallels can be seen in the debate on euthanasia, in both its active and passive forms. The case of active euthanasia immediately raises concerns similar to those associated with suicide and murder. In the case of passive forms, attitudes of Muslim jurists, as well as patients, depend on the perception of whether a particular course of action compromises deeply held religious beliefs about human dignity, the sanctity of life, and the exact timing of death.

Another important topic that is of considerable importance for an Islamic conceptualisation of autonomy is the higher objectives of Sharīʿa. Although discussions on the objectives that the Sharīʿa aims to preserve and protect can be traced to earlier stages of the Islamic juristic tradition, credit for the detailed formulation of this concept is often given to the Andalusī jurist Abū Isḥāq al-Shāṭibī (d. 790/1388). The notion of the higher objectives of Sharīʿa received a great deal of attention in the modern period and was used as the foundation of a new approach for juristic construction, apart from the traditional approach in legal methodology, mainly in the Sunnī tradition, that centred around juristic analogy (Kamali 2009). Although over time these objectives were subject to many classifications, the standard tripartite typology of necessities, needs, and embellishments remained one of the main features in related discussions. The necessary objectives often include five main values: religion, life, intellect, lineage, and property. For the purpose of the present discussion, what is important to note here is the prominent place that "life" occupies in the classifications of these higher objectives, which is gleaned from the numerous Islamic injunctions that are meant to safeguard human life against any form of aggression. Another important point has to do with the particular order within this classification of the higher objectives and whether this order is meant to denote priority in terms of the degree of importance that is attached to each of these values and whether, in this case, a lower value can be sacrificed for the sake of a higher value in cases of conflict. The main example that is of primary concern here is whether life comes after or before religion or any of the other values and whether in case of conflict life can be sacrificed to preserve a higher value. While some jurists gave priority to religion, as it is believed to be the main guide for ultimate salvation in the Hereafter, others reasoned that life takes priority because the right of man takes priority over the right of God in cases of conflict (ʿAṭiyya 2001, 33–34).[7]

Other relevant topics in juristic discussions include themes such as legal responsibility (*taklīf*) as well as legal capacity (*ahliyya*). These discussions tend to concentrate on the qualities of a legally responsible or competent person.[8] Depending on the specific legal context, these qualities often include criteria such as age, mental capacity/competence, free choice, and intent.[9] In general, legal capacity is considered the main criterion for legal responsibility. In juristic discussions capacity is divided into two main categories: original capacity (*ahliyyat wujūb*); and executive capacity (*ahliyyat adāʾ*).[10] The first (original) refers to inherent capability by means of which a human being acquires a distinct identity and becomes subject to legal transactions. It is divided into two main types: incomplete or deficient original capacity, by means of which the person can only acquire certain rights and privileges as is the case with the foetus; and complete or full original capacity, by means of which the person can both acquire rights and discharge duties. The second (executive) type denotes legal capability, by means of which the person becomes able to exercise the different types of religious-legal acts upon reaching the age of maturity. This category is also divided into two main types: deficient executive capacity, by means of which the person acquires limited capability to exercise different religious-legal acts as is the case with minors; and full executive capacity, by means of which the person acquires the capability to exercise all types of religious-legal transactions, which is attained upon reaching full majority (al-Bukhārī 1997, 4:335; al-Zarqā 2012, 2:785; al-Zuḥaylī 2010, 13:550; Kamali 2003, 450–452). The person is considered legally responsible as long as one is

7 In his article on the Islamic Fiqh Academy of India for the *Encyclopedia of Islamic Bioethics*, Waris Mazhari noted that in one of the meetings that was held on the issue of euthanasia, a few scholars argued for the permissibility of mercy killing in the case of a person who, due to psychological problems, may end up uttering blasphemous words. The majority of the convened scholars, however, did not agree with this opinion (Mazhari 2022). This reasoning, however, is quite problematic as it contravenes the basic conditions for legal responsibility.

8 In philosophical discussions on autonomy, a distinction is sometimes made between theories of autonomous persons and theories of autonomous actions (see Beauchamp 2005, 311).

9 In an effort to help Muslim physicians and patients evaluate treatment decisions at EoL, some Muslim clinicians appeal to the ethical-legal literature to assess when a medical intervention becomes obligatory. For example, Padela and Mohiuddin suggest the use of legal responsibility (*taklīf*) as a criterion that justifies the obligation to initiate or continue medical treatment (Padela and Mohiuddin 2015).

10 Kamali translates them as receptive legal capacity and active legal capacity (Kamali 2003, 450).

in possession of full legal capacity, but such capacity can be interrupted either temporarily or permanently due to certain impediments. The jurists discussed these impediments under the rubric of barriers (*ʿawāriḍ*) to full legal capacity, which they divided into two main types: natural (*samāwiyya*) and accidental (*ʿāriḍa*). The former includes six main items: madness, imbecility, fainting, sleep, terminal illness, and slavery.[11] The latter includes items such as intoxication and foolishness.[12] This discussion shows the close connection between legal capacity and personhood, which begins even before birth in the case of the foetus. More particularly, the concept of personhood is associated with the process of ensoulment or the breathing of the soul into the foetus. What is important to note here is that barriers to full legal capacity mostly affect the executive type, which is based on full rational capabilities, but not the original one, which is based on the basic human character. This distinction is relevant in the case of terminal and unconscious patients who would still have original capacity but lack executive capacity in terms of ability to exercise full control over legal and financial affairs.[13]

Contemporary discussions on the place and role of personal autonomy within Islamic bioethics are usually part of larger discussions investigating relevant methodological issues, including potential ethical principles from within the Islamic tradition or evaluating the well-known Principalist approach and its applicability within a Muslim context. For example, some of the questions that Muslim bioethicists raise in connection with this issue include: the extent to which these four principles (autonomy, beneficence, nonmaleficence, and justice) can be justified on Islamic grounds; how the process of balancing and specification should be undertaken in light of the larger Islamic moral structure; and whether an Islamic version of principalism would consist of a different set of principles. In his review of scholarly literature on this issue, Mohammed Ghaly identifies two main approaches, which he refers to as instrumentalist and indigenous. The first refers to efforts to accommodate Western principles within the Islamic ethical structure and the second aims to

11 One of the important reports in this regard is the one narrated by ʿAlī b. Abī Ṭālib (d. 40/661), which states: "The pen (responsibility) is lifted in the case of three: the mad person until he recovers, the sleeping person until he wakes up, and the minor until he reaches the age of maturity" (Abū Dāwūd 2009, 6:452; Ibn Ḥajar al-ʿAsqalānī n.d., 9:388; Kamali 2003, 451).

12 Some scholars add other items such as bankruptcy (al-Zarqā 2012, 833), others add several more such as forgetfulness, ignorance, jesting, mistake, and coercion (Wizārat al-Awqāf 2008, 7:161–167).

13 For more on Islamic conceptualisations of personhood, see Haque 2008; and for more on the legal consequences of terminal illness in Islamic law, see Yanagihashi 1998.

outline possible Islamic principles from within the Islamic ethical-legal tradition that can undergird Islamic deliberations on bioethical issues (Ghaly 2016, 3–39). Out of these four fundamental principles, personal autonomy is often marked as the most controversial one (Ghaly 2016, 34; Sachedina 2009, 3–21). This in turn reveals the importance of examining ethical principles in relationship to specific issues, which can yield useful insights on their potentials and limitations. As the discussion below on suicide and murder indicate, any investigation into the role of personal autonomy has to place it within the larger Islamic ethical-legal framework, which includes other divine and communal considerations as well.

3 Meaning of Euthanasia: General and Islamic Perspectives

The term "euthanasia" is derived from a Greek origin that means good death. The current usage of the term denotes painless termination of the life of a patient who suffers from a painful and incurable disease. Other related terms that are often used as synonyms to euthanasia include: mercy killing, assisted suicide, and physician-assisted suicide. The original usage of the term denotes a smooth, swift, and painless natural (non-induced) death, which was considered a blessing. The term eventually underwent a significant evolution from denoting "physician-aided natural dying" to "physician-induced peaceful death." This development can be traced to the late 19th century following heated debates in Great Britain and the United States over the vindication of this type of induced death. In the first half of the 20th century, the term was used in association with eugenic tendencies to signify the termination of the lives of certain unwanted groups. With the rise of medical technology, the term was also used to refer to the withdrawal of life-sustaining medical measures from terminally ill patients. This latter procedure is also referred to as passive or indirect euthanasia to distinguish it from active or voluntary euthanasia which denotes physician-assisted death (Vanderpool 2004). An important distinction that is often made in ethical discussions is between killing, which is usually associated with active forms of euthanasia, and letting die, which is usually associated with passive forms of euthanasia. The first denotes an act of commission, whereas the second signifies an act of omission. While some researchers find this distinction clear and even intuitive, others deny any meaningful difference between the two as both ultimately violate the principle of avoiding killing (Veatch and Guidry-Grimes 2020, 152–168). The difference between (active) euthanasia and physician-assisted suicide lies in the role that the physician plays and also the intention behind this role. In the case of euthanasia, the intention of the physician is to end the patient's life, whereas in physician-assisted suicide it is primarily to assist the patient in doing so (Keown 2018, 16).

Against the complexity that surrounds the various definitions and uses of the term, some researchers make a distinction between two main ways in which the term is used. The first, broader, meaning includes any action that would lead to death. In this broader use, several adjectives can be added to make it more specific (e.g., active-passive, direct-indirect, or voluntary-involuntary or non-voluntary). The second, more specific, meaning is one that covers only active, direct, and voluntary forms (Broeckaert 2008a, 403–406).[14] The implications of this distinction centre around whether procedures falling under passive euthanasia (e.g., withdrawing or withholding treatment) can be categorised as forms of euthanasia. In Islamic discussions this distinction is not always clear-cut, which can sometimes result in a great deal of confusion (Van den Branden and Broeckaert 2011). For the purpose of this chapter, concentration on the role of personal autonomy in discussions relating to euthanasia assumes that the person making the decision is competent and able to make an independent and free choice. This would apply mostly to cases of active euthanasia, and to passive forms of euthanasia only if the person meets these criteria. The Islamic argument against euthanasia is based on numerous concerns associated with the Islamic theological view of death as well as Islamic legal enactments that both emphasise the sanctity of human life and denounce any form of unjustified attack against it.

3.1 *Background within the Islamic Normative Tradition*

The Islamic attitude towards euthanasia can only be understood within the larger Islamic normative tradition and its view of this world, as well as its conceptualisation of both life and death. This conceptualisation is marked by the interplay of core theological, legal, and moral values, which are reiterated in the foundational sources of Islam. At the theological level, life in this world is considered transient, finite, and bound to end with death (Q 55:26). Yet, despite this inevitability of death, the exact moment of its occurrence remains concealed and unknown to humans (Q 31:34). The predestined nature of death ties it to divine knowledge, which defies any human effort to intervene in this domain. The term *ajal*, which means a specified duration for something, is

14 As an example of this more specific meaning, Broeckaert cites the definition used in both the Netherlands and Belgium, which is: "intentionally terminating life by someone other than the person concerned, at the latter's request" (Broeckaert 2008a, 405; 2008b). Some scholars use other terms such as voluntary active euthanasia, nonvoluntary active euthanasia, and involuntary active euthanasia (Keown 2018, 15).

used in the Qurʾān to denote the specified duration of one's life in this world. It is also used to indicate the expiration of this duration with the occurrence or expectation of death, either due to a fatal cause or old age (al-Rāghib al-Iṣfahānī 2010, 20–21). The exact meaning of the term *ajal* and whether it can change has been debated in classical theological discussions.

In general, while Muslim theologians emphasised the connection between a person's predestined *ajal* and the actual moment of death, they debated several points surrounding the relationship between these two categories. For example, one of the questions that were raised was whether an act of murder cuts short the *ajal* of a slain person. Some theologians, mainly from the Muʿtazilī school, noted that if a slain person were not subjected to an act of murder, he would live longer and therefore the act of murder cuts short one's specified term or *ajal*. Other theologians, on the other hand, held the view that if a slain person were not to die because of a predestined murderous attack, he would still die nonetheless. After listing these two points, the classical Ashʿarī theologian-jurist al-Juwaynī (d. 478/1085) noted that if a person is predestined to die due to an act of murder, such a person would definitely die in this manner. He, however, did not rule out rational speculations about the possibility of survival post a murderous attack for any other reason at the time of such an attack. Al-Juwaynī's discussion underscores two main points: the connection between the exact time of death and the divinely predestined *ajal* for the end of one's life; and the expiration of one's predestined duration in this world at the time of his/her death (al-Juwaynī 2002, 362–363).[15]

These theological values shape and inform a Muslim's moral attitude towards life and death, and consequently towards euthanasia. Life is deemed to be a divine gift that is entrusted to man as a valuable resource, which should be protected and safeguarded. It should be invested through the cultivation of good deeds. Life is the domain of testing, which is used for the verification of one's faith and purification of one's character (Q 67:2). During one's life journey one is bound to encounter different types of challenges (physical, psychological, and moral) and the believer is expected to endure and overcome these challenges, as opportunities on the path towards moral growth and maturity. A Muslim's ideal attitude towards death is captured in a report in which the Prophet indicates that a person should not wish for death due to a harm that befell them. Instead of wishing for death, the report indicates, a person should pray to God to grant them what is better in their situation, either life or death (Ibn Ḥajar al-ʿAsqalānī n.d., 10:127). These guidelines are also reiterated in

15 For more on this point see ʿAbd al-Jabbār b. Aḥmad al-Asadabādī n.d., 11:3–4; al-Māturīdī 2010, 370–373.

numerous passages in the Qurʾān and the Prophetic Sunna, which emphasise patience, perseverance, and trust in God.

At the juristic level, as noted above, life is listed among the five main values that Sharīʿa aims to preserve together with religion, lineage, reason, and property (al-Shāṭibī 2003). Most significantly, Islamic jurisprudence categorises these values among the most fundamental goods deemed necessary for both individual and social wellbeing. Their protection is guaranteed by means of the stipulated punishments or *ḥudūd* for crimes that threaten these values such as murder, adultery, false accusations, and theft. These *ḥudūd* do not only aim to protect the personal rights of individuals but they are also meant to protect the overarching moral order of Sharīʿa and the public good of society. In this respect, they are said to belong to the rights of God either exclusively or in combination with the rights of man. *Ḥudūd* punishments may vary depending on certain considerations. In the case of murder, for example, a distinction is made between premeditated murder or homicide and murder by mistake or manslaughter. The punishment of the former is retribution while the punishment for the latter includes the payment of blood money, in addition to a form of religious expiation.

3.2 *Contemporary Discussions*

Contemporary Muslim discussions on euthanasia often make a distinction between its active and passive forms (Aramesh and Shadi 2007; Sachedina 1999; 2009, 169). The former includes any positive action that results in the termination of life. The latter includes any form of withholding or withdrawal of medical treatment that may result in the death of a terminally ill patient. While the former is unanimously condemned, the latter is deemed subject to further specifications.

This is best illustrated in a famous *fatwā* by the prominent contemporary jurist Yūsuf al-Qaraḍāwī (d. 2022), in which he draws a distinction between active and passive euthanasia (al-Qaraḍāwī 2000, 2:577–582). In the first type (active euthanasia), which he calls active facilitation of death (*taysīr al-mawt al-faʿʿāl*), the physician takes active measures to cause the death of a terminally ill patient with the intent of putting an end to his suffering. It is usually assumed that in these situations the physician would likely be acting on the wishes of a terminally ill patient to end their life. This is considered prohibited killing, despite the benevolent motive behind the physician's action. According to al-Qaraḍāwī, the physician will not be more merciful towards such a patient than his creator. Under the second type (passive euthanasia), which he calls passive facilitation of death (*taysīr al-mawt al-munfaʿil*), he includes two main scenarios: withholding futile medical treatment; and switching off of life support measures. Unlike the first type of active euthanasia, which al-Qaraḍāwī opposes, he makes a careful argument for the permissibility of the two scenarios of passive euthanasia.

The position that al-Qaraḍāwī took in this *fatwā* is often reiterated in the contemporary *fatwā* literature, and across the Islamic normative literature on the issue in general, even though not all scholars use the categories of active and passive euthanasia explicitly. For example, in 2002 the Egyptian Dār al-Iftāʾ issued a similar *fatwā* in response to a question about the notion of "merciful killing" in light of a case in France involving a man who sought permission to end his life, but his request was not granted. In his response, the then head *muftī* Aḥmad al-Ṭayyib (b. 1946), who is the current Grand Shaykh of al-Azhar, emphasised the prohibition of ending the life of a person, whether his/her condition is stable or unstable from the medical point of view. The reasoning he gave was that issues pertaining to life and death are solely in the hands of God and it is not permissible for a physician or anyone else to make such a decision, even if it is motivated by mercy towards a suffering person in order to put an end to the pains that they experience (Dār al-Iftāʾ al-Miṣriyya 2011, 27:191–192). On the other hand, al-Ṭayyib indicated the possibility of switching off of life support measures in the case of a person who is considered "clinically dead" (*al-mutawaffā klīnikiyy*^{an}). Al-Ṭayyib did not provide an exact description of this condition but this designation is most likely used here to describe comatose patients who are diagnosed as brain-dead. According to al-Ṭayyib, removal of life support measures is not in itself an indication of death, but a person can only be considered dead when all signs of life cease to exist, following the removal of these measures. Moreover, removal of organs for the purpose of donation or transplantation can be done only after verifying the death of the patient (Dār al-Iftāʾ al-Miṣriyya 2011, 27:191–192).[16]

Subsequent *fatwās* from Dār al-Iftāʾ generally support this position on the issue of mercy killing. For example, in 2004 a *fatwā* was given by the then head *muftī* ʿAlī Jumʿa (b. 1952) in response to a question about the permissibility of euthanasia. The questioner asked about two scenarios: when a patient seeks the help of a physician to end his/her life in order to get rid of the pain associated with a terminal illness; and when a physician makes an independent determination that ending a patient's life would be more beneficial for him/her than living with pain or disability. The *muftī* noted that euthanasia in both of these cases would be impermissible. According to the *fatwā*, although in the

16 A similar *fatwā* was given also by al-Ṭayyib in 2003 in response to a question about terminal patients or those who suffer from diseases that have no known cures (Dār al-Iftāʾ al-Miṣriyya 2011, 27: 82).

first scenario the patient indicates his/her consent or permission, that would still conflict with the Sharīʿa provisions against any unjustified attack against life. Moreover, ending a patient's life in the second scenario would be categorised as premeditated murder, which is strictly prohibited in Sharīʿa (Q 4:93).[17] Similar *fatwās* by ʿAlī Jumʿa were issued in 2006 and 2007 but they focus more on the issue of switching off of life support measures. These later *fatwās* reiterate the position that al-Ṭayyib indicated above but they provide further information on the definition of the phrase "clinical death," which is used to describe the condition of a terminal patient who is put on medical devices in order to sustain his/her life but without resulting in any improvement in his/her situation (Dār al-Iftāʾ al-Miṣriyya 2011, 30:287–288, 36:167–168).

The position of the Egyptian Dār al-Iftāʾ on the issue of euthanasia is echoed in the opinions of other *fatwā* institutions. Most importantly, a distinction is often made between an intentional act of ending a person's life due to suffering from a terminal illness (whether by the patient himself/herself, by the patient with the help of a physician, or by a physician on the basis of his/her own assessment and initiative); and other acts involving cessation of therapeutic efforts in futile cases such as advanced stages of a terminal illness or switching off of life support measures in the case of comatose patients who are diagnosed as brain-dead. For example, the published collection of the *Fatwā* Committee affiliated with the Kuwaiti Ministry of Endowments and Islamic Affairs, which includes thirty volumes documenting responses from the late seventies until 2014, maintains this distinction by listing these two scenarios under different rubrics. Whereas questions inquiring about intentional efforts to end life are usually located within sections on crimes and punishments, questions inquiring about the permissibility of discontinuing futile treatment are located within sections on medicine and medical procedures.[18]

What is important to note here is that while the committee's responses to questions on merciful killing are quite categorical in emphasising the prohibition of any direct and intentional act aiming at ending life, even if motivated by mercy or kindness, questions on withholding futile therapeutic treatments are less categorical. For example, the committee received a question involving the case of a comatose patient who was already diagnosed as brain-dead and inquiring whether it would be possible to switch off the life support measures.

17 This *fatwā* is published on the website of Dār al-Iftāʾ: www.dar-alifta.org/Home/ViewFatwa?ID=11689.

18 The collection includes several *fatwās* in both sections. For example, for *fatwās* in the crimes and punishment sections, see Idārat al-Iftāʾ 1977–2014, 4:403–404; 15:411–412; and for *fatwās* in the medicine and medical procedures sections, see Idārat al-Iftāʾ 1977–2014, 21:399; 22:459–460; 27:416–417.

In its response, the committee indicated that as long as all the brain functions have stopped completely and irrevocably, as determined by reliable and trusted medical experts according to accepted medical standards, it would be permissible to switch off life-sustaining measures even if some organs are still showing signs of automatic or vegetative life as a result of being attached to these devices (Idārat al-Iftāʾ 1977–2014, 21:399). Other *fatwās* by the committee, however, are extremely cautious when it comes to withdrawing futile treatment in advanced cases of terminal illness even when no known cures are available. In more than one *fatwā*, the committee advised against the removal of artificial resuscitation equipment even when the patient's life is dependent on it. The main condition that is emphasised in these cases is the availability of the required medical equipment (Idārat al-Iftāʾ 1977–2014, 22:459–460, 27:415–417). Part of this seeming ambivalence on the permissibility of withdrawing futile treatment has to do with the attitude of the committee on the issue of brain death and whether it can be used as the decisive criterion to determine death. The committee has consistently maintained that death can be defined only in terms of the total and irreversible cessation of all the vital organs, including the heart (Idārat al-Iftāʾ 1977–2014, 3:449–451, 12:495–496, 30:485).

Availability of necessary medical equipment is occasionally listed as a condition for the continuation of resuscitation or ventilation measures for patients who cannot survive without these measures. For example, the Islamic Fiqh Council in India included this condition in its decree on the permissibility of withholding futile treatment. The decree (no. 68) includes also an explanation of the meaning of death, which it associates with the total cessation of breathing and the appearance of all the known signs of death. With regard to patients who rely on artificial measures to sustain their lives, these measures should continue as long as physicians see a possibility that patients can regain their ability to survive without these measures. However, if these patients or their families cannot afford the expenses of this type of treatment or if treating physicians believe that there is no possibility for these patients to regain their ability to breathe naturally, these measures can be discontinued. Also, in line with the preceding positions, the Islamic Fiqh Council in India issued another decree (no. 69) on the topic of mercy killing, which denounced categorically any unjustified attack against life, even if it is intended to relieve patients from the pains of a terminal illness, or their families from problems associated with medical treatment (Majmaʿ al-Fiqh al-Islāmī bi-l-Hind 2016, 256). The decree does not specify the type of problems that family members may encounter and whether they include financial ability but the phrasing of this decree and, of the preceding one, reveal the difficulty of reconciling moral principles disallowing the predication of life and death decisions on purely financial considerations with the hard realities of life that include, among other things, poverty and the difficulty of ensuring fair and equitable allocation of scarce medical resources.

Some of the main collective discussions that were held to investigate the issue of euthanasia were facilitated by the Islamic Organization for Medical Sciences (IOMS), based in Kuwait. Although the IOMS did not single out euthanasia as an independent topic for one of its seminars, it was often examined in relationship to other larger themes such as the definition of death, scope of medical treatment, and rights of the elderly (al-Jundī 2005, 415–417). Over the past few decades, the IOMS organised two panels to address the various dimensions of euthanasia in light of modern medical advances. The first was part of a seminar that was held in 1988 on health policies (al-Jundī 1997) and the second was part of a seminar that was held in 1999 on the rights of the elderly in Islam (al-Jundī 2001). The first panel consisted of two presentations reflecting both the medical and juristic perspectives, followed by an open discussion with the other participants in the seminar. The first presentation was given by ʿIṣām al-Shirbīnī, a medical consultant in internal medicine at al-Ṣabāḥ Hospital in Kuwait (al-Shirbīnī 1997a, 171–189) and the second was given by a senior scholar from al-Azhar in Egypt, Muḥammad Badr al-Dīn Ḥusām al-Dīn (Ḥusām al-Dīn 1997, 191–209). The second panel was in the form of a plenary session featuring several participants including Yūsuf al-Qaraḍāwī, the Tunisian scholar Muḥammad al-Mukhtār al-Sallāmī (d. 2019), and the Iranian scholar Muḥammad ʿAlī l-Taskhīrī (d. 2020) (al-Jundī 2001, 919–932). Both of these panels and subsequent discussions reiterated the main points in the *fatwā*s above, particularly the distinction between active and intentional acts aiming at ending life on the one hand, and other (in)actions that allow life to take its own course without excessive therapeutic interventions, on the other. The concluding statement of the seminar on the rights of the elderly included a passage on the issue of euthanasia, which denounced all activities that are intended to facilitate or hasten death. The passage indicated that consent by the patient or his family would be immaterial. Moreover, since futile treatment cannot be considered obligatory, withholding or withdrawal of therapeutic procedures in such cases would be permissible, provided that the basic rights of the patient are maintained. These rights include hydration, nutrition, nursing care, and pain relief (al-Jundī 2001, 1287).

The foregoing quick survey of the *fatwā* literature reveals that condemnation of active euthanasia is rooted in the Islamic ban on any unjustified attack against human life, which would include murder but also suicide. They are considered both religious sins and punishable crimes, although for suicide the punishment is in the Hereafter. The case of suicide is particularly important for the discussion on euthanasia because it implies voluntary action on the part of the person, but such voluntary action violates the divine stipulation in favour of the sanctity of human life. On the other hand, the attitude toward passive euthanasia depends on two main points: the legality of seeking medical treatment; and the recognition of brain or brainstem death.

3.3 *Active Euthanasia, Autonomy and Culpability*

Part of the difficulty of assessing the legal status of euthanasia is the perception that it is done voluntarily at the request of a terminally ill patient. But, as noted above with the case of suicide, approval of the person does not remove divine sanctions against any aggression on human life, since it is considered a right of God that cannot be revoked even by the victim's permission. This is the reason euthanasia, especially in its active form, is usually treated as a type of murder rather than suicide, which is evident in the fact that the word for murder (*qatl*) rather than suicide (*intiḥār*) is the one that is used to describe it, although often in combination with other descriptive terms indicating the motivation behind this action such as mercy (*raḥma*) or compassion (*shafaqa*).

3.3.1 Condemnation of Suicide

The Islamic ruling against suicide is rooted in several scriptural passages, in the Qur'ān but more frequently in the Prophetic Sunna. The main reference in the Qur'ān is 4:29: "and do not kill yourselves for indeed God is merciful to you." Although the general meaning of the verse implies prohibition of suicide, classical works of *tafsīr* offer more than one interpretation. In addition to the view that the verse indicates denunciation of suicide, according to a stronger interpretation, the pronoun "yourselves" (*anfusakum*) in this verse means each other rather than your own selves. Although the first (anti-suicide) interpretation is not entirely ruled out, classical commentators often reason that the other interpretation is in line with Arabic usage and is also meant to underscore the sense of solidarity and unity within the Muslim community. This is also supported by the first part of the verse, which includes denunciation of unlawfully consuming each other's wealth (al-Ṭabarī 2001, 6:637–639; Brockopp 2003). Several classical commentators did indeed include supporting arguments for an anti-suicide reading of this verse (al-Rāzī 1981, 10:74; Ibn ʿAṭiyya 2015, 3:120; al-Jaṣṣāṣ 1992, 3:141; and Ibn Kathīr 2009, 2:34). One of the main narratives used to support this interpretation involves the companion ʿAmr b. al-ʿĀṣ (d. 43/664), who is reported to have cited this verse in order to vindicate himself before the Prophet. According to this report, when ʿAmr was sent as the leader of an expedition, known as Dhāt al-Salāsil, he had a wet dream in a cold night. Instead of washing his body, he performed dry ablution and led his companions during the early morning prayer. When they mentioned this to the Prophet upon returning, he asked ʿAmr if he performed the prayer while in a state of impurity (*janāba*). ʿAmr replied by citing the verse, which implied that he feared if he washed his body in that weather he would die. According to the report, when the Prophet heard what ʿAmr had to say, he smiled and did not say anything. Commentators on this report noted that the Prophet's silence in this case indicated tacit approval (al-Khaṭṭābī 2016, 1:168). Modern commentators and scholars also use this verse to emphasise the Islamic condemnation of suicide (Riḍā n.d., 5:38).

Apart from this particular verse, the Qurʾān also includes several other passages indicating the prohibition of an unjustified attack against human life. Muslim scholars often include suicide under this general prohibition of aggression on human life (Shaltūt 2004, 362). The main evidence against suicide, however, usually comes from the Prophetic Sunna, which includes several reports indicating denunciation of the act and severe punishment for the doer in the Hereafter. For example, in one *ḥadīth*, the Prophet is reported as having said:

> whoever throws himself off from a mountain aiming to kill himself, he will be forever throwing himself off in the Hellfire, whoever swallows poison in order to kill himself, he will be holding his poison in his hand and will be forever drinking it in the Hellfire, and whoever stabs himself with a piece of iron in order to kill himself, he will be holding his piece of iron and stabbing himself forever in the Hellfire.
>
> IBN ḤAJAR AL-ʿASQALĀNĪ n.d., 10:247

Commentators on this *ḥadīth* and its various narrations note that it provides important clarifications on the religious-moral status of the suicide and his fate. For example, it is indicated that the *ḥadīth* is meant to single out those who commit the act intentionally, which would exclude those who accidently end up killing themselves (Ibn Ḥajar al-ʿAsqalānī n.d., 10:248).[19] On the other hand, other theologians gave different interpretations, which included: use of

---

19 There are several narrations of this *ḥadīth* in *Ṣaḥīḥ al-Bukhārī*. This narration is included in *Kitāb al-Ṭibb* ("Book of Medicine") (Ibn Ḥajar al-ʿAsqalānī n.d., 10:247). Other narrations are also included in other chapters in *Ṣaḥīḥ al-Bukhārī*. For example, *Kitāb al-Janāʾiz* ("Book of Funerals") includes three reports: "whoever kills himself with a piece of iron, he will be tortured by it in the Hellfire," "once a man was wounded and he killed himself. God said: 'my servant took the initiative to end his life, and therefore I have prohibited Paradise on him,'" and "whoever strangles himself, he will be strangling himself in the Hellfire and whoever stabs himself he will be stabbing himself in the Hellfire" (Ibn Ḥajar al-ʿAsqalānī n.d., 3:226). *Kitāb al-Aymān wa-l-Nudhūr* ("Book of Oaths and Vows") includes one report: "whoever kills himself with something, he will be tortured by it in the Hellfire" (Ibn Ḥajar al-ʿAsqalānī nd: 11:537).

other narrations that do not include reference to the eternity of punishment, that eternity is only the punishment of those who willingly and intentionally perpetrate the act, that it is meant only as a severe warning without being the actual punishment, that reference to eternity is meant to connote length of stay rather than actual eternity, and that such punishment is dependent on God's will (Ibn Ḥajar al-ʿAsqalānī n.d., 3:227–228).

Another *ḥadīth* recounts an incident of suicide among the earlier nations. According to this *ḥadīth* the Prophet is reported as having said:

> among the people before you once a man was wounded. Being upset, he took a knife and cut his hand and as a result he bled until he died. God then said: "my servant took the initiative by killing himself, I have made Paradise prohibited on him."
>
> IBN ḤAJAR AL-ʿASQALĀNĪ n.d., 6:496[20]

Another *ḥadīth*, on the other hand, recounts an incident during the Prophet's lifetime, which is usually quoted to distinguish those who engage in *jihād*, sincerely, from others who may have selfish or worldly motives (Ibn Ḥajar al-ʿAsqalānī n.d., 6:89–90).[21]

---

20 This *ḥadīth* is recorded in *Kitāb Aḥādīth al-Anbiyāʾ* ("Book of Reports of Prophets") in *Ṣaḥīḥ al-Bukhārī*.

21 This *ḥadīth* is recorded in *Kitāb al-Jihād* ("Book of *Jihād*") with a few variations. According to this report, once during a battle that the Prophet had with the disbelievers, a man in the Muslims' camp was spotted fighting extremely hard. People were praising him so much to the extent that they thought no one could be compared to him. The Prophet, however, noted that he was from the people of the Hellfire. One of the listeners decided to follow him to learn more about his situation. Eventually that brave man was severely wounded, but he was impatient and wanted to hasten his death. He put the hand of his sword on the ground and its pointed end between his nipples. He then pushed the sword against his chest and killed himself. Upon seeing this, the man who was following him rushed to the Prophet and informed him about what he saw. The Prophet then said: "a person may do the work of the people of Paradise in front of others while he is actually from the people of the Hellfire. Conversely, a person may do the work of the people of the Hellfire in front of others while he is actually from the people of Paradise." This *ḥadīth* is also recorded with slight variations in *Kitāb al-Riqāq* ("Book of Admonitions") (Ibn Ḥajar al-ʿAsqalānī n.d., 11:330) and in *Kitāb al-Qadar* ("Book of Predestination") (Ibn Ḥajar al-ʿAsqalānī n.d., 11:498–489). Other narrations of this *ḥadīth* are also recorded in *Kitāb al-Maghāzī* ("Book of Excursions") in *Ṣaḥīḥ al-Bukhārī*. These other narrations have small variations and add further information about the incident. For example, according to one narration, the incident took place during the battle of Khaybar (7/628). Moreover, according to another narration, the man killed himself by arrows rather than a sword. Finally, in the other narration, the Prophet is quoted as saying: "only a (true) believer would be admitted into Paradise and God may support the cause of this religion by the work of an

Despite the severe punishment mentioned in these reports in the Hereafter for the suicide, no punishment is indicated in this world – for example, in case of an unsuccessful attempt to end one's life. This absence of a worldly punishment, as compared to the punishment of murder, raised important questions in the legal tradition on the proper treatment of the dead bodies of individuals who take their own lives, and whether they should be treated as Muslims when it comes to the final rites, which include washing, shrouding, offering of the funeral prayer, and burial. Some jurists advanced the view that the supreme leader or *Imām* should not offer the prayer for the suicide, but other Muslims should pray as a way to convey condemnation of the act and also to deter others. This is the view of Aḥmad b. Ḥanbal (d. 241/855) and it is based on a Prophetic report, according to which the Prophet refused to offer the funeral prayer on a person when he knew that he killed himself by a type of broad arrows (*mashāqiṣ*, sing. *mishqaṣ*) (al-Nawawī 1929, 7:47). Some early authorities such as ʿUmar II (d. 101/720) and al-Awzāʿī (d. 157/774) were of the view that no funeral prayer should be offered for the suicide because if the *Imām* does not offer the funeral prayer in this case, no one else should, as is the case with the martyr in the battlefield. Other early authorities, however, such as ʿAṭāʾ (d. *c.*115/733), al-Nakhaʿī (d. *c.*96/714), and al-Shāfiʿī (d. 204/820) were of the view that the funeral prayer should be performed for a Muslim who committed suicide, both by the *Imām* and others due to the Prophetic report indicating that prayer should be held for all who bore the testimony of faith (Ibn Qudāma 1997, 3:504; al-Shirbīnī 1997b, 1:537). Similarly, Abū Ḥanīfa (d. 150/767) is of the view that proper washing and funeral prayer should be offered for the suicide. Only his disciple Abū Yūsuf (d. 182/798) was of the opinion that a suicide's body should be washed but no funeral prayer should be offered in this case (Ibn ʿĀbidīn 2003, 3:108–109).

Similar to Abū Ḥanīfa, Mālik (d. 179/796) held the view that suicides' bodies should be treated in the same way that the bodies of deceased Muslims are treated and they shall answer to God for the sin they committed (Wizārat al-Awqāf 2008, 16:7). Different opinions are reported also within the Mālikī school. According to Ibn Rushd (d. 595/1198), this disagreement has to do with the assessment of the report indicating the Prophet's refusal to offer the funeral prayer on a person who killed himself. Those who considered this report reliable argued against offering the funeral prayer for the suicide while

insolent man." While some commentators argued that these two narrations cover more than one incident, others argued that they document the same incident and accordingly sought to reconcile the details of the two accounts (Ibn Ḥajar al-ʿAsqalānī n.d., 7:471–472).

those who questioned the report argued for the permissibility of offering the funeral prayer on the grounds that although a Muslim who commits suicide would be punished in the Hellfire, according to multiple reports, he will not stay in Hellfire forever because he remains from the people of faith, who would eventually be saved (Ibn Rushd 1982, 1:239–240; al-Zuḥaylī 2012, 2:425).[22]

In the contemporary *fatwā* literature, while scholars usually denounce the act of committing suicide, they often note that the punishment for suicide is in the Hereafter and they advise that the suicide's body should be treated like the body of a deceased Muslim. For example, according to a *fatwā* on the permissibility of performing the funeral prayer on the suicide, the former head *muftī* of Egypt Naṣr Farīd Wāṣil (b. 1937) noted that as long as the person was a Muslim and bore the testimony of faith, he should be treated as such and therefore washing and shrouding his body, as well as offering the funeral prayer in this case would be a collective duty on the Muslim community (Dār al-Iftāʾ al-Miṣriyya 2011, 24:175–177). This foregoing discussion on suicide is important for the topics of autonomy and euthanasia for several reasons. To begin with, an intentional decision to end one's life cannot be tolerated or condoned, in view of Islamic norms concerning the sanctity of human life. Yet, the general ambivalence within the theological-juristic discourses on the fate of the suicide suggests that ultimate judgment should be suspended and relegated to the Hereafter. A distinction is, therefore, made between the religious-moral status of the suicide (*vis-à-vis* God) and their religious-moral standing within the community. While their salvation in the Hereafter is to be left to God to decide, the above outline of the normative discussions on the last rites in their case shows that many jurists recommended treating them (their bodies) as Muslims. An argument for the extension of this distinction between the religious-moral status before God and the religious-moral standing within the community, in the case of those who undergo euthanasia, can be made in light of the ambiguity that surrounds the true motivations behind the two acts of suicide and euthanasia. Such an argument can even be strengthened by the fact that some of the Prophetic reports that are used to condemn suicide indicate that the motivation behind the act was to put an end to pain and suffering, which is also the main motive in the case of euthanasia. This nonetheless would not rule out the fact that active euthanasia would remain a

22 Franz Rosenthal (d. 2003) points out some of the problems associated with the issue of suicide in the Islamic tradition. In addition to the standard treatment of the topic in theological-juristic discussions, he also surveys literary depictions of suicide as well as alleged historical cases of suicide in Islamic history (see Rosenthal 1946).

moral-religious sin and that invocation of personal autonomy would not serve as sufficient grounds to justify it.

3.3.2 Condemnation of Murder

The prohibition of murder is rooted in multiple scriptural references in the Qur'ān (e.g., 6:151; 17:33) and in numerous Prophetic reports banning and disallowing any unjustified attack on human life. Murder is considered one of the major crimes under Sharīʿa for which a stipulated punishment (*ḥadd*) is prescribed. It is also counted as one of the major sins for which severe punishment in the Hereafter is promised (Q 4:93). The majority of jurists distinguish three types of murder depending on the intent of the perpetrator: intentional, semi-intentional, and unintentional or by mistake. The Mālikī school, however, recognises only two types, the intentional (which for them includes the semi-intentional) and the unintentional, and the Ḥanafī school adds two types, which they call semi-unintentional and murder by causation. Still some Ḥanbalī jurists merge these two types into one, so for them there are four types (Ibn Qudāma 1997, 11:445; Wizārat al-Awqāf 2008, 32:323–326).

Intentional murder is one in which three conditions are satisfied: that the victim is a human being who is enjoying a stable life at the time of murder; that murder is the result of attack by the perpetrator(s); and that the perpetrator(s) must have intended to cause the death of the victim (ʿAwda 2003, 2:12).[23] What is important to note in this context is that the jurists did not restrict culpability to the actual perpetrator of the act of intentional murder but they also extended it to a person who causes it (*mutasabbib*). Intentional killing involves the use of a lethal weapon or method such as: a pointed tool (*muḥaddad*) like a sword or knife; use of another tool that is likely to cause death; obstructing breathing by strangling or any similar method; exposing the victim to a situation that is likely to lead to their death; or forcing the victim to swallow poison. Intentional killing by causation includes several scenarios, of which the main one is the case of coercion, when a person forces another to kill someone.

The jurists disagreed on whether a causing (*mutasabib*)/coercing (*mukrih*) agent should receive the same punishment as the actual perpetrator (*mubāshir*)/ coerced (*mukrah*) person. The Mālikī school held the view that only

23 The term "stable life" (*ḥayāt mustaqirra*) is a technical term that is used in the Islamic legal tradition to denote a state of life when man is fully conscious and is also capable of voluntary movement even in case of injury. This state is often contrasted with the state of "continuing life" (*al-ḥayāt al-mustamirra*), which denotes one's state of life from beginning to end, and "life of a slain person" (*ḥayāt ʿaysh al-madhbūḥ*), which denotes a state in which man is not fully conscious or capable of voluntary actions (Ibn al-ʿImād al-Aqfahsī 2009).

the perpetrator should be killed and the causing person should receive a suitable punishment, which is also the view of al-Shāfiʿī, al-Thawrī (d. *c.*161/778), Ibn Ḥanbal, Abū Thawr (d. 240/854) and others. Other jurists, however, held the view that both should be killed in return in case there was no coercion on the part of the causing person (Ibn Rushd 1982, 2:396). On the other hand, if the causing person had a form of authority or coercing power over the coerced person, the jurists were divided into three main groups. The first held the view that only the ordering person should be killed and the ordered person should receive a suitable punishment, which is the view of Abū Dāwūd (d. 275/889) and one of the views attributed to al-Shāfiʿī. The second group held the opposite view; that only the coerced person should be killed and the ordering person should receive a suitable punishment, which is the other view attributed to al-Shāfiʿī. The third held the view that both should be killed, which is the view of Mālik and Ibn Ḥanbal (Ibn Rushd 1982, 2:396; Ibn Qudāma 1997, 11:455). Within the Ḥanafī school several opinions were expressed. According to Abū Ḥanīfa and Muḥammad b. al-Ḥasan al-Shaybānī (d. 189/805), as noted above, only the causing/coercing person should be killed in return because, in this case, the perpetrator/coerced person had diminished agency. Zufar b. al-Hudhayl (d. 158/775) held the opposite view; only the perpetrator should be killed in return because it was him who undertook the act. Still, Abū Yūsuf held the view that none of them should be killed because although each of them carries partial responsibility for the act, none of them can take full responsibility for it. (Ibn Qudāma 1997, 11:444–457).[24] In general, juristic discussions on the respective responsibility of either the perpetrator or the causing agent for the act is based on the exact role that each of them plays in facilitating the act of murder or its performance (al-Zuḥaylī 2012, 6:352).

Apart from the particular case of suicide, where the person takes the initiative to end his own life, the jurists also discuss the culpability of a murderer in case the act of murder is forgiven by the victim prior to his/her death. This is usually covered under the conditions or cases that allow the waiving of retribution (*musqiṭāt al-qiṣāṣ*). In general, the jurists discuss four main reasons for the waiver of retribution: death of the murderer, forgiveness, mutual settlement, and devolvement of the right to exact retribution to someone who cannot execute it, which is usually the case within close family members (al-Zuḥaylī 2012, 6:268). In the case of forgiveness, it is usually sought from the close family

24 Other scenarios of causation include: false testimony that may lead to/cause the death of someone, unjust ruling by a judge who intentionally issues it and that leads to the death of an innocent person, intentionally digging a well or creating an ambush in order to cause the death of someone (Ibn Qudāma 1997, 11:456–457; Wizārat al-Awqāf 2008, 32:325–326).

members of the victim, who have the right to request or demand retribution after the death of the victim.

The jurists disagreed on the possibility that a person in the case of intentional murder can forgive his/her killer before that person's death. The majority of jurists (within the Ḥanafī, Mālikī, Shāfiʿī, and Ḥanbalī schools) were of the opinion that forgiveness by the victim can waive the right to demand both retribution and the blood money. According to this view, since the victim owns the original right to exact retribution and the blood money, his forgiveness can drop these rights (Ibn Qudāma 1997, 11:589–590; Ibn al-Mundhir 2010, 13:122–124; al-Zuḥaylī 2012, 6:274).

Forgiveness by the victim is usually discussed within the context of retribution for injuries, which may eventually lead to or result in death (*sirāya*). The question that the jurists debate in this connection is whether forgiveness would be limited to the injuries in question or whether it would be extended to death in case it happens as a result of these injuries. According to the Ḥanafī jurists, forgiveness by the victim after being injured and prior to death cannot be based on a straightforward analogy (*qiyās*) because forgiveness for murder can only occur after but not before death. It can, however, be permitted on the basis of a juristic preference (*istiḥsān*). Accordingly, although forgiveness was actually expressed before death, it occurred as a result of the leading cause of death in this case, which was the injury that eventually led to the victim's death (al-Kāsānī 2003, 10:291).[25] According to some Shāfiʿī jurists, forgiveness of an injury drops the right to demand retribution or compensation for that injury. If that injury ends up causing the death of the victim, retribution cannot be demanded because the earlier forgiveness for the injury constitutes doubt that prevents the application of retribution in this case (al-Shirbīnī 1997b, 4:67; Wizārat al-Awqāf 2008, 30:177–178).[26]

---

25 According to one view attributed to Mālik, if a person expressed forgiveness for an injury and then eventually died because of it, such forgiveness would not apply unless that person explicitly indicated that he forgave the injurer for this injury and whatever it resulted in (Abū Zahra 2015, 488).

26 According to some Shāfiʿī jurists, if a person gives permission to someone to injure him, that person cannot demand either retribution or compensation for that injury because the prior consent that he gave drops the right to demand these two claims. The same would also apply in case the injury leads to death because prior permission prevents the application of retribution. It is noted, however, that according to another view, blood money must be paid. This disagreement is based on the conceptualisation of the blood money and whether it is originally due to the victim (just prior to death), which is then transferred to the heirs upon death or whether it is originally due to the heirs without any claim for the (dead) victim. According to the former view, the victim has the right to drop it but according to the latter view he does not (al-Shirbīnī 1997b, 4:67; Ibn al-Mulaqqin

Other jurists, however, argued that in the case of intentional murder the victim cannot forgive his killer because this right belongs to the heirs, who are given the right to choose between forgiveness, exacting retribution, or acceptance of the blood money (Ibn Rushd 1982, 2:403). Moreover, according to another view within the Shāfiʿī school and also according to the Ẓāhirī school, retribution is an original right that belongs to the heirs and punishment for the crime of murder cannot be dropped by the victim's approval or forgiveness. They reasoned that the *ḥadd* punishment cannot be waived on the basis of consent as is the case in fornication, which cannot be made licit in case a man and a woman express their consent (Ibn al-Mulaqqin 2018, 12:527; Ibn Ḥazm 2005, 7:622–629).[27] Another question that the jurists debated with regard to premeditated murder, even in the case of prior forgiveness by the victim, is

---

2018, 12:527). Another scenario that was discussed within the Shāfiʿī school was if a person forces someone to kill him. Two views are recorded. The first is that retribution would still apply because murder cannot be permitted even with the consent of the victim, similar to the case of fornication, which cannot be permitted in the case of consent. The second, which is the main view within the school, is that retribution cannot apply due to the doubt created by the victim's consent. As for the exacting of blood money, also two views are recorded, depending on whether it is considered an original right due to the victim during the latest part of his life, which is then transferred to the heirs upon death or whether it is an original right due to the heirs directly. The preferred view of the Shāfiʿī jurists is that it is due to the victim and accordingly in this case no blood money can be requested (al-Shirbīnī 1997b, 4:17). In the commentary of Ibn al-Mulaqqin (d. 801/1404), additional justification is provided for the dropping of both retribution and blood money in this case. It is noted that prior forgiveness by the victim prevents the application of retribution. The addition of coercion to mere consent or forgiveness makes a stronger reason for the dropping of retribution. The same reasoning applies also with regard to blood money. However, another question that relates to this case is whether a coerced person would be liable for the payment of the full amount of the blood money or only its half. If it is half that would be the amount that the coerced person would need to pay. Some jurists, however, held the view that the coerced person would still be liable for the payment of the full amount but in this case, it will be transferred to the inheritance of the victim. Yet, according to these jurists, the levying of the blood money would be pointless (Ibn al-Mulaqqin 2018, 12:402–403). A similar scenario was also discussed by the Ḥanafī jurists; that is, if a person gives permission to someone to kill him. It is noted that in this case retribution does not apply due to the doubt that consent creates here but blood money would still apply because murder cannot be allowed even with prior permission (Ibn ʿĀbidīn 2003, 10:193).

27 These opinions pertain mainly to the case of intentional or premeditated murder. With regard to unintentional murder or one done by mistake, since retribution does not apply and the main punishment is payment of blood money, which should be paid by the agnate relatives (*ʿaṣaba*) rather than by the killer himself, most jurists held the view that in the case of prior forgiveness by the victim it can be paid from the victim's inheritance within the limits of the third only (al-Zuḥaylī 2012, 6:274; Wizārat al-Awqāf 2008, 30:180–181; Ibn Rushd 1982, 2:403). Similar to the case of the intentional or premeditated murder, some

whether the ruler has the right to exact additional punishment. While some jurists held the view that the killer should be punished with one hundred lashes in addition to imprisonment for one year, others argued that no additional punishment should be applied. Still a third group held the view that only in the case of individuals who are known for their bad character, the ruler can implement a suitable punishment (Ibn Rushd 1982, 2:404).

On the face of it, juristic discourses on both the responsibility for murder and forgiveness by the victim seem to push in different directions. While the discourse on the first point seems to enhance the gravity of murder by extending culpability to include causing, not just committing the act, the discourse on the second point suggests that, at least in certain cases, punishment for murder, if forgiven by the victim prior to death, may be suspended or decreased. But, more on the second point, how do we balance these views with the strong condemnation against any unjustified attack against human life? Clearly, these views are primarily concerned with delineating the boundaries of liability and punishment in this world, but they do not rule out moral responsibility for the act in the Hereafter. Even for the views absolving the murderer in case the act is approved or fore-forgiven by the victim, murder remains morally wrong and the perpetrator and the victim will still have to answer to God for violating the sanctity of human life. Moreover, in the case of approval or forgiveness by the victim, other factors would still need to be considered, which cannot be waived by such forgiveness, including the application of religious expiation (*kaffāra*) as part of the rights owed to God in the area of *ḥudūd* (al-Shirbīnī 1997, 4:67) as well as further procedures that can be demanded by the ruler in these cases in order to achieve deterrence (Ibn Rushd 1982, 2:404).

As noted above with regard to suicide, these juristic views on the responsibility and possible punishment for murder can be useful in similar discussions involving determination of liability in the case of euthanasia or assisted suicide. These discussions on prior forgiveness or consent by the victim reveal the role of personal autonomy in the determination of liability. These views show that personal autonomy can play a role in qualifying the criminal responsibility in the case of consensual homicide, and consequently the applicable punishment and other related consequences such as the payment of blood money.[28] They still, however, show that consent of the victim does not change

jurists, mainly the Ẓāhirī school, denied this possibility on the grounds that this is a right due to the heirs rather than the victim himself (Ibn Ḥazm 2005, 7:628).

28 In light of recent efforts, mainly in the US, to increase the scope of intervention to facilitate a terminally ill patient's wish to end their life, some researchers make a distinction between homicide on request and assisted suicide. The main difference lies in the last step in the process. In the case of homicide on request, a physician administers a lethal

the religious-moral status of the act of murder in this case, which remains a sin for which the parties involved would answer to God in the Hereafter.

3.4 *Passive Euthanasia, Medical Treatment, and Brain Death Criteria*

As outlined above, opinions in contemporary Islamic literature concerning passive forms of euthanasia often revolve around withholding (futile) treatment in advanced cases of terminal illness or switching off of life support measures, especially in the case of patients diagnosed as brain-dead. These opinions are usually linked to relevant discourses in the Islamic ethical-legal tradition. While active euthanasia is placed within classical discourses on both murder and suicide, passive euthanasia is anchored in discourses on medical treatment and the definition of death.

3.4.1 Withholding Futile Treatment

The argument for the permissibility of passive euthanasia in the case of futile treatment is based on the attitude towards the question of seeking medical treatment, which, as al-Qaraḍāwī notes, is not deemed obligatory by the majority of jurists but rather remains in the realm of permissibility (al-Qaraḍāwī 2000, 2:579). Only a minority opinion within the Shāfiʿī and Ḥanbalī schools argue for its obligation while others argue that it is recommended. In general, the jurists debate the preferability of seeking medical treatment over exercising patience. Al-Qaraḍāwī, for example, supports the view that seeking medical treatment can be obligatory or recommended in case of severe pain and when recovery or improvement is anticipated according to professional standards and in line with God's law of causality. Otherwise, if medical treatment is expected to prolong illness and increase the suffering of patients and their families, medical treatment cannot be deemed obligatory or recommended. On the contrary, withholding medical treatment in this case could be more recommended. Al-Qaraḍāwī argues that this scenario should not be categorised under euthanasia (*qatl al-raḥma*) but should rather be categorised as refraining from an action that is neither obligatory nor recommended and therefore its omission should not be blameworthy (al-Qaraḍāwī 2000, 2:580–581).

---

injection, while in the case of assisted suicide, a physician may prescribe a lethal drug that the patient can take by himself (Veatch and Guidry-Grimes 2020, 160). Veatch and Guidry-Grimes note that as of 2019, assisted suicide in the case of mentally capable and terminally ill patients is considered legal in a number of states that include: California, Colorado, District of Columbia, Hawaii, Maine, Montana, New Jersey, Oregon, Vermont, and Washington. The practice is also considered legal in a number of European countries such as Switzerland, Germany, the Netherlands, and Belgium.

Al-Qaraḍāwī's view on futile medical treatment echoes the resolution of the International Islamic Fiqh Academy (IIFA), which includes within its membership both Sunnī and Shīʿī scholars, on medical treatment. The resolution was issued at the conclusion of its seventh session in 1992. On the question of medical treatment, the resolution indicated that the ruling could change depending on the specific situation of the patient. For example, it can be categorised as obligatory in case a patient would suffer disability or death if left without treatment. It is also deemed obligatory in the case of communicable diseases. It can be categorised as recommended if lack of treatment would result in weakening of the body but not disability or death. Apart from these two cases, it is generally deemed permissible (*mubāḥ*). On the other hand, medical treatment is deemed reprehensible in case it is anticipated to result in worsening the patient's current condition. With regard to cases of futile treatment, the resolution emphasised the importance of maintaining faith in God's ability to heal all diseases. It encouraged medical professionals as well as family members to provide all necessary support to patients and to work on strengthening their morale. As far as the determination of certain treatments as futile, the resolution indicated that such assessment has to be made by medical experts in light of the established professional standards and in accordance with the specific circumstances of patients (IIFA 1992, 731–744).[29]

In light of these views on the issue of medical treatment, the patient can exercise his will by indicating preference to forgo such treatment when it is deemed futile. This, in turn, illustrates how personal autonomy can play a role in the context of passive forms of euthanasia. This is also perhaps the context that demonstrates the close connection between medicine and faith, especially when therapeutic procedures come close to a dead end. As medical solutions show their limits, faith becomes an important resource for renewed hope in the infinite power and mercy of the divine. The illness experience itself becomes an opportunity for spiritual growth. It also allows a deeper reflection on the transience of existence in this worldly life and the need to keep one's priorities in proper perspective. Recent research by Muslim clinicians in the area of EoL care reveals the potential of these religious discussions on medical treatment in developing more informed attitudes on the part of both care providers as well as patients and their families with regard to EoL decisions.

29 The physician Muḥammad ʿAlī l-Bārr concluded the paper he submitted to this session on the topic of medical treatment with a question about the distinction between active/positive and passive euthanasia. He did not provide a categorical answer to this question in an indication that there was a need for the members of the IIFA to address this issue (al-Bārr 1992, 595).

In particular, they can help in assessing the need for or viability of therapeutic intervention and the possibility of forgoing medical treatment in futile cases (Padela and Qureshi 2017). Similarly, empirical research shows the importance of religious beliefs in the formulation of EoL decisions by Muslim patients, which include withholding or withdrawing medical treatment.

For example, a study on the attitudes of middle-aged and elderly Muslim women of Moroccan origin in Belgium shows that religious convictions play an important role in shaping their opinions on EoL choices (Ahaddour et al. 2018b). In their responses to questions about the possibility of withholding or withdrawing a curative or a life-sustaining treatment, the majority of respondents, about two thirds, were not in favour of prolonging a treatment that is deemed futile. The reasons given are tied to belief in the predestined time for one's death, which is believed to be solely determined by God. On the other hand, about one third of the respondents expressed preference to initiate or continue a curative or life-sustaining treatment. The reasons given are also tied to belief in the predestined time for death but with more emphasis on the importance of taking into account the importance of causes, understood here to include medical treatment. Some of the responses also emphasised God's healing power. What is interesting to note in these responses is that they demonstrate the different interpretations of divine predestination and the assigned time of death. For those who oppose the initiation or continuation of treatment, the onset of the medical condition that is characterised as terminal is perhaps seen as a strong sign for the end or near the end of life. On the other hand, for those who are in favour of initiating or continuing treatment, the exact moment of death remains unknown and only subject to divine will. Moreover, they see almost an obligation on the part of the person to utilise all possible means to preserve life to the extent possible.[30] These responses

30 In his chapter on the concept of the good death in Islamic theology and law, Jonathan Brockopp refers to the notion of *ajal* and that it can play an important role in the ethical-legal evaluation of euthanasia. For example, he notes that because modern medical applications at the end of human life have the capacity to maintain life artificially almost indefinitely, they could end up preventing the predestined *ajal* from coming to term. Accordingly, an argument in favour of passive euthanasia or living wills could be made on the basis of this argument. Moreover, he points out that these medical advances have the potential of reorienting the focus from the actual moment of death to the teleology of death, which can allow for an argument in favour of both active and passive euthanasia (Brockopp 2003, 189). With regard to the first point, as these responses indicate, this will depend on how the concept of *ajal* is understood and whether humans can really change it. On the second point, as the discussions on murder, suicide and active euthanasia illustrate, one can also argue that the Islamic teleology of death cannot be determined in isolation of how one lives his life but also how one dies.

illustrate the freedom-submission tension, mentioned above in the introduction. While the first group's interpretation allows and empowers them to take the initiative to refuse or stop futile treatment and to submit to the divine will, the second group's interpretation equally allows and empowers them to hold on to life to the last moment possible, and for them this would be the best way to submit to God's will.

The value of this empirical research is quite immense not only because it shows how normative views are internalised by individual believers but also because it demonstrates the complexity of real-life situations involving patients, along with their care giver and families, who have to make these difficult decisions and weigh out options. While this confirms the important role of religious beliefs, it also demonstrates that these beliefs are often subject to multiple interpretations. It also shows that these decisions are not always made on the basis of one single factor, but they are often the result of a multiplicity of social, cultural, and economic factors. For example, the study reveals that some of the reasons given by the respondents who oppose life-sustaining treatment include fear of financial burdens on the family. As noted above, some of the juristic pronouncements on this issue already mentioned financial ability to cover the cost of treatment as one of the factors that play a role in the process of decision-making in these situations. This is particularly the case with questions on the continuation of treatment in situations involving those diagnosed as brain-dead who are kept on artificial ventilation, which is discussed in the following section. For the purpose of the present discussion, this empirical research shows that personal autonomy in EoL situations is not always the main determining factor. For example, researchers in the areas of palliative medicine and EoL care warn that other social or economic factors may compel terminal patients to opt for ways to end their life and that such decisions can, in fact, be avoided if the concerns and needs of patients are properly understood and addressed (Broeckaert 2008b, 112).

3.4.2 Brain Death and Switching off Life Support

The second scenario, which is usually subsumed under passive euthanasia, involves the case of (unconscious) patients on life support who are considered medically as brain-dead. Al-Qaraḍāwī argues that this scenario, similar to the previous one, revolves around withdrawing or withholding futile treatment. The main difference between these two scenarios is that in this case the patient may be categorised as already dead according to the brain death criteria (al-Qaraḍāwī 2000, 2:581). Although he does not refer to the debate on brain death, he observes that he shared this view previously at one of the IOMS meetings before a group of jurists and physicians and it was met with approval. Al-Qaraḍāwī refers to a meeting that the IOMS organised to discuss the beginning and end of human life that was held in 1985. This meeting represents one of the earliest attempts in the Muslim world to suggest the adoption of the brain death criteria as the decisive definition of death, which was underscored in the statement issued at the conclusion of this meeting (al-Madhkūr et al. 1985, 677–678). The comment that al-Qaraḍāwī made in one of the open discussions during this meeting concentrated on the difference this new conceptualisation of death would make on two main points: facilitating organ donation; and providing more clarity on the issue of removal of life support measures (al-Madhkūr et al. 1985, 523–525). Over the years the IOMS has confirmed this attitude, especially in a subsequent meeting that was held in 1996, more than a decade after this initial meeting (al-Jundī et al. 2000, 911–921).

This attitude was also supported by the IIFA in 1986, as indicated in the resolution that was issued at the conclusion of its third session. According to this resolution, a person can be considered dead with the existence of one of two signs: if the heart and breathing stopped completely and the physicians declared that this cessation is irreversible; and if all the brain functions became completely and irrevocably disabled, as determined by medical experts, and the brain cells started to deteriorate. According to the resolution, in this case artificial resuscitation can be lifted, even if some of the organs continue to work automatically because of these devices (IIFA 1986, 523; al-Jundī 2005, 358).

Similarly, the Islamic Fiqh Council of the Muslim World League issued a resolution at the conclusion of its 10th session in 1987, which also recognised the brain death criteria, although the phrasing of this resolution was more cautious. For example, it added a stipulation that the diagnosis of brain death has to be confirmed by a committee of three specialists. It also added that death can only be decided according to Sharīʿa after the heart and breathing have stopped completely, following the removal of the resuscitation devices (Rābiṭat al-ʿĀlam al-Islāmī n.d., 214).[31]

Despite the growing acceptance of the brain death criteria, this topic remains quite controversial both at the medical and ethical-legal levels (Krawietz 2003; Moosa 1999; Padela et al. 2013). As noted in the brief survey of the *fatwā* literature above, not all jurists are unanimous and some still insist on

31 The reserved tone of this resolution is also confirmed in the publications of some of the scholars who signed this resolution. For example, in his book on new jurisprudential issues, the Saudi jurist Bakr ʿAbd Allāh Abū Zayd noted that if physicians are in doubt, they should give priority to preserving life. He also emphasised the need for further research on this issue (Abū Zayd 2012, 1:234).

the traditional cardiopulmonary criteria to define death.[32] Consequently, the attitude towards passive forms of euthanasia, if this scenario is categorised as a form of passive euthanasia, would depend, at least in part, on whether the brain death criteria are accepted.

Speaking about the role of personal autonomy in this case might seem irrelevant since patients in these situations are usually unconscious and relevant decisions are made by surrogates. Here again, however empirical research adds important insights on how individuals think about these situations. The study involving Muslim women in Belgium cited above includes a question on what is referred to as "non-treatment decisions" in the case of comatose patients (Ahaddour et al. 2018b, 352).[33] According to the study, the respondents fell into three main categories: about one half were not in favour of switching off life support; about one third were in favour; and about one sixth were undecided. The reasons that the first group gave revolved again around the question of the predestined time for death, which can only be known to God. Some have even indicated the possibility of a divine miraculous intervention in the case of people in deep coma. For the second group, continuation of treatment merely extends life beyond meaningful existence. Similar to the responses on the first question about withholding or withdrawing futile treatment, this group also appealed to the notion of the predestined time for death to indicate that, in the case of people in deep coma who are kept on life support, this time has already come. Some respondents actually noted that artificial prolongation of life delays the process of passing on to the next life. In addition to these religious-theological reasons, some respondents expressed concern over the associated financial costs, which represent significant added burden on the family. Given the grave complexity that these situations entail, respondents in the third group were unable to make a clear decision either way.

---

32 Although IOMS has played a leading role in promoting the concept of the brain death, the *Fatwā* Committee of the Ministry of Endowments in Kuwait has repeatedly noted that death can only be defined on the basis of breathing and heartbeat. The published collection even includes clear reference to letters sent from IOMS to the Committee asking the Committee to align its opinions with the recommendations of the IOMS seminars. The responses from the Committee, however, show that it prefers to base its opinions according to the traditional definition of death rather than on the brain death criteria (Idārat al-Iftāʾ 1977–2014, 3:449–451, 12:495–496, 30:485).

33 The study uses this language to describe the case: "An unconscious patient is artificially kept alive (ventilator, artificial nutrition and hydration). The patient is in a deep and irreversible coma. Should the devices be switched off so that the patient dies? Who should decide about that?" (Ahaddour et al. 2018b, 349).

4 Concluding Remarks

Islamic discussions on the ethical principles that can be used for the examination of (bio)ethical problems are often framed in response to the well-known principalist approach, which emerged in the late 1970s. Some researchers highlight the congruence of these principles with Islamic morality, others underscore significant gaps and areas of discord, or even suggest a different set of principles. While the first approach can result in a false perception of the universality of these principles, the second can be used to emphasise the inevitability of cultural specificity or even moral relativism. Within these discussions, personal autonomy is usually singled out as the most challenging principle, especially when it is formulated to indicate that a patient's right to self-determination constitutes an overriding ethical priority. One way to push this discussion forward and transcend these narrow binaries is, as suggested by prominent Western interlocutors including one of the authors of the principalist approach, to see these principles as dynamic constructs. For example, Tom Beauchamp noted the need to view these principles both in relationship to each other but also in relationship to other pertinent principles (Beauchamp 2016, 96). Moreover, it will be important to see these principles as subject to continuous refinement in light of ongoing developments in (bio)ethics research (Bredenoord 2016, 150–151). Examining these principles in relation to specific bioethical problems can yield useful insights, in light of the substantive details of these cases.

Investigating the scope of personal autonomy within Islamic ethical-legal discussions on euthanasia reveals that it has to be reconciled with other divine and communal considerations. This is indicated in the near consensus on the denouncement of active forms of euthanasia, where personal autonomy is ruled out in view of the Islamic principles on the dignity of the human person and sanctity of human life. This attitude is also rooted in Islamic ethical-legal discussions on suicide and murder. Islamic normative discussions on suicide emphasise the denouncement of the act but they reveal a distinction between the religious status of the suicide before God, on the one hand, and their standing within the community and how they (their bodies) should be treated, on the other. The marked ambivalence in the normative discussions suggests that ultimate judgement should be relegated to God in the Hereafter. As far as human-worldly purposes are concerned, they should continue to be treated as Muslims. An argument for the extension of this distinction to cases of actual or doubtful active euthanasia can be made, especially in light of the fact that some of the recorded cases of suicide in the Prophetic reports were undertaken with the motivation to end pain and suffering. Similarly, Islamic discussions on murder reveal the scope of liability, which includes not only actual perpetrators but also causing agents. While prior permission or consent by the victim may play a role in minimising criminal liability, it does not rule out the moral sin associated with the act of murder.

In the case of passive forms of euthanasia, ethical-legal discussions on medical treatment leave room for patients in certain cases to forgo treatment when it is deemed futile. Ongoing discussions on these issues, however, often emphasise the need for greater precision in the evaluation of these futile cases. As for patients who depend on the initiation or continuation of life-sustaining measures, Islamic juristic discussions often draw on medical expertise in the determination of these cases, which are linked to other issues such as brain death. While several jurists and institutions have endorsed the brain death criteria, others continue to insist on the traditional cardiopulmonary indicators. When these cases are subsumed under the category of passive euthanasia, attitudes would then vary depending on the question of the brain death.

Islamic ethical-legal discussions on the different forms of euthanasia and other EoL issues reveal the wide array of concerns that inform these deliberations, which range from liability, on the one hand, to questions of human dignity and meaning of life, on the other. They clearly show that personal autonomy is hardly the sole determining factor in these situations. At best it can be a factor that has to be considered in some cases together with other pertinent divine and collective considerations. Also, empirical research on Muslim patients and their families along with attending caregivers demonstrates the complexity that surrounds treatment decisions at EoL situations. While it confirms the importance of religious beliefs and values in the formulation of EoL decisions, it also demonstrates that these beliefs and values are often subject to multiple interpretations. Moreover, it also shows that other social and economic factors often play a role in patients' attitudes and choices.

Finally, Islamic discourses on euthanasia reflect the important changes and transformations that advances in medical knowledge and medical technologies at EoL have heralded. These include the scope of medical intervention in advanced stages of terminal illness and also the redefinition of death on the basis of brain function. These developments have blurred the boundaries between life and death and have raised important questions on how such boundaries should be (re)drawn. The foregoing analysis of both personal autonomy and euthanasia reveals the dynamic nature and multiple constructions of both concepts. It shows that, depending on how they are conceptualised, not all forms of autonomy are incompatible with religious authority and that not all types of euthanasia are in conflict with Islamic normativity.

Bibliography

ʿAbd al-Jabbār b. Aḥmad al-Asadabādī. n.d. *Al-Mughnī fī Abwāb al-Tawḥīd wa-l-ʿAdl*, 16 vols. Cairo: n.p.

Abou El Fadl, Khaled. 2014. *Reasoning with God: Reclaiming Shariʿah in the Modern Age*. New York: Rowman & Littlefield.

Abū Dāwūd al-Sijistānī. 2009. *Sunan Abī Dāwūd*, 7 vols. Damascus: Dār al-Risāla al-ʿĀlamiyya.

Abū Zahra, Muḥammad. 2015. *Al-ʿUqūba fī l-Fiqh al-Islāmī*. Cairo: Dār al-Fikr al-ʿArabī.

Abū Zayd, Bakr b. ʿAbd Allāh. 2012. *Fiqh al-Nawāzil: Qaḍāyā Fiqhiyya Muʿāṣira*, 2 vols. Beirut: Muʾassasat al-Risāla.

Ahaddour, Chaima, Stef Van den Branden and Bert Broeckaert. 2018a. "'God is the Giver and Taker of Life': Muslim Beliefs and Attitudes Regarding Assisted Suicide and Euthanasia." *AJOB Empirical Bioethics* 9(1): 1–11.

Ahaddour, Chaima, Stef Van den Branden and Bert Broeckaert. 2018b. "Between Quality of Life and Hope. Attitudes and Beliefs of Muslim Women toward Withholding and Withdrawing Life-Sustaining Treatments." *Medicine, Health Care and Philosophy* 21(3): 347–361.

Aramesh, Kiarash and Heydar Shadi. 2007. "An Islamic Perspective on Euthanasia." *The American Journal of Bioethics* 7(4): 65–66.

ʿAṭiyya, Jamāl al-Dīn. 2001. *Naḥwa Tafʿīl Maqāṣid al-Sharīʿa*. Damascus: Dār al-Fikr.

ʿAwda, ʿAbd al-Qādir. 2003. *Al-Tashrīʿ al-Jināʾī l-Islāmī Muqāran^{an} bi-l-Qānūn al-Waḍʿī*, 2 vols. Cairo: Maktabat Dār al-Turāth.

Ayubi, Zahra. 2019. *Gendered Morality: Classical Islamic Ethics of the Self, Family, and Society*. New York: Columbia University Press.

al-Bārr, Muḥammad ʿAlī. 1992. "Idhn al-Marīḍ wa-ʿIlāj al-Ḥālāt al-Mayʾūs minhā." *Majallat Majmaʿ al-Fiqh al-Islāmī* 7(3): 565–595.

Barry, Vincent. 2012. *Bioethics in a Cultural Context*. Boston, MA: Wadsworth Cengage Learning.

Beauchamp, Tom L. 2005. "Who Deserves Autonomy, and Whose Autonomy Deserves Respect?" In *Personal Autonomy: New Essays on Personal Autonomy and its Role in Contemporary Moral Philosophy*, edited by James Stacy Taylor, 310–329. Cambridge: Cambridge University Press.

Beauchamp, Tom L. 2016. "The Principles of Biomedical Ethics as Universal Principles." In *Islamic Perspectives on the Principles of Biomedical Ethics: Muslim Religious Scholars and Biomedical Scientists in Face-to-Face Dialogue with Western Bioethicists*, edited by Mohammed Ghaly, 91–119. London: World Scientific Publishing.

Beauchamp, Tom L. and James Childress. 2019. *Principles of Biomedical Ethics*, 8th ed. Oxford: Oxford University Press.

Bredenoord, Annelien. 2016. "The Principles of Biomedical Ethics Revisited." In *Islamic Perspectives on the Principles of Biomedical Ethics: Muslim Religious Scholars and Biomedical Scientists in Face-to-Face Dialogue with Western Bioethicists*, edited by Mohammed Ghaly, 133–151. London: World Scientific Publishing.

Brockopp, Jonathan. 2003. "The 'Good Death' in Islamic Theology and Law." In *Islamic Ethics of Life: Abortion, War, and Euthanasia*, edited by Jonathan Brockopp, 177–193. Columbia, SC: University of South Carolina Press.

Broeckaert, Bert. 2008a. "Treatment Decisions at the End of Life: A Conceptual Framework." In *Palliative Care Nursing: Principles and Evidence for Practice*, edited by Sheila Payne, Jane Seymour and Christine Ingleton, 2nd ed., 402–421. Berkshire: Open University Press.

Broeckaert, Bert. 2008b. "Euthanasia and Physician-Assisted Suicide." In *Palliative Medicine*, edited by T. Declan Walsh et al., 110–115. Philadelphia, PA: Saunders.

al-Bukhārī, ʿAlāʾ al-Dīn ʿAbd al-ʿAzīz b. Aḥmad. 1997. *Kashf al-Asrār ʿan Uṣūl Fakhr al-Islām al-Bazdawī*, 4 vols. Beirut: Dār al-Kutub al-ʿIlmiyya.

Colburn, Ben. 2010. *Autonomy and Liberalism*. London: Routledge.

Dār al-Iftāʾ al-Miṣriyya. 2011. *Al-Fatāwā l-Islāmiyya min Dār al-Iftāʾ al-Miṣriyya*, 39 vols. Cairo: Dār al-Iftāʾ al-Miṣriyya.

Fakhry, Majid. 1994. *Ethical Theories in Islam*, 2nd ed. Leiden: Brill.

Faruque, Muhammad U. 2021. *Sculpting the Self: Islam, Selfhood, and Human Flourishing*. Ann Arbor: University of Michigan Press.

Ghaly, Mohammed, ed. 2016. *Islamic Perspectives on the Principles of Biomedical Ethics: Muslim Religious Scholars and Biomedical Scientists in Face-to-Face Dialogue with Western Bioethicists*. London: World Scientific Publishing.

Hague, Ros. 2011. *Autonomy and Identity: The Politics of Who We Are*. London: Routledge.

Hamdy, Sherine. 2012. *Our Bodies Belong to God: Organ Transplants, Islam, and the Struggle for Human Dignity in Egypt*. Berkeley: University of California Press.

Haque, Omar Sultan. 2008. "Brain Death and its Entanglements: A Redefinition of Personhood for Islamic Ethics." *Journal of Religious Ethics* 36(1): 13–36.

Hourani, George F. 1985. *Reason and Tradition in Islamic Ethics*. Cambridge: Cambridge University Press.

Ḥusām al-Dīn, Muḥammad Badr al-Dīn. 1997. "Ḥurmat al-Ḥayāt al-Insāniyya: Mushkilāt al-Shaykhūkha wa-Qatl al-Raḥma." In *al-Siyāsa al-Ṣiḥḥiyya: al-Akhlāqiyyāt wa-l-Qiyam al-Insāniyya min Manẓūr Islāmī*, edited by Aḥmad Rajāʾī l-Jundī, 191–209. Kuwait: al-Munaẓẓama al-Islāmiyya lil-ʿUlūm al-Ṭibbiyya.

Ibn ʿĀbidīn, Muḥammad Amīn. 2003. *Radd al-Muḥtār ʿalā al-Durr al-Mukhtār Sharḥ Tanwīr al-Abṣār*, 13 vols. Riyad: Dār ʿĀlam al-Kutub.

Ibn ʿAṭiyya, Abū Muḥammad ʿAbd al-Ḥaqq. 2015. *Al-Muḥarrar al-Wajīz fī Tafsīr al-Kitāb al-ʿAzīz*, 10 vols. Doha: Wizārat al-Awqāf wa-l-Shuʾūn al-Islāmiyya.

Ibn Ḥajar al-ʿAsqalānī. n.d. *Fatḥ al-Bārī bi-Sharḥ Ṣaḥīḥ al-Bukhārī*, 13 vols. Beirut: Dār al-Maʿrifa.

Ibn Ḥazm, Abū Muḥammad ʿAlī b. Aḥmad. 2005. *Al-Muḥallā*, 11 pts in 8 vols. Cairo: Maktabat Dār al-Turāth.

Ibn al-ʿImād al-Aqfahsī, Aḥmad. 2009. "Al-Farq bayna al-Ḥayāt al-Mustamirra wa-l-Ḥayāt al-Mustaqirra wa-Ḥayāt ʿAysh al-Madhbūḥ," edited by Khālid b. Zayd b. Ḥadhdhāl al-Jabalī. *Majallat al-Sharīʿa wa-l-Dirāsāt al-Islāmiyya* 24(76): 255–329.

Ibn Kathīr, Ismāʿīl b. ʿUmar. 2009. *Tafsīr al-Qurʾān al-ʿAẓīm*, 5 vols. Beirut: Dār Ṣādir.

Ibn al-Mulaqqin, ʿUmar b. Abī l-Ḥasan ʿAlī b. Aḥmad. 2018. *ʿUmdat al-Muḥtāj ilā Sharḥ al-Minhāj*, 16 vols. Doha: Wizārat al-Awqāf wa-l-Shuʾūn al-Islāmiyya.

Ibn al-Mundhir, Muḥammad b. Ibrahīm. 2010. *Al-Awsaṭ min al-Sunan wa-l-Ijmāʿ wa-l-Ikhtilāf*, 15 vols. Doha: Wizārat al-Awqāf wa-l-Shuʾūn al-Islāmiyya.

Ibn Qudāma, Muwaffaq al-Dīn ʿAbd Allāh b. Aḥmad. 1997. *Al-Mughnī*, 15 vols. Riyad: Dār ʿĀlam al-Kutub.

Ibn Rushd, Muḥammad b. Aḥmad. 1982. *Bidāyat al-Mujtahid wa-Nihāyat al-Muqtaṣid*, 2 vols. Beirut: Dār al-Maʿrifa.

Idārat al-Iftāʾ. 1977–2014. *Majmūʿat al-Fatāwā al-Sharʿiyya al-Ṣādira ʿan Qiṭāʿ al-Iftāʾ wa-l-Buḥūth al-Sharʿiyya*, 30 vols. Kuwait: Wizārat al-Awqāf wa-l-Shuʾūn al-Islāmiyya.

IIFA (International Islamic Fiqh Academy). 1986. "Qarār bi-Shaʾn Ajhizat al-Inʿāsh." *Majallat Majmaʿ al-Fiqh al-Islāmī* 3(2): 523. https://iifa-aifi.org/ar/1667.html.

IIFA (International Islamic Fiqh Academy). 1992. "Qarār bi-Shaʾn al-ʿIlāj al-Ṭibbī." *Majallat Majmaʿ al-Fiqh al-Islāmī* 7(3): 731–734.

al-Jaṣṣāṣ, Aḥmad b. ʿAlī. 1992. *Aḥkām al-Qurʾān*, 5 vols. Beirut: Dār Iḥyāʾ al-Turāth al-ʿArabī.

al-Jundī, Aḥmad Rajāʾī, ed. 1997. *Al-Siyāsa al-Ṣiḥḥiyya: al-Akhlāqiyyāt wa-l-Qiyam al-Insāniyya min Manẓūr Islāmī*. Kuwait: al-Munaẓẓama al-Islāmiyya lil-ʿUlūm al-Ṭibbiyya.

al-Jundī. 2001. *Ḥuqūq al-Musinnīn min Manẓūr Islāmī*. Kuwait: al-Munaẓẓama al-Islāmiyya lil-ʿUlūm al-Ṭibbiyya.

al-Jundī. 2005. *Al-Mīthāq al-Islāmī l-ʿĀlamī lil-Akhlāqiyyāt al-Ṭibbiyya wa-l-Ṣiḥḥiyya*. Kuwait: al-Munaẓẓama al-Islāmiyya lil-ʿUlūm al-Ṭibbiyya.

al-Jundī, Aḥmad Rajāʾī, Asmahān al-Shibīlī and Mukhtār Muḥammad Bishr, eds. 2000. *Al-Taʿrīf al-Ṭibbī lil-Mawt*. Kuwait: al-Munaẓẓama al-Islāmiyya lil-ʿUlūm al-Ṭibbiyya.

al-Juwaynī, Imām al-Ḥaramayn ʿAbd al-Malik b. ʿAbd Allāh. 2002. *Kitāb al-Irshād*. Cairo: Maktabat al-Khānjī.

Kamali, Muhammad Hashim. 2003. *Principles of Islamic Jurisprudence*. Cambridge: Islamic Texts Society.

Kamali, Muhammad Hashim. 2009. "Law and Ethics in Islam: The Role of the *Maqāṣid*." In *New Directions in Islamic Thought: Exploring Reform and Muslim Tradition*, edited by Kari Vogt, Lena Larsen and Christian Moe, 23–46. London: I.B. Tauris.

al-Kāsānī, Abū Bakr b. Masʿūd. 2003. *Badāʾiʿ al-Ṣanāʾiʿ fī Tartīb al-Sharāʾiʿ*, 10 vols. Beirut: Dār al-Kutub al-ʿIlmiyya.

Keown, John. 2018. *Euthanasia, Ethics, and Public Policy: An Argument Against Legalisation*, 2nd ed. Cambridge: Cambridge University Press.

al-Khaṭṭābī, Abū Sulaymān Ḥamad b. Muḥammad. 2016. *Maʿālim al-Sunan: Sharḥ Sunan Abī Dāwūd*, 4 vols. Doha: Wizārat al-Awqāf wa-l-Shuʾūn al-Islāmiyya.

Krawietz, Birgit. 2003. "Brain Death and Islamic Traditions: Shifting Borders of Life?" In *Islamic Ethics of Life: Abortion, War, and Euthanasia*, edited by Jonathan Brockopp, 194–213. Columbia, SC: University of South Carolina Press.

Kukla, Rebbeca. 2005. "Conscientious Autonomy: Displacing Decisions in Health Care." *The Hastings Center Report* 35(2): 34–44.

MacIntyre, Alasdair. 2007. *After Virtue: A Study in Moral Philosophy*. Notre Dame, IN: University of Notre Dame Press.

al-Madhkūr, Khālid, ʿAlī Sayf, Aḥmad Rajāʾī l-Jundī and ʿAbd al-Sattār Abū Ghudda, eds. 1985. *Al-Ḥayāt al-Insāniyya: Bidāyatuhā wa-Nihāyatuhā fī l-Mafhūm al-Islāmī*. Kuwait: al-Munaẓẓama al-Islāmiyya lil-ʿUlūm al-Ṭibbiyya.

Majmaʿ al-Fiqh al-Islāmī bi-l-Hind. 2016. *Fatāwā Fiqhiyya Muʿāṣira: Majmūʿ al-Qararāt wa-l-Tawṣiyyāt al-Ṣādira ʿan Majmaʿ al-Fiqh al-Islāmī bi-l-Hind (al-Nadawāt 1–23, al-Qarārāt 1–100, Mā bayna Sanatay 1989–2014)*. Cairo: Dār al-Kalima.

al-Māturīdī, Abū Manṣūr Muḥammad b. Muḥammad b. Maḥmūd. 2010. *Kitāb al-Tawḥīd*. Beirut: Dār Ṣādir.

May, Thomas. 2005. "The Concept of Autonomy in Bioethics: An Unwarranted Fall from Grace." In *Personal Autonomy: New Essays on Personal Autonomy and its Role in Contemporary Moral Philosophy*, edited by James Stacy Taylor, 299–309. Cambridge: Cambridge University Press.

Mazhari, Waris. 2022. "Islamic Fiqh Academy of India." In *The Encyclopedia of Islamic Bioethics. Oxford Islamic Studies Online*, www.oxfordislamicstudies.com/article/opr/t9002/e0290.

Moosa, Ebrahim. 1999. "Language of Change in Islamic Law: Redefining Death in Modernity." *Islamic Studies* 38(3): 305–342.

al-Nawawī, Muḥyī l-Dīn Yaḥyā b. Sharaf. 1929. *Ṣaḥīḥ Muslim bi-Sharḥ al-Nawawī*, 18 vols. Cairo: al-Maṭbaʿa al-Miṣriyya.

O'Neill, Onora. 2003. *Autonomy and Trust in Bioethics*. Cambridge: Cambridge University Press.

Padela, Aasim and Afshan Muhiuddin. 2015. "Ethical Obligations and Clinical Goals in End-of Life Care: Deriving a Quality-of-Life Construct Based on the Islamic Concept of Accountability before God (*Taklīf*)." *The American Journal of Bioethics* 15(1): 3–13.

Padela, Aasim and Omar Qureshi. 2017. "Islamic Perspectives on Clinical Intervention Near the End-of-Life: We Can but Must We?" *Medicine, Health Care and Philosophy* 20(4): 545–559.

Padela, Aasim, Ahsan Arozullah and Ebrahim Moosa. 2013. "Brain Death in Islamic Ethico-Legal Deliberation: Challenges for Applied Islamic Bioethics." *Bioethics* 27(3): 132–139.

Padela, Aasim, Aisha Malik, Farr Curlin and Raymond DeVries. 2015. "[Re]considering Respect for Persons in a Globalized World." *Developing World Bioethics* 15(2): 98–106.

al-Qaraḍāwī, Yūsuf. 2000. *Min Hady al-Islām: Fatāwā Muʿāṣira*, 4 vols. Beirut: al-Maktab al-Islāmī.

al-Qarāfī, Shihāb al-Dīn. 2001. *Kitāb al-Furūq, Anwār al-Burūq fī Anwāʾ al-Furūq*, 4 vols., edited by Muḥammad Aḥmad Sirāj and ʿAlī Jumʿa Muḥammad. Cairo: Dār al-Salām.

Rābiṭat al-ʿĀlam al-Islāmī. n.d. *Qarārāt al-Majmaʿ al-Fiqhī l-Islāmī.* Mecca: Rābiṭat al-ʿĀlam al-Islāmī.

al-Rāghib al-Iṣfahānī. 2010. *Al-Mufradāt fī Gharīb al-Qurʾān.* Beirut: Dār al-Maʿrifa.

al-Rāzī, Fakhr al-Dīn Muḥammad b. ʿUmar. 1981. *Tafsīr al-Fakhr al-Rāzī l-Mushtahir bi-l-al-Tafsīr al-Kabīr wa-Mafātīḥ al-Ghayb*, 32 vols. Beirut: Dār al-Fikr lil-Ṭibāʿa wa-l-Nashr wa-l-Tawzīʿ.

Riḍā, Muḥammad Rashīd. n.d. *Tafsīr al-Qurʾān al-Ḥakīm*, 12 vols. Cairo: al-Maktaba al-Tawfīqiyya.

Rosenthal, Franz. 1946. "On Suicide in Islam." *Journal of the American Oriental Society* 66(3): 239–259.

Sachedina, Abdulaziz. 1999. "Can God Inflict Unrequited Pain on his Creatures? Muslim Perspectives on Health and Suffering." In *Religion, Health and Suffering*, edited by John Hinnells and Roy Porter, 65–84. London: Routledge.

Sachedina, Abdulaziz. 2009. *Islamic Biomedical Ethics*. Oxford: Oxford University Press.

Salvatore, Armando. 2009. "Tradition and Modernity within Islamic Civilization and the West." In *Islam and Modernity: Key Issues and Debates*, edited by Muhammad Khalid Masud, Armando Salvatore and Martin van Bruinessen, 3–35. Edinburgh: Edinburgh University Press.

Shaltūt, Maḥmūd. 2004. *Al-Fatāwā: Dirāsa li-Mushkilāt al-Muslim al-Muʿāṣir fī Ḥayātih al-Yawmiyya al-ʿĀmma*. Cairo: Dār al-Shurūq.

Sharaf al-Dīn, Aḥmad. 1987. *Al-Aḥkām al-Sharʿiyya lil-Aʿmāl al-Ṭibbiyya*, 2nd ed. Cairo: np.

al-Shāṭibī, Abū Isḥāq Ibrāhīm b. Mūsā. 2003. *Al-Muwāfaqāt fī Uṣūl al-Sharīʿa*, 4 prts in 2 vols. Cairo: al-Maktaba al-Tawfīqiyya.

al-Shirbīnī, ʿIṣām. 1997a. "Qatl al-Raḥma." In *al-Siyāsa al-Ṣiḥiyya: al-Akhlāqiyyāt wa-l-Qiyam al-Insāniyya min Manẓūr Islāmī*, edited by Aḥmad Rajāʾī l-Jundī, 171–190. Kuwait: al-Munaẓẓama al-Islāmiyya lil-ʿUlūm al-Ṭibbiyya.

al-Shirbīnī, Shams al-Dīn Muḥammad b. al-Khaṭīb. 1997b. *Mughnī l-Muḥtāj ilā Maʿrifat Alfāẓ al-Minhāj*, 4 vols. Beirut: Dār al-Maʿrifa.

Stammers, Trevor. 2015. "The Evolution of Autonomy." *The New Bioethics* 21(2): 155–163.

Taylor, James Stacy, ed. 2005. *Personal Autonomy: New Essays on Personal Autonomy and its Role in Contemporary Moral Philosophy*. Cambridge: Cambridge University Press.

al-Ṭabarī, Muḥammad b. Jarīr. 2001. *Tafsīr al-Ṭabarī: Jāmiʿ al-Bayān ʿan Taʾwīl Āy al-Qurʾān*, 26 vols. Cairo: Dār Hajr lil-Ṭibāʿa wa-l-Nashr wa-l-Iʿlān.

Timmons, Mark. 2013. *Moral Theory: An Introduction*. New York: Rowman & Littefield Publishers.

Van den Branden, Stef and Bert Broeckaert. 2011. "Living in the Hands of God: English Sunni e-Fatwas on (Non-)Voluntary Euthanasia and Assisted Suicide." *Medicine, Health Care and Philosophy* 14(1): 29–41.

Vanderpool, Harold Y. 2004. "Life-Sustaining Treatment and Euthanasia: II. Historical Aspects." In *Encyclopedia of Bioethics*, edited by Stephen Porter. 1421–1432. New York: Macmillan Reference USA.

Veatch, Robert M. and Laura K. Guidry-Grimes. 2020. *The Basics of Bioethics*, 4th ed. London: Routledge.

Wizārat al-Awqāf, ed. 2008. *Al-Mawsūʿa al-Fiqhiyya*, 45 vols. Kuwait: Wizarat al-Awqāf wa-l-Shuʾūn al-Isāmiyya.

Wolpe, Paul Root. 1998. "The Triumph of Autonomy in American Bioethics: A Sociological View." In *Bioethics and Society, Constructing the Ethical Enterprise*, edited by Raymond DeVries and Janardan Subedi, 38–59. Upper Saddle River, NJ: Prentice-Hall.

Yanagihashi, Hiroyuki. 1998. "The Doctrinal Development of '*Maraḍ al-Mawt*' in the Formative Period of Islamic Law." *Islamic Law and Society* 5(3): 326–358.

Zargar, Cyrus Ali. 2017. *The Polished Mirror: Storytelling and the Pursuit of Virtue in Islamic Philosophy and Sufism*. London: Oneworld Publications.

al-Zarqā, Muṣṭafā. 2012. *Al-Madkhal al-Fiqhī l-ʿĀmm*, 2 vols. Damascus: Dār al-Qalam.

al-Zuḥaylī, Wahba. 2012. *Mawsūʿat al-Fiqh al-Islāmī wa-l-Qaḍāyā al-Muʿāṣira*, 14 vols. Damascus: Dār al-Fikr.

CHAPTER 10

An Islamic Bioethical Framework for Withholding and Withdrawing Life-Sustaining Treatment

Rafaqat Rashid

1 Introduction

Many Muslim clinicians, patients and families look to ethical guidelines on end-of-life decisions sourced within their faith tradition when dealing with withholding and withdrawing life-sustaining treatment (Padela and Mohiuddin 2015). Ethical guidance is sought from Muslim jurisconsults (*muftīs*), who provide authoritative, non-binding expert legal opinions (*fatāwa*) to queries, having analysed past and present juridical rulings from scriptural-based sources.[1] *Fatwās* offered by Muslim jurisconsults related to important bioethical issues at end-of-life care, provide specific legal responses to bioethical cases. It has been argued that sometimes these *fatwās* are vague, have gaps, are scattered, difficult to interpret, and lack a practical focus neglecting healthcare policy implication. As a result, practical difficulties arise when such *fatwās* are used to determine the course of action in end-of-life care to specific cases (Padela, Shanawani and Arozullah 2011; Mohiuddin et al. 2020) It is no wonder that many Muslims around the world still request futile treatment for dying family members, and the shift of focus to palliative care is taken inappropriately late in the course of patients' illness (Mobeireek et al. 2008; Yazigi et al. 2005) This causes unnecessary distress for patients and families and leads to conflict between families and caring physicians. Therefore, it is important that we seek more clarity around the practical implications of the justification criteria mentioned in the *fatwās* for withholding and withdrawing life-sustaining treatments (LST), highlighting where there is a need to revise current Islamic guidelines.

Life-sustaining treatment is any treatment that serves to prolong life without reversing the underlying medical condition. It may include, but is not limited

1 *Fatwā* plural *fatāwā* is an authoritative, but non-binding legal opinion or interpretation on a point of Islamic law given by a qualified legal scholar (known as a *muftī*) or collectively, comprising a number of Muslim scholars with an interdisciplinary team of biomedical scientists. A *fatwā* is usually issued in response to questions from individuals or Islamic courts.

to, cardiopulmonary resuscitation (CPR), mechanical ventilation, renal dialysis, chemotherapy and artificial nutrition and hydration (ANH). Withholding LST is the decision not to make further life-sustaining therapeutic interventions while withdrawing LST is the removal of a LST which has been started in an attempt to sustain life.

An analysis of the *fatwā* literature related to justification criteria for foregoing LST shows that most contemporary Muslim jurists deem it permissible to withhold and withdraw LST in the following situations (Mohiuddin et al. 2020).

1. *Futility* of continued therapy,
2. Diminished neurological state of the patient and,
3. Compounding harms from continued clinical care.

The language and terms used to describe states justifying foregoing treatment, such as "futility," "terminal illness," "depressed neurological state" and "compounding burden/harm," are nuanced and vague, leading to difficulties in interpretation and lack a practical focus, especially because specific clinical examples are mostly avoided in the *fatwās* (Mohiuddin et al. 2020). It is also not clear whether Islam identifies a moral distinction between withholding and withdrawing LST.[2] For example, is a decision not to start mechanical ventilation on a seriously breathless patient, morally distinct to a decision to switch off a ventilator from the same patient after having initiated treatment? Despite wide agreement by Western ethicists that there is no ethical difference between withholding and withdrawing LST, these issues continue to generate considerable debate (Vincent 2005; Weinstein and Fineberg 1980).

The *fatwās* are not explicit about any major distinction between withholding or withdrawing treatment, yet majority of Muslim jurists tend to add more stringent conditions and prohibitions to *withdrawing* LST compared to *withholding* LST. These stringent conditions and prohibitions of withdrawing LST are also scattered and diverse. Most *fatwās* mention that LST can be withdrawn if treatment is *futile* (IIFA 1986, 523) Some generally prohibit the withdrawal of LST and only permit in extreme situations when the patient is brain dead. Others prohibit even when the patient is brain dead, because to them brain death is not "actual" death (al-Jabūrī 2015; Jāb Allāh 2015).

Furthermore, Muslim jurists differentiate between two categories of LST; life-support like CPR and mechanical ventilation, and ancillary interventions like ANH, pain control and antibiotics. They claim that ANH in particular must be maintained as a necessary part of overall care in contrast to CPR and

2 There appears to be little deliberate distinction made between withdrawal and withholding of treatment (see Mohiuddin et al. 2020).

mechanical ventilation (al-Bār 2015; Jāb Allāh 2015; al-Jibrīn 2015, al-Khādimī 2015). It is not clear why such a distinction exists and in what context.

In this chapter, I propose that the nuanced understanding of "futility," that justifies foregoing LST, is best avoided and an alternative approach within the perspective of an Islamic ethico-legal framework be used for withholding and withdrawing LST, framed around "religious duties and obligations" for clinicians, patients and surrogate decision makers. I argue that there is no *moral* distinction between actions of omission and commission when withholding and withdrawing LST. Any distinction claimed between them is not because of acting or not acting, but because of our duty and obligation to rescue patients, which depend on patient prognostic outcomes, and the balance of benefits *versus* compounding harms of treatment, and the underlying patient condition.

The distinction between the two categories of LST; life-support and ANH, exists because of our duties and obligations to treat patients related to outcome of certainty of saving life. ANH is certain to sustain life and thus obligatory, whereas this is not always the case with life-support like CPR and mechanical ventilation.

I propose that the balance of benefit *versus* compounding harms from continued care ought to be assessed using quantitative and qualitative evaluations of life. This serves the best interests of patients by assessing whether treatment will prolong the person's life significantly, alleviate burdens of illness and provide a worthwhile quality of life or meaningful life. The types of harm, the degrees of harm, and the kind of assessment of harm we ought to make, that extends to other considerations of a non-physical nature, like bodily dignity and loss of benefit to afterlife, will all be discussed.

By exploring these concerns using specific clinical situations of withholding and withdrawing LST, it is expected that readers will be better informed about how an Islamic bioethical framework is best implemented practically.

2 From "Futility" to "Duties and Obligations"

There is not enough guidance to inform clinicians, patients and families about what is understood by medical futility in the *fatwās*. Muslim scholars justify withholding and withdrawing LST in patients when treatment is seen *futile*, because the state of the patient is unsuitable, the condition incurable and unresponsive to treatment, or there is inevitable death.[3] The problem

3 For example, the Saudi Permanent Committee for Islamic Research and *Fatwā* issued a statement stating: If the patient's state is unsuitable or non-beneficial (*ghayr ṣāliḥa*) for

is that these descriptions are unclear and do not provide enough guidance for Muslims to apply to policy[4] (Mohiuddin 2020). For example, there is little clarity in these *fatwās* about what Islam would consider an unsuitable state, justifying foregoing LST. Rather, many of these *fatwās* mention the physician as the one who determines unsuitability and therefore decides on the *permissibility* of foregoing LST.

Relying solely on the physician's judgement is problematic. Expert physicians are trained to provide scientific opinions and judgements regarding suitability of treatment, which presuppose moral judgements and often standards of quality of life. Decisions about best interests of a patient involve moral judgements, like what is of value in life, how best to promote the patient's interests, and how different or competing interests should be weighed against each other. Different healthcare professionals and different families may reach different answers about what would be in the best interests of the patient, because they have a different understanding about the relevant facts. They may also disagree because they have different values. Such decisions are influenced and depend on societal values, culture and faith, and are not just scientific judgements. Societal values related to standards of quality of life can change with changing politico-social trends over time.[5] Therefore, reliance on expertise of physicians does not always provide an adequate account of what is *futile*, because futility should also be a moral judgement by Islamic standards.

Moreover, futility descriptions are not clear. Controversy exists about what constitutes futility or futile intervention (Helft, Siegler and Lantos 2000,

---

resuscitation, as agreed by three competent specialised physicians, then there is also no need for any resuscitative measures (second statement).

This is further explained in another one of their statements: If the patient's illness is incurable and unresponsive to treatment (*musta'ṣiyan ghayra qābil al-'ilāj*) and death is inevitable through the witness of three competent specialised physicians then there is also no need for any resuscitative measures (third statement) (al-Lajna al-Dā'ima 1989).

The Saudi Permanent Committee for Islamic Research and *Fatwās* (al-Lajna al-Dā'ima lil-Buḥūth wa-l-Iftā') is a committee established by royal decree in 1971 by King Fayṣal b. 'Abd al-'Azīz (d. 1975) of Saudi Arabia. It issues *fatwās* relevant to all aspects of life (regarding creed, worship, and social issues) both in print and online. Its members are drawn from the most senior Sunnī scholars of *fiqh* in Saudi Arabia. Its head is the Grand Muftī of Saudi Arabia (www.fatwa-online.com/permanent-committee/).

4 The issue of defining "futility" is not just a problem for Muslims but also heavily criticised as being vague in western medical ethics also (see Schneiderman et al. 1990).

5 The proportion of deaths in patients with a decision to withhold/withdraw life-sustaining treatment ranged from 10% in South Asia to 67% in Oceania. Decisions to withhold/withdraw life-sustaining treatment were less frequent in low/lower-middle GNI countries than in high GNI countries (6% vs 14%; P < .001) (see Lobo et al. 2017; Prendergast and Luce 1997).

293–296; Curtis et al. 1995, 124–128). Futility is described as (Baruch and Halevy 1995; Kopelman 1995; Miles 1994; Youngner 1988):

i. *what cannot be performed*
ii. *what is highly unlikely to be efficient* (*statistically the likeliness of success is extremely small*)
iii. *what can only produce low grade insignificant outcome* (*qualitative results are poor*)
iv. *what is more burdensome than beneficial*
v. *what is completely speculative*
vi. *what is of predicted improbable outcome, success*
vii. *what is an unacceptable benefit-burden ratio.*

In other words, futility can mean many things related to the physiological state of the patient, and is best avoided, requiring us to use more precise language (Wilkinson and Savulescu 2011). An Islamic ethico-legal framework for withholding and withdrawing LST ought to be framed around *duties* or *religious obligations* for clinicians, patients and surrogates. These obligations ought to be determined using both scientific and values judgements.

An accurate prognostic outcome measure of the effectiveness of life-saving medical intervention provides decision-makers valuable information about the limitations of treatment choices and their level of benefit. This is a scientific judgement and provides information about, "*what we can do.*" If we know that life support is likely to be 60% effective in a patient whose neurological outcome will be normal, then treatment in such a patient is beneficial. If the patient's treatment is likely to be less than 1% effective with a serious permanently diminished neurological state, then treatment may be described as ineffective or futile and the underlying condition incurable and unresponsive. Scientific judgements therefore provide information about what we can achieve with available treatment options.

Scientific judgements thus assess whether there is any realistic chance of patient's condition improving if life-support is initiated or is continued, and so, inform us of our options and their statistical outcomes. This is expected to be objective, depends on the expertise and accuracy of diagnosis and prognosis. The reliability of technology and clinical testing used, as well as the expert's ability to interpret the results, are essential to attain an accurate account of the outcome. Scientific judgement is important because it informs us of where we are and what we can achieve. However, it should not be considered the sole consideration when justifying foregoing LST.

Value judgements are evaluations of the balance of competing harms and benefits, from the perspective of physician's standards or priorities, when considering the right course of action related to, "*what we ought to do.*" Value judgements assess what we ought to do if the patient's condition does not improve. Should active treatment be initiated, should LST continue, or should it stop, particularly if surrogates do not give permission to withdraw treatment? These are ethical questions, not scientific ones. There are varied views globally about what to do, and they differ amongst different societal cultures, people and faiths. Some favour that resuscitative measures and life-support ought to continue indefinitely for patients who are in this situation, even if there is no chance of improvement. Whereas others may feel that to continue is the wrong thing to do – treatment may prolong life but may be doing more harm than good.

Both scientific judgements and value judgements combined, offer a practical approach to decide whether foregoing LST treatment is justified or not. The decision to use a procedure is based on the product of the probability of success and the quality (utility) of the outcome in terms of quality of life (Weinstein and Fineberg 1980). These factors determine whether it is considered right or wrong to treat, and our obligations to treat. Justifications for foregoing treatment based on definitions or descriptions of *futility* are not helpful, rather what needs to be determined is whether it is a duty or an obligation, optional or wrong to *withhold* or *withdraw* LST, having combined both scientific and value judgements.

So what are obligatory treatments, optional treatments and treatments which should be withheld or withdrawn? The Islamic bioethical legal framework views acts generally on the basis of whether they are obligatory (*wājib*), permissible (*mubāḥ*) or optional, and prohibited (*ḥarām*). Therefore, treatments can be obligatory, optional, or it can be wrong to treat, based on scientific and value judgements. Treatments can be "obligatory to treat" when it is considered wrong not to treat, like when we are able to significantly extend someone's life by initiating life-sustaining measures. It can be wrong if we fail in our duty to attempt to do this and we will be culpable and sinful. It can be wrong to treat when it is considered, "obligatory not to treat," because it seriously violates patient and public interests. Like when it causes severe pain, violates human bodily dignity, when the burden of treatment outweighs the anticipated benefit of brief prolongation of life, or when there are limited resources depriving other sick patients of LST who are in greater need. If we fail in our duty to withdraw treatment, we will be culpable and sinful.

Treatments may be optional to treat when it is neither obligatory nor prohibited, in other words, there is no sin. Usually, such treatments are recommended by physician and can be authorised or refused by a patient or surrogate. Even though treatments may not be obligatory, the ethics of our duty to patients, demands that care is optimised in line with patient wishes or those of surrogates.

If an Islamic ethico-legal framework for withholding and withdrawing LST ought to be framed around "duties" or "religious obligations," then these obligations will remain equally coherent and consistent in both acts of omission and commission; in other words, there is no moral distinction between obligations related to withholding and withdrawing LST.

3 The Withdrawing and Withholding Distinction

Most bioethicists do not draw a distinction between withholding and withdrawing LST. Moral obligations to help, prevent or remove harm are seen morally equal for both. Moral weight is based on the *outcome* of withholding or withdrawing treatment, and so withholding and withdrawing treatment is morally equivalent because of the same effect it causes (Sanchini et al. 2014) For example, if a patient is unable to breathe spontaneously, the "active" decision to stop mechanical ventilation will have the same immediate effect, consequence and outcome as the "passive" decision not to initiate mechanical ventilation. The outcome of the underlying disease or illness of the patient will be the same, i.e., death, because the patient cannot breathe spontaneously, and breathing will not be supported if the ventilator is withdrawn (Vincent 2005) In each case, we decide which treatment is to be applied in the immediate future, to withhold or withdraw, and the immediate result will be the same regardless of the decision (Melltorp 1997).

Even though most guidelines emphasise that there is no ethical difference between withholding and withdrawing LST (GMC 2010a),[6] most health professionals in ICU are of the opinion that there is an ethical difference. Attempts justifying an inherent distinction between withholding and withdrawing seem to be controversial and it is even argued that such a distinction should be considered by recommending a change in emphasis in the professional guidelines (Melltorp 1997). It might be argued that withdrawing LST by the physician interrupts the treatment and this is the direct cause of the patient's death, whereas withholding LST by a physician does nothing to causally contribute to it, rather the illness takes its natural course. Or it may be argued that the moral

6 In the UK withholding and withdrawing treatment are also regarded as legally equivalent. Bolam v Friern HMC [1957] 2 All ER 118.

difference does not exist in the action and omission as such, but it is the conditions in which action and omission take place (Sanchini et al. 2014).

In my opinion, there is no intrinsic moral distinction between withholding and withdrawing LST. If a moral distinction is felt then this is not because of the distinction between acting and not acting that makes us feel this way, rather it is in the conditions in which actions and omissions take place. If treatment is not obligatory and the patient chooses not to start LST, then it is permissible to withhold. If the treatment is started, but the treatment does not succeed in improving the condition, and the odds of effectiveness remain the same, then the non-obligation will remain and the treatment can be withdrawn. If the odds change whilst patient is receiving LST, and it is now very effective due to a very good response from the patient, then it will be an obligation to continue treatment if it is lifesaving. The moral distinction therefore relates to the obligations related to the certainty of effectiveness of treatment as a condition, and not merely actions of omission and commission related to withholding and withdrawing LST. Similarly, if compounding harms due to continued LST significantly outweigh benefits of treatment then these are additional conditions which differentiate withholding and withdrawing LST in certain situations. A thorough evaluation of obligatory treatments in Islam is required, comparing situations and conditions of *withholding* LST with that of withdrawing LST to support this argument. I will relate the obligations related to *certainty of effectiveness of treatment* as a condition, and *compounding harms due to continued LST*.

4 Obligations Related to Withholding LST

In order to know our obligations related to *withholding* LST, it is important to know what our ethico-legal position or duty is when seeking treatment in Islam generally. Are treatments generally obligatory in Islam, and if not, at what stage do they become obligatory, optional or even prohibited? In Islam, medical treatment is encouraged and is promoted as an established practice of the Prophet and is not something which is contrary to trust in God's decree (*tawakkul*). Treatment is therefore seen optional, and generally not an obligation according to all four Sunnī schools of jurisprudence.[7] This is evident from the

7 Sunnī Islam is separated into four main schools of jurisprudence, namely, Ḥanafī, Mālikī, Shāfiʿī, Ḥanbalī. These schools are named after Abū Ḥanīfa (d. 150/767), Mālik b. Anas (d. 179/796), al-Shāfiʿī (d. 204/820), and Aḥmad b. Ḥanbal (d. 241/855), respectively. They emerged in the third/ninth and fourth/tenth centuries and by the sixth/twelfth century

deliberations of classical Muslim jurists. The majority opinion across all four Sunnī schools of jurisprudence hovers around simple permissibility and/or preferability[8] (Ibn al-Humām 2000, 5:355, 360; al-Zaylaʿī 2000, 6:33; al-Bukhārī 2003, 5:373; Ibn ʿĀbidīn 1994, 6:389; al-Ḥalabī 2005, 179; Mawṣīlī 2015, 4:173; al-ʿAynī 2012, 12:271; al-ʿAynī 2007, 471; Qāḍī Khān 2009, 3:251; al-Ramlī 2003, 2:135; al-Haythamī, 2016, 3:182; Ibn Taymiyya 2004, 21:564; Abū Ghudda 1998, 1:73). However, there are other important points which are mentioned in the legal (*fiqh*) text related to situations when treatments do become obligatory.

Consuming food and drink are natural and essential acts and necessities of life and do not fall under the category of taking medicine or treatment. However, Islamic legal texts do refer to consumption of food and drink alongside discussions on obligatory treatments, because they are seen as acts which are obligatory to sustain life and hence are comparable to treatments in this sense. Framed in this sense, Muslim jurists consider the consumption of food and drink an obligation because it prevents death from starvation. This obligation is realised through two indications, both of which relate to *certainty of outcome*. The first certainty of outcome is the "*certainty of death occurring if we abstain*" from food and drink – because death is *certain* to follow from the state of starvation. The second certainty of outcome is the "*certainty of success and effectiveness of using the means*" to overcome death. Food and drink are *certain* (*mutayaqqan*) to save life when a person is at risk of death from starvation and thirst. If you are at a high risk of death due to starvation and you refuse to eat and drink, you will die as a consequence. Because food sustains life, to then abstain from food with the intention of death will be an act of sin. This is because of the verse of the Qurʾān: "Let not your own hands contribute to your destruction…" (Q 2:195) Therefore, it is obligatory for you to consume food and drink to save yourself from starvation.

Muslim jurists mention that when a doctor recommends you take medical treatment and you refuse, and as an outcome you die, you will not be sinful. The reason being that your underlying condition is not *certain* to be life-threatening, like the seriousness of state of starvation, and the medical treatment offered is not *certain* to save your life, like the certainty of food and drink, and hence the treatment is not an obligation and the patient is not culpable (Niẓām al-Dīn et al. 2000, 5:355, 360; al-Zaylaʿī 2000, 6:33; Abū l-Maʿālī

almost all jurists aligned themselves with a particular *madhhab*. These four schools recognise each other's validity and they have interacted in legal debate over the centuries. Rulings of these schools are followed across the Muslim world without exclusive regional restrictions.

8 For a more detailed account in English of the differences amongst the different Sunnī schools see Padela and Qureshi 2016.

2004, 5:373; Ibn ʿĀbidīn 1994, 6:338–389; al-ʿAynī 2007, 471; al-Jamal 2013, 2:135; al-Haythamī 2016, 3:182; al-Qalyūbī 2019, 1:403; Ibn Taymiyya 2004, 21:564; Ibn Mufliḥ 1999, 2:358; al-Buhūtī 1983, 2:76; al-Nawawī 2008, 5:96).

Treatments, however, can be obligatory in certain situations. An example is given in the *fiqh* literature of a person who has severe continual bleeding from a venesection site (*faṣd*) or wound, and there is certainty of death if not treated. The effectiveness of using a tourniquet (i.e., compressing a limb with a cord or tight bandage) to prevent bleeding to death is certain to be effective. In such a situation it becomes obligatory (*wājib*) for the patient to wear a tourniquet otherwise he will bleed to death. If there was little risk of death or the tourniquet was not considered to be very effective, then it would not be an obligation, rather it would be optional due to lack of certainty of death and/or the patient's life being saved. Drinking and eating to prevent death from starvation is obligatory because there is certainty of preventing death. This was not seen to be the case for medical treatment historically, because medicine was not certain in its effectiveness then as is mentioned in the books of *fiqh*. Examples given are cupping (*ḥijāma*), taking honey or humoral treatment, all of which at best have some benefit, but not as lifesaving treatments. Hence, they were not considered obligatory. With current advances in technology, we are able to save lives with certainty, using life support measures like mechanical ventilators.

Medical treatment is therefore obligatory, if (1) there is a certainty of risk of death if no treatment is taken, and (2) the lifesaving treatment offered is certain to save life. Withholding LST in such patients is prohibited and sinful. However, if life cannot be saved at this level of certainty, then LST is not an obligation, but recommended or optional.

Classical Muslim scholars assert that judgements around certainty of treatment outcomes should be based on good empirical evidence (*mutayaqqan bih bi-ʿtibār al-ʿāda*) (al-Zaylaʿī 2000, 6:33). If scientific judgements can accurately predict the prognostic outcome of the treatment, using previously established clinical data related to effectiveness of treatment for similar cases, then this will satisfy what is required to determine whether a treatment is obligatory. Therefore, having knowledge of the prognostic outcome of an underlying condition if treatment is not sought, as well as having the knowledge of the effectiveness of treatment offered, are both essential scientific or clinical judgements which determine whether treatments are obligatory or not.

Muslim scholars describe different degrees of certainty of treatment effectiveness which impart normative obligations (al-ʿAynī 2007, 471; al-Haythamī 2016, 3:182; Abū Ghudda 1998, 1:73). The different degrees of certainty of treatment effectiveness are described as being (1) uncertain (*shakk*), which refers to a treatment outcome where success and failure are equally probable (*istiwāʾ ṭarafay al-shayʾ*). This can be taken broadly as being approximately 50% effective (2) Presumption (*ẓann*) refers to a treatment outcome which is more likely, but treatment failure is significant enough that it cannot be easily dismissed. In other words, failure is possible, but less likely. This can be taken as being between, above half (50%), and below dominant probability, where (3) dominant probability (*ghalabat al-ẓann*), is a dominant successful outcome because treatment failure is predicted to be very unlikely. This can be taken to be approximately above 75% in its effectiveness, as even though the remaining outcome can be dismissed on the basis that it is very unlikely, it cannot be excluded entirely. Dominant probability is at times seen epistemically no different to (4) certainty (*yaqīn*), where certainty is very nearly 100%. Dominant probability achieves a confidence level similar to certainty as a legal proof, even though certainty refers to an outcome that does not entertain any doubt (*wahm*), appreciating that certainty in medical treatment can never be absolute at 100% (al-Ḥamawī 1985, 1:193; Ḥaydar n.d., 1:35–6; al-Nawawī 2008, 5:270). When we turn to Islamic legal authority we can see that the tradition at times uses the term "*yaqīn*" (certainty) when referring to legal issues, yet we know that, in reality, we are unable to achieve this level of certainty, rather recourse is to *ijtihād*, which leads to speculative (*ẓannī*) claims. Therefore, the threshold at which treatment becomes obligatory is at level of dominant probability (*ghalabat al-ẓann*) and not strictly at level of certainty (*yaqīn*), as realistically one cannot entirely exclude the remote possibility that the person may not survive, yet one is quite sure that they will – like when a starving person is given food and drink, he may still die, though very unlikely. Throughout the remaining chapter, any reference to "certainty" of treatment effectiveness will be understood at the epistemic level of dominant probability.

According to all four Sunnī schools, these grades of certainty, related to effectiveness of treatment, are to be determined through expertise and are to be evidence based (*tajriba*) (Ibn al-Humām 2003, 4:378; Mullā Khusraw 2010, 2:491; Ibn Nujaym 1997, 6:229; Ibn ʿĀbidīn 1994, 2:117; al-Ḥaṣkafī 1998, 1:76; Ṭahṭāwī 1997, 1:430; al-Dasūqī n.d., 2:170). Treatment should be based on the most up-to-date clinical evidence and/or appropriate guidelines insofar as these exist. We can therefore determine whether a particular LST is obligatory, based on certainty of outcomes. If LST is not obligatory, then patients who have the capacity to make their own decisions have the right to refuse treatments (including those intended to sustain life), if they are not deemed obligatory, even if physicians regard such treatments in the patients' best interests.

Consequently, what are our obligations when it comes to withholding LST in patients in need of CPR, mechanical ventilation and ancillary interventions like ANH, pain control and antibiotics? Is CPR obligatory and are, "do not resuscitate" (DNR) orders, permissible? The purpose of CPR is to attempt to restart the heart or breathing and restore circulation after a cardio-respiratory arrest. It often includes invasive procedures, for example, obtaining access to the patient's airway and circulation. Its success rate is dependent on circumstance but generally lower than is commonly perceived by the general public. The chance of survival to hospital discharge for in-hospital CPR in older people is low to moderate (11.6–18.7%) and decreases with age (van Gijn et al. 2014). Survival of children and those 18 to 69 years is no more than 45.4% (Zoch et al. 2000; Alsoufi et al. 2007; Danciu et al. 2004). In other words, most patients after CPR do not survive. Therefore, CPR does not qualify as obligatory treatment and is optional. Even though the patient will die if not treated, CPR cannot rescue the patient with certainty, and therefore will not be an obligatory intervention, rather it will be optional. Decisions are therefore left to patients, through advanced directives, or patient's families or other surrogate decision makers about DNR orders. If the patient understands the nature and consequences of his or her decision, is assessed as having capacity to make the decision and is supported by their family, the provision of further LST may no longer be ethically justifiable even if it has the potential to provide some limited clinical benefit.

Similarly, most cases of patients who end up on ventilators have poor prognosis of survival, and majority of the time this treatment is not obligatory as it does not achieve certainty in its effectiveness (Knaus 1989; Esteban et al. 2002). However, each case is to be judged based on pre-illness quality of life to conclude significance of prognosis for long-term survival, combined with additional information about patient's wishes.

Ancillary interventions like pain control and antibiotics will only be obligatory if by withholding them there is certainty that the patient will die. For example, an elderly patient is at risk of death from septicaemia because of non-treatment of urine infection, but the risk of death is not certain, and hence antibiotics are not obligatory treatment (Gharbi et al., 2019) Similarly a patient is very unlikely to die from severe pain even though his quality of life may be severely diminished. Death will be because of the underlying condition. Even though patients may experience severe pain, pain relief will not save life at level of certainty, and therefore it will not be obligatory. In fact, there are concerns about the possibility of certain pain medication hastening death in end-of-life care (Laserna et al. 2020).

Nutrition and hydration are obligatory because it is certain that withholding them will lead to death. However, when there are risks associated with giving food and drink, either by mouth or *artificial* nutrition and hydration, then things can be more complex, because nutrition and hydration can potentially cause more harm, especially if administered through unconventional or artificial routes. All patients have a basic need for food and drink to maintain adequate levels of nutrition and hydration and to prevent the adverse outcomes associated with malnutrition or dehydration. This applies equally to those with life-limiting illness. Giving food by mouth is part of basic care and should be provided for those who can tolerate it without serious risk – for example, choking, aspiration, and who appear hungry and thirsty. A separate assessment of a patient's fluid and nutrition needs should take place alongside assessment of their clinical condition and form a basic part of care. It will determine whether clinically assisted provision of nutrition and hydration is required. ANH is appropriate in many patients, including those with severe impairment or terminal illnesses. This may be through a naso-gastric tube, intravenous infusion, subcutaneous fluids, naso-jejunal tube or by percutaneous endoscopic gastrostomy (PEG) tube and central line etc. Some of these interventions can be invasive and intrusive, leading to hardship, burden and compromise patient dignity. It is therefore not obligatory to continue ANH if the patient is end-of-life, in their last few days of life, or there is evidence that ANH is not effective and unable to bring benefit to the patient, and the harm of intervention outweighs any benefit.

Regarding the prohibition of withholding nutrition and hydration in patients, to contextualise the *fiqh* literature further, this referred to individuals who had the capacity to eat and drink by mouth, unaided or through the help of others. It would have required them to be at least in a state of consciousness, so that they did not aspirate, and hence were in a state to benefit. Withholding food and drink is certain to lead to death if the underlying condition had not taken its toll already. With technological advances we are now able to provide nutrition and hydration to those who are at end-stage of disease, unconscious in their last few days, and are unlikely to benefit from nutrition and hydration. To withhold or withdraw ANH will not cause suffering or be harmful, nor will it be the cause, or contributor to death, but the cause of death will be the underlying illness.

Because nutrition and hydration is essential to sustain life, if evidence suggests with dominant probability that it is of no benefit or even harmful, then it will be permissible to withhold ANH, as then an established certainty (i.e., benefit of ANH) is proven not to be the case in a specific situation. Therefore, the obligations approach to the two categories of LST; life-support and ANH, differ on the basis of certainty of outcome, where ANH is established to be certain in sustaining life, and therefore requires strong proof to the contrary that it is certain that it is of *no* benefit to the patient in a specific situation for it not to be obligatory. In other words, proof is required that there is certainty that ANH will not benefit the patient to justify withholding or withdrawal. This is not the case with life-support like CPR and mechanical ventilation, where they are not certain to sustain life, and require proof that they are certain to save life in specific situations to be obligatory.

ANH was originally developed to provide short-term support for patients who were acutely ill. For patients near the end-of-life, ANH is unlikely to prolong life, and can potentially lead to medical complications and increase suffering (Bruera et al. 2013; Casarett et al. 2005; Koretz 2007; Koretz et al. 2007). In such patients ANH will not be seen as obligatory treatment and may even be prohibited if the harms of ANH far outweigh the benefits.

In conclusion, treatments are therefore obligatory if there is certainty of loss of life due to the underlying condition and the treatment or intervention offered will save life with certainty. However, if the patient cannot be rescued with certainty, then there is no obligation to start treatment, rather it is recommended or optional. ANH can be withheld if there is certainty that it is of no benefit, that it will not cause suffering or that its harms far outweigh its benefits, whereas other LSTs can be withheld if there is no certainty of their benefit.

5 Obligations Related to Withdrawing LST

When deciding to *withdraw* treatment, it is important to know whether it is obligatory to continue LST, because then we are culpable and sinful if we withdraw obligatory treatment. If LST is not obligatory, to withdraw treatment is optional. It can even be prohibited and sinful if we do not withdraw, knowing that the harms due to treatment significantly outweigh the benefits.

It has already been explained that treatment is only obligatory when the condition of the patient is life-threatening and the treatment offered is certain to save life. If these conditions are not met, then it no longer remains obligatory. The same principle applies to withdrawing LST as there is no moral distinction between the two. A patient has an underlying respiratory condition and his breathing has deteriorated significantly. If he is not treated, there will be imminent death. If the use of a mechanical ventilator is certain to save his life, then it becomes obligatory to commence the patient on the ventilator. It remains obligatory to continue ventilation if the odds remain the same, i.e., effectiveness of outcome is certain. If he refuses and dies, he will be sinful. If death is not imminent, or LST is commenced but with no certainty of saving life, then to withdraw treatment will not be sinful, as it is not obligatory to continue. There is no certainty that he will die if LST is removed and there is no certainty that it will rescue him if it is continued. If he dies, then there is no sin, as it was not an obligation to initiate the LST due to its uncertainty. The books of *fiqh* mention that if a doctor recommends treatment and the patient refuses and dies, he will not be sinful because the treatment is not *certain* to save his life (Niẓām al-Dīn et al. 2000, 5:355, 360; al-Zaylaʿī 2000, 6:33; Abū l-Maʿālī 2004, 5:373).

In the situation where effectiveness of LST is not certain and is bordering around 50%, it is good medical practice for all attempts to be made in continuing optimal treatment, as there is reasonable chance of survival. It may also be a medico-legal duty for physicians to maintain LST with such odds of survival ensuring all reasonable approaches are taken to rescue the patient. However, it is incorrect to claim that continuing treatment in such patients is religiously obligatory and that the withdrawal of such treatment is prohibited and sinful, contrary to common belief.

Even when an illness has a reasonable prognosis, is reversible, is not terminal and treatment is not futile, such patients can decide to withhold or withdraw LST against physician advice. They will not be religiously culpable or sinful unless there is certainty that they will die if LST is stopped or withdrawn. It is only with certainty of effectiveness of treatment that continuing treatment remains obligatory for them.

On a practical note, certainty about treatment outcome is rarely possible when making any clinical decision. A relatively high degree of confidence (*ghalabat al-ẓann*) regarding outcomes is required to determine the gravity of the consequences of decisions to limit LST. In acute, emergency situations it is usually necessary to give LST first and to review the decision to continue when more information or expertise is available – like a more experienced and senior clinical opinion, important test results or more time to determine the level of improvement of the clinical state with continuing treatment. In less acute situations it can also be possible to attain higher levels of certainty by continuing to provide LST whilst waiting for more information to be assembled.

When patients in need explicitly refuse life-sustaining emergency treatment that is uncertain, the physician must choose between the undesirable options of foregoing beneficial treatment, and forcing treatment on a competent but unwilling patient, both of which have potential ethical and legal consequences. If treatment is not obligatory, informed consent and informed refusal allow competent patients to choose among treatments in accordance with their values, goals, and priorities for their future. When patients refuse recommended life-sustaining medical treatment, the duty rests with the physician to discern whether the patient has the decision-making capacity to reject treatment. Patients, who have the capacity to make their own decisions, have the right to refuse LST and to have that refusal respected.

Many health care providers believe that any omission of a life-sustaining treatment is tantamount to passive euthanasia or at least assistance in the patient's suicide (Betzold 1992). It may also be the case that the patient is refusing the treatment in an attempt to end his life. Passive euthanasia is, "the intentional ending of one person's life by another, motivated solely by the best interest of the person who dies, through the deliberate [withholding or withdrawing] of a life-preserving substance or procedure."[9] The patient's death cannot simply be an accident, or even an undesired but a tolerated side effect for it to qualify as passive euthanasia. Both in physician assisted suicide PAS and euthanasia, the patient's death is intended, and the interventions are specifically chosen to bring about that outcome. As for the patient, if the patient is refusing treatment in an attempt to end his life, then this will be sinful for the patient. God states in the Qurʾān: "Do not kill yourselves, for God is merciful to you" (Q 4:29), and, "do not put yourself into destruction by your own hands" (Q 2:195). A willingness on the part of caregivers to forego LST does not logically equate a willingness to bring about the patient's death. The foregoing of LST reflects an acceptance of one's limited powers in rescuing the patient. Willingness to bring about the patient's death is the belief that an enacted death is morally preferable to a natural death. Withholding and withdrawing mechanical ventilation is motivated by the health care team's respect of the patient's autonomous decision and is not aimed at bringing about the patient's death (Brassington 2020). But even if the refusal is suicidal, that does not mean the health care team is assisting the patient in his suicide. The team simply has no ethical mandate to start or continue the life-sustaining treatment when a competent patient refuses treatment with uncertain outcome and the treatment is not religiously obligated. Team members should inform the patient, counsel him, negotiate, and use any other respectful means to get the patient to at least try a life-sustaining treatment that is likely to be effective and unlikely to cause severe side-effects. But if a competent patient persists in his refusal, the health care team no longer has a choice in the matter, must abstain from the refused treatment, and cannot be responsible either for the patient's subsequent death (Brassington 2020).

9 For a cogent detailed explanation of definition of passive euthanasia see Brassington 2020. My emphasis added in brackets where author explains that this would refer to both withholding and withdrawing LST.

When treatment is certain to save life, but the burdens of life sustaining treatment significantly outweigh any benefits, in other words the adverse harms of intervention, i.e., hastening death or worsening the severity of other illnesses, outweighs any benefit, then it will be morally wrong and sinful to continue treatment. For example, if removal of a brain tumour is certain to save the life of a child and to prevent death, then this surgery is obligatory. But if the harms of the intervention, i.e., performing brain surgery using general anaesthetic will certainly hasten death or worsen illness, because the child has a serious congenital heart condition and will not tolerate the anaesthetic, then it will be prohibited to continue such intervention.

When treatment is certain to save life and the harm of intervention is equal to its benefit, then it will still remain obligatory to continue. Like when providing artificial nutrition and hydration (ANH) to an elderly patient through a central line because there is no other venous access and he is severely dehydrated.[10] When treatment is not certain to save life and the burdens of the life sustaining treatment significantly outweigh any benefit, then it will be morally wrong and sinful to continue the treatment. If the harm is equal to benefit, then it will not be obligatory or sinful to continue but optional, for example lifesaving surgical operation on an elderly gentleman. Some may attempt to operate on balance of benefit and harm.

The table below shows how approaches to "religious obligations of treatment," when withholding and withdrawing LST, are to be observed in view of certainty of effectiveness of treatment outcome and compounding harm considerations.

Continuing or withdrawing any particular treatment depends on the indication for that treatment and on the justification for limiting LST. It may be appropriate to limit some LSTs but not others on the basis of the burdens of treatment. For example, it may be appropriate to withhold invasive ventilation in a patient with a severe neuromuscular disorder, but obligatory to provide other less burdensome treatments, including non-invasive respiratory support, ANH, antibiotics, or blood transfusions.

Advanced technological application has led to treatments that can sustain life in circumstances where this was previously impossible. However, advanced treatments may be invasive, neither restoring health nor conferring overall benefits to the patient. LST or the underlying condition may produce pain and suffering for the patient and their families. Some of the most challenging and

10 While central venous access is routine in the critically-ill patient, it is not without risk (see Kornbau et al. 2015).

TABLE 10.1 Certainty of medical intervention outcomes and their respective normative rulings

Medical intervention			
Benefit	**Harm**	**Ruling**	
Level of certainty of effectiveness of treatment in saving life	Harm of intervention, in terms of hastening death or worsening severity of illness	Obligation to continue?	Penalty or sinful?
Certainty (*yaqīn*) and dominant probability (*ghalabt al-ẓann*)	No harm or less harm than benefit	Obligatory to continue	Sinful to withhold or withdraw
	Greater harm then benefit	Obligatory not to continue (i.e., prohibited)	Sinful to continue
	Equal harm with benefit	Obligatory to continue	Sinful to withhold or withdraw
Presumption (*ẓann*), uncertainty (*shakk*), doubtfulness (*wahm*)	No harm or less harm than benefit	Not obligatory to continue	Not sinful to withhold or withdraw (i.e., optional)
	Greater harm then benefit	Obligatory not to continue (i.e., prohibited)	Sinful to continue
	Equal harm with benefit	Not obligatory to continue	Not sinful to withhold or withdraw (i.e., optional)

emotionally complex decisions arise in relation to withholding, withdrawing or otherwise limiting treatment that has the potential to sustain life, but which imposes burdens or serious harms to the patient and family. So, how do we balance benefits of LST with that of harms from continued care and the underlying condition? Great progress has been made in obtaining reliable evidence on the beneficial effects of interventions, but developments in the identification, interpretation, and reporting of harmful effects is more challenging (Cuervo and Clarke 2003). What assessment and evaluations of harm should be made which serve patients' best interests?

6 Limiting Treatment

The shorter a person's future life, the less reason there is to provide LST. If the person is end-of-life because of a terminal illness, then certainty of prolonged or extended life cannot be achieved. The patient will soon die and hence it will not be obligatory to start or continue LST. Therefore, there is no obligation to initiate CPR or mechanical ventilation for a patient who is dying from terminal illness and is at end-of-life.

The statement of the Permanent Committee provides details of specific disease conditions that justify withholding life sustaining measures. It states:

> If the patient is physically or mentally incapacitated whilst suffering from a chronic illness, advanced stage cancer, severe cardiopulmonary disease or has had several cardiac arrests, and the decision not to resuscitate has been reached by three competent specialist physicians, then it is permissible not to resuscitate.
>
> AL-LAJNA AL-DĀʾIMA 1989

The Permanent Committee endorses withholding LST when permitting "Do Not Resuscitate" orders (DNR) in end stage chronic or terminal illnesses, with the agreement of three experienced doctors. In other words, if LST is unable or unlikely to prolong life significantly because the illness is terminal or chronically severe, then it is not in the patient's best interests to provide it, i.e., it can be withheld. This describes futility based on the idea that life is limited in quantity because LST cannot prolong life significantly. These justifications can also extend to autonomous decisions of patients, families in cases of non-terminal illness also, when the patient has a serious permanently diminished neurological state and is likely to survive for a prolonged period, like being in a permanent coma, but there is no additional benefit with treatment. Treatment may be able to prolong life significantly but will not alleviate the burdens associated with illness, limiting quality of life (Larcher et al. 2015). This describes futility based on the idea that life is limited in quality or there is no meaningful life.

So, there are two important evaluations of life that require exploring when determining best interests of patients to forego LST:

1. Quantitative evaluations of life – whether the treatment will prolong the person's life significantly.
2. Qualitative evaluations of life – whether the treatment will alleviate burdens of illness to provide a worthwhile quality of life or meaningful life.

These evaluations consist of both scientific and value judgements. When we assess suitability or responsiveness to treatment, we evaluate both the quantitative and qualitative components (Wilkinson 2019). Therefore, treatment becomes obligatory when there is a certainty that the patient's life is significantly prolonged, sustaining a worthwhile life.

7 Quantitative Evaluation of Life and Foregoing LST

If quantity of life is limited because of the underlying condition and there is inevitable or imminent death (Maḥmūd Idrīs 2007), then LST can be withheld or withdrawn because of lack of benefit, as certainty of prolonged or extended life cannot be achieved. Classical Muslim jurists have described different levels or stages of end-of-life.

1. **Legal death:** The stage Muslim jurists refer to as *al-ḥayāt ghayr al-mustaqirra*. This is a state of permanent unconsciousness. Classical Muslim jurists give the example of a person who has been inflicted with serious illness or seriously wounded and is permanently unresponsive. The main diagnostic signs described are permanent loss of cognition, loss of coherent speech (*nuṭq*), sight (*ibṣār*) and voluntary movement (*ḥaraka ikhtiyāriyya*) (al-Jaṣṣāṣ 2010, 5:134; Ibn ʿĀbidīn 1994, 6:455, Ibn al-Humām 2000, 6:6; al-Nawawī 2008, 9:146; al-Zarkashī 2000, 2:105; IIFA 1986, 523). The condition is described as irreversible and analogous to an animal after sacrificial slaughtering (*ḥarakat al-madhbūḥ*), when the sacrificed animal is legally or morally seen as dead even though there may be involuntary movements. This state is referred to as legal death (*al-mawt al-ḥukmī*) (al-Ramlī 2003, 7:263–264; al-Shirbīnī 1997, 4:13; Ibn ʿĀbidīn 1994, 6:544; Ibn al-Humām 2000, 6:4–5; ʿIllaysh 1984, 4:361; al-Kharshī n.d., 8:7–8; al-Nawawī 2008, 2:224; al-Qarāfī 1998, 2:31; Ḥaṭṭāb al-Ruʿaynī 2007, 6:244; al-Nawawī 1991, 5:146).

   In medieval times, consciousness was not understood the way we understand it now, from a physiological or clinical perspective. The descriptions mentioned by classical Muslim jurists suggest that permanent cessation of sensory perception (volition, sentience) and voluntary action (i.e., higher brain functions) are determining factors in considering somebody as legally dead (*al-mawt al-ḥukmī*) or even close to it. Classical Muslim jurists differentiated between somatic signs of permanent loss of consciousness from that of biological or cellular death of the body when providing rulings related to death behaviours and penalties (Rashid 2021).

Starting or continuing LST provides no benefit in such patients and therefore, can be withheld or withdrawn. Death may be diagnosed following cardio-respiratory arrest, or in a permanently unconscious patient, it may be diagnosed following evidence of irreversible cessation of brain stem function. When death is diagnosed following formal confirmation of brain stem death by agreed medical criteria, intensive technological support is no longer appropriate and should be withdrawn.[11]

2. **Imminent death**: This is the stage of *sakarāt al-mawt* (al-Ghazālī 2005, 4:461), which is described as the final moments of death (*nazʿ*) and is the verge of the beginning of the death process when one is about to perish in their last moments. This state is not death and rulings of the living still apply. It is not permissible to speed the dying process through any means as a response to the person's hardship (Ibn ʿĀbidīn 1994, 6:544; al-Qarāfī 1998, 2:31; Ḥaṭṭāb al-Ruʿaynī 2007, 6:244; al-Nawawī 1991, 5:146; al-Ramlī 2003, 7:263–4; al-Shirbīnī 1997, 4:38; Ibn Qudāma 1980, 7:835; al-Buhūtī 1983, 5:516; Ibn Ḥazm n.d., 10:518). This state can be confused as death and treated as such. But reality is, it should not be considered death and should not be confused with legal death. Despite treatment, the patient is physiologically deteriorating. Continuing treatment may delay death but can no longer restore life or health. It is therefore no longer appropriate to provide LST because it is of no benefit and burdensome to do so.
3. **Inevitable demise**: The stage described as *al-ḥayāt al-mustaqirra*, which is during the last stages of life when death is unavoidable. Classical Muslim jurists give the example of a person who may have been inflicted with severe injuries and there is certainty or dominant probability that the patient will die within a few days due to underlying condition. The person has some cognition, can hear, see, talk and has some voluntary actions. This is a state where the soul is seen as having not departed and movements are voluntary (al-Zarkashī 2000, 2:105). This is a state of end-of-life or last days of life in the terminally ill. In some situations, death is not imminent (within minutes or hours) but will occur within a matter of days or even weeks. It may be possible to extend life by LST, but this may provide little or no overall benefit for the patient. In this case, there should be a shift of focus of care from life prolongation to palliation.

11 Recognising that there are different criteria or standards for brain death for more detail see: (Rashid 2021).

8 Qualitative Evaluation of Life and Foregoing LST

In some patients, continuing treatment may prolong life significantly. Yet it may be in the patient's best interests to consider limiting it if there is no overall benefit in prolonging life because of the adverse impact entailed. Other than limited quantity of life, the states of limited quality of life due to underlying condition or illness, bear burden and harm and can also justify foregoing LST. Even when patients can survive for a long time, LST can be withheld or withdrawn when there is lack of ability to derive benefit because we cannot achieve a *meaningful life*. Qualitative evaluations assess the nature of a future life for an individual, the value and meaning that the patient will derive from it and the relative balance of positives and negatives. The positive impact of treatments on the patient's ability to communicate, experience awareness of those around them, experience pleasure, attain goals and be independent, and the negative impact of treatment in terms of *compounding harms* like pain, discomfort, distress, violations of bodily dignity and loss of benefit to afterlife are important factors to be considered.

8.1 *Compounding Harm Considerations*

There are different types of harms and degrees of harm. In the Islamic bioethico-legal discourse, assessment of harm extends to other non-physical considerations like types of bodily dignity and loss of benefit to afterlife. I will first describe the types and degrees of harm and then propose an approach to be taken in considerations of harm expressed to bodily dignity and loss of benefit to afterlife.

Islam has a highly developed and sophisticated legal tradition, and Islamic law is the determining factor that Muslims seek authority from, which allows us to be able to make the right moral decisions (Sherman 2003). The balance and weight of harm outcomes are therefore to be dealt with from an Islamico-legal perspective, as this is what determines the overall permissibility of an act and what we "*ought to*" or "*ought not to*" do. In the Islamic legal tradition, harm is defined broadly when it describes setbacks to peoples' interests related to reputation, property, privacy and liberty. In the legal literature the Arabic word *ḍarar* is commonly used to refer to harms to the physical human body and derives from *ḍarra*, which is mentioned in a number of verses of the Qur'ān either in the form of verb *ḍarra – yaḍurru*, noun *ḍarrun* or adverb *ḍirāran*. In the Qur'ān (Q 25:55, 5:76, 2:231, 20:89, 22:13) it takes a broad meaning, where *ḍarar* is defined as anything that causes damage or danger, and it is the opposite of benefit (*nafʿ*) (al-Rāzī 1986, 379; Fīrūzābadī 2005, 550). *Ḍarar* has been interpreted by Muslim scholars in diverse ways, both in definition and context. *Ḍarar* can connote constriction and constraint (*ḍīq*) (Ibn Manẓūr 2010) or a state of affliction or difficulty. Al-Ṭabarī (d. 310/923)[12] in his commentary describes *ḍarar* as a state of extreme hardship and affliction (al-Ṭabarī 1994, 9:179, 20:170, 221). Al-Qurṭubī (d. 671/1273)[13] and Ibn Kathīr (d. 774/1373)[14] define it as severe poverty and hardship in life *al-faqr wa-l-ḍīq fī l-ʿaysh* (Ibn Kathīr 1999, 3:229; al-Qurṭubī 2004, 6:426). The Qurʾān also describes *ḍarar* as one which extends to emotional states (Q 39:8, 39:49). This is also the view of al-Rāzī (d. 604/1207)[15] who also describes *ḍarar* as grief, distress (*ḥuzn*) (Q 6:17); and extreme fear or adversity (*khawf shadīd*) (al-Rāzī 1981, 12:494, 21:487).

A narrower focus on harm and one which is relevant here is harm considerations which present setbacks to physical bodily interests related to health and survival, and less to a psychosocial interest which are usually subjective and arbitrary (Nathan et al. 2020). Our discussion will address physical harms which are related to pain, psychological distress due to pain, functional disability and death more specifically on causing, permitting death, or risk of death – as the legal text relates harms to life and the human body in this manner.

Pain comes from an injury, either caused by the intervention or due to the underlying condition or illness and leads to diminished quality of life. If pain is severe, then this justifies withholding treatment if there is no benefit in

12 Abū Jaʿfar Muḥammad b. Jarīr b. Yazīd al-Ṭabarī (d. 310/923) was an influential Sunnī Persian Muslim scholar, historian and exegete of the Qurʾān from Amol, Tabaristan (modern Mazandaran Province of Iran). His most influential and best-known works are his Qurʾānic commentary known as *Tafsīr al-Ṭabarī* which immediately won high regard and retained its importance for scholars to the present day. It is the earliest major running commentary of the Qurʾān to have survived in its original form.

13 Abū ʿAbd Allāh al-Qurṭubī (d. 671/1273) was an Andalusī jurist, Islamic scholar and *muḥaddith* (*ḥadīth* expert). He was taught by prominent scholars of Córdoba, Spain and he is well known for his commentary of the Qurʾān named *Tafsīr al-Qurṭubī*. The most important and famous of his works, this 20-volume commentary has raised great interest, and has had many editions. It is often referred to as *al-Jamīʿ li-Aḥkām*, meaning "All the Judgments." Contrary to what this name implies, the commentary is not limited to verses dealing with legal issues but is a general interpretation of the whole of Qurʾān with a Mālikī point of view.

14 Abū l-Fiḍā ʿImād al-Dīn Ismāʿīl b. ʿUmar Ibn Kathīr al-Qurashī l-Damishqī (d. 774/1373), known as Ibn Kathīr was a highly influential Sunnī historian, exegete and scholar during the Mamluk era in Syria. An expert on *tafsīr* (Qurʾānic exegesis) and *faqīh* (jurisprudence), he wrote several books, including a fourteen-volume universal history and his famous commentary on the Qurʾān named *Tafsīr al-Qurʾān al-ʿAẓīm*.

15 Fakhr al-Dīn al-Rāzī (d. 604/1207) was a Persian polymath, Islamic scholar and a pioneer of inductive logic who made various works in the fields of medicine, chemistry, physics, astronomy, cosmology, literature, theology, ontology, philosophy, history and jurisprudence. One of his outstanding achievements was his unique interpretive work on the Qurʾān called *Mafātīḥ al-Ghayb* ("Keys to the Unseen") and later nicknamed *Tafsīr al-Kabīr* ("The Great Commentary").

treatment for the patient (Raffaeli and Arnaudo 2017). Whilst the Islamic tradition rewards individuals who bear pain during illness, supporting the notion that forbearance with pain is rewarded, the Prophetic statement in Islam states that there should be no harming or reciprocating of harm (*lā ḍarar wa-lā ḍirār*), which informs us that serious and irreversible harm from treatment should also be removed (Padela 2016). The psychosocial and functional consequences of chronic pain disorders are well documented as having significant effects on responsiveness to and participation in treatment, on functional disability, and health-related quality of life (Turk et al. 2016). Therefore, pain is an important physical factor which impacts our *psychological* and *functional* wellbeing, and in turn, affects treatment efficiency and outcome as well as our quality of life.

In the Islamic legal literature, competing harm considerations extend beyond the dimensions of personhood related to the physical body described in secular bioethics (Addis 2020). They also encompass events external to personhood, such as the sanctity of the human body. Actions such as tampering and violating the *integrity dignity* (*ḥurma*) of the human body are also recognised harms. For this reason, Muslim jurists commonly prohibit post-mortem autopsies and medical research on the human cadaver (Rispler-Chaim 1993). Classical Muslim jurists relate cases where violation of the sanctity or dignity of the human body is seen as a competing moral harm. Examples include the prohibition of dissecting a dead mother's abdomen to extract a foetus when attempts of rescue are futile. Also the prohibition of dissecting and extracting another's valuable property from the abdomen of a dead person who has swallowed the possession of another, and the prohibition of eating the human flesh of the dead even in a state of extreme starvation for survival (al-Kāsānī 2003, 5:129–130, 7:177; Ibn al-Humām 2003, 2:102; Saḥnūn 2014, 1:264; al-Dasūqī n.d. 1:429; al-Nawawī 2008, 5:270, 9:42–43; Ibn Qudāma 1980, 3:497–498, 13:338–339). In each of these cases the violation to the *integrity* dignity and sanctity of the dead human body through dissection, is for some, a weightier competing harm compared to other competing moral considerations like futile attempts at rescuing a foetus, the loss of the right of ownership of another, or even when rescuing self from starvation (Ibn Qudāma 1980, 2:413–414; Ibn Nujaym 1999, 88). The legal reasoning applied in the classical literature draws on legal maxims, where the sanctity and dignity of the violation of the body is weighed against other competing harms (*aḍrār*), when deciding which dominant harm is to be removed. Therefore, in an Islamic ethico-legal framework related to harm associated with LST, the sanctity and dignity of the human body must be preserved as much as possible when weighing harms and benefits of treatment.

Respect for bodily sanctity, dignity and integrity is generally viewed from two diverse views – the *person*-orientated and the *body*-oriented view (Rashid 2018). Modern bioethics gives more weight to the *person*-orientated view, which is based on respect of persons and autonomy (Rendtorff 2002). The body is of *instrumental* value and not *essential value*, and if mental life could survive outside the body, then the body would have no moral significance.[16] Its value only exists in relation to the body being inhabited by the person. Once the person is removed, the body is just a shell that can be potentially used for other goods. This view employs an extrinsic value to the physical body. The *body*-orientated view refers mainly to duties to one's own body rather than others. As a result, it can conflict with the *person*-orientated view, in that it is not always consistent with personal autonomy and self-determination. This intrinsic value to bodily integrity implies that our body is not entirely owned by us and that we are prohibited in doing certain things to our body that violate its dignity (*karāma*). This *body*-orientated approach is found mainly in religious doctrine such as the monotheistic traditions of Judaism, Christianity and Islam. It is also found in classical Greek and Roman thought, as well as in the works of philosophers such as Aquinas (d. 1274) and Kant (d. 1804) (Dekkers 2009, 340). This intrinsic value to the body view employs sacredness (*ḥurma*) to the body in a sociopolitical order, which extends to its natural, biological order (Ramsey 1970). The value of the body both living and dead is a sign of our dependence on it. It is a gift to be cherished and respected as inseparable from human dignity (Kass 1985, 278–294).

The Islamic legal tradition describes the human body as possessing *karāma* (dignity) and *ḥurma* (inviolability). Both these terms are described as closely related concepts (Padela 2016), and sometimes due to an inability to differentiate between the two, are used synonymously. Their distinction exists in their usage where *karāma* is a "right" conferred by God in the Qurʾān, which stresses that, "We have honoured (*karramnā*) the sons of Adam … and conferred on them special favours [i.e., rights], above a great part of our creation" (Q 17:70). Whereas *ḥurma*, a verbal noun of *ḥaruma* relates to an "obligation or duty not to harm or violate" (i.e., prohibition) as the Qurʾān states: "And do not kill the soul which Allāh has forbidden (*ḥarram Allāhu*), except for just cause" (Q 17:33). A right is an entitlement not to be harmed whereas an obligation is something that one must do because of a law, necessity, or because it is a duty. Just as something may enjoy a right, there is an obligation on others towards it. The human body has a right or entitlement (*karāma*) not to be harmed or violated, and there is an obligation or prohibition (*ḥurma*) not to harm or violate.

16 Two recognised rejectors of the significance of the human body are the theologian Joseph Fletcher (d. 1991) and the philosopher Tristram Engelhardt (d. 2018) (see Murray 1987, 1063–1067).

We are concerned with obligations related to harm to human bodily dignity which are physical harm considerations or violations (*ḥurma*) against the human body, through medical intervention. These come in many forms and are not to be seen as just a single broad concept. For example, Muslim jurists differentiate between different types of violations of dignity of the body. For example, dissection of the human body is seen morally different to using human body parts (i.e., as implants or transplants). The latter demands more stringent conditions compared to the former. Muslim jurists describe three main types or classifications of violations (*ḥurma*) to human body dignity in the *fiqh* literature, but there are more which hold less relevance to our discussion.[17]

1. The "integrity" *ḥurma*: This is normally described as mutilation (*muthla*) of the body. In other words, the human body is not to be physically mutilated and/or to be unjustly tampered with. Dissection, excision or removal of an organ or parts from an individual's body, when there is no benefit for him, is considered mutilation (Sanbhalī 1994, 1:188). This act, if it serves no purpose or benefit to the one whose body is violated, is prohibited in normal circumstances. The offence of mutilation extends to the dead corpse also, where both the dead and alive are equal in *ḥurma*. This is what is meant by the *ḥadīth* of the Prophet Muḥammad who said: "Breaking the bones of the dead is akin to breaking the bones of the living" (Abū Dāwūd 2000, 1464; Ibn Māja 2000, 2573), and "causing injury to a dead believer is similar to causing him injury when he is alive" (Sanbhalī 1994, 1:188). There is general consensus amongst most contemporary scholars that such an act, if not excused in the Sharīʿa, is strictly prohibited (*ḥarām*) or at least disliked enough to be impermissible (*makrūh*) (al-Qāḍī ʿIyāḍ, 5:463; al-Mawwāq 1994, 4:548; al-Nawawī 2006, 12:37; al-Shīrāzī 1992, 3:282; Ibn Qudāma 1980, 9:327). Al-Shawkānī (d. 1255/1839)[18] comments regarding the *ḥadīth* about breaking bones of the dead, that this *ḥadīth* identifies the caution required in ensuring that due care is taken in performing the ritual bath, shrouding, burial and other related acts, and that this applies to both Muslims and non-Muslims. He further states: "… if sin is committed against the cadaver, then there is no

17 There are also other prime descriptions related to the violation of human bodily dignity, such as bodily modesty *ʿawra*, ensuring the private parts of the body are always covered, but these descriptions are less relevant to the topic.

18 Muḥammad al-Shawkanī (d. 1255/1839) was a Yemeni scholar of Islam, jurist and reformer and called for a return to the textual sources of the Qurʾān and *ḥadīth*. He is credited with developing a series of syllabi for attaining various ranks of scholarship and used a strict system of legal analysis based on Sunnī thought.

doubt that this is impermissible (*fī taḥrīm*). And if there is injury, then just as it is prohibited to cause injury to the living, it is prohibited to cause injury to the dead" (al-Shawkānī 2006, 4:34). To mutilate the human body is a culpable offence, and it is an obligation to refrain from this. Any kind of invasive intervention is to be considered a violation of the integrity component of human bodily dignity, requiring moral justification.

2. The "functional" *ḥurma*: This is normally described as harm (*ḍarar*) to the body, but the term *ḍarar* also refers to broader considerations including violations of mutilation to the body. Life is a gift from God and no one has the authority to destroy it without a justified cause acceptable to God. The functional component of our bodily dignity preserves life, and if the *ḥurma* of this functional component is harmed, then our life will suffer. God states in the Qurʾān: "Do not kill yourselves, for God is merciful to you" (Q 4:29), and "do not put yourself into destruction by your own hands" (Q 2:195). Suicide or any direct attempt to harm self is therefore prohibited, as this violates the functional dignity *ḥurma* of the human body. Allowing others to harm self, when there is no benefit for self or others, is also prohibited because the bearer of life cannot authorise to destroy self without the behest of the originator of life (God) (al-Qurṭubī 2004, 2:361, 5:150). The importance of preserving the functional component of bodily dignity is evident in many concessions (*rukhṣa*) that the Sharīʿa grants in times of hardship.[19] An example of such a concession is the permissibility of dry ablution (*tayammum*), as a prerequisite to daily prayers, in place of the obligatory wet ablution (*wuḍūʾ*). This is in cases where water is scarce or harmful and serves the purpose of preventing potential detriment to health. All these concessions are granted in the Sharīʿa to preserve the functional component of our bodily dignity.[20]

19 Q 2:185: "During the month of Ramaḍān the Qurʾān was sent down as a guidance to the people with Clear Signs of the true guidance and as the Criterion (between right and wrong). So those of you who live to see that month should fast it, and whoever is sick or on a journey should fast the same number of other days instead. Allāh wants ease and not hardship for you so that you may complete the number of days required, magnify Allāh for what He has guided you to, and give thanks to Him."

And Q 22:78: "Strive in the cause of Allāh in a manner worthy of that striving. He has chosen you (for His task), and He has not laid upon you any hardship in religion."

20 Another example is the dispensation given to the frail, the pregnant and the ill, in keeping obligatory fasts, so as to preserve health and prevent harm. It is considered permissible for individuals to consume wine, to the extent necessary to avert harm. This is for the one who is choking whilst eating if no other drink is available. Other concessions are given for those who are weak and ill in performing their obligatory prayer and pilgrimage, and for the ill to consume unlawful medication when alternate forms of therapy are unavailable.

Pain and psychological trauma can be viewed as a functional harm if it interferes with a person's quality of life by diminishing their functioning capabilities (Breivik et al. 2008).

Distinctions exist between the integrity component and the functional component of human bodily dignity, because the dead do not have a functional component. Their body has ceased to function in the worldly sense. This suggests that the functional component is specific only to the living.

An important distinction is the strength of the functional component compared to the integrity component.[21] Violation of the integrity component to bodily dignity (mutilation) is tolerated and justified in order to preserve or maintain the functional component to bodily dignity on medical grounds if it is proven to be of benefit to the individual, i.e., having a surgical operation.[22]

3. The objectification *ḥurma*: This is claimed on the basis that the entire universe has been created for the benefit of mankind. Within reason, man can use its resources to his benefit. "Indeed, We honoured mankind" (Q 17:70) and "It is He (God), who created for you, all that which is on the earth" (Q 2:29). It is undignified, if man's body or body parts are used, other than what God had ordained, as this would violate human bodily dignity and sanctity (Sayf Allāh 2004, 5:70; al-Sarakhsī 2005, 128). The Ḥanafī jurist Ibn Nujaym (d. 970/1563), states that, "… it is not permissible to sell or make use (*intifāʿ*) of human hair. This is because man is honoured (*mukarram*) and he is not to be defiled (*mubtadhal*). Therefore, it is not permissible that any part of his body is objectified in an undignified way (*muhānan mubtadhalan*)" (Ibn Nujaym 1997, 6:88). This description of harm to bodily dignity is extensively discussed in debates on organ transplantation and is not as relevant here.

Obligations of preventing harm do not just relate to obligations not to harm another, but also include obligations not to impose *risks* of harm, particularly with regards to treatment and non-treatment decisions. There are many examples of this in the *fiqh* literature, and legal maxims[23] are used to guide

---

Many other concessions are present to prevent physical and functional harm to our body (see Ibn Nujaym 1999, 64–65).

21 The *ḥurma* of the living is weightier than the *ḥurma* of the deceased (see Jād al-Ḥaqq 1983, 10:3702–3715).

22 Male circumcision is a religious ritual, which is also considered a weightier factor than the inviolability of the *integrity* component to bodily integrity.

23 Unless they re-affirm a ruling of the Qurʾān or Sunna, the legal maxims do not bind the jurist in delivering a judgment, but they do provide an important influence in exercising *ijtihād* in arriving at legal decisions (*ḥukm*) and opinions (*fatwā*). Legal maxims, like legal theories (*naẓariyyāt fiqhiyya*), are designed to elucidate a refined understanding of the subject matter rather than address enforcement. The legal maxims are not similar to *uṣūl*

TABLE 10.2 Maxims that relate to harm considerations

1.	Harm should be removed to what is possible (*al-ḍarar yudfaʿ bi-qadr al-imkān*)
2.	Harm should not be removed by another harm or by the same [degree of] harm (*al-ḍarar lā yuzāl bi-l-ḍarar, al-ḍarar lā yuzāl bi-mithlih*)
3.	A more severe harm is to be removed by a lesser harm (*al-ḍarar al-ashadd yuzāl bi-l-ḍarar al-akhaff*)
4.	Harm to an individual is tolerated in removing a public harm (*yutaḥammal al-ḍarar al-khāss li-dafʿ al-ḍarar al-ʿāmm*)
5.	Avoiding [harm] detriment takes precedence over bringing about benefit (*darʾ al-mafāsid awlā min jalb al-maṣāliḥ*)

how competing harms ought to be evaluated and judged (Ibn ʿAbd al-Salām n.d., 1:64–65). It is commonly accepted that there are five leading maxims in Islamic jurisprudence and one of them relates to harm principles, "harm must be eliminated" (*al-ḍararu yuzāl*) or otherwise described as, "there is to be no harm and no reciprocating harm" (*lā ḍarar wa-lā ḍirār*), which have subsidiary maxims (Ibn Nujaym 1999) (see Table. 10.1).

Classic Muslim jurists are all agreed on these principles of harm and associated maxims, but they differ in their application. The moral weight given to the violation of the dignity of the body varies in view of the facts relevant to each case (Yaseen 1990, 49–87, 56–57). For example, in the case of the mother who dies, and whether it is permissible to dissect her abdomen and rescue the foetus in her womb, Muslim jurists come to different conclusions from their legal reasoning. Either an attempt is made to rescue the foetus, by dissecting the mother and tolerating the violation of the integrity dignity of her body, or the integrity dignity of her body is not violated and the foetus not extracted, because rescuing the foetus is futile and serves no benefit. Violation of the integrity dignity of the mother's body is seen an important competing moral feature, even when she is dead. Muslim jurists draw their conclusion using the maxim, "severe harm is to be removed by a lesser harm" (*al-ḍarar al-ashadd yuzāl bi-l-ḍarar al-akhaff*). The Ḥanafī and Shāfiʿī jurists permit the dissection of the mother to extract the foetus because even though the chance of survival

al-fiqh (principles of Islamic jurisprudence) since maxims are based on the *fiqh* itself and represent rules and principles that are derived from the detailed rules of *fiqh* on various issues. *Uṣūl al-fiqh* is concerned with the sources of law, the rules of interpretation, methodology of legal reasoning, dealing with the meaning and implication of commands and prohibitions and so on. On the other hand, a maxim is defined as "a general rule, which applies to all or most of its related particulars" (Kamali 2012).

of the foetus is small, attempts should be made because the preservation of the life of the living (i.e., functional dignity of the foetus) is weightier than that of the integrity dignity of the body of the dead (al-Samarqandī 1994, 3:345). Most of the Mālikī and Ḥanbalī jurists differ, because rescuing the foetus is of no benefit, and dissecting the mother serves no purpose except it violates her bodily dignity. However, if the mother is alive and the foetus is known to be dead, then all agree not to dissect the mother to extract the foetus, even if it means, dissecting and mutilating the foetus to extract it, as the functional *ḥurma* of the living supersedes the integrity *ḥurma* of the dead (Jād al-Ḥaqq 1983; Ibn al-Humām 2003, 2:142; Saḥnūn 2014, 1:264; al-Shīrāzī 1992, 1:257; ʿIllaysh 1984, 1:532; Ibn Qudāma 1980, 2:410). Preserving the life of the mother supersedes preserving the integrity *ḥurma* of the dead foetus. There are other similar cases in the Islamic legal literature, where these harm maxims are used to determine normative opinions, after evaluating the moral weight of the *ḥurma* of the body to specific cases.

In summary, the human body has intrinsic value, which is an important competing harm consideration compared to what is seen in western bioethics. There is an obligation not to harm, where harm is seen more broadly in Islamic legal literature associated to violations of human bodily dignity related to the integrity and functional component. Diminished functioning due to physical harm, disability, pain and psychological trauma can all impact the functional *ḥurma* of the body, and the integrity component can only be violated if it benefits the functional component.

So how do these harm considerations relate to discussions around foregoing LST?

8.2 *Harms and Burdens of Treatment*

There is an obligation to maintain the functional component of bodily dignity at the cost of the integrity component if treatment benefit is certain. If there is uncertainty, but harms are minimised, then it is optional to continue LST. The use of invasive measures like mechanical ventilation in patients who will not benefit, swings the balance of harm, making the integrity dignity a weightier component to preserve. This is because there is little if any benefit to the functional component, or in fact the functional component may be diminished (Figure 10.1).

Duties associated with withdrawing LST fundamentally revolve around competing natures of preventing risk of harm, with the aim of providing functional benefit to the patient at the cost of tolerating violation to the integrity component of human bodily dignity. If there is no functional benefit and there is actual functional harm due to burden of intervention, leading to severe

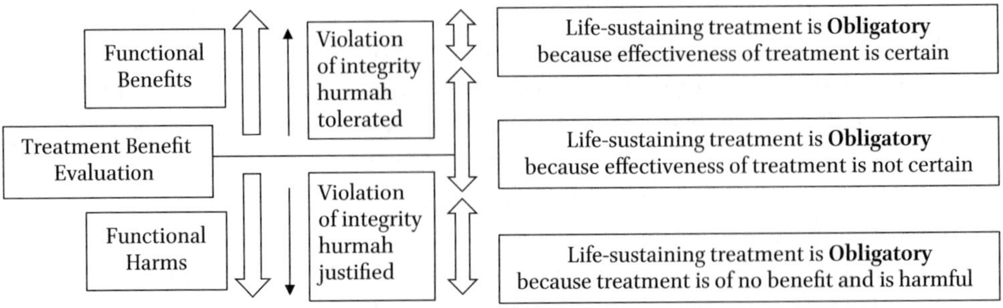

FIGURE 10.1 Balancing benefits and harms of treatment

pain or other adverse effects, then the violation of the integrity component is no longer justified Rendering such an intervention normatively neutral, wrong and even prohibited. An example would be withholding CPR in the frail and elderly, which is not free from its burdens and risks.[24] Decisions of DNR orders may be encouraged or may even be obligatory if harm significantly outweighs benefit. Both CPR, and the physiological process leading up to cardio-respiratory arrest, may have adverse consequences, for example, hypoxic brain damage and poor neurological outcomes. If it is unsuccessful, it may mean that death occurs in a traumatic and undignified manner and often in the absence of family.

Some forms of medical treatments in themselves cause pain and distress, which can be physical, psychological and emotional. If a patient's life can only be sustained, but at the cost of significant pain and distress it may not be in their best interests to receive such treatment, especially if such treatment is not obligatory, for example, the use of invasive mechanical ventilation in severe irreversible neuromuscular disease in children.[25] It is important that all options to relieve or overcome the negative effects of treatment are explored before proposing that it should be limited. However, if such treatment can only be delivered at the expense of compromising the patient's consciousness, for example, by deep sedation, its potential benefit may be significantly reduced.

24 CPR and resuscitative measures are with burdens and risks and include harmful side effects such as rib fracture and damage to internal organs; adverse clinical outcomes such as hypoxic brain damage; and other consequences for the patient such as increased physical disability. If the use of CPR is not successful in restarting the heart or breathing, and in restoring circulation, it may mean that the patient dies in an undignified and traumatic manner (see GMC 2010b).

25 Chronic pain is a significant problem in youths with neuromuscular disease NMD. Data strongly supports making comprehensive pain assessment and management an integral part of the standard of care for youths with NMD (see Engel et al. 2009).

Other examples of particularly high impact treatments include extracorporeal membrane oxygenation (ECMO), renal dialysis and, sometimes, intensive chemotherapy.

The professional duty to preserve life is not an absolute one that applies at all costs. Treatments should only be provided when they are in the patient's best interests. Treatment which is medically inappropriate and cannot achieve its intended purpose, in preserving a meaningful life or restoring health, is no longer in the best interests of the patient, because its burdens outweigh the benefits.

8.3 *Harms and Burdens of Underlying Condition or Illness*

Life support is not treatment but just buys time. Life support and resuscitation refer to interventions, techniques and procedures to maintain life by artificially replacing the function of vital organs if needed. The objective is to buy time for patients so that they can be treated for the underlying cause or are able to recover on their own. Treatment becomes obligatory when there is certainty that the patient's life is significantly prolonged, maintaining a *worthwhile life*. If the patient is not able to recover with life support to achieve a *worthwhile* or *meaningful life* with certainty – a life that can benefit the patient's afterlife – then it no longer remains obligatory to continue. Therefore, treatment becomes obligatory when there is certainty that the patient's life is significantly prolonged, maintaining a *worthwhile* or *meaningful life* and not merely just to rescue from death. Advances in technology allow us to keep patients' vital organs sustained mechanically for prolonged periods, yet the patient does not benefit because his life has no meaning due to a severely diminished neurological state. The objective of LST is not to unduly prolong lives of patients in this state, nor is this something that the Sharīʿa demands. The Sharīʿa demands that we rescue patients so that they can live to benefit their afterlife by leading a life which is worthwhile and meaningful.

In Islam, a meaningful life suffices that the patient is able to be brought to a state of cognitive consciousness, where at the minimum, there is sustained volition, sentience and an ability to enjoy and interact with the world, even if cognitive functioning is diminished to the degree that the patient is not legally accountable in religion for his or her actions. This may be due to an incomplete legal cognitive capacity (*ahliyyat al-adāʾ al-nāqiṣa*) by Sharīʿa juristic standards. *Ahliyyat al-adāʾ al-nāqiṣa* relates to a state of cognitive functioning where a person is not culpable and obligated to act on God's commands. This is because their cognitive functioning has not matured for them to make their own decisions and to understand the implications of those decisions. They may have the ability to differentiate between good and bad (*tamyīz*) but do not have the capacity to grasp the wider implications of their decisions. Even though this term specifically relates to legal culpability of children who have not achieved a level of maturity, i.e., when they have reached puberty (*bulūgh*), it is also used to describe both children and adults with reduced cognitive capacity (*maʿtūh*) like those with autism or dementia and would fall into the same ruling (*ḥukm*). In other words, it is not essential for the level of cognition to achieve a state of *mukallaf*[26] where the patient is legally accountable for his actions, possessing *ahliyyat al-adāʾ al-kāmila* (qualified legal cognitive capacity). Rather the state of incomplete legal cognitive capacity would also require us to rescue patients using LST.[27]

It is only an obligation to initiate or continue resuscitative measures in patients where at least this minimum state of *ahliyyat al-adāʾ al-nāqiṣa* can be achieved with dominant probability (*ghalabat al-ẓann*) (al-Zuḥaylī 1989, 4:2968; Mullā Khusraw 2017, 2:441; Ibn al-Humām 1999, 2:176; al-Bukhārī 2009, 2:1394; Ibn ʿĀbidīn 1994, 5:100; Taftāzānī 1957, 2:168). If this level of certainty cannot be achieved, at this level of cognitive functioning and independent life,

26 A *mukallaf* in Islamic legal literature is described as the addressee of the Sharīʿa (*mukhāṭab al-sharīʿa*) who is obligated to act by the commands of God because they have the capacity to follow the instructions of God in the Sharīʿa and understand its implications. They have the cognition and will to do the right thing and the physical bodily means to act. This is to be differentiated from *ahliyyat al-wujūb*, which refers to rights one possesses and not obligations. *Ahliyyat al-adāʾ al-kāmila* (qualified cognitive capacity) refers to the level of capacity required to be considered *mukallaf*.

27 In response to Padela and Mohiuddin (2015), I would not recommend using the state of *mukallaf* here, as wilful actions can still occur in those not cognisant of their potential afterlife ramifications and conditions of God's commands. *Mukallaf* actually refers to a legal state premised on the basis that an individual's primary duty is to recognise and worship God and to gain reward in the afterlife. It is argued that this minimal religious utility is achieved when the person is able to distinguish between what is beneficial and harmful (*tamyīz*) and there is an adoption of righteous character (*rushd*). To consider such a state as the minimal standard obligated, to restore a person to a state of meaningful life, is problematic. First, there are potential harmful ramifications, i.e., slippery slope, when considering anyone who has a cognitive functional state below *mukallaf* as a life not worthwhile saving. Second, introducing broad exceptions to overcome this, such as using another end goal for children specifically, and those who have a non-*mukallaf* state prior to injury, doesn't remove the idea that one is still accepting a non-*mukallaf* state as a life not worthwhile living /saving. Third, there are gaps and problems with such a construct related to *mukallaf* state, that the author recognises, but to then compensate by distorting the use of the term *mukallaf* to suit a status beyond just accountability of worship, and to include all worldly acts that gain divine pleasure and reward, renders the term *mukallaf* unsuitable for its actual original description coined by Muslim scholars.

TABLE 10.3 Quantitative and qualitative reasons which permit foregoing LST (see Larcher et al. 2015)[a]

Quantitative evaluation of life and when foregoing treatment is permitted	
Brain death (*al-mawt al-ḥukmī*)	Permanent loss of capacity for consciousness
Imminent death (*sakarāt al-mawt*)	Physiological deterioration with expected death within minutes to hours
Inevitable death (*al-ḥayāt al-mustaqirra*)	Expected death despite treatment within days to weeks
Qualitative evaluation of life when foregoing treatment is permitted	
Burdens of treatment	Life is sustained at the cost of significant functional harm and violation of the integrity *ḥurma*
Burdens of illness or underlying condition	Severity or impact of underlying condition leads to inability to achieve dominant probability of a meaningful life and independence from life-saving medical intervention

a This guideline was co-authored by Dominic Wilkinson, who provided the original draft taxonomy and has been adjusted to suit ideas expressed in this chapter.

then to forego LST and resuscitative measures in such patients will be permissible, optional and not culpable.[28]

A life is no longer meaningful if the person is unable to perceive, respond or engage with his/ her environment indefinitely. To maintain or initiate resuscitative measures in such patients is of no value in fulfilling a worthwhile life as the patient is unable to achieve the minimum cognitive capacity or conscious state which is worth preserving. Higher functions of volition and sentience (*idrāk*) must be preserved, which are indications of the presence of the soul and a state when a person can engage with their environment. These higher functions are biologically attributed to the brain and not other parts of the body (Rashid 2021). To live such a life suffices one to enjoy life and be rewarded for acts of worship even though there is no obligation or culpability (al-Zuḥaylī 1989, 4:2968). They have voluntary movements, speech, vision,

28 This description also coheres with the description proposed by Schneiderman, Jecker and Jonsen that, "if a treatment merely preserves permanent unconsciousness or cannot end dependence on intensive medical care, the treatment should be considered futile" (Schneiderman et al. 1990).

sensory perception and cognition. This would therefore, exclude permanent vegetative states (PVS)[29] and permanent minimally conscious states (MCS)[30] because these patients have severely diminished neurological states which fall far below the minimum standard required for incomplete legal cognitive capacity (*ahliyyat al-adāʾ al-nāqiṣa*). It is therefore not an obligation to continue LST in these patients.

8.4 *Harms and Burdens to Others*

Value judgements related to LST extend to concerns of best interests for individuals and for society. Such concerns depend fundamentally on the normative balance of benefits and harms related to resource allocation of LSTs and its limitations at a societal level. There are only a finite number of specialist intensive care beds in health systems. Prolonged use of an intensive care bed after resuscitation may mean that another patient is unable to be admitted to intensive care. When a patient has an extremely low chance of ever recovering to benefit from that treatment, prolonged intensive care may be ethically difficult to justify. Those sorts of concerns can be very different in health systems that are privately funded, though even in those systems, resources are not infinite. The Islamic tradition views this from the perspective of individual rights (*ḥaqq al-ʿabd*) of the patient *vis-à-vis* rights related to public interests, i.e., rights of other patients who are also in need. Public rights are viewed from the perspective of God's rights (*ḥaqq Allāh*), because God's rights require us to uphold some of our obligations to others or the public, even at the cost of our self-interest.[31]

The human body is a joint right (a right of God and the individual),[32] and any intervention that provides little or no benefit at the cost of significant harm, in

29 PVS is when it's been more than 6 months if caused by a non-traumatic brain injury, or more than 12 months if caused by a traumatic brain injury.

30 MCS is when a person shows clear but minimal or inconsistent awareness. They may have periods where they can communicate or respond to commands, such as moving a finger when asked. A person may enter a MCS after being in a coma or vegetative state. In some cases a minimally conscious state is a stage on the route to recovery, but in others it's permanent. As with vegetative state, a continuing minimally conscious state means it's lasted longer than 4 weeks. But it's more difficult to diagnose a permanent minimally conscious state. In most cases, a minimally conscious state isn't usually considered to be permanent until it's lasted several years.

31 The rights of God are not for the benefit of God, as He is above all wants, but they relate to public interest (*al-nafʿ al-ʿāmm*). Their reference to God is because of their significant moral weight (*ʿiẓam khaṭarih*) and their general overall beneficial outcome (*shumūl nafʿih*) in public welfare in comparison to other considerations.

32 Imām al-Sarakhsī (d. 490/1090) has classified these rights to four categories (al-Sarakhsī 2005, 2:289–300) (1) acts which are exclusively the rights of Almighty God (*ḥuqūq Allāh*

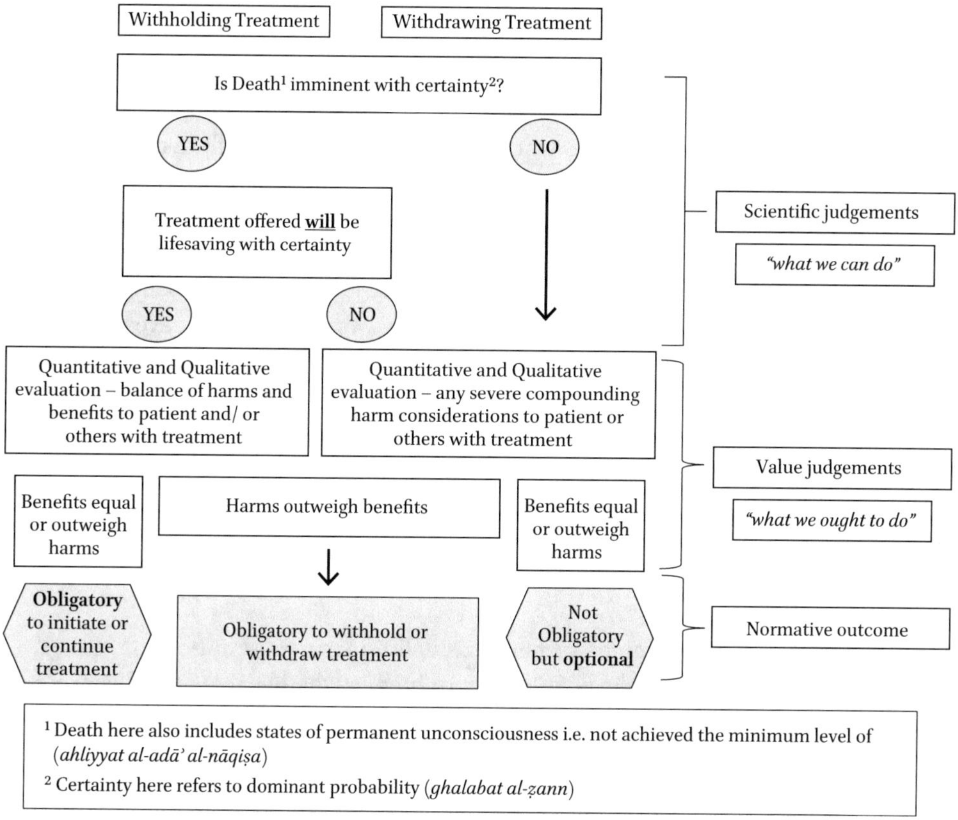

FIGURE 10.2 Flow chart showing a decision algorithm related to obligations of withholding and withdrawing LST

terms of pain, burden or distress, can potentially be seen as something wrong and culpable. Patient autonomy may be limited when seeking extreme measures which have little or no benefit to the patient, and the surrogate decision can be refused if it is seen that it is against the best interests of the patient, or even public interest if resources are limited. The balance of these rights will determine whether we can withhold or withdraw live saving treatment for patients. This balance is pivotal on factors which determine outcomes for the patient related to effectiveness of treatment relative to public need.

---

al-khāliṣa), (2) acts which are exclusively the rights of the individual, (3) acts where the rights of God (as public interest) and the rights of the individual, are combined but public interest supersedes, and, (4) acts where the rights of God (as public interest) and the rights of the individual are combined, but individual interest supersedes.

Questions of what treatments are in the patient's clinical best interests must be separated from questions of available resources. Costs are an irrelevant consideration if a particular treatment clearly cannot provide overall benefit and is not in the patient's best interests. Resource implications of providing treatment may be relevant in cases where the overall clinical benefit to the patient is open to debate and where provision of the treatment may pose significant risks of harm to the patient. Healthcare teams may therefore not be justified in providing treatments that are highly expensive or limited in availability and that appear to offer little benefit to the patient. Ideally, decisions to limit treatment should be based on clear and consistently applied policies developed at the institutional, local or community level. Any decisions to prioritise patients and treatments should be fair and based on the patient's ability to benefit and should avoid discrimination, for example, race, age, gender, social status (Padela et al, 2021).[33]

9 Conclusion

Justifications for foregoing LST based on definitions or descriptions of futility are not helpful. What needs to be determined is whether it is an obligation, optional or wrong to withhold or withdraw LST, framed in duties or religious obligations for clinicians, patients and surrogate decision makers.

There is no *moral* distinction between actions of omission and commission when withholding and withdrawing LST. Any distinction claimed between them is not because of acting or not acting, but because of our duties and obligations to rescue patients, which depend on patient prognostic outcomes, and the balance of benefits *versus* compounding harms of treatment and the underlying patient condition.

The distinction that exists between duties and obligations to treat differentiating the two categories of LST – life-support and ANH, is associated with certainty of outcome of saving life, where ANH is certain to sustain life, whereas this is not always the case with life-support like CPR and mechanical ventilation.

The balance of benefit *versus* compounding harms from continued care ought to be assessed through *quantitative* and *qualitative* evaluations of life. This serves best interests of patients by assessing whether treatment will

33 For a more detailed overview of the Islamic stance to resource allocation of LST, see article on resource allocation (Padela et al. 2021).

prolong the person's life significantly and alleviate burdens of illness, harm to others and provide a worthwhile quality of life or meaningful life.

Classical Muslim jurists have described states where there is seriously limited quantity of life and hence foregoing treatment is justified, because extending life is not certain. When patients are to survive for a prolonged period, LST can also be withheld or withdrawn when there is lack of ability to derive benefit, and the burdens of treatment illness or the underlying condition demand that we forego treatment.

It is only an obligation to initiate or continue resuscitative measures in those patients if the minimum state of *ahliyyat al-adāʾ al-nāqiṣa* can be achieved with dominant probability (*ghalabat al-ẓann*). If this level of certainty cannot be achieved at this level of cognitive functioning and independent life, then to withhold or withdraw LST treatment and resuscitative measures will be permissible, optional and not culpable.

Prolonged use of an intensive care bed after resuscitation may mean that another patient is unable to be admitted to intensive care. Where a patient has an extremely low chance of ever recovering to benefit from that treatment, prolonged intensive care may be ethically difficult to justify.

In many cases where treatment is of little or no benefit, redirection of management from LST to palliation represents a change in aims and objectives of treatment and does not constitute a withdrawal of care. If this is the case, then appropriate and effective palliative care should continue to be provided and it is not permissible for healthcare professionals to take active steps that are intended to end the life of a patient.

What is important is social acceptance of such redirection in management within an Islamic ethico-legal framework. Informed consent should be obtained and should include honest, caring, and culturally sensitive communication with family members, explanations of how interventions will be withheld, strategies for assessing and ensuring comfort, information about the patient's expected length of survival, and solicitation of feedback and strong preferences about end-of-life care.

If the duty and obligations rationale is to be applied to withholding or indeed withdrawing medical interventions, practice guidelines for its use should be developed, and education about this approach ought to be incorporated into medical school, residency training, and continuing medical education programs. Muslim theological positions should also be incorporated recognising that not all LST are obligatory. If treatment is not obligatory, informed consent and informed refusal allow competent patients to choose among treatments in accordance with their values, goals, and priorities for their future (Curtis et al. 1995).

Bibliography

Abū Dāwūd. 2000. *Sunan Abī Dāwūd, Kitāb al-Janā'iz, ḥadīth* no. 3207. Riyad: Dār al-Salām.

Abū Ghudda, ʿAbd al-Sattār, ed. 1998. *Qarārāt wa-Tawṣiyyāt Majmaʿ al-Fiqh al-Islāmī lil-Dawrāt 1–10, al-Qarārāt 1–97*. Damascus: Dār al-Qalam.

Abū l-Maʿālī. 2004. *Al-Muḥīṭ al-Burhānī*, 9 vols. Beirut: Dār al-Kutub al-ʿIlmiyya.

Abū Sulaymān, ʿAbd al-Wahhāb Ibrāhīm. 1423 AH. *Fiqh al-Ḍarūrat wa-Taṭbīqātuh al-Muʿāṣira. Āfāq wa-Abʿād*. Jedda: al-Maʿhad al-Islāmī lil-Buḥūth wa-l-Tadrīb.

Addis, Adeno. 2020. "Dignity, Integrity, and the Concept of a Person." *ICL Journal* 13(4): 323–372. DOI: 10.1515/icl-2019-0015.

Alsoufi, Bahaaldin, Osman O. Al-Radi, Rakan I. Nazer, Christopher A. Caldarone, Desmond G. Bohn and Glen S. Van Arsdell. 2007. "Survival Outcomes After Rescue Extracorporeal Cardiopulmonary Resuscitation in Pediatric Patients with Refractory Cardiac Arrest." *Journal of Thoracic and Cardiovascular Surgery* 134(4): 952–959. DOI: 10.1016/j.jtcvs.2007.05.054.

al-ʿAynī, Badr al-Dīn. 2007. *Minḥat al-Sulūk fī Sharḥ Tuḥfat al-Mulūk*. Doha: Wizārat al-Awqāf wa-l-Shu'ūn al-Islāmiyya.

al-ʿAynī, Badr al-Dīn. 2012. *Al-Bināya Sharḥ al-Hidāya*, 13 vols. Beirut: Dār al-Kutub al-ʿIlmiyya.

al-Bārr, Muḥammad. 2015. "Al-Tadāwī Qurb Nihāyat al-Ḥayāt wa-l-Inʿāsh al-Qalbī l-Ri'awī." Paper Presented at the 22nd session of the International Islamic Fiqh Academy (IIFA), Mecca, 10–13 May. http://ar.themwl.org/sites/default/files/Fiqh22 0405.pdf.

Baruch, A. Brody and Amir Halevy. 1995. "Is Futility a Futile Concept." *Journal of Medicine and Philosophy* 20: 123–144.

Betzold, Michael. 1992. "'Suicide Doctor' Cleared Again." *Sun Journal*, July 22, 1–8. http:// news.google.com/newspapers?nid=bcT4vkklUMwC&dat=19920722&printsec =frontpage&hl=en.

Brassington, Iain. 2020. "What Passive Euthanasia Is." *BMC Medical Ethics* 21: no. 41.

Breivik, H., P.C. Borchgrevink, S.M. Allen, L.A. Rosseland, L. Romundstad, E.K. Hals, G. Kvarstein, A. Stubhaug. 2008. "Assessment of Pain." *British Journal of Anaesthesia* 101(1): 17–24.

British Medical Association. 2007. *Withholding and Withdrawing Life-Prolonging Medical Treatment: Guidance for Decision Making*, 3rd edition. London: BMA Publications.

Bruera, Eduardo, David Hui, Shalini Dalal, Isabel Torres-Vigil, Joseph Trumble, Joseph Roosth, Susan Krauter, Carol Strickland, Kenneth Unger, J. Lynn Palmer, Julio Allo, Susan Frisbee-Hume, Kenneth Tarleton. 2013. "Parenteral Hydration in Patients with

Advanced Cancer: A Multicenter, Double-Blind, Placebo-Controlled Randomized Trial." *Journal of Clinical Oncology* 31: 111–118. DOI: 10.1200/JCO.2012.44.6518.

al-Buhūtī, Manṣūr b. Yunus. 1983. *Kashshāf al-Qināʿ ʿan Matn al-Iqnāʿ*, 6 vols. Beirut: ʿĀlam al-Kutub.

al-Bukhārī, ʿAlāʾ al-Dīn. 2009. *Kashf al-Asrār ʿan Uṣūl Fakhr al-Islām al-Bazdawī*, 4 vols. Beirut: Dār al-Kutub al-ʿIlmiyya.

al-Bukhārī, Burhān al-Dīn b. Māza. 2003. *Al-Muḥīṭ al-Burhānī*, 9 vols. Beirut: Idārat al-Qurʾān.

Casarett, David, Jennifer Kapo and Arthur Caplan. 2005. "Appropriate Use of Artificial Nutrition and Hydration – Fundamental Principles And Recommendations." *The New England Journal of Medicine* 353(24): 2607–2612. DOI: 10.1056/NEJMsb052907.

Cudney, Paul. 2014. "What Really Separates Casuistry from Principlism in Biomedical Ethics." *Theoretical Medicine and Bioethics* 35(3): 205–229. DOI: 10.1007/s11017-014-9295-3.

Cuervo, Luis Gabriel and Mike Clarke. 2003. "Balancing Benefits and Harms in Health Care." *British Medical Journal* 327(7406): 65–66. DOI:10.1136/bmj.327.7406.65.

Curtis, J.R., D.R. Park, M.R. Krone and R.A. Pearlman. 1995. "Use of the Medical Futility Rationale in Do-Not-Attempt-Resuscitation Orders." *Journal of the American Medical Association* 273: 124–128.

Danciu, Sorin C., Liviu Klein, Maziyar Mir Hosseini, Lamia Ibrahim, Bryan W. Coyle and Richard F. Kehoe. 2004. "A Predictive Model For Survival after In-Hospital Cardiopulmonary Arrest." *Resuscitation* 62(1): 35–42. DOI: 10.1016/j.resuscitation.2004.01.035.

al-Dasūqī, Muḥammad b. ʿArafa. n.d. *Ḥāshiyat al-Dasūqī ʿalā l-Sharḥ al-Kabīr*, 4 vols. Beirut: Dār al-Fikr.

Dekkers, Wim. 2009. "Viewing the Person through the Body: The Relevance of Philosophical Anthropology to Medical Education." *Korean Journal of Medical Education* 21(4): 340.

Engel, Joyce M., Deborah Kartin, Gregory T. Carter, Mark P. Jensen and Kenneth M. Jaffe. 2009. "Pain in Youths with Neuromuscular Disease." *The American Journal of Hospice & Palliative Care* 26(5): 405–412. DOI:10.1177/1049909109346165.

Esteban, Andrés, Antonio Anzueto, Fernando Frutos, Inmaculada Alía, Laurent Brochard, Thomas E. Stewart, Salvador Benito, Scott K. Epstein, Carlos Apezteguía, Peter Nightingale, A lejandro C. Arroliga and Martin J. Tobin. 2002. "Characteristics and Outcomes in Adult Patients Receiving Mechanical Ventilation: A 28-Day International Study." *Journal of the American Medical Association* 287(3): 345–355. DOI:10.1001/jama.287.3.345.

al-Fayyūmī, Aḥmad b. Muḥammad. 2016. *Al-Miṣbāḥ al-Munīr fī Gharīb al-Sharḥ al-Kabīr*. Cairo: Dār al-Maʿārif.

Fīrūzābadī, Muḥammad b. Yaʿqūb. 2005. *Al-Qāmūs al-Muḥīṭ*. Cairo: Muʾassasat al-Risāla.

Frankena, William K. 1973. *Ethics*, 2nd edition. Englewood Cliffs, NJ: Prentice-Hall.

Gharbi, Myriam, Joseph H. Drysdale, Hannah Lishman, Rosalind Goudie, Mariam Molokhia, Alan P. Johnson, Alison H. Holmes and Paul Aylin. 2019. "Antibiotic Management of Urinary Tract Infection in Elderly Patients in Primary Care and Its Association with Bloodstream Infections and All Cause Mortality: Population Based Cohort Study." *British Medical Journal* 364: l525. DOI: 10.1136/bmj.l525.

al-Ghazālī, Abū Ḥāmid. 2005. *Iḥyāʾ ʿUlūm al-Dīn*, 4 vols. Beirut: Dār al-Kutub al-ʿIlmiyya.

GMC (General Medical Council). 2010a. *Treatment and Care towards the End of Life: Good Practice in Decision Making*. London: General Medical Council.

GMC (General Medical Council). 2010b. "Treatment and Care towards the End of Life: Good Practice in Decision Making, Cardiopulmonary Resuscitation (CPR)," note 128. www.gmc-uk.org/ethical-guidance/ethical-guidance-for-doctors/treatment-and-care-towards-the-end-of-life/cardiopulmonary-resuscitation-cpr.

al-Ḥalabī, Ibrahīm b. Muḥammad. 2005. *Multaqā l-Abḥur fī l-Fiqh ʿalā Madhhab al-Imām al-Aʿẓam Abī Ḥanīfa al-Nuʿmān*. Damascus: Dār al-Bayrūtī.

al-Ḥamawī, Shihāb al-Dīn. 1985. *Ghamz ʿUyūn al-Baṣāʾir fī Sharḥ al-Ashbāh wa-l-Naẓāʾir*, 4 vols. Beirut: Dār al-Kutub al-ʿIlmiyya.

al-Ḥaṣkafī, ʿAbd al-Raḥmān. 2002. *Durr al-Mukhtār Sharḥ Tanwīr al-Abṣār wa-Jāmiʿ al-Biḥār*. Beirut: Dār al-Kutub al-ʿIlmiyya.

al-Ḥaṣkafī, Muḥammad b. ʿAlī. 1998. *Majmaʿ al-Anḥur fī Sharḥ Multaqā l-Abḥur*, 4 vols. Beirut: Dār al-Kutub al-ʿIlmiyya.

Ḥaṭṭāb al-Ruʿaynī. 2007. *Mawāhib al-Jalīl li-Sharḥ Mukhtaṣar Khalīl*, 8 vols. Beirut: Dār al-Kutub al-ʿIlmiyya.

Ḥaydar, ʿAlī. n.d. *Durar al-Ḥukkām Sharḥ Majallat al-Aḥkām*, 4 vols. Beirut: Dār al-Kutub al-ʿIlmiyya.

al-Haythamī, Ibn Ḥajar. 2016. *Tuḥfat al-Muḥtāj bi-Sharḥ al-Minhāj*, 4 vols. Cairo: Dār al-Ḥadīth.

Helft, P.R., M. Siegler and J. Lantos. 2000. "The Rise and Fall of the Futility Movement." *New England Journal of Medicine* 343(4): 293–296.

Ibn ʿAbd al-Salām, al-ʿIzz. n.d. *Qawāʿid al-Aḥkām fī Maṣāliḥ al-Anām*, 2 vols. Beirut: Dār al-Maʿārif.

Ibn ʿĀbidīn. 1994. *Radd al-Muḥtār ʿalā al-Durr al-Mukhtār*, edited by ʿĀdil Aḥmad ʿAbd al-Mawjūd and ʿAlī Muḥammad Muʿawwaḍ, 14 vols. Beirut: Dār al-Kutub al-ʿIlmiyya.

Ibn Ḥazm. n.d. *Al-Muḥallā bi-l-Āthār*, 12 vols. Beirut: Dār al-Kutub al-ʿIlmiyya.

Ibn al-Humām, Kamāl al-Dīn. 1999. *Al-Taqrīr wa-l-Taḥbīr*, 3 vols. Beirut: Dār al-Kutub al-ʿIlmiyya.

Ibn al-Humām, Kamāl al-Dīn. 2003. *Fatḥ al-Qadīr*, 10 vols. Beirut: Dār al-Kutub al-ʿIlmiyya.

Ibn Kathīr. 1999. *Tafsīr al-Qurʾān al-ʿAẓīm* (*Tafsīr Ibn Kathīr*), 8 vols. Riyad: Dār Tayba.

Ibn Māja. 2000. *Sunan Ibn Māja, Kitāb al-Janāʾiz, ḥadīth* no. 1616–1617. Riyad: Dār al-Salām.

Ibn Manẓūr. 2010. *Lisān al-ʿArab*, 15 vols. Beirut: Dār Ṣādir.

Ibn Mufliḥ. 1999. *Al-Ādāb al-Sharʿiyya*, 3 vols. Beirut: Muʾassasat al-Risāla.

Ibn Nujaym, Zayn al-Dīn b. Ibrāhīm. 1997. *Al-Baḥr al-Rāʾiq Sharḥ Kanz al-Daqāʾiq*, 9 vols. Beirut: Dār al-Kutub al-ʿIlmiyya.

Ibn Nujaym, Zayn al-Dīn b. Ibrāhīm. 1999. *Al-Ashbāh wa-l-Naẓāʾir ʿalā Madhhab Abī Ḥanīfa al-Nuʿmān*. Beirut: Dār al-Kutub al-ʿIlmiyya.

Ibn Qayyim al-Jawziyya. 2004. *Iʿlām al-Muwaqqiʿīn*, 7 vols. Beirut: Dār al-Kutub al-ʿIlmiyya.

Ibn Qudāma, ʿAbd Allāh b. Aḥmad. 1980. *Al-Mughnī*, 15 vols. Beirut: Dār al-Fikr.

Ibn Rushd, Abū l-Walīd. n.d. *Bidāyat al-Mujtahid wa-Nihāyat al-Muqtaṣid*, 4 vols. Beirut: Dār Ibn Hazm.

Ibn Taymiyya. 2004. *Majmuʿ al-Fatāwa*, 37 vols. Doha: Wizārat al-Awqāf wa-l-Shuʾūn al-Islāmiyya.

IIFA (International Islamic Fiqh Academy). 1986. "Qarār bi-Shaʾn Ajhizat al-Inʿāsh." *Majallat Majmaʿ al-Fiqh al-Islāmī* 3(2): 523. https://iifa-aifi.org/ar/1667.html.

ʿIllaysh, Muḥammad. 1984. *Sharḥ Manḥ al-Jalīl ʿalā Mukhtaṣar al-ʿAllāma Khalīl*, 9 vols. Beirut: Dār al-Fikr.

Jāb Allāh, Aḥmad. 2015. "Īqāf al-ʿIlāj ʿan al-Marīḍ al-Mayʿūs min Barʾih." Paper presented at the 22nd session of the Islamic Fiqh Academy (IIFA), Mecca, 10–13 May. http://ar.themwl.org/sites/default/files/Fiqh220404.pdf.

al-Jabūrī, ʿAbd Allāh. 2015. "Īqāf al-ʿIlāj ʿan al-Marīḍ al-Mayʿūs min Barʾih." Paper presented at the 22nd session of the Islamic Fiqh Academy (IIFA), Mecca, 10–13 May. http://ar.themwl.org/sites/default/files/Fiqh220403.pdf.

Jād al-Ḥaqq ʿAlī Jād al-Ḥaqq. 1403/1983. "Naql al-Aʿḍāʾ min Insān ilā Ākhar." In *al-Fatāwā al-Islāmiyya min Dār al-Iftāʾ al-Miṣriyya*, vol. 10, *fatwā* no. 1323, 5 December 1979. Cairo: al-Majlis al-Aʿlā lil-Shuʾūn al-Islāmiyya.

Jackson, Sherman A. 2003. "Shariʿah, Democracy, and the Modern Nation-State: Some Reflections on Islam, Popular Rule, and Pluralism." *Fordham International Law Journal* 27(1): 88–107.

al-Jamal, Sulaymān. 2013. *Ḥāshiyat al-Jamal ʿalā Sharḥ al-Manhaj*, 8 vols. Beirut: Dār al-Kutub al-ʿIlmiyya.

al-Jaṣṣāṣ, Abū Bakr. 2010. *Sharḥ Mukhtaṣar al-Ṭaḥāwī lil-Jaṣṣāṣ*, 8 vols. Dār al-Bashāʾir al-Islamiyya.

al-Jibrīn, ʿAbd Allāh. 2015. "Īqāf al-ʿIlāj ʿan al-Marīḍ al-Mayʿūs min Shifāʾih." Paper presented at the 22nd session of the Islamic Fiqh Academy (IIFA), Mecca, 10–13 May. http://ar.themwl.org/sites/default/files/Fiqh220402.pdf.

Jonsen, A.R. 1991. "Casuistry as Methodology in Clinical Ethics." *Theoretical Medicine* 12(4): 295–307.

Kamali, Mohammad Hashim. 2003. *Principles of Islamic Jurisprudence*. Cambridge: The Islamic Texts Society.

Kamali, Mohammad Hashim. 2012. *Shariʿah Law: An Introduction*. Oxford: Oneworld.

al-Kāsānī, Abū Bakr b. Masʿūd. 2003. *Badāʾiʿ al-Ṣanāʾiʿ fī Tartīb al-Sharāʾiʿ*, 10 vols. Beirut: Dār al-Kutub al-ʿIlmiyya.

Kass, Leon R. 1985. *Toward a More Natural Science*. New York: Free Press.

al-Khādimī, Nūr al-Dīn. 2015. "(Qatl al-Raḥma) wa-Īqāf al-ʿIlāj ʿan al-Marīḍ al-Mayʾūs min Barʾih: Ḥukmuh wa-Mudrakātuh." Paper presented at the 22nd session of the Islamic Fiqh Academy (IIFA), Mecca, 10–13 May. http://ar.themwl.org/sites/default/files/Fiqh220401.pdf.

al-Kharshī, Muḥammad. n.d. *Al-Kharshī ʿalā Mukhtaṣar Khalīl*, 8 vols. Cairo: al-Maṭbaʿa al-Amīriyya al-Kubrā.

Knaus, W.A. 1989. "Prognosis with Mechanical Ventilation: The Influence of Disease, Severity of Disease, Age, and Chronic Health Status on Survival From an Acute Illness." *The American Review of Respiratory Disease* 140 (2 Pt 2): S8–13. DOI: 10.1164/ajrccm/140.2_Pt_2.S8.

Kopelman, Loretta M. 1995. "Conceptual and Moral Disputes about Futile and Useful Treatments." *Journal of Medicine and Philosophy* 20(2): 109–121. DOI: 10.1093/jmp/20.2.109.

Koretz, Ronald L. 2007. "Should Patients with Cancer Be Offered Nutritional Support: Does the Benefit Outweigh the Burden?" *Eurpoean Journal of Gastroenterololgy & Hepatology* 9: 379–382. DOI: 10.1097/MEG.0b013e3280bdc093.

Koretz, Ronald L., Alison Avenell, Timothy O. Lipman, Carol L. Braunschweig and Anne C. Milne. 2007. "Does Enteral Nutrition Affect Clinical Outcome? A Systematic Review of the Randomized Trials." *The American Journal of Gastroenterology* 102: 412–429. DOI: 10.1111/j.1572-0241.2006.01024.x.

Kornbau, Craig, Kathryn C. Lee, Gwendolyn D. Hughes and Michael S. Firstenberg. 2015. "Central Line Complications." *International Journal of Critical Illness & Injury Science* 5(3): 170–178. DOI: 10.4103/2229-5151.164940.

Kuczewski, M. 1998. "Casuistry and Principlism: The Convergence of Method in Biomedical Ethics." *Theoretical Medicine and Bioethics* 19: 509–524. DOI: 10.1023/a:1009904125910.

al-Lajna al-Dāʾima lil-Buḥūth al-ʿIlmiyya wa-l-Iftāʾ. 1989/1420. "ʿAdam Tanfīdh Ijrāʾāt al-Inʿāsh lil-Marīd alladhī lā Yurjā Shifāʾuh," *fatwā* no. 12086. www.alifta.gov.sa/Ar/Magazine/Pages/issues.aspx?cultStr=ar&View=Page&PageID=8073&PageNo=1&BookID=2.

Larcher, Vic, Finella Craig, Kiran Bhogal, Dominic Wilkinson and Joe Brierley. 2015. "Making Decisions to Limit Treatment in Life-Limiting and Life-Threatening Conditions in Children: A Framework for Practice." *Archives of Disease in Childhood* 100: s1–s23. DOI: 10.1136/archdischild-2014-306666.

Laserna, Andres, Alejandro Durán-Crane, María A. López-Olivo, John A. Cuenca, Cosmo Fowler, Diana Paola Díaz, Yenny R. Cardenas, Catherine Urso, Keara O'Connell, Clara Fowler, Kristen J. Price, Charles L. Sprung and Joseph L. Nates. 2020. "Pain Management during The Withholding and Withdrawal of Life Support in Critically Ill Patients at the End-Of-Life: A Systematic Review and Meta-Analysis." *Intensive Care Medicine* 46(9): 1671–1682. DOI: 10.1007/s00134-020-06139-7.

Lobo, Suzana M., Flavio H.B. De Simoni, Stephan M. Jakob, Angel Estella, Sonali Vadi, Andreas Bluethgen, Ignacio Martin-Loeches, Yasser Sakr and Jean-Louis Vincent. 2017. "Decision-Making on Withholding or Withdrawing Life Support in the ICU: A Worldwide Perspective." *Chest* 152(2): 321–329. DOI: 10.1016/j.chest.2017.04.176.

Maḥmūd Idrīs, ʿAbd al-Fattāḥ. 2007 "Ḥaqīqat al-Ḥayāt wa-ʿAlāmātuhā wa-l-Āthār al-Mutarattabat ʿAlayhā." *Midād*, 27 Shawwāl 1428 (8 November 2007), http://midad.com/article/199575/حقيقة-الحياة-وعلاماتها-والآثار-المترتبة-عليها.

Mawṣilī, ʿAbd Allāh. 2015. *Al-Ikhtiyār li-Taʿlīl al-Mukhtār*, 5 vols. Beirut: Dār al-Kutub al-ʿIlmiyya.

al-Mawwāq, Muḥammad b. Yūsuf. 1994. *Al-Tāj wa-l-Iklīl li-Muktaṣar Khalīl*, 8 vols. Beirut: Dār al-Kutub al-ʿIlmiyya.

Miles, Steven H. 1994. "Medical Futility." In *Health Care Ethics: Critical Issues*, edited by John F. Monagle and David C. Thomasma, 233–244. Gaithersburg, MD: Aspen Publishers.

Melltorp, G. and T. Nilstun. 1997. "The Difference between Withholding and Withdrawing Life-Sustaining Treatment." *Intensive Care Medicine* 23(12): 1264–1267. DOI: 10.1007/s001340050496.

Mobeireek, A., F. Al-Kassimi, K. Al-Zahrani, A. Al-Shimemeri, S. al-Damegh, O. Al-Amoudi, S. Al-Eithan, B. Al-Ghamdi and M. Gamal-Eldin. 2008. "Information Disclosure and Decisionmaking: The Middle East versus the Far East and the West." *Journal of Medical Ethics* 34(4): 225–229. DOI: 10.1136/jme.2006.019638.

Mohiuddin, Afshan, Mehrunisha Suleman, Shoaib Rasheed and Aasim I. Padela. 2020. "When Can Muslims Withdraw or Withhold Life Support? A Narrative Review of Islamic Juridical Rulings." *Global Bioethics* 31(1): 29–46. DOI: 10.1080/11287462.2020.1736243.

Mullā Khusraw. 2010. *Durar al-Ḥukkām Sharḥ Ghurar al-Aḥkām*, 2 vols. Karachi: Mīr Muḥammad Kutub Khāna.

Mullā Khusraw. 2017. *Mirʾāt al-Uṣūl fī Sharḥ Mirqāt al-Wuṣūl*. Beirut: Dār al-Kutub al-ʿIlmiyya.

Murgic, Lucija, Philip C. Hébert, Slavica Sovic and Gordana Pavlekovic. 2015. "Paternalism and Autonomy: Views of Patients and Providers in a Transitional (Post-Communist) Country." *BMC Medical Ethics* 16(1): 65.

Murray, Thomas H. 1987. "On the Human Body as Property: The Meaning of Embodiment, Markets and the Meaning of Strangers." *University of Michigan Journal of Law Reform* 20(4): 1055–1088.

Nathan, Rajan, Jonathon Whyler and Peter Wilson. 2020. "Risk of Harm to Others: Subjectivity and Meaning of Risk in Mental Health Practice." *Journal of Risk Research* 24(10): 1228–1238. DOI: 10.1080/13669877.2020.1819389.

al-Nawawī, Yaḥyā b. Sharaf. 1991. *Rawḍat al-Ṭālibīn*, 12 vols. Beirut: Maktabat al-Islāmī.

al-Nawawī, Yaḥyā b. Sharaf. 2006. *Ṣaḥīḥ Muslim bi-Sharḥ al-Nawawī*, 9 vols. Beirut: Dār al-Kutub al-ʿIlmiyya.

al-Nawawī, Yaḥyā b. Sharaf. 2008. *Al-Majmuʿ fī Sharḥ al-Muhadhdhab*, 23 vols. Jedda: Maktabat al-Irshād.

Niẓām al-Dīn et al. 2000. *Al-Fatāwā al-Hindiyya*, edited by ʿAbd al-Laṭīf Ḥasan ʿAbd al-Raḥmān, 6 vols. Beirut: Dār al-Kutub al-ʿIlmiyya.

Nyazee, Imran Ahsan Khan. 2006. *Islamic Jurisprudence*. New Delhi: Adam Publishers.

Padela, Aasim and Afshan Mohiuddin. 2015. "Ethical Obligations and Clinical Goals in End-of-Life Care: Deriving a Quality-of-Life Construct Based on the Islamic Concept of Accountability before God (*Taklīf*)." *The American Journal of Bioethics* 15(1): 3–13. DOI: 10.1080/15265161.2014.974769.

Padela, Aasim and Omar Qureshi. 2016. "Islamic Perspectives on Clinical Intervention near the End-of-Life: We Can But Must We?" *Medical Health Care and Philosophy* 20(4): 545–559. DOI: 10.1007/s11019-016-9729-y.

Padela, Aasim, Hasan Shanawani and Afshan Arozullah. 2011. "Medical Experts & Islamic Scholars Deliberating over Brain Death: Gaps in the Applied Islamic Bioethics Discourse." *The Muslim World* 101(1): 53–72. DOI: 10.1111/j.1478-1913.2010.01342.x.

Padela, Aasim, Mansur Ali and Asim Yusuf. 2021. "Aligning Medical and Muslim Morality: An Islamic Bioethical Approach to Applying and Rationing Life Sustaining Ventilators in the COVID-19 Pandemic Era." *Journal of Islamic Ethics* (advance online). DOI: 10.1163/24685542-12340061.

Prendergast, T.J. and J.M. Luce. 1997. "Increasing Incidence of Withholding and Withdrawal of Life Support from the Critically Ill." *The American Journal of Respiratory and Critical Care Medicine* 155(1): 15–20. DOI: 10.1164/ajrccm.155.1.9001282.

al-Qāḍī ʿIyāḍ. 1998. *Ikmāl al-Muʿlim bi-Fawāʾid Muslim*, 9 vols. Cairo: Dār al-Wafāʾ.

Qāḍī Khān, Fakhr al-Dīn. 2009. *Fatāwā Qāḍī Khan*, 3 vols. Beirut: Dār al-Kutub al-ʿIlmiyya.

al-Qalyūbī and ʿUmayra. 2019. *Ḥāshiyatā l-Qalyūbī wa-ʿUmayra ʿalā Sharḥ al-Muḥallā ʿala Minhāj al-Ṭālibīn*, 4 vols. Beirut: Dār al-Kutub al-ʿIlmiyya.

al-Qarāfī, Abū l-ʿAbbās Aḥmad b. Idrīs. 1998. *Anwār al-Burūq fī Anwāʿ al-Furūq*, 4 vols. Beirut: Dār al-Kutub al-ʿIlmiyya.

Qāsimī, Qāḍī Mujāhid al-Islām. 1994. *Ḍarūrat wa Ḥājat ka Aḥkām Sharʿī may Iʿtibār*. Karachi: Idārat al-Qurʾān wa-l-ʿUlūm al-Islāmiyya.

al-Qurṭubī, Muḥammad b. Aḥmad. 2004. *Al-Jāmiʿ li-Aḥkām al-Qurʾān*, 24 vols. Beirut: Dār al-Kutub al-ʿIlmiyya.

Raffaeli, William and Elisa Arnaudo. 2017. "Pain as a Disease: An Overview." *Journal of Pain Research* 10:2003–2008. DOI: 10.2147/JPR.S138864.

al-Ramlī, Shihāb al-Dīn. 2003. *Nihāyat al-Muḥtāj fī Sharḥ al-Minhāj*, 8 vols. Beirut: Dār al-Kutub al-ʿIlmiyya.

Ramsey, Paul. 1970. *The Patient as Person*. Newhaven: Yale University Press.

Rashid, Rafaqat. 2018. *Organ Transplantation an Islamic Perspective to Human Bodily Dignity and Property in the Body*. Bradford: Al-Balagh Academy Publication. www.academia.edu/38829745/organ_transplantation_an_islamic_perspective_to_human_bodily_dignity_and_property_in_the_body.

Rashid, Rafaqat. 2021. "The Intersection between Science and Sunnī Theological and Legal Discourse in Defining Medical Death." In *Islam and Biomedicine*, edited by Aasim Padela and Afifi Al-Akiti, 223–241. Dordrecht: Springer.

al-Rāzī, Fakhr al-Dīn. 1981. *Mafātīḥ al-Ghayb: Tafsīr al-Rāzī*, 32 vols. Beirut: Dār al-Fikr.

al-Rāzī, Muḥammad b. Abī Bakr. 1986. *Mukhtār al-Ṣiḥāḥ*. Beirut: Maktabat Lubnān.

Rehman, K.L. 1993. "Cardio-Pulmonary Resuscitation and Life Support: The Current Laws and the Muslim Perspective." *Journal of the Islamic Medical Association of North America* 25: 20–22.

Rendtorff, Jacob D. 2002. "Basic Ethical Principles in European Bioethics and Law: Autonomy, Dignity, Integrity and Vulnerability – Towards a Foundation of Bioethics and Biolaw." *Medicine, Health Care and Philosophy* 5: 235–244. DOI: 10.1023/a:1021132602330.

Rispler-Chaim, Vardit. 1993. "The Ethics of Postmortem Examinations in Contemporary Islam." *Journal of Medical Ethics* 19(3): 164–168. DOI: 10.1136/jme.19.3.164.

Saḥnūn, Ibn Saʿīd. 2014. *Al-Madawwana al-Kubrā*, 16 vols. Riyad: Wizārat al-Awqāf al-Suʿūdiyya.

Saiyad, Saleem. 2009. "Do Not Resuscitate: A Case Study from the Islamic Viewpoint." *Journal of the Islamic Medical Association of North America* 41(3): 109–113. DOI: 10.5915/41-3-4477.

al-Samarqandī, ʿAlāʾ al-Dīn Muḥammad. 1994. *Tuḥfat al-Fuqahāʾ*, 3 vols. Beirut: Dār al-Kutub al-ʿIlmiyya.

Sanbhalī, Burhān al-Dīn. 1994. "Aʿḍā ki Paiwandkārī." In *Jadīd Fiqhī Mubāḥith*, edited by Qāḍī Mujāhid al-Islām Qāsimī. Karachi: Idārat al-Qurʾān wa-l-ʿUlūm al-Islāmiyya.

Sanchini, Virginia, Cecilia Nardini and Giovanni Boniolo. 2014. "The Withholding/Withdrawing Distinction in the End-of-Life Debate." *Multidisciplinary Respiratory Medicine* 9: art. no. 13.

al-Sarakhsī, Abū Bakr Muḥammad b. Aḥmad. 2005. *Uṣūl al-Sarakhsī*, 2 vols. Beirut: Dār al-Kutub al-ʿIlmiyya.

al-Sarakhsī, Abū Bakr Muḥammad b. Aḥmad. 1997. *Sharḥ al-Siyar al-Kabīr*, 5 vols. Beirut: Dār al-Kutub al-ʿIlmiyya.

Sayf Allāh, Khālid Raḥmānī. 2004. *Jadīd Fiqhī Masāʾil*. Karachi: Zam Zam Publishers.

Schneiderman, L.J., N.S. Jecker and A.R. Jonsen. 1990. "Medical Futility: Its Meaning and Ethical Implications." *Annals of Internal Medicine* 112(12): 949–954. DOI: 10.7326/0003-4819-112-12-949.

al-Shāṭibī, Abū Isḥaq. 2001. *Al-Muwāfaqāt fī Uṣūl al-Sharīʿa*, 6 vols. Beirut: Dār al-Iḥyāʾ al-Turāth al-ʿArabī.

al-Shawkānī, Muḥammad. 2006. *Nayl al-Awṭār*. Beirut: Dār al-Kutub al-ʿIlmiyya.

al-Shīrāzī, Abū Isḥāq. 1992. *Al-Muhadhdhab fī Fiqh al-Imām al-Shāfiʿī*, 6 vols. Beirut: Dār al-Shāmiyya.

al-Shirbīnī, al-Khaṭīb. 1997. *Mughnī l-Muḥtāj*, 4 vols. Beirut: Dār al-Maʿrifa.

al-Ṭabarī, Ibn Jarīr. 1994. *Tafsīr al-Ṭabarī: Jāmiʿ al-Bayān ʿan Taʾwīl Āy al-Qurʾān*, 7 vols. Beirut: Muʾassasat al-Risāla.

al-Taftāzānī, Saʿd al-Dīn Masʿūd b. ʿUmar. 1957. *Al-Talwīḥ ʿalā al-Tawḍīḥ*, 2 vols. Cairo: Dār al-ʿAhd al-Jadīd lil-Ṭibāʿa.

al-Ṭahṭāwī, Aḥmad b. Muḥammad. 1997. *Ḥāshiyat al-Ṭahṭāwī ʿalā al-Marāqī l-Falāḥ*. Beirut: Dār al-Kutub al-ʿIlmiyya.

Turk, Dennis C., Roger B. Fillingim, Richard Ohrbach and Kushang V. Patel. 2016. "Assessment of Psychosocial and Functional Impact of Chronic Pain." *The Journal of Pain* 17(9): 21–49. DOI: 10.1016/j.jpain.2016.02.006.

van Gijn, Myke S., Dionne Frijns, Esther M.M. van de Glind, Barbara C. van Munster and Marije E. Hamaker. 2014. "The Chance of Survival and the Functional Outcome after In-Hospital Cardiopulmonary Resuscitation in Older People: A Systematic Review." *Age and Ageing* 43(4): 456–463. DOI: 10.1093/ageing/afu035.

Vincent, Jean-Louis. 2005. "Withdrawing May be Preferable to Withholding." *Critical Care* 9(3): 226–229. DOI: 10.1186/cc3486.

Weinstein, Milton C. and Harvey V. Fineberg. 1980. *Clinical Decision Analysis*. Philadelphia, PA: Saunders.

Westra, Anna E., Dick L. Willems and Bert J. Smit. 2009. "Communicating with Muslim Parents: 'The Four Principles' Are Not as Culturally Neutral as Suggested." *Eurropean Journal of Pediatrics* 168(11): 1383–1387. DOI: 10.1007/s00431-009-0970-8.

Wilkinson, Dominic. 2019. "Expert Reaction to the Tafida Raqeeb Case." *Science Media Centre*, 11 September. www.sciencemediacentre.org/expert-reaction-to-the-tafida-raqeeb-case-2/.

Wilkinson, D.J.C. and J. Savulescu. 2011. "Knowing When to Stop: Futility in the ICU." *Current Opinion in Anaesthesiology* 24(2): 160–165. DOI: 10.1097/ACO.0b013e328343c5af.

Yaseen, Mohammad Naeem. 1990. "The Rulings for the Donation of Human Organs in the Light of Sharīʿa Rules and Medical Facts." *Arab Law Quarterly* 5(1): 49–87. DOI: 10.2307/3381562.

Yazigi, A., M. Riachi and G. Dabbar. 2005. "Withholding and Withdrawal of Life-Sustaining Treatment in a Lebanese Intensive Care Unit: A Prospective Observational Study." *Intensive Care Medicine* 31: 562–567.

Youngner, Stuart J. 1988. "Who Defines Futility?" *Journal of The American Medical Association* 260(14): 2094–2095. DOI: 10.1001/jama.1988.03410140106033.

al-Zarkashī, Badr al-Dīn. 2000. *Al-Manthūr fī l-Qawāʿid*, 2 vols. Beirut: Dār al-Kutub al-ʿIlmiyya.

al-Zaylaʿī. 2000. *Tabyīn al-Ḥaqāʾiq Sharḥ Kanz al-Daqāʾiq*, 7 vols. Beirut: Dār al-Kutub al-ʿIlmiyya.

Zoch, T.W., N.A. Desbiens, F. DeStefano, D.T. Stueland and P.M. Layde. 2000. "Short- and Long-Term Survival after Cardiopulmonary Resuscitation." *Archives of Internal Medicine* 160(13): 1969–1973.

al-Zuḥaylī, Wahba. 1989. *Al-Fiqh al-Islāmī wa-Adillatuh*, 10 vols., 3rd edition. Damascus: Dār al-Fikr.

CHAPTER 11

Artificial Nutrition and Hydration at the Terminal Stage of Dementia from an Islamic Perspective

Hadil Lababidi

1 Introduction

Religious assessments of novel medical procedures are complex and end-of-life nutrition in the context of dementia is a contested topic from both a clinical and an Islamic perspective. The terminal stage of dementia in particular is characterised by difficulties in swallowing, malnutrition, and loss of appetite which usually lead to weight loss and dehydration. Consequently, this chapter aims to analyse the advantages and disadvantages of artificial nutrition and hydration (ANH) in consideration to Islamic law. It considers whether the latter perspective permits artificial nutrition and hydration in the terminal phase of dementia. Finally, this chapter aims to contribute to the Islamic discussion on end-of-life care while emphasising the need to consider all cases in their individual contexts and advising that the view presented here does not represent the entire spectrum of Islamic sects.

2 Dementia

Dementia (Ar., *kharaf*; al-Ḥifnī 1992, 842) is an umbrella term that refers to a large number of types of progressive cognitive decline such as Alzheimer's disease (Ar., *maraḍ alzhaymar*), which is the most common form of dementia. The common features of the different types of dementia,[1] such as Alzheimer's disease, cause a progressive deterioration in cognitive and memory functions which is associated with communication problems, changes in personality, and motor disorders. In classical and modern Arabic, the verb *kharifa* describes the process of becoming old and experiencing the typical cognitive changes (Lane and Lane-Poole 1955, 725) that are part of the ageing process.

1 Other common types are vascular dementia, dementia with Lewy bodies, and frontotemporal dementia. A subset of people has a mixed dementia, which is a combination of Alzheimer's disease and another type of dementia.

Old age is associated with a high risk of dementia. At advanced ages (75+ years), the risk of developing dementia is about 30–50% (Radman 2010, 18). The Alzheimer's Association estimates that more than 50 million people were living with dementia in 2019 and expects that the number of dementia cases will triple by 2050 (Alzheimer's Disease International 2019, 13).[2] There is no treatment to reverse the loss of cognitive functions experienced in dementia. Some studies show that cognitive training and medication are likely to preserve cognitive functions or at least slow the progress of the disease down.[3] The symptoms intensify as the disease runs its course, and the person living with dementia needs increasing levels of care and support. The caregiver faces the challenging task of finding the right balance between supporting the persons concerned by encouraging them to continue to do things for themselves without overstraining their capacity. People with dementia lose abilities but with assistance are still able to make use of those they retain.

The upcoming text will describe the stages of Alzheimer's disease, as it is the most widespread type of dementia. The most common signs of this type include memory loss, difficulties in performing familiar tasks, and changes in mood, behaviour or personality (Engel 2006, 11). Life expectancy after the diagnosis varies between approximately 2 and 20 years (Engel 2006, 29). The development of dementia is usually divided into three stages that merge into one another (WHO-ADI 2012, 7). At the early stage, the patients face problems with short-term memory and have mood swings, along with experiencing word-finding difficulties; communication is increasingly challenging (Laabdallaoui and Rüschoff 2009, 90). Further early signs are difficulties with solving problems and performing daily tasks, such as cooking meals and driving a car. The affected patients are aware of the changes and often withdraw from social life or conceal their difficulties from others. For this reason, relatives, friends, or the individuals themselves often misrecognise this stage and may consider the patients to be suffering from depression or simply experiencing the effects of older age (Radman 2010, 24). In the middle stage, it is no longer possible for the individuals to conceal the changes because they find themselves experiencing considerable difficulties in everyday tasks and personal care. The impairment of long-term memory increases, but actions learned early in life remain available and can be used in the individuals' care (Radman 2010, 27). People at this stage can live semi-independently with assistance provided. Though, they may

2 Alzheimer's Disease International is the global umbrella organisation of all Alzheimer's Associations.

3 On medical interventions, see Fellgiebel 2008, 45–48; for non-medical interventions see Stoppe and Maeck 2007, 33–36.

struggle to articulate themselves verbally in the correct context (Laabdallaoui and Rüschoff 2009, 90). Notably, changes in behaviour such as aggression and activity at night ("sundown syndrome") occur. People with dementia may be tired in the daytime and awake at night; they may want to go for walks and call for their caregiver, interrupting their sleep (Fellgiebel 2008, 46).

People with late-stage dementia are often bedridden and their speech is impaired, which makes articulation virtually impossible. They "are typically unable to walk or to feed themselves, they are incontinent and aphasic, and they have lost the capacity to have relationships with other people" (Gillick 2000, 206). In addition, difficulties in swallowing or incontinence occur (Radman 2010, 25). Loss of appetite and desire for food is likely to lead to lower food intake, malnutrition, and consequent weight loss, and ultimately to difficulties for caregivers in ensuring they take in a sufficient amount of food and liquids (Laabdallaoui and Rüschoff 2009, 90f.), notwithstanding the reduced need for both in people in old age with low activity levels (Vilgis, Lendner, and Caviezel 2015, 14–16). Assistance with eating counters malnutrition in moderate dementia. However, artificial nutrition and hydration (ANH) is an option at the late stage. In many cases, people in this terminal stage of dementia die from infections (Laabdallaoui and Rüschoff 2009, 91). It should be noted that death certificates in many countries do not record dementia as a cause of death because of the difficulty of assessing whether dementia or the accompanying illness(es) were the key causal factor(s) (WHO-ADI 2012, 12).

3 Artificial Nutrition and Hydration at the End-of-Life

Food intake, swallowing, and drinking are considered among the last everyday activities to be impaired in people with dementia. The results are malnutrition, difficulties with swallowing, pneumonia, and food refusal (Volkert et al. 2015, 3). Artificial nutrition and hydration is the most common medical intervention in advanced dementia. This section of the chapter discusses the drawbacks of this treatment and situations in which it may be suitable, before going on to consider it from an Islamic perspective.

In the advanced stage of the disease, people with dementia "no longer know what they are supposed to do with the food and/or utensils put in front of them, behavioural problems emerge and eating skills are lost" (Volkert et al. 2015, 3). The malnutrition that may result from a decrease in food intake causes weight loss and a decline in muscle strength which then heightens the risk of falls (Knels, Lauer, and Schrey-Dern 2018, 143). Studies show that a low BMI increases the mortality of people with dementia (Volkert et al. 2015, 3).

However, food refusal may additionally be related to other factors. A distracting environment, for example, or a poorly fitting dental prothesis causing pain or gum inflammation may impact food intake (Vilgis, Lendner, and Caviezel 2015, 4). In advanced dementia, a functional impairment in swallowing (dysphagia) leads to aspiration before, during and after swallowing (Volkert et al. 2015, 3). Dysphagia causes choking and increases the risk of pneumonia when bacteria enter the lungs. Pneumonia is one of the common causes of death in people with dementia (Volkert et al. 2015, 3). A medical procedure that is finding more and more use in this case is artificial nutrition and hydration (ANH), which can be given through a gastrostomy tube or a nasogastric tube. The latter is used to bridge temporary periods of insufficient nutrient consumption. As soon as it is foreseeable that tube feeding is needed in the long term, the patient receives a PEG (percutaneous endoscopic gastrostomy) after consideration of the individual case (Knels, Lauer, and Schrey-Dern 2018, 155). The Saudi Commission for Health Specialties, for instance, declares that artificial nutrition is to be used in cases when natural food intake is impossible, regardless of the type or duration of the illness (SCFHS n.d., 32).

Furthermore, artificial feeding is claimed by some physicians to satisfy hunger. Mohammed Ali Al-Bar (Muḥammad ʿAlī l-Bārr, b. 1939) and Hassan Chamsi-Pasha (Ḥassān Shamsī Bāshā, b. 1951) argue that "[i]f hydration and feeding is stopped the patient does not die peacefully and comfortably. He suffers dehydration and hunger for 10–14 days" (al-Bar and Chamsi-Pasha 2015, 250). However, in the case of end-of-life, both take a decreased food intake into consideration. Referring to the *ḥadīth* which discouraged forcing the sick to take food and drink, al-Bar and Chamsi-Pasha see the importance to inform the families about occurring biological changes that lead to the loss of weight. They recommend reducing the amount of nutrition and justify that:

> [T]he reason for this approach is to prevent the potential feelings of guilt and sorrow that could be experienced by the family if nutrition or hydration support was withdrawn or withheld completely.
>
> AL-BAR and CHAMSI-PASHA 2015, 254

Notably, al-Bar and Chamsi-Pasha disagree with the complete discontinuation of basic nutrition because this would mean starvation to death which is a sinful act from an Islamic view (al-Bar and Chamsi-Pasha 2015, 254). Studies in palliative care show, however, that many persons at the end-of-life do not feel hungry and thirsty and consequently do not starve (Vilgis, Lendner, and Caviezel 2015, 44; Sitte 2016, 34). A dry mouth is not in and of itself a sign of thirst (Vilgis, Lendner, and Caviezel 2015, 71). The dying person may suffer from a painfully dry mouth, and oral care is essential to alleviate the suffering (Stiefelhagen 2018, 14). In fact, dehydration and reduced food intake support the dying process because they aid the release of endogenous opiates in the brain, which is likely to make the patient's state more comfortable (Post and Cicirella 1995, 105; Sitte 2016, 34). Hence, it is argued that in palliative caring one should consider both on a case-by-case basis in order to balance pain management and actual needs (Sitte 2016, 21). Gillick regards the necessity to raise awareness of the effectiveness of dehydration and contends that withholding tube feeding can be considered as a part of palliative care (Gillick 2000, 209).

Dehydration could be an accessible component of palliative care in view of the lack of availability of end-of-life care, such as in the Middle East. In a survey conducted among Muslim medical staff, Al-Awamer and Downar found that

> [i]n the Middle Eastern model, PC [palliative care] practitioners faced a shortage of skilled medical staff, limited drug availability, limited availability of home care, and [the challenge of] integrating services across care settings.
>
> AL-AWAMER and DOWNAR 2014, 3255

When considering the availability of palliative care for Muslims, it is crucial to consider the geographic distribution of the majority of Muslims who live outside the Middle East and North Africa. The comparative study on palliative care and especially the use of medication in Muslim-majority countries by Aljawi and Harford shows that there is a "virtually nonexistent consumption," except for Turkey and Saudi Arabia which are on a very low level, although a *fatwā* in Saudi Arabia exists, supporting the use of opioid analgesics for relief of physical pain. They identify not only a lack of palliative service, but also religious barriers such as the fear of diversion from opioid use (Aljawi and Harford 2012, 143). However, palliative medication is no modern invention. Physicians such as Ḥunayn b. Isḥāq (d. 260/873) recommended certain extracts of plants as well as opium to alleviate severe pain and to cause lethargy (Klein-Franke 1982, 104). Furthermore, cultural factors play a role as well. For example, Muslims in non-Muslim majority countries may feel that inferior care is offered to them because of their religion or ethnicity (Hedayat 2006, 1288).

The availability and barriers to accepting palliative care are important when considering that the request for treatment at the end-of-life, such as ANH, reflects a strong hope in its effectiveness, but the survival rate with ANH is controversial. Compared to assisted hand feeding, Chou and colleagues show that nasal feeding could not significantly lower the mortality rate in late dementia (Chou et al. 2020, 4). Proponents of this therapy argue that ANH reduces the risk of pneumonia. However, Chou and his colleagues have shown that there is no significant evidence that ANH decreases the incidence of pneumonia (Chou et al. 2020). Another problem with ANH is its elimination of the social component of food consumption. Chou et al. suggest that tube feeding leads to isolation and that "an adequate environment setting (e. g., removing distractions and scheduling mealtime with family) could make patients enjoy their social time, as opposed to isolated tube feeding" (Chou et al. 2020, 6).

Considering that food intake is one of the last activities people with dementia can undertake in the context of their loss of cognitive skills, the withdrawal from social life which may take place with artificial feeding is a concern, as is the important therapeutic measure of retention of routines – such as mealtimes – within the structure of the patient's day. Therefore, Gillick recommends oral food intake for people with dementia in the terminal stage of their disease (Gillick 2000, 208; Post and Cicirella 1995, 96–109; Chou et al. 2020).

Further disadvantages of artificial nutrition outweigh its few advantages in the dementia context. Artificially fed dying persons have stomach and bowel content which leads to vomiting, nausea, and diarrhoea. They suffer pain and discomfort during connection, repositioning, and disconnection of the tube. Tubes may become blocked or infected, and fixation is needed to avoid the patient manipulating them (Stiefelhagen 2018, 14). Other side-effects are risks of bleeding and traumata to abdominal organs, whose prevention may necessitate the use of restraints and chemical sedation. Moreover, changing tubes requires an invasive procedure in a hospital, which can be stressful in advanced dementia (Alibhai 2008, 46). Hence, Alsolamy contends that the complications of ANH, as detailed above, should be accepted as the "lesser of the two evils" due to the greater harm, from a religious point of view, caused by responsibility for a person's starvation (Alsolamy 2012, 99). This point is to be discussed later.

Swallowing problems can be treated by non-invasive methods. There are three ways to encourage independence in eating: 1) assisted hand feeding (AHF, assistance with eating and drinking); 2) adjusting the setting of meals and the position of the patient during feeding (Chou et al. 2020, 6); 3) modification of food texture (Vilgis, Lendner, and Caviezel 2015, 137–248). What follows is a concise discussion of these three methods, in order.

1) Assisted hand feeding, that is the assistance of another person with food intake, is a favourable alternative to ANH. AHF requires nursing staff or carers as opposed to medical intervention, and therefore represents an instance of interpersonal interaction for people with dementia. This form of food intake is time-consuming and makes significant demands on staff or caregiver time which engender a high cost in staffing or in loss of earnings for economically

active caregivers. When AHF is possible and the person ingests enough food, from a medical point of view ANH is not necessary. In cases where AHF ceases to be viable or food and/or liquid intake is insufficient despite AHF, ANH can be considered, provided that its benefits are likely to outweigh any potential harm (Osterfeld, Lababidi, and Langfeldt 2018, 497). Alibhai contends that AHF is often not possible at this stage (Alibhai 2008, 40). The question arises whether AHF is unfeasible due to swallowing problems or impracticable due to a lack of staff or carer resources for the more time-consuming process of AHF.

2) A noisy environment might be distracting to the person receiving feeding, and their physical position and posture affect their swallowing function. The chin tuck position and head rotation toward the weaker side can facilitate food intake (Chou et al. 2020, 6).

3) Swallowing problems can arise from the texture of the food offered, where it requires physical effort when chewing, and fluids are difficult to control. Modification of the physical features of the food, such as mashing, thickening and foaming can make food appetising and serve as an opportunity to increase enjoyment when eating, as well as countering swallowing difficulties.

Difficulties with swallowing can be treated using invasive and non-invasive methods. The latter are preferable, but not always possible. However, the medical and psychological side-effects of ANH should be considered.

4 An Islamic Perspective on Artificial Nutrition and Hydration of People with Late-Stage Dementia

Nutrition at the end-of-life is a controversial topic. Clearly, starvation is an ethically unacceptable route. The weight loss and loss of appetite often experienced – for various reasons, as discussed above – by people at the terminal stage of dementia appears to call for the administration of food to prevent starvation. Offering too little food or drink can be viewed as neglect, and relatives in particular may feel a sense of co-responsibility for the death of their family member. Some relatives may understandably opt for ANH to avoid feelings of guilt at inactivity in the face of their loved one's state which may overcome them if they withhold or withdraw ANH (al-Shahri and al-Khenaizan 2005, 434). It is believed that the fear of the death (*al-khawf min al-mawt*) of this person may indeed induce physical pain in those left behind; Ibn Ḥazm (d. 456/1064) recounts various stories in which unrequited love or the loss of loved ones lead to grief (*ḥuzn*), physical weakening, and even to the death of the loving person (Ibn Ḥazm 1943, 179–187).

The following chapter discusses the permissibility of artificial nutrition and hydration at the end-of-life from an Islamic perspective, including a look at studies on the advantages and disadvantages of ANH.

4.1 Qatl al-Ṣabr *Analogy*

The Islamic Fiqh Academy (IFA), affiliated with the Muslim World League, declared in 2015 that continuing feeding is "significant" for the care of a patient (IFA 2015). Hence, refusing or withdrawing ANH would be equal to (quasi-intentional) homicide.[4] This conclusion derives from the following precedent of the prohibition of killing detainees (*qatl al-ṣabr*) (Ghaly et al. 2018). It was reported by Khālid ibn al-Walīd (d. 21/642) that Prophet Muḥammad prohibited to confine someone to die (Ibn Ḥibbān n.d.). The analogy is questioned because the underlying situation differs. The killing of a detainee is an active act which certainly leads to death.

There are a few *fatwā*s discussing the permissibility of refusal of ANH. *Fatwā*s as an "expression of the religious-Islamic law and Islamic jurisprudence" are requested to examine not yet specifically regulated situations, acts, and circumstances for their godliness (Krawietz 1991, 21, 29) – which is the case in the majority of medical issues. Sachedina criticises this approach in tackling bioethical questions. In his view, moral reasoning in Islamic ethico-legal deliberations on medical interventions should not be limited to *fatwā*s alone. He states:

> Instead, [...] this emerging discipline needs to define its epistemic parameters and develop both a methodology and a justificatory mechanics of moral reasoning that explore and open venues for deriving ethical "recommendation (*tawṣīya*)" rather than "judicial opinion (*fatwā*)" on issues that confront human health and medical research in Muslim societies.
>
> SACHEDINA 2009, 13

However, Sachedina points out not to dismiss juridical opinions which could serve as basis for further moral discussions (Sachedina 2009, 13f.). The search for a similar precedent can support the ethical deliberations on a present problem in order to extract the underlying moral purpose. Hence, research in Islamic bioethics should bear in mind that the specific medical problem(s) may change with new medical technology and the ethical consideration constitutes only a preliminary evaluation.

---

4 Intentional homicide (*qatl ʿamd*) involves the use of a lethal weapon in contrast to quasi-intentional killing (*shibh ʿamd*), see on another three types of homicide and bodily harm (*qiṣāṣ*), Hallaq 2009, 320.

The limitation of the juridical approach appears from the *fatwās* which address the refusal of ANH as a form of killing. On the one side, it is contended that the physician would cause the death by terminating tube feeding. For example, in a *fatwā* from Kuwait it is argued that if the physician terminates any treatment, he would be guilty of unlawful killing (Krawietz 1991, 106). He should rather act out of inner motivations, such as mercy, to save the life and leave it in the hands of God, whether healing will occur (Krawietz 1991, 106). In the same vein argues another *fatwā* which denies a patient who has an artificial lung and about 1% probability to improvement his or her right to die. Otherwise, the physicians would be liable for assisted suicide. If they cannot convince the patients to continue – even futile – medical treatment and the patient demands for letting die the physicians should not be involved in any related act (IslamWeb 2002). On the other side, the underlying disease – and not the act of the physician – is considered to cause the death (Ilkilic 2016, 97). Hence, it cannot be regarded as voluntary active euthanasia because the intention here is to allow a person to gain release from an untreatable suffering and no lethal injection is administered (Sachedina 2009, 169–171).

In the precedent, the focus is on the moral responsibility of the guardian. Does it differ when the detainee decides to refuse food? The main argument – why medical treatment is not obligatory – is based on the assumption that the therapeutic benefit is speculative (Padela and Qureshi 2016). Furthermore, from Prophetic sayings such as the duty to seek healing but also receive reward from being steadfast and trustful (*tawakkul*) in God as the sole healer (Q 26:80) it can be concluded that there be either a recommendation or obligation to seek medical treatment, but also some reward for abstaining (Padela and Qureshi 2016, 598).

Padela and Qureshi elaborate on how the jurists of the four Sunnī law schools differ in their view on the compatibility of *tawakkul* and receiving medical treatment. The majority of legal scholars representing the Ḥanafī, Shāfiʿī and Mālikī law consider medication as a confirmation of the trust in God if the effectiveness is certain and regard the refusal in this case as a lack of *tawakkul*. Only a few Ḥanbalī jurists preferred the trust in God over a medical treatment (Padela and Qureshi 2016, 599–604). Patience as general command should be the stance during suffering, especially in futile cases (Krawietz 1990, 97–101). Notably, the Ḥanafī jurists al-Mawṣilī (d. 683/1284) and Ibrāhīm al-Ḥalabī (d. 956/1549) differentiate between the consequences of refusal of food and medication in the hereafter. They agree upon that the one who fasts and starves to death is sinful whereas the one who refuses medical treatment until he dies does not commit a sin (Padela and Qureshi 2016, 599). The juristic argument is agreed upon that the human being who does not take food and starves to death is sinful because the prevention of harm is certain by nutrition – in contrast to medical interventions (Kellner 2010, 150). In contrast, al-Ghazālī (d. 505/1111) emphasises the role of the patient in deciding to refuse medication. He contends that if sick persons realise that they reached the end-of-life and, hence, every medical treatment is futile, they can decide to refuse all kinds of medications (Klein-Franke 1982, 126).

Starvation for a higher objective is viewed differently. It is still possible that the detainee starves even though he has been offered food and drink. Hunger strike could represent a means of resistance. For example, Muḥammad Aḥmad Ḥusayn (b. 1966), *muftī* of Jerusalem and the Palestinian Territories, legitimised the hunger strike of Palestinian prisoners in 2015 and declared that the victims of force-feeding were "martyrs" (Al Jazeera 2015). In this context, resisting force-feeding is permitted and is not considered as suicide.

However, the analogy of *qatl al-ṣabr* is contested in the case of refusal of ANH, i.e., when no tubes are placed. If the person or his relatives decided not to undergo ANH, then refusal of this is permitted because refusing a medical treatment not warranting to prevent death is not forbidden. For example, a *fatwā* released in 2017 states that refusing treatment (from fatal disease) is not considered suicide (IslamWeb 2017). Whereas, if they wish ANH to be administered, then it is permitted, too.

Another ruling derived from Islamic ethico-legal deliberations applies in this case: the tenet of "no harm, no harassment" (*lā ḍarar wa-lā ḍirār fī l-Islām*), which functions both as a principle and a source for the rule that "hardship necessitates relief" (*al-mashaqqa tajlib al-taysīr*). According to Sachedina, it means that there can be no legislation, promulgation, or execution of any law that leads to harm of anyone in society. For that reason, in derivation of a legal-ethical judgment the rule is given priority over all primary obligations in the Sharīʿa. In fact, it functions as a check on all other ordinances to make sure that their fulfilment does not lead to harm (Sachedina 2009, 228).

In a nutshell, the analogy has shortcomings: the intention (*niyya*) in the precedent is to confine someone to die who would normally continue living if not confined. Whereas the intention in refusing or withdrawing ANH is to let someone die who has no chance of improvement with any medical treatment. Rather, considering the higher objectives of the Sharīʿa (*maqāṣid*) would serve better in this novel situation. The Sharīʿa promotes the safeguard of three universal goals: 1) essential needs (*ḍarūriyyāt*), 2) necessary needs (*ḥājiyyāt*), 3) secondary needs (*taḥsīniyyāt*). The common good (*maṣlaḥa*) in applying the universal goals in the context of public health care is to ensure essential needs are met and probable harm is averted (see Raissouni 2016). Both, withdrawing and refusal of ANH permits a natural course of dying for patients with dementia at the end-of-life. The majority argues that neither the physician, nor the family members are morally responsible for the death of the person concerned because the underlying disease and not the act itself caused the death. Withdrawing and refusal of ANH can support the dying process appropriately because reduced food and liquids intake releases hormones that eases pain, whereas food intake causes discomfort and infections.

4.2 *Medical Treatment or Nutrition?*

It is debated whether ANH is considered a medical treatment or a kind of nutrition at the end of life. Muḥammad Aḥmad al-Shāṭirī claims that the person who restrains another one's food and liquids so that it leads to death is to be penalised with retaliation and thus is guilty of murder. He is also a fervent opponent of switching off ventilators. This he deems even graver than starvation because a human being may live without nutrition and hydration for a certain period of time, but not without oxygen (Kellner 2010, 150). The IFA does not share this view and allows withdrawal of respirators in futile cases.

According to a *fatwā* that follows the IFA ruling on ANH – as stated above – removing resuscitation devices is allowed in a child with cancer in an incurable stage, after three specialist doctors have testified that death is certain. However, nourishing him is not permissible to stop (IslamWeb 2019).

Sachedina criticises that previous bioethical researchers in Islam consider bioethics a subcategory of Islamic jurisprudence, pursuing the overall goal to determine the permissibility or prohibition of a certain medical treatment. However, the reasoning why something is permitted or prohibited from an ethical perspective does not concern them (Sachedina 2009, 18). The Islamic scholar Yūsuf al-Qaraḍāwī (d. 2022) argues in the same vein. Stemming from the conviction that medical care is not obligatory, he has a different view on ANH. In a *fatwā* he raised the question if therapeutic substances – e.g., nutrition in the form of injection – extends the duration of the illness and suffering, then it apparently is neither obligatory nor preferable (Kellner 2010, 149). It becomes obvious that al-Qaraḍāwī envisions a different approach on bioethical dilemmas weighing up the benefits against the potential harm of a specific medical procedure. The principle of *maṣlaḥa*[5] (public or common good) serves as a useful tool "in providing solutions to the majority of novel issues in biomedical issues" (Sachedina 2009, 47). Sachedina states that legal scholars from all law schools have met on a regular basis and established common decisions, often prioritising the common good. Besides, they applied the principle of

5 See Opwis on the definition and understandings of *maṣlaḥa* in the Islamic ethico-legal tradition and in contemporary discussions (Opwis 2005).

proportionality (*tanāsub*) in rulings on individual and social interests of the community whereby in a few cases collective interests set aside the interests and rights of an individual (Sachedina 2009, 48).

The same controversial discussion on artificial nutrition and hydration can be found in Judaism. On the one hand, Rabbi Moshe Feinstein and Rabbi Shlomo Zalman Auerbach contend that ANH is imperative and may be administered involuntarily even if the patient is suffering from it. On the other hand, Rabbi Hershel Schachter and Rabbi Horowitz argue that ANH is a medical procedure which may rightfully be refused by terminally ill patients (Schostak 1994, 97f.). Standing between those opposing poles, Rosin and Sonnenblick demand to consider the ethical questions to assess the benefits of ANH against the risks and suffering caused to the patient (Rosin and Sonnenblick 1998, 45).

In Catholicism, ANH is rather discussed in the context of persistent vegetative state. Opponents of ANH raise awareness of the serious side-effects which should be considered when evaluating the procedure as proportionate care. Proponents of ANH, such as Pope John Paul II (d. 2005), state that ANH is basic nutrition – rather than a medical means –, hence obligatory and always proportionate (Zientek 2013, 151f.).

The question remaining is whether it is considered to prevent death or satisfy appetite. To what extent does one speak of nourishing in artificial feeding, or could it rather be regarded as a medical treatment? At this juncture, the ethico-legal question of whether artificial feeding via injection (*ḥuqna, ibra*) during Ramaḍān breaks the fasting is highly debated (IslamOnline n.d.) and may help reflection on ANH. One form of parental nutrition is probably addressed where the feeding takes place intravenously only to support the intake of nutritional components such as glucose – not the complete replacement of nutrition. The discussion mainly focused on the two issues: entry and the circulation in the human body, whereas the contemporary debate addresses the question of the overarching goal of fasting.[6] The use of a nourishing injection is normally intended to restore health and not for the satisfaction of hunger. Al-Qaraḍāwī contends that although the substance infiltrates the blood, it does not break the fasting rule because it does not satisfy the appetite (Krawietz 1991, 303f.). However, as shown above, this is not necessary at the end-of-life. Finally, the person with advanced dementia may remove the tube because of the lack of understanding its purpose. Hence, artificial feeding should not be obligatory.

6 See Krawietz on contemporary ethico-legal deliberations on injections during Ramaḍān and the cited precedent in classical literature (Krawietz 1991, 298–313).

4.3 *"Duty to Feed" Whom?*

Proponents of ANH argue that the refusal of artificial nutrition and hydration would lead to death by starvation. Islamic scholars and physicians are therefore inclined to allow artificial food intake when the patients are not able to eat and drink by themselves (as mentioned above). The view outlined above ultimately stems from the Qur'ānic directive to save life, as is expressed in numerous verses on the duty to feed poor, hungry, and needy individuals (see, for example, Q 90:12–18; Alibhai 2008, 43–45). It is obvious that this imperative implies the giving of drinks and could be interpreted as a basic human right to access to food and drink. Does the duty to feed as a necessity imply artificial nutrition and hydration? Does the duty to feed apply to the end-of-life when the dying person refuses food and liquids? The context of withdrawal of feeding in the terminal stage of dementia differs from that of the hungry person outside of this situation. The dying person does not feel hungry or thirsty because this is part of the dying process, while the non-dying person aims to survive. Furthermore, the question remains who is meant to be provided with food. Here, the person in need of food lives in privation and has no access to it because of financial reasons. In the final analysis, the Qur'ānic "duty to feed" those wanting to be fed cannot be applied in the end-of-life context.

I would argue, however and furthermore, that if the person expresses hunger or is able to eat with assisted hand feeding, then AHF is acceptable, and he or she should not be force-fed. Gillick argues that the fixation of tubes to people with advanced dementia is ethically unjustifiable with respect to the disadvantages of ANH and the lack of understanding of the process in people with dementia (Gillick 2000, 207). They cannot comprehend why tubes are attached to their stomach and may try to pull them out. This procedure can lead to stress and aggressive behaviour which makes the use of restraints and chemical sedation necessary. According to the Islamic tradition, there should be no constraints placed upon a sick person. Ibn Qayyim al-Jawziyya (d. 751/1350) refers to a *ḥadīth* which states that one should not force sick people to eat or drink because God gives them food and drink (Ibn Qayyim al-Jawziyya n.d., 70f.). This understanding stems from the Islamic view that the mental disposition of a person influences the physical healing process, as the human mind and body are considered to form a unit (Haque 2004, 357–377). Additionally, the directive to refrain from applying force emphasises the moral agency of sick persons. The Islamic tradition asserts the Prophet Muḥammad's concern that the needs of people in illness be met. In a Prophetic saying reported by Ibn ʿAbbās (d. *c.*68/687), the Prophet visits a sick person and asks him what he would like to have. The man answers: "Wheat bread." The Prophet says that whoever has wheat bread, should give it to the sick person. He adds that whenever someone is sick and has appetite for something, then he or she should eat it (Aksoy and Elmali 2002, 216). This raises the question of what serves the "best interest" of a sick person. The bioethicists Aksoy and Elmali argue that even if there is something harmful in the food itself (from a religious perspective), it would bring a benefit and may heal the sick person, and would be less harmful than if the individual ate something they did not wish to eat – even if it were in their best interests from a medical perspective (Aksoy and Elmali 2002, 217).

In this view, the focal issue should be the will of the person with dementia and whether it is ethically justifiable. Jaworska argues that the wishes and desires of people with dementia must be considered because the capacity for appreciation remains functional even in the terminal stage of the disease. For example, a person recognises the work of another person which is addressed but because of communication problems it is difficult to understand. A person closely associated with him or her could assist in translating the expression of appreciation (Jaworska 2010, 71–96). In this case, such consideration would mean respecting the expression of the individual's need or refusal to eat. However, understanding these needs is challenging for caregivers and medical staff and may sometimes only be the "best interpretation" of what is known about the patient's former and present wishes (Flynn 2018, 157–174). Given that the capacity to act is rooted deeply in the Islamic tradition (Ghaly 2019, 257–261), Advance Care Planning (ACP) represents a useful instrument for the recording of personal preferences. ACP is a method in end-of-life care which enables a step-by-step approach to questions of life, death, and life-sustaining measures with the involvement of the individual concerned. This would relief the family members from the burden of moral responsibility. In the case of dementia, there is a need to provide understandable information and to involve relatives and other caregivers (Voß and Kruse 2019, 286). However, in the actual situation, the patient's wishes are often ignored, with a concomitant impact on the rights of the person affected by dementia. Current regional initiatives aim to promote the rights of older people and to enshrine them in legislation. For example, the Beirut-based Institute for Development, Research, Advocacy and Applied Care (IDRAAC) seeks to raise awareness of the rights of people with dementia and in old age and has launched a national awareness campaign using the slogan "Even if you lose yourself, you don't lose your rights" (*ḥattā law ḍayya'at, mā tuḍayyiʿ ḥaqqak*) (IDRAAC n.d.).

4.4 *Prolonging Death*

The ability to take in food and liquids independently is one of the last activities to be lost at the terminal stage of dementia. It is likely that ANH prolongs the dying process of people with dementia. From an Islamic view, it is rejected to manipulate the natural course of dying. As outlined above, and in this context, ANH cannot be considered a curative treatment in terminally ill dementia patients. Opinions diverge on the application of ANH from ethico-legal perspective in both Sunnī and Shīʿī Islam, but a consensus is apparent on the discontinuation of therapy where the intervention proves futile (Alsolamy 2012). Islamic law permits the refusal of futile medical treatments at the end-of-life when there is no hope of restoring health (Sachedina 2009, 170f.). This tenet stems from the Prophetic saying that God sends remedies for all illnesses except for death (Ibn Qayyim al-Jawziyya n.d., 57f.).[7] From this position one can conclude that once the terminal stage has begun, it is permitted to refuse life-extending measures, as they may be considered an interference with the divine plan. Islam holds that the time of death is fixed by God (*ajal musammā*, i.e., Q 7:34). However, *ajal* is not the terminal point of existence and should not be viewed pessimistically; it is rather a threshold into eternal life (*khulūd*) (Izutsu 2002, 138). The prolonging of life or of the end-of-life phase with artificial resuscitation postpones death; delaying of death, then, may appear as a manipulation of the process of dying (Krawietz 1991, 109). Al-Bar and Chamsi-Pasha point to the limitations of medicine in the terminal stage:

> Islam acknowledges that death is an inevitable phase of the life of a human being; medical management should not be given if it only prolongs the final stage of a terminal illness as opposed to treating a superimposed, life-threatening condition.
>
> AL-BAR and CHAMSI-PASHA 2015, 244

The physician is not liable for prosecution after the withdrawal of a medical treatment if the decision of letting the patient die has been decided and confirmed from the patient and stakeholder (Sachedina 2009, 169). ANH may appear as opposing to the authority of God as He is the only authority that can give and take life. In the Islamic belief system, God is the One who brings beings into life and lets them die (Q 2:258). Thus, withdrawal or withholding of ANH means accepting that only God is the author of life and death. As discussed above, food refusal cannot be regarded as active euthanasia because accepting the natural course of dying is in accordance with the divine will. However, the question of delaying the appointed time of death (*taʾjīl al-mawt*) is contested. It is stated that from an Islamic perspective, it is not possible to hasten or postpone the death (Krawietz 1991, 109). Yet, ANH could be considered as prolonging the end-of-life phase.

---

7 Another version has it that God sends remedies for all illnesses except for old age.

From an Islamic perspective, survival and death are equivalent because both are contingent to the will of God. Neither of them has an intrinsic value. The purpose of death is the induction of created beings to eternal life in the hereafter. A *ḥadīth* sets out that believers should not seek for death or induce their premature death by refusing effective remedies (Brockopp 2003, 188). Once the time of death has come, however, the Islamic faith prescribes the adoption of a passive role (Brockopp 2003, 188), which nevertheless permits the alleviation of pain via palliative care. Lastly, artificial feeding cannot change the appointed time of death but rather prolong suffering in the dying phase. Therefore, it should be permissible to refuse ANH and to alleviate pain by palliative care.

5 Concluding Remarks

Artificial hydration and nutrition at the terminal stage of dementia should not be the preferred therapy from a medical and an Islamic perspective, respectively. ANH can be a reasonable intervention for short-term use in situations where a person with dementia has lapsed into a coma and is unconscious. However, ANH should not be obligatory in the terminal stage of dementia if the patient or the relatives refuses it. Hence, it is crucial that at least two physicians agree upon the dying phase having started and any treatment being futile. I therefore strongly advocate the provision of greater resources for assisted hand feeding and palliative care, particularly in light of the argument – which I hope to have supported convincingly in this chapter – that the disadvantages of ANH at the terminal stage of dementia outweigh the benefits.

Besides the medical considerations, the ethical arguments from an Islamic perspective have been discussed on four topics. In my view, the precedent of the prohibition of the killing of a detainee (*qaṭl al-ṣabr*) cannot support the ethical deliberation on ANH. Rather, considering the higher objectives of the Sharīʿa (*maqāṣid*) would serve better in novel medical situation (Raissouni 2016, 220–223). Furthermore, the Qurʾānic imperative of the "duty to feed" may apply only to the terminally ill dementia patient who still shows interest in food and can eat with assisted feeding rather than with ANH. Where a patient with dementia does not wish to eat with assistance, the duty to feed does not apply because the perspective of Islamic law would consider force-feeding non-permissible; instead, the patient's comfort should be ensured, and pain relief provided if the patient or a stakeholder request it after an informed consent. The Qurʾānic "duty to feed" cannot be applied in the end-of-life context; the majority position in the Islamic scholarship agrees that there is no moral responsibility for the death on the physician or the family members. Finally,

ANH could be considered as prolonging the end-of-life phase, not as postponing death but rather extending the dying period.

At the terminal stage of dementia, weight loss, decreased food intake and food refusal, and swallowing difficulties signal the approaching end-of-life. From an Islamic ethical perspective, acceptance of this dying process is permitted. Letting the patient die in futile cases does not interfere with the moral duty of a physician to save life. The duty is rather to allow the person to die with dignity. On this note, I will conclude by stressing the ongoing need for intensified research in palliative care to the end of raising awareness of its effectiveness, necessity, and permissibility.

Acknowledgement

Publication of this chapter has been made possible through the generous support of the Academy for Islam in Research and Society (AIWG) at Frankfurt University.

Bibliography

Aksoy, Şahin and Abdurrahman Elmali. 2002. "The Core Concepts of the Four Principles of Bioethics as Found in Islamic Tradition." *Journal of Medicine and Law* 21(2): 211–224.

Al Jazeera. 2015. "Muftī l-Quds: Ḍaḥāyā al-Taghdiya al-Qasriyya Shuhadāʾ (The Mufti of Jerusalem: Victims of Forced Feeding Are Martyrs)." 2015. www.aljazeera.net/news/humanrights/2015/8/10/مفتي-القدس-ضحايا-التغذية-القسرية.

Alibhai, Shabbir M.H. 2008. "The Duty to Feed in Cases of Advanced Dementia. Scientific Challenges and a Proposed Islamic Ethical Response." *Journal of Religious Ethics* 36(1): 37–52.

Aljawi, Deena M. and Joe B. Harford. 2012. "Palliative Care in the Muslim-Majority Countries: The Need for More and Better Care." *Contemporary and Innovative Practice in Palliative Care*, edited by Esther Chang and Amanda Johnson, 137–150. n.p.: InTech.

Alsolamy, Sami. 2012. "Islamic Views on Artificial Nutrition and Hydration in Terminally Ill Patients." *Bioethics* 28(2): 96–99.

Alzheimer's Disease International. 2019. *World Alzheimer Report 2019*. London: n.p.

Al-Awamer, Ahmed and James Downar. 2014. "Developing a Palliative Care Service Model for Muslim Middle Eastern Countries." *Support Care Cancer* 22: 3253–3262.

al-Bar, Mohammad Ali and Hassan Chamsi-Pasha. 2015. *Contemporary Bioethics. Islamic Perspective.* Cham: Springer Open.

Brockopp, Jonathan E. 2003. "The 'Good Death' in Islamic Theology and Law." *Islamic Ethics of Life. Abortion, War, and Euthanasia*, edited by Jonathan E. Brockopp, 177–193. Columbia, SC: University of South California Press.

Chou, Hsiao-Hui, et al. 2020. "Nasogastric Tube Feeding versus Assisted Hand Feeding In-home Healthcare Older Adults with Severe Dementia in Taiwan: A Prognosis Comparison." *BMC Geriatrics* 20(60): 1–8.

Engel, Sabine. 2006. *Alzheimer & Demenzen. Die Methode der einfühlsamen Kommunikation*, second edition. Stuttgart: Trias.

Fellgiebel, Andreas. 2008. "Medikamentöse Therapie neuropsychiatrischer Symptome bei Alzheimer-Demenz." *Die Psychiatrie* 5(1): 45–48.

Flynn, Eilionoir. 2018. "Legal Capacity for People with Dementia: A Human Rights Approach." *Dementia and Human Rights*, edited by Suzanne Cahill, 157–174. Bristol: Bristol University Press.

Ghaly, Mohammed. 2019. "The Convention on the Rights of Persons with Disabilities and the Islamic Tradition: The Question of Legal Capacity in Focus." *Journal of Disability and Religion* 23(3): 251–278.

Ghaly, Mohammed, Randi R. Diamond, Maha El-Akoum and Azza Hassan. 2018. *Palliative Care and Islamic Ethics: Exploring Key Issues and Best Practice.* Doha: World Innovation Summit for Health.

Gillick, Muriel R. 2000. "Rethinking the Role of Tube Feeding in Patients with Advanced Dementia." *The New England Journal of Medicine* 342(3): 206–210.

Hallaq, Wael B. 2009. *Sharīʿa. Theory, Practice, Transformations.* Cambridge: Cambridge University Press.

Haque, Amber. 2004. "Psychology from Islamic Perspective: Contributions of Early Muslim Scholars and Challenges to Contemporary Muslim Psychologists." *Journal of Religion and Health* 43(4): 357–377.

Hedayat, Kamyar. 2006. "When the Spirit Leaves: Childhood Death, Grieving and Bereavement in Islam." *Journal of Palliative Medicine* 9(6): 1282–1291.

al-Ḥifnī, ʿAbd al-Munʿim. 1992. *Mawsūʿat al-Ṭibb al-Nafsī. Al-Kitāb al-Jāmiʿ fī l-Iḍṭirābāt al-Nafsiyya wa-Ṭuruq ʿIlājihā Nafsiyyan* ["Encyclopedia of Psychiatry"], vol. 2. Cairo: Maktabat Madbūlī.

Ibn Ḥazm al-Andalusī, Abū Muḥammad ʿAlī. 1943. *Halsband der Taube. Über die Liebe und die Liebenden* [*Ṭawq al-Ḥamāma*], translated by Max Weisweiler. Leiden: Brill.

Ibn Ḥibbān. n.d. *Ṣaḥīḥ Ibn Ḥibbān*, "Bāb al-Nahy ʿan Qatl al-Ṣabr" ["Prohibition of *Qatl al Ṣabr*"], *ḥadīth* no. 1660. https://al-maktaba.org/book/901/950.

Ibn Qayyim al-Jawziyya, Abū ʿAbdallāh Shams al-Dīn Muḥammad b. Abī Bakr. n.d. *Al-Ṭibb al-Nabawī.* Beirut: Dār al-Fikr.

IDRAAC (Institute for Development, Research, Advocacy and Applied Care). n.d. *The Rights of the Elderly Campaign*. www.idraac.org/home/awareness/awareness-campaigns1/toward-the-human-rights-protection-of-a-vulnerable-population-the-elderly-of-lebanon.

IFA (Islamic Fiqh Academy). 2015. *Īqāf al-ʿIlāj ʿan al-Marīḍ al-Mayʾūs min Barʾih* ["Withdraw Treatment for a Terminally Ill Patient"]. http://almoslim.net/node/233659.

Ilkilic, Ilhan. 2016. "Menschenwürde und ethische Bewertung von Entscheidungen am Lebensende am Beispiel innerislamischer Positionen." *Zeitschrift für Evangelische Ethik* 60(2): 88–101.

IslamOnline. n.d. "Athar al-Ḥaqn ʿalā al-Ṣiyām wa-l-Mufaṭṭarāt min al-Adwiya" ["The Effect of Injections on Fasting and Breaking the Fast through Medications"]. https://fatwa.islamonline.net/1739.

IslamWeb. 2002. "Patient's Right to Die," *fatwā*-no. 84065. www.islamweb.net/en/fatwa/84065/patients-right-to-die.

IslamWeb. 2017. "Refusing Treatment (from Fatal Disease) Is not Suicide," *fatwā*-no. 357055. www.islamweb.net/en/fatwa/357055/refusing-treatment-from-fatal-disease-is-not-suicide.

IslamWeb. 2019. "ʿIlāj aw Īqāf ʿIlāj man Lā Yurjā Shifāʾuh" ["Treating or Withdrawal for the Terminally Ill"], *fatwā*-no. 405700. www.islamweb.net/ar/fatwa/405700/علاج-أو-إيقاف-علاج-من-لا-يرجى-شفاؤه.

Izutsu, Toshihiko. 2002. *God and Man in the Qurʾan. Semantics of the Qurʾanic Weltanschauung*. Karachi: Royal Book Company.

Jaworska, Agnieszka. 2010. "Ethische Dilemmas bei neurodegenerativen Krankheiten: Respektierung von Patienten mit schwindender Autonomiefähigkeit." *Herausforderung Demenz. Spannungsfelder und Dilemmata in der Betreuung demenzkranker Menschen*, edited by Markus Christen, Corinna Osman and Ruth Baumann-Hölzle, 71–96. Bern: Peter Lang.

Kellner, Martin. 2010. *Islamische Rechtsmeinungen zu medizinischen Eingriffen an den Grenzen des Lebens. Ein Beitrag zur kulturübergreifenden Bioethik*. Würzburg: Ergon.

Klein-Franke, Felix. 1982. *Vorlesungen über die Medizin im Islam*. Wiesbaden: Steiner.

Knels, Christina, Norina Lauer and Dietlinde Schrey-Dern. 2018. *Sprache und Ernährung bei Demenz. Klinik, Diagnostik und Therapie*. Stuttgart: Georg Thieme.

Krawietz, Birgit. 1991. *Die Ḥurma. Schariatrechtlicher Schutz vor Eingriffen in die körperliche Unversehrtheit nach arabischen Fatwas des 20. Jahrhunderts*. Berlin: Duncker & Humblot.

Laabdallaoui, Malika and Ibrahim Rüschoff. 2009. *Ratgeber für Muslime bei psychischen und psychosozialen Krisen*. Mössingen: Edition Bukhara.

Lane, Edward William and Stanley Lane-Poole. 1955. *Arabic-English Lexicon*. New York: F. Ungar.

Opwis, Felicitas. 2005. "*Maṣlaḥa* in Contemporary Islamic Legal Thought." *Islamic Law and Society* 12(2): 182–223.

Osterfeld, Margarete, Hadil Lababidi and Marina Langfeldt. 2018. "Einhaltung der Menschenrechte in der Psychiatrie. Nationale und internationale Kontrollmechanismen – verbunden mit einem interkulturellen Exkurs zur Demenz im Islam." *Fortschritte der Neurologie Psychiatrie* 86(8): 493–499.

Padela, Aasim I. and Omar Qureshi. 2016. "When Must a Patient Seek Healthcare? Bringing the Perspectives of Islamic Jurists and Clinicians into Dialogue." *Zygon* 51(3): 592–625.

Post, Stephen Garrard and Margaret M. Cicirella. 1995. "Dying with Dignity. The Case against Artificial Nutrition and Hydration." In *The Moral Challenge of Alzheimer Disease: Ethical Issues from Diagnosis to Dying*, edited by Stephen Garrard Post, second edition, 96–109. Baltimore/London: John Hopkins University Press.

Radman, Ivana. 2010. "Demenz: Medizinische Fakten zu einem komplexen Problem." In *Herausforderung Demenz. Spannungsfelder und Dilemmata in der Betreuung demenzkranker Menschen*, edited by Markus Christen, 17–52. Bern: Peter Lang.

Raissouni, Ahmed. 2016. "Ethics in Medicine: A Principle-Based Approach in the Light of the Higher Objectives (*Maqāṣid*) of Sharia." In *Islamic Perspectives on the Principles of Biomedical Ethics. Muslim Religious Scholars and Biomedical Scientists in Face-To-Face Dialogue with Western Bioethicists*, edited by Mohammed Ghaly, 211–231. London: World Scientific Publishing.

Rosin, Arnold J. and Moshe Sonnenblick. 1998. "Autonomy and Paternalism in Geriatric Medicine. The Jewish Ethical Approach to Issues of Feeding Terminally Ill Patients, and to Cardiopulmonary Resuscitation." *Journal of Medical Ethics* 24: 44–48.

Sachedina, Abdulaziz Abdulhussein. 2009. *Islamic Biomedical Ethics. Principles and Application*. Oxford: Oxford University Press.

SCFHS (Saudi Commission for Health Specialties). n.d. *Medical Ethics*. www.scfhs.org.sa/en/elibrary/DocsLibrary/versions/Documents/Medical%20ethics.pdf.

Schostak, Rabbi Zev. 1994. "Jewish Ethical Guidelines for Resuscitation and Artificial Nutrition and Hydration of the Dying Elderly." *Journal of Medical Ethics* 20(2): 93–100.

al-Shahri, Mohammad Zafir and Abdullah al-Khenaizan. 2005. "Palliative Care for Muslim Patients." *Journal of Supportive Oncology* 3: 432–436.

Sitte, Thomas. 2016. *Die Pflegetipps. Palliative Care*, sixteenth edition. Fulda: Deutscher PalliativVerlag.

Stiefelhagen, Peter. 2018. "Keine künstliche Flüssigkeitszufuhr in der Sterbephase." *Fortschritte der Medizin* 160(14).

Stoppe, Gabriela and Lenhard Maeck. 2007. "Nicht-pharmakologische Therapie bei Alzheimer-Demenz." *Die Psychiatrie* 4(1): 33–36.

Vilgis, Thomas A., Ilka Lendner and Rolf Caviezel. 2015. *Ernährung bei Pflegebedürftigkeit und Demenz. Lebensfreude durch Genuss*. Wien: Springer.

Volkert, Dorothee et al. 2015. "ESPEN Guidelines on Nutrition in Dementia." *Clinical Nutrition* 34(6): 1052–1073.

Voß, Henrike and Andreas Kruse. 2019. "Advance Care Planning im Kontext von Demenz. Entwicklung eines Instruments zur Exploration von Perspektiven der Betroffenen." *Zeitschrift Gerontologie und Geriatrie* 52 (S4): 282–290.

WHO-ADI (World Health Organization and Alzheimer's Disease International). 2012. *Dementia: A Public Health Priority*, 13. http://apps.who.int/iris/bitstream/10665/75263/1/9789241564458_eng.pdf?ua=1.

Zientek, David M. 2013. "Artificial Nutrition and Hydration in Catholic Healthcare: Balancing Tradition, Recent Teaching, and Law." *HEC Forum* 25(2): 145–159.

CHAPTER 12

Child Loss in Early Pregnancy

A Balancing Exercise between Islamic Legal Thinking and Life's Challenge

Beate Anam

Sabir and Zahra[1] live in Leipzig (Saxony), Germany. Zahra was in her 8th week of pregnancy, when in June 2019 her child died through spontaneous miscarriage.[2] Both parents wished for an Islamic funeral, therefore Sabir asked the *imām* at the mosque he attended as to whether the child could be buried in the Islamic burial ground.[3] His request was rejected by both the *imām* and his representative on the grounds that the deceased child was merely a "piece of flesh," as the soul was only "breathed into it on the 40th day or 120th day." The child could therefore simply be left in the hospital, buried in a park, or – if available – in one's own garden. An Islamic burial, however, could not take place.[4] Sabir and Zahra were rather disappointed about the answer. When Sabir searched for

1 For the protection of the individuals concerned, their names are anonymised.

2 Following German legislation (Bundesrepublik Deutschland 2008 [Personenstandsverordnung (PStV), Ordinance on Personal Status], § 31), a miscarriage is understood to occur when the child – irrespective of the cause of the miscarriage – shows no signs of life at birth (par. 2), when the child has a maximum weight of 500 g at birth (par. 2, sentence 1) and when the birth occurs before the 24th week of pregnancy (par. 2, sentence 2). If the child dies prenatally before the 16th week of pregnancy, it is called an early abortion (Schulze 2013, 72).

3 There has been a Muslim burial ground at the Ostfriedhof (East cemetery) since 1997, as in Germany, Muslim organisations are generally not allowed to set up their own Muslim cemeteries, which is due to their basically non-existent status as a public corporation (Bundesrepublik Deutschland 1949 [Grundgesetz (GG), Constitution], § 140 in connection with the Weimar Constitution of 1919 [Deutsches Reich 1919], § 137). The Saxon Burial Act (Sächsisches Bestattungsgesetz [SächsBestG]; Sächsische Staatskanzlei 1994) is currently (26 April 2022) under revision. A first draft bill is reportedly to be presented to the cabinet in the second quarter of 2022 (MDR Sachsen 2022) and might bring along some facilitation, for example for Muslims, that might see the lift of the obligatory coffin (*Sargpflicht*; SächsBestG § 16 par. 1 and 2) already implemented in other federal states (for example North Rhine-Westfalia in 2000). The explicit reference to federal state law, and not nation state law, is due to the fact that according to GG § 74, par. 1, sentences 1–33 in connection with § 72, the burial legislation falls under the legislative competence of the individual federal states.

4 Interview with Sabir, 16 June 2019.

DOI:10.1163/9789004459410_014

further information on the internet, he learned that the shape of the child gave information about whether it was already a human being (and had to be buried accordingly) or not yet. He seemed to accept the answer and told Zahra that if the child would have a human shape, a burial should be made. Otherwise, it would not matter where the child was left. Zahra, however, was shocked by this line of arguments, even though she understood Sabir's underlying motivation: he was concerned about the observance of religious rules in the case of their prematurely deceased child. For Zahra, there was never a doubt that the child gets buried, preferably in the Muslim burial ground.[5] In the course of the necessary medical aftercare, Zahra came to know about the possibility of having the child buried together with other prematurely deceased children in the so-called Ruhegarten für Schmetterlingskinder.[6] As Zahra was not sure whether such a burial was permissible from a religious point of view, she sent a (textual) request to the aforementioned *imām* concerning this matter. Her enquiry, however, remained unanswered.[7] The parents had thought through the ways of burial put forward by the *imām* and his representative, however they did not want their child to be buried in a public place or in a garden. Consequently, they had unanimously decided against it and resolved to bury the child communally in the Ruhegarten für Schmetterlingskinder. Following this decision, Zahra told me that she wanted to have a dignified funeral for her child. The notion to bury the child somewhere in a park where it could be dug up and eaten by an animal or a passer-by's dog caused Sabir and her great discomfort. As regards a burial in a garden, the parents did not want to burden the relatives in question with a dead child in their yard, as they themselves did not have their

5 Interview with Zahra, 17 June 2019.

6 Literally: "resting garden for butterfly children"; an area set aside for children that died during pregnancy (miscarriage and stillbirth), irrespective of their religious belonging, in the Leipzig-Lindenau cemetery. The communal funeral is organised three to four times per year by the Working Group Schmetterlingskinder.

For a definition of miscarriage see above. As far as a stillbirth is concerned, according to PStV § 31, this applies if the child shows no signs of life at birth (par. 2), has a minimum weight of 500 g (par. 2, sentence 1) or has a maximum weight of 500 g, but the birth takes place after the 24th week of pregnancy (par. 2, sentence 2) or if – in deviation from par. 2, sentence 2 – the miscarried child is part of a multiple birth in which at least one child is certified as a live birth or as a stillbirth (par. 3).

7 Interview with Zahra, 17 June 2019.

own garden.[8] In the time after their misfortune, the parents took different paths in dealing with their grief over the loss of their child. Neither Sabir nor Zahra made use of professional grief counselling. While Sabir turned to God and kept repeating that God had decided it that way and that he would accept this decision, Zahra, who also accepted God's decision, chose to actively deal with what had happened. She made inquiries about the reason for her child's death and informed herself about miscarried children and their parents, inter alia with regard to the legal status of the child (both religious and non-religious).[9] She came across the possibility of getting an official certificate acknowledging the existence of a miscarried child.[10] Such a certificate was issued to Zahra by the local registrar's office in July 2019. Finally, in November 2019, the child found its final resting place in the Ruhegarten für Schmetterlingskinder.

∴

1 Introduction

Although spontaneous termination of early pregnancy (miscarriage) takes place quite often,[11] it still seems to be a highly tabooed issue. In her publication *Tabuthema Fehlgeburt* ("Taboo Issue Miscarriage"),[12] Miriam Funk states that this taboo may be linked to a widespread perception that the physical appearance of the deceased human being is considered to not yet be of a "real child." Based on the lack of appreciation, those affected by the loss are usually forced to retreat in mourning in the sense of an isolated and silent grief (Funk

8 Interview with Zahra, 18 June 2019.

9 Participant observation, June 2019 to June 2020.

10 Based on PStV § 31 par. 3 out of which, however, does not arise any legal entitlements except for the registration in the family register.

11 The number amounts to 7% of all known pregnancies, whereby the number of unreported cases is probably much higher (Schulze 2013, 72).

12 It can be generally observed that publications on spontaneous miscarriages and their social psychological consequences for the individuals affected are mainly found in the so-called popular science literature. Some of which were written as reference books for the affected themselves, but also for counsellors, grief counsellors, midwives and the like (for example Wolter 2015; 2017). In contrast, there is a wide spectrum of publications on medically or socially induced abortions (Rosner 2001, 176, who notes this across religions).

2017, 7f.).[13] My own empirical findings in Germany[14] showed parents of the decedent face an extraordinary wide range of challenges after the loss. These range from renouncing a funeral to psychologically repress one's own grief. Here, my research focus lies on Muslim contexts and how believers coped with their individual religiosity. In doing so, I also included external actors assisting those affected. These actors reported a raising number of persons who seek bereavement counselling, regardless of whether the child was lost as a result of miscarriage (*isqāṭ*), abortion (*ijhāḍ*), or stillbirth (*wilāda mayyita*). Although a growing number of Sharīʿa based scholarly publications and *fatwā*s are available on these issues, an in-depth approach to the individual perspective of those challenged with the situation in daily life is missing in the debate. Doctrinal approaches dealing with methodological aspects of abortion (see Katz 2003; Sachedina 2009, 125–144) or the legal and moral status of embryos (see Sachedina 2009, 139–141) do not, in most parts, answer what is needed in practice. Yet, the intellectual discourse should not become an end in itself but must engage much more with the taboo in its consequences on the ground.

The point of departure is that Muslim legal scholars (*ʿulamāʾ*, sg. *ʿālim*) have been and still are expressing themselves within the context of their respective (Muslim) society and time. With that said, there is no doubt that nowadays living conditions are different to those in the past and most probably will be different to those in the future. In addition, one should keep in mind that today, an increasing number of Muslims are living in a non-Muslim majority country. The way of living differs therefore, not only in time of a certain society, but also in terms of its overall religious setting. Within this heterogeneous setting, believers negotiate everyday matters – such as those on the end-of-life care of prenatally deceased children – between norms and expectations that are shaped by religion and those of the non-Muslim society they live in. Answers to everyday questions of life are thus found primarily through discussions with other believers and not necessarily on the basis of what has been expressed in scholarly works or *fatwā*s. This does not imply, however, that scholarly and intellectual discourse is, *per se*, contradictory to non-doctrinal individual approaches of those affected. None of both should be given preference over the other. As Thomas Eich and Jonathan E. Brockopp (2008, 2) rightly point

13 There are still no scientifically or empirically sound studies available for Germany on the reasons and the degree of the respective taboo. My finding concerning the taboo in this article is based on my conversations with those affected and their families, midwives, grief counsellors and morticians, as well as on a review of publications in various genres.

14 Interviews with affected parents, midwives, and grief counsellors on various occasions, summer 2020–2022.

out for the field of medical ethics and practice, the bottom-up analysis of individual cases is essential to bridge gaps between theory and practice.

2 Case-by-Case Analysis

In doing so, let us recapitulate the main aspects of the aforementioned case of Sabir and Zahra, which are:

- The funeral, especially 1) the question of burial due to age, 2) the burial place and 3) the question of individual vs. communal burial.
- How Sabir and Zahra themselves coped with the death of their child.

2.1 *Funeral*

2.1.1 Burial Due to Age

As to the first aspect, the majority of *ʿulamāʾ* across all schools of jurisprudence (*madhāhib*, sg. *madhhab*) hold the opinion that the entitlement to vested personal and legal rights (and, thus, also to a proper burial) begins with the ensoulment (*nafkh al-rūḥ*) of the child, which occurs on the 120th day of gestation (Eich 2020, 354).[15] In this regard, however, Hamza Yusuf (2018) points out that

> [t]he basis for 120 days, if taken from the hadith in its standard interpretation, would mean that the hadith contradicts today's medical views that are based upon unshakeable biological evidence.
>
> YUSUF 2018

---

15 The embryonic development according to the scripture can be found *inter alia* in Q 22:5, 23:12–14 and the Sunna, for example al-Bukhārī 1422, nos. 3208, 3332, 6594, 7454, as well as Muslim n.d., nos. 1616, 1617. For an analysis of classical or contemporary majority views, see Ghaly 2012 with further reference; Mittelsdorf 2019.

By way of comparison: In Judaism, the 40th day represents a crucial point: Thus, a miscarried child born up to the 40th day after conception is not buried because it is not yet formed and therefore does not yet have an identity. If, however, the child is born after the 40th day, it must be buried and mourned (Rey-Stocker 2006, 126f.). As far as Christianity is concerned, the Catholic Church already recognises the zygote as human life, which has a right to life and is also entitled to personal rights. In the Protestant Church, there are different positions which see the starting point of becoming human either in fertilisation or in completed implantation. In either case, the fertilised egg is not given the same person status and the same rights as the born human being (Rey-Stocker 2006, 132). If we look at individual cases in practice, we find that the burials by the Schmetterlingskinder at the Leipzig Ostfriedhof are always conducted by one Catholic and one Protestant pastor. A Jewish rabbi or a Muslim *imām*, however, are missing.

Yusuf refers to the opinion of the Mālikī *madhhab* that the individual passes through each phase in utero as a human being (for example Q 75:36–38; see also Ghaly 2012, 185). With ensoulment, the (bodily) human being is elevated to a spiritual being which "most likely relates to and initiates human brain activity that will eventually develop into the capacity for human thought" (Yusuf 2018). Furthermore, the Mālikī interpretation does not see a consecutive sequence in 40-day steps in the verses in question, but a concurrent sequence of all phases *within* the first 40 days. Referring to *aḥādīth* of Muslim b. al-Ḥajjāj al-Naysābūrī (d. 261/875) and Abū Dāwūd al-Sijistānī (d. 275/889), Yusuf consequently argues that the ensoulment already takes place after about six weeks, that is after the lump phase (*muḍgha*), when the child takes shape.

Yusuf is not alone in his view to take medical or biological findings into account. Several other participants in the current debates on the question of the actual beginning of human life, like the physician[16] Ḥassān Ḥatḥūt (d. 2009), also argue that "biomedical and scientific knowledge should be given precedence over the opinions expressed by classical Muslim religious scholars" (Ghaly 2012, 181). Advocates of this view hold that the relevant scripture is in principle open to interpretation and not definite (*qaṭʿī*), thus also allowing metaphorical interpretations (*taʾwīlāt*, sg. *taʾwīl*). These different interpretations should be taken into account; however, no interpretation should be given precedence over another (Ghaly 2012, 187).

In the case at hand, the *imām* refused an Islamic burial of the prematurely deceased child on the grounds that its soul was only "breathed into it on the 40th day or 120th day." It is striking that the *imām* refers explicitly to two points in time regarding the ensoulment, which indicates that he is probably aware of the respective debates among Muslim scholars. Why then did he deny the parents the wish for an Islamic burial? Information about this could be provided by discussions that I have had with Muslim believers that attend the respective mosque.[17] The information obtained suggests that Islamic norms are only implemented eclectically by the *imām*. Their adaptation to the reality of life in a non-Muslim majority society is done opportunely with a view to the advantage of the Muslim concerned. This opportunism sometimes violates the law in force. This was exemplified in the answer to a Muslim believer's question as to whether it was permissible for him from an Islamic perspective to

16 On the involvement of external experts in questions of bioethical relevance apart from *ʿulamāʾ*, see Ghaly 2015. The joint decision-making process takes place by means of collective independent reasoning (*ijtihād jamāʿī*; Gad Makhlouf 2018).

17 2020 until 2022.

work illegally. The *imām* answered the question in the affirmative, stating that the German state does not support Muslims living here either.[18]

If we return to the actual topic of this chapter, the question arises as to how German legislation positions itself on the burial of miscarried children. It can first be stated, in general terms, that the law with regard to the entitlement to personal and legal rights at the beginning of life is informed by biomedical findings. Thus, the weight limit of 500 g at birth that marks the beginning of the child's potential viability outside the uterus in the event of a premature birth decides over the child's legal status. Hence, a child that dies prior to the 24th week of pregnancy with a birth weight of below 500 g is usually referred to as a miscarriage and it is not registered under civil status law (PStV § 31 par. 2, sentence 2). The mentioned weight limit is also relevant in the funeral service as the SächsBestG provides for a burial of the deceased to qualify as a corpse, which is tied to a birth weight of at least 500 g (SächsBestG § 9, par. 1), while miscarried children are not classified as corpse (SächsBestG § 9, par. 2). Consequently, there is no *obligation* to bury a miscarried child, but there is a *right*, which Sabir and Zahra exercised when they had their child buried in the Ruhegarten für Schmetterlingskinder.

2.1.2 Burial Place

The question of the burial place (*maqbara*) is another aspect where divergences became clear from the case study at hand. Referring to ethico-moral Islamic values, Ḥasan Khālid (d. 1989) points to the necessity to respect the dignity (*ikrām*) of the deceased, which results in the imperative to bury her/him properly and not simply leave her/him behind so that birds or wild animals may eat her/him (Khālid 1986, 2:120, quoted in Krawietz 1991, 152). The latter is also referred to by Wahba al-Zuḥaylī (d. 2015) (al-Zuḥaylī 1989, 2:251, quoted in Krawietz 1991, 152). The *imām*'s statement, however, that Sabir's and Zahra's miscarried child could, for example, be buried in a park or in one's own garden, is diametrically opposed to the views of Khālid and al-Zuḥaylī. Apart from the fact that the *imām*'s statement not only lacks any reference to the dignity of the deceased, it also leads to the conclusion that the miscarried child is unworthy of recognition as a human being. This may also be deduced from his statement that the deceased child is merely a "piece of flesh."

The concept of dignity as a *sine qua non* of a burial can also be found in the respective state legislation. Here, the place of burial is based on a general obligatory burial in a cemetery (*Friedhofspflicht*; SächsBestG § 1 par. 1). These are subject to the condition that the places of burial comply with human dignity,

18 Personal information from the respective Muslim believer, April/May 2020.

general moral concepts and recognised social orders[19] (SächsBestG § 1 par. 2 sentence 1); in addition, they must *inter alia* guarantee the peace of the dead (SächsBestG § 1 par. 2 sentence 2). What is striking here is that "moral concepts and recognised social orders" are formulated in the plural, but without further elaboration on what exactly is meant by those rather abstract concepts. The same applies to the aforementioned concept of dignity, which at first glance shows similarities to Khālid's view.

And what about burial outside the official cemeteries as had been put forward by the *imām*? According to SächsBestG, burial in a private burial ground is only permitted with permission of the relevant authority (§ 3 par. 4 sentence 1) and only provides for the burial of ashes of deceased persons (SächsBestG § 3 par. 4 sentence 2). It is also subject to the condition that a dignified arrangement and maintenance of the burial place are ensured during the minimum resting period[20] (*Mindestruhezeit*; SächsBestG § 3 par. 3 sentence 2). Any violation of the stipulations, be it intentionally or negligently, is sanctioned according to SächsBestG § 23, *inter alia* if contrary to SächsBestG § 1 par. 3 a burial place is created, extended or re-occupied without official permission (SächsBestG § 23 par. 1 sentence 1), if contrary to SächsBestG § 3 par. 4, a corpse is buried on a private burial ground without permission of the relevant authority (SächsBestG § 23 par. 1 sentence 2), or if contrary to § 18 par. 6 sentence 1 misscarried children are not buried, not buried in time or not buried properly (SächsBestG § 23 par. 1 sentence 14). Following these legal provisions, it can be deduced that we find ourselves in a legal grey area regarding the statement of the *imām* and his representative to bury the child in a park or a garden, as the explicit prohibition in this regard only applies to deceased persons qualified as corpses.

2.1.3 Individual vs. Communal Burial

Another aspect that requires consideration is the question (posed by Zahra but left unanswered on the side of the *imām*) of whether it is permissible to bury miscarried children jointly. The Sharīʿa-based scholarly literature provides information on the basic requirement that the deceased should be buried individually and must face Mecca. In the case of joint burial, there must be sufficient space for each deceased as well as a partition between them. Joint burials are permissible for members of a family, and exceptionally also

19 In the original: "Bestattungsplätze müssen der Würde des Menschen, den allgemeinen sittlichen Vorstellungen und den anerkannten gesellschaftlichen Ordnungen entsprechen."

20 Which is 10 years for miscarried, still born, and those children who died before the age of 2 years and apart from that 20 years (SächsBestG § 6 par. 2 sentence 1).

for Muslims who are not members of a family, provided that the burial of each deceased in an individual grave is difficult, as in the case of war. In contrast, communal burial with non-Muslims (namely: Christians) is forbidden if the bodies cannot be kept apart. In this case, the communal burial should be carried out in a Muslim grave, with the Muslim retaining the upper hand (Krawietz 1991, 153–155). The literature consulted did not provide information on whether the aspects presented are also valid for miscarried children. If that were the case, the communal burial of the miscarried child in the Ruhegarten für Schmetterlingskinder might be forbidden from a religio-legal point of view.

Sabir and Zahra were not aware of these normative details when they decided to bury their child together with other miscarried children. Nor were they aware that according to SächsBestG § 18 par. 2, they would have been entitled to an individual burial apart from the collective and anonymous one (SächsBestG § 18 par. 6 sentence 2) they finally decided for. In view of the *imām*'s refusal to bury the child in the Islamic burial ground, the municipal cemetery would have been the only option for an individual burial. In this respect, however, Birgit Krawietz notes a fundamental tendency in the *fatwā*s she analysed (albeit with gradual differences in argumentation) to the effect that the burial of a Muslim in a Christian cemetery is tantamount to insulting the dead (Krawietz 1991, 156). That Sabir and Zahra, as Muslim believers, are not alone in their decision for a communal burial, however, became evident by my (participant) observation at a communal burial in which other affected Muslim parents participated as well.[21]

To sum it up, we see a discrepancy between scholarly knowledge and those of the affected parents. Furthermore, deficient support by the religious authority lead to the creation of own ways of coping with the misfortune. Often, as the case reveals, not in the constraints of religious regulations. This cannot be in the interest of either the *imām* or those seeking religious guidance. The struggle to legitimise one's individual way leads to the concept of dignity (*ikrām*) of the dead. This approach should, preferably, be considered by the religious authority.

2.2 *Coping with the Child's Death*

If we would break these considerations down to our case and Sabir's and Zahra's different ways of coping with the death of their child, we would have to consider to what extent their individual

21 Participant observation, 2 November 2019. The chairperson of the Working Group Schmetterlingskinder also confirmed the participation of Muslims in the communal funerals. Personal information, 27 May 2020.

1) biography,
2) psycho-mental disposition,
3) socio-emotional ties to the child,
4) perceived or actually available framework for action influences, drives and shapes their thinking and behaviour.

2.2.1 Biography

In the course of her/his life, a person is exposed to different experiences, all of which have an influence on how she/he thinks and acts in the present and future, such as education, socialisation, migration, conversion, cultural and/or religious values (Scherr 2016). Biography also includes experiences of loss and grief. In case of acute grief, losses that have already been experienced can erupt and make it more difficult to cope with the current grief. Knowledge of the individual's past can thus be a calculable factor, ideally a resource, for the person affected in coping with the misfortune.

2.2.2 Psycho-Mental Disposition

A person's psycho-mental disposition is part of her/his personality. Anita DeLongis and Susan Holtzman studied the interplay of stress, social support and personality in coping. They conclude that the individual character influences and shapes the event itself, the appraisals, the coping and the outcomes (DeLongis and Holtzman 2005, 1635). The individual psycho-mental disposition thus influences the emotional, physical, cognitive, behavioural and spiritual reaction (Himmelrich 2015, 76–80) of the individual to the event. It also influences the form in which the affected person grieves which ranges from intuitive to instrumental (Himmelrich 2015, 81–84).

2.2.3 Socio-Emotional Ties to the Child

The bond between the parents and the child does not only begin with the child's birth, but long before. In the case of the mother, the prenatal bond develops through the physiological and hormonal interaction of mother and child as well as through sensory perception on the part of the child. Accordingly, even the spontaneous miscarriage of a child at the beginning of pregnancy can cause great shock and grief. Integrating this event into one's life can prove no less challenging than in the case of a child who died peri- or postnatally.

2.2.4 Framework for Action

Framework of action relates on the one hand to the state-legal, religio-legal and institutional context in which a person affected finds herself/himself. On the other hand, it refers to her/his network of relationships (Schäfers 2016,

23), that includes the spousal partner, the family, the Muslim community, but also Muslim authorities like an *imām*. The relationship and interaction of the person affected within her/his network of relationship plays a key role in the grieving process (see DeLongis and Holzman 2005; Himmelrich 2015, 123–135). In the best case, the network can prove to be supportive, but it can also lead to the opposite result if those affected are not perceived or taken seriously in their grief.

3 Current Challenges

3.1 *Shift from Burial to Cremation*

In the summer of 2021, the Working Group Schmetterlingskinder organising the communal burial of prematurely deceased children decided to change from burials to cremations due to the limited space allocated for the Ruhegarten für Schmetterlingskinder, which is now running short after its establishment in 2005. Due to this, it was decided to switch from burial in two coffins to burial in one urn starting January 2022.

From an Islamic religio-legal point of view, there is a general obligation to burial on the basis of the scripture itself (for example Q 77:25–26), which does not only include dead bodies as a whole but also parts of it, such as organs (Krawietz 1991, 150). In her publication *Die Ḥurma*, Krawietz discusses the assessment of the burning of corpses regarding miscarriages or stillbirths in two *fatwā*s. Concerning the qualitative specification of the dead body, she states that

> [d]er möglicherweise besondere Charakter der körperlichen Qualität ungeborenen Lebens … in diesem Zusammenhang in den Fatwas nicht weiter aufgeworfen [wird]….
>
> KRAWIETZ 1991, 120[22]

In principle, however, the *muftī*s of the *fatwā*s in question were in favour of a prohibition on burning foetuses (miscarriage and stillbirth), regardless of whether the pregnancy's termination was spontaneous or induced and regardless of whether a human form was recognisable or not (Krawietz 1991, 123–125). Thus, Ḥasan Ma'mūn (d. 1973) (Ma'mūn 1955) decided for the prohibition of burning a miscarried child while Aḥmad Ṣabrī Ghabjūqa (in an unpublished

22 "… the possibly special character of the physical quality of unborn life in this context is not raised further in the *fatwā*s she examines" (own translation).

fatwā) decided for the obligation to bury the unborn child (Ghabjūqa 1985, *fatwā* no. 1946, cited in Krawietz 1991, 125).

The prohibition of the burning of corpses, which can be derived from various passages in the scripture (Q 6:151; Sunna, for example al-Albānī n.d., no. 3207), is closely connected to the human right to bodily integrity (*ḥurma*) and the belief in bodily resurrection (Q 80:21–22, 82:5) on the Day of Resurrection. Furthermore, it is connected to the belief that God alone has power over fire (Q 82:14–16; Sunna, for example al-Albānī n.d., no. 2673). Accordingly, also from this religio-legal perspective, affected parents would no longer be allowed to have their prematurely deceased child buried jointly.[23]

3.2 *Institutional and Knowledge Gap*

Let us leave the religio-legal and state-legal realm and turn to the institutional network to support affected parents as part of their child's end-of-life care. In this respect – and this may already be anticipated at this point – there still exists a gap as to the institutional and knowledge-based end-of-life care with respect to the affected parents in focus.

In institutional terms, Germany resembles a patchwork quilt when it comes to supporting those affected, as services in this regard are not available in equal measure everywhere, but primarily in cities and conurbations rather than in rural areas. Furthermore, the relevant services offered do not reflect the social reality and are aimed at affected people of all social classes and all religions uniformly, which is why in some cases there is a lack of knowledge to be able to counsel people appropriately.

Counselling Muslim parents in their grief is commonly assigned to Muslim counselling (*Seelsorge*) and within that to emergency counselling (*Notfallseelsorge*). However, the network of professional Muslim bereavement counselling in Germany varies in extent with, for example, more established structures in the West and South-West of Germany (Şahinöz 2018), whereas there is a lack of sufficient support in the East of Germany, such as Leipzig.[24] Moreover, Muslim counsellors (*Seelsorger*) are only gradually being trained, whereby the particularities of counselling parents of prematurely deceased children are not yet taken into account, or at least not to a sufficient extent yet,

23 The change from burial to cremation is, however, unobjectionable from the point of view of Saxon law, as the SächsBestG basically provides for the options of burial and cremation (§ 18 par. 4 sentence 1).

24 Experience from empirical research, 2019 to 2021. In Leipzig, however, structures for the counselling of specifically Muslim parents are gradually developing, for example in the registered association Nur al-Hayat.

while common topics (such as illness, death of a relative, suicide or accident; Lemmen, Yardim and Müller-Lange 2011, 84–123) clearly dominate.

Consequently, there is an explicit need for Muslim social workers, grief counsellors, and undertakers in Leipzig, especially if they have sound knowledge of the religio-legal and ethico-moral canon of norms and values and are familiar with the relevant legal requirements of (federal) state law. However, as the final decision rests with the parents, as Eich and Brockopp indicate (Eich and Brockopp 2008, 2), the parents must be provided with the appropriate knowledge to make informed decisions. Therefore, it is advantageous for the counsellor to be knowledgeable not only about the respective commonly held majority views of Muslim scholars, but also about the views that might only be hold by a minority of *ʿulamāʾ*. So, what is needed here is person-centred, well-founded end-of-life care based on individual support, not only with reference to religious phrases, but also with the integration of epistemological results, for example from psychology, palliative care, etc. It is important to take those affected seriously without implying a disparagement of religious norms and values at the same time (Anam 2022). A sustainable integration of events (especially those at the borders of life) can only take place through a profound examination of the event itself and the factors influencing the negotiation and decision-making process on the side of the individuals concerned.

The knowledge gap, however, relates to the termination of pregnancies in general. Nevertheless, it can be observed that the religio-legal specifications and requirements become clearer the older the child is at the time of passing away. In contrast, a great deal of uncertainty can be observed in the case of children who died in early pregnancy. This is due, in large part, to the fact that the respective literature as well as the differentiated, topic-specific debates that are being conducted in Islamic countries, especially in the field of bioethics and medical ethics, are hardly known outside the Arabic-speaking world (an outstanding example in this regard is Ghaly 2012). However, the availability of translated information in the aforementioned sense would also support non-Muslim actors (undertakers, counsellors, clinical staff for example obstetrics and gynaecologists) who are also willing to counsel Muslims appropriately while incorporating their specific religio-legal and ethico-moral canon of norms and values.[25]

25 Personal information from an undertaker, 3 June 2021, and from a trainer of bereavement counsellors, 13 March 2022. The latter also told me about an increase in the number of affected Muslim parents seeking bereavement counselling.

4 Future Prospects

As to the future, the following concrete approaches for action can be identified regarding end-of-life care at the beginning of life: It is of utmost relevance to engage in a much more intensive interdisciplinary and bottom up discourse, that is from individual cases and singular patterns of explanation, when considering Muslim negotiation processes and actions, instead of assuming that Muslim thoughts and behaviour are monolithic in nature (see Elliesie 2014, 5). Thus, the assessment of the question,

> ob im konkreten Einzelfalle auch wirklich eine Abweichung von den durch Brauch und Sitte, Recht und Ritus vorgeschriebenen normenkonformen Verhaltensweisen vorliegt, würde eine ins Detail gehende Untersuchung und Darstellung der jeweils gebotenen Vorgehens- und Verfahrensweise notwendig machen.
>
> KRAWIETZ 1991, 148[26]

Another aspect that deserves reconsideration is the still widespread phenomenon of grief often being thought of as typically female. Yet it has long been known that women and men both grieve, but differently. We have to keep in mind here that the father has also lost a child and might need bereavement counselling, but is facing a lack of corresponding offers targeted at Muslim men.[27]

A desideratum that needs to be addressed is the translation of relevant Arabic texts and their accessibility in German. In this respect, there is a great need to make relevant works by Muslim scholars on bereavement counselling accessible (for example al-Suyūṭī 1407/1978). Having such material readily available should not only help parents to make informed decisions. As said before, it would also be of great help to those who counsel Muslims in end-of-life issues and who lack relevant knowledge.

---

26 "… whether in a specific individual case there is really a deviation from the norms of conduct prescribed by custom and usage, law and rite, requires a detailed examination and presentation of the respectively required approach and procedure" (own translation).

27 When doing research in Düsseldorf (North Rhine-Westphalia, October 2019 to March 2020), one female interlocutor, who's sister's child had died sometime after its birth for health reasons, told me how much the behaviour of the child's father had changed since the child's death and that he was no longer accessible since then. The search for respective offers as to bereavement counselling specifically for Muslim men ended unsuccessfully. Rihm and Rihm (2013) also point to the desideratum of missing offers for grieving men regardless of religious affiliation.

Furthermore, more importance should be given to (bereavement) counselling at the prenatal end of life in the education of Muslim counsellors. Here the responsible theologians are on duty to prepare counsellors (especially community counsellors, *Gemeindeseelsorger*) for this task by including appropriate content in their education. Additionally, access to support services for those affected also requires further development. There are several reasons for the limited accessibility to offers concerning end-of-life issues, for example factual unavailability of relevant offers or language barriers. There is also a lack of information on both sides: on the part of those affected about the institutional and legal provisions and options available in Germany as well as about the wide-ranging views of Muslim scholars; on the part of the actors about relevant support services specifically dedicated to Muslims (if available) as well as the inner-Islamic range of opinions and normative specifications.

Apart from these desiderata and notwithstanding the diversity of infrastructure for Muslims across the country, one can basically assume a slow but positive development to do justice to the reality of an increasing number of Muslims through corresponding offers: accordingly, for example, Islamic cemeteries are also increasingly being established as a counselling specifically for Muslims. There is also increasing awareness on the part of non-Muslim actors regarding a religion-sensitive counselling of Muslims, which is already being included in some training courses.[28] It is also encouraging that the growing awareness of the need for specific support for Muslims in end-of-life issues has led to the creation of fora to overcome the disciplinary boundaries that still prevail and to enable a truly interdisciplinary and multidisciplinary exchange.[29]

5 Conclusion

To sum it up, the preceding discussion of Sabir's and Zahra's case may be considered exemplary in several respects:

1. The non-majority Muslim setting in Germany presents Muslims with special challenges when it comes to end-of-life issues as different normative systems – including the comparison of individual concepts of

28 For example, with the registered association Hope's Angel Foundation in the training of grief counsellors. Personal information from the head of training on various occasions during 2021.

29 To this end, the Working Group Medizinethik und Islam (Medical Ethics and Islam) at the Erlangen Centre for Islam and Law in Europe EZIRE has dedicated itself to networking scientific and practical actors.

norms and values with those of third parties – must also be included in the considerations.

2. The case of Sabir and Zahra reflects the individuality of negotiation processes and to what extent the framing conditions must be taken into account as influencing factors. However, it also shows that a truly multidisciplinary approach, which takes a holistic view of the affected individual in her/his specific setting, is necessary for the examination of negotiation processes and factual decisions on end-of-life issues.
3. A comparison of individual case-specific decisions with the relevant *fiqh*–treatises and –debates might point to existing discrepancies between legal-theological views and factual application in real life. To what extent a development of religio-legal norms *sui generis* can be derived from this in the context of non-majority Muslim societies must be left to further qualitative research, which ideally starts from the very people concerned as a bottom-up approach.
4. Regardless of the religio-legal guidelines, however, I consider it essential to rethink the way miscarried children are dealt with, which also takes the relationship and the grief of the parents into account and seriously. After all, end-of-life care does not only include the care of the child who deceased prematurely, but also the parents who are confronted with the end of their child's life. Only then the tabooing social tone can be counteracted and changes could be brought, but for this, the topic has to be addressed and made public, both in non-Muslim majority society and within Muslim communities.
5. In view of the action-guiding function of religion, an ambivalent picture and thus a certain oddity regarding the miscarried child can be ascertained from the sources and scholarly debates, but also from life practice itself: Although some Muslim authorities – scholars as well as the *imām* in the case study – do not recognise the miscarried child as a human being, it is equally forbidden to be burned. At least in practice, there is also the discrepancy that the child can simply be thrown away, although the sources provide for a dignified burial. Consequently, it seems that the current Islamic practice – at least in the case at hand – is closer to the atheistic materialistic way of thinking on this issue, including just throwing away the "piece of flesh".
6. In the *fiqh*-literature as well as in the *fatwā*s, there are different views on a single issue, which – in a very abbreviated form – are held by a majority of *ʿulamāʾ* or by a minority. Often, however, it is only the majority opinions that are known to Muslims or conveyed to them. I consider it important

to impart knowledge about the broad spectrum of views so that those concerned can make an informed decision. With that said, I strongly advocate taking advantage of the flexibility of interpretation enshrined in the Sharīʿa and the given possibilities for adapting the underlying principles to time and space, in order to offer those affected the best possible support in end-of-life care at the beginning of life.

Acknowledgements

I sincerely thank Mohammed Ghaly, without whose generous offer this contribution would not have come into being. I also thank the anonymous reviewers and Hatem Elliesie for their critical remarks and valuable suggestions that improved the final version of this contribution.

Bibliography

al-Albānī, Muḥammad Nāṣir al-Dīn. n.d. *Ṣaḥīḥ wa-Ḍaʿīf Sunan Abī Dāwūd*. Alexandria: Markaz Nūr al-Islām li-Abḥāth al-Qurʾān wa-l-Sunna, https://al-maktaba.org/book/1755.

Anam, Beate. 2022 (in preparation). *Lebensweltliche Alltagspragmatik von Musliminnen und islamische Normativität: Exemplarisch dargestellt anhand der Bedeutung von amāna und gender ǧihād*. PhD thesis, Leipzig University.

al-Bukhārī, Muḥammad b. Ismāʿīl. 1422. *Al-Jāmiʿ al-Musnad al-Ṣaḥīḥ al-Mukhtaṣar min Umūr Rasūl Allāh*. n.p.: n.p. https://al-maktaba.org/book/33757.

Bundesrepublik Deutschland. 1949. *Grundgesetz für die Bundesrepublik Deutschland…, das zuletzt durch Artikel 1 u. 2 Satz 2 des Gesetzes vom 29. September 2020 (BGBl. I S. 2048) geändert worden ist*. www.gesetze-im-internet.de/gg/BJNR000010949.html.

Bundesrepublik Deutschland. 2008. *Personenstandsverordnung vom 22. November 2008 (BGBl. I S. 2263), die zuletzt durch Artikel 19 des Gesetzes vom 28. März 2021 (BGBl. I S. 591) geändert worden ist*. www.gesetze-im-internet.de/pstv/BJNR226300008.html.

DeLongis, Anita and Susan Holtzman. 2005. "Coping in Context: The Role of Stress, Social Support, and Personality in Coping." *Journal of Personality* 73(6): 1633–1656. https://delongis-psych.sites.olt.ubc.ca/files/2017/12/Coping-in-context.pdf.

Deutsches Reich. 1919. *Die Verfassung des Deutschen Reiches („Weimarer Reichsverfassung") vom 11. August 1919, geändert durch Gesetz vom 6. August 1930 (RGBl. S. 1566) … sowie einige verfassungsdurchbrechende Reichsgesetze, ohne formale Änderung des Verfassungstextes*, www.verfassungen.de/de19-33/verf19-i.htm.

Eich, Thomas. 2020. "Zur Abtreibung in frühen islamischen Texten." *Zeitschrift der Deutschen Morgenländischen Gesellschaft* 170(2): 345–360.

Eich, Thomas and Jonathan E. Brockopp. 2003. "Introduction: Medical Ethics and Muslim Perspectives." In *Muslim Medical Ethics: From Theory to Practice*, edited by Thomas Eich and Jonathan E. Brockopp, 1–16. Columbia: University of South Carolina Press.

Elliesie, Hatem. 2014. *Binnenpluralität des Islamischen Rechts: Diversität religiöser Normativität rechtsdogmatisch und -methodisch betrachtet*. Berlin: SFB 700.

Funk, Miriam. 2017. *Tabuthema Fehlgeburt: Ein Ratgeber*. Frankfurt am Main: Mabuse.

Gad Makhlouf, Ahmed. 2018. *Das Konzept des kollektiven* iǧtihād *und seine Umsetzungsformen: Analyse der Organisation und Arbeitsweise islamischer Rechtsakademien*. Berlin: Peter Lang.

Ghabjūqa, Aḥmad Ṣafar. 1985. "*Fatwā* no. 1946/n." Unpublished *Fatwā* on Dead Foetuses, 28 May.

Ghaly, Mohammed. 2012. "The Beginning of Human Life: Islamic Bioethical Perspectives." *Zygon: Journal of Religion and Science* (47)1: 175–213.

Ghaly, Mohammed. 2015. "Biomedical Scientists as Co-Muftis: Their Contribution to Contemporary Islamic Bioethics." *Die Welt des Islam* (55)3–4: 286–311. DOI 10.1163/15700607-05534P03.

Himmelrich, Nathalie. 2015. *Trauernde Eltern: Wie ein Paar den Verlust eines Kindes überlebt*. n.p.: Reach the Sky.

Katz, Marion Holmes. 2003. "The Problem of Abortion in Classical Sunni *Fiqh*." In *Islamic Ethics of Life: Abortion, War, and Euthanasia*, edited by Jonathan E. Brockopp, 25–50. Columbia: University of South Carolina Press.

Khālid, Ḥasan. 1986. *Al-Islām wa-Ruʾya fīmā baʿd al-Ḥayāt*. Beirut: Dār al-Nahḍa al-ʿArabiyya.

Krawietz, Birgit. 1991. *Die Ḥurma: Schariatrechtlicher Schutz vor Eingriffen in die körperliche Unversehrtheit nach arabischen Fatwas des 20. Jahrhunderts*. Berlin: Duncker & Humblot.

Lemmen, Thomas, Nigaro Yardim and Joachim Müller-Lange, eds. 2011. *Notfallbegleitung für Muslime und mit Muslimen: Ein Kursbuch zur Ausbildung Ehrenamtlicher*. Gütersloh: Gütersloher Verlagshaus.

Maʾmūn, Ḥasan. 1955. "Ḥarq al-Saqṭ Ḥarām." *Fatāwā Dār al-Ifāʾ al-Miṣriyya*. http://books.islam-db.com/book/فتاوي_دار_الافتاء_المصريه/3259.

MDR Sachsen. 2022. "Gesetzentwurf: Sachsen will Sargpflicht lockern" *MDR.de*, 13 January. www.mdr.de/nachrichten/sachsen/politik/sachsen-gesetzesvorhaben-lockerung-sargpflicht-100.html.

Mittelsdorf, Jakob. 2019. *Das ungeborene Leben im Islam: Ein Beispiel kultureller Wertetradierung von Spätantike bis Gegenwart*. Wuppertal: Societas Verlagsgesellschaft.

al-Naysābūrī, Muslim b. al-Ḥajjāj. n.d. *Al-Musnad al-Ṣaḥīḥ al-Mukhtaṣar bi-Naql al-ʿAdl ʿan al-ʿAdl ilā Rasūl Allāh*. Beirut: Dār Iḥyāʾ al-Turāth al-ʿArabī. https://al-maktaba.org/book/33760.

Rey-Stocker, Irmi. 2006. *Anfang und Ende des menschlichen Lebens aus Sicht der Medizin und der drei monotheistischen Religionen Judentum, Christentum und Islam*. Basel: Karger.

Rihm, Melanie and Dominik Rihm. 2013. *Die vergessene Trauer der Väter*. Norderstedt: Books on Demand.

Rosner, Fred. 2001. *Biomedical Ethics and Jewish Law*. Hoboken, NJ: KTAV Publication House.

Sachedina, Abdulaziz. 2009. *Islamic Biomedical Ethics: Principles and Application*. Oxford: Oxford University Press.

Sächsische Staatskanzlei. 1994. *Sächsisches Gesetz über das Friedhofs-, Leichen- und Bestattungswesen [Sächsisches Bestattungsgesetz – SächsBestG] vom 8. Juli 1994*. www.revosax.sachsen.de/vorschrift/4526-Saechsisches-Bestattungsgesetz.

Şahinöz, Cemil. 2018. *Seelsorge im Islam: Theorie und Praxis in Deutschland*. Wiesbaden: Springer VS.

Scherr, Albert. 2016. "Sozialisation, Person, Individuum." In *Einführung in Hauptbegriffe der Soziologie*, edited by Hermann Korte and Bernhard Schäfers, 9th edition, 49–77. Wiesbaden: Springer Fachmedien Wiesbaden.

Schulze, Susanne. 2013. *Mediscript Kurzlehrbuch Embryologie*, 2nd edition. München: Urban & Fischer / Elsevier.

al-Suyūṭī, Jalāl al-Dīn. 1407/1978. *Tasliyat al-Ābāʾ bi-Fuqdān al-Abnāʾ*. Al-Zarqāʾ: Maktabat al-Manār.

Tietze, Nicola. 2001. *Islamische Identitäten: Formen muslimischer Religiosität junger Männer in Deutschland und Frankreich*. Hamburg: Hamburger Edition.

Wolter, Heike. 2015. *Mein unsichtbares Kind: Begleitbuch für Frauen, Angehörige und Fachpersonen vor und nach einem Schwangerschaftsabbruch*. Salzburg: Edition Riedenburg.

Wolter, Heike. 2017. *Mein Sternenkind: Begleitbuch für Eltern, Angehörige und Fachpersonen nach Fehlgeburt, stiller Geburt und Neugeborenentod*. Salzburg: Edition Riedenburg.

Yusuf, Hamza. 2018. "When Does a Human Fetus Become Human?" *Renovatio: The Journal of Zaytuna College*, 18 June. https://renovatio.zaytuna.edu/article/when-does-a-human-fetus-become-human.

al-Zuḥaylī, Wahba. 1989. *Al-Fiqh al-Islāmī wa-Adillatuhu*. Damascus: Dār al-Fikr.

فهرس

آدم 98
الآملی، علاء الدين حسين 92
الإبداع الأدبي 110
ابن سينا 86، 92
ابن العديم. راجع كمال الدين أبي القاسم عمرو بن أحمد
ابن عربي، محي الدين 112–113
ابن الفارض 111
أبيقور 83، 85
إبيكتتوس 83، 85
اجتياح المغول 110، 124
أخلاق الجلالية 92
أخلاق المنصورية 92
أخلاق ناصري 91–92
أخلاقيات الألم والمعاناة 119–120
الأدب الصوفي 110–112
الأدب الصوفي، العصر الذهبي في 111
الأدب الصوفي القديم 111
الأدب الفارسي 111–112
أدلة الخوف من الموت 89
الأذى 87
أرسطو 91
استكمال الإنسان 120–121
أسرار نامه 112
أسر الزمان 117
الاغتمام 93
أفلاطون 83
الأفلاطونية المحدثة 93
الألم 85، 94، 109–123
الألم، أسباب 116–117
الألم الأصيل 117–118
الألم الطارئ 118
ألم الفراق والابتعاد عن المعشوق الأزلي 117–118
الألم. الناحية الأنطولوجية 115–116
الألم، أنواع 117–118
الألم، صور 115
ألم في الموت 89، 96
الألم كقضية وجودية 110
الألم كلطف من قبل الله 115–116
الألم كمقولة ذاتية 116
الألم، مفهوم 114–115
الألم، مكوّنات 115
الألم والراحة، المصدر هو الله 119
الألم وجوديًا 115–116
إلهيات الموت 97
أمين، نصرت 91
الأنا 116–117، 120
أنين الناي 117
الإهمال 118–119
أورليوس 83
أورنج زيب 92
أوصاف الأشراف 92
أوغسطينوس 83، 98
أولسن، روبرت 98
اونامونو 83
أونامونو، ميجل ديه 90–91

برهان الدين محقق الترمذي 112–113
برهانپوری الغياثي، عبد الرحمن بن عبد الكريم 92
بغداد 112
البقاء 99
بوسويه 90

التبريزي، شمس الدين 118
تجاهل التفكير في الموت 90
التجربة الروحانية الوجدانية 111
تحديد نسبة النفس والموت 94–95

تحليل نفساني للمصابين برهاب الموت 93–94
التركب والتكثّر 116
التسليم بقضاء الله 120
التضرع إلى الله 120
التفكير بالانتحار 88، 90
التفكير بالموت 91
التفكير في الموت 85، 90، 101
تقويمية الموت 97
تهذيب الأخلاق 92–93، 95
تهذيب الأخلاق من جهة أخرى 93
تهذيب الأخلاق وتطهير الأعراق 91
توضيح الأخلاق 92

جامع السعادات 92
الجامي، عبد الرحمن 112
الجنيد 111
جهاد النفس 120
الجهل بحال معاد النفس بعد الموت 95–96، 101

حبّ جلال الدين للشمس 113–114
الحزن 98
الحضرة الإلهية 111
حقيقة الموت 94–95، 97
الحكمة المتعالية في الأسفار الأربعة العقلية 99
حلب 113
حلبي، علي أصغر 91
الحموي، سعد الدين 113
حياة ذات معنى 90

الخضِرْ، النبي 119
الخلود 88، 97
خوف الموت 93
الخوف وأنواعه 93

دافنشي 84
الدراسات البينية 102
الدراسات المتعددة التخصصات 102
درّة التاج 92
دفع الغمّ من الموت 92
دمشق 113
الداوني، جلال الدين 92
ديناني، ابراهيمي 91
ديوان شمس التبريزي 114
ديوجانس 98

الذات الربانية 111
ذنوب 96
ذي النون المصري 111

رابعة العدوية 111
الرازي، أبو بكر محمد بن زكريا 86–91
راسل، برتراند 84
الرؤية الصوفية 111
الرباعيات 114
الرحمة 122–123
الرسائل 114
الرعاية التلطيفية 103، 109
الرعاية الروحية، تأصيل إسلامي 109
ركن الدين السّجاسيّ 113
رُكن الدّين الجرجاني 91
رهاب الموت 83، 85–87، 89–90، 92–93، 99–102
الرواقية، المدرسة الإغريقية والرومانية 98
رواقيون 85–86
الرومي، جلال الدين 110–111

الزهد 111

سارتر، جان بول 83، 900
سبينوزا، باروخ 83، 85، 88–89
سقراط 84
سُكر الوجود 117

سلطان ولد 114
السنائي، الحكيم 111
السهروردي، شهاب الدين 112
السيرة الفلسفية 90
سينيكا 83، 85–86

الشاه صفي 92
الشبستري، محمود 112
شرّ الموت 84–85، 90، 98
شرح أخلاق ناصري 92
الشعر الفارسي 111–112
الشفاء من خوف الموت ومعالجة داء الاغتمام به 92
شكوك بشأن معتقداته الدينية 109
شلر 83
شهاب الدين السهروردي 112
شوبنهاور، أرتور 83–84، 90
الشيرازي، حافظ 112
الشيرازي، صدر الدين 86
الشيرازي، قطب الدين 92
الشيرازي، محمد بن إبراهيم القوامي 99–101

الصبر 120
صرف الفكر عن الموت 89
صفاء النفس 122

الطبّ الروحاني 86–88
الطبّ النفساني 93
الطريق إلى الله 111
الطريقة الفلسفية بالحكمة المتعالية 99–101
الطوسي، نصير الدين 86، 91–92

ظاهرات الموت 97

العاملي، أبو المعالي 92
عبد القادر الجيلاني 111
عزام، عبد الوهاب 112
عطاء الدين تديّن 113
العقاب بعد الموت 96
علاء الدين 114
عليم الله جالند هري 92
عوارف المعارف 112

الغزو المغولي 112
الغفلة 123–124
الغمّ من الموت 93
غياث الدين الدشتكي 92

فردانية الإنسان في مواجهة الموت 101
فريد الدين العطّار 111–112
فساد البدن 89
فساد الجسد 87
فضل الله، محمّد صادق 91
فلاسفة المدرسة البراغماتية (pragmatism) 84
الفلسفة التحليلية المعاصرة 89–90
الفلسفة الوجودية 90
الفناء 99
الفوز الأصغر 94–95
فويرباخ 98
الفيزيائي (physicalism) 97–98

قدر 118–119
قطب شاه، عبد الله 92
قلق الموت 83–87، 90
قوس الصعود 101
قوس النزول 116–117
القونوي، صدر الدين 113
قونية 112–114

الكرماني، أوحد الدين 113
كمال الدين أبي القاسم عمرو بن أحمد 113
كوربين، هنري 99
كيركيغارد، سورن 83، 90
كندورسة 84
الكينونة الأصيلة 90–91
الكينونة والزمان 90–91

لارَندَه 112
لايبنتس، غوتفريد 119
اللذة 85–88
لق الموت 85–86
لوكريتيوس 83، 85
ليوناردو دا فينشي 83، 98

ماركوس أورليوس 85
المثنوي 114، 117–118، 122
المجالس السبعة 114
محاكمة سقراط 84
محاورة فايدون 84
محبة الله 111
محمد بن الحسين بهاء الدين ولد 112
المدرسة الحلاوية 113
المدرسة المقدسية 113
المذهب الوجودي 88
مريم 121–122
مسكويه، أبو علي أحمد بن محمد بن يعقوب 86، 91–99
مصير النفس 94
المعاناة لدى الإنسان 114–124
معراج السعادة 92
معنى في الحيات 90
مفارقة الإدراك 89
مفارقة النفس للبدن 93
مفتاح الأخلاق 92
الموت كمرحلة انتقالية 101
"موتوا قبل أن تموتوا" 95
موسى 124
موقف حدّي 116

ناغل، توماس 90
النراقي، أحمد 92
النراقي، مهدي 92
النراقيَين 86
النظرية الأبيقورية عن اللذة والشرور 85
نظرية الفلاسفة المشائيين عن الموت 94–95
النفس 87–90، 92–96، 99–100، 103، 106، 120
النفس كجوهر روحاني 94–95
نقاء القلب 122
نيتشه 83–84، 90، 98
نيسابور 112

هيجل 97–98
هيدجر، مارتن 83، 90، 97، 101
هيسه، هرمان 124

وحدة لا كثرة فيها 116
ويكنز 92

ياسبرز، كارل 116
يوسفَ 119

Index

Abāẓa, Nizār 155
ʿAbd al-Ḥamīd al-Qanawātī 166
ʿAbd Allāh, ʿAbd Allāh Muḥammad 182
ʿAbd al-Qādir al-Khānī 166
ʿAbd al-Qādir Quwaydir 164
ʿAbd al-Raḥmān 158
ʿAbd al-Raḥmān b. Mahdī 157
abortion (*ijhāḍ*) 354
Abū Bakr 158
Abū Dāwūd (al-Sijistānī) 145, 264, 356
Abū Ḥanīfa 261, 264
Abū l-Dardāʾ 158
Abū Thawr 264
Abū Yūsuf 221, 261
Abū ʿUtba al-Khawlānī 137
academic bioethics literature 52
accountability before God (*ḥisāb*) 19
acting (*ʿamal*) 128, 148
Adam, Prophet 55
Advance Care Planning (ACP) 343
al-Afghānī, ʿAbd al-Ḥakīm 164–165
after-death period in the grave (*barzakh*) 26
afterlife (*ākhira*) 19–20
agonies (*sakarāt/ghamarāt*) 19
Aḥmad b. Ḥanbal 22, 261
Aksoy, Şahin 61–63
Alizamani, Amir Abbas 5
allopathic healthcare 53
Alzheimer's disease 330–331
ʿAmr b. al-ʿĀṣ 258–259
ʿAmr b. Maymūn 158
ʿAmr b. ʿUthmān al-Makkī 160
analgesics 15, 189–193
Anam, Beate 9
al-Anṣārī, Muḥammad b. Zakariyyā 128
al-Anṣārī, Muḥyī l-Dīn Yaḥyā 128
al-Anṣārī, Zakariyyā b. Muḥammad 5, 127–149
antibiotics 193
Antichrist (*dajjāl*) 128, 148
anti-treatment position 31
appointed time of death (*taʾjīl al-mawt*) 19, 27, 252, 344
ʿAqīda ("Creed") 148
al-ʿAqqād, Ṣāliḥ 165
Aquinas 306
Arezaei, Hamed 4
ars moriendi (the art of dying) 6, 153
artificial nutrition and hydration (ANH) 6–9, 15, 177, 180, 186–189, 197, 283–284, 298, 318, 330, 332
  as medical treatment 340–341
  at End-of-Life (EoL) 332–336
  at late-stage dementia, Islamic perspective 336–344
  views in Catholicism 341
  views in Judaism 341
  withholding of 293–295
Asad b. Mūsā 24
Asadi, Asma 4
asceticism (*zuhd*) 31
al-Ashqar, Muḥammad Sulaymān 71
assisted hand feeding 335–336, 342
assisted suicide 267
ʿAṭāʾ 261
Aṭāʾ al-Salīmī 159
al-ʿAṭṭār, Bakrī 165
Auerbach, Shlomo Zalman 341
autonomy 317
  as defining characteristic of Western modernity 241–242
  conceptions of 245
  in context of passive euthanasia 269–270
  Islamic conceptualisation of 246–247
  position in in Islamic (bio)ethics 245–250, 274–275
  position in secular bioethics 243–245
  secular perspectives 241–243
awe (*hayba*) 160
al-Awzāʿī 221, 261

Badhl al-Māʿūn fī Faḍl al-Ṭāʿūn 129
bad news 193–197
Badr al-Dīn al-Ḥasanī 164, 166
al-Bārr, Muḥammad ʿAlī 179–180, 185–187, 333
Bauer, Thomas 167
al-Bayhaqī 24, 38

Bedir, Ahmet 61–63
beginning of human life 356
behaviours surrounding death 56–57
Beiträge zur Eschatologie des Islam 20
belief (*īmān*) 128, 148
belief in prophethood (*nubuwwa*) 27
belief in the hereafter (*maʿād/ākhira/qiyāma*) 27
belief in the unity of God (*tawḥīd*) 27
benefit (*nafʿ*) 303
bereavement counselling 9
bereavement, Islamic perspectives 224–225
al-Bidlīsī, Idrīs 138
Bilāl b. Rabāḥ 161
bioethics, contemporary Islamic perspective 187
biographical dictionaries on Islamic scholars 155
biographical literature 156
Bishr al-Ḥāfī 160
Bishr b. al-Ḥārith 158
al-Bīṭār, ʿAbd al-Razzāq 155, 163
bloodletting (*faṣd*) 139, 141–142
blood money (*diya*) 188, 221, 266
bodily dignity 305–307, 309, 311
bodily integrity (*ḥurma*) 362
bodily sanctity 305–306
brain death 182–184, 255, 271–273
  criteria for 58
  Islamic bioethical literature on 52
  Islamic scriptural evidence 64–66
brain function 55
Brockopp, Jonathan E. 354
al-Bukhārī 22–24, 36–40, 136
burial place for deceased premature children 357–359
al-Būʿazīzī, Muḥammad 227

Cairo 128
cardiopulmonary function 55
cardiopulmonary resuscitation (CPR) 6–7, 15, 56, 68, 177, 180–186, 197, 283, 293, 312
catastrophe (*muṣība*) 34
cemeteries, Islamic 365
Chamsi-Pasha, Hassan (Shamsī Bāshā, Ḥassān) 187, 333, 344
child loss in early pregnancy 9
chin tuck position 336
cognitive capacity 313–314
collective religio-ethical reasoning (*ijtihād jamāʿī*) 178
communal burial 358–359
compassion 195, 226
competing harms (*aḍrār*) 305
compounding harm 303–311
confessing (*qawl*) 128, 148
consciousness 301
consent (*riḍan*) 142
consolation of people with calamities (*tasliyat ahl al-maṣāʾib*) 34
consumption of food and drink 290
contentment on the deathbed 166
contentment (*riḍā*) 30, 155, 160
conviction (*yaqīn*) 139
coping with the death of a child 359–361
Coppens, Pieter 6
Council of Senior Religious Scholars (*Hayʾat Kibār al-ʿUlamāʾ*) 179, 185–186
counselling approach to suicide by muftis and imams 215–216
cremation of deceased premature children 361–362
cupping (*ḥijāma*) 291
curative medical treatment 176

dafʿ al-halaka (warding off death) 182
Daiber, Hans 5
al-dār al-ākhira (abode of the hereafter) 20
Dār al-Iftāʾ 254–255
al-Dārānī, Abū Sulaymān 158
ḍarar (physical harm) 303–304
David, Prophet 130
Dāwūd al-Ṭāʾī 162
Day of Reckoning (*yawm al-ḥisāb/yawm al-taghābun/yawm al-tanād* 19–20
death
  anxiety. *See* fear of death
  as a “single irreversible event” 64
  behaviours 4
  criteria for 55–61
  declaration 4
  illness (*maraḍ al-mawt*) 71
  imminent 302
  legal (*al-ḥayāt ghayr al-mustaqirra*) 301–302
  legal indicants 66

death (*cont.*)
  medicalisation of 6
  m-w-t 19
  nature and definition 54–58
  neurological criteria for 59
  penalty (*qiṣāṣ*) 188
  physical signs 62
  Prophet Muḥammad's thoughts on 20
  purposes of 57
  Qur'ānic references to 20
decreased awareness 189
dehydration 333–334
deliverance-after-hardship (*al-faraj ba'd al-shidda*) 34
DeLongis, Anita 360
dementia 330, 332
demise, inevitable (*al-ḥayāt al-mustaqirra*) 302
deterioration in cognitive and memory functions 330
Dhāt al-Salāsil 258
Dibs wa-Zayt, 'Abd al-Wahhāb 167
dignity bestowed on man 246–247
dignity (*ikrām*) of the dead 357, 359
dignity integrity 305–309
disability and bioethics 28
discretionary punishment (*ta'zīr*) regarding suicide victim 220
disobedience against God 147
distress (*ḍarrā'*) 131
divine decree (*qaḍā'*) 128, 142, 148
do not resuscitate (DNR) 186, 293, 300, 312
Doomsday (*yawm al-qiyāma*) 19, 21
double effect principle (DEP) 16, 192
Durkheim, Emil 210
duty to feed 9, 342–343, 345
du'ā' 127, 146
Dworkin, Gerald 242
dying process (*iḥtiḍār*) 19, 185
  medicalisation of 16, 19, 23–26, 58

ecstasy (*wajd*) on the deathbed 161–162
education of Muslim counsellors 365
Eich, Thomas 351
Elzamzamy, Khalid 7
emotional ambiguity 160–162
emotional communities 154–155
emotions as constructs 154–155

Encyclopaedia of the Qur'ān 21–22
ensoulment (*nafkh al-rūḥ*) 355–356
EoLC
  in the Sunna 22–23
  Islamic legal theory (*uṣūl al-fiqh*) 32–33
  issues, fiqh 33
  decisions, importance of religious beliefs 270–271, 275
epidemic (*wabā'*) 130
epistemology, Islamic legal 53, 61
eschatological manuals 23–26
eschatological perspectives in early Islamic history 28
eschatological terms, metaphorical use of 32
eschatology in Sufi literature 31–32
essential needs (*ḍarūriyyāt*) 339
Ess, Josef van 28
eternal life (*khulūd*) 344–345
etiquettes
  of dealing with pre-death sickness 23
  of dying 31
  of the physician (*adab al-ṭabīb*) 195
European Council for Fatwā and Research (ECFR) 178, 184, 192
euthanasia (*qatl al-raḥma*) 6, 8, 192, 268
  active 258–267
  contemporary Muslim discussions on 253–257
  Islamic normative tradition regarding 251–253
  meaning of 250–251, 256
  passive 268–273, 297
  passive versus active 250–251
  passive versus active (Islamic perspective) 253–256
executive capacity (*ahliyyat adā'*) 248–249
expiation (*kaffāra*) 221
external (*ẓāhir*) 30
"extreme Sufis" (*ghulāt al-ṣūfiyya*) 31

Fakhr al-Dīn Ibn 'Asākir 227
Fatwā Department (*Idārat al-Iftā'*) 179
fatwās
  medical (*fatāwā ṭibbiyya*) 13
  on bioethical issues at end-of-life care 282–283
  on the topic of suicide 216

favour (*niʿma*) 128, 147
fear of death 4, 14–15, 24, 31, 127, 147, 336
fear for punishment 159
Feinstein, Moshe 341
fettering (*taṣfīd*) 130
forgiveness (*maghfira*) 130, 160, 210
  by murder victim 264–267
  of God 29
forgoing treatment (*tark al-tadāwī*) 184
for the cause of God (*fī sabīl Allāh*) 127, 130, 133
Frankfurt, Harry 242
freedom of choice 242
Freud, Sigmund 14
funeral
  of deceased premature children 355–359
  prayer for suicide victim 261
  prayer (*ṣalāt al-janāza*) 221
  rites of suicide victims 221–222
  farḍ kifāya 227–228
Funk, Miriam 353
futile treatment 8, 180, 184, 256, 338–340, 344
  description of 285–286
  of LST therapy 283–287
  withholding of 268–271
al-Futūḥāt al-Ilāhiyya 148

general anaesthesia 191
Ghabjūqa, Aḥmad Ṣafar 361
Ghaly, Mohammed 3, 7, 249
al-Ghazālī, Abū Ḥāmid 25, 27–31, 40, 129, 198, 339
gift of life 210
God's acceptance (*marḍāt*) 127, 131–132, 146–147
God's benevolence 20
God's decree (*tawakkul*) 289
God's reward (*thawāb*) 136
good manner (*adab*) regarding afflicted by plague 142–143
grace (*luṭf*) 161
gratitude (*shukr*) 30
grief of fathers 364
grief therapy 223
Günther, Sebastian 21

ḥadd punishment 253, 263, 266–267
al-Ḥāfiẓ, Muḥammad Muṭīʿ 155
hagiographical literature 155–156, 158
Hague, Ros 244
al-Ḥajjāj b. Yūsuf 158
al-Ḥalabī, Ibrāhīm 338
Hamad Medical Corporation (HMC) 186
Hamdy, Sherine 64
Ḥanbalī-Sufi school 128, 148
happiness (*sarrā'*) 131
Haque, Omar Sultan 62
al-Ḥārith al-Muḥāsibī 24
harm and burden to society 316–318
harmfulness (*ba's*) 130
Harm versus burden of treatment 311–315
al-Ḥasan b. ʿAlī 161
Hastings Center 66
Ḥathḥūt, Ḥassān 356
al-ḥayāt ghayr al-mustaqirra (legal death) 301
Ḥayy Ibn Yaqẓān 29
heaven (*janna*) 19–20
hellfire (*nār/jahannam/jaḥīm*) 19–21
hierarchy of personal motivations 242
Higher Objectives of Sharīʿa (*maqāṣid al-Sharīʿa*) 182, 193, 247
al-Ḥijjāwī 226
ḥikma 127
Ḥilyat al-Awliyā' 6, 155, 157
Ḥilyat al-Bashar fī Tārīkh al-Qarn al-Thālith ʿAshar 6, 155
History of Emotions 154
Holtzman, Susan 360
holy war (*jihād*) 128, 148
hope (*raja'*) 160
Horowitz (*Rabbi*) 341
Ḥudhayfa 160
human intellect (*ʿaql*) 31
humor on the deathbed 161
al-Ḥumṣī, Ṣāliḥ 164
ḥurma (violation/inviolability) 306–311
Ḥusām al-Dīn, Muḥammad Badr al-Dīn 257
Husayn, Muḥammad Aḥmad 339
Ḥusn al-Ẓann bi-Llāh ("Thinking Good of God") 24
hypocrite (*munāfiq*) 133, 136

Ibn Abī l-Dunyā 24–25, 30, 34, 41–42
Ibn Abī Dāwūd 24
Ibn Ḥajar al-ʿAsqalānī 129–130, 132, 138
Ibn Ḥanbal 264
Ibn Ḥazm 29, 228, 336
Ibn Ḥibbān 136, 144–145
Ibn Kathīr 304
Ibn al-Mubārak 31
Ibn al-Nafīs 127, 130, 146
Ibn Qayyim al-Jawziyya 132, 147, 342
Ibn Qudāma al-Maqdisī 148
Ibn Rajab al-Ḥanbalī 25
Ibn Rushd 27, 42, 261
Ibn Sīnā 29, 62, 127, 130, 139, 141, 146
Ibn Taymiyya 226
Ibn Ṭufayl 29
Ibn ʿAbbās 342
Ibn ʿAjība 163
identity in light of personal autonomy 244
idiot (*aḥmaq*) 31
Iḥkām al-Dalāla ʿalā Taḥrīr al-Risāla 129
Imam Aḥmad 136
incision (*sharṭ*) 139, 141–142
incontinence 332
incurable disease (*la yurjā bar'uh*) 182–186
independence (*ghaniya*) 128
indignation (*sukhṭ*) 130
inner (*bāṭin*) 30
inner space 168
inqādh (saving) 182
Institute for Development, Research, Advocacy and Applied Care (IDRAAC) 343
Institution for issuing *fatwās* (*Dār al-Iftā'*) (Jordan) 181
integrity dignity (*ḥurma*) 305
integrity of the human body 247
intentional homicide (*al-qatl al-ʿamd*) 181
intention (*niyya*) 128, 133, 146, 148
intercultural sensitivity 152–153
International Islamic Code for Medical and Health Ethics (*al-Mīthāq al-Islāmī al-ʿĀlamī lil-Akhlāqiyyāt al-Ṭibbiya wa-l-Ṣiḥḥiyya*) 178, 184
International Islamic Fiqh Academy (IIFA) 178, 180, 183, 185, 187, 269, 272
interreligious sensitivity 152–153
intrinsic human value 242

invisible world (*ghayb*) 31
al-Iṣfahānī, Abū Nuʿaym 155, 157
Islamic Code of Medical Ethics (*al-Dustūr al-Islāmī lil-Mihna al-Ṭibbiya*) 178, 182, 195
Islamic Fiqh Academy (IFA) 178–179, 183, 337, 340
Islamic Fiqh Council (India) 256
Islamic modernity 155
Islamic moral view on suicide 205–206
Islamic Organization for Medical Sciences (IOMS) 178, 180, 183, 185, 192, 257, 272
Islamic Psychology 205
Islamic suicide discourse 215

al-Jabūrī, ʿAbd Allāh 181–182
Jalāl al-Dīn al-Rūmī 5
al-Janā'iz (lit. "Funerals" or "Funerary Practices") 33
al-Jazā'irī, Ṭāhir 165
jinn 132–133
John Paul II, Pope 341
journey (*sayr*) 30
Jumʿa, ʿAlī 59, 254–255
al-Jurayrī, Abū Muḥammad 160
juristic ethics 178

Kant 306
Kantian version of autonomy 242
al-Karam 204–205
karāma (dignity) 306
Khālid, Ḥasan 357
Khālid b. al-Walīd 337
al-Kharrāz, Abū Saʿīd 161
Kholwadia, M. Amin 59
killing detainees (*qatl al-ṣabr*) 188–189, 337–339, 345
al-Kindī 29, 38–39, 43
King Faisal Specialist Hospital and Research Center 186
Kuftārū, Muḥammad Amīn 164
Kuftārū, Ṣāliḥ 164
kutub al-zuhd (books on renunciation) 153

[illegible], Hadil 9
Lange, Christian 21
late-stage dementia 9, 332, 334
legal capacity (*ahliyya*) 33, 248
and personhood 249

legal responsibility (*taklīf*) 248
legal thresholds for human death 55
Leget, Carlo 168
Life-Sustaining Treatments (LSTs) 6–8, 15, 177, 179–189
  advanced technologies 298–299
  distinction between withholding and withdrawing 288–289
  effectiveness of 296–299
  judging effectiveness of 286–287
  obligations related to withdrawing 295–299
  obligations related to withholding 289–295
  obligatory (*wājib*) 287
  permissible (*mubāḥ*) 287
longing to meet God 158
loss of cognitive skills 335
loss of consciousness 189–191, 197
love of God 161
Luṭfī, Ṣafwat 64

al-Maʿarrī, Abū al-ʿAlāʾ 29
Mahdavi, Shahaboddin 5
Maḥmūd Ḥamza 166
make a good end (*ḥusn al-khātima*) 26
Makḥūl al-Shāmī 158
Mālik 261, 264
Mālik b. Dīnār 160, 162
malnutrition 332
Maʾmūn, Ḥasan 361
martyrdom (*shahāda*) 130, 133, 146
  degrees of 133–137
martyr (*shahīd*) 27
Maududi, Abul Aʿla 55
al-Mawṣilī 338
al-Mawsūʿa al-Fiqhiyya 218
meaningful life 303, 313, 315, 319
mechanical ventilation 177, 180–186, 283, 293, 311
mediation (*shafāʿa*) 128, 130, 148
medical treatment (*ʿilāj*) 141
Mehrdeutigkeit (ambiguity) 167
mental capacity (*istiṭāʿa ʿaqliyya*) 32
Mental Health Action Plan 207
mental illness 226
mercy killing. *See* euthanasia, meaning of
mercy (*raḥma*) 128, 130, 147
methodology in EoL care studies 3–4
miscarriage (*isqāṭ*) 9, 353–354
miserable (*ḥaqīr*) 128
Miskawayh 4, 29
moral agency of patients 16
moral relativism 53
al-Muḥallā 228
Muḥammad, Prophet 149, 221–222, 224, 226, 307, 337, 342
al-Muhayzaʿ 226
Mullā Ṣadrā 29
Multilevel Interdisciplinary Paradigm (MIP) 205
murder (*qatl*) 27, 187, 197, 205–206, 258
  coersion to 264
  intentional 263
  Islamic condemnation of 263–267
Muslim b. al-Ḥajjāj al-Naysābūrī 22, 356
Muslim counselling (*Seelsorge*) 362–363
mutilation (*muthla*) 307
Muʿādh b. Jabal 158

al-Nakhaʿī 261
names and attributes of God 28
natural forces (*dahr*) 19
necessary needs (*ḥājiyyāt*) 339
niyya 127–128
non-physical aspects of EoLC 16
North West Armed Forces Hospital (NWAFH) 186
al-Nūrī, Abū l-Ḥusayn 161
nutrition and hydration (withholding of) 293–295

ontology 53
opioid drugs 189, 191, 193, 334
organ donation 64
Organization of Islamic Cooperation (OIC) 178
organ transplantation 59–60
original capacity (*ahliyyat wujūb*) 248–249
O'Shaughnessy 21

Padela, Aasim 3, 338
pain (*wajaʿ*) 4, 13, 130, 304–305, 335
  control 293
  ladder 190
  vs. pleasure 28

palliative care (PC) 7, 176, 186
palliative sedation 15, 190
panic (*jazaʿ*) 31
paradise and hell in Islamic traditions 21
paradise and hell, Sufi perception of 32
paradise, Qurʾānic portrayal 21
patience (*ṣabr*) 30, 127, 132, 138, 142, 146, 148
patient's awareness/consciousness 15
peace of the dead 358
percutaneous endoscopic gastrostomy 333
Permanent Committee for Scholarly Research and Issuing Fatwās (*al-Lajna al-Dāʾima lil-Buḥūth al-ʿIlmiyya wa-l-Iftāʾ*) 179, 185–186
personal autonomy and religion 244
personhood 63, 305
physical capacity (*qudra badaniyya*) 32
physical part (*jasad*) 30
piercing (*ṭaʿn*) 130
plague (*ṭāʿūn*) 4–5, 128, 130, 133
  in Mecca and Medina 137
pneumonia 333, 335
post-death time in the grave (*barzakh*) 19
power (*qahr*) 161
predestination (*qadar*) 138, 142, 212
predictive medical treatment 175
Presidential Commission on Bioethics 66
preventive medical treatment 175–176
pricking (*wakhz*) 130
principalism 243
principalist approach to autonomy 249–250
principle of veracity 194
private burial ground 358
process of resurrection (*baʿth*) 27
prohibition of harmful lifestyles 210
prohibition of suicide 212
  in Islam 215
prohibition of the burning of corpses 362
prolonging of death 343–346
prophetic medicine 146
prudent (*ʿāqil*) 31
psyche 204
psychological distress [illegible]6
psychological "therapeutics" 29
punishment (*ʿadhāb, rujz, rijz*) 130
  for murder 267
  for suicide 262
purification of the soul 132

qaḍāʾ 128
al-Qaraḍāwī, Yūsuf 227, 253, 257, 268–269, 272, 340
Qarmaṭiyya sect attack on Mecca 160
Qāsim, ʿAbd al-Raḥmān b. Muḥammad b. 226–227
qawl 128
Qazi, Faisal 64
quality of life 13, 303–311, 318
quantity of life 301–302, 318
Qureshi 338
al-Qurṭubī 25, 46–47, 304
al-Qushayrī, Abū l-Qāsim 129, 155, 157, 160
Quṭb, Sayyid 21

al-Rabīʿ b. al-Khaytham 159
Rady, Mohammed 64
rāḥa (rest) 149
Ramaḍān 130
al-Ramlī 221
Rashid, Rafaqat 8
al-Rāzī, Abū Bakr 4, 29
Raz, Joseph 242
reason (*ḥikma*) 131
reckoning (*ḥisāb*) 20
refusal of medical treatment, permissibility 290–291
refusal of medication and nutrition 159–160, 166, 337–339
regret 132
rehabilitative medical treatment 176
relations with family and friends on the deathbed 165
religion and suicide 210
religious exhortation (*mawʿiẓa*) 130
religious expiation (*kaffara*) 267
religious leaders working in a healthcare-related capacity 71
religious liberties 64
religiously commendable practices (*ʿibādāt*) 31
religious obligation (*taklīf*) 33
religious professionals serving the patient 69
remembrance (*dhikr*) 198
remembrance of death 31
renunciant (*zāhid*) 158
renunciation of this worldly life 29–30
repentance (*tawba*) 30, 127, 146, 155

research 343
restlessness in this-worldly life 159
resurrection 19, 158
retribution 265–266
rights of God 246–247
rights of man 246–247
right to self-determination 243
Risāla fī l-Taṣawwuf 6, 155
Risālat al-Ghufrān 29
Risālat al-Ibāʾ ʿan Mawāqiʿ al-Wabāʾ 138
Rosenwein, Barbara 154–155
Routledge Handbook on Sufism 32
Rüling 20

Sachedina 337, 339–340
Salama al-Ghuwayṭī 158
al-Sallāmī, Muḥammad al-Mukhtār 257
sanctity of human life 182, 212, 247
Scale (*mīzān*) 20
scarcity of LSTs resources 185
Schachter, Hershel 341
scope of religious sciences (*al-ʿulūm al-sharʿiyya*) 178
secondary needs (*taḥsīniyyāt*) 339
self-creation, concept regarding autonomy 242
self-immolation 210
sense of meaning 210
sentience (*idrāk*) 301, 313, 315
serenity (*sukūn*) 160
Shabana, Ayman 8
Shaddād Ibn Aws 143
shafāʿa 128
al-Shāfiʿī 261, 264
shahāda (testimony of faith) 26, 191
Shamsī Bāshā, Ḥassān (Chamsi-Pasha, Hassan) 187, 333, 344
al-Shāṭibī, Abū Isḥāq 247
al-Shāṭirī, Muḥammad Aḥmad 340
al-Shawkānī 307
al-Shaybānī, Muḥammad b. al-Ḥasan 264
al-Shiblī 161
al-Shirāzī, Ṣadr al-Dīn 4
al-Shirbīnī, ʿIṣām 257
al-Sibāʿī, Muṣṭafā 166
sincerity (*ṣidq*) 133
Islamic Fiqh Academy of the Organization of Islamic Conference (now Cooperation) (OIC-IFA) 71
smart person (*kayyis*) 31
sobriety in deathbed emotions 163
social constructionism 53
social realism 53
societal responsibility regarding suicide 213
sorrows and anxieties (*aḥzān/humūm*) 28
soul 62, 204–205, 249
  departure of 56, 62, 65
spiritual development 212–213
spiritual discourse on suicide 216
states (*aḥwāl*) 30
stations (*maqāmāt*) 30
steadfastness in acts of obedience and teaching 155, 163–164
stigma related to suicide 210
stillbirth (*wilāda mayyita*) 354
subjective reality of death 53
submission (*taslīm*) 128, 148
Sufi hagiographical literature, 20th century 162–166
Sufi hagiographical literature, formative period 156–161
Sufism, role in spiritual care for muslim terminal patients 5
Sufyān al-Thawrī 157, 160, 163
Suhrawardī 29
suicidal thoughts 203–204
suicide (*intiḥār*) 7–8, 29, 258
  aftermath of 217–229
  Islamic condemnation of 258–262
  loss survivors 222–224
  postvention 202
  prevention 202, 207–217
  protective role of religion 214
  punishment against the corpse 218
  punishment against the properties 218
  statisics 202, 206–207
  victims, theological and moral status of 218–220
Sunnī legal views on *tawakkul* and medical treatment 338
support within the religious community 210
al-Suyūṭī 25, 47–48
swallowing difficulties 332–333, 335

al-Ṭabarī 304
Ṭanṭāwī, Muḥammad Sayyid 58
al-Taskhīrī, Muḥammad ʿAlī 257

Tawheedic Paradigm 205
al-Ṭayyib, Aḥmad 254
Ta'rīkh 'Ulamā' Dimashq 6, 155
teaching on the deathbed 164–165
temptations (*fitan*) 127, 146
terminal illness 255
terminal sedation 190–191
testament creation on the deathbed 165
Thābit b. Aslam al-Bunānī 159
thanatophobia *See* fear of death
al-Thawrī 264
The Death of Ivan Iljitsch 152
theodicy 28
theological prohibition of suicide 210
this-worldly life (*dunyā*) 20, 159
al-Tirmidhī, Abū 'Īsā 133, 144–145
Tolstoy, Lev 152
translation of Arabic texts on bereavement counselling 364
transnational Islamic institutions 178
treatment outcomes, certainty of 291–292
trial (*balā'*) 130
tribulation (*fitna*) 156–158, 212, 224
true Healer (God, *al-Shāfī*) 182
trust (in God) (*tawakkul*) 30, 138, 148, 155, 177
truthfulness (*ṣidq*) 194
tube-feeding 9, 335, 338, 342
al-Ṭufayl al-Dawsī 219, 226
Tuḥfat al-Rāghibīn fī Bayān Amr al-Ṭawā'īn 5, 128–129

'Umar b. al-Khaṭṭāb 158, 163, 194–195
'Umar b. 'Abd al-A'zīz (or 'Umar II) 161, 221, 261
universality of moral principles 242
unsuitable state (foregoing LST) 285–286
'Urwa b. al-Zubayr 190
al-Usṭuwānī, Muḥammad 165
'Uthmān Ibn Abī l-'Āṣ 142

Vereindeutigung (disambiguation) 167
viceregency (*khilāfa*) 245
Vielfalt (pluriformity) 167
visiting a patient (*'iyāda*) 147
vivisection 60
volition 301, 313, 315
vulnerability to suicide 209

waiving of retribution (*musqiṭāt al-qiṣāṣ*) 264–265
wariness (*taḥarruz*) 141
Wāṣil, Naṣr Farīd 262
wayfarers (*sā'irūn*) 30
al-Wā'ī, Tawfīq 182
weakness to perform pious acts 158–159
weight limit for legal beginning of life 357
welfare (*naf'*) 132
WHO 213–215
"whole person" 13, 16, 35
will of the person with dementia 343
wishing for death 156–160, 163
woman in childbed (*nafsā'*) 137
works on eschatology 24
World Health Organization (WHO) 7, 190, 202, 207
worthlessness of worldly life 32

Ya'qūb, Prophet 224
Yāsīn, Muḥammad Na'īm 59
Yāzīd b. Abī Muslim 158
Yusuf, Hamza 355–356

al-Zarkashī 141
al-Zarw al-Tamīmī 226
Zufar b. al-Hudhayl 264
al-Zuḥaylī, Wahba 357